The Life of
Walter Scott

BLACKWELL CRITICAL BIOGRAPHIES

General Editor: Claude Rawson

The Life of
WALTER SCOTT
A Critical Biography

John Sutherland

BLACKWELL
Oxford UK & Cambridge USA

First published 1995

Blackwell Publishers
108 Cowley Road
Oxford OX4 1JF
UK

238 Main Street
Cambridge, Massachusetts 02142
USA

British Library Cataloguing in Publication Data

A CIP catalogue record for this book is available from the British Library.

Library of Congress Cataloging-in-Publication Data
Sutherland, John, 1938—
The life of Walter Scott / John Sutherland.
p. cm. — (Blackwell critical biographies ; 6)
Includes bibliographical references (p.) and index.
ISBN 1-55786-231-1
1. Scott, Walter, Sir, 1771-1832—Biography. 2. Authors,
Scottish—19th century—Biography. I. Title. II. Series.
PR5332.S87 1995
828'.709—dc20
[B]   95-25769
CIP

Typeset in 10 on 11pt Baskerville
by Best-set Typesetter Ltd., Hong Kong
Printed in Great Britain by Hartnolls Ltd, Bodmin

This book is printed on acid-free paper

Contents

Illustrations

Acknowledgements

For expert advice on illustrations I am grateful to Francis Russell (author of *Portraits of Sir Walter Scott*, 1987). Mrs Susanna Kerr of the Scottish National Portrait Gallery has been very helpful in tracking down illustrations. Part of this book was written on study leave supplied by the Sherman Fairchild Foundation to whom I am grateful. I am grateful, too, to the Huntington Library, where I did most of my research. For much help with the text I am grateful to Rosemary Ashton, Jane Dietrich, Andrew McNeillie, Karl Miller, Claude Rawson and Guilland Sutherland.

Abbreviations used in the Text

Where multiple references are restricted to a single chapter, the abbreviated reference is indicated in the chapter's end note.

<table>
<tr><td>ACLC</td><td>T. Constable, Archibald Constable and his Literary Correspondents, 3 vols (Edinburgh, 1873).</td></tr>
<tr><td>Allan</td><td>George Allan (continuing work begun by William Weir), Life of Sir Walter Scott, Baronet (Edinburgh, 1834).</td></tr>
<tr><td>Ball</td><td>Margaret Ball, Sir Walter Scott as a Critic of Literature (New York, 1907).</td></tr>
<tr><td>Butt</td><td>John Butt and Geoffrey Carnall, The Mid-Eighteenth Century (Oxford, 1979).</td></tr>
<tr><td>Byron, Lett.</td><td>Lord Byron: Letters and Journals (ed.) Leslie A. Marchand, 12 vols (London, 1973–81).</td></tr>
<tr><td>Chambers</td><td>Robert Chambers, Memoir of Sir Walter Scott (Edinburgh, 1872).</td></tr>
<tr><td>Clark</td><td>Arthur Melville Clark, Sir Walter Scott: The Formative Years (New York, 1970).</td></tr>
<tr><td>Cook</td><td>Davidson Cook (ed.), New Love Poems (Oxford, 1932).</td></tr>
<tr><td>Corson</td><td>James Corson, Notes and Index to Sir Herbert Grierson's Edition of The Letters of Sir Walter Scott (Oxford, 1979).</td></tr>
<tr><td>Critical Heritage</td><td>John O. Hayden, Scott: The Critical Heritage (London, 1970).</td></tr>
<tr><td>Curry</td><td>Kenneth Curry, Sir Walter Scott's Edinburgh Annual Register (Knoxville: Tennessee, 1977).</td></tr>
<tr><td>Daiches</td><td>David Daiches, Sir Walter Scott and his World (London, 1971).</td></tr>
<tr><td>Dobie</td><td>M. R. Dobie, 'The development of Scott's Minstrelsy: an attempt at a reconstruction', Transactions of the Edinburgh Bibliographical Society, 2, 1, 1940.</td></tr>
<tr><td>Dryden</td><td>The Works of John Dryden, (ed.), Walter Scott, 18 vols</td></tr>
</table>

(Edinburgh, 1808; revised George Saintsbury, London, 1882–83).

EAR   *Edinburgh Annual Register.*

EJ   Edgar Johnson, *Sir Walter Scott: The Great Unknown*, 2 vols (New York, 1970).

Emerson   O. F. Emerson, 'The early literary life of Sir Walter Scott', *JEGP*, 23, Jan. 1924, 28–62; Apr. 1924, 241–69; July 1924, 3, 89–417.

EQ   Eric Quayle, *The Ruin of Sir Walter Scott* (London, 1968).

Gordon   Robert C. Gordon, *Under Which King?* (Edinburgh, 1969).

Greig   James A. Greig, *Jeffrey of the Edinburgh Review* (London, 1948).

Griggs   Samuel Taylor Coleridge, *Collected Letters* (ed.), E. L. Griggs, 6 vols (Oxford, 1956–71).

HG   Herbert Grierson, *Sir Walter Scott, Bart.* (London, 1938).

Hart   Francis R. Hart, *Lockhart as Romantic Biographer* (Edinburgh, 1971).

Hew.   David Hewitt, *Scott on Himself* (Edinburgh, 1981).

JB   John Buchan, *Sir Walter Scott* (London, 1932).

JLR   *Scott: Poetical Works* (ed.), J. L. Robertson (Oxford, 1894).

Jrnl.   *The Journal of Sir Walter Scott* (ed.), W. E. K. Anderson (Oxford, 1972).

Lamont   Claire Lamont, (ed.), *Waverley* (Oxford, 1982).

Lett.   *The Letters of Sir Walter Scott* (ed.), H. Grierson, 12 vols (London, 1932–7).

Lock.   J. G. Lockhart, *Memoirs of the Life of Sir Walter Scott*, 5 vols (Boston and New York, 1902).

Mack   Douglas S. Mack (ed.), *James Hogg's Anecdotes of Sir Walter Scott* (Edinburgh, 1983).

Mem.   Henry Cockburn, *Memorials of his Times* (New York, 1856).

Millgate   Jane Millgate, *Walter Scott: The Making of the Novelist* (Toronto, 1984).

MSB   *The Minstrelsy of the Scottish Border*, with notes and index by Sir Walter Scott, revised and edited by T. F. Henderson, 4 vols (Edinburgh, 1932).

Osb.   J. M. Osborn, *Dryden: Some Biographical Facts and Problems* (New York, 1940).

Pearson   Hesketh Pearson, *Sir Walter Scott* (New York, 1954).

Postbag   *Sir Walter Scott's Postbag* (ed.), Wilfred Partington (London, 1932).

PLB   *The Private Letter Books of Sir Walter Scott* (ed.), Wilfred Partington (London 1930).

Prose	*The Prose Works of Sir Walter Scott*, 6 vols (Edinburgh, 1832).
Rog.	Charles Rogers, *Genealogical Memoirs of the Family of Sir Walter Scott, Bart.* (Edinburgh, 1877).
Shattock	Joanne Shattock, *Politics and Reviewers* (Leicester, 1989).
SLJ	*The Scottish Literary Journal.*
SLE	Jane Millgate, *Scott's Last Edition* (Edinburgh, 1987).
Smout	T. C. Smout, *A History of the Scottish People* (New York, 1969).
Southey, NL	Kenneth Curry (ed.), *New Letters of Southey*, 2 vols (New York, 1965).
SSL	*Studies in Scottish Literature.*
Sultana	Donald Sultana, *The Siege of Malta Rediscovered* (Edinburgh, 1977).
Wilt	Judith Wilt, *Secret Leaves: The Novels of Walter Scott* (Chicago, 1985).

References to Scott's novels are abbreviated from the 'Border Edition' of the *Waverley Novels* (ed.) Andrew Lang, 48 vols (Edinburgh, 1892–94).

1

Scott among the Scotts (1771–1783)

He desired to plant a lasting root, and dreamt not of present fame, but of long distant generations rejoicing in the name of Scott of Abbotsford.

Lockhart

Scott begins his unfinished autobiography[1] as all biographies of Sir Walter dutifully begin, with a dissertation on 'parentage' – the webs of kinship that extend backwards to heroic border chieftains of the middle ages and laterally into powerful modern patrons like the ducal Scotts of Buccleuch. As Scott forages tirelessly into his remote lineage, the reader is dragged headlong through thickets of homonymic ancestors. The mind swims as Walter Scott – the son of Walter Scott – tells us that 'my father's grandfather was Walter Scott, well known in Teviotdale by the surname of *Beardie*. He was the second son of Walter Scott, first Laird of Raeburn, who was the third son of Sir William Scott, and the grandson of Walter Scott, commonly called *Auld Wat*, of Harden' (Hew. 2).

As he tells us, 'Beardie' (1653?–1729) was one of Walter Scott's favourite Walter Scotts. The old warrior's bewhiskered visage occupied a place of honour on the study wall in Scott's home of Abbotsford, looking down on his descendant's mild feats of penmanship. Beardie was a fierce Jacobite and had his nickname from a rash vow in 1688 never to shave until the House of Stuart was restored to the British throne. The 1715 rebellion ruined him and nearly cost him his head. But the hirsute Jacobite held fast. Anne, Duchess of Buccleuch and Monmouth successfully interceded for her kinsman's life. But for her kindness, the poet Walter Scott would never have happened.[2] He repaid the debt with a starring role for Anne Scott as Lady Bountiful in the framing narrative of *The Lay of the Last Minstrel*. In the sixth canto of *Marmion* a jovial pen portrait is given of the hairy old loyalist who 'The banished race of kings revered, And lost his land – but kept his beard.'

The Walter Scott dearest to Walter Scott's heart at all periods of his life was the 'freebooting' chieftain, Auld Wat (?1550–?1629), one of the border heroes of the mythic age before the shrink-wrapping of Scotland in John Knox's grey reforms and the impact of the 1707 Act of Union. He represented that primal freedom which Freud tells us all civilized men yearn to recover. A borderer in the literal sense of straddling the frontier between savagery and civilization, Auld Wat's exploits consisted mainly in murder, wholesale cattle-rustling, doubtless some insignificant rapes, and poaching of the king's game, for which he was nearly branded outlaw. His first wife was Mary Scott, the much-sung 'Flower of Yarrow'.

Auld Wat's son and heir, William, was the occasion of one of Scott's merriest genealogical anecdotes. In his youth, William was wild and undertook a raid on the lands of Sir Gideon Murray of Elibank, Treasurer-Depute of Scotland. He was captured and brought back to the Murray castle to be hanged at leisure. But Lady Murray intervened. They had, she pragmatically reminded her husband, 'three ill-favoured daughters unmarried'. The young man was given the choice of the noose or meikle-mouthed Meg Murray, 'the ugliest woman in the four counties' – a kind of reverse rape in which the man had the option of death or sexual dishonour:

> The lady was so very ugly, that Sir William, the handsomest man of his time, positively refused the honour of her hand. Three days were allowed him to make up his mind; and it was not until he found one end of a rope made fast to his neck, and the other knitted to a sturdy oak bough, that his resolution gave way, and he preferred an ugly wife to the literal noose. It is said, they were afterwards a very happy couple. (*Lett.* 1. 144–5)

Scott loved this (wildly apocryphal) legend, and embroidered on it in various versions during his life.[3] He liked to think that he had inherited something of Meg's 'characteristic feature', a large, rather drooping mouth. He had a cartoon of his ancestor's forced wooing executed for another spot on the wall at Abbotsford.

Scott's biographer Lockhart – who was not romantic by nature – frankly implies that his father-in-law was something of a bore on the subject of pedigree and the derring-do of his Border forebears. Lockhart had evidently heard these tales more often than amused him. But it was the old gentleman's hobby-horse, and must be indulged. And in an astute aside, Lockhart suggests that Scott's mania was a compensation for his being a cripple: 'his physical infirmity was reconciled to him, even dignified, by tracing it back to forefathers who acquired famousness in their own way, in spite of such disadvantages' (Lock. 1. 54). But what after all was this 'famousness'? – so much thuggery glorified. Twentieth-century Scottophiles like Herbert Grierson have been frankly baffled by Sir Walter's infatuation with 'Auld Wat of Harden and other Border champions, whose life, when stripped of feudal glamour, does not really differ essentially from that of the gun-men of Chicago' (HG 4–5).

Whatever else, it is clear that Scott did not – would not – see himself as a respectable lawyer's son, the grandson of a distinguished university professor and of a modestly prosperous sheep-farmer and tacksman. This was not what he understood by 'parentage'. Walter Scott was the product of subtler and more remote mixtures. It was a foible with him (one that Lockhart dutifully repeats) that he looked nothing like his mother and father, he was a 'throwback' to earlier, greater generations of Scotts. Abbotsford, his house, was in one sense the physical embodiment of Scotland; a national history told in stones, armorial relics, old books, and such memorial bric-a-brac as Robert Bruce's skull and Rob Roy's long gun (as likely to be spurious, one guesses, as medieval splinters of the Cross). But at its heart, Abbotsford was a shrine to his family. Scott's house was the House of Scott. In the hall of Abbotsford (the room where he was brought to die) Scott had emblazoned the ceiling with the heraldic devices of every house or clan to whom he could claim familial connection. The lower walls were covered with portraits of heroic forebears and his immediate family. After death, he arranged to have his body laid to rest with pomp in the ruins of Dryburgh Abbey – a (purchased) 'privilege' of his family on his mother's (Swinton) side.

The dynastic backdrop to Scott's death was as insubstantial as a Drury Lane stage set – one of his many powerful fictions. Abbotsford is a wholly synthetic structure. Even its name was an invention of the 'Dunroamin' variety. When in 1811 Scott bought the land on which his baronial residence eventually reared itself, it was occupied by a farm with the unprepossessing (but authentic) name of 'Clarty Hale' – or dirty hole. It was not that Scott invented his romantic ancestries or all the feats of his great namesakes – there are no less than seven notable Walter Scotts, his relatives, entered in the *DNB*. But such connections were meaningless in the nineteenth century, with the replacement of kinship systems by the bureaucratic apparatus of the modern state. Those (mainly Highland) families who remained powers in the land after 1745 did so – like the Countess of Sutherland – by denying obligations of traditional kinship (Smout, 353). They evicted their clansmen by means of legal instruments (provided by the British Parliament) to make way for sheep and the more rapid amassing of personal wealth.

Nor did Scott, as he craved, found a 'line' – the Scotts of Abbotsford. His son and heir, Walter, outgrew some modest gambling vices to become a respectable middle-ranking officer in the peacetime British army before dying prematurely and childless in 1847 – following what seems to have been a notably unsuccessful tiger hunt in India. Lieutenant-Colonel Scott did not make the *DNB*. Scott's second son, Charles, died prematurely and childless in 1841 after an aimless career in the Foreign Office. Scott's line of the family – carried on through his sole married daughter – dissolved into the respectable British middle classes. Scott's son-in-law, principal confidant and biographer, Lockhart, never did the great things expected of him. The House of Scott dies with Sir Walter (1771–1832), swallowed up in the septs of Lockhart, Hope and Maxwell. There was nothing shameful; simply a decent petering out. Abbotsford remains, a literary shrine administered by trustees.

The mythic genealogy that Scott drew from his antiquarian research descends from the outlaw to the lawyer: from the reiver Auld Wat expropriating his neighbour's cattle by force of arm to the scrivener Walter Scott *père*, Writer to the Signet, dutifully legalizing the return of Jacobite estates and property after the 1784 amnesty and enriching himself in the process. Scott accepted the circumstance that he lived in a lawful world; was indeed himself a lawyer. A 'son-in-law' (another lawyer) was to be his memorialist, not a son in blood. The law was good to Scott. Without his sinecurial sheriff's stipend and later his far-from-onerous clerkship to the Court of Session he could never have indulged his early literary aspirations. But for all its usefulness, the professional respectability of the wig and pen chafed him. Ancestral Walter Scotts had lived realer lives. He complains in 1808 that his life has had no events, merely 'circumstance'. He was afflicted with an infuriating sense of having missed history, of having arrived too late on the Scottish scene.

Perhaps the only consolation in the great crash that Scott's fortunes suffered in 1826 was that its unimaginable awfulness released him from legal prudence. By the letter of the law, he could have done what his friends, his lawyer and his own professional instincts advised him to do – namely, declare bankruptcy and compound with his creditors at a few shillings in the pound. Or he might have accepted the generous loans which admirers offered. Famously, Sir Walter Scott was in his darkest hour not prudent but chivalric. His debts, he declared, should be debts of honour; he would pay them in full – every last penny and unaided. Scott reacted to his predicament with the vaunt of a border chieftain facing impossible odds – 'Time and this hand . . . we two against the world' – magnificent, but hardly the act of a lawyer.

The bankruptcy and the heroic clearing of his debts is arguably the one 'event' of Scott's life; the only occasion when he transcended circumstance and historical chronology to become something more than a passed-over lawyer who wrote bestselling novels and concealed the fact under a mask of anonymity. But grand as it was, the crash was only an episode. Carlyle shrewdly observes that Scott seemed to exist somehow 'parallel' to his real self. This alienation can plausibly be linked to Scott's mania with pedigree, his neverending hunt for his true identity in the identity of others. For the genealogist, there is nothing – however 'out of character' – that cannot be explained by reference to a predecessor. It was an ingrained habit in Scott to think in this genealogical way. Lockhart reports his father-in-law gazing at his family portraits as one might explore a mirror:

> Often, when moralizing in his latter days over the doubtful condition of his ultimate fortunes, Sir Walter would point to 'Honest Robin' [i.e. his paternal

grandfather, Robert] and say, 'Blood will out: – my building and planting was but his buying the hunter before he stocked his sheep-walk over again.' 'And yet,' I once heard him say, glancing to the likeness of his own staid calculating father, 'it was a wonder too – for I have a thread of the attorney in me.' (Lock. 5. 444)

He was in this way a genetic plaid, or tartan – every square and line of which could be explained genealogically. But where, in the complex quarterings and many ancestral residues, was the essential Walter Scott?

FAMILY

Genealogical curiosity and pride of family (Scott was possessed of both) can trace the name back to the tenth century, when 'a branch of the Scots, a Galwegian clan, settled in the county of Peebles' (Rog. x). Uchtred Fitz-Scott, or Filius Scott, found favour at the court of King David I in the 1120s, and from this date the family was 'gentle' and bobs in and out of various chronicles over the centuries. Some main strands, named in the Lowland manner after their estates, predominate – the Scotts of Harden, of Raeburn and, grandest of all, of Buccleuch.

We can start with grandparents. Male Scotts has an unhappy habit of rebelling against their fathers and the faiths of their fathers. Robert Scott (1699–1775), Walter's paternal grandfather and a second son, was sent to sea by the redoubtable Beardie. But young Robert was wrecked on his first (rather modest) voyage, near Dundee, and refused to set sail ever again. Beardie – whose own rebellions did not render him tolerant of rebellion in his sons – was infuriated. He refused any further help to Robert who 'turned Whig on the spot, and fairly abjured his father's politics and . . . poverty'.[4] Disowned by his father, the young man turned to patrons. One of the 'chiefs' of the family, Scott of Harden, gave the newly respectable young Whig the lease of a farm at Sandy Knowe, some thirty miles from Edin-burgh, in the 'South country' by the ruined fort of Smailholm. Here he might raise sheep and by industry make himself a yeoman farmer – a tacksman. Unless and until he owned land, he was cut off from higher social rungs. He reportedly started his farming career without any capital whatsoever, but a deferential shepherd called Hogg 'out of respect for his family' loaned Robert his life savings of some thirty pounds. Instead of buying a flock, Robert blew this retainer's nest-egg on a 'mettled hunter' (Hew. 4). The bargain was irretrievable. Master and shepherd returned sheepless from the fair to Sandy Knowe. As Scott records, 'In the course of a few days however, my grandfather who was one of the best horsemen of his time attended John Scott of Harden's hounds on this same horse, and displayed him to such advantage that he sold him for double the original price' (Hew. 4).

Having had his fling, Robert was extremely cautious. On the proceeds of his horse trade, the Sandy Knowe farm was stocked. Robert went on to prosper in the droving business (the driving of cattle from the Highlands to the northern counties of England) and by selling produce locally to the expanding city of Edinburgh. Farmers like to marry early and Robert chose for his wife Barbara Haliburton, second daughter of Thomas Haliburton of Newmains. They married in 1728. She was twenty-two years old (he six years older) and from a landed family. It was a good and prudent match. At the time of the wedding, Robert was described as a 'tacksman [lessee] of Sandy Knowe'. She doubtless added to Robert's financial well-being. Marriage was very much a man's market in this unsettled period and bargains could be driven by likely-looking husbands. Of Haliburton's six daughters four died spinsters.

In the healthy environs of Smailholm, the Robert Scotts had eight surviving children (four sons, four daughters), of whom the eldest, Walter, was born in May 1729, a bare ten months after his parents' marriage. After his brief school education, Walter did not take over the farm – indeed none of the legitimate sons did. It is clear that Robert wished to lift his branch of the family above the modest point he himself had reached. The hope, of course, was that eventually the Sandy Knowe Scotts might be landed, not tenants. City money was needed for the acquisition of land. Young Walter, as the hope of the Scotts, was duly sent off to Edinburgh where he applied himself to the law. It was a shrewd move on Robert's part. A career in law qualified the young man for Buccleuch patronage. The law as a profession was at once prestigious (much more so than school teaching, or the ministry) and open to all talents. It had rungs which extended from the lowest scrivener to the President of the Court of Session.

Did young Walter Scott aspire to reach the highest level? Even if he did not, a range of good careers were available in law, fitting all varieties of intelligence and character. Only advocates (equivalent to English barristers) could plead in Edinburgh's supreme civil court (the Court of Session). Theirs was the more honorific branch. But advocacy required money, a university training, contacts, and – once qualified – superior powers of eloquence and public address. For those who preferred the pen to the wig there was a distinguished legal corporation of solicitors called Writers to the Signet. They represented the highest rung of solicitorship, and the title carried with it the privilege of appearing (though not of pleading) in the Court of Session. In standing Writers to the Signet were below advocates, but not as far divided as English solicitors from barristers. Their training – by apprenticeship – was less costly than that of advocates and they could buy into partnerships so as to prosper early in their careers. It was as a WS that Walter was apprenticed.

Robert supported his son through his years of apprenticeship, and afterwards bought him a partnership with a 'respectable solicitor' called George Chalmers. (Robert may have sacrificed all chance of ever owning a farm of his own to do so.) Walter was steady and rose to the rank of Writer to the Signet in 1755, aged twenty-five. He had powerful family connections. Walter Scott WS was well set to make a fortune – but didn't. He was undeniably comfortable in his later career, but never rich. By 1774 (after twenty years living in poky Old Town tenements) he could afford to buy for himself a spacious house (which also contained his business office) in George Square, and at the same period he had some £5,500 to offer for a piece of land around the ruins of Dryburgh Abbey (he was outbid; HG 7). He was prosperous enough to set his older sons on a higher rung than his own had been. But nevertheless, Walter Scott WS never made the pots of money that his father, Robert Scott, had reasonably hoped for.

Scott dwells in the 1808 section of his *Memoir* on the perverse quirks in his father's character, a character which 'in some degree unfitted him as a lawyer'. If we believe Scott, his father was unfitted for most roles in life, including fatherhood. 'Uncle Toby', Scott remarks, 'could not have conducted himself with more simplicity than my father.' Walter Scott WS allowed clients to rob him. He became unprofessionally sympathetic with them. And he neglected to keep records, which meant uncollected fees. Walter Scott WS reserved his scrupulosity for religious affairs. His accounts with Heaven were kept very straight. His domestic character was dourly Knoxian–Calvinistic, undemonstrative, and self-punitively abstemious. One anecdote recalls that if a diner at his table commented approvingly on the richness of the broth, Walter Scott WS would promptly dilute his bowl with water. He reportedly lost at least one important client (a farmer from Haddington) by refusing to talk business on a Sunday. Sabbaths in the Scott household were 'days of penance', dreary with long domestic readings from holy text and prayer. The father of the house was not, on Sunday or any other day, a reader of novels.

Viewed in terms of the social demands of his profession, Walter Scott WS had a hard family burden imposed on him. Lawyers were the elite of Edinburgh society, but the majority of them started professional life with advantages denied the farmer's boy from Sandy Knowe. Of the Writers to the Signet who qualified between 1750 and 1789, the bulk were from landowning families (41) and lawyer families (20). Only three – Walter Scott among them – had fathers who were humble tenant farmers (Smout, 375). The top echelon of lawyers in Edinburgh had been educated at the University, had travelled or studied abroad and moved freely among the many clubs and societies that flourished in the city. Walter Scott WS had none of this cultural breadth. There were no books in his father's house, other than the Bible and some volumes of verse for the girls. By the standards of the day and his profession he was a narrow, hidebound, limited man. It was his duty to provide a foundation for future generations; this was the extent to which he might rise.

Walter Scott duly married in April 1758 – aged a prudent twenty-nine years. He was by now four years set up in his profession and could afford a family. His bride was carefully chosen to advance an Edinburgh lawyer's career. She was Anne Rutherford, the eldest daughter of Dr John

Rutherford. They brought different things to the union. Walter was 'uncommonly handsome' (Hew. 6). As Lockhart notes, Anne was 'short of stature, and by no means comely, at least after the days of her early youth' (Lock. 1. 66). At twenty-six she was past that reputed period of comeliness. Presumably the dowry was the greater. There were other inducements. Anne on her maternal side was related to the powerful Swinton family which 'produced many distinguished warriors during the middle ages and which for antiquity and honourable alliances [might] rank with any in Britain' (Hew. 8). Walter Scott had married even better than his father. The marriage agreement, 25 April 1758, describes Walter as 'the eldest lawful son' (Rog. xlvi) of Robert Scott. Unless this is a neutral legalism, it is possible that Robert had a natural son older than Walter. A bastard would not have entirely surprising, given Robert's love of hunting, his jockey hat and his generally 'fast' character in his youth.

John Rutherford, Walter Scott WS's new father-in-law, was far more impressive than Robert Scott, the Sandy Knowe tacksman. Rutherford was born a younger son in 1695. After graduating from the University of Edinburgh, he took a degree at Rheims in 1719 and studied at Leyden under Boerhaave, the greatest authority on the new science of clinical medicine. Rutherford returned to Edinburgh, where he proposed the setting up of a school of medicine, attached to the university. This came about in 1726 and he was appointed professor. He held the post until 1765, living on in retirement until his eighty-fourth year. Rutherford married twice. Scott's mother Anne was the only surviving child of his first marriage, in 1731, to Jean Swinton.

Walter Scott's marriage was good for his long-term family fortunes but probably slightly uncomfortable for himself. His wife was more refined than he; she read modern poetry and kept elegant volumes of Shakespeare's plays in her dressing room. Her religion was also more refined – Episcopalian rather than Presbyterian. In death, the Scotts were divided. He was buried in Greyfriars (a few yards from where the National Covenant had been signed in 1638); she was buried in St John's Chapel, at the fashionable West End of Princes Street. During young Walter's upbringing there seem to have been two regimes in the family home in George Square. The father loomed over dreary Presbyterian Sundays and daily prayers. The mother encouraged the children in amateur theatricals. The father liked to lock himself away and read works of Calvinist theology. His uncle once found young Walter (aged seven) reading *Tristram Shandy* – a book which must have come from Mrs Scott's private library. The cultural friction between the parents was hardly Lawrentian, but Walter bore marks of the division through life.

Walter Scott's relationship with his father lasted twenty-eight years and went through many phases. But dominating all else was the awareness that he was not an important child. Never during his father's life did he outgrow this sense of inferiority. Much of it focused on his relationships with his male siblings. Robert – the oldest boy, and the hope of the family – did not, like his brothers, attend the High School, but was removed to a 'superior boarding school'. Unlike young Walter he had the freedom to pick his profession. When he chose a career at sea – inspired allegedly by John Paul Jones's daring dash up the Forth in 1779 – Mrs Scott actually employed a sea-captain to come and tell him blood-curdling tales. With youth's perversity, Robert was excited rather than terrified by what he heard and insisted on the Navy. John Scott, the other elder brother, had a commission, expensive uniform and accoutrements bought for him for his career in the army. Doubtless he too was consulted about which profession he desired to follow.

Young Walter, by contrast, was a third son. He was set to work in the 'old shop', as a clerk in his father's business with the measly prospect of a Writership to the Signet and a junior partnership ('and son') – if he proved industrious. He cannot have been consulted on the matter of his career. In rebellion against his brothers' fine uniforms he affected an ostentatious shabbiness in dress as a young man. His last quarrel with his father (who was paralysed by a series of strokes in the late 1790s) concerned the arrangements for his marriage, at the age of twenty-seven, with Charlotte Charpentier. The father declined to be generous, giving as his reason that he wanted to purchase a majority and some land for John. Over the years, Scott must have experienced thousands of such slights.

Walter was the ninth child to arrive, at a time when five of his siblings had already moved on to the churchyard. Another died when he was five months old. His mother at the time of his birth was thirty-nine, his father forty-two, and both of them well past any extravagant feeling at the arrival (or departure) of little strangers. The child's sense of unimportance was increased by the Scotts' parsimony in the matter of Christian names, which were passed on from the dead to the living. There were three Roberts, two Annes, two Johns. Walter was, of course, the name of names for a Scott. But it had earlier been bestowed on a sibling, who was born and died in 1766.

Inherited names are one thing; second-hand names another. And then there was the mystery of the birthdate. Extraordinarily, Walter Scott seems not to have been entirely sure of the year of his birth (Clark, 1–7). In his autobiographical fragment he declares offhandedly, 'I was born, as I believe, on the 15 August 1771.'[5] There is evidence (although not overwhelming) that he may have been born in 1770. In 1808, when he wrote this section of the *Memoir*, his mother was still alive and sharp-witted. But she presumably had forgotten the detail. The vagueness is symptomatic. There were so many births, so many deaths in the household. Scott writes in one place that he 'believes' (Hew. 8) that his parents had 'no fewer than twelve children', in another that they had thirteen (which seems the truer figure). Baptism was a perfunctory private ceremony carried out at home and no authoritative register of babies' comings and goings was kept. Scott's parents must have been wary of investing too much love in so fragile a thing as a child of their loins. There was no deep warmth between parents and children in the Scott family. After the fashion of the time Mrs Scott did not nurse Walter, and of his first eight years, six were spent away from home.

Scott had complex and – over the years – changeable feelings towards his father. When he penned his portrait in the autobiographical fragment of 1808 he was plainly vexed and out of temper. Walter Scott WS had died in 1799, aged seventy. He had lingered in his final illness, and been tyranically peevish to his daughter Anne, driving her to a premature death shortly after his. (Oddly, his son was to do the same with his *own* daughter Anne, thirty years later).[6] He had left his legal affairs in disorder. The trust he left behind him took some fifteen years to untangle – an extraordinary mess for a successful Edinburgh solicitor to have perpetrated.

Writing in 1808, Scott portrays his father as a passive, neurotically withdrawn man. His complexion had been pale and bloodless; his habitual expression blank; his garb presbyterian black with snowy white ruffles. Walter Scott WS was everything that the young Scott wanted *not* to be. He was neurasthenic and stolid by nature. It was not his choice, presumably, to be a lawyer. But once the decision was made for him, he stuck to it like a limpet.

Fathers in Scott's narratives present a variety of characters – most of them negative. Richard Waverley is culpably indifferent, and leaves the bringing up of his son to his brother. In *Rob Roy* the father is a tyrant. In *Harold the Dauntless*, the excessively religious ('priest-led') Witikind disowns his son. The most friendly portrait, as biographers note, is in *Redgauntlet*. One could extend the list, but the variety of father-figures is itself indicative. It seems clear that for all the severity of his religious views, Walter Scott WS lacked any great power of personality. None of his sons took after him – even in the forms of religion. Robert became a sailor, a quarreller, and (as Herbert Grierson guesses) drank himself to death. John, after a career in the army, devoted himself to whist ('gambling') and drink. Of their younger brothers, Daniel was a wastrel and a drinker, while Tom was lucky not to end up in prison for embezzlement.

Uncharismatic as his father was, Scott never completely escaped the burden of real and imagined paternal disapprovals – something that went back to the grim Sundays of his early childhood. In all externals, Scott fashioned his adult personality by straight opposition to him. His father was a Calvinist; he would be Episcopalian. His father was a Whig – Scott would be a Tory. His father was a Writer to the Signet, Scott would be a writer of lays and novels. His father yearned back to the days of Knox, he would celebrate the dissolute era of James V. His father built for himself an austerely classical New Town house, Scott would erect a Gothic castle. At any number of points in his life, one can see Walter Scott defining himself by willed difference from Walter Scott WS. And yet – as he confessed – there remained in him an ineradicable thread of the attorney.

Walter Scott, his parents' ninth child and seventh son, was born in a tenement at College Wynd, off the Cowgate in Edinburgh, on 15 August

1771 (as he believed). The Scotts had begun their married life in 1758 further down the High Street hill, at Anchor Close. They remained in this 'dirty narrow alley' until 1767–8. College Wynd (wynds being narrow alleys that descended steeply) was less dirty than most, however, and the Scotts' flat was on the desirable third floor. Their wynd was also the main access to the old buildings of the College of Edinburgh. Students must have been in and out all the time and many professors lived in the Scotts' tenement. One of their near neighbours (known to them socially through the Rutherford connection) was Joseph Black, the world-famous chemist.

Although picturesque, the Old Town of the eighteenth century – with its legendary warning cry of 'Gardey Loo!' – was famously insanitary. John Buchan's nose twitches eloquently in imagining what life in College Wynd must have been like in 1771: 'The house stood in the corner of a small court, the flats were reached by a foul common stair, and the narrow windows looked out upon wynds where refuse rotted in heaps, and pigs roamed as in a farmyard, and well-born children played barefoot in the gutters' (JB 24). In the off-street closes and wynds, heaps of human dung lay uncollected for days. The Scotts' domestic sanitation would have been supplied by a sand-closet by the front door and by water brought up by servants and watermen from a common pump. By the time it reached the third floor it was a precious commodity.

Walter Scott WS has been criticized – not least by his son – as an infanticide for presuming to raise a family in this midden. But Edinburgh's explosive growth in the 1750–80 period was a direct consequence of the compactness of its parts. Some 60,000 people were crammed into the core of the Old Town. Within two hundred yards of where Walter Scott WS lived were the Court of Session, the College, the High Kirk of St Giles, the Tron Kirk, the Castle, Holyrood House and some of the worst slums in Europe.

It was too compressed to last and Edinburgh soon broke up into a more rationally segmented city. In the 1770s, the Town Council had just embarked on a huge speculative building boom, whose most dramatic sign was the draining of the Nor Loch and the emerging of the New Town across its dried-out bed. Like others of his professional class, Walter Scott WS would in 1774 'flit' from his Old Town flat for something more suburban and salubrious on the south side of the city. It was his childrens' bad luck that half-a-dozen of them arrived just too early to benefit from the bourgeois diaspora from Old to New Town.

College Wynd did its best to kill young Walter. As he records:

I was an uncommonly healthy child [he means by comparison with his dead siblings] but had nearly died in consequence of my first nurse being ill of a consumption, a circumstance which she chose to conceal, though to do so was murder to both herself and me. She went privately to consult Dr Black, the celebrated professor of chemistry, who put my father on his guard. The woman was dismissed, and I was consigned to a healthy peasant. (Lock. 1. 12)

It's a telling example of how democratic the city was; in Edinburgh a wet nurse might consult one of the premier medical authorities in Europe. But it is also an example of bourgeois solidarity. Black's primary allegiance was not to his suffering patient (who lost her post and was thus hastened to a wretched death) but to his fellow professional, Walter Scott WS.

The baby was transferred to the nipple of the above 'healthy peasant' (Scott kept in touch with her until her death some forty years later). Young Walter continued healthy until he was 'about eighteen months old' when a three-day teething fever, as it was diagnosed, kept him in bed. On his recovery, while he was being bathed, it was discovered that he had lost the power of his right leg. Scott never knew what had afflicted him – 'infantile paralysis'. (During his life, most of his contemporaries believed that he had been dropped by a careless nurse as a baby.) A battery of clinical and folk-medicine remedies were applied to what was already a hopeless case. The baby boy was blistered, dosed and pummelled in the vain hope of reviving his limb. He would be badly lamed – though not wholly crippled – for the rest of his life. Helpless as he was to cure his grandson, Dr Rutherford gave the sound advice that the lad should be removed to his other grand-parents at Sandy Knowe, to recuperate in the countryside's 'free air and liberty', some thirty miles from the city. His mother was pregnant again, and could not cope with a sickly child. He should go to the country to get better or die.

SANDY KNOWE

Scott must have gone to his grandfather's farm at Sandy Knowe in spring 1773, aged a little over a year-and-a-half and still unconscious of his where-abouts. His anecdotes about his preconscious self all stress his narrow escapes from death – whether in the form of tubercular wet nurses or the unnameable diseases swirling through fetid College Wynd. He could have died, and never have known he lived. His stay at Sandy Knowe began with another near-run thing. The maid sent by Mrs Walter Scott to accompany the baby ('that I might be no inconvenience') had been seduced in Edinburgh. This girl contracted a secret hatred of young Walter 'as the cause of her being detained at Sandy Knowe'. It is likely that she was pregnant, or feared she was, and had a hysterical phobia about babies. In her 'delirious affection' she carried Wattie up to the crags which rose dramatically from the farm at their foot to the old ruined keep at their crest, 'meaning, under a strong temptation of the Devil, to cut my throat with her scissors and bury me in the moss'. She later confided her homi-cidal urges to the Sandy Knowe housekeeper. 'She was dismissed of course', Scott coldly notes, 'and I have heard became afterwards a lunatic' ('after-wards' is a nice touch). It's a powerful story, but one should note that Scott added it to his *Memoir* in 1826; it may be fictional spice.

'Wattie' (as he was fondly called) remained at Sandy Knowe until January 1775 – from the age of eighteen months to three-and-a-half. He soon recovered his health. But it remained convenient for his parents to keep him in the country. They were in the throes of moving into their grand new establishment at 25 George Square. In addition, Mrs Scott had new and more durable babies to worry about. In all this turmoil, it was a help not to have to worry about a limping toddler like Walter.

It was at Sandy Knowe that the boy had his 'first consciousness of existence', which he recalls humorously in his autobiography:

> Among the odd remedies recurred to, to aid my lameness, some one had recommended that so often as a sheep was killed for the use of the family, I should be stripped and swathed up in the skin, warm as it was flayed from the carcase of the animal. In this tartar-like habiliment I well remember lying upon the floor of the little parlour in the farm-house, while my grandfather a venerable old man with white hair, used every excitement to make me crawl. (Hew. 12)

It was as good a remedy as any for the nerve-dead leg, and kinder than blistering and cupping. Kindness in fact was all around the child during these two years. He was a general favourite in and out of the farm house, and systematically spoiled. The young female ewe-milkers 'delighted . . . to carry him about on their backs among the crags.' The formidable cow-bailie 'Auld Sandy Ormistoun' would also carry the bairn on his shoulders, as he went about his foreman's work. Among this general amity Scott even claimed to have 'a fellowship . . . with the sheep and lambs'.

Indoors he was similarly indulged. He was an only child among old people (Robert and Anne Scott were in their seventies; his two maiden aunts, Jane and Mary, were forty and thirty-six respectively in 1773). Wattie was treated with extraordinary gentleness and each babyish accomplishment was hailed as a prodigious advance. He was taught to walk by his shrewdly sensible grandfather, who would take him out on fine days to the crags and rocks where the sheep were grazing and lay him in the grass: 'The impatience of a child soon inclined me to struggle with my infirmity, and I began by degrees to stand, to walk and to run' (Hew. 15). Skilled in the making of crooks, the old sheep-farmer fashioned a crutch-cum-staff for his grandson which served him until the weakened right leg could bear his weight. Infantile paralysis responds well to physiotherapy and it is likely that the activity restored more of his leg's function than had he been cooped up in an Edinburgh town house. Everyone encouraged the child to talk, which he did incessantly. His upbringing was taken in hand by his aunt, Janet Scott. 'Aunt Jennie' had a temper, but over the next six years she was Wattie's foster mother and first teacher. (She was born in 1733 and he was the only child she would be in a position to mother.) Before he could master the letters himself, she would read aloud to him during the evening or on tedious winter days from 'two or three old books which lay in the window seat', for the women of the family. Among the boy's favourites was

Ramsay's *Tea-table Miscellany*, with its collection of old Scottish ballads. As Scott remenbers, his aunt

> used to read these works to me with admirable patience, until I could repeat long passages by heart. The ballad of Hardyknute I was early master of to the great annoyance of *almost* our only visitor, the worthy clergyman of the parish, Dr Duncan, who had not patience to have a sober chat interrupted by my shouting forth this ditty. Methinks I now see his tall thin emaciated figure, his legs cased in clasped gambadoes, and his face of a length that would have rivalled the Knight of Lamancha's, and hear him exclaiming, 'One may as well speak in the mouth of a cannon as where that child is.' (Hew. 13–4)

It's a comical and revealing scene. Walter was clearly allowed to interrupt the minister – a dignitary in the little world of Sandy Knowe – by his fond aunt and grandparents. The boy's precocity was not to be suppressed (as it could easily have been with a cuff round the ear and a command to be seen and not heard) even for the cloth. One can't believe that the infantile cannonade would have been suffered at College Wynd.

Sandy Knowe probably had no more books than other small farms in the Borders. And of this library, probably only one text, the Bible, was much thumbed. But, in compensation, there was a rich oral culture. Wattie 'imbibed' songs and tales of the Jacobites. During the evenings in the parlour – literally a talking-place – his grandparents would tell tales handed down to them years before. The boy's juvenile partiality for the House of Stuart was fanned by 'stories told in my hearing of the cruelties exercised in the executions at Carlisle and in the highlands, after the battle of Culloden. One or two of our own distant relations [i.e. Campbells] had fallen on that occasion and I remember detesting the name of Cumberland with more than infant hatred' (Hew. 13). His grandfather had lived through the anxious days of 1745, and could even remember the '15, when his father, Beardie, had come to grief.

Wattie's grandmother, 'in whose youth the old border depredations were matter of recent tradition used to tell me many a tale of Wat of Harden, Wight Willie of Aikwood, Jamie Tellfer of the fair Dodhead, and other heroes' (Hew. 13). The boy learned the history and lore of the landscape around the farm, in which 'every field has its battle and every rivulet its song.' His own family lore was intermixed with historical legend. He actually learned to read from 'a rhyming chronicle history of his own family' (EJ 15).

In January 1775 Robert Scott died, aged seventy-six. Wattie was only three-and-a-half at the time but he told Lockhart that 'he distinctly remembered the writing and sealing of the funeral letters, and all the ceremonial of the melancholy procession as it left Sandy Knowe' (Lock. 1. 72). It was a difficult period for his grandmother (hale as she was) and for his aunt. Robert was a lessee, not a landowner, and decisions had to be made. The old lady determined to continue running the farm, with the assistance of her son Thomas Scott, a factor at nearby Crailing.

In the circumstances, young Walter was best out of the way, at least for a few months. He was bundled back to Edinburgh. The homeward journey must have been a tense eight hours. In effect, he was going to meet his parents and siblings for the first time. He was also seeing Edinburgh for the first time with conscious eyes. No record remains of how the three-and-a-half year old Wattie survived the encounter. His mother was always kind to him (it was apparently arranged that he should sleep in her dressing room at George Square, rather than with his older brothers on the top floor). But Mrs Scott was distracted by the demands of her new house and her newer children. There were now Robert (aged eight), John (six), Anne (three) and Thomas (one), with Daniel (born in 1776) to come. It seems that young Walter found the roughness of his elder brothers (particularly the imperious Robert) and the city-bred servants something of a shock. As he recalled more than once in later life, he could never cross the Meadows (the drained swamp behind George Square) without a pang at seeing the stile where 'a cross child's-maid' had upbraided him with his infirmity 'as she lifted me coarsely and carelessly over the flinty steps which my brothers traversed with shout and bound' (Lock. 1. 84).

His parents were also conscious of the mysteriously defective leg and still hoped that it might be mended. A specialist was consulted who 'advised that the Bath waters might be of some advantage'. The advice indicated, if nothing else, that the Walter Scotts were rising in the world (he was now head of Chalmers' firm). And it is likely that there was no great objection to having Wattie out of the way again. Aunt Jennie (now free of the care of her aged father) was recruited to accompany him, and the couple set off by boat from Leith in the summer of 1775, after only a few weeks stay at George Square.

In Bath the Scotts stayed in lodgings. Wattie 'acquired the rudiments of reading at a day school, kept by an old dame' in the neighbourhood, and his aunt gave him extra lessons at home. They evidently lived a retired life. But, as a highpoint, they were visited by Robert Scott, Wattie's uncle, home on furlough from India. Even at this early stage, his nephew seems to have been a favourite with the Captain who took Walter to his first play, *As You Like It.*

Wattie acquired an English accent at Bath and learned to read very well, but his leg obstinately refused to mend. In the summer of 1776, he returned to George Square for a few weeks. Such stays were 'not happy' (Lock. 1. 74). One problem – at least with his elder brothers – must have been the oddness of his speech; neither the rustic Border burr nor the repugnantly genteel Bath accent can have gone down well, especially with his brother Robert, who was a bully (Scott emphasized this point in his 1826 emendations to the *Memoir*). Mrs Scott had borne another baby son, Daniel, during Walter's year away and had her arms full again.

Wattie returned to Sandy Knowe, 'Thus', he recalls, 'the time whiled away till about my eighth [amended to 'seventh'] year' (Hew. 17). His parents' concern for their boarded-out son seems to have concentrated neurotically, if intermittently, on his leg. Now it was thought that sea-bathing might help. Walter and the long-suffering Aunt Jenny were duly dispatched to Prestonpans, by the Firth of Forth.

Walter and his aunt remained at the little resort for some weeks. There were no children for him to play with and Wattie made two superannuated friends. One was an old half-pay ensign, 'Captain' Dalgetty. Wattie would listen to the veteran's tales of the wars and discuss the progress of the current American rebellion. Dalgetty also conducted his young friend over the field of the Battle of Prestonpans (later to feature in *Waverley*). The other, more influential friendship was with a retired lawyer and friend of his father, George Constable, who was courting the forty-two-year-old Aunt Jennie (she was now presumably known as the inheritrix of her parents' wealth). The gentleman was 'of course very kind to me', Scott recalled in 1826, and 'was the first person who told me about Falstaff and Hotspur, and other persons in Shakespeare' (Lock. 1. 20). Constable was later immortalized as the curious antiquarian, Jonathan Oldbuck.

By November 1777 the boy was again briefly – and again unhappily – at George Square, before returning for a last spell to Sandy Knowe. He was now a prince in the old farm house, and his Uncle Thomas gave his nephew a Shetland pony. On this beast – 'not so large as many a Newfoundland dog' – the boy cantered among the crags and the beast, as much a pet as its young master, would walk into Mistress Scott's house at will. Lockhart suggests that news of his son's horsemanship persuaded Walter Scott WS that some school discipline was in order. Wattie returned to Edinburgh for good 'probably in early 1778', as Edgar Johnson surmises (EJ 26; correcting Scott's 'about my eighth year' – i.e. 1779).

A number of themes recur in Scott's account of his Edenic, five-year-long interlude at Sandy Knowe. At College Wynd he had been one of many Scott children, most of whom were already dead having made no mark on the world. At Sandy Knowe he was an only child, and his survival, well-being and tuition were paramount concerns. Fresh milk and fresh air helped his physical survival. But as important was the self-worth produced by his grandparents' and aunt's attentions. His parents' attention was well-meaning enough, but remote. After he left College Wynd until his eighth year, Wattie spent no more than nine months with his parental family.

A striking feature in Scott's account of his early years is his prodigious and precocious memory. He was evidently conscious of his physical surroundings at an unusually early age. More than this, his memory seems to have been photographic. Lockhart notes, for instance, that Scott never again visited Bath after his fourth year. Yet his memory of the terrifying Abbey Church statues is as sharp as if he had seen them every day of his adult life. Most children do not form coherent stores of memory until five or six; and then only rarely with Scott's sharpness of circumstantial detail. Lockhart records other impressive juvenile and later feats testifying to Scott's 'portentous tenacity of memory' (Lock. 1. 131) and adduces it as evidence of an almost magical power of mind, proof that Scott was indeed, as his contemporaries knew him, a 'Wizard of the North'.

Some of the anecdotes celebrating Scott's memory are demonstrably false, exaggerated or of dubious authenticity. The much repeated episode of Scott in Malta, a few months before his death, mechanically reproducing page after page of the Abbé Vertot's *Knights of Malta* which he had read fifty years before, has been shown to be an invention.[7] More plausible are the frequent accounts of Scott's being able to memorize – on only one hearing – a ballad. But it is likely this was a learned skill. There remains a close account of Scott gathering a ballad ('Auld Maitland') from James Hogg's mother, and it is clear that in such circumstances he could not make his source repeat, or slow down. He had to store the text in his mind. His companion on the Liddesdale raids in the 1790s, Robert Shortreed, recalls that Scott used a peculiar mnemonic system, involving notches on twigs, for memoranda.[8] It would seem that Scott, rather like repertory actors who can memorize a part on one reading, trained his memory to a high pitch of efficiency.

This capaciousness and readiness of memory can be traced to the culture of Sandy Knowe. As an author Scott inhabited the border between oral and literary narrative. His novels characteristically define themselves as things told verbally by an old to a younger person, who writes them down ('Tales of my Landlord', for example). Scott was fixated on oral tale-tellers, whether bard, minstrel, grandfather, balladeer, Wandering Willie, or merely some garrulous Edinburgh burger. Scott's powers of memory and orality are plausibly linked. He saw himself as both an aural–oral and a literary artist. And in the former character, memory was a main element of his art. The minstrel (as in *The Lay of the Last Minstrel*) has his poem not as a text, or prompt copy, but in his head. He learns through hearing, and performs from memory – and is free to improve what he remembers, or to fill in where memory fails. Scott's seed-time at Sandy Knowe confirmed this sense, which he later cultivated, of being a novelist of the nineteenth century drawing on the creative resources of a balladeer of the seventeenth.

In his essay on Lockhart's *Life*, Carlyle notes dismissively that until 'the age of thirty, Scott's life has nothing in it decisively pointing towards Literature, or indeed towards distinction of any kind.' There is some truth in this. After he returned to Edinburgh at his father's summons in 1778, Walter became an ordinary, bright but not brilliant schoolboy and apprentice lawyer. But during his Sandy Knowe period, he seems to have been indeed brilliant. There is a vignette of the boy which supposedly occurred during his brief stay at George Square in November 1777, following his return from Prestonpans. It is recorded by Mrs Cockburn, herself an amateur poetess and a relative of Anne Scott. In a letter home to her minister in Galashiels, she wrote:

I last night supped in Mr Walter Scott's. He has the most extraordinary genius of a boy I ever saw. He was reading a poem [William Falconer's *The Shipwreck*, 1762] to his mother when I went in. I made him read on; it was the description of a shipwreck. His passion rose with the storm. He lifted his eyes and hands. 'There's the mast gone,' says he; 'crash it goes! – they will all perish!'[9]

After his agitation, he turns to me. 'That is too melancholy,' says he; 'I had
better read you something more amusing.' I preferred a little chat, and asked
his opinion of Milton and other books he was reading, which he gave me
wonderfully. One of his observations was, 'How strange it is that Adam, just
new come into the world, should know everything – that must be the poet's
fancy' . . . Pray, what age do you suppose this boy to be? Name it now, before
I tell you. Why, twelve or fourteen. No such thing; he is not quite six years old.
(Lock. 1. 75)

He was, as Lockhart asserts, a little over six, but still small for his age. This
attractive story has all the signs of having been embroidered by Lockhart so
as to counter the modesty of Scott's own account of his juvenile literary
attainments in the *Memoir*. The description of the poetry-loving Walter
seems more properly to belong to a couple of years later. As the *Memoir*
records, it was not until he returned to Edinburgh in late 1778 that his
mother had him read to her Pope's translation of Homer, which was – as he
recalls – the first 'real' poetry he had encountered. Before that date, he had
read nothing 'except a few traditionary ballads and the songs in Allan
Ramsay's *Evergreen*' (Hew. 19). It is hard to square this with the six-year-old's
intelligent discourse on Milton, and his familiarity with a fashionable modern poet like Falconer. The choice of *The Shipwreck* itself suggests that this
episode may date from the period after September 1779, when Mrs Scott
was trying to frighten her elder son Robert from going to sea.

CONFINEMENT

From Prestonpans, Scott was 'transported' (his word) back to George
Square, which was to be his domestic base for the next eleven years. It was
now autumn 1778 (by the best guess we can make) and he was seven years
old. Scott remembers that he 'internally experienced . . . agony' at this
homecoming. He was a lame, undersized boy of solitary disposition and
quaint mannerisms. Both countrified and precocious, he was cast as the
family misfit. Order at 25 George Square was imposed formally by patriarchal authority, particularly on Sundays. The Scotts observed a Presbyterian
sabbath, dominated by Walter Scott's prohibitions, his sermons, catechiz-
ing, cold food, uplifting reading, and extended family prayers. Informally,
the younger children were kept in line by Robert Scott's bullying. He
'kicked and cuffed without mercy' Scott recalled bitterly (Hew. 9).
  'I found much consolation during this period of mortification', Scott
recalls, 'in the partiality of my mother. She joined to a light and happy
temper of mind a strong turn to study poetry and works of the imagination.
She was sincerely devout but her religion was, as became her sex, of a cast
less austere than my father's' (Hew. 19). He took root in this cranny
between his parents' degrees of piety, playing on his mother's cultural
pretensions and on his physical handicap to become a favourite and pam-

pered. On weekdays his 'hours of leisure were usually spent in reading aloud to my mother Pope's translation of Homer.' This, as he recalls, was the first real poetry he had encountered.

Exercises in Popeian translation were prominent on the syllabus at the High School, and it is possible that Mrs Scott took advice from their George Square neighbour, Mr Adam, the school's admired Rector. The culture of George Square, or at least its maternal aspect, was formed on Enlightenment principles, and put a high premium on cultivation. Walter also found some volumes of Shakespeare in his mother's dressing room, where he slept – kept there, it would seem, away from her husband's gaze. He devoured the books guiltily, and all his life recalled 'the rapture with which I sate up in my shirt reading them by the light of a fire in her apartment until the bustle of the family rising from supper warned me it was time to creep back into my bed where I was supposed to have been safely deposited since nine o'clock' (Hew. 26).

This secrecy (both his mother's and Walter's) was something new and significant in the formation of his literary character. At Sandy Knowe, ballads and tales had been common property, public things to be openly enjoyed and transmitted by the traditional machinery of oral recitation. They were shared by master, mistress, milkmaid and farmhand. Walter would bawl out his 'Hardyknute' for the delectation of assembled company and hang on his grandparents' much-told stories in the evening parlour; the girls who milked the ewes would sing to each other. The few volumes of Scottish ballads were to be found in the living room, for all to dip into, and to be read aloud by the most lettered member of the company to those less able. There was, in short, a common literary culture. Here, at George Square, literary pleasure was private and closeted. Wives had different tastes from husbands; masters from servants; one brother from another. Literature was something for Walter to relish *à deux* with his mother or, as often, by himself, almost furtively.

He was now a quiet boy, when not reciting, and enjoyed the privilege of occupying adult regions of the house on the seen-and-not-heard principle. His character was temporarily that of the mother's pet. When, for example, his uncle Robert – the sea-faring man who had a particular soft spot for Walter – asked him if he would not like to be out of doors, playing with his fellows, he replied, 'No, uncle. You cannot think how ignorant those boys are; I am much happier here reading my book' (HG 13). It was a prig's reply calculated to please adults – who duly enshrined it in family lore. And this, one should remember, was the young lout who a year before rode his pony into his grandmother's kitchen. At this slightly later period, Wattie had graduated from his mother's dressing room and evidently had a bedroom which he shared not with his elder brothers (as would have seemed normal) but with a fifteen-year-old maid called Becky, 'who could look after him if he was ill or suffered from bad dreams at night' (EJ 33). According to Lockhart, Mrs Scott 'dreaded, and deferred as long as she could, the day when he should be exposed to the rude collision of a crowd of boys' (Lock.

1. 78). Other mothers might have worried about his nightly collision with naked pubescent female flesh.

The Scotts were meanwhile in the throes of rapid gentrification. Edinburgh was almost overnight dividing into two cities: one was the central Old Town, the other the New Town to the north and its genteel satellite, south Edinburgh. As Cockburn notes: 'It was the rise of the New Town that obliterated our old peculiarities with the greatest rapidity and effect. It not only changed our scenes and habits of life, but, by mere inundation of modern population, broke up and, as was then thought, formed our prescriptive gentilities' (*Mem.* 29).

As a result of middle-class migration to the urban fringe a whole new style of more spacious life had to be learned. Families like the Walter Scotts – accustomed for generations to the cramped amenities of the Edinburgh flat and the common staircase – now found themselves living in large, airy, well-lighted, three-storied, terraced households of austere beauty. Twenty-five George Square was part of the first phase of Brown's development; the house had Craigmillar stone facings, Adam features, and an especially fine fanlight which is noted in the 1951 Royal Commission survey of Edinburgh's architecture. The George Square project was begun in 1766 and its sixty houses were finished around 1785. The Scotts – who took up residence around 1774 – were early settlers in the square, itself one of the first settlements of the New Town expansion. The family must have experienced something of the thrill of pioneers, and were obliged to master a whole new set of skills. For the first time they had the management of cellars, stables, and live-in servants' quarters (in the double attic top floor). Young Walter could find hidden copies of Shakespeare in his mother's dressing room because she now had a separate dressing room – something that was certainly absent at College Wynd, where bedchambers were probably shuttered recesses during the day.

Household inventories, routines and budgets were correspondingly more complex. George Square had a handsomely laid-out garden in its centre (it was fenced, and entry was by houseowner's key). Sanitation was vastly improved; there was clean water, a decent sand-closet privy and numerous sash windows to allow the movement of air. With meadows and open land to its south, the prevailing winds blew Edinburgh's famous (and deadly) reek away from the Square. The next logical step in the Walter Scotts' gentrification was for him to become a lawyer–laird with the purchase of an estate in the country. To his son's everlasting regret, his father neglected to make this last all-important step.

Arguably this rapid embourgeoisement of his family was the most formative event in Scott's childhood. But he barely mentions it in his autobiographical fragment. His family moved to George Square, he observes in passing, as if it were a neutral fact. Nor, oddly enough, did Scott ever write about the 'great flittin' directly in later life. Young Wattie fitted into the scheme of his parents' gentrification, but he was not central to it. He was not, for one thing, the family heir but third in line. Nor was he robust enough – as his parents must have thought – to carry the family destiny up and onward. That would be the task of his stronger siblings: the boys by professional achievement, the girl – Anne – by good marriage.

However minor a cadet, Wattie must still have the education of a gentleman. Over the year 1778–9, he was prepared for entry to school by a series of private tutors. The High School, for which he was destined, was an educational hothouse and required that entering pupils should be already literate and numerate. Scottish, and more particularly Edinburgh, education was at this period the best to be had in Britain. Scots were themselves inordinately proud of the fact. As T. C. Smout notes, 'It is hard to think of any subject on which Scots were so united as this determination to praise and attribute wonder to the national tradition of education' (Smout, 449).

The High School which Scott attended was not the present classicized structure, which was opened in 1829 by Calton Hill. In the 1770s the school was housed near the present University in a simpler, rather barn-like building. The four classes were huge and were kept in line by choral teaching and drills. There was only the most cursory personal attention. While Scott was at the High School it was – like the city of Edinburgh – in a state of vigorous expansion. There were some 200 pupils in 1760, 500 in 1783, and by 1790, it was estimated to be the largest secondary school in Britain (Smout, 378).

Academically, the High School was run on strictly competitive and egalitarian principles. Classes were organized as 'forms' which were highly fluid and reflected the boys' current intellectual performance or 'place'. Notionally all pupils aspired to be 'top of the form' – or 'dux'. Dunces would sink shamefully to the bottom. Classes remained in the care of the same teacher or form master over a number of academic years. There were four such masters, under the superintendence of a Rector, or headmaster. Usually boys would spend up to four years with a class teacher, then one or two years with the head. A prudent parent would weigh up which of the quartet of teachers would suit his child best. Discipline was a factor; teachers flogged at the High School, some to the degree that – as Henry Cockburn put it – they would have earned transportation as violent criminals in a later age. Mr and Mrs Scott felt strongly that Wattie should be kept well away from William Nicol, a master reckoned to be a good classicist but notoriously savage and sarcastic (Clark, 15). To avoid this ogre, Wattie was jumped into the second class (i.e. second year) in the care of the milder Luke Fraser. He spent only two years under Fraser and thence proceeded to some final polishing up at the scholarly hand of the Rector, Dr Alexander Adam (Clark, 19).

The High School curriculum was obsessively concerned with mastering Latin. Grammar, translations and proses were the boys' principal exercises in all four years, and were the main business of the Rector's top classes. Significantly, the earliest extant example of Scott's literary efforts is a Popeian translation of Etna's eruption from Virgil, preserved by Mrs Scott as 'My Walter's first lines, 1782' (EJ 45). Cicero was the staple author studied. Mathematics and some Greek were also part of the school syllabus. Dr Johnson visited the school in 1773 (shortly before Scott's attendance) and approved of what he found. But he observed that Scottish education – at school and college – was designed to achieve what he termed (unpejoratively) 'mediocrity'; that is, a broader-based curriculum than in England.

It was usual for the school's core curriculum to be supplemented by private lessons, which parents would arrange and pay for themselves. Edinburgh University provided a supply of tutors available by the hour. An impressive range of adjunct subjects was on offer. French, German, geography, drawing, mathematics, the science of fortification (for boys going into the army, or civil engineering) and music were favourites. Young Walter was evidently tutored in all these subjects at various times. For a period around 1782–3 (Clark, 26) Walter Scott WS recruited a live-in tutor for his boys called James Mitchell. Mitchell was a strict Presbyterian, a Whig, and a loyalist. As Scott recalls, he affectionately twitted Mitchell (as he did not dare twit his Presbyterian, Whig, loyalist father) by a schoolboyish ostentation of Jacobite and pro-Cavalier sentiments.

Walter entered the High School in October 1779, aged just eight. It was unfortunate that he skipped the first year (his duller brother John, by contrast, was held back a couple of years). Walter was mentally precocious enough and had evidently been sufficiently crammed by his tutors to handle the academic work of the class. But physically and emotionally the young Scott must have been at a disadvantage to boys a year or more older than himself and constitutionally more robust. Socially, too, he was an outsider; most of his fellows had been together for a year when he joined them and had forged their schoolboy alliances.

Scott goes over his early school experiences in some detail. He was judged to be 'rather behind the class . . . in years and progress' and duly placed at the rear or 'bottom'. He had difficulty in advancing himself from this position. Occasionally he 'glanced like a meteor from one end of the class to another', but his position was generally middling to low: 'I did not make any great figure at the High School or at least any exertions which I made were desultory and little to be depended on' (Hew. 21). The class prizes and duxships went to steadier children, working at their own pace and within their abilities.

Walter Scott had already assumed several characters in his passage through boyhood. At Sandy Knowe he was a bucolic child of nature. He was the infant prodigy during his early visits back to his family at George Square – the frail mother's pet who would rather read a book than play outside. Now, if we believe him, he assumed the role of the robust schoolboy, a champion of the yards. Walking through the High School grounds, forty years later, he reminisced to Lockhart 'that he had scarcely made his first appearance there, before some dispute arising, his opponent remarked that "there was no use to hargle bargle with a cripple."' According to Scott, an older boy proposed that the two 'tinklers' (their voices had not yet broken) should be put to fight tied sitting on a deal board. The cripple reportedly gave as good as he got and went on to win other 'pugilistic trophies [in] such sittings in banco'. Lockhart comments, 'Considering his utter ignorance of fear, the strength of his chest and upper limbs, and that the scientific part of pugilism never flourished in Scotland, I daresay these trophies were not few' (Lock. 1. 84). There are other recollections of Scott risking his life climbing Salisbury Crags and the Castle Rock's 'kittle nine stanes' to impress his fellows and fighting in the savage class wars ('bickers') that the boys of George Square conducted against the oicks of neighbouring Bristo Street. In these battles, the young gents of the Square were encouraged by their elders. As Scott recalls in his 1829 *Waverley* apparatus, 'a lady of distinction' presented them a 'handsome set of colours' under which to fight their class foes. By Scott's account, blood was spilled. As Lockhart surmises, this running himself into danger compensated in part for Scott's (the cripple's) sense of physical inferiority.

Scott would have us believe that he impressed his peers more than his masters. 'I made a brighter figure in the yards than in the class,' he concludes. And his account of his time at the High School is retrospectively imbued with the British schoolboy's traditional philistinism and loathing of the swot. He narrates acts of high-spirited sabotage against teachers' favourites – those whose main reward was the approval of the authorities. Scott's attachment was to the school's champions. He describes himself as the prized tale-teller or 'minstrel' for the chieftains of the yards: 'In the winter play hours when hard exercise was impossible my tales used to assemble an admiring audience round Lucky Brown's [the sweet-seller's] fireside and happy was he that could sit next to the inexhaustible narrator. I was also though often negligent of my own task always ready to assist my friends and hence I had a little party of staunch partizans and adherents, stout of hand and heart, though somewhat dull of head' (Hew. 21).

Scott's account of his schooldays was written in 1810–11, at a buoyant period of his life. He was a bestselling author, a happily (and prosperously) married man. He had apparently overcome all the handicaps of his youth – the physical disability, his patchy education, the endless burden of the lawyer's drudgery which his father had imposed on his boyhood. He was an officer in the Edinburgh Light Horse at a time when Scottish valour in the Napoleonic wars had become legendary. His sense of manly achievement casts a rosy glow over the *Memoir*. What had happened to the little prodigy that Mrs Cockburn describes? the child who had bad dreams and could not sleep alone nor with his rough brothers? the prig who told his Uncle Robert that he had much better things to do than play outside with those same rough boys? His schooldays had their rubs but they were on the whole good fun, we gather from his 1808–11 account. In his journal, eighteen years later, Scott passed a more sober judgement. 'Did I ever pass unhappy years anywhere?' he asks himself: 'None that I remember, save those at the High School, which I thoroughly detested on account of the confinement' (Jrnl. 124–5). He was not a boarder, so confinement here does not mean

physical durance. He refers, presumably, to the never-ending lessons
and 'discipline'.

In his last six months as a schoolboy his health, as he recalls, had
'become rather delicate from rapid growth' (Hew. 24). In June 1783, he was
sent off to stay six months with his favourite aunt Janet at Kelso in the
country, where he might recover from what was evidently a breakdown.
Kelso was 'the most romantic village in Scotland' (EJ 54) and his aunt's
house had a fine location by the churchyard and seven or so acres of
grounds extending down to the Tweed. While he lived with the kind aunt
(now fifty) who had nursed him through most of his early health crises,
Walter attended the village grammar school four hours a day. It was here
that he met the brothers James and John Ballantyne, who were to play
central roles in his later career. The Kelso school was not arduous after the
High School. Walter was far enough ahead of the others to serve as an
usher, teaching the junior classes their lessons. Academically he coasted.
And his course of 'desultory' omnivorous reading continued. In contemplating it, the older Scott adopts a tone of self-castigation:

> If my studies were not under any direction at Edinburgh, in the country it
> may well be imagined they were less so. A respectable subscription library, a
> circulating library of ancient standing and some private bookshelves were
> open to my random perusal and I waded into the stream like a blind man into
> a ford without the power of searching my way unless by groping for it. My
> appetite for books was as ample and indiscriminating as it was indefatigable
> and I since have had too frequently reason to repent that few ever read so
> much, and to so little purpose. (Hew. 27)

Among the much that he read was Percy's *Reliques of Ancient English
Poetry*. Scott remembers first reading the *Reliques* in Edenic surroundings
'beneath, a huge platanas tree in the ruins of what had been intended for
an old fashioned arbour ... The summer day sped onward so fast that
notwithstanding the sharp appetite of thirteen [he was in fact just twelve] I
forgot the hour of dinner, was sought for with anxiety and was still found
entranced in my intellectual banquet' (Hew. 28). During this convalescence, he also read Richardson, Smollett, Fielding, Mackenzie 'and some
other of our best novelists', whose work he had from the local circulating
library. Aunt Jennie was evidently not censorious about her young nephew's
reading.

It was also at this period that Scott claimed to have formed his taste for
Scottish landscape. Kelso has a famously romantic aspect, situated as it is at
a confluence of the Tweed and Teviot rivers. The town is dominated by the
picturesquely ruined abbey. The ruin of Roxburgh Castle is distantly visible.
'From this time,' Scott notes, 'the love of natural beauty more especially
when combined with ancient ruins or remains of our fathers' piety or
splendour, became with me an insatiable passion' (Hew. 29). Lockhart –
who is not without his puncturing shrewdness – makes some rather jaundiced comments about Scott's recollections. Kelso, or at least his aunt's

household, was not quite as idyllic or as extensive as he recalls it to be. Scott was only eleven-and-three-quarters years old in July 1783. The idea that he could have had these essentially adult and precociously romantic responses to landscape is hard to credit.

Scott returned to Edinburgh in November 1783, evidently restored in health. He was duly matriculated at the University. Only twelve and a couple of months, it was an extraordinarily young age for him to go up. His school education had been interrupted and incomplete. He was physically frail, as his protracted convalescence at Kelso indicated. Why, then, was he sent to university in 1783? It is true that in the eighteenth century childhood was a less time-wasting affair than it is now. This was partly a function of life-expectancy. People lived shorter lives and could not linger over education. It was also the case that Scottish undergraduates were then, as now, younger than their English counterparts. Byron was at school until he was eighteen and could write, before he was twenty, a volume of verse called *Hours of Idleness* (1807). There were no such hours of idleness in Scott's education. He was rushed through school and university at the earliest decent age. One assumes it was Walter Scott WS's conscious decision that his son's education should be scrambled in this way.

2

Student and Apprentice (1783–1790)

Walter Scott passed his first period of study at Edinburgh University from late 1783 to mid-1786. Scott enrolled for a degree in Humanities (effectively a classics, logic, moral philosophy tripos). It was a popular option, and he was one of about 500 Humanities undergraduates, about a third of the university's student population. The college functioned in one of its main aspects as a sixth form (as it would now be) for the neighbouring High School. The main difference between the two establishments was in discipline. At school, the masters – aptly named – kept their pupils strictly in line; by corporal punishment if necessary. (Scott was once struck to the ground by one of his more physical teachers.) The College operated on a system of lectures given in English which presupposed voluntary good behaviour by the students and minimal coercion by the lecturers. Good behaviour was not, however, automatic or universal. Scott frankly called his university classes a 'riot', in which seventy-or-so unruly lads paid as much or as little attention as they liked. Scott was of the inattentive party and confessed that as an undergraduate he did not 'relish labour'.

The classics component in Humanities comprised Greek as well as Latin. Walter had evidently missed all tuition in the older classical language in his absences from the High School. He made no attempt to catch up. He scorned the well-meaning offer of assistance from a sheepfarmer's son which, as the grandson of a sheepfarmer, Walter Scott felt was beneath him. Scott became known among his fellows as 'the Greek blockhead'. But for all his self-castigation (all these stories about his doltishness originate with him), one should not leap to conclusions based on today's educational standards. Poor classics scholar as he may have been, Scott seems to have had no difficulty reading Latin in later life.

Scott's studies at university were interrupted during his second session in 1784, when he fell ill[1] and required bed rest and convalescence at Kelso. As a result Walter missed much of the logic and metaphysics taught in his second year, 1784–85. He seems nonetheless to have made a good impression on his philosophy teachers, John Bruce and Dugald Stewart. During his absences for sickness Scott improved his chess, read romances and poetry. And over time he fell further back in his studies, losing even his command of the Greek alphabet. Scott's father, however, seems not to have worried much about his son's classical derelictions. He did, however, think that a future lawyer should be able to understand accounts and Walter was enrolled into a class in mathematics. The teacher was ancient and largely useless.

In March 1786 Scott was apprenticed to his father for five years. He was still only fourteen-and-a-bit. The ever-cautious Walter Scott WS decided that his curiously wayward son should qualify – like himself – as a Writer to the Signet, not as an Advocate. So Scott's formal 'education' came to an end, after a mere seven years, of which around two were lost to illness. He entered the High School at seven, the university at twelve and graduated at fourteen.

Walter Scott at fourteen was not an educational success; at least not by the criteria of the day. His knowledge was too patchy. Scott saw it as a moral fault in himself that he had not benefited from his opportunities and in later life frequently berated himself for his 'desultoriness' as a pupil and student. 'It is with the deepest regret', he writes in his *Memoir*, 'that I recollect in my manhood the opportunities of learning which I neglected in my youth, that through every part of my literary career I have felt pinched and hampered by my own ignorance and that I would at this moment give half the reputation I have had the good fortune to acquire if by doing so I could rest the remaining part upon a sound foundation of learning and science' (Hew. 31).

There are some points to be made against Scott for Scott. The first is that the important decisions about his formal education were taken not by the boy but by the father. Walter Scott WS rushed his son through the forms of a gentleman's education; presumably just so that it could be said that he had done his fatherly duty in this respect. But it was a hopelessly accelerated course of study – more so given young Walter's frequent absences for sickness. There was little chance that the boy could take full advantage of the educational opportunities that flashed by him.

It was true that in eighteenth-century Scotland students often went to university very young. The example of David Hume, who matriculated at twelve-and-a-bit, is often cited. But fourteen was the normal age of Walter's peers (that was the age, for instance, at which Cockburn went to Edinburgh University). And there was nothing in the boy's school performance to warrant his being treated like an infant prodigy and worthier even than David Hume of accelerated progress. He skipped one year at school; two at university. The handicap this imposed can be shown in the career of one of Scott's close friends and contemporaries at the High School, William Rae. Rae was three years older than Scott, but in the same educational cohort. The two young men were subsequently advocates of the same vintage, and both members of the select 'Club', in 1788. They had many tastes in common, and Rae was certainly not the more gifted intellectually. In 1797, Scott and Rae were fellow members of the same volunteer cavalry troop. Able to pace himself, Rae went on to outstrip Scott in his later career. In 1819, he was ahead of Scott in the competition for a vacant judgeship and in fact became Lord Advocate that same year. This was a top position, far above the Clerkship of the Court of Session, where Scott's legal career had stalled. In 1826, when it seemed that Scott might again get his 'baron's gown', Rae was again ahead of him. Of course there were other factors (not least that Rae inherited a title). But it seems nonetheless clear that Scott the lawyer could never make up the three years' difference that separated him from Rae.

Walter Scott WS wanted to get his son's education over with by the time the boy was fifteen, so that he could be apprenticed to the law at the right age. He would have, effectively, the education of a gentleman and the training of an apprentice. Scott would have needed two childhoods (and better health) to fulfil all his father expected of him. His blame against himself in these circumstances is certainly misplaced. In defence of Walter Scott WS, it should be said that the years 1783 – 6 were extremely troubled. In June 1784 there were bread riots in Edinburgh. In such times, a wise father might well want to place his physically disabled son in a 'safe' line of work, as near home as possible. Coincidentally the period immediately after the 1784 disannexation act was golden for Writers to the Signet. The revocation of forfeitures meant vast amounts of the paperwork Walter Scott WS specialized in. Rather than recruit a new clerk to help with this work it may have seemed prudent to indenture his own son, a lad who was unusually deft with his pen.

Even in the seven years of imperfect education that he had, Scott revealed an extraordinary ability to wedge open periods of time in which he effectively educated himself. In some cases solitude was forced on him: as when, for instance, he fell ill. But on other occasions he clearly created his own intellectual spaces and freedoms. 'The chief enjoyment of my [College] holidays', he recalls in the 1829 'General Preface' to *Waverley*, 'was to escape with a chosen friend, who had the same taste with myself, and alternately to recite to each other such wild adventures as we were able to devize' (Lamont, 349). The friend was John Irving, also a lawyer in embryo. The two young men steeped themselves in 'romances of knight errantry' and gothic tales acquired from James Sibbald's Edinburgh Circulating Library. Scott and Irving devoured Spenser together. They learned Italian to the point that they 'could both read it with fluency' and enjoy the poetry of Ariosto, Dante and Matteo Boiardo in the original (EJ 60). Every Saturday they wandered over Salisbury Crags or other nearby hills daydreaming and story-telling. Their weekday evenings must have been occupied by cramming modern languages. If Lockhart is to believed (and it stretches credulity) the fourteen-year-old Walter in the space of a few months, in the intervals of office work, taught himself – in addition to 'fluent' Italian – French well enough to read *Gil Blas* and Spanish well enough to read *Don Quixote*. Throughout later life, as we have seen, this amazing juvenile linguist never ceased castigating himself for incorrigible 'idleness' at this period of his youth. It smacks of one of Lockhart's flights of invention, designed to counteract the modesty of Scott's own account in the *Memoir* of his early intellectual development.

APPRENTICE LAWYER

One of the features of Scott's personality that perplexes modern admirers is his pliability to authority. No poet in his youth had, it seems, less *non serviam*. By allowing himself to be indentured as a WS Scott was – while pleasing his WS father – substantially lowering the rung he might reasonably reach in life. Perplexing too is the young Scott's knee-jerk Toryism (more so as there were robust strands of Whiggism in the Scott family background). But in his true-blue politics Scott was a child of the time. Particularly for a professional man who wanted a share of the good things of life, obedience was in order. Associate yourself with a patriciate (like the Buccleuchs), attach yourself to a patron, was the prudent motto.

The principal dispenser of Scottish patronage was Henry Dundas, subsequently Lord Melville, Pitt the younger's ally and chosen proconsul. Dundas, his family and his Tory satraps throttled any incipient independence and 'managed' Scotland as their fiefdom. A nod from Dundas could promote any loyal lawyer. Henry Cockburn, Scott's Whiggish friend, wryly describes the more than feudal subservience of Edinburgh's professional classes under the 'absolute dictator of Scotland' – also known as 'the uncrowned king of Scotland', and 'Henry the Ninth of Scotland'. 'The pulpit, the bench, the bar, the colleges, the parliamentary elections, the press, the magistracies, the local institutions', Cockburn recalled, 'were so completely at the service of the party in power, that the idea of independence, besides being monstrous and absurd, was suppressed by a feeling of conscious ingratitude' (*Mem.* 86). There was, according to Cockburn, no future in law for a Whig at the end of the eighteenth century. Such a man might get his living, but he would never rise to the top.

The experience of living in an undemocratically 'managed' state during his formative years explains a vein of subservience that runs through even Scott's greatest novels. It mars his most widely read work, *The Heart of Midlothian*. Justice in that novel – the salvation of innocent Effie from execution – is conspicuously not achieved by rebellion. The assault by the citizenry on the Tollbooth produces only riot and the prospect of horrific reprisal by the English authorities. No more is justice achieved by the Edinburgh law court, the institution to which Scott devoted his professional career. Despite a humane judge and sympathetic advocates, no legal instrument or process can save Effie from capital punishment. The law must take its obtuse and bloody course.

What does save Effie is some personal lobbying at court (the Royal court, not the legal) by the Duke of Argyle (i.e. John Campbell, 1678–1743), a particular favourite of Queen Caroline. Argyle – like Dundas – is one of those Scots who manage Scotland on behalf of England. (He was also, distantly, a kinsman of Scott's.) In 1715, General Argyle had been instrumental in putting down Mar's insurrection, thus crushing the Jacobite revolt. He thereafter worked for full implementation of the 1707 Union. He was – when not slaughtering his rebellious countrymen – the kind of paternalistic Scottish landowner Scott most admired and aspired himself to be at Abbotsford. Great narrative prominence is given to Argyle's setting up Effie's father and her sister Jeanie as his tenants on his model estate. Argyle was doubtless a great man and kind to little people like the Deanses. But it does seem wrong that Effie could not have been reprieved by the agency of law, or the heroism of her lover, rather than by a blue-blooded sycophant and a royal prerogative which can benignly flout the law of the land. Viewed dispassionately, Effie is not saved by her sister's heroic pilgrimage, but by the grace and favour of rich, unelected potentates who happen to be charmed by Jeanie's rustic virtue and simplicity. Had Jeanie been afflicted with a wart on her nose, cross eyes, and a rude manner, her sister would have been doomed.

In his youth, Scott's attitude to the profession of law was tinged with a strong cynicism. He saw no more than the labour and clerical chores it represented. And at the end of all that drudgery, he would be a rusty, black-coated pettifogger with ink in his veins like Walter Scott WS or an eccentric old-before-his-time recluse like George Constable WS. To his friends, the young Scott spoke of his profession as more of the 'confinement' he had already suffered at the High School; another prisonhouse. 'A dry and barren wilderness of forms and conveyances' (Lock. 1. 36) stretched before the fifteen-year-old boy.

In his later life, after rising in his profession, Scott came to love the forms of Scottish law passionately and saw them as the embodiment of 'old Scotland'. He bitterly resented such post-1808 reforms as jury trial in civil cases, and the reduction (or abolition) of such dubiously useful posts as his own clerkship to the Court of Session. But for all his affection for the old rituals of Scottish law, Scott seems never to have been much attracted by the grand philosophico-legal dissertations of such great minds as David Hume, Viscount Stair, or Adam Smith. For him the law was primarily an instrument of control: the means by which state authority exerted its will. The legal measure to which he returns most often is the Heritable Jurisdictions Act of 1748. After the Rebellion, England suppressed Scotland not by sowing its fields with salt, laying its cities waste, raping its women, distributing small-pox-infested blankets or hanging every tenth Scotsman. They passed a coercive law at Westminster abolishing the old principle of allegiance on which the clan system depended. The 1748 Act was an elegant example of the law as an instrument of imperial discipline. Scotland was subjugated by Geo. iv. 7. as much as by Cumberland's dragoons. It is significant that

Waverley ends not with Culloden, or the Pretender's flight, but with the trials (in England) at which the rebels were legally convicted and executed, by due process. For Scott, final solutions are legal solutions.

Nearer home and his own time, the lawyer Scott most admired – and to whom he dedicated his advocate's thesis – was 'the Jeffreys of Scotland', Lord Braxfield. Robert Macqueen (as he was born) made his name as counsel for the crown in the legal forfeitures after 1745. 'A coarse, and illiterate man' (spectacularly drunken to boot) who loved to use broad dialect on the bench, he was promoted to Lord Justice Clerk (i.e. head of the Scottish criminal justice system) in 1776: the ennoblement as Lord Braxfield came with the appointment. For the next twenty years he literally lorded it over the Scottish legal system. Braxfield made himself hated (and earned his 'Jeffreys' nickname) in the brutal repression of the Duns rioters over which he presided, 1793–4. His conduct was, Cockburn declared, a 'disgrace to the age'. And it was this bogeyman, this brute in a wig, that Scott took as his legal role model and whom he thanked later for having shown him particular favours.

Biographers tend to skirt Scott's attachment to Braxfield – an attachment that he never revoked. It is said, in Scott's defence, that the Scottish law in which he was trained did not – like the English – ground itself in notions of age-old rights and freedoms, enshrined in 'common law'. Scotch law was more Roman (or 'civilian') in its philosophy, conceiving itself as the expression not of primal 'rights' but present social order. Political judges were not necessarily anomalous. But it was also in Scott's nature to subordinate himself to authority figures like Dundas, Braxfield, and – in the 1780s – his own father. Whether they were brutes like Braxfield or benign dictators like Dundas was immaterial.

On one thing Scott and Cockburn would have agreed. Lawyers were men of high standing in turn-of-the-century society. As Smout notes, the lawyers were 'the real leaders of Edinburgh society . . . they formed a cultural elite' (Smout, 373–4). There were, of course, lawyers and lawyers. When he talks of a 'cultural elite' Smout primarily means the top-dog advocates and lawyer – lairds, not work-a-day scriveners. Nevertheless some of the lustre of the profession spread even to the humblest pen-driving clerk in High Street chambers, such as Scott was in 1786.

Scott started in 1786 as the lowest of the legal low, a copying clerk. But even this – measured by its monetary rewards – was far from menial. Clerks were paid threepence a page for everything they copied for court use. This is an astonishingly high rate of pay. The young Scott, as he told Lockhart, managed on occasion to write 120 pages in a single day, earning himself 30*s* (Lock. 1. 118). This much repeated legend – which originated with Scott in late life – must surely be exaggerated. It is inconceivable that Walter Scott WS, a cautious man, would have paid an apprentice (a class of worker universally underpaid and exploited) more than a WS and many an advocate, while fellow citizens starved in the street. But it is safe to assume that Scott earned what was, for a fifteen-year-old, a handsome wage. This was his own money, to be spent on books, medals or other collectibles. And however deficient Scott's Greek and maths may have been, he had clearly taught himself a fluent and legible hand. The scrivener's readiness ('the Old Shop', as he called it; EJ 59) stayed with him throughout life, as did the neat copperplate writing and the lawyer's terminal flourishes at the foot of every page (designed to prevent insertions). Throughout his life, writing came as easily as talking to Scott. He has left more letters (typically chatty letters) than is practicable to edit and print.

While making himself a black-coated, confidential lawyer, as apparently imperturbable as any of his kind, young Walter was cultivating in a separate area of his mind a wholly unlawyerly passion for the visually picturesque. Any number of manuals – refining the codes of Thomson's *Seasons*, with imagery derived from Claude Lorrain's pastorals – instructed the late eighteenth-century person of taste on these matters. Scott evidently picked up the language of sensibility from the standard sources and from emulation of his richer friends around 1786–8 (not, as he claimed, at Kelso three years earlier). At about the same period he dabbled in landscape painting, but discovered that he had no artistic ability.

A main influence on the evolution of Scott's sensibility was claustrophobia; the fact that he was confined to Edinburgh and its environs. This limitation of scenic range gave the young enthusiast's sense of landscape an unusual twist. The approved means of cultivating one's appreciation of the picturesque was tourism – preferably foreign tourism. But travel was inhibited nationally by the Napoleonic Wars and for Scott personally by his father's ineradicable provincialism. Walter Scott WS would evidently as soon have eaten human flesh, roast on Sunday, as go abroad (i.e. out of Midlothian) for his vacations; if – apart from Sabbath rest – he took vacations. There is no evidence that Walter Scott WS ever crossed over the borders of Scotland, even for his son's wedding. It was not until he was twenty-five – two years before his father's death – that Walter went even as far afield as the Lake District (his involuntary year in Bath, aged four, on doctor's orders, does not count).

Nor had Scott seen much of his own country. Apart from his time in Bath, he had never, until his fifteenth year, been farther afield than he could walk in a day or two from George Square. But as it happened, Edinburgh was the starting point for the approved Scottish tour – something that had become very popular with the closing of the Continent. Nearby sites like Roslin Castle (Scott's favourite spot; EJ 58) were the conventional tourist's first 'views'. If Scott had to be confined to a thirty-mile range (i.e. what he could walk in a weekend) there were worse places to be confined.

It is possible that in later life Scott exaggerated the range and frequency of these expeditions. There is an odd anecdote told by Scott's friend Guthrie Wright. On being shown an early draft of *Marmion* in 1807 Wright suggested that the opening episode of the hero's journey into Scotland should include a stay at the dramatic castle of Tantallon, on the Lothian shore opposite the Bass Rock. Scott was excited by the suggestion:

He then asked if I had ever been there, and upon saying I had frequently, he desired me to describe it, which I did; and I verily believe it is from what I then said, that the accurate description contained in the fifth canto was given – at least I never heard him say he had afterwards gone to visit the castle. (Lock. 2. 11)

Tantallon is probably the most dramatic ruined castle in the environs of Edinburgh, and easily reached by road, just a few miles on from Prestonpans. It is extraordinary that Scott (in his thirty-sixth year) did not know it.

However inspirational to a poetically inclined young man, the excursions Scott made on foot to Cramond, Prestonpans or Roslin were a poor substitute for the amenities of the grand tour, or even the humbler Highland Tour. It was therefore an epoch in his life when 'in the first autumn of his apprenticeship' (EJ 62–4) Walter Scott WS entrusted his son to take a journey 'on a pony of my own' to visit a Highland client, Alexander Stewart of Invernahyle. A Jacobite veteran of 1715 and 1745, Invernahyle had fought a broadsword duel with Rob Roy, and evidently liked to reminisce about it. There is some doubt about the exact date and details of this trip but Scott's description of his first experience of the Highlands (recalled four decades later in the opening pages of *The Fair Maid of Perth*) rings true. He emerged, as he remembers, from a narrow cleft, after transversing a long, flat, boring landscape. It was a natal moment. Beneath him was the Vale of Perth, threshold of the Highlands. He glutted himself on the view:

> I recollect pulling up the reins, without meaning to do so, and gazing on the scene before me as if I had been afraid it would shift, like those in a theatre, before I could distinctly observe its different parts, or convince myself that what I saw was real. Since that hour, the recollection of that inimitable landscape has possessed the strongest influence over my mind, and retained its place as a memorable thing, while much that was influential on my own fortunes has fled from my recollection. (Lock. 1. 124)

It was clearly a milestone on Scott's growth to maturity, his 'makin of himsell'. And one wonders how his personality would have been differently made had he plodded through the regimented tour of the Wye or Rhine, reproducing as he went all the conventional responses to picturesque scenery.

If one can credit Scott's retrospective account, he was – while swooning at the scenery – singularly immune to the charm of the peasantry. He seems, at this stage of his life, to have shared the fanatically anti-Celtic John Pinkerton's contempt for the degraded condition of the Highland aborigines. Lockhart recalls some of Scott's recollections of the natives he met on his first visits to the Highlands:

> On reaching the brow of a bleak eminence overhanging the primitive tower and its tiny patch of cultivated ground, he found his host and three sons, and perhaps half-a-dozen attendant *gillies*, all stretched half asleep in their tartans

upon the heath, with guns and dogs, and a profusion of game about them; while in the courtyard, far below, appeared a company of women engaged in loading a cart with manure . . . he discovered, on descending from the height, that among these industrious females were the laird's own lady, and two or three of her daughters. (1. 125)

These were not the picturesque peasants of Claude's landscapes; nor the romantic highlanders of *Waverley*. One cannot picture Flora MacIvor squishing her toes among the cow pats.

In Edinburgh during the leisure of the evening, the weekend, and the vacation, Walter studiously trained his voracious literary appetite into literary taste. Besides subscribing to Sibbald's Circulating Library, he bought chapbooks, which he later had bound. But his main literary efforts were towards poetry, which required relatively few actual books, but much intense reading and memorization. He bought Thomas Evans's *Old Ballads* when it came out in four volumes in 1784 and devoured its saccharine contents. As a teenager, he loved the lilt of balladic verse and would recite passages over and over again, for the pleasure of the sound alone. It was, as he later noted in the preface to *Kenilworth*, the mark of an 'immature taste'.

Scott developed in the mid-1780s a particular (as he would later think, particularly immature) enthusiasm for the lyrics of Mickle (or 'Meikle'), whose career may have helped form the young lawyer's idea of what a modern poet was. Born in 1735 in Dumfriesshire, the son of a poor minister, William Julius Mickle worked his way up the brewery business. When his firm went bankrupt, he turned to literature, settling in London. From 1771–8 he worked on a translation of Camoens's *Lusiads*. This work eventually appeared with a pugnacious preface by Mickle, in defence of 'Commerce.' The translation earned Mickle £1,000 (Scott was not, as is sometimes alleged, the first to earn this sum for a poem), membership of the Royal Academy of Portugal and a fair degree of British fame, which he has since entirely lost. Encountering further financial setbacks, Mickle – who seems to have been a dauntless fellow – went to sea and won much prize money in the wars with France, but his later years were embittered by speculations that went wrong, by the misdoings of his banker, and by a chancery suit. He died in 1788. Scott loved Mickle's 'Cumnor Hall', particularly the haunting first stanza:

> The dews of summer night did fall –
> The Moon, sweet regent of the sky,
> Silvered the walls of Cumnor Hall,
> And many an oak that grew thereby.

The young Scott was also steeped in the long-narrative verse of John Langhorne (1735–79). This forgotten poet was the occasion of Scott's only contact with Burns, in the winter of 1786–7, at the house of Professor Adam Ferguson, the philosopher and father of Walter's close friend of that name. David Daiches tells the story:

Burns was twenty-eight, and Scott a boy of fifteen, sitting silent in the background while his elders conversed with the famous poet. Burns was struck by some lines of verse inscribed under the picture [by H. W. Bunbury] of a dead soldier being mourned by his widow and child. Scott later recalled the scene for Lockhart. Burns 'asked whose the lines were, and it chanced that nobody but myself remembered that they occur in a half-forgotten poem of Langhorne's called by the unpromising title of "The Justice of the Peace". I whispered my information to a friend present, who mentioned it to Burns, who rewarded me with a look and a word, which, though of mere civility, I then received with very great pleasure.' (Daiches, 39)

This is evidently an improved version of what actually happened. As later critics have pointed out, Langhorne's name is clearly printed beneath the verses in Bunbury's print. It seems that Scott overdramatized this meeting, and his own brilliant intervention. But that he knew the work of Langhorne shows that at a very early age he was abreast of the latest thing in 1780s poetry – more particularly Scottish (or in Langhorne's case pro-Scottish) verse produced by petty bourgeois poets of the same class background as himself. Langhorne was born in Westmoreland, the son of a clergyman. He took up employment himself as a schoolteacher, then as a curate, and finally drifted into letters. He was always indigent. In 1765 his *Poetical Works* appeared. Edinburgh University gave him a D.D. for *Genius and Valour* (1764), 'a Scotch Pastoral'. The work was written on behalf of the Scottish people against Charles Churchill's Scotophobic *Prophecy of Famine* (1763). In the early 1770s, the worthy Langhorne was made a Justice of the Peace, which led to the writing of his sentimental tales in verse, *The Country Justice* (1774–7), which were admired by Wordsworth. Langhorne was subsequently dogged by various kinds of misfortune and laid low by his own 'intemperate habits'. He died in 1779.

Regarding the formation of Scott's taste, it is significant that the first poem that we know him to have read (apart from ballads like 'Hardyknute', picked up at Sandy Knowe) is William Falconer's *The Shipwreck*, from which Mrs Cockburn heard him recite. Falconer was born in Edinburgh in 1732, the son of a poor barber. As a boy he went into the navy, and at the age of eighteen (by now a second mate) was shipwrecked trading off the Levant. He published his first poem in 1751, but remained at sea even after the popular reception of his major work, *The Shipwreck*, in 1762. The poem is written in Crabbe-like couplets, and was seriously compared to the *Odyssey* and the *Aeneid* by contemporary reviewers. In September 1769 (by which stage the poem was in its third edition) Falconer went to sea for the last time, and was never heard of again. It seems clear that Mrs Scott (who evidently gave the poem to young Walter) had a lively interest in contemporary Scottish poetry, which she passed on to her precocious son. Scott's more mature enthusiasms for Burns, Southey, Wordsworth, Byron, and, most enduringly, Crabbe are well known. But it is clear that his character as a poet may have been influenced by the examples of the less canonical Mickle, Falconer, and Langhorne –

Scottish (or pro-Scot) poets who combined the muse with trade and professional career.

According to Lockhart Walter was 'a frequent guest' (Lock. 1. 122) at the villa of John Home (1722–1808), the clergyman-poet, who lived near Edinburgh at this retired period of his long life. In the 1745, Home had served as a 'volunteer' (i.e. pro-Hanover) and was captured at Falkirk (Scott used this episode in *Waverley*). In later years Home was renowned as the author of the nationalist tragedy *Douglas* which (after being rejected by Garrick) was performed with huge success at Edinburgh in 1756. There had been some furore at a minister writing for the stage. Nonetheless Home was now regarded as Scotland's greatest living author, and had a strong connection with the same border lands as Scott's own family. He was also a main promoter of James Macpherson, the creator, and self-proclaimed discoverer, of the allegedly ancient Scottish 'Ossian' poems.

One of the most direct influences on young Scott was that of the blind poet, Dr Thomas Blacklock, at whose house he became a 'frequent and favoured guest'. He was introduced to Blacklock by his friend Adam Ferguson (EJ 61). Blacklock is an interesting but now wholly forgotten writer. The son of a humble Dumfriesshire bricklayer, he had no sight from the age of six months, after an attack of smallpox. Nevertheless, in his childhood he was recognized as a poetic prodigy and was later befriended by David Hume. A gentle, ineffectual man, he 'would have been made a professor of Greek at Aberdeen', according to the *DNB*, 'but for a timidity which disqualified him from teaching boys.' Since 1764 Blacklock had lived in Edinburgh, where he tutored boarding pupils. He died in 1791 aged seventy, and when Scott knew him he was frail and known as 'the blind bard'. But 'the kind old man opened to me the stores of his library and through his recommendation I became intimate with Ossian [another blind bard] and Spenser.' Ossian's 'tawdry repetitions' eventually disgusted him, Scott claimed, but Spenser 'I could have read for ever' (Hew. 26).

Scott was certainly disgusted by the 'Ossian' hoax in later years. And perhaps, as he implies, he was never entirely persuaded by the 'Celtic Homer'. Certainly when he wrote an article on the subject in the *Edinburgh Review* in July 1805, he was not fooled. But in the 1770s and 1780s, some of the most level-headed of Scots were taken in. Lord Kames, for instance, the philosopher, who declared Ossian to be greater than Homer – a much echoed boast at the time. Professor Adam Ferguson, the father of Scott's particular friend, was a firm believer in Ossian's authenticity. It was through the Fergusons – a family of great literary cultivation – that Scott had his personal introduction to poets like Burns and Blacklock. It is hard to believe that the immature young man – consorting as he was in 1780s with pro-Ossianists – was immune to the fever that possessed his betters. Would he, a fifteen-year-old apprentice, have dared contradict Professor Ferguson, or the Reverend Home, or even the meeker Dr Blacklock on the subject? Had he done so, would they have allowed the young puppy into their salons again?

Scott's career as an apprentice WS was a short but formative interlude. This phase of Scott's life came to a close with what seems to have been his most serious bout of illness since the original crippling fever of 1773. Details as to exact date are somewhat vague, Scott himself locating it at 'about the second year of my apprenticeship' (i.e. 1787–8).[2] For some time, as Scott records, 'my health . . . from rapid growth and other causes had been . . . rather uncertain and delicate' (Hew. 34); a blood vessel broke in his lower bowels and he almost died. His uncle, Dr Rutherford, thought his recovery 'miraculous' (Lock. 1. 39). Nor does the treatment seem to have been designed to assist his survival. He was bled, blistered and starved, 'till I scarcely had a pulse left'. A bland vegetarian diet was prescribed, consisting mainly of boiled rice. He was forbidden all speech and movement. He was left under a thin counterpane with the windows open to cold spring weather. The aim apparently was to slow his metabolism. He read, and played chess silently with John Irving. (Although he was evidently good at the game, Scott disliked chess for the rest of his life.) He went to convalesce at his uncle's villa at Kelso, Rosebank – which, like Sandy Knowe, was a rural tonic that worked better than Edinburgh medicine.

Scott's latest and most severe illness raises the question of what credence we should give to his own and Lockhart's picture of a robust, rock-climbing, street-fighting, schoolyard-brawling, one-handed anvil-lifting, thirty-mile-walking 'young Hercules'. Scott's portraiture of himself in boyhood stresses his toughness in the face of handicap. But the list of serious ailments he suffered in childhood is awesome: infantile paralysis at one-and-a-half (1773); a relapse at four which led to a year in Bath (1776); an illness at school which led to his missing two terms (1783); in his second year at college another severe illness that lost him several months of tuition (1784–5); and in the second year of his apprenticeship, a near-fatal haemorrhage which needed months of bedrest and convalescence (1787–8). Scott himself refers to long-lasting periods of 'delicacy' around puberty, as a result of 'rapid growth'. There are also revealing glimpses of a milk-sop Scott: the little boy terrified of sleeping by himself, telling an uncle that he did not 'want to play with rough boys', his mother's nervousness about exposing him to the rough and tumble of the High School may be significant. There is now no way of getting at the truth, but one should perhaps be more sceptical than some biographers have been about Scott's boast that he was 'a roaring boy in my youth, a desperate climber, a bold rider, a deep drinker, and a stout player at single stick' (Jrnl. 290). He may also have been a tall talker.

The year 1787–8 was not happy for Scott. But it brought what may be seen as a perverse stroke of luck. His brother Robert – the son on whom most of the family's hopes were resting – died. Robert projects a suspiciously shadowy image in the small corner of Scott biography that he occupies. The date of his birth is uncertain (1763 or 1767?), as is the date on which he entered the navy (1779 or 1781?). There seems no dispute, however, that Robert served at the Battle of Martinique in April 1782, with

Admiral Rodney. The battle was won magnificently. But after the Peace of
Paris there was, Scott says, no hopes of promotion 'for those who had no
great interest; and some disgust which his proud spirit had taken at harsh
usage from a superior officer, combined to throw poor Robert into the East-
India Company's service, for which his habits were ill adapted. He made
two voyages to the East, and died a victim to the climate in . . .' (Scott gives
no date; Lock. 1. 10). John Buchan sums up Robert's career in a brisk
executionary sentence: 'He entered the Navy, fought under Rodney, quarrelled with his superiors, joined the East India Company's service, and died
of malaria at forty-one' (i.e. 1804, or 1808; JB, 28). Johnson – drawing on
marine records – does not concur. In February 1784 Robert sailed as fourth
mate on the *Neptune* (an East India Company vessel). And 'a little less than
three years later [i.e. January 1787], as third mate on the *Rodney*, at the age
of twenty-three, Robert died on a voyage from Madeira to Bengal and was
buried at sea some 1,000 miles south of Ceylon' (EJ 55–6). Grierson agrees
with this date, and implies that heavy drinking precipitated Robert's death.

What is clear from the autobiographical fragment is that Scott did not
entirely love his brother Robert: 'His temper was bold and haughty, and to
me was often checkered with what I felt to be capricious tyranny . . . When
in bad humour . . . he kicked and cuffed without mercy.' (The last detail
was added in 1826, after the death of Scott's mother; Hew. 9). There seems
to have been some disgrace in Robert's leaving the King's service (something more, that is, than mere unemployment after an inconvenient peace
treaty). Did the 'disgust which his spirit had taken at harsh usage from a
superior officer' have something to do with the young officer's love of
pushing the bottle round too often? Are these the 'habits' alluded to? Nor
does the promotion from fourth to third mate (by the age of twenty-three
as Johnson calculates) suggest any meteoric rise in his three years in the
civil marine.

Robert's death was momentous for Walter. The oldest son was evidently
the *protégé* of his namesake, Captain Robert Scott. It is likely that Captain
Robert helped his nephew Robert with the expenses of his naval career and
marked him as his prospective heir. Shortly after young Robert's death (or
possibly just before – dates are hazy) Walter went to stay and convalesce
with his uncle Robert. This gentleman had long had a soft spot for his frail
younger nephew. They had interests in common. Robert was an antiquarian and apparently bookish. They visited castles together, shot over
Rosebank's twenty acres, fished on its Tweedside bank, read the same
volumes. Scott spent the large part of his summer breaks from 1788 to 1792
at Rosebank, and did legal work there – which suggests that he had a study
in the house. He and his uncle must have become very intimate. One can
only guess, but Robert probably encouraged Walter to rebel against his
father's Presbyterian narrowness. He may even have breathed a little nautical free-and-easiness into the young man's ideas about sex. (It is hard to
believe that he – or his sister Janet who lived nearby – did not know it when
in 1788, or thereabouts, Walter began courting a local Kelso girl, 'Jessie'.)

Scott filled the heir's vacancy left by his brother Robert, and in June 1804 duly came into all his dead uncle's property.

There remained one other brother between Walter and the senior son's position. John, born in 1768, was three years older. Few details of John's career have survived. 'He addicted himself to the military service,' Scott wrote in 1808, 'and is now brevet-major in the 73rd regiment' (Hew. 9). In 1809, through Scott's influence with the War Office, John was belatedly promoted major. Almost immediately, John sold out, his health 'totally broken' – by drink, as Grierson assumes (*Lett.* 1. liv). Although he seems to have been reasonably well-off, John's military career was evidently far from glorious. He died prematurely in 1816.

Not to make Scott a monster, he was evidently fonder of his (worthless) younger brothers Daniel and Tom than of his (worthier) older brothers Robert and John. His obituary remarks on Robert (whose date of death he has trouble remembering) strike one as perfunctory. John he seems to have liked more (he is portrayed fondly enough as the veteran half-pay officer in *Paul's Letters*). But there seems to have been no warmth in the relationship.

Back to School

In the winter term of 1789 (Clark, 184) Scott returned to the University to attend lectures on Civil Law. It was not yet certain that he would be anything more than a Writer to the Signet, but his options were expanding. Members of the Civil Law class routinely progressed to the higher rank of advocate. Now eighteen years old, he was intellectually mature for his age, and had a winning presence. As Lockhart puts it: 'He had outgrown the sallowness of early ill-health, and had a fresh, brilliant complexion . . . His figure, excepting the blemish in one limb, must in those days have been eminently handsome; tall, much above the usual standard, it was cast in the very mould of a young Hercules . . . his conversation must have been such as could have dispensed with any exterior disadvantages, and certainly brought swift forgiveness for the one unkindness of nature' (Lock. 1. 144–5).

Much has been built on these remarks, whose glowing terms are recycled by Edgar Johnson. They originated with 'a lady of high rank [i.e. the Countess of Sutherland], who well remembers [Scott] in the Assembly Rooms' – some forty years later. They should be taken with other less biased accounts, such as that of Lady Shelley: 'His first appearance is not prepossessing. A club-foot, white eyelashes, and a clumsy figure. He has not any expression when his face is in repose; but upon an instant some remark will light up his countenance, and you discover a man of genius.'[3] Shelley describes the mature Scott (in 1815), but like observers at all periods of his life she was struck by the degree of lameness, the inert expression and the bleached colouring.

Scott chose his particular friends from the better-connected and more ambitious members of his class. His old companions John Irving and Adam Ferguson were classmates. A new friend – soon to be his *fidus Achates* – was William Clerk of Eldin, the son of John Clerk (1728–1812), the naval theoretician. Others of the Clerk family were distinguished lawyers. Lockhart records a coterie of friends made at this crucial period of Scott's life 'which opened to him abundantly certain advantages . . . from which he had hitherto been in great measure debarred in consequence of the retired habits of his parents' (Lock. 1. 130). They included: George Cranstoun (later Lord Corehouse), George (later Lord) Abercromby, John James Edmonstone of Newton, Patrick Murray of Simprim, Sir Patrick Murray of Ochtertyre.

These young men's friendship was not – as with Ferguson and Irving – bookish. Least bookish of all was Charles Kerr of Abbotrule (a friend of his son's whom Walter Scott WS particularly disliked). Four years older than Scott, Kerr became a WS in 1789, then embarked on a life of debauchery and sloth that ended with exile first to the Isle of Man (where he made an injudicious marriage) and to the West Indies. Scott helped Kerr through some of his early scrapes. He became Scott's first serious drinking partner and they indulged in the 'juvenile bacchanalia' which, as a prim Lockhart notes, 'were then indulged among the young men of Edinburgh, whether students of law, solicitors, or barristers, to an extent now happily unknown' (Lock. 1. 130). Adolescent drinking is prone to heroic exaggeration, but there is reliable evidence that Scott drank to the point of having blackouts (EJ 85) and he recalls in his journal, years later, drinking as much as three bottles at a sitting.

Scott's consorting with friends who could offer him 'certain advantages' looks like snobbery. Those who were directly exposed to this snobbishness were sometimes unforgiving. His father's apprentices – recently his comrades and, as they fondly thought, equals – upbraided Walter for 'cutting' them for the sake of 'dons like William Clerk' who looked down on mere lawyer's clerks. The accusation was evidently made at the firm's annual dinner and must have somewhat dampened the jollity. According to Scott, he retorted in high style:

> Gentlemen, I will never *cut* any man unless I detect him in scoundrelism; but I know not what right any of you have to interfere with my choice of my company. If any one thought that I had injured him, he would have done well to ask an explanation in a more private manner. As it is, I fairly own, that though I like many of you very much, and have long done so, I think William Clerk well worth you all put together. (Lock. 1. 140)

The speech looks more at home in eighteenth-century drama than at an informal Edinburgh supper. Nor is it easy to imagine an eighteen-year-old carrying off the 'Gentlemen' tone of address without pomposity. But it clearly enough records Scott's rise in the world and his determination not to be held back by low associations. It was about 1790, as Clerk noticed, that his friend laid aside 'that carelessness, not to say slovenliness, as to dress, which used to furnish matter for joking at the beginning of their acquaintance. He now did himself more justice in these little matters' (Lock. 1. 144).

Around 1790 his father offered Walter a partnership in the family firm. The offer was flattering. Young Walter was barely nineteen, nor had he sought the promotion. The old man's motives can only be guessed at. It may have been a tacit appeal for help. He was over sixty, and his health was failing. The business was not apparently doing as well as it had in the busy days of the mid-1780s. (Under Tom, who accepted the partnership that Walter declined, it was to go sharply downhill.) It is possible too that the father was worried about the gap growing between him and his son. He is recorded making grumpy remarks about Walter's gipsy-like wanderings through the countryside with wild friends like Kerr. After his son had been out for days, walking and drinking who knew where, Walter Scott WS declared with a telling lapse into the dialect of his boyhood 'I doubt, I greatly doubt, sir, you were born for nae better than a *gangrel scrape-gut*' (Lock. 1. 134). Why offer this vagrant fiddler a partnership in the respectable firm of Chalmers and Scott? Presumably so that early hours, regular appointments, and professional discipline might make him as amenable to paternal discipline as he had been in the past.

If Walter Scott WS had his own reasons for offering the partnership, his son had his for declining. To throw in his lot with his father would mean Scott's remaining a Writer to the Signet. He would in all probability end his career like his father, still Walter Scott WS after thirty-five years. His father was richer, but fixed in the same middling rank of life as he had been in 1755. Walter wanted more elevation. And, as Johnson observes, 'he did not like the element of subservience in the relationship of a Writer to his clients.' The young man chose instead to continue his studies and aim at making himself an advocate. It is a mark of how far he had come in three years that he could go against his father's desires so directly. More so as Walter Scott WS would have to pay for his son's studies.

Scott's second spell at college lasted from autumn 1789 to 1792. It is one of the few periods in which one can see his ideas being formed directly by single intellectual influences. The influences were stronger since he was fortunate enough to be a student in an era when the university had particularly luminous teachers. They were also, as it happened, relatively young, only a generation ahead of Scott. Among them was David Hume (1757–1838, nephew to his better-known namesake) who was appointed professor of Scottish law in 1786. Scott copied Hume's 1790–1 lectures out twice, giving his father one set. Another lecturer, Dugald Stewart (1753–1828), had succeeded Adam Ferguson (the father of Scott's friend) in 1785, and could claim to be Scotland's greatest living philosopher. He was a charismatic teacher. Cockburn claimed for himself in his *Memorials* that Stewart's views on the 'ethics of life' had changed his nature. Graham McMaster in *Scott and Society* (1981) makes a powerful case for the young man's being saturated in eighteenth-century rationalism, with its overriding faith in progress. Scott was not, McMaster insists, the 'mildly eccentric antiquarian' that Lockhart invented, but an orthodox child of Scottish Enlightenment. And he took in this enlightenment at its fount, Edinburgh University, in the early 1790s.

Scott was evidently liberated from his apprentice's office drudgery at this period, and there are records of much walking, fishing and conviviality. 'His health was fully established,' as Grierson notes. 'In the freshness of the morning he could lift a smith's anvil by the horn. His amazing energy was coming into full play as he launched into the social – and convivial – life of young Edinburgh lawyers' (HG 19). Much of the amazing energy was reserved for the freshness of the evening. By his own account, Scott – so recently the pale romance-reading invalid languishing on a plain rice diet – was by night a roaring boy, a devotee of 'Bacchus, Venus, and Mars' (EJ 86). One morning he reported to Clerk 'and exhibiting his stick all cut and marked, told him he had been attacked in the streets the night before by three fellows, against whom he had defended himself for an hour' (Lock. 1. 132). The length of time may have been, like Falstaff's rogues in buckram, heroically exaggerated. But clearly Scott was breaking out of his father's narrow notions of gentlemanly conduct. The father would have called his son's single stick duel so much street-brawling. Lockhart is almost comically nervous that no-one should suspect his father-in-law of sexual delinquency at this (or any other) period of his life, although he concedes that 'in this season of hot and impetuous blood he may not have escaped *quite* blameless' (Lock. 1. 143). Edgar Johnson builds on the concession, noting roguishly that after a night's roistering 'there were plenty of wenches to be boarded in the purlieus of Blackfriars' Wynd' (EJ 86). Scott, that is, used prostitutes.

There were more decent nocturnal activities than fighting and wenching. Scott took full advantage of the students' multifarious clubs and societies. These institutions expressed the peculiarly Scottish 'democratic intellect' and at the same time served as a kind of freemasonry which lasted after members went on to their professional careers. More immediately, the clubs formed character. It was Edinburgh's debating clubs, Cockburn noted, that 'gradually hardened me into the man I became'. Scott belonged to clubs principally devoted to debates and essay-writing. He claimed – over-modestly, one suspects – to have made 'no great figure' in either activity, although 'the odd lumber of my brain, especially that which was connected with the recondite parts of history, did me, as Hamlet says, "yeoman's service"' (Lock. 1. 40).

By far the most significant of Scott's memberships was to the Speculative Society – a club devoted to discussing current affairs, philosophy, politics and literature. Scott applied and was accepted in December 1790. Founded in 1764, the 'Spec' had strong links with the university, all the professors being members. 'The legal element was strong', Melville Clark notes (Clark, 204). While Scott was a member, political discussion (strong at other periods) was inhibited by alarm about the French Revolution. Nevertheless, admission to this prestigious Society was a red-letter day for young Scott. Over the next five years, he 'hardly ever missed a meeting'. His clerk's training made him useful to its officers. He was elected librarian in 1791 and subsequently became secretary and treasurer of the society.

Scott wrote and read out a number of essays (the texts of which are lost) for the Spec over the years, whose subjects reflect both the nature of proceedings and the growth of his mind – more particularly its drift towards antiquarianism. Between November 1791 and 1796 he spoke on 'The Origin of the Feudal System', 'The Authenticity of the Poems of Ossian' (twice), 'The Origin of Scandinavian Mythology'. As Melville Clark calculates, Scott spoke in no less than twenty-one debates at the Speculative Society between 1791 and 1796. Around a dozen members were usually present and the votes indicate the highly conservative nature of the club at the period: they were for capital punishment (three debates), against the provision of relief for the poor (two debates), for the corn laws, against the national debt, against divorce, and for national religion. It is a fair assumption that these votes reflect the young Scott's prejudices.

An important function of these intellectual societies was to give Scott access to the culture of Europe – something which, as a stay-at-home, he could not obtain at first hand. The most important of these European influences was that of German literature. German Romanticism had fallen like a thunderbolt with Henry Mackenzie's lecture on German theatre to the Royal Society of Edinburgh in April 1788. Translations from the German became the rage. In 1792 Scott and a group of friends hired themselves a German tutor, Dr Anthony Willich. Skipping the dull business of learning the language accurately, they rushed on to the fascinating masterpieces of Schiller and Goethe. Another surge of German mania was provoked by Mrs Barbauld in 1795. At a Dugald Stewart soirée she read Bürger's 'Lenore' in William Taylor's translation, to an 'electrified audience'. Bürger's ballad (1775) tells the story of a dead lover who returns from the grave to reclaim his beloved. It became wildly popular in Britain, and inspired a whole genre of lurid imitations and a fad for charnel-house horrors. Scott was not at the Stewarts' to hear Mrs Barbauld. A friend – who had been at the event – recited Taylor's translation to him. Even at second-hand, Scott was entranced. German books were extremely hard to come by at that period – particularly in Edinburgh. However he managed to obtain that year (1795) a copy of the original 'Lenore' from a German kinswoman, Harriet Scott (née von Brühl), who had recently married Hugh Scott of Harden, a diplomat (EJ 113).

Scott confessed himself to be 'German mad' at this period. A shared passion for German literature led to the forging of one of the most important friendships of his life, with William Erskine. Two years ahead of Scott (he qualified as an advocate in 1790), Erskine guided Scott through his early reading of German drama and romance, and encouraged his friend's own efforts in poetic translation.

The years 1788–92 were a phase of major intellectual and character growth for Scott. He also found his professional vocation. He was examined in the summer of 1791, and qualified as an advocate the following July. William Clerk recalled the newly qualified Scott and himself standing like a couple of journeywomen (or whores) waiting to be hired, outside the Tron Kirk. More respectably, Scott told Clerk that it was 'a sort of wedding day' (EJ 80). In fact, ideas of love and marriage were forming in his mind now that he had a profession.

3

Getting Forward (1790–1797)

Looking back, Scott saw the turn his life took around 1790 as crucial. Then it was that he determined to stop being a 'mere dreamer' and 'get forward'. He would do something with his life. From now on Scott was – as his friend and Liddesdale guide Robert Shortreed put it – 'makin himsell a' the time'. Scott's life in this self-making phase – from 1792 when he qualified as advocate until his marriage in 1797 – was dominated by three activities: 'expeditions', career-building, and finding a wife. Each of these activities may be examined in turn.

Scott's expeditions at their simplest were walks away from George Square into the countryside that began on the other side of the Meadows, Arthur's Seat, and the Pentlands. The rambles over Salisbury Crags with John Irving became with adolescence more ambitious, often involving several members of his young lawyer set – jovially called 'the Mountain' or 'the Montagnards'. These companions were wilder – and a social cut above – the undemonstrative Irving, who was no longer the bosom friend of schooldays. Scott's earliest surviving letters have to do with these expeditions, which he apparently undertook with Pitscottie, or some other authority on Scottish history, in hand (*Lett.* 1. 19). When he had gained regular use of one of his father's horses, Scott ranged further afield. In his early twenties Scott might be away from home for as long as ten days, staying with his extended network of relatives or in houses to which his well-connected friends gave him an introduction. Adam Ferguson, for instance, arranged for the two of them to stay with families in 'some of the finest districts of Stirlingshire and Perthshire'. George Abercromby introduced Walter Scott to his family and the young man 'lingered some time at Tullibody, the seat of the father of Sir Ralph Abercromby [George's grand-father] and heard from the old gentleman's own lips his narrative of a journey which he had been obliged to make, shortly after he first settled in Stirlingshire, to the wild retreat of Rob Roy' (Lock. 1. 193). Lockhart plausibly locates many details of the subsequent poems and novels in Scott's jaunts in the early 1790s. He walked over Flodden field – which furnishes the grand climax to *Marmion* – on an early excursion, in August 1791. In autumn 1793, he returned to Loch Katrine, the main setting for *The Lady of the Lake* (Lock. 1. 194). On the same trip, he stayed with the Rattrays in Perthshire, relatives of William Clerk's, whose house Craighall evidently inspired Tully-Veolan.

Convivial, sometimes riotous, occasionally lecherous (Lockhart hints) as parts of these expeditions were, Scott was all the time storing his mind (and his small parlour at George Square) with mementoes of the antique past. He had no idea at this period of writing novels but he evidently collected with kleptomaniac intensity. He loved what he called 'technical history', objects that one could handle and which conjured up the past through the fingers that held them. For seven years (1792–9) he made annual 'raids' – as he called them, in honour of his Border ancestor Watt of Harden – into Liddesdale, the (then) desolate area around Jedburgh in the southern corner of Roxburghshire. These raids took place in the long summer vacation. Scott's booty was sometimes archaeological (an old Border war horn, for instance; Lock. 1. 180). Some of the peasants he met furnished 'originals' for the later novels (Dandie Dinmont was supposedly inspired by Willie Elliot, an upland sheep-farmer, at Millburnholm). But mainly, Scott's booty was philological and folkloric, and fed indirectly into the *Minstrelsy of the Scottish Border*, his first major work.

Scott had as his guide on these raids Robert Shortreed, Sheriff-Substitute of Roxburghshire. Scott had met this gentleman – nine years his senior – in Jedburgh shortly after being admitted to the bar in 1792, through Charles Kerr of Abbotrule, a kinsman of Shortreed's. Scott and Shortreed subsequently ranged up and down Liddesdale, which was as yet unspoiled by Edinburgh's expansion into the Lowlands. Shortreed left a memorandum in 1824 and some oral recollections for Lockhart, which have been seized on by later biographers for their vernacular raciness and their extravagantly sentimental portraiture of Scott as a young man for all seasons: 'Eh me, sic an endless fund o' humour and drollery as he then had wi' him,' Shortreed recalled:

> I've seen him in a' moods in these jaunts, grave and gay, daft and serious, sober and drunk . . . but drunk or sober he was aye the gentleman. He looked unco heavy and stupid when he was fou, but he was never out o' gude-humour . . . He was the youldest [most active] young chield I ever saw, and could beat us a' at walking or louping across moss-hags, and especially at coming down a hillside. He took sich spangs as ye can hardly imagine. (Lock. 1. 179, EJ 92, 93)

Shortreed was a lawyer and, like Scott, an educated man. Why he should have lapsed into this broad Lallans is mysterious. It should also be remembered that these recollections were put down thirty years after the event, when Scott was a living legend – the young man may not have been as invariably 'gentlemanly' as Shortreed protests. Nor – given later accounts of his lameness – is it entirely credible that he could outrun his companions.

Looking back, Shortreed evidently conceived Scott's raids into Liddesdale as essentially aimless – undertaken, like the drinking, for the 'fun' of it all. In fact, there was method in the raids and they show the young man consciously playing the antiquary. The term – as Scott understood it – needs some elaboration. 'Antiquarian' is now used almost entirely pejoratively, suggestive of 'Dr Jonas Dryasdust' (Scott's own ironic caricature of the type) and incorrigible lovers of old junk. But in the eighteenth century, antiquarianism was a respectable and in many ways an admirable historical technique.

As a historian, Scott had at least two personalities, of which that of the antiquary was more consistent and deeper rooted. He had, of course, been thoroughly exposed to 'philosophic history', during his second spell at the University of Edinburgh. Enlightenment writers like Stewart, Hugh Blair, Adam Smith had formed his mind. Philosophical historians like Alexander Tytler, David Hume and Adam Ferguson imbued him with a sense of history mapped out conceptually against vast backdrops of time. He was trained in the rationalist analysis of social institutions. With this analysis went a firm belief in 'progress' from feudal to commercial civilization. Scott absorbed all this Enlightenment thinking efficiently enough and his early essay on feudalism, delivered to the Speculative Society, reflects it. Scott's thesis – as outlined to his uncle Robert – is that feudalism is not a local, or accidental social state. It is universally the basic condition, or ground, in which all subsequent progress to the mature commercial civilization anatomized by Adam Smith is rooted.

Scott in this philosophical frame of mind is (despite his Toryism) highly congenial to Marxists like Georg Lukács. But Scott's other 'antiquarian' personality – the hoarder of coins, suits of armour, old manuscripts and heroic relics – was, arguably, more *Scott*. This was the Scott who lovingly mounted Rob Roy's dirk and pouch on his wall and made his chair from wood of the house where Wallace was killed. The Scott who could not resist antique armour from London salerooms – even though his credit was strained to breaking and there remained not a square foot on his walls to cover.

It is a lost opportunity that, as Joseph Levine notes, narrative history never learned how to profit from the accumulations of the antiquaries.[1] The two species despised each other and went their separate scholarly ways: one to the ivory tower of the university history department, the other to the antique shop and Sotheby's. Arguably, Walter Scott brought the two profitably together in his novels. Scott is much reprinted, and the Edinburgh University Press is publishing, starting from 1994, a new edition based on the most approved principles of modern textual theory. But for enjoyment Scott is best read in one of the many Black reprints of the late nineteenth century, with their multitudinous marginal, terminal, and intra-textual embellishments. On one page there will be a reproduction of a coin from the reign of Richard; on another page, a depiction of Bruce's dagger runs down the margin; a bracket from the column-work of Melrose Abbey or some appropriate medal will fill up a convenient white space left at the end of a chapter; a whole page will be given to a facsimile of some ancient document. Every gathering has its engraving on steel of some Scottish or other appropriate ruin. The raw power in Scott's fictions lies in their presentation of surfaces, textures of the past that Scott has felt in his hand, heard in the accents of some old peasant or nobleman, apprehended from the view of some crumbled tower. To read Scott thus is to experience a direct transfusion of his antiquarian's enthusiasm.

One of the main attractions of antiquarianism was that it could happily coexist with – and even dignify – a professional career. Lord Elgin for instance was a diplomat. Following this example, Scott did not let his legal prospects suffer for what were, after all, his gentlemanly hobbies. The early 1790s were a period in which he worked hard at establishing himself as an advocate. In November 1792, Scott and Clerk began their regular attendance at the Parliament House, where the Court of Session was housed. Scott was mainly employed – on those few occasions when he was employed – to write 'informations': that is, summaries or briefs. The bulk of these commissions apparently came from or through the good offices of his father. He handled humble cases of persons suing 'in forma pauperis' – legal aid clients. It was another apprenticeship, and correspondingly underpaid. His main income, and his board, continued to come from his (occasionally grouchy) father.

The defence for a delinquent clergyman, M'Naught, which Scott undertook before the General Assembly of the Kirk in May 1793 for a fee of five guineas, is quoted extensively by Lockhart for its comic aspects. The defendant – a manifest rogue – was accused of 'habitual drunkenness, singing of lewd and profane songs, dancing and toying at a penny-wedding with a "sweetie wife" [and] promoting irregular marriages as a justice of the peace'. The comedy lay in the fact that these offences were (with the exception of the impersonation) exactly what Scott and his young lawyer friends got up to of an evening. The 'Club' were there in strength in the gallery to hear Scott's arch plea which hung on some super-ingenious distinction drawn between *ebrius* and *ebriosus*. As Lockhart (who evidently had the story somewhat embellished from Scott in later life) records:

> When, by and by, he had to recite a stanza of one of M'Naught's convivial ditties, he breathed it out in a faint and hesitating style; whereupon, thinking he needed encouragement, the allies in the gallery astounded the Assembly by cordial shouts of *hear! hear! – encore! encore!* They were immediately turned out, and Scott got through the rest of his harangue very little to his own satisfaction. (Lock. 1. 191)

He emerged wretched from his ordeal, and was dragged off by his unrepentant friends to a neighbouring tavern for a night's 'high jinks'. His stumbling performance was prophetic. Scott – so fluent, quick-witted, and able in every other verbal activity – could never shine in courtroom pleading.

Scott handled other small felonies, some of which opened up to him the darker side of life. He defended a murderer in July 1795, for instance (Lock. 1. 210). But in the main it was very small stuff. In his first year as an advocate (1792–3) he earned 23 guineas; in his second year (1793–4) he earned 55 guineas; in his third year (1794–5), his income rose to a still unimpressive £84 (EJ 105). Barristers are accustomed to wait for their first success but for someone with Scott's contacts the lack of fees was ominous. Nor did it make things easier at home. As Edgar Johnson notes, by 1795, Walter Scott WS was no longer the indulgent parent he had been in 1792, and Walter was finding his father's harsh and carping austerity more and more trying. Presbyterian sabbaths were particularly trying for the twenty-four-year-old no longer young man who must sometimes have had a throbbing head from the night before.

Over these three years, 1792–5, Scott evidently realized that he had poor prospects as a courtroom advocate. He sensibly invested his future hopes in what patronage might do for him. He would look for one of the near-sinecure salaried appointments which were open to likely young Edinburgh lawyers. This would mean catching the eye of powerful men who could do things for him.

The powerful men of the time – like Dundas and Lord Braxfield – were uncompromisingly authoritarian. Scott's views fell into line. Over this period, his political attitudes hardened. As an advocate, with whatever ineptitude, he had defended the poor. As a freshly qualified advocate it had pleased him, however jestingly, to assume with his companions the Jacobin nickname 'Montagnards'. By 1793, however, revolutionary Jacobinism was no longer a joke, what with the French declaration of war on Britain, the guillotining of Louis XVI, and the enthronement of a prostitute in Notre Dame as his successor. Any tincture of Whiggism (let alone sansculottism) would be death to Scott's hopes of preferment in the regime of Dundas.

It is, of course, extremely unlikely that Scott had ever been seriously tempted by radicalism, however temporarily. He had dedicated his thesis to Braxfield in 1792 and had considered assisting him in a junior capacity with the prosecution of the Duns rioters (EJ 90). In 1794 there were new targets for Braxfield's persecutory zeal. In 1792 a reform society had been estab-lished in Scotland called, provocatively, 'The Friends of the People'. By October 1793 this society had held three 'general conventions' of a moder-ately agitational nature. Initially, the society enjoyed middle-class support (particularly from Edinburgh's lawyers). Edinburgh had been seething with popular resentment since the grain riots of 1783–4. By 1793–4, there were 11,000 of the populace being fed by charity.

Increasingly the 'Friends of the People' drew strength from the people: radical artisans and workers. The bourgeois element dropped away in alarm, and had largely disappeared by the time of the third convention. Nevertheless the effective leader of the Society remained Thomas Muir, a respectable Glasgow advocate who had qualified at about the same time as Scott. Muir was subsequently arrested for 'sedition' (i.e. peacefully advocat-ing universal suffrage and annual parliaments) and was sentenced at the

High Court of Judiciary in Edinburgh by the implacable Braxfield after a travesty of a trial in 1793 to fourteen years' transportation in Botany Bay. An English Unitarian Minister, Thomas Fyshe Palmer, was also sentenced to deportation by Braxfield. In summing up against Muir, Braxfield declared that: 'This is the question for consideration. – Is the [prisoner] guilty of sedition or is he not? Now, before this can be answered, two things must be attended that require no proof: First, that the British constitution is the best that ever was since the creation of the world, and it is not possible to make it better.'

There were various small riots provoked by the Society, but nothing to justify the government's subsequent iron repression. A 'Treason Act' and a 'Sedition Act' (an offence new to Scotland) were passed in 1795. Cockburn saw it all as a witchhunt. He deplored the 'absolute straining for convictions' and the awful punishment. 'These trials,' he recalled in his *Memorials*, 'sank deep not merely into the popular mind, but into the minds of all men who thought.'

The most sensational development occurred in 1794, when a cache of arms was discovered in Edinburgh. The arsenal was traced to Robert Watt, 'a self-deluded former government spy' who evidently fantasized an uprising against the authorities. Desperate plans to seize the Castle, the banks, and the judges were discovered. Conspiratorial contacts had been made between the 'Society of United Scotsmen' and the 'United Irishmen'. Watt was publicly hanged as a traitor in November. As a traitor, his head was cut off and held aloft to the people of Edinburgh. Scott was there. 'It was a very solemn scene,' he told his aunt, Miss Christian Rutherford, 'but the pusillanimity of the unfortunate victim was astonishing considering the boldness of his nefarious plans. It is a matter of general regret that his Associate Downie should have received a reprieve.' Scott wanted more heads and exulted in the overthrow of 'our friends the democrats' and their 'Great Plan' (*Lett.* 1. 131). Fortified with 'some cold meat and a bottle of wine', he had earlier attended the trial of 'the Ednr. Traitors . . . which displayed to the public the most atrocious and deliberate plan of villainy which has occurred perhaps in the annals of G. Britain' (*Lett.* 1. 37).

It reads like facetious overstatement, but it was written in all sincerity. Excessive and bloodthirsty reaction to any sign of popular uprising was to be a regular feature of Scott's politics (HG 27). He was also on occasion physically violent at this stage of his life. In April 1794, Scott and a band of like-minded young advocates attended the Edinburgh Theatre armed with staves to ensure the singing of the National Anthem was not interrupted or mocked. A brawl broke out with some democratically inclined Irish medical students. Heads were broken (Scott boasted that he split three himself). Scott and his friends were arrested, and bound over to keep the peace. (Interestingly, it was Scott's uncle Robert – not his father – who warned the young man against this too boisterous expression of his political views.)

Partly as a reaction to the feared Jacobin rebellion, partly as a general mobilization against the French successes in Holland, a volunteer Edinburgh force was raised. Scott was mad with military zeal. He wrote to his uncle at Kelso, asking for a strong gelding 'such as would suit a stalwart dragoon' (i.e. himself). He was even prepared to sell his coin collection for the purpose. His lameness, however, was against him. His younger brother Tom joined up in late 1794 as a grenadier. John, of course, was already serving in the regular army. Over the next few years there was a general militarization of Scottish society. Edinburgh, as Cockburn said, became less a city than a camp. Burns – the erstwhile laureate of liberty – joined the Dumfries Volunteers, and turned his pen to poems such as 'Does Haughty Gaul Invasion Threat?' New regiments were raised. Scott was in an agony of frustration until 1797, when he too could take up arms. Agony is not too strong a term. There is a relevant boyhood anecdote told by Robert Chambers:

> It is the tradition of the family . . . that Sir Walter wished at this period to become a soldier. The illness, however, which had beset his early years rendered this wish bootless, even though his parents had been inclined to gratify it. His malady had the effect of contracting his right leg, so that he could hardly walk erect, even with the toes of that foot upon the ground. It has been related by a member of his family that, on this being represented to him as an insuperable obstacle to his entering the army, he left the room in an agony of mortified feeling, and was found some time afterwards suspended by the wrists from his bedroom window . . . On being asked the cause of this strange proceeding, he said he wished to prove to them that, however unfitted by his lower limbs for the profession of a soldier, he was at least strong enough in the arms. He had actually remained in that uneasy and trying posture for upwards of an hour. (Chambers, 23)

JESSIE, GREEN MANTLE AND MRS SCOTT

Scott's wife – a financial prize and a strikingly attractive woman – was expertly wooed and won over a whirlwind three weeks in early autumn 1797. By this stage in his life the twenty-six-year-old Scott – since 1790 a 'squire of dames' – was a seasoned lover. No part of his life is more unknown, but there survive patchy accounts of two previous affairs which reveal something of Scott in love and learning how to love to advantage – and, arguably, how to seduce. Writing in 1832 – with access to living gossip – Scott's first biographer, George Allan, claims to 'possess undeniable evidence that Scott was concerned . . . in at least one illicit amour' (Allan, 181).

The first of Scott's affairs we know about – that with 'Jessie' – has resisted the sleuthing efforts of all biographers, and remains tantalizingly shadowy.

(Lockhart is absolutely silent.) From an unpublished and coy memoir, written after Sir Walter was world-famous, some facts have emerged, and others may be conjectured (see *Lett.* 1. 8).[2] Jessie was a shopkeeper's daughter in Kelso (EJ 71). The young couple seem to have fallen in love during Scott's convalescence at his uncle's house, Rosebank, 1787–8. Scott would have been around seventeen at the time; old enough to lose his heart, but certainly not old enough to think seriously of marriage. In Kelso – if not in the greater world – young Walter Scott would have been seen as a catch; his aunt Janet and uncle Robert were both prominent land-holding members of the community and Walter was probably known to be heir to Rosebank. A future Writer to the Signet might well take a well-trained country girl for his wife once he was on his feet (so at least Jessie must have thought). Jessie was evidently 'a year or two' Walter's junior; old enough to lose her virginity, but still under the legal age of consent. Her father was 'an austers Presbyterian', and was kept in the dark as to his daughter's lover. The easier-going Captain Scott may have known, and conceivably even have encouraged his nephew's apprentice philandering. The young couple evidently had a mutual interest in ballads, which may have been their public cover for meeting.

The affair supposedly went on 'three or four years at least'. The source notes that the young people ignored the 'mischievous tendency of their conduct' (Cook, 2) and Johnson takes the hint that at some point the affair was 'consummated'. (Allan's phrase 'undeniable evidence' hints at a bastard child). But it seems to have been unable to develop into a mature relationship. Scott was often at Kelso, but more often in Edinburgh. His life was undergoing changes with the return to university. There was a long interval, during which – unknown to Scott – Jessie was actually at the house of a sick and deaf aunt in Edinburgh, a few hundred yards away from George Square. They met by accident on a common stair, and the affair resumed. But in the city it seems that the tradesman's daughter's rustic charms did not show to advantage. Grierson suggests that Scott felt 'snobbish' qualms now that he was an advocate in the making. Jessie herself apparently believed that she had a rival. For whatever reason, Scott gave up his 'humble blue-eyed Kelso beauty' (EJ 67). Her deaf aunt died, she inherited a small property, married a medical student, emigrated to London, and nursed a lifelong 'resentment' for Walter Scott – her putative seducer (EJ 68–71).

The 'rival' thesis has on the face of it some support. As Edgar Johnson puts it with his usual gallantry 'only a little later [than the end of the Jessie affair] we learn that a certain pair of eyes shaded beneath a green mantle have made their fateful entrance on the scene' (EJ 67–71). The eyes and the green mantle belonged to Williamina Belsches, the *amour fou* of Scott's life. Melodramatic significance is invested in this affair. It left, according to Edgar Johnson, 'a wound whose scar never disappeared' (EJ 124). The suffering however had its benefits as a rite of passage:

'When he disciplined his pain, it left him a man'. Scott himself encouraged by judicious hints a portentous interpretation of the Green Mantle episode. In his journal – which he intended one day to be published – he referred to its having made a crack in his heart which 'will remain till my dying day' (Jrnl. 43).

We learn about Green Mantle's fateful entrance around the time of Jessie's presumed exit (i.e. 1790) from two sources. In the revised (1848) version of his biography Lockhart refers indirectly to Williamina. The context, however, is tendentious. The nineteen-year-old Scott, Lockhart claims, was protected from 'low and vulgar debaucheries' or 'the remotest dream of tampering with female innocence' by 'a secret attachment, which continued, through the most perilous stage of life, to act as a romantic charm in safeguard of virtue' (Lock. 1. 143–4). Lockhart evidently had in mind the fifty-or-so brothels in Edinburgh's High Street in whose risky neighbourhood Scott was regularly drinking to excess.

One might be sceptical, and think that this is another dab of Lockhartian whitewash. But the 1790 date is confirmed by William Clerk. In a letter to Sophia Lockhart in 1835 (three years after Scott's death), he wrote:

> Your father's penchant for the lady [i.e. Green Mantle] began I think in the year 1790 (her mother Lady Jane was an acquaintance of his mother which led to a visiting acquaintance) it was a prodigious secret at first which I discovered by observing that [Walter] wore a sort of medallion in the style of Tassie's heads about his neck which had been made for him by a Mons. Guildbert, a french tutor, and shortly afterwards he told me all about it, he certainly was very much attached to her. (HG 29)

Clerk was Scott's *fidus Achates* at this period, and they were 'daily companions' (EJ 74). The date – 1790 – would have stuck in his mind.

Lockhart quotes the following guarded remarks from a letter, 'among the first' in a series from a friend that began in 1788: 'Your Quixotism, dear Walter, was highly characteristic. From the description of the blooming fair, as she appeared when she lowered her *manteau vert*, I am hopeful you have not dropped the acquaintance' (HG 29). Lockhart makes the obvious connection between this and 'Lady Green Mantle' in *Redgauntlet* – the beautiful young woman Darsie falls in love with. The 'blooming fair' is, presumably, the 'Green Mantle' that less discreet biographers than Lockhart have eagerly identified by name as Williamina Belsches.[3] Edgar Johnson goes so far as to speculate about the exact costume details: 'The green mantle was Williamina's walking cloak of silk, fancifully embroidered, and with a deep hood shadowing her rose-tinted pallor'.

Lockhart adds another detail of the early relationship with Williamina, which has been much seized on by biographers (and at least one romantic novelist):

I believe, however, that the 'pretty young woman' here specially alluded to had occupied his attention long before he ever appeared in the Edinburgh Assembly Rooms, or any of his friends took note of him as 'setting up for a squire of dames' [i.e. long before 1790]. I have been told that their acquaintance began in the Greyfriars' churchyard, where rain beginning to fall one Sunday as the congregation were dispersing, Scott happened to offer his umbrella, and the tender being accepted, so escorted her to her residence, which proved to be at no great distance from his own. To return from church together had, it seems, grown into something like a custom, before they met in society, Mrs Scott being one of the party. It then appeared that she and the lady's mother had been companions in their youth, though, both living secludedly, they had scarcely seen each other for many years; and the two matrons now renewed their former intercourse. (Lock. 1. 144–5)

It makes a charming picture. The 'young Hercules' looming protectively with his umbrella over the pretty young girl, demurely dressed for church with a green mantle covering her head. The rain falls around them, their heads decently but excitingly close under the umbrella's hood. Meanwhile the mothers exchange friendly civilities, fondly remembering their own girlhood intimacies. Edgar Johnson lets his imagination rip in gilding Lockhart's version: 'Walter talked animatedly, no doubt about Ariosto and Launcelot and Baldur the Beautiful and Border ballads, and Williamina's cheek glowed and her lips curved in laughter' (EJ 109).

Unfortunately, there are some facts which don't fit. Williamina's mother was twenty years younger than Anne Scott. They cannot have been girl friends together, as Lockhart implies. Even more perplexing are Williamina's dates. Scott did not propose to her until August 1795, when she was just nineteen, and he did not get a definite reply until a year later. At the time of the supposed meeting in Greyfriars churchyard, she was fourteen – taking Clerk's date of 1790. But Lockhart states his belief that Scott's tender feelings 'long' precede 1790 and offers a 1788 date for of the '*manteau vert*' allusion, which gives us Scott making sheep's eyes at a twelve-year-old. And it is secret passion for this nymphet which supposedly acts as a sovereign prophylactic against the High Street's ladies of the night for five years, and through some epic drinking during which even the most steadfast lover might lapse. Meanwhile, somewhere in the background, is his 'three or four years at least' relationship with Jessie (1787–91? 1788–92?). Most damningly, James Corson points out that a letter to Jessie dated tentatively by Grierson '1787–9' must in fact (by reference to the dates of ballads cited) be dated 1792 or later (Corson, 3). Other letters to Jessie follow. If the Jessie letters are not forgeries, Scott was making passionate love to her (physical love, if Johnson's 'consummation' thesis is accepted) while he was madly and purely in love with fifteen-year-old 'Green Mantle' Williamina.

Edgar Johnson does his best with this awkward chronology. The relationship began, he suggests, as a casual 'boy and girl' thing in the rain in 1790. (He cannot bring himself to give up the Greyfriars meeting, although he jiggles with the date by two years so as to make her age plausible.) 'Little by little,' Johnson surmises, 'in the course of 1791 and 1792 we find [Scott's] feelings warming and deepening' (EJ 109). The evidence for this is very slight. In September 1792 Scott wrote to Clerk, 'I have no prospect of seeing *ma chère adorable* till winter, if then' (HG 123). Who the adored one is, he does not say. In 1793, on a visit to St Andrews, he is supposed to have carved Williamina's name on the turf beside the castle gate (would that he had carved it on a young oak for his later biographers' benefit). Other than this, it is not easy to find the 'feelings warming and deepening' that Johnson describes. But we have to suppose the warming and deepening continued until 1795, when it reached white heat and volcanic force, and a madly-in-love Scott proposed, was rejected, and desperately contemplated suicide.

One is in a realm of cobwebby speculation. But nonetheless, there are scenarios that knit the few known facts together rather better than Johnson's cradle-snatching Scott. Most likely, Scott continued his liaison with Jessie well into the 1790s. It was her necklace that Scott wore, and his love-making with her – as Lockhart surmises – did preserve him from too frequent recourse (or any recourse) to whores. But with his qualification as an advocate, Scott conceived for himself a higher class of wife. She was cast off – not necessarily unkindly – and Scott began methodically to look for someone more in keeping with his elevated station in life.

What is certain, is that around 1795–6 Scott became very interested indeed in Williamina Belsches. It is likely that his head as well as his heart was involved. He was now twenty-four and looking for a wife. She was eminently eligible – the daughter of a baronet, Sir John Belsches (Sir John Stuart after 1798, when he assumed his wife's name) and the granddaughter of an earl. Sir John was an MP and had enriched himself in the service of the East India Company. His wife, Lady Jane Stuart, brought a large estate in Fettercairn, Kincardineshire, to the marriage. Williamina was herself an heiress, and might bequeath a baronetcy to any male child she bore. She was, in short, of much loftier station than a briefless advocate, the son of a Writer to the Signet, and the grandson of a tenant farmer.

Williamina – who had evidently come out in her eighteenth year – went 'a good deal into public' (EJ 111) over the winter and early spring 1794–5, and one assumes that she and Scott met and flirted. Scott, apparently urged on by Clerk, proposed to Williamina by letter in summer 1795, after she had returned to Fettercairn, the Edinburgh season being over. Scott received a reply in early August which has not survived. Clerk confided to Sophia Lockhart in 1835 Scott's reaction, which was that Williamina's letter was 'highly flattering and favourable', but ultimately non-committal, advocating a 'prudent line of conduct' (HG 30). It did not, evidently, entirely preclude an eventual (long) engagement. She may have been playing with the young man, as Matilda plays with the poetry-writing Wilfrid in *Rokeby*. It is likely that even at this early date, however, Williamina and her parents were aware of the interest of a 'rich young laird and banker', William

Forbes (HG 31). Among his other attractions, Forbes (two years younger than Scott) was the heir to a baronetcy. Scott was apparently left on tenter-hooks for the remainder of 1795 and early 1796. The evidence is scanty, but it seems that Williamina did not go much into public in this year.

Scott was aided in his wooing of Williamina by two confidantes – Jane Anne Cranstoun (the sister of his friend George) and his youthful half-aunt Chritty Rutherford who knew the Stuart-Belsches family well. It was Jane, apparently, who advised Scott to call in aid his newly honed poetic skills. Over one night in March 1796 (EJ 115) Scott allegedly dashed off sixty-six stanzas of his translation of 'Lenore'. At Jane's suggestion and with her help, he had an early copy specially printed and bound for Williamina, languishing in Kincardineshire (EJ 114). After some anxiety, he was invited (after hanging around the area hopefully) to stay for seven days at Fettercairn at the end of April.

Scott languished over the summer without apparently seeing Williamina or hearing from her. But dire rumours about the progress of his rival, 'Don Guglielmo', came to his ears. On 12 October her engagement to William Forbes was announced. Friends feared for Walter's life and reason: 'This is not good news,' one wrote. 'I shudder at the violence of his irritable and most ungovernable mind' (HG 39). Wilfrid, it will be remembered, dies of frustrated love in *Rokeby*, expiring in the church before the altar where he nobly surrenders Matilda to his rival. Scott is generally supposed to have recalled his feelings of October 1796 in *Rob Roy*, when Frank supposes (wrongly) that he will never see Di Vernon again and weeps the only tears of his manhood, experiencing the 'hysterica passio of poor Lear'.

In a cooler but no less black mood Scott made sarcastic reference to Forbes as 'dot and carry one' (i.e. a mere ledger-drudging bank clerk). One could, of course, retort that Walter Scott, former apprentice Writer to the Signet, was more of a clerk than William Forbes, heir to one of the greatest banks in Edinburgh. But Scott evidently believed that it was a match of convenience – Williamina was not marrying a man, she was marrying a financial institution and a prospective title. In a notebook poem presumably composed in the dark days of October 1796 Scott declared: 'For grandeur, for wealth your poor friend you resign' (HG 40). He evidently (and rightly) suspected that Williamina's mother had influenced her daughter's choice. Matilda in *Rokeby* is a very passive creature and obedient to her elders. One of the few poems Scott is known to have written for Williamina – 'The Violet' – suggests by its very title a retiring nature. In a letter, he refers to her adorable 'meekness'. But having examined Williamina's surviving correspondence Grierson and Edgar Johnson are inclined to believe that the young lady had some backbone, and 'made up her own mind' (EJ 120). She unmeekly preferred William to Walter. But the young peoples' parents seem nonetheless to have meddled quite unromantically in the affair. Lady Jane, mother of the long dead Williamina, confessed bitter remorse to Scott in 1827 for having cut him out.

She was not alone. 'Long afterwards', as he claimed, Scott discovered that his father had warned Sir John about the affair with a view to spiking his son's guns. Since Walter Scott WS was incapacitated by a stroke in 1795–6, one assumes he interfered at some point in late 1794 or early 1795, when his son's intentions became manifestly earnest. It is possible that they discussed and even quarrelled about the matter. The father's intervention was almost certainly inspired by the anxiety that he could not afford the settlement such a match would involve. On his part, Sir John was financially embarrassed in 1796, and a connection with the banking house of Sir William Forbes would be extremely useful.

It was Scott himself who gave currency to the received view that the Williamina affair was cataclysmic – by hints to his biographer and in his journal, and by recreations of it in his narratives. Johnson states as something incontrovertible that 'To his dying day [Scott's] suffering left its mark on his entire being' (EJ 123). But there are grounds for being suspicious. Whatever intimacies Scott enjoyed with the young Williamina in 1794–5, the fact that he was effectively barred from her presence after his proposal in August 1795 must have dampened his hopes well before October 1796 when his rejection was confirmed. Did he really think that she was going to elope with him in defiance of her parents? He must have realized – even if his father did not tell him, as he surely did – that he was not an ideal suitor in the eyes of the lady's parents. And if Scott was so violently upset that his friends feared some act of blood or madness why did he, four months later, join with William Forbes to form the Light Dragoons? Given the smallness of the troop, the two young men must have been constant mess-mates – and this at a period when Forbes was just returned from his honeymoon. When Forbes died in 1828, Scott wrote to a friend, Sir Alexander Wood, who had been a close companion of both young officers in the 1790s:

> In him [i.e. William Forbes] I feel I have sustained a loss which no after years of my life can fill up to me. Our early friendship none knew better than you; and you also well know that if I look back to the gay and happy hours of youth, they must be filled with recollections of our departed friend. In the whole course of life our friendship has been uninterrupted as his kindness has been unwearied. (*Lett.* 11. 26)

One would think that robbing Scott of the only woman he ever really loved might interrupt friendship, at least for a month or two. But it seems not to have done. Williamina and William were married on 17 January 1797. The Light Dragoons in which Walter and William were fellow officers was formed on 14 February. There must have been toasts to the beautiful Mrs Forbes in the mess, and Scott must have drunk them with his comrades – unless he wanted to provoke a duel. (Just twelve months later, William was in a position to drink to the beautiful Mrs Walter Scott, and presumably did so.) It is hard to believe that some manly conversation on the lines of 'the best man won . . . no hard feelings' did not take place.

According to one account Scott rushed up to Fettercairn in October, 'was rejected by Williamina in person and left her presence in a rage, saying that he would be married before her' (Pearson, 35). Since she married in double haste in January 1797 (possibly to forestall any more changes of mind) Walter failed to make good his threat. But he did not fail by much. On Christmas Day 1797 Walter Scott was a married man. Hardly an hour was wasted. As soon as the Court of Session rose in July, he and his brother John (now a captain in the British army) and his fellow-volunteer Adam Ferguson went on a horseback expedition (Scott mounted on his ominously named steed, Lenore) over the Border into the English Lake District. From there, the three young raiders eventually landed up in Gilsland, a watering place just south of the Border. It was exactly the kind of summer resort where young people might find marriage partners.

Scott was clearly on the lookout for a Mrs Scott. He duly met and won her in the shape of Charlotte Carpenter. 'Miss Carpenter's charm', as Johnson gallantly puts it, 'was less that of ideal beauty than of a vivid bloom' (EJ 139). But she was undeniably a catch: attractive, mature, sophisticated, and extraordinarily well connected. There was, however, an insoluble mystery about Charlotte Carpenter, or Marguerite Charlotte Charpentier, as she had been born. She was almost a year older than Scott and, in her twenty-seventh year, not as young as many brides of her class (she was considerably older than Williamina, for instance, and felt obliged to misrepresent her age to Scott by several years; EJ 149). She had a marked French accent, and made numerous phonetic mistakes in writing English. One account says she was in the Lakes so as to be kept away from a suitor of whom her guardians disapproved. This rustication, her relatively advanced age, and her dashing looks, suggest that she was not, like Green Mantle, a shrinking violet nor, like Jessie, easily seduced. If, as eventually transpired, her guardians were quite happy to have her marry – on the strength of two weeks' acquaintance – a penniless Scottish advocate, wholly unknown to the family, what must the unsuitable suitor have been like? There was no father in tow at Gilsland, and no clear information as to her background.

Lockhart's version is beautiful, but erroneous, deliberately so, one assumes. Charlotte, as Lockhart's *Life* tells us, was the daughter of Jean-François Charpentier, the 'Ecuyer du Roi de l'Académie' in Lyons (i.e. the director of the military academy in the city). A staunch Royalist, Charpentier hedged against the coming revolution by investing £4,000 in English securities and a mortgage on one of the Downshire estates. The son of the Marquess of Downshire, Viscount Fairford, who was to inherit his father's title in 1793, was a personal friend. According to Lockhart, Charpentier died at the beginning of the Revolution and 'Madame Charpentier made her escape with her children, first to Paris, and then to England, where they found a warm friend and protector in the late Marquis of Downshire [d. 1801], who had, in the course of his travels in France, formed an intimate acquaintance with the family, and indeed spent some time under their roof' (Lock. 1. 247). According to Lockhart, Madame Charpentier was a Protestant and at her insistence her children were brought up in that faith.

This goes beyond the tantalizingly little that Charlotte (with some prodding) told Scott about her background in the lovers' premarital correspondence. In a disingenuous reply to the enquiries of the Scott family, who were suspicious of Walter's French fiancée, she merely claimed that her father and Fairford had been close friends and the Viscount had become her guardian when her father died in her very early girlhood 'before she knew him'.

It is likely that Lockhart invented his lurid melodrama of threatened guillotines and tumbrils to square with some unpleasant versions of Charlotte's background that were already current in Edinburgh as he wrote his biography. Weir, for instance, in his life of Scott mentions 'whispers (never substantially contradicted) that her nominal guardian, the Marquis of Downshire, stood in a closer affinity to [Charlotte]' (Allan, 184). Robert Chambers in an account of Scott's life published serially in *Chambers's Edinburgh Journal* 1832–3 (i.e. five years before the publication of Lockhart's *Life*) alleged that the young Viscount Fairford, having been introduced to M. Charpentier in France by a mutual friend, eloped with Mme Charpentier. A 'liaison' ensued. No dates were given for this episode, leaving open the paternity of Charlotte. She and her brother Jean-David were subsequently taken care of by Fairford, Chambers informed his readers. Charlotte was educated in a convent, and Jean-David was helped by the Viscount's interest to a lucrative post in the East India Company, on the understanding that he remit £200 a year for the support (and dowry) of his sister. It is not known where Chambers got his account, which contains a surprising amount of true detail.

Lockhart's account clearly attempts to supply a preferable alternative to Chambers's and to throw a romantic haze over what it cannot explain away. (Lady Scott was, after all, his mother-in-law.) But the major element in Lockhart's version – M. Charpentier's investments in England – has never been substantiated. The presumption is that Lockhart made up the £4,000 and the business arrangement with Downshire. Twentieth-century research has supplied new facts, most of which swing the balance Chambers's way, but not entirely. It is presumed the Charpentiers married in 1769–70 (HG 49). There are three known children of their marriage; Charlotte (b. 1770), Jean-David [later renamed Charles] (b. 1772) and a Noel (b. 1775), who probably died in infancy. There is no evidence that Mme Charpentier was a Protestant. M. Charpentier was some twenty years older than his wife.

One of the oddities about the Charpentier household is that it seems to have been much frequented by British tourists. Grierson's guess, which seems plausible, is that a young Welsh spendthrift, Wyrriot Owen, who stayed with the Charpentiers in the late 1770s, was to blame for the immediate break-up of the Charpentier household. Owen left Charlotte's mother some money in trust in 1778, shortly before his bankruptcy and

premature death a year later. It may have been repayment of a debt, or
reparation for having seduced her. It is one of the many oddities in this
matter that the money was never claimed by Mme Charpentier, for the
good reason that she did not know about it. (Scott's interest in the accrued
sum, in later life, is the clue that eventually led researchers to Owen.)
Another oddity is that the Charpentiers still seem to have been living
together a year after Owen's death (EJ 147).

The assumption is that the young Viscount Fairford succeeded Owen as
Madame Charpentier's 'protector' and supported her, either in London or
Paris, or both places for some years after 1780. Mme Charpentier is known
to have been in England – possibly with her children – in 1785. Fairford
married nobly in 1786. It was a period of new responsibilities in his life. In
1793, when his father died, he assumed the Marquisate of Downshire. With
his marriage he may have wished to put his private life in order and – as
kindly as possible – sweep any French mistresses under the carpet or across
the channel.

Around the same date as her protector's marriage, 1786, Mme
Charpentier returned to Paris, where she continued to receive an allowance from her English protector (possibly on condition that she stay away
from England). Her life in France, on the evidence of one surviving letter,
seems to have been mildly dissolute and irregular. Charlotte and her
brother Jean-David [Charles] were meanwhile baptized into the Church of
England in May 1787. The Charpentier children became thoroughly Angli-
cized, even in name: Charlotte and Charles Carpenter. The reason for the
change, according to Charlotte, was the unpopularity of her race during
the French Revolutionary Wars. It may also have been done to sever any
lingering connection with the now disreputable Mme Charpentier. She
died, French to the end, in 1788; a year before the Revolution which
Lockhart pictures her fleeing. Her daughter seems not to have seen her
mother in later years.

It is recorded that on her deathbed, Charlotte muttered something that
could be construed as 'Lord Downshire' and 'father'. Was Downshire the
children's father? He certainly seems to have acted with paternal benevolence. In March 1789, he arranged Charles's appointment with the East
India Company on condition – as Chambers correctly records – that he pay
his sister £200 a year from his salary. This could be thought suspicious. But,
as Edgar Johnson notes, Viscount Fairford was born in 1753. There is no
record of his having been in France the year before Charlotte's birth, when
he would have been sixteen or seventeen. That he was her father at this
early age is unlikely.

The nagging question is, why did Fairford go to such lengths to look
after these children if they were not his own? Why would he pay their
mother a quarterly allowance in France? Innocent explanations are possible. He may, as Charlotte claimed, have been a very kind marquess.
Charlotte's other explanation was that her father and Fairford were close
friends. But, as Johnson points out, there was a large age gap – thirty years

between the two men, as well as a language. What could they have had in common? The most plausible assumption is that Mme Charpentier knew Fairford as a young man and after the breakup of her marriage became his mistress for a few years. On his marriage he pensioned her off generously and remained kind to her children whom he brought up to be more respectable than the mother whom he had helped make unrespectable.

Another conundrum is – what was Charlotte doing between May 1787, when she was baptized into the Church of England (aged seventeen), and August 1797 when, as Johnson puts it, 'a blue-eyed, flaxen-polled, young lawyer fell desperately in love with her brown eyes and dark hair' (EJ 148). Although at the time of her death in Paris Mme Charpentier was described as a 'widow', five years later in 1791 M. Charpentier is recorded as living as an *émigré* in Alsace with his daughter Charlotte. (Her statement to Scott in October 1797 that her father died before she had a chance to know him was evidently a falsehood; EJ 1. xii, 45). What seems likely is that Charlotte was kept at a convent until she was sixteen or seventeen (i.e. 1787). At this point she was brought to London, where her mother was living as Fairford's mistress, and baptized. When she was twenty-one (1790–1) Fairford conceived his responsibility to her was fulfilled, and she was sent to her father, currently a refugee from the Revolution in Alsace. Charpentier died in the early 1790s, and Charlotte – reluctant to return to the Parisian Terror – came to England where, now an orphan, she threw herself on the mercy of Fairford. It was a period when there was a great deal of philanthropy towards the French *émigrés* who were flooding across the channel. In London Charlotte was connected with a well-established French *émigré* family, headed by Charles Dumergue (he was a fashionable dentist by profession and had known the Charpentiers in Lyons, when they were still an intact family). Fairford, by now Marquess of Downshire, may well have made arrangements for Charlotte to stay with them and to go into society under their aegis. A woman of some experience, Charlotte was currently (in 1797) under the superintendence of a companion – Miss Jane Nicolson. The two of them were in the Lake District because Miss Nicolson (and presumably the Marquess her guardian) had disapproved of some suitor of Charlotte's in London, where they normally lived. And who was Miss Nicolson? – probably another 'cast mistress' of Downshire's.

The mystery is compounded by the fibs Scott told his own family about Charlotte after he had been accepted. On 6/7 October he had written to Charlotte enquiring rather nervously about 'your father's country and profession' (*Lett.* 1. 71). Late in the same month he wrote to his half-aunt Chritty Rutherford (a trusted confidante in his affairs of the heart) stating that though Charlotte 'was born in France her parents were of English extraction, the name Carpenter . . . though born in France, she has the sentiments and manners of an Englishwoman and does not like to be thought of otherwise – a very slight tinge in her pronunciation is all which marks the foreigner . . . She was baptized and educated a protestant of the Church of England.' Charlotte's (ostensible) parents were entirely French;

she had a pronounced French accent; and was baptized at the age of seventeen, having (probably) been educated in a Catholic convent. It is possible that Scott was diplomatically playing down the French-Catholicism in deference to the susceptibilities of his Presbyterian father. But it is clear that from the first he was willing to protect his wife by a shield of lies.

In later life Scott affected not to know or to be at all curious about his wife's early history. Writing in 1827 to Lockhart, shortly after Lady Scott's death, he tersely noted that 'there was, I believe, domestic distress and disagreement between Made. Charpentier and her husband – at least I have conjectured so much' (EJ 146). Grierson claims that we know more about Charlotte 'than Scott himself ever knew' (HG 46). This is questionable. Someone as fascinated by genealogy and as ambitious for his 'race' as Walter Scott would surely have made discreet enquiries over the years. He would certainly have wanted to know what blood was in his children's veins. He was a lawyer skilled in investigations into delicate matters. He made a habit of staying with the Dumergues in London when Charlotte was not present. It would have been natural to have asked a question or two. Scott's silence on the subject – like Lockhart's fabrications – suggests something needed to be covered up.

Scott swept Charlotte off her feet in his three weeks at Gilsland. She apparently put up some resistance to his overtures, but 'the whirlwind of his desire swept away her resistance' (EJ 140). Whirlwinds aside, their choice of each other speaks much for Scott's and Charlotte's Austenish good sense. Scott, as he pointed out to Charlotte in an early letter, was turning his new contacts in the Light Dragoons to excellent advantage. His comradely connexion with the offspring of the Duke of Buccleuch (Lord Dalkeith) and Lord Melville (Robert Dundas) had been particularly advantageous. He was already promised by his patrons a sheriff's position worth £250 a year, when one became vacant. The Marquess of Downshire would be another invaluable patron.

Comments on Lady Scott in later life are mixed, and some of them very hostile – alleging that she was a shrew, too fond of the bottle, and an opium addict. But in 1797 she was right for Scott. Charlotte Charpentier was a woman of strong character, vivacious appearance, possessed of money and noble connections. More importantly, she embodied the glamorous greater-than-Edinburgh world that Scott longed to occupy. On her part, it was astute of Charlotte to penetrate the provincial shell of her suitor and to see that he was, in fact, a more promising man than his two dashing companions on the expedition to Gilsland. He had 'great expectations', she told Downshire. Nor did he misrepresent himself to her; in a letter before she had committed herself he confessed that he had no money and was 'only the second brother of a large family' with no prospect of inheriting money. All he had to offer was his abilities. It seems likely that she could have taken the safer, older brother, John, had she so wanted and perhaps even the more obviously eligible Ferguson (EJ 138).

Once Charlotte had accepted him Scott wrote a number of supremely tactful letters to Downshire and received gracious assent to his proposals. The Marquess did not require to see him, being satisfied merely by the 'manly' tone of the young lover's correspondence. This is slightly odd – Scott could easily have been summoned. Perhaps Downshire felt that at twenty-seven Charlotte might not have too many more eligible suitors. It was a nerve-wracking interval. Although ostensibly Scott was asking Downshire's permission for Charlotte's hand, the real point at issue was her money allowance. If this allowance were not continued from the Marquess (or his *protégé* Charles Carpenter) they could not marry. Scott was no longer, as he had been with Williamina, a reckless lover.

Scott's own family were also sticky. The Frenchness of Charlotte was a problem. So too was money. Walter Scott WS, paralysed by strokes and querulous, made difficulties. He wanted to reserve what wealth he had for John, the elder son and heir, who needed his majority (which would have to be purchased) and a piece of land to retire to. The word 'imprudent' was bandied about. Having interfered behind his son's back with Williamina Belsches, Mr Scott seemed determined to ruin his son's marriage chances yet again. Walter at one particularly frustrated state of the negotiations threatened to decamp to the West Indies. All was made straight, however, when Charles Carpenter vouchsafed a raised pension for his sister of £500 a year from the income of the Indian post (Commercial Resident at Salem) which the Downshire interest had procured for him (*Lett.* 1. 61). According to Chambers there was another discordant voice. 'It chanced . . . that one of Mr Scott's female friends, who did not, however, entertain [Downshire's] respectful notion of him, hearing of some love adventure in which he had been entangled at Gilsland, wrote to [Mrs Bird] with whom she was acquainted, inquiring if she had heard of such a thing, and "what kind of a young lady was it, who was going to take Watty Scott?"' (Chambers, 40).

The wedding took place in Carlisle on Christmas Eve, 1797. Although the couple had his consent and full approval, the ceremony was not graced by the Marquess of Downshire's presence. Pressing business in his Irish estates detained him. Nor were Walter Scott WS or Mrs Scott present – presumably by reason of his sickness. The Scotts did not meet their daughter-in-law until after the ceremony nor does there ever seem to have been any closeness between the older and the younger Mrs Walter Scott. John Bird, a Carlisle clergyman, was a witness at the wedding. According to Chambers, it was the Revd. Bird who had initially introduced Fairford to the Charpentier family in France.

Over the years, the Scotts' marriage does not seem to have been based on any great passion. According to Weir, Scott when twitted by a friend on his choice of wife declared 'she would bring him bairns, and not interfere with his work, and that was all he cared for' (Allan, 184). The general verdict is that it was at best a prudent, mutually affectionate union. Scott himself summed up his marriage relationship tepidly to Lady Abercorn (with whom he had an epistolary flirtation) after ten years of wedded life:

> Mrs Scott's match and mine was of our own making and proceeded from the most sincere affection on both sides which has rather increased than diminished during twelve years' marriage. But it was something short of Love in all its forms which I suspect people only feel *once* in their lives folks who have been nearly drownd in bathing rarely venturing a second time out of their depth. (Hew. 80)

'To Horse, To Horse!': German Poems and Light Dragoons

The period of Scott's search for a wife (1794–7) coincides with his first serious attempts at authorship. In autumn 1795 he caught the infection of German balladry which was sweeping Edinburgh. In April 1796 his first significant composition – the imitation of Bürger's 'Lenore', retitled 'William and Helen' – was (supposedly) specially printed for Williamina. As part of a 'thin quarto' the poem was given to the wider world (or at least some Edinburgh friends) in late August 1796. All the while that he was courting Charlotte in late 1797 Scott was reading, translating, and imitating German drama and poetry. He was aided by the scholarly William Erskine and by a new friend whom he made in 1796, James Skene, 'an Aberdeenshire laird four years his junior who had just returned from two years in Saxony and was now about to be called to the bar' (EJ 130). Possessed of a good German library, Skene 'also shared Scott's love of horseback exercise'. Scott had material assistance from his new German kinswoman, Scott of Harden's wife, who got for him German texts of Goethe, Schiller, and other authors hard to come by in Edinburgh. In March 1799 Scott's first gainful publication, a translation of Goethe's *Götz von Berlichingen*, appeared and he was an author indeed.

Scott's early German efforts are customarily deprecated as literary infantilism – 'a transient subjection to foreign literary models'. While undeniably minor and immature, Scott's experiments in the German mode merit more than dismissal or neglect. And read symptomatically, Scott's early German imitations record an important liberation from the 'confinement' which plagued his youth. This liberation took two forms. First, German poetry gave Scott an eloquent language of grand emotions and a repertory of grand theatrical gestures – something that the pinched Presbyterianism of his fathers denied him. (His ultra-Wertherian reaction to Williamina's cruelty is a case in point.) Secondly, the German poems reveal how vital the horse was to Scott's sense of transcending his 'disability' – his lame right leg.

More than with most authors, we know what beasts Scott possessed during his life – it is, after all, his favourite dog not his wife who lies with him in stone under the Princes Street monument. We are particularly well informed about the four-footed friends who bore Scott on their backs. He evidently had a 'dwarf shetland pony' (EJ 26) at Sandy Knowe and was given the loan of a family horse when, as a teenager, he undertook work for his father in Perthshire and elsewhere outside Edinburgh. There were prob-ably other household beasts he could borrow in his adolescence. But it would seem that Walter got a horse of his own at about the age that many young men today get their first car, in 1792 when he qualified as an advocate. Then it was he began his 'raids' into Liddesdale. In 1794, he asked his uncle for a strong gelding 'such as would suit a stalwart dragoon'. Not long after he acquired a mare, which he (meaningfully) called Lenore.

Scott's imitation of Bürger's 'Lenore' climaxes on a vividly described gallop to a grisly wedding ceremony cum interment. The poem contains the immortally bad lines:

> Tramp! tramp! along the land they rode,
> Splash! splash! along the sea.

'The Chase' (otherwise 'The Wild Huntsman'), which was published along with 'William and Helen' in Scott's first volume, is a translation of Bürger's 'Wilde Jäger'. The 'Wildgrave' of the title is encountered on horseback, accompanied by two strangers, one fair one dark. He is encouraged by his dark companion to various acts of brutality as he rides on his way. As a consequence, the Wildgrave is cursed to ride his horse forever, as an equestrian Flying Dutchman. 'The Erl King', a translation from Goethe, comprises a mad gallop, mimetically described, as a father, his young son behind him, tries, unsuccessfully, to outride a demon. 'Frederick and Alice', a loose translation from Goethe, was first published in Matthew Lewis's *Tales of Wonder* (1801) but written (apparently) like 'The Erl King' in autumn 1797. At this period, anxiously awaiting approval of his marriage plans, Scott's only pastimes were galloping on Leith Sands and at night making translations from the German. In 'Frederick and Alice' he dis-honours her, she curses him and dies. Frederick is subsequently visited by her vengeful wraith and flies off, galloping as fast as he can for seven days and nights.

What all these poems have in common – in addition to the crude romanticism that Daiches deplores – is an obsession with heroic or doomed feats of equestrianism. If Scott was 'German mad' in the 1790s he was also horse mad. Scott was later to refine this mania into two of the finest passages of his poetry: Deloraine's devil-take-the-hindmost gallop to Melrose in *The Lay of the Last Minstrel* and James's horseback chase of the stag at the beginning of *The Lady of the Lake*. But what these immature poems of 1796–7 communicate is sheer exultation in mobility: the lame man's discovery that he can run, run, run. The mad gallop was evidently for Scott what the Hellespont was to Byron – an athletic arena in which he was not lame. German poetry fused with this intoxicating mobility. At the same time it fused with his romantic 'raids' into Liddesdale, his growing obsession with 'riding ballads' (which were to make up the mass of *The Minstrelsy of the Scottish Border*) and, above all, with the bounding sexual desires of Walter Scott in love. (It is significant that the first time Scott met Charlotte they were both on horseback.) In his essay on 'Chivalry', written for the *Encyclopaedia Britannica* in 1817, Scott declares that merely *being* on horseback raises a man's morality and general humanity.

There was another liberation for Scott associated directly with the horse. He had always longed to be a soldier. John Scott had gone into the regular army. It was a bitter blow in 1794 when his younger brothers, Tom and Daniel, were accepted for the Volunteers, but he – because of his bad leg – was rejected. In December 1796 there was another invasion scare and a serious attempt by the French to land a force in Ireland. This emergency revived the Volunteer spirit. And, as Johnson puts it:

> In Edinburgh the idea of a volunteer force of light horse broached almost three years earlier was revived again. Scott's lameness made it impossible for him to serve on foot, but mounted! – all the belligerence of his moss-trooper forebears flamed up in him at the thought. On horseback he could cut and slash with any man. Soon he had fired Skene and a group of other friends with his glow. (EJ 131)

Scott was the moving spirit behind the formation in February 1797 of a body of light cavalry, comprising Edinburgh gentleman of the officer class mounted and uniformed at their own expense (at his uncle's expense in Scott's case). They constituted a kind of rich man's *posse comitatus*. In April the King gave his consent that Scott's gentleman posse be called the Royal Edinburgh Volunteer Light Dragoons. Scott was appointed quartermaster, secretary and paymaster of what grew to two troops of fifty men apiece. (As in the 'Spec', and his later service on the boards of companies, Scott's office training with his father stood him in good stead.) He was also the unit's bard, and composed a rousing 'War Song' – adapted from a German *Kriegslied* – which begins 'To Horse! To Horse!'

All through the spring, the dragoons laboriously drilled (typically before breakfast) while the country seethed with expectation of invasion and civil insurrection. It is clear from anecdotes that Scott's first forays into long narrative verse were initially done for the delectation of his cavalry comrades. This may explains his later addiction to what he called the 'light horse stanza' and the octosyllabic line – ideal for lively recitation but limited in its literary range.

In March 1797 Scott informed his friend Murray of Simprin (a professional soldier) that he too was 'quite a military man' (*Lett.* 1. 64). By all accounts, Scott was intoxicated with his new military status – so much so that some of his lawyer friends found his trooper airs obnoxious (EJ 133). But for Scott becoming a horseman was coterminous with becoming a complete man. From a career point of view, forming the Light Dragoons was a shrewd move. It put him into comradely connection with the Buccleuch and Dundas families (sons of whom were Scott's fellow officers) and led directly to his first important legal promotions.

The Light Cavalry can be seen as having opened many doors for Walter Scott, Advocate. But Lieutenant Scott's motives were not primarily careerist. The dragoon officer's gorgeous red and blue uniform and the exhausting cavalry exercises were an emotional fulfilment – they erased his disability, the 'club foot' as strangers called it. Cockburn gives a sarcastic picture of Scott the cavalry officer, and hints at the needs within him which a horse, a uniform and a sword satisfied:

> It was not a duty with him, or a necessity, or a pastime, but an absolute passion, indulgence in which gratified his feudal taste for war, and his jovial sociableness. He drilled, and drank, and made songs, with a hearty conscientious earnestness which inspired or shamed everybody within the attraction. I do not know if it is usual, but his troop used to practise, individually, with the sabre at a turnip, which was stuck on the top of a staff, to represent a Frenchman, in front of the line. Every other trooper, when he set forward in his turn, was far less concerned about the success of his aim at the turnip, than about how he was to tumble. But Walter pricked forward gallantly, saying to himself: 'Cut them down, the villains, cut them down!' and made his blow, which from his lameness was often an awkward one, cordially, muttering curses all the while at the detested enemy. (*Mem.* 187–8).

In his lover's correspondence with Charlotte, Scott recurs to the horse and his volunteer duties again and again. Borderers like himself, he tells her, are born into the saddle. Riding is as natural as walking. He hopes he will not have to give up Lenore once he is married. He is determined not to give up his connection with the Light Dragoons (EJ 152). Soldiering (more particularly the cavalry) remained for Scott the most glamorous of occupations. His son and heir, Walter, was groomed from earliest years for the dragoons. Scott raised equestrian exercise to the level of a religious devotion for his young children.

Running through Scott's career are a series of mythic and dramatically significant feats of horsemanship. One suspects that a couple, at least, were improved in the telling to Lockhart. The biographer, for instance, records that in 1805, while enjoying a second honeymoon with his wife at Gilsland in the Lakes, Scott learned of a threatened invasion by the French in Scotland. The volunteers were mustered:

> He was not slow to obey the summons. He had luckily chosen to accompany on horseback the carriage in which Mrs Scott travelled. His good steed carried him to the spot of rendezvous, full a hundred miles from Gilsland, within twenty-four hours . . . it was during his fiery ride from Gilsland to Dalkeith, on the occasion above mentioned, that he composed his 'Bard's Incantation' first published six years afterward in the *Edinburgh Annual Register*:
>
>> The forest of Glenmore is drear,
>> It is all of black pine and the dark oak tree, etc.

and the verses bear the full stamp of the feelings of the moment. (Lock. 1. 452–3)

The 'Incantation' is certainly a rousing poem. But Scott (who edited the *Register*) wrote as subtitle, 'written under the threat of invasion in the autumn of 1804'. In autumn 1804, Scott was living only a few miles from Dalkeith, where the volunteers were mustered.

Another gallop, which has entered Scott lore, is that described by Lockhart as occurring in summer 1809, as Scott began serious work on his Highland poem, *The Lady of the Lake*. According to Lockhart:

> On the rising of the Court in July [1809], he went, accompanied by Mrs Scott and his eldest daughter, to revisit the localities, so dear to him in the days of his juvenile rambling, which he had chosen for the scene of his fable. He gave a week to his old friends at Cambusmore, and ascertained, in his own person, that a good horseman, well mounted, might gallop from the shore of Loch Vennachar to the rock of Stirling within the space allotted for that purpose to FitzJames. (Lock. 2. 130)

From the testimony of the letters, however, Grierson shows that Scott did not visit the Highlands in July–August 1809 (HG 101). He did make a short visit at the end of August – but other circumstantial details given by Lockhart do not fit. Grierson concludes, 'Lockhart's tale may be due to some slip of Scott's memory in later years.' (Johnson compromises by transposing Scott's 'swift ride' to the end of August, and otherwise accepting Lockhart's details.) It is unlikely that Scott invented these mid-life gallops which are so reminiscent of the equestrian heroics of the early German poems. But it seems likely he may have embellished them in the telling and retelling over the years.

Scott's physical decline can be charted by his connections with the horse. When he returned from his visit to Waterloo in 1815 – an experience which had a sobering effect on his view of war – Scott discovered that his charger, Daisy, would no longer bear him. Thereafter, he never rode a war-horse again, sticking to hunters and peaceable beasts. In 1825, the last hunt before his financial crash, Scott took a bad fall at the Catrail (a massive ditch). Thereafter, he was too disabled to control full-size mounts. In later life, in his financial ruin, Scott was restricted to a very docile pony, called Douce Davie (after Jeanie's father in *The Heart of Midlothian*). The Presbyterian name was ironic, with all its recollections of the early confinement which – in his manhood – the horse had allowed him to escape.

4

The Minstrelsy of the Scottish Border (1798–1802)

On their return to Edinburgh in January 1798 the newly wed Scotts set up at 50 George Street in the New Town, a house they rented at 10 guineas a month for six months. It is clear that the vivacious Charlotte made significant changes in her husband's lifestyle. Even the tactful Lockhart admits that there was little in common between the two Mistresses Scott and much to divide the provincial, narrowly religious Scottish matron from her worldly, foreign, London-fashionably-dressed, Anglican daughter-in-law. This incompatibility and the hellish domestic atmosphere created at George Square by the dying Walter Scott WS (which was to drive Scott's sister Anne to an early grave) evidently broke whatever ties there remained between Scott and his parental family. Charlotte began a small salon in her new home. The open-house hospitality which all commentators note as a feature of Abbotsford began with Charlotte's regime at 50 George Street. One of the very few facts which we know about the Charpentier household in Lyons where she was brought up was that many interesting strangers seem to have dropped in. So too did people drop in on the Scotts in the New Town and at the houses they later kept in the country. Charlotte's religion was less morally oppressive than anything Scott had hitherto experienced and he embraced its freedom. She loved novels and – above all – the theatre. 'I doubt if they ever spent a week in Edinburgh without indulging themselves in this amusement', Lockhart writes (Lock. 1. 267). Before she was brought down by child-bearing and chronic illness Charlotte effervesced Scott's life and social habits in ways that a younger Scottish wife bred to respectable Edinburgh ways might not have done.

In October 1798, the Scott's first child – a boy – was stillborn. In March 1799 Scott's first gainful publication, a translation of Goethe's *Götz von Berlichingen*, appeared in London, earning him 50 guineas. Although Scott's errors in translating have caused merriment, *Götz* is a landmark. Scott's is the first translation of Goethe's 1771 play to be listed in the British Museum catalogue. The baronial melodrama – set in the sixteenth century

– had a clear influence on Scott's baronial poems, and elements of *Götz's* plot, as Lockhart notes, resurface as far away as *Ivanhoe* and *Anne of Geierstein*. The work, the payment, and the praise it received raised Scott's hopes for a literary career. At this period, under his wife's cosmopolitan influence, he seems to have seen that career as one which would draw him to London and the Drury Lane stage.

Scott and Charlotte went to London in the same month, March 1799, that his play appeared in print. It was not an easy trip – the roads were snowbound, Charlotte was newly pregnant. It was the longest journey Scott had undertaken as a grown man. In London he made a determined attempt to push himself as an author. Scott's main contact was Matthew Lewis ('Monk Lewis', as he was nicknamed, after his notorious novel). Lewis – physically diminutive but devilishly handsome – pioneered the cult of youthful genius later exploited by Byron. He was barely twenty years old when the scandalous *Ambrosio, or the Monk* (1795) made him a celebrity. In 1796 he was elected to the House of Commons. In 1798 his play *Castle Spectre* ran for sixty nights at Drury Lane. For all his early flare, Lewis's vogue was soon extinguished. By 1800 his gothic horrors and Germanic pastiche were looking cheap and vulgar. But in 1799, Monk Lewis was still enjoying his moth's heyday and was able to introduce his (somewhat antique) Scottish friend into the 'fashionable and literary society' of which he was currently the youthful ornament.

Scott and Lewis had first met in Edinburgh in summer 1798. William Erskine had shown Lewis the translations of 'Lenore' and 'The Wild Huntsman', and he was impressed enough (and astute enough) to invite Scott to contribute to a proposed *mélange, Tales of Wonder*. It was Lewis who had arranged for a London publisher, Bell, to take Scott's *Götz of Berlichingen* and – wonder of wonders – pay for the translation. Lewis strongly encouraged Scott in writing 'original ballads', but then rather chilled his protégé's flow with objections about rhyme words (Scott's 'Scotticisms' and his uneven measures grated on Monk's metropolitan ear – an organ which was famously sensitive).

During his 1799 spring visit to London, Scott was also composing a dark and gothic drama – *The House of Aspen* – which he clearly hoped would enjoy the same Drury Lane success as Lewis's *Castle Spectre* the year before (*Lett*. 1. 247). Its main action concerns a baroness who has poisoned her first husband. She is tried by a secret tribunal (or 'Vehm') and stabs herself. The action takes place against the ominous background of a hemlock marsh and dire prophetic dreams. After it failed to make him famous and Kemble turned it down for Drury Lane Scott affected to be very dismissive of his 'Germanized brat' (*Lett*. 1. 123). Had it succeeded – as in 1799 he clearly wanted it to succeed – his whole literary career would have been different.

Lewis – 'the good natured fopling' as Lockhart calls him – has only a walk-on part in standard Scott biography and biographers invariably have a sneer at his expense. But Lewis's influence (combined with the cosmopolitanism brought into Scott's life by Charlotte) was important. It might have been all-important had *The House of Aspen* been taken by Kemble (as the work of Lewis's disciple). Conceivably, Scott and Charlotte might have moved to London in those circumstances.

In the event, Scott made little immediate impact on the world of London letters and theatre. And whatever ambitions he had were interrupted when his father died in mid-April, aged seventy. Walter took the loss very calmly, telling his mother to remember that 'the removal of my regretted parent from this earthly scene is to him, doubtless, the happiest change' (*Lett.* 1. 90). The situation of Charlotte's health 'in its present delicate state prevented me from setting off directly for Scotland' (*Lett.* 1. 91), he informed her. Charlotte's pregnancy had not, however, prevented him travelling down through mud and snow to London a couple of weeks earlier to keep an appointment with the Marquess of Downshire. Furthermore, Scott added, 'the situation of my affairs detain me here for a few days more' (*Lett.* 1. 90–1). He would miss the funeral. The frigidity of this letter (the only one which survives from the London trip) suggests that Scott had not forgiven his father for the obstructions put in the way of his marriage in 1797. Or perhaps the old man, in the rage of his final illness, had said something offensive about Charlotte Scott's French origins and English religion.

Somewhat tardily, Scott returned to Edinburgh, without having succeeded in his campaign to conquer literary London. Financially his affairs were improved by the prospect of inheriting a portion of his father's wealth (although the estate was left in disorder which it took an extraordinary fifteen years to untangle). Scott's prospects were further consolidated in December 1799, when through the influence of his 'kinsman' the Duke of Buccleuch and the goodwill of Henry Dundas, he was appointed Sheriff-Depute of Selkirkshire, at a salary of £250 (later raised to £300). The promotion was the outcome of patronage, pure and simple. As Lockhart puts it, Buccleuch and Dundas 'had both seen Scott frequently under their roofs, and been pleased with his manners and conversation.' The duties of the office, Lockhart adds, 'were far from heavy; the district small, peaceful, and pastoral, was in great part the property of the Duke of Buccleuch; and he turned with redoubled zeal to his project of editing the ballads, many of the best of which belonged to his very district of his favourite Border' (Lock. 1. 296). It was, of course, a moot point whether as sheriff Scott might dabble any more in the London stage – even if any manager wanted *The House of Aspen*, which seemed increasingly unlikely. But his recently deceased predecessor, Andrew Plummer, had been an antiquarian, and inquiry into Border minstrelsy was quite in order. (Plummer was also a ballad hunter, whose name appears a number of times in the notes to the *Minstrelsy of the Scottish Border.*)

Scott's duties as a sheriff – a post which he held from 16 December 1799 until his death – have been authoritatively described by John Chisholm K. C., himself a sheriff of Roxburgh, Berwick and Selkirk. It was in large part a sinecure (which is why incumbents like Plummer and Scott held it until death – long after either of them was competent as a judge). Most of

Scott's actual work was done by a Sheriff Substitute who – unlike his principal – was obliged to reside in Selkirk, the principal seat of the Court (the autumn assizes were held at Jedburgh). In March 1800 Scott appointed Charles Erskine, a Melrose solicitor, to be his Substitute. Scott normally resided in Edinburgh or, later, at Abbotsford. Scott had cases sent to him from Selkirk and made written judgements which he sent to Erskine. Only very rarely was Scott obliged to go to Selkirk in person.

The nineteenth-century legal code had its horrific aspect – some 220 offences for which the death penalty was applied. When Edie Ochiltree finds he has accidentally come by Dousterswivel's pocket book his first thought is that he may be hanged. Nonetheless, the Sheriff-Depute of Selkirkshire was no Braxfield. As Scott wrote in his journal, 12 December 1825, 'Very few cases come before the Sheriff Court of Selkirkshire that ought to come anywhere' (Jrnl. 35). In fact there seem to have been very few defended cases *tout court*. (Undefended actions were dealt with by the Substitute and did not trouble the Sheriff.) Scott, as Chisholm computes, dealt personally with 114 legal processes, or 112 law suits, in 33 years – over which period he received some £10,000 in salary. The cases, as abstracted by Chisholm, are astoundingly petty – affiliation (i.e. determining parenthood of disputed babies), 'wrongous' dismissal, trespass, sabbath-breaking, toll disputes, disputed boundary lines. In December 1810 a gentleman illadvisedly fishes in close season, and is fined. In 1827 a poacher sues to have his gun returned by a gamekeeper – the court turns down his request. Such was the law the 'Shirra' Scott administered.

LASSWADE

Scott entered the nineteenth century as a man whose life was comfortably set in its mould. His character, Lockhart notes, 'was completely formed and settled.' He took a 'calm delight in his own pursuits' (Lock. 1. 317). If we believe his son-in-law (not everyone does) Scott had grown up to be a model of Augustan equanimity – a Scottish Addison. Whatever religious zeal he inherited from his father was calmed. When he attended service, it was the Episcopalian church of his mother (and now his wife). Not that he felt strongly about such things. As Johnson points out, at Abbotsford he read from the Scottish Prayer Book on Sundays (EJ 1. xvi). Like his admired Dryden, Scott seems not to have put much importance on the mere forms of religious devotion.

The heyday in Scott's blood was tame. His strongest passion is alleged by Lockhart to have been 'patriotic enthusiasm'. This enthusiasm was now directed against the Radical as well as the Gallic foe. Poorer Scots were starving in large numbers. Many of them were less happily reconciled to their poverty than Edie Ochiltree, and Scott's volunteer troops were periodically mobilized for police action. The Walter Scotts were not poor. From its various sources, the family income now amounted to between £1,000 and £1,500 a year (EJ 174). Scott was happily married, and his wife – despite some ominous ill-health – was both a comfort and an ornament. There were four surviving children between 1799 and 1805: Sophia was born in 1799, Walter in 1801, Anne in 1803 and the last, Charles, in 1805. Scott had not made his father's mistake of having too many sons. Nor did Charlotte make the other Mrs Scott's error of wearing herself out with continual annual childbirth – the babies were well spaced out.

The Scotts established themselves in town and country residences – adapting to the annual sessions of the Court and the 'seasons' of Edinburgh's upper classes. Scott was well on the way to being a 'lawyer-laird'. He rented a 'cottage' (i.e. a small country house) at Lasswade in summer 1798, and for five years thereafter. Handsomely situated on the Esk, it cost only £30 a year and belonged to the family of Walter's oldest friend, William Clerk. At Lasswade, the Scotts had some grand neighbours, notably at Dalkeith Palace – the principal Buccleuch residence. The Scotts were frequent guests: the Earl of Dalkeith, Scott's exact contemporary, became his friend and in future years a major patron. It was at the Palace that Scott first met, among others, Lady Louisa Stuart, a woman of remarkable literary sensibility. Scott's ménage at Lasswade was far from palatial. But it allowed him to indulge his love of walking, shooting, fishing, of dogs (his favourite in 1801 was a bull-terrier, Camp) and of riding his beloved mare Lenore. In town, after 1801, the Scotts lived at 39 North Castle Street – a main-door terraced house, just up the hill from George Street. They remained there twenty-five years in all, longer than in any of their other residences.

Scott's legal work was light, varied and dignified. He was normally in Edinburgh during the three terms of the Court of Session – which occupied well under half the year. During the lengthy spring, summer and Christmas breaks he would normally be at Lasswade. Unfortunately this was not in the immediate vicinity of Selkirk or Jedburgh. But he could ride there when he had to. (He had acquired a fine new beast for his Sheriff's duties, called Brown Adam, after a famous Border outlaw.) The day-to-day chores of Sheriffdom were efficiently handled by Charles Erskine.

In March 1801, Scott began what was to be a long and friendly correspondence with George Ellis, a retired diplomat with West Indies wealth in his background. It was a mutual interest in antiquarianism that brought the two men together, and from the first Scott was keen for Ellis's good opinion. Scott knew, of course, that Ellis was, with George Canning, a founder of the *Anti-Jacobin*, a Tory satirical magazine that ran from November 1797 to July 1798. Although its political views were highly congenial to Scott, the *Anti-Jacobin* was spittingly hostile to Germanico-gothic literature, which it attacked as conducive to radical sentiments. Ellis, together with the Tory political wits John Hookham Frere, William Gifford and George Canning, composed a corrective parody of Schillerian drama, entitled 'The Rovers; or the Double Arrangement' which made a huge impact. It was with

the likes of Canning, Gifford, Frere and Ellis (all later friends and collaborators) that Scott particularly wished to associate himself. He could not do
so as the author of the type of mush the 'Rovers' mocked. From this point
on in his literary life, Scott became a witheringly sarcastic commentator on
his early 'German mad' productions, of which he had once been so proud
as to make a love-gift to Williamina Belsches.

What, then, having spurned his *Gesamtwerk* up to 1799, was Scott to write?
It was a complication that, easy as his juridical work was, it nonetheless tied
the Shirra down. He could not, like his countrymen James Thomson and
Tobias Smollett, hie off to London to make his fortune. The patrons who
had acquired him his Sheriffdom were too civilized to require much actual
work of him; but they expected him to remain in their demesne. So did his
wife and children. Even if he had continued to indulge his German mania
Scott could not, like Coleridge and Wordsworth in 1798–9, spend a
Wanderjahr in Germany. Scott had some hard choices if he wanted to
fulfil his professional duties and do anything more than amateur literary
dabbling.

Instead of becoming a Lakelander, a London lion, a Burnsian ploughman or a Weimar sage, Scott modelled himself – the literary part of himself,
that is – on a charismatic new friend whom he met in 1799. Richard Heber
was a mild-mannered Oxonian, Croesus rich, a connoisseur, a closet homosexual, and – above all – a bibliomane. Heber is estimated to have spent
£100,000 on his library of 150,000 books. Nor was he just a collector; he had
a profound knowledge of the literary monuments of the middle ages. A
man of immense cultivation, Heber did translations of the classics, and was
a none-too-earnest MP for Oxford. It was his books he lived for.

Heber was one of the pioneers of the cult of the bibliophile which took
hold in the early nineteenth century. It was a gentleman's – more specifically a rich gentleman's – pursuit. (The most famous exponent was John
Ker, third Duke of Roxburghe, 1740–1804, in honour of whom the
Roxburghe Club was formed in 1812.) The bibliophile connoisseur, like
Heber or Roxburghe, had a well-defined relationship to literature. They
were not creators, nor patrons. In a sense, they were curators: they valued
and preserved literature as a set of beautiful and curious objects. It was on
such men that Scott now modelled himself. At this period he cut himself off
from the egalitarian university circle, and its club and drinking life.

In 1800 it was by no means irrational for Scott to expect wealth. Prospects looked very good for a young hopeful in the right party. Dundas at the
1802 General Election fixed it so that only two Whigs were returned in the
forty-five Scottish constituencies. On 24 December 1802 he was created
Viscount Melville. When Pitt returned to power in 1804, Melville was created first Lord of the Admiralty. Behind the scenes, the invisibly powerful
Buccleuch was also crescent. It was very likely that with his friends' help
Scott would have become a Baron of the Exchequer, and possibly even
President of the Court of Session. And even if the highest office eluded
him, he might still fall heir to wealth. In three years – between 1797 and

1800 – his income had risen tenfold. Was it not reasonable to expect that someone as well connected, gifted and fortunate as himself could expect further increase?

THE MAKING OF THE *MINSTRELSY*

On their introduction in summer 1799 Heber and Scott hit it off immediately. Scott admired the younger man's scholarship, which was more academically trained than his. Not that Heber was standoffish: the relationship – although largely conducted by correspondence about intricate antiquarian matters – was soon affectionate. In August 1800, Scott used Heber to purchase on his behalf a coach for Mrs Scott. She was ill with the influenza and had 'set her heart on a phaeton'. Even more usefully, Heber became Scott's adviser on the *Minstrelsy*, a project which had been formulated in late 1799 with his old schoolfriend from Kelso, James Ballantyne.

Initially, Scott seems to have had in mind a slim volume of ballads on the lines of Bishop Thomas Percy's *Reliques of Ancient English Poetry* (1765; by 1794 in its fourth bestselling edition) which would combine popularity (at a modest 5*s*) with the more strenuous standards applied by scholars like Percy's critical antagonist, Joseph Ritson. The collection would be thematically organized around the 'riding' (or 'raiding') ballad. Scott took as his starting point Percy's Border ballad 'Hawarden' and the comment in his accompanying 'Essay on Minstrelsy' that the Borders were the cradle of Scottish balladry.

Scott's venture – which eventually became the multi-volume and much-revised *Minstrelsy* – was founded on a controversial theory of ballad composition. Like Percy, he firmly believed that these surviving ballads were originally the single creation of bards or minstrels in the employ of a king or chief. They were, in origin, acts of duty and homage to their lord by peculiarly gifted followers. Scott would have disdained the theory – later popularized by Andrew Lang – that ballads are the spontaneous production of simple communities in a state of nature (with the corollary that women, too, might have a hand in their manufacture). Rural communities, as historical backwaters, might usefully preserve these minstrels' compositions in an eroded condition, Scott believed. But they did not generate them. The *Volk* was a receptacle not an author. In this respect even the title was tendentious – not 'Ballads of the Scottish Border', 'Reliques of Ancient Scots Poetry', or 'Songs and Metrical Romances of the Borders' but 'Minstrelsy'.

Not surprisingly, the aristocratic heads of Scottish society were addicted to the minstrelsy theory of balladic composition. Poetry – like the land and everything else worth having – had once belonged to them. They were nostalgic about their ancient poetic property. There was a tradition of Scottish nobility collecting, improving and even inventing ballads. Lady

Wardlaw and Lord Hailes were well-known examples of this cult. As John
Butt notes, 'in [aristocratic Scottish] families the tradition of singing old
Scots songs and ballads was still surviving' through the mid-eighteenth
century (Butt, 153). Scott himself – as Laird of Abbotsford – was to revive
the quaint practice. James Hogg recalls that 'Mrs Lockhart [i.e. Sophia
Scott] was always his darling . . . I shall never forget with what affection she
used to look up in his face as he hung over her while singing the old
Scottish ballads at the harp or piano' (Mack, 34–5). Although he did not
lumber his old minstrels with pianos Scott liked to think that (as in *The Lay
of the Last Minstrel*) they were harpers or pipers.

There were other comforting aspects to the minstrelsy theory for gentleman collectors like 'Walter Scott, Esq., Advocate', in 1800. It presumed
'authentic' ballads to be dignified productions, by trained artists with an
elevated position in a clearly defined social hierarchy – professional gentlemen, in a word. Such men as the minstrels would, of course, no more stoop
to indecency than a New Town advocate. Bawdy ballads and comedian
pieces of the kind which Burns scurrilously anthologized in 'The Merry
Muses of Caledonia' could be ignored by the antiquarian collector and
effectively written out of the archaeological record. Scott's strong preference was for 'riding ballads' which memorialized some historical battle,
skirmish, spectacular act of outlawry, or a martial hero. It was only as a
second thought that he included 'romantic' ballads, dealing with love. And
there are no comic ballads in the *Minstrelsy* whatsoever. And certainly no
ball at Kirriemuir.

Scott's great trick as a ballad collector was his ability to foster collaboration – something that came very hard to the antiquarians. Although it is
not evident from the title page (where 'Walter Scott, Esq., Advocate' has
sole billing) the *Minstrelsy* integrated many scholars' activities in a team
effort. Scott showed extraordinary skill in binding a host of assistants to his
editorial cause. Almost all these assistants remained friends for life. They
included his equals (or betters) in station like Heber and Ellis; inferiors like
James Ballantyne, his Sheriff-Depute Charles Erskine, and the Ettrick
locals James Hogg and William Laidlaw; and impoverished students like
Henry Weber and John Leyden. Even when he poached Scott did it so
charmingly and with such generous compensation that the victim felt
honoured and made over his research and sources with the best will in the
world.

An antiquary who was a somewhat equivocal help to Scott on the
Minstrelsy was Robert Surtees. Surtees – like Heber, Oxford-trained –
devoted his life to collecting materials for his *History of Durham* (1816–40).
He persuaded Scott to include as original his spurious 'The Death of
Featherstonhaugh'. (Surtees also concocted another contribution to the
Minstrelsy, 'Barthram's Dirge', which he claimed came to him from an old
lady who weeded his garden.) Nearer home was Charles Kirkpatrick Sharpe
(?1781–1851) another Oxford-trained recluse who now lived in Edinburgh
– a city he loved passionately, and whose monuments he helped preserve.
Scott made Sharpe's acquaintance in 1802, while preparing his third vol-

ume. Sharpe was not an easy man to get to know, and even harder to like. Scott apparently managed both. A gifted artist, gossip-monger (and like Heber probably homosexual), Sharpe specialized in the discovery of historical scandal (preferably obscene). He contributed 'The Twa Corbies' to the third volume of the *Minstrelsy* – one of its most popular items, but also one about which commentators are most sceptical.

Antiquaries worked on their magna opera with legendary slowness. Coincidentally, and fortunately for their researches, most of them were extraordinarily long-lived. Surtees's devotion of thirty years' study to his history of Durham is typical. Most of them were monied or had well-paid sinecures and could work at their research full time. Typically, they were bachelors, allowing a monastic concentration on their work. Scott by contrast achieved his *Minstrelsy*, a huge and definitive project which has never been surpassed, in something like five years, newly married with a growing family, while bustling as a lawyer eager to make a good impression on his patrons. No other antiquary of the age achieved his great work, as did Scott, in his early thirties. The first two volumes took him just over three years. The third volume was prepared and put through the press in just one year.

It is clear that Scott delegated most of the leg-work involved in locating, from oral sources in the countryside, the patches and variants for his composite texts. His principal aide was John Leyden, whom he met in the winter of 1799–1800 through Richard Heber. Heber had himself first run across Leyden – a notoriously odd sight – rummaging at Archibald Constable's High Street bookshop. Leyden was a student when Scott first took him on but – if contemporary accounts are to be believed – he was unlike any other student at Edinburgh University before or since. He was an autodidact and polyglot of legendary brilliance. These qualities had raised Leyden from the poor shepherd's cottage 'in one of the wildest valleys of Roxburghshire' where he was born in 1775. In 1800, he seemed doomed to study eternally. He was formally enrolled for the ministry, but boasted that he could master any course the university offered and seemed set to work through the whole curriculum. He was poor, grotesquely shabby and uncouth. But he was a genius and he had two great passions: Border ballads and the travels of Mungo Park (1771–1806), the Selkirk explorer (and ballad collector) whose exploits Leyden yearned to emulate.

Leyden attached himself to Scott as an assistant. He was certainly paid some stipend, and Scott was in a position to do something for his career in the longer term. Leyden cannot, however, have been easy to work with, and Scott – as Lockhart tells us – treated him as affectionately and condescendingly as he would a favourite but not entirely house-broken dog. In return Leyden loved Scott with dog-like fidelity. Scott introduced Leyden as a noble savage into 'the best society of Edinburgh, where his strange, wild uncouthness does not seem to have at all interfered with the general appreciation of his genius' (Lock. 1. 300). Part of that genius was poetic. Leyden's 'Imitations of the Ancient Ballads' – particularly 'Lord Soulis' – are among the finest things in the *Minstrelsy*.

In 1802, after work on the *Minstrelsy* was over, Scott prevailed on his Dundas patrons to find something for his peculiar assistant in India. The vacancy which was found for him was as a surgeon's assistant. Leyden duly set to, and took a degree in medicine in six months, four years being the usual term of study. In India, he made himself within seven years one of the country's leading Orientalists. He died prematurely in 1811. Scott lamented his death in *The Lord of the Isles* (4. 11) and wrote a memoir for the *Edinburgh Annual Register* (1811).

In addition to field work, Leyden was invaluable in transcription: not only was he extremely literate, his ear was from birth attuned to the accents of the region. He was also puritanically opposed to forgery (he was, for instance, very suspicious of James Hogg). It was Leyden who (according to Lockhart) persuaded Scott to enlarge the scope of the *Minstrelsy* from the five-shilling volume he originally proposed to Ballantyne. 'Dash it,' Leyden asked scornfully, 'does Mr Scott mean another thin thing like Goetz of Berlichingen? I have more than that in my head myself; we shall turn out three or four such volumes at least' (Lock. 1. 303).

That 'we shall' is interesting. The caricature history of Leyden – autodidact zany – originates with Scott and is amplified by Lockhart. It climaxes with Edgar Johnson, whose portrait leaves one wondering whether Scott's assistant – 'a wild-looking scarecrow-figure with unshorn sandy hair and staring eyes' – properly belonged in a zoo or a lunatic asylum (EJ 167). There are a number of reasons for suspecting tendentious exaggeration. Take the autodidacticism. Scott asserts (in a letter of recommendation to Charles Carpenter in India, 6 March 1803) that Leyden 'had so little education that at 12 years old he did not know how to write' (*Lett.* 1. 176). As he was to do with James Hogg, Scott was indulging conventional myths about rural poetic genius. Lockhart (who never met Leyden) embellishes the myth: 'Few can need to be reminded that this extraordinary man, born in a shepherd's cottage in one of the wildest valleys of Roxburghshire, and of course almost entirely self-educated, had, before he attained his nine-teenth year, confounded the doctors of Edinburgh by the portentous mass of his acquisitions in almost every department of learning' (Lock. 1. 300).

In fact, as Grierson indignantly points out, Leyden was a living testament to the efficiency and democratic universality of the Scottish education system:

> Leyden was *not* entirely self-educated. Born of humble parents in 1775, taught to read from the Bible by his grandmother, he was sent to the village school at the age of nine. His striking abilities pointing to the Church, he received some special training in Latin and Greek from a Cameronian minister, and entered Edinburgh University in 1790. There he studied till 1797, and after a year in St Andrews was licensed in 1798. (*Lett.* 1. 111)

Leyden, in other words, was a scholarship boy, helped by the system every step of the way to fulfil his remarkable talents. Nor does his career, either before or after he left Scott, suggest the madman of the biographical record. He was at a loose end in 1799 when Scott met him because, like many would-be ministers without money or powerful friends, he could not get a parish. Moreover, he wanted to travel – preferably in Africa. Scott's employing him was a useful stopgap. His helping him to a good position overseas was even more useful. In India, Leyden prospered brilliantly and was soon earning £1,000 a year with fifty men under his authority. The buffoon painted by Lockhart and Johnson would have had difficulty finding the subcontinent.

Although both Lockhart and Johnson gloss over the fact, Leyden had published more than Scott. In addition to various pieces for the Edinburgh journals, which he had been putting out since 1794, he was the author of a learned book, on Europeans in Western Africa (1799). While the *Minstrelsy* was going forward, he published an edition of *The Complaynt of Scotland* (1801) and a volume of *Scottish Descriptive Poems*. More important, as M. R. Dobie points out in the most authoritative account we have of the composition of the *Minstrelsy*,[1] Leyden was the project's workhorse and its architect. Although Scott claimed that Leyden did not become involved with actually collecting for the *Minstrelsy* until 1802, it is clear that his influence was formative from his arrival on the scene in winter 1799.

Initially, Scott wanted to restrict the *Minstrelsy* to what were later categorized as 'Historical Ballads'. As early as April 1800, when he was making his first overtures to James Ballantyne, he had the historical section much as we know it. Shortly after (around May), he learned about Anna Brown's collection of romantic ballads. And on a walking tour at this same period Leyden obtained from a bookseller at Carlisle the manuscripts of Riddell of Glenriddell. These two new sources were the basis on which the *Minstrelsy* was enlarged. But there was a complication. In summer 1800 there appeared on the scene Robert Jamieson, an English collector, who was well ahead with Mrs Brown material. Leyden was away at the time – walking in the Highlands. Scott made a treaty with Jamieson. He (Scott) would restrict himself to Border 'Raiding' ballads, and Jamieson could have the romantic ballads. But on his return, Leyden persuaded Scott into a more ruthless policy. Leyden had 'no great opinion of Jamieson', and he induced Scott to break the agreement (Dobie, 74). By October 1800, the romantic ballads were incorporated into the *Minstrelsy* scheme. Jamieson (a mere schoolteacher, and less gifted a ballad-collector than Scott or Leyden) was easily overawed. Scott made it up to Jamieson with subsequent kindness – but it was sharp practice. Over 1801, the final building blocks were put in place, as Scott (urged by Leyden) expanded his conception to a third volume, for which Leyden embarked on a vigorous programme of fieldwork. This final part would also incorporate a corpus of original 'imitations' (in which Leyden again seems to have been influential).

The expansion from the gentlemanly slim volume to the majestic three-volume second edition of 1803 was the direct result of Leyden's contribution as collector and planner. His name should have been on the title page as joint-editor. Scott, of course, repaid his 'assistant' by interceding with

Melville and others to place him in India. (In the same way, he found Jamieson a suitable post in Register House.) Doubtless Leyden was more than happy with the arrangement. But the pattern of exploiting collaborators is one that would recur in Scott's early literary career. It testifies to a streak of authorial ruthlessness. In the caricature of Leyden that he propagated for posterity Scott was, I suspect, subconsciously justifying his shabby treatment of his co-editor.

Scott's fellow antiquaries – potential rivals and critics – needed to be treated with extreme diplomacy. Scott's skill in this department is witnessed by his managing to correspond simultaneously with Bishop Percy and Joseph Ritson, the age's two greatest adversaries. Scott wrote to Percy in 1800 with exquisite tact. The old gentleman was now seventy and had been Bishop of Dromore since 1782. He answered Scott's queries on various fine points and – more importantly – intimated his general approval. Joseph Ritson was harder to approach than Percy, but ultimately more useful. Lockhart applauds Scott's suavity in winning Ritson over: 'This narrowminded, sour, and dogmatical little word-catcher had hated the very name of a Scotsman and was utterly incapable of sympathizing with any of the higher views of his new correspondent. Yet the bland courtesy of Scott disarmed even this half-crazy pedant' (Lock. 1. 307).

The quarrel between Percy and Ritson had centred on three issues. Ritson objected that in the *Reliques* Percy had romanticized the role of the minstrel. Percy saw these artists as descending in a direct line from the bards, and ultimately the 'Skalds' of the teutonic races. In Percy's view, minstrels were both the composers and performers of their lays, or poems. Percy was convinced that his ballads – deformed and eroded as they might be – originated with the true minstrels of prehistory – single creators. He claimed that his texts came from a folio manuscript which he discovered at a friend's house which constituted a direct link over the corrupting generations of modern history. These happily resurrected poems connected the modern age with a 'common teutonic stock' and the founding 'Danish tribes' of British civilization. Percy, as he complacently thought, had reconstructed 'poetry in a state of nature'.

The younger Ritson was very dubious about the sociology of Percy's minstrelsy. He took the occasion of the publication of the fourth edition of *Reliques* (1794) to renew his attack. The history of ballad composition was, Ritson argued, a ragged and diffuse thing. Many of the 'English' ballads and lays were in fact bastardized versions of French originals rather than direct shoots from the common teutonic stock. 'Minstrels' were typically hack musicians and vagabond performers, not authors. Ballads themselves were much more the product of current local conditions. The obscene, bawdy and rugged aspects of ballads must be respected. The people were not the mere repository of ballads temporarily put in store by their betters; they were often the ballads' begetters. All this talk of archetypes, single original versions, and ancient druidic Homers stalking the land like Gray's 'Bard' was too convenient.

Secondly, Ritson objected that Percy took unscholarly liberties with his materials. He unethically improved his poems giving them 'an air of antiquity, which they were not entitled to'. Even more objectionably, he invented sources. In his attack on the 1794 edition of the *Reliques*, Ritson bluntly accused Percy of lying in claiming that he had manuscript warrant for his texts. Produce the manuscript, Ritson challenged. It was 'Ossian' all over again – 'fraud, forgery, and imposture'. Thirdly, Ritson condemned Percy as an armchair editor. He – Joseph Ritson – had gone on a walking tour through the north of Scotland in 1786–7 to gather his material, first hand, from living sources.

Scott – as a ballad theorist – was pulled both ways. He tended strongly towards Percy's romantic idea of the minstrel-author (this is the whole framework of *The Lay of the Last Minstrel*, which can be read as a fantasia on Percyan themes). Like Percy, he tended to think of ballads as having single, not corporate, authorship; and as being aristocratic not proletarian in their origins. He had a passionate affection for the *Reliques* as poetry – dating from his epiphanic experience under the great platanus tree in Kelso. On the other hand, Scott admired the strenuous puritanism of Ritson's walks through the wilds. This was exactly what he had done in his Liddesdale raids. He differed in this from his Selkirk predecessor, Andrew Plummer, who felt that a stroll from the drawing room to the garden once a day was all the exercise an antiquarian needed. In his 1810 review of Evans's *Old Ballads* (1777–84, repr. 1808) Scott was politely scornful of the fact that Evans (a bookseller) had done his collecting 'from rare copies and manuscripts'. The real ballad collector, Scott implied, needed to get his boots muddy.

Scott's editorial practice was similarly ambivalent and verges at times on the confused. To Burns's biographer, Dr Currie, he insisted in July 1805 that 'I have made it an invariable rule to attempt no improvements upon the genuine ballads which I have been able to recover' (*Lett.* 1. 120). Yet as Grierson notes (and amply demonstrates):

> Scott composed his texts by a process of combining different versions, correcting and improving the phraseology, the rhythm and the rhyme, heightening by occasional words the archaic flavour, rewriting and supplying whole stanzas, lending to an often prosaic version the animation of his own eager and buoyant temperament. (HG 75)

Scott's most famous primary source among the Border peasantry was James Hogg. A self-proclaimed genius, the 'Ettrick shepherd' had been impatiently awaiting discovery for some years. He was in fact a year older than Scott. The son of a sheep-farmer ruined when young Hogg was six, 'Jamie the Poeter', as his rustic neighbours called him, had spent only two three-month periods at school (Mack, 6). Following the example of other rural geniuses Hogg taught himself to read from odd books he found. He learned to play the fiddle the same way. He was employed as a shepherd by a cousin of his mother Margaret Hogg (née Laidlaw). It was the Laidlaws who instructed Hogg in the higher skills of reading and writing and who introduced him to such formative texts as Allan Ramsay's kitsch Scots pastoral, *The Gentle Shepherd.*

Scott came across Hogg indirectly. The Sheriff-Depute at Selkirk, Charles Erskine, had introduced Scott to his cousin William Laidlaw, the well-educated son of a local Ettrick farmer, a man who was later to become Scott's factor at Abbotsford and lifelong confidant. Laidlaw, being in turn related to the Hoggs, told Scott that Margaret Hogg had some ballads, notably 'Auld Maitland', which he dearly wanted for the third volume of the *Minstrelsy.* Laidlaw claimed to have heard from a servant girl the first stanzas of the ballad and wrote about it to Hogg, who sent back a whole copy from his uncle, Will Laidlaw, corroborated by his mother (Chambers, 118). Margaret and Will had allegedly learned it from their father – yet another Will Laidlaw. According to Chambers, Laidlaw then showed Scott and Leyden a manuscript copy of the ballad, on a visit to the Hoggs' house.

Another version of this episode, deriving from Hogg, has the famous recitation and conversation with Margaret herself. According to this more dramatic version, when Scott and Laidlaw (less Leyden) arrived at her cottage 'In Ettrick's bleakest, loneliest sheil' Mrs Hogg supplied the material willingly enough. But like those modern native Americans who complain that there are more anthropologists than Indians at their rain dances, she showed herself quite familiar with the needs of gentleman collectors, and displayed formidable expertise on the niceties of transcription. Other antiquarians had wholly mangled the texts of 'my sangs', she complained. They had 'prentit' them in a way which was 'nouther richt spell'd nor richt setten down'. More significantly she undermined the whole basis on which the *Minstrelsy* was compiled by asserting that her ballads 'were for singin' an' no for readin'.[2]

In her article 'Odd characters: Traditional Informants in James Hogg's Family', Elaine E. Petrie argues that there are reasons 'why Margaret Laidlaw's reputation as a competent, practised source of traditional material should be treated with caution.'[3] Neither was Jamie the happy bard of legend (his own carefully manufactured legend). He had written and published his first poem in October 1794 (some time before Scott himself was in print). He had embarked on a five-act comedy – *The Scotch Gentleman* – in 1795, which he finally gave up in 1801. His *Scottish Pastorals, Poems, Songs, etc.* was published (to little acclaim) in 1801. Moreover, Hogg had swathed his literary evolution in myth (or, less politely, lies). He claimed, for example, that he first encountered Burns's work in 1797 and wept because he realized – in the face of such genius – that he, James Hogg, could never be a poet. Edith Batho shows this must be untrue (for one thing, Hogg had been publishing in metropolitan Edinburgh journals for three years by 1797 – not to have heard of Burns, the most famous Scottish writer living in 1796, is preposterous).

The literary sophistication of James Hogg and his mother – their being *au fait* with the work of the scholars who came to examine them as reservoirs of unspoiled poetic heritage – suggests that the Borders were not as much out of Edinburgh's metropolitan orbit in 1800 as Scott intimates. And 'Auld Maitland', the superbly preserved ballad which Mrs Hogg gave Scott, has been suspected of being fabricated. Scott himself seems to have been slightly suspicious. 'It is a curious circumstance,' he notes in his preface, 'that this interesting tale, so often referred to by ancient authors, should be now recovered in so perfect a state' (*MSB* 1. 239).

There are certainly grounds for being curious. Hogg's first meeting with Scott was not as happily accidental as he implies in his memoir. James had by 1802 seen the first two volumes of the *Minstrelsy*, and had corresponded with Scott, enclosing copies of versions of ballads. In fact Hogg had been hunting up ballads for Scott as early as July 1801, though they did not actually meet at this date. Scott first met Laidlaw (who was also hunting out original ballads for him) in April or May 1802 (it was at this point, presumably, that Laidlaw showed him manuscript fragments of 'Auld Maitland' to whet his appetite). Scott then seems to have had a brief meeting with Hogg for the first time in Edinburgh shortly after. Hogg is misleading in claiming that the meeting with his mother and Scott took place in summer 1801 – it was 1802. And Hogg is doubly misleading in reporting that this encounter on the afternoon when 'Auld Maitland' was recited was his first encounter with Scott. In addition to the meeting in Edinburgh a couple of months earlier, Hogg saw Laidlaw and Scott on the day before they called on his mother.

It is in fact possible that Scott's 'discovery' of Hogg was stage-managed by William Laidlaw. Both Hogg and Laidlaw in 1801–2 seem to have marked Scott as a man who would be a useful patron. When Willie first intimated to Scott – apparently artlessly – that they might have something for him in the ballad way, it is likely that Mrs Hogg (and James) had an idea what was coming when the collector dropped in at their Ettrick home. Did Mrs Hogg learn the sixty-five stanzas (some of them very dreary) from her son who composed them for the occasion? Such gross dishonesty seems unlikely. Or did Mrs Hogg elaborate on a shorter, and more fragmentary ballad? Scott himself made much of certain antique words of 'chivalry and war' (e.g. 'portcullize') which – as he supposed – a peasant woman could not have invented, or even known the meaning of. But clearly Mrs Hogg was shrewd enough to collate printed with oral versions of her ballads. She may well have had a larger vocabulary than Scott gave her credit for. And certainly some parts of the text seem very like the padding a not-very-gifted balladeer might come up with on the spur of the moment – the description of Edward's army on the rampage, for example:

> As they fared up o'er Lammermore,
> They burned baith up and down,

Until they came to a darksome home,
Some call it Leader-Town.

Both Laidlaw and Hogg by summer 1802 knew Scott's fetish for complete-
ness. It is quite within the realm of possibility that the three of them (or the
two Hoggs) put some finishing touches to an imperfect poem, with a view
to dazzling their powerful new acquaintance.

Whatever his private doubts, Scott went on to accept the authenticity of
Mrs Hogg's 'Auld Maitland' and made it the centre-piece of his third
volume. He also accepted James as 'a brother poet' and introduced him
into Edinburgh society (as he had Leyden) 'under the garb, aspect, and
bearing of a rude peasant' (Lock. 1. 306).

THE PUBLISHING OF THE *MINSTRELSY*

The printing of Scott's first major work by a local Scottish, rather than a
London firm is a crucial event in his authorial career. The links which the
Minstrelsy forged with James Ballantyne's Border Press were to lead – via the
publishing company of John Ballantyne – directly to Scott's literary glory
and, ultimately, his financial doom.

Scott had formed his early friendship with the Ballantyne brothers when
they were all boys at school together in Kelso in 1783. Both James and John
went to Edinburgh University in the early 1790s, and must have kept up
relations with their old grammar-school friend. Scott was a frequent visitor
to Rosebank (possibly the Ballantynes knew about Jessie) and their paths
would have crossed in the small town. James returned to Kelso in 1795 to
start a solicitor's practice; his younger brother went his own wilder way.
Then, in the political excitement of 1796, James launched a newspaper –
the *Kelso Mail* – 'devoted to the Tory interest' (EQ 21). Scott would have
found such an organ politically congenial. The *Mail* published Scott's
translation from Goethe, 'The Erl King', on 1 March 1798. This seems to
have been their first recorded collaboration as author and printer – although there may be more buried in the anonymous pages of Ballantyne's
newspaper.

By April 1800, Scott was urging James Ballantyne to move to Edinburgh,
where he might operate on a larger scale and do justice to the proposed
Border ballads 'which are now in some forwardness'. The letter in which he
made the invitation is unusual. Scott (quite sober) wrote it in a room
alongside a drunkenly sleeping fellow lawyer – a solicitor called Joseph
Gillon (the events by which Scott discovered himself in this situation are
mysterious). On behalf of himself and Gillon, Scott proposed that
Ballantyne should 'migrate from Kelso to this place'. Three kinds of work
are available in Edinburgh, he tells the printer: they might start a Tory
newspaper, or set up a Scottish equivalent to the *Annual Register*, and

Ballantyne could take over the printing of Session (i.e. Civil Court) papers. The current contractor for these is less than competent and in ill health. 'I daresay,' Scott adds, 'if wanted, pecuniary assistance might be procured to assist you at the outset' (*Lett.* 1. 97). Gillon subsequently disgraced himself and was forced to leave Edinburgh. He dropped out of the proposed partnership. And the business about Session papers may explain why Scott's subsequent partnership arrangement was secret. As an advocate – more particularly as a Principal Clerk of Session, which is what he intended to be – it would have been improper (and possibly illegal) for Scott to have exploited the processes of the Court for commercial gain.

A more plausible explanation for the secrecy in which the Scott – Ballantyne relationship was hatched, and in which it was shrouded for twenty-five years, was the men's involvement in Freemasonry – an interesting and neglected area of Scott's biography.[4] Scott's father was made a Mason in St David's lodge (based in Hyndford Close, just off the High Street) in January 1754. He was aged twenty-five, and qualified as a Writer to the Signet the following year, 1755. Then, as now, membership was seen as an advantage by young lawyers. Walter Scott WS was evidently a very keen Mason and rose through the steps of his lodge hierarchy. He also used his connections. The two main tutors whom we know Walter to have had in his childhood – James French (who taught him Latin, 1778–9) and James Mitchell (who boarded at George Square in 1782) – were both members of the St David lodge.

In December 1785, Walter Scott WS inducted his eldest son, Robert – aged nineteen – into his lodge. Walter Scott WS died in April 1799. The fact that Walter, by then the dominant son in the family, was not made a member of his father's lodge suggests resistance on the son's part and confirms that relations between them were strained. Walter did, however, join St David's at the age of thirty, on 2 March 1801. His motive was not piety to the memory of his two-year-dead father. The reason for joining was attachment to his 'chief', the Earl of Dalkeith, a Grand Master whose mother lodge was St David's. In 1801, Scott saw his future as inextricably entwined with the house of Buccleuch.

Membership brought, or renewed, other connections. James and John Ballantyne were keen Masons in their home town. 'The brethren Ballantyne of Kelso Lodge' were also popular and regular guests at St David's at this period by virtue of their 'elegant manners and musical powers'. Meetings were apparently convivial, and the Ballantynes were very jolly company. Scott loved the brothers' singing talent and the general fun they brought with them. Joseph Gillon was another member of the St David's lodge (as had been Andrew Plummer – Scott's predecessor as Sheriff). Scott was, in the early years of his membership, a frequent attender at St David's and in 1816 became an honorary member at Kelso (on James's nomination, presumably). His later relations with Freemasonry seem less enthusiastic. In 1819 he gave what looks like a very hostile, if oblique, account of the society in his depiction of the Knights Templar in

Ivanhoe. And in 1823 he declined to be put up as 'Grandmaster of the Knights Templar' in Edinburgh, on the grounds of age and health.

It is the nature of Freemasonry to be mysterious. But at the very least, one may speculate that the rituals of the 'brotherhood' were partly responsible for the intense intimacy and conspiratorial clandestinity surrounding the Ballantyne – Scott connection for over two decades. Masonic loyalty might also explain why Scott should so irrationally connect his financial affairs with John Ballantyne (a crook) and Joseph Gillon (a hopeless drunk) – partners from whom any prudent businessman would have run a mile.

James Ballantyne was evidently tempted by Scott's April 1800 invitation, but there seems to have been a hitch. He did not, in fact, set up in business in Edinburgh until late 1802 – eighteen months later. James, a very cautious man where his own money was concerned, needed the time to train a third brother, Sandy, in running the *Kelso Mail* (EQ 24). Meanwhile the first two volumes of the *Minstrelsy* appeared in January 1802 (EJ 187). The work was published by Cadell & Davies in the Strand and printed (very handsomely – to the amazement of London's 'amateurs of typography') in Kelso. Eight hundred copies were produced as the first edition, fifty on large sheets of paper. The cost for the regular copies was 18*s*, a guinea for copies in boards (EJ 187). The edition sold out in a year, yielding £78 10*s* profit to Scott. The *Minstrelsy* earned praise from, among others, Joseph Ritson who reportedly told Scott it was 'the most valuable literary treasure in his possession'. Ritson went mad and died the following year. It is likely that he did not study his presentation copy. Had he been himself, Ritson would have been appalled to find that Scott had embraced the Percy heresy on the vexed minstrel question.

Praise and sales encouraged Scott to produce his 'threatened third volume', which duly appeared on 25 May 1803. On the eve of its publication, Scott came down to Oxford, where he found himself something of a literary lion. He stayed with Heber and visited Woodstock where he stuffed his head with a jumble of old monuments. He was also lionized in London, where he met Samuel Rogers and attended a rather decadent party of Monk Lewis's graced with the capital's leading courtesans.

The third volume was again printed by Ballantyne and published by Longman. The newly edited and added-to collection was reissued as a three-volume set costing 10*s* 6*d* a volume. A thousand copies of the first two volumes were printed, and fifteen hundred of the new third volume for those who wished merely to supplement their 1802 set (EJ 194). Scott then accepted £500 for the copyright from Longman – which, since the ballads were in the public domain, was cool enough. According to Scott, writing in 1830, the reprint did not sell well, but as Lockhart points out, he was comparing it with the unprecedented sales of his later narrative poems. Judged for what it was – a work of literary-historical scholarship – the *Minstrelsy* was outstandingly successful. It was in its fifth three-volume edition by 1812, representing a sale of around 10,000. (Scott, incidentally, used almost every new edition to revise or insert new material.)

The *Minstrelsy* divided its contents into three categories: historical ballads, romantic ballads, and 'original' – or pastiche – ballads by modern hands. All three varieties have points of interest, but it is clear that Scott's particular fondness was for the bloodier historical ballads. Violence is prefigured by the epigraph on the title page which promises:

> The songs to savage virtue dear,
> That won of yore the savage ear,
> Ere Polity, sedate and sage,
> Had quench'd the fires of feudal rage.

In reading the *Minstrelsy* one should picture the period in which it was assembled (1796–9) and the mood of that period. Scott was belligerent, war-mad one might say, over these years. His historical introduction portrays a Borders culture in which warfare was the normal way of life. The archetypal ballad is a war song. 'As remarked by Lesley,' Scott notes, 'the music and songs of the Borders were of a military nature, and celebrated the valour and success of their predatory expeditions' (*MSB* 1. 157). The modern reader may tire at verse interminably glorifying cattle-rustling, revenge raids, tribal skirmishing, and a neverendingly bloody surge of invasion and counter-invasion in the 'debateable land'. It may be that Scott is historically correct in asserting that this was the story of everyday life over the centuries in the Borders. But it seems as likely to have been a reaction to the invasion alarms and militaristic frenzy of the 1796–1802 period. 'At the blaze of the beacon fires,' Scott tells us, '[the Borderers] were wont to assemble 10,000 horsemen in the course of a single day' (*MSB* 1. 130). This wholly incredible assertion (which is covered by poetic licence when repeated in the *Lay* and *The Lady of the Lake*) is explained by the excitement Scott felt at the mustering of the Edinburgh Light Cavalry in 1797 to repel expected French invasion. Lest we miss the point, he adds in his historical introduction that 'the habits of the Borderers fitted them particularly to distinguish themselves as light cavalry' (*MSB* 1. 130). Scott is, of course, thinking of a certain quartermaster.

5

Ashestiel and *The Lay of the Last Minstrel* (1802–1805)

The *Minstrelsy* did very well for Scott. Why then did he give up collecting and editing ballads? For others it was a lifetime's passion. One reason may have been the loss of Leyden – Scott had so many commitments (not least young children) that with his departure fieldwork became impossible. Scott may also have been influenced by the low opinion some of his new literary friends had about ballads. Anna Seward (with whom he made acquaintance in 1802) denounced the form's 'squalid dress of language', its 'rude' and 'valueless' nature (*Lett.* 1. 144–5). The 'Swan of Lichfield' was perhaps thinking of such performances as 'Sir Hugh Le Blond', where false Rodingham makes a lewd proposal to the Queen, who repulses him with a volley of plain speaking:

> Away, away, O Rodingham!
> You are both stark and stoor,
> Would you defile the King's own bed
> And make his queen a whore?

Yes, it emerges, Rodingham would do just that. In retaliation he souses a 'plook' leper in drink, and deposits the stinking wretch in the royal bed, telling the King that 'Your queen's a false woman.' She is eventually rescued from her husband's wrath by the noble Sir Hugh.

Around the same period (1800–2) Scott was visited by the young doctor and lover of Romantic poetry John Stoddart, who informed him of the experiments in long poetry which that 'eccentric and admirable poet' (*Lett.* 1. 146) Coleridge had recently embarked on. This may have opened up new vistas. As Wordsworth discovered, the ballad – strictly adhered to – imposes crippling limitations on the Romantic sensibility, as does the natural language of men. Scott, looking back in 1830, himself notes the 'flatness and insipidity which is the great imperfection of ballad poetry'. This imperfection may have begun to chafe as he prepared the third volume of the *Minstrelsy*.

The crucial texts in Scott's transformation are the 'Imitations of Ancient Ballads', which proliferated in the three-volume second edition of the *Minstrelsy* of 1803. In these imitations one can see Scott transcending 'the flatness and insipidity . . . of ballad poetry' while at the same time inventing the elaborate narrative machinery out of which *The Lay of the Last Minstrel* would emerge. Of the imitations, 'Cadyow Castle' and 'Thomas the Rhymer' are particularly noteworthy.[1] Apart from anything else, 'Cadyow Castle' was probably Scott's most admired and widely read poem to date. He circulated the poem among his friends at the period like a calling card.

A primary motive for writing 'Cadyow Castle' is found in Scott's social activities in the interval between finishing the first version of the *Minstrelsy* and embarking on the three-volume revision. He spent Christmas 1801 at 'the hospitable halls of Hamilton' (*Lett.* 1. 125) in Lanarkshire, by the River Evan. Scott was unaccompanied by his wife and was the guest of Lord Archibald, Hamilton and Lady Anne Hamilton. The relationship with his hostess was significant. At this period of his life, Scott embarked on a series of intimate friendships with fascinating, powerful, often aristocratic, sometimes beautiful women. In addition to Lady Hamilton (to whom he was introduced by Lady Charlotte Campbell), these women friends included the young Countess of Dalkeith (later Duchess of Buccleuch), Lady Louisa Stuart (whom he had come to know closely at Bothwell Castle in autumn 1799), the poet Anna Seward, and – rather later – Lady Abercorn. Scott was again, it seemed, the Squire of Dames. At the same period, Mrs Scott was beginning her long career of chronic sickness. Their last child, Charles, was born on Christmas Day 1805.

As Lockhart notes, Lady Anne Hamilton particularly admired 'Glenfinlas' and 'The Eve of St John'. She apparently asked ('commanded') him to write something along the same lines for her on the theme of her ancestor Bothwellhaugh's assassination of Regent Murray. Scott duly went away and wrote 'Cadyow Castle' over the next few months. His first letter to Lady Anne, after their Christmas encounter, opens on a note of sexual flattery. He quotes some hyperbolic lines of Thomas Campbell's on female beauty: 'O thou by whose expressive art / Her perfect image Nature sees.' Scott adds '[the lines] are I think exquisitely beautiful and the subject entitles them in a very particular manner to your ladyship's peculiar notice' (*Lett.* 1. 127). It is an unusual compliment for a married man to pay a married woman. In a subsequent letter of 23 February, Lady Anne is addressed with new intimacy as 'my fair friend'. In passing, Scott mentions 'the Bothwell anecdote' and ends 'Did I ever tell you that my Ancestors were armour bearers to the Douglases, so that my attachment to you and all your family is feudal and hereditary' (*Lett.* 1. 137). On 29 July 1802 he sent 'Cadyow Castle' to Lady Hamilton with the flourish 'Inclosed the long promised Ballad kisses your Ladyship's hands' (*Lett.* 1. 149).

'Cadyow Castle' has a number of features which mark it as a bridge to *The Lay of the Last Minstrel.* As Lockhart notes, it is the first verse narrative

Scott composed on a theme from Scottish history. More strikingly, as Jane Millgate notes, 'Cadyow Castle' anticipates the *Lay* with the device of Scott as a modern minstrel commanded by a noble lady, Lady Anne Hamilton (the Countess of Dalkeith in the *Lay*), to write ('tune my harp of border frame') on the theme of her 'princely abode', now decayed (Cadyow Castle in the ballad, Branxholm in the *Lay*).

In 'Cadyow Castle' the minstrel Scott dutifully obeys his lady's command and tells a sixteenth-century tale of bloody murder, feud and revenge in the 'wild Borders'. Regent Murray sacks Bothwellhaugh's castle and kills his wife, Margaret, while her husband is away. The poem alludes to, but does not specify the gratuitous brutality of the historical event in which the lady – recovering from childbirth – was 'turned out naked, in a cold night, into the open fields'. She went mad under her ordeal, and later died. As the poem continues, the bereaved husband lies in wait for Murray with his 'hackbut bent' (cocked musket) as the proud murderer parades in triumph through Linlithgow. In a nice little aside, the odious bigot Knox, foe to all ballads, smiles at Murray's triumph. Bothwellhaugh shoots the Regent dead, then eludes capture to gallop back and tell his Hamilton clansmen what he has done, interrupting their wild bull hunt among the 'huge oaks of Evandale'. 'Murray's fallen, and Scotland [is] free,' he tells his followers. The episode fades out ('the minstrel vision fails') with the hunters' savage applause and the scene melts into the ivied ruins of Cadyow Castle, as it now is.

'Cadyow Castle' reads like a vivid trailer for one of Scott's six-canto narratives. 'Thomas the Rhymer' is a more complex effort. The ballad's subject is the career of the most fabulous of the Border minstrels, Thomas of Ercildoune – 'the Merlin of Scotland'. (The modern form of Ercildoune, or 'Hersildoune' is Earlston – a village some five miles from Sandy Knowe.) Scott was to devote a huge amount of the next three years to this bafflingly elusive Thomas. Like the wizard Michael Scott in *The Lay of the Last Minstrel*, the Rhymer inhabits two irreconcilable spheres. One is historical (see, for example, the *DNB*'s 'Erceldoune, Thomas of, fl. 1220?–1297?'). The other Thomas – with whom Scott's ballad is primarily concerned – is folkloric. Popular legend had it that the folkloric Thomas was abducted into faeryland for seven years by a demon lover. He returned 'to enlighten and astonish his countrymen' by his minstrelsy and his prophecy of such events as the death of Alexander III, Bannockburn, and the union of the thrones of England and Scotland, before being summoned back to Faerie by his peremptory elfin mistress.

Scott's poem opens with an 'ancient' section, dealing with the Rhymer's seduction by the Queen of fair Elfland on Huntley Bank, underneath the Eildons. This section is based on original versions which Scott records as getting from a 'lady' near Ercildoune and from the well-known Aberdeen-shire source, Anna Brown. Charmingly, Thomas's faery queen addresses her victim in broad Scots:

'Harp and carp, Thomas,' she said,
'Harp and carp along wi' me;
And if ye dare to kiss my lips,
Sure of your bodie I will be.'

The two subsequent sections of 'Thomas the Rhymer' – dealing with the wizard-minstrel's feats of minstrelsy, prophecy, and his return to Faerie – are 'modern', that is, in contemporary English diction. This ability to switch at will between ancient and modern dialects (English and Lowlands vernacular) was an important breakthrough for Scott the poet. But before he could arrive at *The Lay of the Last Minstrel,* he had to make a considerable detour, one that detained him at least a year. This was his edition of *Sir Tristrem.*

Scott came on the *Sir Tristrem* material indirectly. The text (a 1450 copy of a poem probably written 150 years earlier) had been discovered in the Auchinleck MS by Joseph Ritson in 1792. The manuscript was held in the Library of the Faculty of Advocates in Edinburgh. Ritson, around 1800, evidently put the exciting idea into the heads of John Leyden (to whom he was close) and of Scott that the *Sir Tristrem* in the Auchinleck MS was the composition of 'Thomas the Rhymer'. It is likely that Ritson's visit to Lasswade in summer 1801 had to do with a proposed edition of *Sir Tristrem.* But Ritson sickened in 1802 and died a year later.

Scott did not, however, inherit the *Sir Tristrem* project directly from Ritson. Initially George Ellis intended to include the romance in his *Specimens of Ancient Poetry* (1805). But Ellis ceded the poem to his friend Scott on the grounds that 'the honour of Scotland' (*Lett.* 12. 174) required a Scottish editor for Thomas of Ercildoune's poem (Ellis, like Scott and Ritson, accepted that the Rhymer was *Sir Tristrem*'s author).

In the *Minstrelsy* note to 'Thomas the Rhymer', Scott announced that he had already 'undertaken the superintendence of a very limited edition of this curious work' which he claimed would be 'the earliest specimen of Scottish poetry hitherto published' (Millgate, 11). He was assisted by Leyden who seems to have begun transcribing in early 1801. (Scott was allowed to borrow the Auchinleck MS for use in his own home; Johnston, 179.) While Leyden copied, Scott edited the text and prepared notes. Most of the transcription was complete before Leyden left for India.

Although Scott made a typically gracious acknowledgement to his coadjutor in the preface, Leyden again received no title-page billing. Allegedly, after transcribing 1,000 or so lines and effectively preparing the edition, Leyden came across the word 'queynt' ('cunt') in the text (Johnston, 180). He was a minister – if only formally – and he felt it was improper to have his name attached to such a profanity. Similarly the Duke of Roxburghe, although he argued as an antiquarian for retaining the indelicacies, would not, as a gentleman, accept the dedication Scott offered. Scott himself – despite his prominence on the title page ('Walter

Scott, Esq., Advocate') – was made of firmer stuff (although he allowed himself to be forced into one small 'castration' of his text). As he had in 'Thomas the Rhymer', Scott finished the incomplete poem off with a short conclusion (not as Grierson claims a whole 'fytte', or book; HG 76) of his own composition in medieval pastiche.

Scott's original intention was to include *Sir Tristrem* in the *Minstrelsy*. But he decided it would 'hang too heavy on the skirts' of that collection of short pieces. It was sold as a separate item to Constable. Constable did not desperately want *Sir Tristrem,* but he did want to woo Scott from Longman (who bought the copyright of the *Minstrelsy* for a handsome sum, and who, around the same time, undertook to buy the long original poem Scott had in mind). By October 1802, *Sir Tristrem* was set up in type and might easily have been published by Christmas. But Scott remained nervous about his scholarship – more so without Leyden by his side. It was almost two more years before the edition was released to the public, during which time the editor frantically strove to reassure himself and convert his antiquarian friends to his thesis.

Scott's introduction begins with a bold proclamation: 'The Romance of *Sir Tristrem* was composed by THOMAS OF ERCILDOUNE, called THE RHYMER, who flourished in the 13th century.' Scholarship records that this assertion and what Scott built on it are wrong on every score. Thomas the Rhymer was not the author of *Sir Tristrem.* Nor was any Scot. *Sir Tristrem* did not originate in Scotland. Probably the Auchinleck version which Leyden transcribed was the work of a London scribe, condensing a garbled North of England version, itself mangled by intermediate oral transmission. And at the end of the line *Sir Tristrem* was not originally composed by any minstrel (historically a much lower caste of artist than Scott – following Percy – took them to be). *Sir Tristrem* had an 'ultimately literary origin'. It was not the effusion of some harpist (Scottish or Breton) in a state of vatic transport but was written on paper by some learned 'clerk', or author.

Scott's error about the composition of *Sir Tristrem* supported a mass of further ingenious error. Thomas's poem, he insisted, was the *ur*-Arthurian text. It pioneered the idea of 'an association of knights assembled around one mighty sovereign'. Thus was the Arthurian cycle begun, and the code of chivalry born, just a few miles from where Scott had passed his boyhood and where he now lived. To bolster this theory, Scott ascribed to 'Thomas the Rhymer' and his Berwickshire colleagues a batch of other Arthurian romances and rewrote great swathes of British prehistory. Since Sir Tristrem is a Celtic hero, Scott theorized that there had been a Celtic kingdom, Welsh in origin, in the dark ages in south west Scotland, which as it went under left dynamic elements of Celtic – or 'Briton' – culture 'floating' into the middle ages (i.e. early thirteenth Century) when 'Thomas the Rhymer' ('probably of Saxon origin') picked them up. By these acrobatics Scott proved to himself that 'the first classical English romance was written in part of what is now called Scotland.' And that English romance was, of course, essentially Welsh.

Scott has a staunch ally in Edgar Johnson, who informs us that 'parts of Scott's argument have been overthrown by the more detailed knowledge available to more modern scholarship and its more scientific methodology ...At the time he published the poem, none of his arguments were seriously challenged' (EJ 222). This is not true. The antiquarian Francis Douce discovered a fragment of a French *Sir Tristrem*, attributed to Thomas of Brittany, which he made available to Scott before publication. Douce pressed the obvious deduction that the Auchinleck version represented a secondary version.

Scott circumvented Douce's contrary evidence by the sophistical argument that the Auchinleck manuscript contained not a literal transcription of Thomas the Rhymer's original poem, but its 'essence' – an essence which predated and inspired the French versions. Despite manifest chronological implausibility, he suggested that Thomas the Rhymer and Thomas of Brittany were one and the same Thomas. Another of Scott's contemporaries, William Taylor of Norwich (a well known balladist), argued cogently against the originality of *Sir Tristrem*, again pointing to the earlier Norman versions. Scott must have read this. In 1807, Scott's assistant Henry Weber brought more contrary evidence to his notice. Finally, Richard Price demolished Scott's arguments in 1824 (Johnston, 186–7).[2] On scholarly grounds, Scott was holed below the water line several times during his own lifetime. Nevertheless, he obstinately stuck to his guns. He was, as Jane Millgate puts it, 'obsessive and simply stubborn' on the subject (Millgate, 12).

Sir Tristrem was eventually published by Constable & Co. on 7 September 1804. Archibald Constable had graduated from the High Street bookshop where Heber had met Leyden four years before and was now Edinburgh's principal publisher. He had just made a great hit with the launch of the *Edinburgh Review* and was to be Scott's partner in most of the great literary projects that lay ahead. Constable's hallmark was lavishness (25 guineas a sheet for *Edinburgh* contributors, for instance). But his treatment of *Sir Tristrem* was extravagantly cautious. Only 150 copies were printed, and the none-too-fat volume was priced at a prohibitive two guineas. Printing costs (involving antique types) may have been partly responsible. A more likely explanation for the high cost and low print run was the scandalously sexual nature of the narrative. The custodians of public morals have always been more indulgent of pornography in de luxe editions. On the strength of Scott's later fame *Sir Tristrem* went into three more editions (1806, 1811, 1819) before being absorbed into Scott's collected poetry.

ASHESTIEL

Scott's domestic and public lives continued serenely over the years 1802–5. Historically the period was anything but serene. After the brief interval of peace following the Treaty of Amiens in 1802, Buonaparte seized Italy, and war was again declared against France in May 1803. Invasion was again feared (paranoiacs expected the Gallic horde would come by tunnel from the Continent). Martello Towers were raised and Scott's militia held its 'voluntary brand' in full readiness. There was another levy of volunteers.

In her study of British patriotism, *Forging the Nation* (London, 1992), Linda Colley marks 1804 as a particularly formative year and adds that the Scots (notably the Scots of Selkirk) were even more enthusiastic in their patriotism than the English. There were, however, crosscurrents. Twenty years later Scott confessed to Lockhart that his internal security duties at this period had been distressing to him. Slashing at starving countrymen was not the glorious cavalry action he had foreseen in 1797. Passing through Portsburgh in 1824, he recalled an episode there in 1802 when a bread shop was looted during the Meal Riots:

> Scott, whose troop was attempting to restore order had nearly been killed by a brickbat, which made him reel in the saddle; he spurred his horse to cut down the fellow who had thrown it, but when the man cried, 'Upon my soul I did not mean it for you,' he only gave him a stroke with the flat of his sword, for 'Truth to say it was a dreadful feeling to use violence against a people in real and absolute want of food'. (EJ 869)

Scott's uncle Robert died in June 1804, leaving his favourite nephew a handsome bequest (*Lett.* 1. 224). The old gentleman's fortune was divided equally among nine of the family, yielding Walter a £600 share. More substantially, he was the sole inheritor of his uncle's Rosebank Villa and its twenty acres. He might have lived there, but Kelso was too tamely genteel a burgh for Scott's taste, and he promptly sold the property for £5,000 (EJ 223). At around the same time, Charles Carpenter married and made a handsome final settlement on his sister.

Housing posed a problem. Scott had been reminded by the Lord Lieutenant of the county, Francis Lord Napier, that regulations required the Sheriff to reside four months of the year in Ettrick Forest. It was 'nervous fidget', as Lockhart puts it: Napier was a fusspot, we are to understand. Johnson falls in line by terming Napier 'a finicking old gentleman' (he was, in fact, just forty-five and had seen active service in the American War rather more hazardous than brickbats at Portsburgh). Scott, when annual duty called him to his jurisdiction in the Ettrick Forest, usually put up at the Clovenford Inn (an establishment later to make its fortune on its association with the author of *Waverley*). Napier, reasonably enough, felt this did not constitute residence. But his underlying concern was Scott's increasing neglect of his Sheriffdom for literary pursuits and military duties. Plummer had been wholly idle, but wholly secluded (and secluded in Ettrick Forest). Scott was swaggering around Edinburgh in his gaudy volunteer's uniform lacking, as he told Ellis, only a 'pipe and a *schnurbartchen* to convert me into a complete hussar' (*Lett.* 1. 204). He was also one of Edinburgh's literary lions, the *Minstrelsy* having come out under his name.

As it happened, Scott did need a new house for his growing family. He could kill two birds with one stone. In summer 1804 the Scotts duly moved from Lasswade to a larger country residence in Ashestiel, with a spectacular setting, only half-a-dozen miles from Selkirk. The new house belonged to distant relatives of Scott's on his mother's side and was rented at a moderate £325 a year. The family was to stay at Ashestiel eight years – the only uninterruptedly happy phase of Scott's life, as John Buchan guesses. It was – apart from anything else – a good place for young children to grow up, affording plenty of the healthy exercise in the countryside that Scott himself had benefited from in Sandy Knowe.

Scott described Ashestiel as a 'decent farm-house overhanging the Tweed and situated in a wild pastoral country'. It was, in fact, strikingly lovely, if then bare of the trees which the new occupant began to plant as soon as he arrived. There was no Dalkeith Palace nearby; but among the Scotts' more interesting neighbours was Mungo Park, the African explorer. Together with the house Scott took over an adjoining farm. It added to his already sizeable repertory of roles: lawyer, antiquarian, bard, soldier, and now Lowland gentleman farmer. Recent trends had transformed farming from a humble to an eminently respectable occupation. Fifteen years earlier Scott had turned down help with his Greek at university because the would-be helper was a mere sheep-farmer's son. Tending cattle was no longer a disgraceful calling. The Napoleonic Wars inaugurated an unprecedented boom in agriculture. Rich profits could be had from products like corn and wool, and from rents. During the same period, 'improving' landlords – like Coke of Norfolk and the Duke of Buccleuch – introduced new systems of scientific farming, stock-breeding and land-management.

Sheep were the principal business of Ashestiel, as they were of Scottish farming generally at the time. Scott plunged into the complicated business of animal husbandry and set himself to learning all about long sheep, short sheep, tups, and gimmers and hogs and dinmonts (*Lett.* 1. 222). John Buchan claims that he was not a good farmer and in later life Scott himself claimed to 'hate' the work. But there was no lack of enthusiasm in 1805. He had some idea of hiring James Hogg as his shepherd. Instead he hired a local man, Tom Purdie. According to Lockhart, Purdie first came to Scott's notice as a poacher who gave the bench such a pathetic account of his domestic problems that the compassionate Sheriff not only dismissed the charge but took him on as an employee (Lock. 1. 396.) Edgar Johnson casts cold water on this legend, which must, however, have originated with Scott (EJ 230). True or not, Purdie became the most devoted of retainers, and eventually served Scott as a factotum: shepherd, foreman, gillie, Man Friday. On his part, Scott became inordinately fond of his Tom and drew on him in the depiction of the peasantry and their dialect in his Scottish novels.

Scott's remarkably efficient authorial habits were formed at Ashestiel. His doctor had advised him against writing late at night. He therefore made it his habit to rise early – at farmer's daybreak – around five o'clock. Before the rest of the house was stirring he would write from six to nine. It was a crotchet first to feed his horses and to dress for the day before sitting down to his desk in the dining room, with his dogs happily couched at his feet (EJ 231). The remainder of the day and evening he could apply to social intercourse, legal work, farming or reading. Scott was a Trollope before Trollope. And it was this early-to-rise routine which enabled him to take on at this Ashestiel stage of his life a new role as reviewer for magazines such as the *Edinburgh Review* and, later, the *Quarterly Review.*

Preparing for a Literary Career

It is a cliché of the romantic literary career that writers woke and found themselves famous. How much did Scott crave success? To what extent did he seek it? Or was it accidental and wholly unsought? Lockhart is in no doubt that fame was thrust upon Scott. This is in keeping with his conception of his father-in-law as an essentially modest and stoic man. Eric Quayle – with an eye on the early financial dealings – discerns a more calculating face under the masks. In the early Ashestiel years, Quayle notes, Scott was 'comfortably settled in life, happily married, with a healthy young family, and surrounded by a large circle of friends. Yet he was already consumed with financial ambitions that stemmed from an innate greed, perhaps prompted by a sense of insecurity brought about by his physical disability which had made him the butt of coarsely shouted facetious remarks for much of his early childhood'(EQ 24).

In his 1830 afterword to the *Lay* Scott gives his own reasons for writing and publishing the poem. They do not constitute 'innate greed', although financial self-interest certainly comes into it ('honourable provision' for his family, is how he puts it). The success of the *Minstrelsy* had, he recalls, reduced his income from law. Advocates who are known to have a time-consuming sideline – whether it be golf or old ballads – tend not to be trusted by fee-paying clients. There were other difficulties. Tom Scott's mismanagement stopped the flow of commissions from their father's old firm. Scott was not a fluent speaker on his feet in court – a necessity for any advocate ambitious for big commissions from strangers. By Johnson's reckoning, he seems never to have earned much more than £200 in fees in any year from 1792 to 1804. If, as he says, the success of the *Minstrelsy* reduced even this pittance it must have been a very clear signal as to Scott's professional prospects.

That Scott had long-term strategies for himself outside law is clear from a remark to Wordsworth, on the Lake poet's visit to Scotland in September 1803. He could, Scott told Wordsworth, always 'if he chose, get more money than he should ever wish from the booksellers' (EJ 215). Scott's intention to diversify his sources of income (and insure himself against future short-age of legal income) is also deducible from the secret arrangements he had made with James Ballantyne. When the Kelso printer was finally persuaded to move to Edinburgh in late 1802, Scott advanced him £500 as a loan, to help set up new premises in the city: money that probably came from the windfall sale of the copyright of the *Minstrelsy* in November 1802.

Scott had saved most of his uncle Robert's inheritance with the idea of eventually buying a mountain farm, or an estate of some kind. But Ashestiel continued to serve his purposes very well at a very modest cost. He conse-quently invested another £1,500 in Ballantyne's firm, making a total of £2,000. This was in May 1805, when the printer was experiencing cash flow problems. He had just moved to new and larger premises, in the Canongate. He needed new plant and extra labour quickly to meet the orders flowing in (principally for the *Lay*). It was agreed in the new (and secret) contract that Ballantyne would have one third of all ensuing profits; the remaining two-thirds being divided between the partners. On his part, Scott would put printing work Ballantyne's way. More than this, he would actively drum up business for his partner.

Why did Scott put so much money into Ballantyne's business? His mo-tives are never easy to uncover, although several suggest themselves. He was, of course, an old friend from their days together in Kelso. But his second tranche of investment went well beyond mere friendliness. Scott was en-trusting the printer with his family nest-egg. Eric Quayle, for whom Scott is a villain, ascribes the secret investment to 'his impatient need to acquire the wealth that would enable him to maintain a position to which he imagined he was fully entitled by reason of his illustrious forebearers that honoured the family name' (EQ 24). Scott, that is, wanted to get rich quickly. There may be something in this, although one needn't like Quayle see it as evidence of Scott's utter moral depravity. But on balance it seems more likely that Scott was not eager for quick wealth, so much as secure income. He wanted to cushion himself against the notoriously fickle fortunes of literature. He expected, quite rationally, that literary fame would injure his career as a lawyer – which in any case seemed not very promising. He needed something to guarantee a steady source of money, year-in, year-out, should the public taste turn against him leaving him nothing but his fees to live on. As he put it in a much quoted comment, literature must be his staff not his crutch.

Even those who accept that it was sensible for Scott to become a partner in Ballantyne's firm question the secrecy of the arrangement. Edgar Johnson will have none of it. 'Much nonsense has been written about the fact that Scott did not blazon this business venture to the world', he exclaims (EJ 233). Scott was no more obliged to publicize his contract with the printer than a modern lawyer to divulge his share holdings to the outside world. Johnson goes on to assert that it is 'absurd . . . to imagine that those in the Edinburgh book trade were not aware of the arrangement

. . . Of course Constable and Longman knew.' His publishers over the years must have noted their author's insistence that only Ballantyne print Scott's works. And sharp-eyed readers must surely also have noted the invariable imprint. 'Gradually,' Johnson surmises, 'if not to every friend or fellow advocate, certainly to the business world, Scott's association with Ballantyne became well known'(EJ 234).

For all his indignation, Johnson chooses his words carefully. When he says 'fellow advocates' he is thinking particularly of the inconvenient instance of Henry Cockburn. Cockburn was one of the 'select friends' who were to penetrate the mystery of Scott's anonymous authorship of *Waverley*. Cockburn knew Edinburgh and its secrets better than any man living. 'Harry' Cockburn had been friends with Scott for over twenty years. Yet the revelation of the Ballantyne connection in 1826 was a 'thunderbolt' to him. 'The idea that his practical sense had so left Scott as to have permitted him to dabble in trade had never crossed our imagination,' Cockburn recorded years later (*Mem.* 405). His amazement ('our amazement' as he says) is very convincing. And it is worth specifying what exactly shocked Cockburn, and Edinburgh gentry like him. He would have quite agreed with Edgar Johnson that Scott was not ethically obliged to have his partner hang out a sign in the Canongate proclaiming 'Ballantyne, Ballantyne, and – would you believe it? – Walter Scott, Advocate'. What amazed Cockburn was Scott's 'impracticality'. Scott was not merely an investor in Ballantyne's business, nor acting as a sleeping partner. He was, from beginning to end, a co-manager of the operation and the prime mover. This was as irresponsible and fraught with disaster as James Ballantyne's pleading a client's case in the Court of Session would have been.

THE LAY OF THE LAST MINSTREL

The anecdotes recording the genesis and composition of *The Lay of the Last Minstrel* all testify to its 'accidental' origins and the ease with which it flowed from Scott's pen. It was written, he said, 'to discharge my mind'. By his own account twenty-five years later, the project began with a hint from 'the young and beautiful' Countess of Dalkeith (whom Scott adored) that he might write a ballad on the Gilpin Horner legend – a sorcerer's apprentice fable about a goblin page who steals, but cannot entirely control, a magician's book of spells. According to this version (drawing on Scott's 1830 afterword) the Countess had recently become a member of the Buccleuch family by marriage, and was collecting local legends connected with her new domain (in fact, she had married her husband, the Earl of Dalkeith, in 1795). It was the command of a 'chieftainess' to her loyal minstrel (something echoed in the structure of the poem).

On examination, modern critics do not accept Scott's assertion (offered in 1830) that the poem *began* with the Countess's command. Her Gilpin suggestion was apparently communicated to Scott in late January 1803, by which time the composition of the poem was in full swing (the goblin page does not, in fact, appear in the narrative until almost half way through the narrative). On 30 November 1802 – some three months earlier – Scott had told Anna Seward that 'I am at present busy with the second edition of the Minstrelsy and preparations for the third volume particularly a sort of Romance of Border Chivalry and inchantment which will extend to some length' (*Lett.* 1. 166). As Jane Millgate plausibly argues, the Gilpin Horner material was probably grafted into the poem as an afterthought.

According to Edgar Johnson, Scott began composition of the *Lay* 'during the summer or autumn' of 1802. By his own account he soon after recited some early stanzas to a couple of friends, William Erskine and George Cranstoun (EJ 197). Their blank looks dismayed him and he impulsively burned the manuscript. It later turned out that Scott's comrades had, after all, rather liked what they heard, but did not know how best to respond. The *Lay* was on again.

Later in the autumn of 1802 (as Johnson calculates) a horse kicked Scott while he was at Portobello on his cavalry exercises (this may be the inspiration for Deloraine's being wounded and restlessly *hors de combat* in Canto 3 of the *Lay*). Scott was laid up for three days at nearby Musselburgh and he embarked on what later became the first canto in earnest (*Lett.* 1. 188–9). By January 1803 Scott had received his 'command' from the Countess of Dalkeith, which (it is supposed) led him to complicate the poem with the Horner subplot. It is clear from a letter to Ellis at the end of the month that by this date he had the framing device firmly in place. The poem, Scott told Ellis, was put 'in the mouth of an old bard who is supposed to have survived all his brethren and to have lived down to 1690. The thing itself will be very long' (*Lett.* 1. 175). Scott consulted various other friends and the poem was subsequently dashed off 'at the rate of a canto per week' – or so Scott alleged in his 1830 afterword. Jane Millgate sums up the whole sequence of starts, stops and careless sprints sceptically as a 'fable of creation' (like the famous tale of the *Waverley* manuscript found accidentally with the fishing tackle). She notes 'this narrative of happy accidents represents the origin of the *Lay* as a natural and inevitable process almost beyond Scott's personal control, each stage connected to the next by intervention not of choice but of chance' (Millgate, 16). Scott's account of the genesis of the poem as something dashed down on the spurs of various moments should be taken as fiction, like the poem itself. It seems more likely that, as Johnson records, Scott worked 'steadily' on the *Lay* throughout 1803 and most of 1804, finishing in August of that year (EJ 224).

If one follows Millgate and discounts elements of Scott's 'train of accidents' account, it seems likely that he was driven to write the *Lay* primarily by the military excitement of the time. It is an excessively belligerent and war-glorifying poem. And its climax – the mustering of 10,000 Border Scotsmen and horse to repel the lightning raid of the English invader – clearly allegorizes the mobilization of the Edinburgh Light Cavalry at

Musselburgh, to fight Boney on Portobello's beaches. Scott's blood was boiling for an honest fight. This pugnacious excitement heats up the poem, which is all gallop, sword-play, and lusty after-the-battle wassail. There is, for instance, a telling (and oddly prophetic) moment in the fifth canto when the English (suddenly outnumbered three-to-one) prudently agree to trial by single combat. The opposing armies throw down their weapons, embrace,

> And some, with many a merry shout,
> In riot, revelry and rout,
> Pursued the foot ball play. (V. 6)

War dissolves into the first international soccer match. Battle is sport by another name.

In its framework the *Lay* picks up themes that Scott had been chewing over in *Sir Tristrem* and *Thomas the Rhymer*. A minstrel in a time when minstrelsy has all but decayed under puritan oppression recites a last poem for a great lord's lady (a queen, in her own esteem). For all his feebleness, the minstrel represents an apostolic link with that period when, as Scott put it in his 1824 essay on 'Romance', 'poets were the historians and often the priests of their society' (*Prose* 6. 163). The lay – which takes some time to arrive at – tells of love and war in the mid-1500s Border country. The plot is a mixture of historical, romantic and 'Border raider' ballad material laced with 'inchantment' (Scott – like Shakespeare – typically sees supernatural forces as something released during times of civil unrest). Generically, the *Lay* draws on metrical Arthurian romance and Ellis's *Specimens of Early English Romances in Metre* (1805). Elements of Scott's early passion for Goethe's baronial melodrama (particularly *Götz*) resurface. Further back, one catches echoes of Scott's juvenile passion for Spenser.

But most of all, the poem draws on Scott's indefatigable genealogical research into his own family background. It is an act of fealty to the family 'chief' – Henry, third Duke of Buccleuch. The various septs of Scotts feature in the *Lay* as fanatically loyal and brave liegemen to the House of Buccleuch (see Canto IV, ix–xi). At its root, the *Lay* is a family affair. All this is in line with Scott's idea of *Urpoesie*. In the golden age of minstrelsy romance was essentially an effusion of the 'vanity of the tribe' (*Prose* 6. 135).

Technically the *Lay* is, for 1805, a startlingly innovative poem. But its novelty did not emerge from nowhere. In his 1830 afterword, Scott acknowledges the influence of Southey's *Thalaba* (1801), an Oriental tale which brought exotic raw material under the control of modern English verse forms and diction. In the same afterword, Scott admits a more plausible and troubling debt to 'Christabel'. The first part of Coleridge's poem was written in 1797, the second in 1800, after the poet's return from Germany. Never completed, no part of 'Christabel' was published until 1816, a decade after the *Lay*. Scott came by Coleridge's poem in circumstances that have led to persistent and damaging charges of plagiarism.

According to Edgar Johnson, John Stoddart, a doctor, visited Scott at Lasswade during a tramp through northern England and Scotland in 1800. A fanatic admirer of the *Lyrical Ballads*, Stoddart knew the Lake poets personally and he recited 'Christabel' – still being written. Scott – whose ear was trained by his tracking down ballads from oral sources – memorized the poem on one hearing, and had it in his repertoire for the rest of his life. (Thirteen years later, in coversation with Byron, Scott was still able to recite 'Christabel' from memory.) Two years after listening to Stoddart, as the *Lay* grew in his mind, half-consciously Scott wove elements of Coleridge's poem into his design.

So at least runs the official version. The Coleridgeans have a different account. As Earl Griggs summarizes, in his edition of Coleridge's *Letters*, 'Coleridge gave Stoddart a copy of "Christabel" presumably in 1801. Subsequently, in 1802, Stoddart recited the poem to Scott' (Griggs 2. 1191–2). The date is significant. If Scott began the *Lay* immediately after hearing 'Christabel' the allegation of plagiarism is that much stickier. And demonstrably, Johnson's summer 1800 must be wrong. On 26 December 1800 Stoddart wrote to Scott that 'Coleridge is engaged on a poetical Romance called *Christabel* of very high merit' (*Postbag*, 12). Clearly Scott did not know of the poem before this point and certainly he did not know it by heart.

As Southey noted, Scott borrows most heavily from 'Christabel' in the early sections of the minstrel's lay. The gothic quality of Branksome Castle is stressed and – in this early section – there is a clear forecast (not carried out) that 'the magic of the lady' (that is, the French widow of Lord Walter, who is portrayed as half-witch) will figure as centrally as that of Geraldine. Scott also lifted elements of Coleridge's phraseology almost verbatim. But the most powerful stimulus to Scott was Coleridge's unorthodox scansion. 'Christabel' is written in what Hopkins later termed 'sprung rhythm', a metre that works by stress not syllable count. This was an innovation in Romantic poetry, entirely original with Coleridge. His friends – Southey, Lamb and the Wordsworths – were upset on his behalf by the prior publication of the *Lay*. As Dorothy Wordsworth put it, 'My brother [i.e. William] and sister think that the *Lay* being published first, it will tarnish the freshness of *Christabel*, and considerably injure the first effect of it.' His friends were more upset, as it appeared, than Coleridge himself was, since he seems not to have bothered to read Scott's poem until 1807 when he generously observed that he saw 'no dishonourable or avoidable resemblance to *Christabel*' (Griggs 1191).

Scott's behaviour was more equivocal. In September 1803, when the Wordsworths visited Lasswade, they found, to their consternation, that Scott knew 'Christabel' by heart and they 'were struck with the resemblance' to the *Lay*, parts of which he recited to his guests. But Scott told the Wordsworths that he had begun the *Lay* before Stoddart introduced him to the other work 'and was much delighted to meet with so happy a specimen of the same kind of irregular metre which he had adopted.' That is, he had made the invention before Coleridge and independently. This must have

been an untruth. As Southey pointed out there are exact verbal echoes (e.g.
'Jesu Maria, shield her well'; *Lay* I. 1) which could not have been accidental.
The issue of Scott's unauthorized borrowing from 'Christabel' was to
rumble on for decades until Scott finally admitted in the 1830 afterword to
the *Lay* that he was indebted to 'Christabel', as 'the pupil to his master'.

The opening section of the *Lay* enacts prosodically Scott's liberating
discovery of Coleridge. The poem begins with an introduction written
in the most leaden Hudibrastics. The octosyllabic lines carry their iambs
like leg-irons:

> The way was long, the wind was cold
> The minstrel was infirm and old;
> His wither'd cheek and tresses gray
> Seem'd to have known a better day;
> The harp, his sole remaining joy,
> Was carried by an orphan boy.

The limp march of these lines aptly conveys the time's 'iron bigotry' against
verse and the minstrel's weariness. Then, after some diffident twanging of
the harp, the minstrel begins his lay. Suddenly the poem breaks into sprung
verse: lines of variable syllabic length, each with four asymmetrical stresses:

> The feast was over in Branksome Tower,
> And the Ladye had gone to her secret bower;
> Her bower that was guarded by word and by spell,
> Deadly to hear, and deadly to tell –
> Jesu Maria, shield us well! (I. 1)

Read coldly, it is tushery of the kind that one laughs at in Poe. But in Scott's
poem the effect, not to exaggerate, is like switching from black and white
to technicolor film. On the ears of the age – accustomed as they were to
orthodox poetic metre – the effect was sensational.

The poem which follows is – like all Scott's narrative verse – undemand-
ing and wonderfully enjoyable. But it principally asks to be read as an
obsessional exercise in name narcissism, a fantasia on what it is to be a
'Scott' – more particularly, one of the powerful women of the clan. The
Countess of Dalkeith, Harriet Scott (future Duchess of Buccleuch) commands her minstrel Walter Scott to write a poem. An infirm minstrel (an
apologetic version of Walter Scott, son of Anne Scott, brother of Anne
Scott, and father of Anne Scott) arrives at a castle which is the home of
Anne Scott, first Duchess of Buccleuch. Her husband James Scott is better
known to posterity as the Duke of Monmouth. He was executed some years
earlier, in 1685, for trying to make the Scotts kings of England and
Scotland. At the Duchess's command, the minstrel recites a lay about Janet
Scott, widow of another 'assassinated' leader of the family, Walter Scott of
Buccleuch. She summons the rugged moss-trooper William of Deloraine –
a fictional personage, but Earl of Deloraine was one of the titles of Henry

Scott, the son of Monmouth: we are to assume that Deloraine is an illegitimate Scott. He is to go to the grave of Michael Scott, the fabulous wizard
– one of the mythic founders of the family – and disinter his book of spells.
According to the poem, Lady Janet knew Michael while he lived. This is
poetic licence, since the historical Michael Scott – an alchemist and astrologer – died in the 1240s. But Walter Scott was particularly attracted to him,
as a Scott whose power was – like his own – manifested in 'books' of various
kinds: like the minstrel, the wizard is a version of the poet.

What witchery Lady Janet Scott intends to do with Michael Scott's book
and its 'grammar' [magic] is never known. Like Geraldine's plot in the
incomplete *Christabel*, it is left hanging. The unexpected English invasion
unites the feuding Scots, as does Cranstoun's heroism in single combat and
his fifth-canto union with Margaret Scott. The conclusion skitters off into
various subplots (Gilpin Horner, the abduction of the Buccleuch heir, etc.)
But the core of the narrative is Walter Scott's extraordinarily convoluted
genealogical play with his family history. The *Lay* is less a poem than a
totem pole in verse. It inescapably recalls the book of doggerel verse from
which the infant Walter learned his letters: *The History of the Right Honourable Name of Scott* (EJ 15).

Why did Scott write this fantasia on his right honourable name? It seems
to have been part of his quest to recover for the modern poet the dignity of
the minstrel – an entertainer who had once enjoyed high rank. In a more
practical way, Scott wanted patronage for his legal career. The *Lay* is a poem
which flatters women and solicits favours from powerful men. Scott had
identified the Duke of Buccleuch – and his new friend and comrade the
Earl of Dalkeith (the heir to Buccleuch) – as the ladders by which he would
rise in the world. Scott's loyalty to his chief, and to his chief's demesne, is
reiterated at a number of points in the poem. At the end of the fifth canto,
the ladies ask the minstrel why – as such a gifted harpist – he does not travel
to the 'more generous Southern land', where he will become rich. This
inspires by way of retort the magnificent patriotic lyric 'Breathes there the
man, with soul so dead.' Scott is here asserting his own disinclination to go
to London and make his fortune. He will (like the minstrel) attach himself
to his patron(ess).

The poem ends with what looks like a naked request that 'the minstrel'
(i.e. Walter Scott) be given a house on the Buccleuch estate:

> Hush'd is the harp: the Minstrel gone.
> And did he wander forth alone?
> Alone, in indigence and age,
> To linger out his pilgrimage?
> No; close beneath proud Newark's tower.
> Arose the Minstrel's lowly bower

Scott was house-hunting at this period and – as Lockhart reports – had his
eye on a property at Broadmeadows, 'close beneath proud Newark's tower',

in the grounds of one of the Buccleuch castles (Lock. 1. 410). It would seem, on the face of it, a fairly broad hint. He did not, apparently get his house and had to content himself with the Sheriffdom and the Clerkship which (among many lesser favours) the Buccleuch interest helped secure him over the years.

He might have had more. It is quite likely that Scott would have risen very high indeed by his attachment to the Buccleuchs had not the family suffered a quite appalling series of premature deaths. Henry, the third Duke (to whom Scott owed his sheriff's post) died in 1812. Harriet, Scott's beloved Duchess, the inspirer of the *Lay*, died in 1814. Charles, the fourth Duke, Harriet's husband, Walter's particular friend and comrade-in-arms, the dedicatee of the *Lay*, died in 1819, leaving a thirteen-year-old fifth Duke in whom Scott took an avuncular interest, but who clearly could do nothing in the patronage way.

The *Lay*'s 'family' narrative centres on two disasters which nearly destroyed the House of Buccleuch (as the House of Douglas was destroyed in the fifteenth century) but from which – Scott implies – it recovered to occupy its foremost position in Scotland of the nineteenth century. Women were instrumental in both recoveries. The first crisis (embodied in the *Lay* itself) was precipitated by the assassination of Walter Scott by the Kerrs in 1552. At this period, the family was intent on establishing itself – principally by violence and strategic marriage. Walter's marriage in 1543 to his French bride Janet Beaton (the 'Lady' in the *Lay*) was his third (and hers as well). They had two sons and three daughters, including one called 'Margaret' of whom nothing is known (it is into this vacancy that Scott inserts his Margaret – Cranstoun love plot). Lady Buccleuch was popularly believed to be a witch. But it was solely due to her indomitable force of character (her 'masculine spirit' as Scott's 'Note *ix*' puts it) that the house survived the catastrophe of having its head killed.

In the Newark framework of the poem, Scott flirts daringly with the just-missed greatness of the house of Buccleuch, and the second major setback in the family's history. Lady Anne Scott (born 1651) succeeded on the death of her sister in 1661 to the family's titles and estates. But as a ten-year-old girl she was a weak link. In 1663, aged only twelve, she was married to the fourteen-year-old James, Duke of Monmouth (1649–85), a natural son of Charles II. The King made over a huge sum (£40,000) and James took over his wife's surname, Scott, and the title 'first Duke of Buccleuch'. On the death of Charles II, Monmouth raised a rebellion. Had he succeeded in his attempt to make himself James III the Buccleuchs would have been a royal dynasty and Walter Scott would have been minor royalty. But the uprising failed. Monmouth was captured, tried and executed as a traitor.

On his death, it fell to Anne (still only in her mid-thirties) to rescue the family fortunes. Their English estates and his dukedom were, of course, forfeited. The Duchess retreated to Scotland, where she was allowed to retain her Buccleuch honours and to pass the ducal title on. 'One of the wisest and craftiest of her sex' (as John Evelyn called her), she contrived to ensure succession to the traitor's children. In 1688 (only three years after Monmouth's execution) she married Charles, Lord Cornwallis. In later life, she assumed royal airs, terming herself 'Mighty Princess', and insisting on being served on the knee. But the longer she lived the more distance she put between her successor and Monmouth's disaster. Anne died aged eighty-one, and was succeeded in 1732 by her grandson Francis, the second duke of Buccleuch.

The recovery of the House of Buccleuch was all owing to Anne. This formidable woman – by guile and sheer durability – preserved the Buccleuch fortunes through four reigns. Scott's depiction of her is a tribute to the Buccleuch women, saviours of the line. In the interests of romance, however, he blurred some of the Duchess's less flattering traits – her haughtiness, the unhappiness of her marriage with Monmouth (which presumably began with her childhood devirgination), and her opportunistically quick remarriage to Cornwallis. Scott's Anne, Duchess of Buccleuch, is a gentle, infinitely faithful widow, suffused with poignant recollections of matrimonial bliss.

The dedication of the poem to Charles, fourth Duke apparent, alludes to the long recovery of the House of Buccleuch from the disgrace into which Monmouth's adventurism had plunged it. Francis, the second Duke (1695– 1751, succeeded 1732) was ostentatiously loyal to his monarch. During the uprising of 1745 he commanded his tenantry to man the walls of Edinburgh (to comically little effect, unfortunately). He was succeeded by his grandson, Henry, the third Duke (1746–1812), Scott's dedicatee in the *Minstrelsy*. Henry devoted his long tenure as Duke to keeping a low profile, acquiring property, improving estates, and unswervingly supporting the King, Dundas, and the Tory party. By 1805 – as the largest landholder in Scotland – he could safely be said to have presided over the Buccleuchs' complete rehabilitation.

Everyone was delighted by the *Lay*. Critics universally applauded William of Deloraine's night gallop and good-naturedly deplored the Gilpin Horner business ('the capital deformity of the poem', as Francis Jeffrey called it). Ballantyne's business took off like a rocket with the work's publication in January 1805 under Longman's and Constable's imprint. (The Scottish publisher had astutely bought a share of the copyright). Within five years, it is estimated, 15,000 copies were sold (Lock. 1. 419). As Edgar Johnson notes, 'In the entire history of English poetry there had never been anything like the popularity of the *Lay*' (EJ 225). The Prime Minister, Pitt, himself enthused, and told William Dundas to 'look to' Walter Scott in the future: 'He can't remain where he is' (EJ 226). Scott, who was still slightly green about the value of his literary property, sold the copyright for £770 – a mistake he would not repeat. But he could expect to recoup the loss, and more. In January 1807, Constable offered him a thousand guineas for his next, as yet unwritten, poem.

'My Staff but not my Crutch'

According to David Daiches, 'Scott never really knew where he was going in his literary career' (Daiches, 84). This is in line with the gentleman amateur, 'Wizard of the North' image which Scott (aided by Lockhart) wanted to project to his public and posterity. Nevertheless at a more private level one discerns a Walter Scott prone to plan his moves. In the period after the *Lay*'s triumph one sees him methodically laying the ground for a whole range of future eventualities. The favour of the public he sensibly took to be 'proverbially capricious' (although in fact he was never to lose it until long after his death – when it went with a vengeance). He and Charlotte visited the Wordsworths in summer 1805, and Scott was struck by the poverty of the Lake poets, especially the politically congenial Southey, who starved on his high reputation and his lofty unreadables like *Thalaba* and the Welsh epic, *Madoc*. Scott took precautions against any such plight; not for him greatness in a cottage with boiled mutton for supper.

In fact by mid-life Scott's means were ample for an Edinburgh gentleman of moderately retired habits. Just before the publication of *Marmion* he estimated his total worth as around £10,000 (EJ 273). But he had four children; he had a wife with social aspirations well above his current station; he had two needy younger brothers; and a widowed mother whose money was bogged down in an interminable trust. Most of all he was possessed of a driving ambition to become a laird – to climb up the ladder of his family pedigree. ('Laird' was, tellingly enough, the family nickname for young Walter Scott, the heir. Among his advocate friends Scott had attracted the telling nickname 'Earl Walter'.)

It was clear that briefs and courtroom brilliance would not make Scott rich and an earl. After a dozen years at the bar he was still only earning a little over £200 a year from that source. One *Lay* – the pleasurable work of six weeks – could earn him as much as ten years of law drudgery. But there was no guarantee that literary popularity would last. Scott rationally decided that literature would henceforward be his staff – 'but not my crutch', he cautiously added. He knew about walking aids.

He would, in fact, rely on two crutches for year-in, year-out 'safe' income. Law (not necessarily advocacy) was one. Another was his dividend from the Ballantyne partnership. To keep this healthy Scott fed the Canongate presses a torrent of legal, literary and historical material. At this stage of his life he proposed to an insatiable James Ballantyne and an increasingly nervous Constable some of the most ambitious publishing schemes since Johnson's *Dictionary*.

The Ballantyne – Scott partnership yielded almost £1,000 profits in 1807 and had estimated capital resources of over £7,000 (EJ 263). According to Eric Quayle, Scott was in the habit of drawing interest on his loans to the company at 15 per cent interest, which must have made a handsome addition to his income. His other support was the Ettrick Shrievalty. This

yielded £300 a year, which was comfortable (not least because it would last
all his life) but hardly munificent. It was not, to play on his image, a staff on
which Scott could put much weight. He accordingly formed the resolution
around this period to make himself a Principal Clerk of Session (EJ 249).
This post, if he could secure it, involved between four and six hours' work
in the forenoon, four or five days a week, for the six months a year that the
Court of Session sat. Not much was required of the half-dozen Clerks
beyond signing their names to documents and parking their bodies at the
table prominently set out for them.

Clerkships yielded (at this date) £800 a year with unchallenged life
tenure. The only thing that could interfere with this arrangement was
Whiggish reform of old Scottish ways – something that gave Scott occasional nightmares. Mental or physical incompetence need be no bar to
holding the position, as Scott's stone-deaf predecessor demonstrated. In
these circumstances, a low-paid substitute could be employed. Not surprisingly, vacancies were hotly competed for. (At one point, Scott found himself
in competition with one of his old university teachers, David Hume.) Scott
had certain advantages over his rivals. Being known as a poetical lawyer
might hurt him with clients but it helped him with the political patrons in
high places who had clerkships in their gift. He had attracted the Tory
administration's attention as someone who might be useful – or at least an
ornament – to the party.

The *Lay* had mightily impressed the Prime Minister, Pitt, who 'expressed
a wish to my personal friend, the Right Honourable William Dundas now
Lord Clerk Register of Scotland, that some fitting opportunity should be
taken of service to me' (JLR 171–2). The Duke of Buccleuch also intervened personally on Scott's behalf with the other Dundas, Viscount
Melville. (EJ 249). The Earl of Dalkeith, Scott's comrade-in-arms, since
1793 a Pittite MP, and dedicatee of the *Lay* was also on his side. To be thus
picked out by the most powerful patrons in Britain was gratifying. But there
was, infuriatingly enough, no convenient prize for his friends to award
Scott. No principal Clerk of Session had died recently.

Scott was extremely nervous about delay. Pitt–the nation's Palinurus –
was frail (he eventually died in January 1806). There were ominous
grumblings against his great patron, Melville. Scott feared (with some
justice) that the administration that he had served would be washed away
before he could be paid off. As he later admitted, had he been surer of the
Tories holding on to power he would have aimed higher than a mere
Clerkship – or have been more patient for his reward.

Ingenuity supplied a solution. There was, as it happened, one superannuated, deaf incumbent who was, Scott noted (with a rueful reference to
his own disability), 'as capable of discharging his duty as I am of dancing a
hornpipe' (EJ 249). George Home of Wedderburn – a longstanding friend
of the Scott family – had been thirty years a Principal Clerk of Session. In
return for the 'survivorship' of the post, Scott offered to take over all its
duties, gratis, until Home should die. The older man would continue to

draw his salary until death, which was tactfully presumed to be imminent. Negotiations were satisfactorily concluded between Scott and Home. The Duke of Buccleuch's influence was used to persuade the relevant authorities to approve a 'dual commission', by which Scott would do the work and Home collect the cash.

6

The Scott Brothers and *Marmion* (1806–1809)

The cosy arrangement about the Clerkship came under threat with Pitt's death on 23 January 1806. As Scott had feared, the Tory government fell. The Whigs came in with their 'Ministry of all the talents' and a declared intention to root out the bad old ways. Melville was impeached and charged with having mishandled Navy estimates some years earlier. 'Poor Lord Melville! . . . my heart bleeds when I think on his situation', Scott told Ellis (*Lett.* 1. 280). The Whigs were clearly in a vindictive mood. As Scott glumly noted, the new administration would surely 'provide for the Whiggish children before they throw their bread to the Tory dogs' (EJ 250).

Scott had three causes for immediate alarm. There had been a clerical error in the drawing up of the official document about the Clerkship. Instead of assigning him and Home dual responsibility it had named Scott alone. Although Scott (in the 1830 afterword to *Marmion*) and Lockhart suggest that his principal anxiety was for Home, in the event of his (i.e. Scott's) predeceasing the old man, it is evident that Scott was also worried for himself. If the document were declared invalid, a 'Tory dog' like himself might all too plausibly be ousted on the technicality of an improperly drawn-up commission. The government might well refuse to renew an arrangement made by their corrupt predecessors. In a larger way, Scott and Tory lawyers like him feared that the whole structure of Scottish law might be reformed. In this root-and-branch operation, such antiquities as the sinecurial Clerkships might well be abolished. On a third count, Scott was concerned that the Clerkship might mean his having to resign his Sheriff's post at Selkirk.

Scott went down to London in early February 1806, to supplicate in person for the redrafting of his Clerkship appointment. In the event, the enemy acted generously – more generously than their Tory predecessors might have done. Advance lobbying by George Ellis smoothed the way. The commission was duly redrawn and the agreement with Home was let stand. Scott took up his duties in May 1806. Scott's friends rejoiced. The tutor to the Duke of Buccleuch's children, the Revd. John Marriott, wrote a poem with the McGonagallesque title 'On Mr Walter Scott's Retiring from the Bar'. It described its subject as 'The captive bird from irksome durance freed . . . No more to plod in Mammon's toilsome road'.

Before returning to Edinburgh and Mammon's toilsome road, Scott went on a round of junketing with his high Tory friends. 'Sallying out from his hotel at 79 Jermyn Street', Johnson records, 'he went nightly to receptions and dinners. He met the witty George Canning and John Hookham Frere' (EJ 251). During this Whig administration (an interregnum, as it turned out) Scott became a more aggressively political animal and 'made himself conspicuous as a leading instrument of his party' (Lock. 1. 489). His poem-in-progress, *Marmion*, was strung around the founding idea of 'epistles dedicatory' to this coterie of Tory grandees (and the loyal Revd. Marriott, by way of gracious acknowledgement).

The Tories proved resilient. Melville was acquitted in mid-June 1806. Scott (now back in Edinburgh) expected appropriate jubilation. But, as Johnson puts it, 'the Magistrates of Edinburgh cravenly turned down an application that the town be illuminated in celebration.' (There were riots against the acquittal in other parts of the country – Melville was clearly culpable and Edinburgh's governors were acting quite properly.) Scott dashed off a triumphant drinking song, 'A Health to Lord Melville', which was widely printed and bellowed out at party meetings. A copy was sent to Canning, via Scott's new Tory friend, William Stewart Rose (EJ 257).

Grierson plausibly suggests that the crude partisanship of 'A Health' (more particularly the aggressive printing of it, so that it might give offence outside partisan circles) was intended to impress the leaders of his party that Scott had not been 'bought' by the Whigs. It nonetheless lost him friends, such as the Countess of Rosslyn (who thereafter considered Scott a 'beast') and his old teacher, Dugald Stewart (HG 91). Scott got his Clerkship and (with the fall of the Whigs in spring 1807) the lifetime financial security that went with it. But there was to be a large fly in his ointment. George Home, despite his great age and frailty, obstinately lived on six more years. An exasperated Scott nicknamed him the 'Old Man of the Sea'. In 1811 Home – clearly flourishing in his retirement – was finally induced to give up his income in return for a massive pension (to which Scott contributed; EJ 383). Scott at last had his stoutest staff – £800 a year for life.

In later life Scott kicked himself for having sold himself to his party so cheap. He candidly explained his mistake to his brother-in-law Charles Carpenter in February 1808 as a loss of nerve, precipitated by the calamity of Pitt's death:

> [It] was rather a hard bargain but it was made when the administration was dissolved upon Pitts death: all was going to pieces and I was glad to swim ashore on a plank of the wreck in a word to be provided any how ere the new people came in. Nobody to be sure could have foreseen that in a years time my friends were all to be in again. (*Lett.* 2. 18)

It was some compensation that he was not, after all, obliged to give up his Sheriff's position. For a while it seemed as if he might have to. The Earl of Dalkeith pointedly wrote to Scott after his successful intervention with the Whigs that 'You are now to snap your finger at the Bar . . . We shall expect much from your leisure' (EJ 250). Scott did not intend (despite the broad hint) that his leisure be augmented by giving up his Sheriff's stipend. He successfully intervened with the Duke of Buccleuch (via the Marquis of Abercorn, his new patron) to be allowed to keep his Sheriffdom. It was an extraordinary piece of pluralism – even by the lax standards of the age, and clearly Scott could in no way fulfil the attendance requirements Napier had insisted on, if he were a full-time official in the Edinburgh Court of Session. Nonetheless it was let stand.

In February 1807 the Whigs, as Scott feared they would, turned their reforming attention to Scottish law. Grenville introduced a bill into the House of Lords proposing sweeping changes – a new tricameral structure, trial by jury in civil cases, and the possible elimination of the Clerks of Session. The appalled Clerks of Session sent down one of their senior colleagues, Colin Mackenzie, to lobby Westminster for compensation in the event of their posts being abolished. When Mackenzie fell ill Scott (already marked as the most vigorous member of the Clerks' table) was dispatched to replace him. He arrived in London on 20 March and to his relief found the new government already on the way out, falling on a (laudable) bill to allow Catholics to hold commissions in the army. Britain was not ready for such radical reforms as Catholic lieutenants or the abolition of Clerks of Session. Scott and his country breathed again. 'The Law of Scotland', he exulted to Charlotte, 'will remain as it was or at least be touched with a respectful and lenient hand' (EJ 266).

The new (Tory-dominated) Parliament, under Lord Eldon, retained the earlier reform bill in modified form. It resulted in an appropriately respectful and lenient 'Commission on the Administration of Justice in Scotland' (EJ 285). On 5 February 1808, Scott used his contacts with the Marquis of Abercorn (more effectively with the Marchioness, who was infatuated with him) to solicit his appointment as Secretary to this Commission. The 'job' was arranged, through Melville, a couple of days later (*Lett.* 2. 9). The recommendations of the Commission duly became law in July 1808. Among the reforms were a division of the Court of Session into two, and an increase of the Clerks' stipend to a salary of £1,300 a year (plus pension) instead of £800 a year, paid out of fees. It is evident that, as secretary, Scott had exercised a powerful influence. And since the Commission sat in London, he further strengthened his links with powerful people in the Tory party. It is also evident from letters to the Marchioness of Abercorn that he had hopes that their interest might secure him his Clerk's salary before Home's death. He even hinted in one letter to the Marchioness that a Barony (judgeship) might be appropriate. It seems the Abercorns did indeed plead Scott's case to Melville, without immediate result.

FRIENDS AND RELATIONS

Scott's work as a legal lobbyist entailed his longest sustained sojourns in London. The author of *The Lay of the Last Minstrel* was a literary lion and he drank the 'cup of blandishment', as Lockhart puts it. He made powerful and glamorous friends – including Caroline, the Princess of Wales. He developed a particular skill in charming literary ladies. Joanna Baillie, 'the poetess of Hampstead', was a notable conquest. Scott revered Baillie's arid dramas, and seriously ranked her with Shakespeare. She was ten years older than her admirer and would outlive him by twenty. Originally Scottish, she had a father who had been a minister at Bothwell, and who could claim a distant connection with William Wallace. Her *Plays on the Passions* had started to come out anonymously in 1798. They caused considerable stir – not least on the question of who their mysterious author might be. Scott was one of those who identified her hand behind the plays (and perhaps stored away the ruse for his own use, later). Now in her mid-forties, Baillie was living in a Hampstead cottage. When they met, she was initially slightly disappointed at Scott's less than 'ideal' appearance. But they hit it off, and Scott would subsequently do his best – against all the odds – to promote her as Scotland's great living dramatist. Scott also became strongly attached to another woman poet at this period, Anna Seward, the 'Swan of Lichfield'. Thirty years older than him, she had been lame since her mid-twenties (although she remained, like Scott, robustly active).

Despite his celebrity, Scott was careful to keep up his interchanges with the antiquarians who still regarded him principally as the editor of the *Minstrelsy* and *Sir Tristrem*. George Ellis (who had been so helpful about the Home business) was his constant correspondent and literary adviser. Scott also visited Heber in Oxford. He became acquainted at this period with J. B. S. Morritt. A gentleman-scholar of private means, Morritt had devoted much of his life to the study of Homer and the site of Troy (about which he developed ingenious and wrong-headed theories). An MP and a renowned traveller who founded the Travellers' Club in London, Morritt was possessed of a fine estate at Rokeby Park in Yorkshire. According to Lockhart, Morritt was the last intimate friend that Scott made – thus closing a phase that had begun with his return to university in 1788.

As Scott's social network widened his relationships with his surviving siblings soured and narrowed. And in the period 1805–9 his family affairs were a cause of severe vexation. Walter's eldest surviving brother, John Scott, sold out from the army as a Major on half-pay after his long-delayed promotion in 1809. This was the same promotion that had almost scuppered Walter's marriage plans in 1797. What had gone wrong? The auguries for success in his career had been excellent. In 1808, John Scott had been in the army for over fifteen years; Britain had been almost continuously at war, a situation in which promotion in the forces is accelerated; he had been posted abroad, where promotions were typically awarded on merit not connection; John's background was reasonably well-off. In 1797, John Scott had evidently been a promising young officer on a fast track (it was expected he would attain field rank by the age of thirty). In 1808 he was a washed-up, passed-over, forty-year-old captain on the brink of premature retirement. Grierson alludes to the 'unhealthy, even decadent strain' in the Scott personality – by which he means a tendency to early alcoholism. This it was that presumably held John Scott back.

Scott was angling over 1808 to get 'Jack' a home garrison posting or a safe berth in an 'invalid battalion'. His majority was acquired for him in 1809 by the influence of Canning (to whom Walter had been introduced by the politician and author John Wilson Croker, whom in turn he had met through Ellis). John's promotion was transparently a pay-off for the political epistles in *Marmion*. Since John loaned his brother quite considerable sums of money in the next few years and made Walter his principal heir, there may have been some charge by Walter for his intercession in 1809. Being able to sell a majority (rather than a captaincy) substantially increased John's wealth and half-pay. He retired very comfortably off. On his discharge, 'Major' John lived with the widowed Mrs Scott. His health had by now totally collapsed and he was considered by Walter to be a whist-playing dullard. His life was over, and he was no distinction to the Scott family. John and Walter evidently kept civilly out of each other's way. Scott gives a moderately affectionate pen-portrait of his brother as the half-pay veteran in *Paul's Letters to his Kinsfolk* (1816). John Scott died, still in his forties, in 1816, of 'exhaustion'.

Daniel Scott could not be ignored. Daniel evidently began his adult career promisingly, as a teenage officer in the volunteers in the mid-1790s (his bastard son William apparently referred to his dead father through life as 'Lieutenant Daniel Scott'). It would seem that he was educated in 'the mercantile line', and he may have worked for a while in London. In an early letter of reference, Scott reports that Daniel 'is a very good-natured young man [who] writes and figures very decently.'

Whatever commercial business Daniel began in, it clearly did not prosper. Grierson deduces that in 1799 he was sent off for a brief stay in the southern states of America, but soon returned (HG 99). At some point around the turn of the century Daniel was placed in the Custom House in Edinburgh. Notoriously (as with Robert Burns – the most unlikely exciseman in British history) such posts were distributed by patronage. It seems probable that Scott exercised his influence to acquire this safe berth for his younger brother. According to the same letter of reference (which may, like many, be rosier than the facts warranted) Daniel 'had a good chance of promotion [in the Custom service] had he not formed an imprudent connexion with an artful woman which was likely to end in a *mesalliance*' (*Lett.* 12. 246).

This seems rather too soluble a pickle for what happened next. Daniel was hurried out of Edinburgh to Liverpool, where he was apparently instructed to look for something suitable in America, or the colonies. He was evidently supported, *pro tem*, by a remittance from his sheriff brother. He was, however, strictly forbidden to tell anyone that he was Walter Scott's brother – a prohibition Daniel evidently observed, despite heavy drinking. In writing his letter of reference, to one of his closest friends, Scott only went so far as to say that Daniel was a 'relation'. Exile and shameful anonymity would seem a drastic reprisal for a threatened *mésalliance*. Daniel was over twenty-one; like the other Scott sons he inherited £600 on his uncle Robert's death in June 1804. He could expect thousands more when his father's estate was cleared up. Johnson, following Grierson, building on ambiguous remarks of Lockhart's and what looks like a misdated letter, assumes that there was a bastard son born in 1800. But even if there were an out-of-wedlock child born at some point between 1800 and 1804, embarrassing as it would have been for the Presbyterian Scotts, it should not have forced Daniel (still in his early twenties) to give up a safe, honourable post and go into hiding in a port town south of the border. What seems more likely is that there was some criminal malefaction at the Custom House which Walter Scott hushed up. Later events suggest that even at this early date Daniel was already in an advanced condition of alcoholism. Professional misconduct would seem a logical assumption.

A couple of months passed and nothing turned up for Daniel in Liverpool. In clear desperation, Scott prevailed upon his connections with Ellis to help his unidentified 'relation'. Ellis's wealth came from the Caribbean and in May 1804 he succeeded in finding a place for Daniel with a West Indies plantation owner, called Blackburn. Scott was profoundly grateful. On his part, Blackburn was unimpressed when Daniel (whom he did not know to be Walter Scott's brother) arrived in Jamaica in December 1804. There followed over the months a series of ominous comments on Daniel's 'idleness' and his addiction to rum (*Lett.* 12. 280).

What occurred next is found only in Lockhart's account, written thirty years later. In late 1805, 'being employed in some service against a refractory or insurgent body of negroes, Daniel exhibited a lamentable deficiency of spirit and conduct. He returned to Scotland a dishonoured man' (Lock. 2. 135). There was, in fact, an uprising of slaves in Jamaica in 1805, following the dramatic rebellion in neighbouring Haiti, and the British military did not, apparently, respond firmly enough. There were court martials, and reprisals. It seems that Daniel was among the colonials held responsible. Perhaps he was unwilling to use the discipline of terror necessary to restore order in a slave state. Whatever the mitigating circumstances, Walter Scott was not inclined to be merciful. On his return to Edinburgh in disgrace (presumably in early 1806) his mother took the reprobate in. 'Scott, to whom cowardice was almost the one unforgiveable weakness, would not even see him,' Johnson reports, echoing Lockhart's high moral tone (EJ 257). Since Castle Street was only a stone's throw from their mother's lodgings in George Street the brothers' paths must have crossed, but Walter presumably cut his relation when they met in the street.

This state of affairs evidently continued for a few months. Then, in a letter of May 1806 which survives (unlike most concerning Daniel) to his Substitute in Selkirk, Charles Erskine, Scott wrote: 'My mother is anxious to have Daniel's business finished and is willing to agree to the terms last proposed by them which though high are I think little enough for getting rid of such a scrape. The money is ready in Sir William Forbes's [bank] . . . I do not care to be seen in [the matter] myself' (*Lett.* 1. 295). Grierson notes that this is 'probably a reference to the [payment] for Daniel's natural child'. That is, Scott was making provision for his illegitimate nephew but would not have any personal dealings with the scapegrace father.

After May, Daniel's affairs wound up quickly. His health collapsed, 'shattered by dissolute indulgence, and probably the intolerable load of shame' as Lockhart conjectures (Lock. 2. 135). He drank himself to death (or conceivably committed suicide) a few weeks later in mid-July 1806. The next episode in one of the most famous in Scott's career. 'The poet refused either to attend his funeral or to wear mourning for him like the rest of the family. Thus sternly, when in the height and pride of his blood, could Scott, whose heart was never hardened against the distress of an enemy, recoil from the disgrace of a brother' (Lock. 2. 135). When, by contrast, his beloved terrier Camp died in March 1809, Scott was grief-stricken. The beast was buried with the whole family standing damp-eyed around the grave at Castle Street and Scott cancelled his social engagements on the grounds of the 'death of a dear old friend' (EJ 312). The dog, of course, was courageous.

Lockhart (whose pomposity in recording these events is stomach-turning) adds a touching final detail. 'It is the more pleasing part of my duty to add, that [Scott] spoke to me, twenty years afterwards, in terms of great and painful contrition for the austerity with which he had conducted himself on this occasion [i.e. Daniel's death]. I must add, moreover, that he took a warm interest in a natural child whom Daniel had bequeathed to his mother's care; and after the old lady's death, religiously supplied her place as the boy's protector' (Lock. 2. 135). This occasion, twenty years later, was the composition of *The Fair Maid of Perth*, and the central part given Conachar, the congenital coward. His 'secret motive' in portraying Conachar, Scott told his son-in-law, 'was to perform a sort of expiation to my poor brother's *manes*. I have now learned to have more tolerance and compassion than I had in those days' (Lock. 5. 166).

It is a stirring, pathetic and pretty story from which Scott – for all his severity – comes out very well. His faults are those of the Roman patriarch, for whom honour and the martial virtues outweigh all personal consideration. Yet, with time, the more charitable side of his nature wears through – he forgives, and makes an expiation in the years of his own greatest suffering. This pretty story is, however, somewhat contradicted by other facts which have surfaced. The first fact is that Daniel's natural son was born not before his father's exile in December 1804 (as Johnson assumes) but six weeks after his father's death in Scotland, in July 1806. What then was the disgrace that drove Daniel out of Scotland in early 1804? Drink was certainly part of it, and dishonesty at the Custom House may (as I surmise) have been another. But Scott specifically mentions an 'artful woman' who threatened to trap his 'soft' brother into a misalliance, or 'imprudent connexion'.

Who was this harlot? It emerges that she was Miss Currie Lamb, the daughter of a prosperous seedsman in Selkirk. Moreover, 'she appears to have been well educated and of good character and altogether a worthy daughter of an honest and much respected citizen of the town.'[1] Walter Scott was, of course, the Sheriff of that same town. In what sense would a connection with Miss Lamb be an 'imprudent connexion' for a young man himself brought up in the 'mercantile line'? The answer is found in Miss Lamb's position as housekeeper to the Marquis of Abercorn, at Duddingston. At the same period Tom Scott, Walter's brother, was Abercorn's agent at Duddingston (more of which later). This, presumably was how Currie and Daniel fell in each other's way. More importantly, Scott was on visiting terms with the Marquis and Marchioness – who were, in fact, to become his most distinguished friends over the years 1806–9. Scott, one is led to assume, did not want his brother marrying the *housekeeper* of a noble household where he was a regular guest – being shown into the drawing room at Duddingston, for instance, by his sister-in-law.

Daniel had clearly done something else which gave Walter the authority to order him out of Scotland. But – other things being equal – there would seem to have been no imprudence in a match with Currie Lamb. It may well be that Daniel 'showed the white feather' in the West Indies, but this again would not necessarily explain why he should return to Scotland, rather than go on to America or Canada, supported by some small remittance from the family. If the bastard son (William Mitchell [Scott]) was born in September 1806, he must have been fathered almost the minute Daniel returned. It was, one can guess, love which brought him back to the arms of Currie. But marriage was still, apparently, not an option – or, at least, public marriage was not. (In later life William's mother told her son that she and Daniel had been joined in a secret ceremony.) When the pregnancy was discovered there must have been huge family rows. In the May 1806 letter to Charles Erskine, it is clear that Scott is paying off Currie (who has returned to Selkirk to bear her child). The payment was evidently in return for breaking off entirely with the Scotts and taking the child away. The sum may have been handsome. In 1810, after four years of 'widowhood', Currie married 'Thomas Mitchell of Selkirk, a gentleman of no inconsiderable standing in his native town' (King, 103).

One should also add some modification to Lockhart's epilogue about Scott's 'religiously' taking over the care of William after Mrs Scott's death in 1819. In October 1821 Scott supplied £100 for the boy (now fifteen, presumably) to be apprenticed for seven years to a clothier in Edinburgh's High Street. Thereafter, Scott made over another £30 a year, to meet the young man's indentures. But in 1827, just eighteen months short of completion, Scott informed William that – due to his bankruptcy – he could not continue the payments. The young man was cast adrift, with only a £10 note and a letter of introduction from Scott to a West End tailor in London. His mother in Selkirk could not (or would not) help William either – although it was at this point she informed her son about the 'secret marriage', and his legitimacy (which may well not have been true). Thereafter, the unfortunate young man's life went all to the bad. This casting adrift of William occured at exactly the period (1827–8) that Scott was making his heartwarming 'expiation' to Daniel in *The Fair Maid of Perth*.

Tom Scott had always been Walter's favourite ever since they fought shoulder to shoulder in boyhood 'bickers'. He insisted on believing that his younger brother was prodigiously gifted and capable of better things than being a mere WS and his father's junior partner. But when the family law firm descended into his hands, Tom (who had finished the WS training that Walter started) failed badly. Nor could he blame adverse circumstances. Tom had inherited from his father a profitable business built up over many years of service. It included the agency for the city of Aberdeen and the stewardship of the Marquis of Abercorn's estate at Duddingston. These contracts should have had been gold in Tom's pocket for life. He certainly had need of steady income. He had married imprudently in 1799 and by 1807 had five children to support. But so slovenly was Tom at keeping accounts that clients dropped away and within six years of his father's death the firm was on the rocks (EJ 273).

More seriously, Tom became involved in a complicated business with some brickworks on the Duddingston estate. (A Tory grandee, the Marquis spent most of his time in London.) It seems that, just as Walter was doing with the Ballantyne Printing Office, Tom hoped to enrich himself quickly by trade. Committing one of the most serious offences in the solicitor's profession, Tom misappropriated some of Abercorn's rents to pay outstanding bills incurred by his personal investments.

When this criminal act came to light around July 1807 Tom went into hiding under an alias, leaving his wife (just delivered of a new child) and his children to face the shame and his brother Walter to repair the damage – if he could (EJ 273). Tom was subsequently disqualified from practising law in Edinburgh. It seems likely that he was not prosecuted by his guild, on condition that he left the profession and Edinburgh. His peculations were initially estimated at something over £3,000 – a huge sum. To raise money to guarantee Tom's debts, Scott records that he was obliged to rush *Marmion* into print before its time. What seems more likely is that anxiety forced him to make a highly injudicious (but highly remunerative) agreement with Constable to edit the works of Swift, a chore that would lie like a millstone on his writing career over the next few years. There is no question, however, that worry on Tom's account blighted the composition of the last stages of *Marmion*, and robbed Scott of time and mental energy he would have liked to devote to the work.

At this period – which followed Daniel's death and coincided with the sense that something must be done for John – Scott suffered agonies of shame, humiliation and violent headaches. He evidently received practical assistance from the Marquis and comfort from the Marchioness. In May, she offered her 'powerful mediation' (*Lett.* 1. 363) in rescuing Tom (from her husband's wrath, presumably). Scott confessed to her on 20 July 1807 that – despite all their efforts – Tom had absconded. 'Who could have thought this miserable young man would have behaved so cruelly ill after your Ladyship and the Marquis remonstrating so kindly with him', Scott declared (*Lett.* 1. 370).

Putting things right was not easy. Walter was obliged to make himself responsible for Tom's debts (thus allowing the embezzler to slink back to his family in Edinburgh). Two of Tom's farms on the Abercorn estate were sold off. The Marquis evidently owned a tenth share of the brickworks and he offered to buy Tom's portion for £3,000. Lockhart deduces that Abercorn was further squared by the promise of Tom's share of his father's inheritance (some £5,000, as Grierson calculates).

As Johnson notes, 'two of [Tom's] creditors, named Gillon and Riddell, proved especially rapacious, possibly because Gillon himself was going bankrupt' (EJ 274). This, apparently, was the same Gillon who had been a co-partner (and fellow Mason) with Scott and Ballantyne, in 1800. (Gillon did indeed go bankrupt in 1810, and like Tom was forced to leave Edinburgh.) Scott evidently smoothed things over. Tom conceived a particular dislike towards another solicitor called Guthrie Wright, who took over one of his farms and the Duddingston agency. Walter also had long associations with Wright, who was a fellow member of the Light Cavalry and a 'relation and intimate friend of Mr Erskine' (Lock. 2. 10). Scott was most flattering to Wright, letting him see the manuscript of *Marmion* and suggest improvements. Scott also allowed the Marquis of Abercorn to see the manuscript, and actually to insert lines. Scott's motives were clearly diplomatic (Abercorn seems to have been a stupidly vain man, and there is no reason to suppose that Scott respected his intellect or sensibility). It would seem that Scott went to immense lengths to rescue his favourite brother, pulling every string that he could lay his hand on. Scott's next poem, *The Lady of the Lake*, was gratefully dedicated to the Marquis of Abercorn who had relieved the worst of his problems with Tom, and whose wife probably helped sort out the Daniel Scott imbroglio.

Having preserved the family honour from public disgrace, Scott packed Tom and his family off to the Isle of Man. Since his debts could not pursue him, his Edinburgh debtors would be that much more inclined to settle, as they eventually did for 10s in the pound (EJ 274). After the composition, Scott apparently sold Tom's house for £2,000 (EJ 329) All the while, he presumably supplied money to his brother on the Isle of Man.

In his offshore refuge Tom toyed with the idea of taking orders, joined the Manx Fencibles, and toyed with writing a history of the island. Scott meanwhile succeeded in procuring for his brother an 'extractorship' – an absentee sinecure which nominally involved 'extracting' (i.e. summarizing) court reports. The post was worth £250 a year – a small portion of which was paid over to the hack who actually did the work. Lockhart blurs this 'job' by implying that the appointment had been made well before Tom left Edinburgh, when he still enjoyed the reputation of an honest man. On his part, Johnson also dates it as occurring 'at the beginning of Tom's troubles in 1807' (EJ 330).

It is an important detail. As far as one can work out the dates, Tom's troubles began in July 1807, when he was discovered misappropriating Abercorn funds. By August, he had gone into hiding. Scott was appointed Secretary of the Judicature Commission in February 1808 (through the good offices of the Abercorns). At some point around February – March 1808, Tom and his family went to the Isle of Man. In June 1808, he received his commission in the Manx Fencibles (it is likely that Scott was helpful in this appointment). As James Corson has shown, a vacancy occurred on 4 April 1808 for a Deputy Clerk in the Edinburgh Court of Session. An extractor was appointed to this post, creating a vacancy which was in Scott's gift, and which was filled by Tom in late spring or early summer 1808. This was a full year after 'his troubles began', and at a period in which he was a debt-exile, and a serving officer abroad.

Stripped of the Lockhart – Johnson mitigating circumstances, Scott's putting Tom in this post must be seen as cynical. There was a follow-up. Tom was discharged from the Fencibles in May 1810, when the defence force was reduced to peace-time level. Tom's only remaining source of income was his Edinburgh sinecure. In December 1809, the Judicature Commission (on which Scott had been sitting for over a year) recommended the abolition of Extractorships (EJ 330). But in fairness to those who (like Tom's predecessor) had worked years in the post they awarded a compensatory pension to the incumbents. Tom – who had done no actual work at all in the position, and had held it only a year – was thus guaranteed £130 a year for life. Scott was accused by political enemies of jobbery – which it undoubtedly was.

Tom Scott never returned to Scotland, which may have been prudent. In October 1811 he was secured the post of paymaster in the 70th Regiment, serving abroad. This was as the result of further jobbery by a military relative of his wife, and intervention by Heber and Ellis at the War Office (EJ 380). Two sureties of £1,000 were required. Scott supplied £500 and his mother made up the balance of one bond. Another relative declined – on the sensible ground that Tom was not a fit person to be a paymaster. Finally yet another relative (on his wife's side) chipped in. The whole episode witnesses to Scott's extraordinary personal loyalty to his brother and his incorrigibly poor judgement. As a proven embezzler, Tom Scott should never again have been allowed to manage money. Inevitably he got into more trouble.

MARMION COMMISSIONED

Scott records in 1830 that he began writing *Marmion* with what was for him unusual care, having 'formed the prudent resolution to endeavour to bestow a little more labour than I had yet done on my productions and to be in no hurry again to announce myself as a candidate for literary fame.' But, Scott regretfully recalls, 'the misfortunes of a near relation and friend, which happened at this time, led me to alter my prudent determination, which had been, to use great precaution in sending this poem into the world' (JLR 172).

There are reasons for regarding this protestation as defensive and not entirely true. Scott evidently began writing *Marmion* on 6 November 1806 ('November' is the first word in the poem). In his early conceptions of the poem – during winter 1806 – he was evidently in a dilemma as to whether he was writing two works or one. The *Lay* had been devised with a framework (the minstrelsy business) which is inseparable from the narrative. The corresponding framework surrounding the feudal matter of *Marmion* (or 'Flodden Field', as it was first conceived) is a set of six 'epistles' to (predominantly) English friends of Scott in the present day. These epistles, modelled on Dryden's verse letters, are generally concerned with contemporary politics and are (in many places) aggressively pro-Tory. They are eminently separable. Even Scott's party-political friends thought the epistles were extraneous. Southey spoke for many readers when he frankly told Scott that 'I wished them at the end of the volume, or at the beginning – anywhere except where they were'.[2] Ellis (one of the addressees) frankly termed them 'interruptions'.

Scott's initial dilemma is reflected in two letters written on the same day, 13 January 1807. One was to Anna Seward. Mentioning his newly-conceived 'Flodden Field', Scott told his friend that 'each canto is to be introduced by a little digressive poem which for want of a better name may be calld an epistle' (*Lett.* 1. 347). But on the same day Scott wrote to Longman (still going great guns with the *Lay*) offering them a volume to be entitled 'Six Epistles from the Ettrick Forest'. What was going through Scott's mind was a Scottish poem about Flodden Field, published and printed in Edinburgh by Constable and Ballantyne, and a set of 'Epistles from the Ettrick Forest [to London]' to be published by Longman in London. The reply from the London publisher was, however, discouraging.

Scott meanwhile was evidently deep in negotiation with Constable about 'Flodden Field' and may even have used Longman's interest in his poetry to jack up any offer the Edinburgh publisher cared to make. On 31 January Scott wrote to Constable in response to 'our previous communing' on the subject of 'one thousand guineas for the poem' (*Lett.* 1. 349). Scott accepted the munificent offer. And at the same time he evidently accepted that his two enterprises must become one. The 'Epistles from Ettrick Forest' are heard of no more.

In the early and middle months of 1807, when the bulk of *Marmion* was written (four cantos were complete by September) there was no hint that Scott intended to hold back his production, as he later alleged in 1830. On 15 May Scott gaily informed Lady Abercorn that *Marmion* 'will have the honor of kissing [your] hand at Christmas having adjourned his introduction to public life till that period' (*Lett.* 1. 362). Scott builds this conclusion into the fabric of the poem with the yuletide Mertoun House episode which makes up the last Epistle. Anticlimactically, *Marmion* did not in the event appear until February 1808. Nor can Tom's misfortunes be said to have *hurried* or rushed *Marmion* into print, as Scott claimed in 1830. That affair did not blow up until mid-July 1807. By this time Scott had apparently received his full payment and there would have been no financial advantage in hurrying. If anything the effect of Tom Scott's embarrassments was to delay the publication of *Marmion* rather than accelerate it, by distracting Scott and provoking a crisis in his health. (Lockhart – with his usual pragmatism about chronology – covers Scott's tracks by pushing Tom's troubles back a year, to 1806.)

It may well be true that looking back Scott *wished* he had spent more time on *Marmion*. It may also be the case that he felt that the promise of Constable's guineas – the 1,000 guineas for *Marmion* in January 1807 and the 1,500 guineas for the Swift edition the following year – had distorted the natural course of his artistic development. There was certainly unhappiness among Scott's friends at what they took to be his propensity to waste his talents on literary 'drudgery' and to think more about money than the muse. (Scott dramatizes their unease in the 'Epistle to Erskine' which opens the third canto.)

Scott was, in fact beset by conflicting advice as to what he should do as a poet. Erskine and Seward wanted him to study greatness, and emulate the English classics – Shakespeare, Milton, Dryden. His coterie of noble female admirers – Lady Abercorn, Lady Anne Hamilton, the Countess of Dalkeith – urged and flattered him towards elegant drawing-room verse. His comrades in the Light Horse Cavalry, to whom he routinely recited his work in progress, wanted lusty *Kriegslieder*. His political friends in London wanted political missiles in verse. Ballantyne wanted bestsellers – poems that would sell 20,000 copies a year and make them all rich.

Seen in this light, the two modes of *Marmion* represent a crossroads in Scott's poetic career. In one direction lay cool, Drydenesque, political verse. Scott was saturated in the Restoration poet in 1807, and had all his works at his fingertips. (In framing *Marmion*'s introductions he seems particularly to have been influenced by the delightful Epistle 'To my Honor'd Kinsman John Driden'). Scott's first epistle (sent to Lady Abercorn in February 1807) is so much better than anything else he had written to date as to be almost startling. Particularly effective is the bleak portrait of Ashestiel in winter:

> The shepherd shifts his mantle's fold,
> And wraps him closer from the cold;
> His dogs no merry circles wheel,
> But shivering follow at his heel;
> A cowering glance they often cast,
> As deeper moans the gathering blast.

The epistle modulates into lament over the deaths of Pitt and Fox –
Britain's winter. Had he continued in this vein and accepted the Laureateship when it was offered him in 1813 Scott might have done for nineteenth-
century political poetry what he subsequently did for the novel.

Scott, however, chose not to develop this vein, restricting it to the level of
the semi-attached preface. Tempted by Constable's guineas, he dedicated
the main part of the poem, 'Flodden Field', to superheated romance. The
action sections of the poem contain lines so bad and careless that only the
breakneck pace of the narrative can excuse them. This is the Scott who
airily told Anna Seward (who had advised him to aim for greatness):

> As for poetry it is very little labour to me indeed 'twere pity of my life should
> I spend much time on the light and loose sort of poetry which alone I can
> pretend to write. Were all the time I wasted on the Lay put together for it was
> laid aside for long intervals I am sure it would not exceed six weeks – the last
> Canto [of the *Lay*] was written in three forenoons when I was lying in quarters
> with our Yeomanry. I leave it with yourself to guess how little I can have it in
> my most distant imagination to place myself upon a level with the great bards
> you have mentioned [Chaucer, Spenser, Dryden] the very latchets of whose
> shoes neither Southey nor I are worthy to unloose. (*Lett.* 1. 353–4).

Scott's modesty is infuriating to his supporters since it gives such easy
ammunition to his enemies. There is a defence which can be made on his
behalf. Scott may have dashed off his final cantos of the *Lay* and *Marmion*
with the nonchalance of a child blowing bubbles, as he disarmingly confesses. But underlying the narratives is a lifetime's gruelling reading. Rose
Marie Grady, in a heroic survey of the sources of the eight long poems,
calculates that Scott makes 3,000 references to authorities 'exclusive of
glossarial notes, illustrative passages, and cross references, which are numerous'.[3] Six hundred of these are to manuscript sources, and Scott ranges
between no less than 1,000 different authorities. And these are only the
sources Scott bothers to cite. Infinitely more lie invisible beneath the
surface.

It is with *Marmion* that Constable enters Scott's life as a major force.
Constable's payment for the poem was sensational. Similarly unusual was
the mode of payment. Advances were an innovation in the book trade of
1807 and felt to be somewhat disgraceful by authors of quality like Byron.
Constable was in as much of a hurry as Scott to reach the top of the tree. As
Cockburn put it, Constable had abandoned 'the old timid and grudging
system [and] stood out as the general patron and payer of all promising

publications . . . he made Edinburgh a literary mart' (*Mem.* 164). Constable distinguished himself from the timid ruck by laying out 'unheard of prices to authors' – and making sure that everyone heard about them.

Constable's genius went beyond his purse. One can draw up a catalogue of achievements which qualify him as the most innovative publisher of the century. He founded the nineteenth-century quarterly magazine with the *Edinburgh Review* in 1802. The 25 guineas a sheet (i.e. 16 printed pages) that he paid effectively established the profession of higher journalism as something for gentlemen. Constable inaugurated the three-volume, guinea-and-a-half novel (with *Kenilworth*) on which the major achievements of Victorian fiction, and the circulating library system, came to be based. Constable devised a sophisticated form of the mixed list, on which British general trade publishing has since generally relied. It involves a cross-subsidizing mix of fast and slow selling items (Scott's novels and the *Encyclopaedia Britannica*, for instance). Constable pioneered many of the arts of modern publicity and although he did not invent the 'Great Unknown' ploy, he exploited it to the full. Constable bought up Scott's copyrights, after 1819, for the purpose of collective reissue (with apparatus) of a living author's works – pioneering one of the great sales schemes of the nineteenth century. Constable made himself the most successful exporting publisher of his age. (Of the first 1,000 of *Waverley*, 700 went to England.) Just before the 1826 crash, Constable was planning his great 'miscellany' experiment; cheap books for the millions.

A number of contemporaries (including Lockhart) found Constable to be a crass man and in his later years offensively drunken. But he was a publishing genius – as gifted in his line as Scott was in his. It is a nice question as to whether either man would have reached the heights without the other or would have fallen, had each not been caught up in the other's towering ambitions. Constable's origins were lower than Scott's, although not as degraded as *The Life of Scott* suggests (Lockhart is sarcastically amused at the thought of Constable – a mere tradesman – setting himself up with a country house, as if he were a laird, or a lawyer).

Constable had been born the son of a land steward on the estate of Kellie, in 1774. According to his autobiographical fragment, the young Archibald was attracted magnetically to the bookseller's trade, even as a boy. On leaving parish school (at the age of twelve or thirteen) he was apprenticed in Edinburgh to a bookseller at Parliament Close. (He and Scott must have jostled shoulders many times in the High Street before they knew each other.) Out of his apprenticeship in January 1795, young Archibald set up for himself in the High Street, as a dealer in 'scarce old books' (*ACLC* 1. 20) and prudently married a daughter of the trade who brought with her £300 worth of stock as dowry.

Constable's shop became a resort for rich cultivated collectors and university men. He evidently prospered (largely, according to Carlyle, by disposing of gentlemen's libraries) and amassed more capital than he needed for his bookshop. He began publishing theological and religious pamphlets on commission. By 1801, he had acquired some small periodicals such as *The Farmer's Magazine* and *The Scots Magazine*. He was already known as a keen Whig and in 1802 the coterie that founded the *Edinburgh Review* approached him to be its publisher. His initiative in breaking with the amateur traditions of the Edinburgh literary club and paying contributors as if they were professionals contributed to an extraordinarily successful venture, intellectually, politically and commercially. In 1802 Constable was able to take a quarter share in the *Minstrelsy* – his first business contact with Scott. In 1804 he further consolidated his financial base by taking on a monied partner – Alexander Gibson Hunter.

   Their opposite politics in a period of political struggle (and possibly Scott's aversion to Hunter – a man he later came to detest) kept Constable and Scott apart until the astonishing bid for *Marmion* in January 1807. Constable followed it some eighteen months later with an offer of 1,500 guineas for an edition of Swift. Together these sums represented almost ten years' salary as Sheriff of Selkirk. Constable's intention was to make Scott the sole property of Constable and Co. Thereafter, despite the rift of 1809–14 (provoked by Scott's resistance to being Constable's property) the two men's destinies were inextricably connected as twin colossi of the Scottish book world.

MARMION

Scott had originally thought of a Highland subject for his new poem. But he wanted a tremendous international battle – something appropriate to the wartime mood of the country. August 1805 had seen the climax of the invasion panic in Britain. In November Trafalgar was fought – the most momentous battle since 1066. 'Flodden Field' was, consequently, *Marmion*'s early provisional title. It did not, of course, escape Scott's Edinburgh critics that the narrative is founded on a devastating *English* victory over Scotland. Any troubled Scottish patriot would hardly be reassured by the first Epistle. It is addressed to the English grandee William Stewart Rose. The son of a rising Tory statesman, George Rose, William was educated at Eton, progressed directly to Parliament, took the Chiltern Hundreds in 1800, and retired – through his family influence – to a sinecure in the House of Lords. As a rich gentleman of leisure, Rose devoted himself to poetry. Like George Ellis, he had caught the prevailing passion for medieval romance, and translated *Amadis of Gaul* into English rhyme. Scott had met Rose in 1803 in London through mutual antiquarian friends. And it was through Rose that he met Morritt, and through Rose that he learned of Pitt's admiration for *The Lay of the Last Minstrel* – which in turn led to Scott's panegyric on Pitt in the opening Epistle of *Marmion*. In March 1807, Scott visited Rose at his villa, Gundimore, in Hampshire (EJ 268). The poem which he was in the midst of writing is saturated in Tory politics, and reflects this hobnobbing with grandees of the party. The exquisite opening on the death of Pitt – addressed to the son of a rising Tory cabinet minister, and 'improved' by a senior Tory peer (Abercorn added a couple of lines) – show Scott in his bluest colours, the party laureate and the London politico.

Scott wrote early sections of *Marmion*'s narrative (and four of the Epistles) at Ashestiel. As he remembered, his favourite spot was beneath a large oak on the banks of the Tweed (it must have been brisk in November). He also recalled to Lockhart in later life, as they rode across the hills around Ashestiel, 'Oh, man, I had many a grand gallop among these braes when I was thinking of *Marmion*' (Lock. 2. 5–6). The later sections of the poem were done with even more brio and less thinking. According to his friend and fellow militia-man, James Skene, Scott wrote the climactic Flodden section ('The Battle') while training with his cavalry troop in autumn 1807, 'in the intervals of drilling'. The last canto was written in four days 'and sent piece meal to the press as the ink dried on the paper'. The breakneck pace of composition shows. Some of the later couplets have rhymes William McGonagall would have thought twice about. The most derided is:

> Charge, Chester, charge! On, Stanley, on!
> Were the last words of Marmion. (VI. 31)

Scott's contemporaries loved the poem, bad rhymes notwithstanding: the 13,000 copies sold (5,000 at a guinea-and-a-half) within six months of publication, confirming the shrewdness of Constable's judgement. After the initial sales frenzy, the poem held its esteem with a class of respectable, if sometimes unsophisticated, readers for over a century. In the 1920s, for instance, Robert Graves records visiting Thomas Hardy in the company of T. E. Lawrence:

> Hardy's taste in literature was certainly most unexpected. Once when Lawrence had ventured to say something disparaging against Homer's *Iliad*, he protested: 'Oh, but I admire the *Iliad* greatly. Why, it's in the *Marmion* class!' Lawrence could not at first believe that Hardy was not making a little joke.[4]

Lawrence's amazement and Graves's amusement indicate a less friendly climate of opinion.

Marmion has always presented problems to its more discerning readers. It is a very vexing poem. Why, one may ask, did Scott build his poem around the greatest catastrophe in Scottish history: 'Flodden's fatal field, where shiver'd was fair Scotland's spear'? It was something that annoyed the critic Francis Jeffrey, who went on to accuse Scott of lack of patriotism. Scott's 'neglect of Scottish feelings' would, however, seem to have been in the service of a higher patriotism towards Britain. Flodden is one of many points at which one can plausibly locate the extinction of Scotland. Scott saw this extinction as less a tragic loss than the opportunity for a new sense of country – something that he enlarges on in the opening Epistle and political elegies. This overture powerfully evokes the autumnal Scottish landscape (there is much reference to 'glens', the Tweed, heather, and a sonorous roll-call of Border place-names.) But the section – for all its celebration of place – is constructed around a notable silence where the words 'Scotland' and 'Scottish' ought to be. Instead, in the first Epistle, there are no less than twelve usages of 'Britain' and 'British' (and one 'English'). This elimination of Scotland is reflected in *Marmion*'s idiom. The poem – even in its Scottish sections and the speeches of Scottish characters – is written in pure English.

Harder to account for are two perplexing features in the core plot of *Marmion* – both of which relate to the titular hero. Most perplexing is the fact that Marmion – Lord of Fontenaye, of Lutterworth, of Tamworth tower and town – is such a rat. He persuades poor Constance to break her vows and serve him, 'crimson'd with shame', in double office as 'a horseboy in his train' and as concubine, for three years. Having deflowered and debauched her nun's purity, he deserts Constance for 'young Clara . . . of broadlands the heir'. When Clara takes refuge from him in a convent Marmion shows himself perfectly ready to ravish another nun, whose betrothed he has cold-bloodedly slaughtered. Scott's heroes are nowhere else so clearly reprobates. Byron made much of Marmion's dubious character in *English Bards and Scotch Reviewers*:

> Next view in state, proud prancing on his roan,
> The golden-crested haughty Marmion,
> Now forging scrolls, now foremost in the fight,
> Not quite a felon, yet but half a knight.

Speculatively, one can suggest that some of the explanation for Marmion's caddishness may lie with Byron himself. Scott had spent spring and summer 1807 based in the West End of London. At that season, the whole town was buzzing with gossip about the new literary celebrity, currently based at Dorant's Hotel. The young Lord was plunged into debauchery, disastrous dealings with money lenders, and sexual adventures of amazing licentiousness. He was already notorious for his practice of passing off his harlot-lovers as pages – or young boys – so that they might visit him anonymously, and at the same time indulge the bisexual ambiguities that were sauce to his sexual appetite. As Louis Crompton records, 'Though his involvements were overwhelmingly heterosexual, various stories circulated, all at second hand, about how he passed off his inamoratas as boys to deceive his mother and others'.[5] It seems likely that Scott heard some of these stories, and was excited enough by them to devise the Constance subplot to *Marmion*.

Marmion was published in late February 1808. It was tremendously popular, outselling the *Lay*. Even as a guinea-and-a-half 'splendid quarto', it sold wonderfully.[6] Two thousand were sold in two months, 8,000 in three months (EJ 279). The second edition in octavo format went almost as fast. There were, in all, six editions by the end of the year. Constable had

Raeburn paint Scott's portrait – in full poetical fig, by the ruins of Hermitage Castle, with the mountains of Liddesdale in the background, and his terrier Camp at his feet. He also gave his star author a hogshead of claret – in allusion to the laureate's pipe of port. Scott was drinking bumpers of 'Marmion' for months after.

For all the acclaim *Marmion* did, however, elicit more criticism, and weightier criticism, than its predecessor. Coleridge was offended by what he took to be *Marmion*'s cheap appeal to the mass public. Byron also accused Scott of selling out. The most painful review, however, was that nearest home in the *Edinburgh Review* – a journal which Scott himself wrote for. His friend Francis Jeffrey – the scourge of Romantic poets – wrote the piece. It was the anachronism of *Marmion* that he principally attacked. 'To write a modern romance of chivalry', Jeffrey maintained, 'seems to be much such a phantasy as to build a modern abbey, or an English pagoda' (Greig, 117). In fact, Scott might have retorted, such follies were much to Regency taste (as Abbotsford and the Brighton Pavilion were to demonstrate). As Johnson guesses, underlying Jeffrey's pique was a Whig distaste for war, particularly in the bloody forms in which Scott glorified it. Jeffrey's party was for domestic reform; Scott's was for imperial war abroad against Napoleon. Scott saw Whig opposition to the Peninsular War as wretched appeasement. Jeffrey went on to make his more enigmatic objection that Scott had 'neglected Scottish feelings', done the dirt on his country. James A. Greig plausibly glosses what was meant by this: 'Jeffrey wanted to see in Scott's poetry . . . a realisation that there is more in love of country than love of its picturesqueness and more in history than the flash of ancient weapons and colourfulness of antique costume' (Greig, 120). It boils down to the standard objection that there is something cheap and flashy about *Marmion* – too much 'rust and tinsel', as Southey put it (behind Scott's back).

Jeffrey had been invited to dinner at the Scotts' a few days before his notice was to appear in the *Edinburgh Review*. Scott – who had seen the offending piece in proof – was affability itself. But Mrs Scott gave Jeffrey a tart farewell: 'Well, good-night, Mr Jeffrey – dey tell me you have abused Scott in de *Review,* and I hope Mr Constable has paid *you* very well for writing it' (EJ 283). (Constable was in the odd position of having paid Scott a thousand guineas for writing *Marmion* and Jeffrey twenty-five guineas a sheet for cutting it to pieces.) For his part Scott maintained a public mask of indifference against criticism like Jeffrey's, but privately he chafed. William Erskine, who knew him most intimately at this period, correctly judged he was 'much hurt' (*Lett.* 2. 102). He maintained a nominal connection with the *Edinburgh Review* after Jeffrey's attack; but it was very uneasy. Jeffrey's barbs sharpened Scott's sense that he should found a Tory alternative to the *Edinburgh* – which he did with the *Quarterly Review,* in early 1809. A dislike for Jeffrey's kind of deep-delving criticism (which was also a criticism of Walter Scott) may also have predisposed him in later years to protective anonymity as the 'author of *Waverley*'.

Dryden and 'By Jobs'

Within the gloom of his general posthumous eclipse, Scott the poet and
Scott the novelist have totally overshadowed Scott the editor and biographer. Nonetheless, Scott's achievements in the editorial department are
remarkable, more so as they were done with such speed and in company
with so much else. Scott's eighteen volumes of Dryden's verse and drama
and the accompanying 'Life' (1808) complement Malone's four volumes of
the author's prose (1801), and surpass Johnson's biographical sketch in his
Lives of the Poets. Scott's life of Dryden is arguably the first social-critical
biography of any British author. He sets out to understand Dryden and his
poetry in terms of his age, his politics and his material circumstances. Scott
uses his subject's life and works as a point of entry into a 'general view of the
literature of the time'. Scott's investigations into literary climate and the
sociology of authorship were equally innovative.

Scott had his *parti pris*. Dryden (like Swift after him) appealed principally as a Tory satirist. One of the aims of the edition was to raise this most
political of poets to the status of Milton, Shakespeare and Spenser. Dryden
– as Lockhart notes – was also the model Scott took for himself as man of
letters. He admired the other poet's habitually sceptical line on strong
doctrine, his willingness to serve party, his Augustan equanimity, his 'brave
neglect' of minutiae. Above all, what attracted him was Dryden's 'elasticity'
and his 'rapidity of conception'. Dryden's robust commercialism was also to
Scott's taste. 'He whose bread depends on the success of his volume', Scott
noted with Johnsonian suavity, 'is compelled to study popularity' (*Dryden*
1. 4). The rule applied as much to himself as Dryden. Scott also wanted to
emulate Dryden's role with *The Medall* as the scourge of all Whigs. It is not
coincidental that Scott went straight from the publication of *Dryden* to the
formation of *his* anti-Whig organ, the *Quarterly Review*.

In early 1805 Scott declared that 'an edition of Dryden has been a hobby
of mine for some time' (*Lett*. 1. 246). By the part-owner of a printing press,
such hobbies could now be turned to business. As James Osborn has shown,
the Dryden idea originates in the early phase of Scott's publishing ambitions, when he was thinking of a series of magna opera (*Lett*. 1. 245). The
edition of Dryden (which was the earliest of these schemes) preceded the
project of 'a complete edition of British Poets ancient and modern . . . At
least a hundred volumes, to be published at the rate of ten a-year' (*Lett*.
1. 248). The grandeur of Scott's conceptions in 1805 is breathtaking – more
so when put alongside the parallel schemes for British drama and the
British novel. What he was proposing was no less than a revised reissue of
the whole of the national literature. 'There is a scheme for you!', as he
exultantly told James Ballantyne through whose presses the hundreds of
volumes would pass.

Clearly such titanic schemes could not be achieved single-handed – even
by Scott in the strength of his prime. In devising work-teams for his magna

opera Scott typically went through the same routine. First he would enter into relations with a potential co-editor, or partner. Then, as details were thrashed out, the partner would one way or another fall by the way. Scott would then proceed to execution of his plan as sole head, with a group of hard-working assistants. When Scott decided to edit Dryden in spring 1805 he found another editor in the field well ahead of him – the London-based clergyman Edward Forster. (There was also the fear that Edmund Malone – the doyen of Dryden studies – might supplement his 1800 *Life*, which Scott hoped to supplant.) Scott and Forster had evidently met socially (*Lett.* 1. 244). Scott quickly suggested a joint editorial effort – with himself as junior partner. Initially, Scott went so far as to indicate that he would work anonymously (EJ 236). An advantage of this arrangement was that Forster would be better placed to collect materials 'both from the Museum [i.e. the BM] and private hands' (Osb. 73). In a letter of 17 March 1805, Scott outlined the 'pecuniary' arrangements to Forster – 'from 30 to 40 guineas a volume'. Whichever of them did the 'life and general critique' should get £100 and 'I would willingly undertake to do the Drama at 20 guineas a volume' (EJ 236). Scott was now putting himself forward as an equal partner, with equal title-page billing.

The circumstances in which Forster was then edged out are murky. Without telling Forster that Ballantyne was in his pocket, Scott informed his fellow-editor that the printing must, of course, be done in Edinburgh and that he (Forster) must deal with the Scottish printer direct 'and make the best bargain you can' (Osb. 73). Ballantyne then put in a bill for printing that was so high that Forster despaired. It is inconceivable that Ballantyne and Scott did not collaborate on this. But the London clergyman never knew of his partner's other partnership (legally contracted on 14 March 1805, at exactly the period Scott was negotiating with Forster). It seems that shortly after, William Miller, the London publisher, voiced the opinion that Forster's name on the project would not be an asset. The name of the author of *The Lay of the Last Minstrel* (published a few months earlier) clearly would. Ballantyne, doubtless speaking for his invisible partner, retorted that in that case retaining Forster would be 'madness'. In other words, he (as printer) was encouraging the publisher to discard Forster. As James Osborn records: 'Before many weeks [i.e. by September 1805] had elapsed Forster was squeezed out by the pincer-like pressure'. Scott shed some crocodile tears in a letter of condolence to his erstwhile collaborator (Osb. 73–4). Forster never realized, of course, that it was Scott – with Ballantyne as his catspaw – who was engineering his ejection from his own project. In Osborn's opinion, 'Scott's part in the negotiations is not the most creditable page in his biography' (Osb. 74). Even Edgar Johnson concedes that Scott was 'not absolutely blameless' in the affair (EJ 238).

It would be easier to exculpate Scott in his dealings with Forster were it not that at exactly the same time he did much the same thing with Thomas Campbell. In 1804, Cadell & Davies had made an agreement with the other poet for a panoramic 'Specimens of the British Poets'. Knowing of

Campbell's arrangement, Scott in mid-1805 approached Constable with his proposed hundred-volume edition of the British poets, 'ancient and modern', which would entirely supersede Campbell. Campbell (who had received favours from Scott and expected more) promptly offered to withdraw ('I rejoice that the plan is taken from me by a hand so powerful. I really do my dear Scott')[7]. Scott went on to suggest that they join forces. Campbell – whose career was not going well – humbly agreed. The project was first encouraged by Constable (who was keen to bind Scott to him) and then discouraged on grounds of impracticality. It was revived in 1806 by Murray (who also wanted to recruit Scott) who then also developed doubts. Scott did other things. But had he gone forward as originally planned in 1805, one cannot but think that Campbell would have gone the way of Forster.

Scott worked steadily on his edition of Dryden between 1806 and 1807. The eighteen volumes were published by William Miller (of Albemarle Street, London) as 'The Works of John Dryden, now first collected' in May 1808, just three months after *Marmion*, at 40 guineas a volume (i.e. 720 guineas in toto), payment to the editor (EJ 291). According to Scott, the edition sold £2,000-worth in one day in London and earned another £1,500 in country orders. It was an extraordinary achievement, and not least so because Scott's edition is, by the standards of its day, sound in its scholarship (something that rather surprised friends like George Ellis). The life – Johnsonian in tone and manner, but more wide-ranging in method – was able to stand independently as a book by itself and was twice republished in Scott's lifetime. It formed the basis of Saintsbury's edition and biography, which has lasted until virtually the present generation of scholarship.

Coming only seven years after Malone's massively researched life, Scott's was necessarily dependent on the other scholar. According to Osborn, if Scott had been scrupulous about citation Malone's name 'would occur in every other paragraph' (Osb. 76). The fact that it appears only every third page or so Osborn regards as slightly unethical on Scott's part. This, however, is outweighed by the 'transcendant structure' of Scott's achievement. Osborn (while noting some factual thinness in Scott's original work) particularly commends two things: first, Scott's inwardness with Dryden's works and his brilliance as a critic; second, Scott's creativity: 'Almost every page is vitalized by his historical imagination, the power that later found its proper medium in the novel. The biography of Dryden is the first fruit of one of the most productive geniuses in the history of all literature' (Osb. 82).

In the nooks and crannies of time left to him between *Marmion* and Dryden, Scott did enough incidental things – 'by-jobs' as he called them – to have occupied most authors full time. These by-jobs included a collection of his lyric verse, published by Longman in 1806; the 'Ashestiel' fragment of autobiography, not published in his lifetime; an edition of the state papers of the Elizabethan diplomatist Sir Ralph Sadler (Scott did the preface, the 'Life', and the notes); a start on a comprehensive edition of

'Somers's Tracts' (eventually published in 1812, this collection of political papers ran to thirteen quarto volumes; Scott received 100 guineas a volume, in addition to his cut from Ballantyne, who printed the collection). Scott also completed Joseph Strutt's historical novel, *Queenhoo Hall,* for Murray in 1808. In the same year he wrote prefaces for memoirs by Captain Carleton and Robert Cary – both of which involved research. He was besieged by booksellers, who wanted to attach his name to their productions, and he toyed with innumerable projects such as a series of 'tales of wonder' (EJ 288), and the encyclopaedic editions of the British novelists and poets mentioned above. His new assistant, the German (and half-crazed, as it turned out) Henry Weber had meanwhile embarked on monumental editions of ancient metrical romances and Jacobean dramatists under Scott's direct superintendence.

Constable – perceiving Scott's tendency to lose himself in a multitude of projects – cemented him to his house with a contract for a nineteen- or twenty-volume edition of Swift, at 1,500 guineas, £500 in advance. It was twice what Miller had given for Dryden. Friends like Ellis and Lady Abercorn worried that Scott was spreading himself too thin, and warned him to reserve his powers for worthwhile projects. 'Surely, the best poet of the age ought not to be incessantly employed in the drudgeries of literature. I shall lament if you are effectually distracted from the exercise of the talent in which you are confessedly without a rival', Ellis scolded (Lock. 2. 54). Looking back in later years, Scott told Lockhart, 'Ay, it was enough to tear me to pieces, but there was a wonderful exhilaration about it all: my blood was kept at fever pitch – I felt as if I could have grappled with anything and everything' (EJ 290).

7

The Complete Author (1809–1811)

Scott wanted a rest after *Marmion*. With an image drawn from his new commitment to tilling the land he told Lady Abercorn that 'I know as a small farmer that good husbandry consists in not taking the same crop too frequently from the same soil and as turnips come after wheat according to the best rules of agriculture I take it that an edition . . . will do well after such a scourging crop as *Marmion*' (*Lett.* 2. 32). He would concentrate his efforts on Swift. The contract stipulated delivery in two years – during which time Scott intended to collect ideas for his 'Highland poem' (i.e. *The Lady of the Lake*) which, he told Lady Abercorn in February 1808, 'I intend to begin two years hence.' He mentioned the poem frequently at this period, as his enthusiasm for things Highland grew with the progress of the Peninsular War and the battle triumphs of the Scottish regiments.

Scott, who loved to be doing many things at once, meanwhile turned his attention to Edinburgh, a city which sadly needed some cosmopolitan touches. Principally, Scotland's capital lacked a theatre to rival London's. It still does and probably always will except for a few festival weeks every summer. In his plans for an Edinburgh theatre Scott 'was plentifully encouraged by his domestic *camarilla*; for his wife had all a Frenchwoman's passion for the *spectacle*' (Lock. 2. 147). Rather improbably Lockhart and Johnson also suggest that Scott was primarily inspired by civic and philanthropic incentives. But it is clear from evidence cited by Grierson from the Melville papers, that Scott was also driven by commercial motives (*Lett.* 2. 46).[1]

The 'patent' or licence for the existing Edinburgh theatre was due to expire in September 1809. Getting the next five-year lease transferred required favours from the usual powerful friends and some intricate manoeuvring. A committee was formed, dominated by Scott and his friends William Erskine and Henry Mackenzie. A new board of trustees was assembled, headed (irresistibly) by the Duke of Buccleuch. The next step was to cut out the previous owners of the patent – the Jackson family and their ally Mr Rock – who, as Scott told his patron Robert Dundas, 'are under-handedly endeavouring to get the Patent renewed in their name' (*Lett.* 2. 76). Ultimately, the previous patentees (who evidently had a good case in law and current possession of the Theatre Royal) had to be part bought out and part levered out by Melville and other friends in high places. The amount of compensation paid the Jacksons was a millstone for Scott's theatrical project.

There is no doubt that Scott's artistic motives were higher than his commercial predecessor. He wanted to raise the theatre in Scotland above 'the garbage of melodrama and pantomime' (*Lett.* 2. 118) into which it had sunk. He intended to create a national repertoire and – in his wildest moments – to build a new £20,000 establishment (*Postbag*, 50). It would have been possible to invent a national theatre around the achievements of national playwrights like Home. But despite the chauvinistic vaunt from the stalls, 'Whaur's yer Wullie Shakespeare noo?', neither Home nor any other home-based dramatist was good enough. Nor was there a classic Scottish drama or theatrical tradition to build on. Instead, Scott set about trans-planting theatre ready-made from London, in the hope that it would take root in the other capital. He prevailed on Henry Siddons to take over the management of the Edinburgh Theatre when its licence expired, hoping thereby to lure star London players – like Siddons's relatives, the Kembles – into coming north. Scott, in his capacity as lawyer, arranged all the patent and property lease business. He also purchased a share in the new theatri-cal venture and in June 1809 became a trustee (EJ 322). Henry Mackenzie – the Grand Old Man of Scottish letters, the 'Addison of the North' – was another.

As Christopher Worth points out, 'what Scott and his friends did not have initially, as a result of difficulties over compensation to the Jackson family, was a theatre.' Temporarily they used Corri's Rooms, in Broughton Street. Eventually they moved into the refurbished Theatre Royal, which stood in Shakespeare Square, on the site now occupied by the Post Office. With Scott's takeover, the Theatre Royal (founded in 1769) was to enjoy a brief flowering. It opened under its new management on 14 November 1809 and its early Shakespearian productions were well received. But Scott was determined to go beyond the English classics. After the rejection of *The House of Aspen*, he evidently had no serious ambitions in the play-writing line himself. Instead, he touted as Scottish masterworks the plays of his new friend, Joanna Baillie, who had stayed with the Scotts on a longish visit in February–March 1808, while the theatre scheme was hatching. Baillie was a Scot (Glasgow-born), although her family had emigrated to London in 1784, when she was twenty-two. Her 'Plays of the Passions' – which began to come out in 1798 – had earned her wide fame. Scott believed her 'certainly the best dramatic writer whom Britain has produced since the days of Shakespeare and Massinger' (*Lett.* 2. 29).

Scott's intention was to promote Baillie as *the* Scottish dramatist. In November 1808 he wrote to her, expressing his hope to put the new theatre on a 'most classical footing', adding, 'my great ambition will be to get up some of your dramas and shew the people what plays ought to be' (*Lett.* 2. 118). For the first season of the new Edinburgh Theatre, he particularly desired her tale of Highland feud, *The Family Legend,* which he apparently first read around April 1809 and which she may well have written at his instigation. By late 1809, Scott – by a mixture of flattery and urgency – had persuaded Miss Baillie to release rights for the performance of this 'story of my motherland' to Siddons (*Lett.* 2. 219).

The Family Legend declares itself 'A Fable founded on Fact'. Set princi-pally on the island of Mull, the plot centres on a blood feud in the fifteenth century between the (Highland) Macleans and the (Lowland) Argylls. Scott's new passion for tales of 'romantic Caledon', and the 'aboriginal' Celts had two origins. Like most middle-class Lowland Scots (of 'Gothic' descent), he was immensely proud of the gallantry of the new Highland regiments in the Peninsular War. He was also probably aware of the clear-ances that were currently depopulating the Highlands and destroying its ancient clan culture for ever. 1809 was the 'year of the burnings', and the overture to ten years of ruthless persecution. Scott made serious visits to the Highlands in 1809–10. His celebration of the clan way of life was given poignant force by the coffin boats leaving every week for the New World, crammed with uprooted Highlanders.

Scott visited rehearsals of *The Family Legend,* and gave detailed advice on the proper costuming of the Highlanders in the 'garb of old Gael'. He evidently wrote to all the chiefs of the Highland clans, inviting them to the first night, to make it a 'great Scottish occasion' (an anticipation of the 'gathering of the clans' in Edinburgh which he was to mastermind in 1822). Scott seems to have seen no problem in the play's depiction of the inveter-ate treachery of Highlanders; although, out of deference to the Macleans, their clan name was changed in the performance text to 'Duart'. Scott penned a preface, and Henry Mackenzie contributed an epilogue.

The Family Legend began what was to be a fourteen-night run on 29 January 1810. It was well received although, as the *Edinburgh Annual Register* reported, the houses were no more than 'respectable'. Scott did his best. 'We wept till our hearts were sore,' Scott told Morritt, 'and applauded till our hands were blistered' (*Lett.* 2. 307). Despite this applause and all Scott's subsequent efforts the new Edinburgh Theatre never did take root. Henry Siddons, beset by money problems, died in 1815. Under his widow's management, the theatre limped on another fifteen years. It is unlikely that it made any substantial earning for the trustees.

The best thing that came out of the Edinburgh Theatre, from Scott's point of view, was his introduction to Daniel Terry, who had played a minor part in *The Family Legend.* A young architect turned actor, Terry subsequently became Scott's most fervent admirer, and the agent for his acquisition of historical bric-a-brac in the London sale houses. It was Terry who largely contributed to the elaborately theatrical aspect of Abbotsford's decor.

THE BREAK WITH CONSTABLE

Scott had better luck setting up publishing houses than theatres. Having made his agreement with Constable for Swift, and taken a large part of his advance, he began to feel uncomfortably as if the publisher owned him. 'It is not with inclination that I fag for the booksellers; but what can I do?' he asked Louisa Stuart in June 1808; 'my poverty and not my will consents' (*Lett.* 2. 73). Poverty was hardly the right word for a still-young man with £10,000 net worth and an income of around £1,500. But Scott was aiming his sights high. Not to be rich was to be poor. Why not, then, set up a publisher to 'fag' for Walter Scott? Preferably a publisher who was not a Whig, like Constable and the detestable Hunter. Scott broke the news to Morritt in January 1809 that 'I have prepared to start [against Constable and Hunter] at Whitsunday first the celebrated printer Ballantyne . . . in the shape of an Edinburgh publisher with a long purse and a sound political creed' (EJ 304). To front his new publishing outfit, Scott had chosen James Ballantyne's brother, John; another old Kelso friend and Masonic brother. The long purse was, of course, Scott's.

Scott's pretexts for breaking with Constable were just that – pretexts. He claimed to have been insulted by Constable's 'bearish' partner, Alexander Gibson Hunter. Hunter was a hard-drinking, rough-mannered Whig. According to Lockhart, his 'intemperate language' had given offence. In fact, what evidence there is suggests that Hunter was affable and shrewd in his personal dealings with the poet (*ACLC* 3. 12–3). Scott had chosen to be enraged for strategic purposes. Hunter's main offence (apart from his politics) was that he had quite reasonably questioned the huge amount of money (his money) the firm had sunk in the Swift venture, and the slow delivery of that work (promised in two years, it took a provoking six).

Towards the end of 1808, when the *Edinburgh Review* people had caught wind of Scott's setting up a Tory quarterly, Hunter evidently made some injudicious remarks – perhaps about treachery, perhaps about Scott's infidelity to the house of Constable. Scott construed this as 'extreme incivility' (*Lett.* 2. 146). In fact, Constable & Co. had quite reasonable grounds for complaint – Scott was setting up a rival magazine, with a rival publisher (Murray), while taking thousands of pounds from Constable and not delivering on time. In high dudgeon Scott demanded back the Raeburn portrait of him which Constable had commissioned. The publisher refused, declaring 'it is my private property' (*Lett.* 2. 155). Nevertheless, Constable was careful (unlike his partner) not to be incivil either to Scott or to Murray. And neither would he be provoked – as Scott clearly hoped he would – into releasing his author from the Swift contract.

In January 1809 (the legal arrangements were finalized a few months later) Scott set up a rival publisher to Constable in premises a few hundred yards away. John Ballantyne was launched with the Edinburgh distribution rights for a Tory imitation of Constable's *Edinburgh Review* and advertisements for a new poem by Constable's star author, the author of *Marmion*. Worse, Scott founded his new publishing house with what Constable conceived to be an act of literary theft. William Davies, of Cadell & Davies, had proposed a Scottish rival to the *Annual Register* to Hunter, who was visiting London in spring 1807. Hunter duly passed the idea on to his partner in Edinburgh in a letter of 18 March. Constable replied four days later, cautiously describing the idea as 'not unpromising' and wondering who the editor should be. On this decision 'the success of such a work would depend' (*ACLC* 1. 117). Hunter's preference for editor was Brougham; Constable evidently hankered after Scott.

Hunter met Scott later in March, and mentioned the idea of an *Edinburgh Annual Register* 'in strict confidence'. The project fell through, however, because Constable could not prevail on his writers for the *Edinburgh Review* to participate (Curry, 5–6). But Scott stored Hunter's blueprint in his mind. And in December 1808, he announced that John Ballantyne would publish an *Edinburgh Annual Register*, as one of the new firm's flagship ventures. Constable was mortified. In March 1809, he was reported to be consulting his lawyers (Curry, 9). Objective observers have found Scott's behaviour in this matter sharp. As Emerson puts it, 'Doubtless Scott, who had been told in confidence of Constable's plan, justified his somewhat unethical procedure by his intense and sincere patriotism' (Emerson, 415). Loyal as ever, Edgar Johnson describes Constable's indignation as 'deluded'. But it seems self-evident that Scott should, at the planning stage, have cleared his project with its moral owner, Constable.

Under all this provocation, Constable seems to have acted with forbearance (EJ 318–9). Jeffrey wrote no more 'ticklers', giving Dryden and *The Lady of the Lake* respectful notices in the *Edinburgh Review*. Constable & Co. even gave John Ballantyne assistance on printing matters. Constable himself stoically declared that the *Quarterly* was a good journal, and 'cannot harm us' (the sales of 800 or so must, however, have come at the expense of the *Edinburgh Review*). Constable's only recorded complaint about the defection of his bestselling author was a more-in-sorrow-than-in-anger anecdote: ' "Ay" he would say, stamping on the ground with a savage smile, "Ay, there is such a thing as rearing the oak until it can support itself".'

Scott wanted a publisher more pliant than Constable, more deferential than Hunter and more Tory than both. He wanted to publish by command – by whim if he so desired. At the same time, he was badly bitten at this period by the speculative bug (the same fever that had brought Tom Scott to grief, with his brickworks on the Duddingston estate). If the theatre did not make him rich, surely a publishing house would? It was not an irrational calculation. Scott knew about books. What was irrational was his choice of partner. John Ballantyne was not a publisher in Constable's class. In fact until Scott took him up he was not a publisher at all. At Kelso John (who probably did not finish his law studies at the university) had gone into the family's haberdashery business. Inevitably, this brought him into contact with the Volunteers. With over half of the country's able-bodied males mobilized and wearing some form of ad hoc military uniform, the period 1797–1805 was a bonanza for tailors. John Ballantyne reportedly supplied breeches for local cavalry units.

But John, ominously, did not prosper in his Kelso establishment. He married young and against his father's wishes. He compounded his filial rebellion by setting up a clothier's shop in opposition to his father's, a few yards away, in Kelso High Street. Poor business habits, drinking, hunting, gaming and wenching (especially the last) brought John Ballantyne to early ruin by 1805. At the low point of his fortunes he contemplated going to the West Indies (following the ignominious trail blazed by Daniel Scott). This desperate remedy was forestalled when in 1806 the eminently respectable James took the prodigal on as a clerk in his Edinburgh printing works. (James was later to take his father on, when the older Ballantyne also drank himself out of the clothier's business.)

John had 'great *apparent* dexterity in book-keeping', Lockhart cattily notes (Lock. 2. 80). He was employed by his brother James as a clerk on the strict condition that he go back to his deserted wife and mend his morals – at a salary of £200 a year. Lockhart thought that the day that brought John Ballantyne into contact with Scott 'was the blackest in his calendar.' But this charming wastrel did not – as Lockhart implies – *drift* into Scott's life. He was selected to be the author's publisher. Scott did not *have* to pour thousands into the publishing firm of John Ballantyne – it was his calculated decision to do so. (It is estimated that Scott invested some £9,000 in the Ballantyne firms between 1805 and 1810.) Nor was Scott for a moment unaware of John Ballantyne's defects of character – he had been up with Kelso gossip for twenty years.

John did not reform his ways in Edinburgh. If anything, his misconduct became even more flagrant. Publishers like John Murray soon refused to exchange bills with the firm, on the very reasonable grounds that John Ballantyne was not to be trusted (Emerson, 399). Why then did Scott trust him? Why would anyone, and he a lawyer, knowingly entrust his fortunes and those of his family to such a one as John Ballantyne?

Perhaps Scott intended a Caligula's-horse gesture. Scott expressed his low opinion of the 'trade' pungently in a letter of September 1807 to Anna Seward: 'A Butcher generally understands something of black cattle, and woe betide the jockey who should presume to exercise his profession without a competent knowledge of horse flesh. But who ever heard of a Bookseller pretending to understand the commodity in which he dealt?' (*Lett.* 1. 379).

'John Ballantyne & Co., Booksellers to the Regent' was set up in Hanover Street, in January 1809 (EJ 307). The phrase 'to the Regent' is interesting. While writing *Marmion*, Scott had been (in line with other senior Tories) very much in the Princess of Wales's camp. She, of course, was bitterly estranged from her husband, who was aligned with the Whigs. Scott, having met the Princess in 1806, introduced a florid compliment to her father, the Duke of Brunswick, into his poem (Lock. 2. 6). Caroline was sent an early presentation copy. But by 1809, Scott seems to have moved round to an attachment to the Prince Regent (although they were not to meet until 1815). It may be that some intermediary, such as Murray or Canning, was responsible for the change of affiliation.

John Ballantyne fronted the firm which bore his name, but was actually co-partner and manager at an annual salary of £300. It was a significantly small sum. Scott – as unnamed (but far from sleeping) partner – put in a half-share of the firm's start-up capital. James and John came up with a quarter apiece. Effectively, Scott's £1,000 investment (plus a loan of £1,500) got the firm off the ground (EJ 306). Since he financed the operation Scott 'had the last word in all matters of importance including the vital one of which titles the company should market' (EQ 43). His current preference was for antiquarian reprints – subsidized by his bestselling poems.

There was now no professional check on Scott's insatiable enthusiasm for vast collected editions of dramas, transcriptions of historical documents, and reprinted tracts. John Ballantyne & Co. was an antiquarian's dream come true. Whenever he had broached these gigantic schemes to Constable or Murray, they diplomatically fobbed him off. (There is an amusing anecdote of Murray estimating, to his horror, that one of Scott's magna opera would cost over £20,000 in printing costs.) The month before he set up John, Scott engaged himself even more heavily in James Ballantyne's printing business, making himself the dominant partner in that operation as well. 'Thus', Grierson gloomily notes, 'began to flow the strong undercurrent of financial activity, which was, more and more as time went on, to influence all the activities of Scott's life literary and social' (HG 89).

The rupture with Constable predisposed Scott to the other momentous innovation of 1809. He was increasingly out of temper with the *Edinburgh Review* – partly because of Jeffrey's treatment of *Marmion*, partly because of a political quarrel with the magazine's Whig line on the Peninsular War. He went so far as to cancel his subscription on reading in the October 1808 issue Jeffrey's article 'Don Cevallos on the Usurpation in Spain' (EJ 300). Jeffrey argued for appeasement. Scott's (and his party's) thinking about Napoleon's takeover of Portugal and expansion into Spain was unequivocally adventurist. The Corsican must be met with force, and bled to death in foreign fields, lest he invade Britain. Scott forecast to Ellis that 'the Whigs will . . . lay the country at the feet of Buonaparte for peace' (*Lett.* 2. 248). History proves Scott to have been justified in his belligerence; the 'Spanish ulcer' debilitated Napoleon, setting him up for his final defeat at Waterloo and Britain's century of imperial triumph.

John Murray skilfully exploited this rift between Scott and their former ally Constable by proposing a rival quarterly. He had nursed the idea for some time, as a logical outgrowth from the *Anti-Jacobin* and its coterie of Tory wits. There was room for another quarterly. By Scott's (probably overoptimistic) reckoning 9,000 copies of the *Edinburgh* were printed quarterly ('and no genteel family *can* pretend to be without it, because, independent of its politics, it gives the only valuable literary criticism that can be met with', he added; EJ 300). These subscribers were not linked to the *Edinburgh Review* by party loyalty, merely by the high journalistic quality of the product. Scott estimated that not one out of twenty who read the magazine was a Whig and that large numbers would defect to a journal of the opposite party.

Murray made his first overtures to Scott through the Canongate printers. Ostensibly, he was enquiring about the 'Novelist's Library', a project in which Scott had nursed an interest since 1805. But this was merely bait. In October 1808 the London publisher came up to Edinburgh to lay down definite plans for a rival journal to the *Edinburgh* – happily for him it coincided with the Don Cevallos explosion.

The *Quarterly Review* – as it was unimaginatively titled – would be edited by William Gifford (1756–1826), an *Anti-Jacobin* veteran. Scott (who was the architect of the venture) declined the editorship – which is what Murray had in mind – but offered himself 'as a sort of Jackal or Lion's provider' (EJ 301). It was a typical tight-rope walk of the kind Scott was now expert in. He wanted to control the operation, but he did not want to be seen to be in control. His jackal work was impressive. Scott had no less than four articles in the magazine's first issue and was the dominant contributor in the journal from 1809 to 1811. There were two subsequent gaps in his string of contributions in 1811–5 (caused by Murray's row with John Ballantyne) and in 1818–24 (caused by Scott's chronic sickness, and over-production of novels in these years).

The *Quarterly Review* was to be based, like Murray's publishing house, in London. Thus, it was hoped, the magazine could cabal directly with senior ministers, like Canning (EJ 302, 311). Scott proposed his Tory friends – George Ellis, the Hebers, W. S. Rose, Southey – as key contributors. He had definite ideas about the tone of the new organ: 'I think, from the little observation I have made, that the Whigs suffer most deeply from cool sarcastic reasoning and occasional ridicule' (Lock. 2. 995). For maximum impact Scott wanted the project to be kept secret and intended that it should burst among the Whigs 'like a bomb' in March 1809 (EJ 301).

By 1810, the circuit was closed: Scott was the completest of authors. He could write his books, publish his books, print his books, sell his books and – if he were daring enough – review (or have friends review) his books in *his* journal.[2] Each of his subsequent major poems was reviewed in the *Quarterly* by Ellis. A more friendly critic it would be harder to imagine. In the abstract one can see Scott's 1809 activities as a fascinating experiment in professional writing. He had closed all the gaps – or 'gateways' – across which literature habitually jumped or fell. At the same time Scott, by setting himself up as a publisher, was blundering into areas in which he was inexpert. Amateurs in the printing and publishing business – even wealthy and intelligent amateurs like Scott – tend not to last long. Grierson quotes

James Ballantyne's hard-earned wisdom on the matter: 'Nothing, in my conviction, can supply the place of long, creeping, cautious experience. Theory will as soon make a good general as a good bookseller' (HG 115).

THE LADY OF THE LAKE

Scott mentioned his intention of writing a Highland poem as early as 1805. The idea seems to have originated in a long and very judicious piece he wrote for the *Edinburgh Review* in July of that year on the long-running investigation into the 'Nature and Authenticity of the Poems of Ossian'. He referred to his Highland poem a number of times thereafter as a future project. One knows less about its genesis than other works, but Scott probably started to compose *The Lady of the Lake* in his mind on a short Highland holiday with Charlotte and his elder daughter in late August 1809 (Lock. 2. 130). He finally began to 'thread verses' together into what became *The Lady of the Lake* in September 1809 (EJ 316). By November he had the title – which either contains a sly joke or represents a provincial blunder on the poet's part.[3] Scott had the first two cantos sufficiently complete to show Lady Abercorn in March 1810. By mid-April, he had five cantos done and, printing as the sections were finished, the whole poem was published in early May 1810.

The Scotts had penetrated as far north as Loch Katrine – the lake of the poem's title – a year earlier in June 1808 (Lock. 2. 65–6). It was a memorable holiday. 'We had most heavenly weather, which was peculiarly favourable to my fair companions', Scott told Louisa Stuart (*Lett.* 2. 73). One of his fair companions was Lydia White, a Welsh 'blue stocking' (EJ 293–4) with a passion for drawing. Miss White infected Charlotte with her enthusiasm for landscapes and picturesque decor. Scott commented on the ladies' zeal for sketching everything they came across 'from a castle to a pigeon house'. He affected a bluff masculine irritation at their swooning reactions to the Highland scenery. They drew like cart-horses, he tartly punned. But it is clear that he too caught the scenic infection from Miss White. His own poem emerged as heavily pictorial. 'He sees everything with a painter's eye', Ellis wrote approvingly in his *Quarterly* review of *The Lady of the Lake*. It was a new stress in Scott's poetry. There are fewer old castles in the new poem and many more striking long views of landscape.

As one of its many cultural offshoots – which range from the Western movie, through the rituals of the post-Civil War Ku Klux Klan, to the tartan shortbread tin – *The Lady of the Lake* pioneered a tie-in industry of ancillary decoration of the poetry of Walter Scott. Albums of unauthorized 'illustrations' were produced by opportunistic artists, and pictorially encrusted reprints followed throughout the century. Landseer's career was largely built on the opening stag hunt and its associated Highland romanticism. (See, for instance, his 'Monarch of the Glen', 1851.) Lavishly scenic theatrical productions also testified to the pictoriality of *The Lady of the Lake*. According to Robert Cadell, Scott's Highland poem – together with Telford's new road systems – was primarily responsible for turning northern Scotland into a mass tourist resort. Miss White had planted a powerful seed.

The Lady of the Lake was Scott's first extended treatment of the 'aboriginal' Scots, the Gaels who were (as Scott thought) displaced by civilized Saxons from the south and pushed progressively north to the barren highlands. Thus Dhu proclaims the doom of his evicted race, looking south with King James:

> These fertile plains, that soften'd vale,
> Were once the birthright of the Gael;
> The stranger came with iron hand,
> And from our fathers reft the land. (V. 7)

In this passage, Scott seems to have swallowed the propaganda of the Highland Societies, that the Celts were an indigenous Scottish race pushed north, not immigrants from the Irish west who had percolated south. His fellow feeling for the Gael did not, however, stem from shared blood or heritage, but shared misfortune. As the Highlanders had been pushed north, so the Borderers (Scott's quite different race) had been pushed south by the same 'civilized' Scots of the Glasgow–Edinburgh midlands. The Borderers and Highlanders represented pockets of Scottish aboriginality squeezed to either end of the country's habitable territory. They were partners in persecution. Hence, in the poem, the unlikely alliance between Dhu, Highland Chief, and Douglas, Border Baron – both persecuted by James.

Scott turned to his Highland theme in a mood of elegiac sympathy. Meanwhile the historical reality – indigenous Highland culture – was in irreversible decline. A number of factors had combined to produce this extinction: the failure of the 1745 Rebellion, the Heritable Jurisdictions Act of 1748, the improved road systems laid down after 1806 (which allowed families like the Scotts to tour the Trossachs), the death of the last Pretender in August 1807, the clearances (which peaked in 1809), 'improvements' in agriculture. Scott initially toyed with the idea of *The Lady of the Lake*'s being told to the Chevalier after Culloden (EJ 321), which would have been too obvious (and too Jacobite) a device. Instead, he cut out almost entirely the 'prologuizing' framework which had encumbered *Marmion*. The poem begins with a very perfunctory apostrophe to the 'Harp of the North'.

Scott never quite reconciled his emotional attachment to outlawry (his Wat of Harden heritage) with his office as a sworn agent of the King's law. While glamorizing the noble savagery of Dhu (and to a lesser degree Graeme) the poet clearly identifies himself with James/Snowdon, the bringer of law and order to the 'debatable lands' of Scotland. James (who died at the age of twenty-nine, about ten years younger than Scott, himself thirty-nine, makes him in the poem) was a famous – if famously ruthless – peacemaker. In 1529, based at Edinburgh, James savagely pacified the Borders which had grown insubordinate during his minority. He swept through Ettrick Forest, hanging rebels as he went. His victims included that hero of the *Minstrelsy*, John Armstrong, and Adam Scott of Tushielaw, the 'King of the Borders'. The blood of Border reivers ran through Scott's veins, and he loved to sing their exploits, but he was also Sheriff Depute of Selkirkshire, with the responsibility of keeping the King's peace in Ettrick Forest – with sword and rope if necessary.

Marmion was a poem which in large part served the Tory party – a Pittite work. *The Lady of the Lake* marks a significant shift of political affiliation to the country's heir apparent. The poem is centred on a monarch – the first of Scott's major narratives to take a king as hero. James V comes out very well in the story; he is a middle-aged but gallant ruler with an eye for the ladies. It is a telling detail, however, that when James proposes to Ellen, it is not to make her his wife, but his mistress – his Mrs Fitzherbert:

> I'll place thee in a lovely bower
> I'll guard thee like a tender flower. (IV. 18)

James cannot offer more than a bower because he already has a wife – the French princess Magdalen whom he married in 1536 (Scott pointedly refers to James's French trips, but not his spouse). James V enjoyed a folkloric reputation as a cheerful amorist – nicknamed 'The Gaberlunzie Man,' and 'the Jolly Beggar'. In fact, some of his historically recorded acts were far from jolly. According to David Lindsay, James once raped a servant maid who saucily emptied a brewing vat over his head. He took the 'duddron in the puddle' the two of them 'swettering like swine' in the spilled beer, as the disgusted annalist records. The historical James would have had Ellen's petticoats over her head the moment she stepped out of her little boat. As part of a general whitewash, *The Lady of the Lake* completely reverses James's behaviour to the Douglas family, which was vindictive in the extreme. There was no such gracious reconciliation as is found at the end of Scott's narrative. Nor was sixteenth-century Scotland the cultural centre Scott makes it out to be in the Stirling cantos. The Papal ambassador to James V was probably nearer the mark when in 1530 he declared Scotland to be 'the arse of the world'.[4]

While conceding that the monarch has an eye for the ladies, Scott never lets his James descend to ungallantry. He is portrayed conscientiously making the acquaintance of his remote northern territories and their inhabitants with a view to forging his kingdom into national unity. One can imagine this going down extremely well at Carlton House with the very distant descendant of James V of Scotland.

Published as it was by the self-proclaimed 'Bookseller to the Regent', it seems obvious that Scott was aiming his poem at a royal patron. Royal approbation was confirmed in 1812 when Byron reported to the other poet that the Prince Regent indeed preferred Scott 'to every bard past and present'. *The Lady of the Lake* had particularly pleased. When Byron called Scott 'the poet of *Princes*, as *they* never appeared more fascinating than in *Marmion* and *The Lady of the Lake* [the Prince Regent] was pleased to coincide and to dwell on the description of your [i.e. Scott's] Jameses as no less royal than poetical' (EJ 392). In 1813, when Henry Pye died, Scott was duly offered the Poet-Laureateship – a signal honour for a Scottish writer.

The other main tribute in *The Lady of the Lake* is to the Highland Regiments, currently distinguishing themselves in the Peninsular Campaign. The roll call of their tremendous military achievements is familiar. Between 1740 and 1800, some fifty Highland battalions were raised. These regiments served abroad with distinction in various actions, but most brilliantly in Spain and Portugal. *The Lady of the Lake* marks a major act of historical revision, by Scott and more generally by his class of traditionally Anglophile Lowland gentry. The northern bandits, thieves, or caterans of traditional Lowland lore are now pictured as wholly admirable 'British' soldiers of the King. The first appearance of Roderick Dhu and his boat-borne comrades on the breast of Loch Katrine (literally the 'lake of thieves') is a striking illustration of the Highland warrior's new image:

> Nearer and nearer as they bear,
> Spears, pikes, and axes flash in air.
> Now might you see the tartans brave,
> And plaids and plumage dance and wave:
> Now see the bonnets sink and rise,
> As his tough oar the rower plies;
> See, flashing at each sturdy stroke,
> The wave ascending into smoke;
> See the proud pipers on the bow,
> And mark the gaudy streamers flow
> From their loud chanters down, and sweep
> The furrow'd bosom of the deep,
> As, rushing through the lake amain,
> They plied the ancient Highland strain. (II. 16)

These are not bare-legged bandits, but a disciplined regiment: the pride of their country. In 1810 Scott wanted to go in person to the Peninsular front lines. It would have been his first trip abroad (and would doubtless have produced some excellent war reporting). When the project fell through, he went to the Highlands instead. The poem travelled where its author could not. Scott's old friend Adam Ferguson, now in the Peninsula with Wellington, recited the battle scenes from *The Lady of the Lake* to keep his company of 'Black Cuffs' steady while under enemy fire (Lock. 2. 25).

The Lady of the Lake was published by John Ballantyne in May 1810, with a quarter share sold to the London publisher William Miller (EJ 335). The first issue of the poem was a quarto edition of 2,050 copies 'with every accompanying grace of typography' – supplied, of course, by the other Ballantyne. The volume was embellished with an engraved reproduction of Saxon's portrait of Scott and cost a whopping two guineas. It was nonetheless snapped up at unprecedented speed. Four editions followed and total sales by the end of the first year were 30,000 or more (EJ 335). In return for the copyright Scott 'nominally' received 2,000 guineas; but his profit-sharing and loan agreements with the Ballantynes yielded much more. His income was probably around £10,000 in 1810 – ten times what it had been in 1800. He had, as he said, put a nail in Fortune's wheel.

The Lady of the Lake was reviewed well by Ellis in the *Quarterly*, which was no surprise. Less predictably Francis Jeffrey – the scourge of *Marmion* – was warmly approving in the *Edinburgh Review*. He may have been reined in by Constable, still playing a waiting game for the return of Scott to his list. Jeffrey declared himself charmed to find in *The Lady of the Lake* 'a diction tinged successively with the careless richness of Shakespeare, the harshness and antique simplicity of the old romances, the homeliness of vulgar ballads and anecdotes, and the sentimental glitter of the most modern poetry'. He claimed to like the slick smooth-rhyming octosyllabic couplets in which the bulk of the poem moves.

Modern readers tend not to like the poem's Hudibrastic 'dog trot' varied with the 'hop step and jump' of the interjected songs (Scott's self-deprecating descriptions, to Southey). Why did Scott not opt, like the other Romantics, for decasyllabics or blank verse? When Ellis politely asked the question in his *Quarterly* review Scott offered an interesting defence. He conceded that the short line left no room for the 'epithets of Homeric poetry' – or any ambitious poetic device (Lock. 2. 182). But the octosyllabic measure created a sense of speed and allowed the 'Pindaric' effects which Scott particularly relished. Historically, the metre looked back to the octosyllabic line of John Barbour (*c.*1320–95), author of *The Bruce* and the father of Scottish national verse.

The truth is, Scott's octosyllabics go together with a helter-skelter mode of writing. It results in gaping holes in the poem's narrative. What actually happens to James Fitzjames after his arrival at the Clan-Alpine camp? Why is he allowed to leave? Why exactly do the Clan Alpine and the Earls Mar and Moray do battle with each other? Surely, even in medieval Scotland, armies did not slaughter each other just for the hell of it? What will happen to the clan after the happy-ever-after episode at Stirling?

Scott disarms questions of this kind by constantly deprecating even his best works of poetry as unworthy of serious attention. His comments invariably stress how casually he composed or how *lucky* he was to hit the fickle public's taste with such incredibly shoddy wares. His description of his major poems as so many 'soap bubbles' finds no equivalent in other major poets of his time. Can one, for example, imagine Wordsworth confessing that 'my poetry has always passed from the desk to the printer in the most hurried manner possible, so that it is no wonder I am sometimes puzzled to explain my own meaning'? (Lock. 2. 184–6).

Scott was very firm with James Ballantyne when he dared compare his verse with Burns (EJ 336). But at times Scott's deprecation passes well beyond a show of modest amateurism to naked self-contempt, almost as if he intended to do his worst enemies' work for them. In his 1830 afterword to *The Lady of the Lake* he writes: 'As the celebrated John Wilkes is said to have explained to [King George the Third] that he himself, amid his full tide of popularity, was never a Wilkite, so I can, with honest truth, exculpate myself from having been at any time a partisan of my own poetry, even when it was in the highest fashion with the million.' Did ever poet so disrespect his work? When James Ballantyne asked the poet's daughter Sophia how she liked *The Lady of the Lake*, Miss Scott replied: 'Oh, I have not read it; papa says there's nothing so bad for young people as reading bad poetry' (EJ 336).

The modesty trope is common enough among authors, but we have to accept that in his heart Scott really did not think poetry was a serious occupation for serious men. As Lockhart observes:

> It is impossible to consider the whole course of [Scott's] correspondence and conversation, without agreeing in the conclusion of Mr Morritt, that he was all along sincere in the opinion that literature ought never to be ranked on the same scale of importance with the conduct of business in any of the great departments of public life. (Lock. 2. 214)

This conviction relates directly to the battles and combats which form the climaxes of all his major poems. Scott lived the formative years of his life during the longest war modern Britain has ever been engaged in. War was the greatest 'department of life' in the period 1792–1815. Scott had always wanted to be a soldier, but his 'disability' prevented him. What right had he to chronicle fighting, war, daring deeds, single combat to the death? Was he anything more than a lawyer with a limp, a lively imagination, and a happy knack with words? Other men were dying, or winning glory, in his place. Scott was addicted to spilling blood across his verse. No rhymer of the nineteenth century until Kipling is so fond of battle. But it seems that Scott – for all his verbal sabre-rattling – felt increasingly uneasy at a belligerence whose only risk was a cutting review from Francis Jeffrey.

THE RISE AND FALL OF JOHN BALLANTYNE & CO.

The Lady of the Lake made thousands of pounds for all concerned; most of all for the author who happened also to be the poem's co-publisher and co-printer. But the expenses of James Ballantyne's press (in fact now eleven presses – with plans for fourteen; EJ 360) drained the firm's profits. Scott's break with Constable, while securing publishing commissions, had robbed the Printing Office of business. At the best of times Constable did not think much of James Ballantyne as a printer.

John Ballantyne did not, as was fondly hoped in January 1809, overmatch Archibald Constable & Co. as Edinburgh's leading publisher. By 1812 the publisher to the Regent was looking something of a lame duck and by 1813 he was a hopeless casualty. What the Hanover Street firm printed and published via brother John since the secret pact of 1809 was – other than *The Lady of the Lake* – a catalogue of worthy duds from the sales point of view. Anna Seward's collected poems – for instance – were left for Scott to bring out when the 'the Swan of Lichfield' died in 1809. He gallantly accepted the responsibility, producing in 1810 a 'formidable monument of mediocrity' (Lock. 2. 208) in three volumes. In general, the tone of the John Ballantyne list was soporifically stuffy, with the exception of the poems of his own which Scott published through the firm (*The Vision of Don Roderick, The Lady of the Lake, Rokeby*).

The ulcer that sapped the strength of John Ballantyne and Co. was the *Edinburgh Annual Register* – a work upon which Scott vowed he would 'pawn his life' (EJ 362) when he set up the firm. The *Register*, like other of the house's products, was a good idea which was mishandled by Ballantyne and neglected by Scott.[5] Scott initially lined up strong contributors for the *Edinburgh Annual Register* – notably himself and Robert Southey for the 'History of Europe' section (Southey was paid £400 for his contribution – a stipend which reflects Scott's high expectations). Scott and Ballantyne composed a prospectus which committed the journal to a range of contributions that Diderot himself might have thought twice about: (1) A History of Europe (2) A Catalogue of State Papers (3) A Chronicle of Remarkable Events (4) A History of Literature (5) A History of Science (6) A History of the Fine Arts (7) A History of the Useful Arts (8) A History of the Atmosphere (9) Commercial, Financial, and Statistical Tables.

The *Edinburgh Annual Register*'s ruinous failure can be put down to three errors. First, it was made a two-volume publication, unlike its English model, the *Annual Register*. More damagingly, most of the original essays for which the second volume was created never appeared and those that did were dashed off by Scott himself, with the sole aim of filling pages. This failure arose (as Kenneth Curry states) from the lack of any clear editorial strategy. James Ballantyne and Scott shared the editorship between them as a chore to be done on the side. Most damagingly, the *Edinburgh Annual Register* never appeared on time. The first edition, for the year 1808, did not appear until the end of July 1810. In a foreword the proprietor (John Ballantyne) claimed that motives of 'delicacy' prevented him from giving any explanation. He hinted darkly at having been let down by his contributors. This may have been so, but the *Edinburgh Annual Register* did not improve in punctuality in its subsequent issues. It was always two years late and, as Curry puts it, 'Every volume of the *Register* has a certain air, if not of desperation, at least of hurried, last-minute arrangements' (Curry, 10).

The proprietors' third mistake was to make the *Edinburgh Annual Register* the vehicle of party interests. Articles which Scott wrote himself (on the Judicature Commission, and the present state of poetry and periodical criticism) were strongly and at times violently partisan. While Toryism might sell a quarterly, it alienated a good part of an annual register's potential market. That market lay in the south. The *Edinburgh Annual Register* never got the foothold it needed in the London bookshops. When in December 1812 John Murray withdrew his one-twelfth share, it was a death-knell for the *Register*. Southey reckoned that for every ten copies of *Edinburgh Annual Register* sold in Scotland, only one sold in England (Curry, 10).

The *Edinburgh Annual Register* was, as Curry records, 'the single heaviest loser on the Ballantyne list' (Curry, 12). He reckons that John Ballantyne printed 3,000 two-volume sets a year for the first eight years. This must have been less than they originally projected, but of these it is likely that they did not sell much above half and probably even most of those at a heavily discounted price. By 1812, the *Edinburgh Annual Register* was losing at least £1,000 a year (as Constable later reckoned; EJ 415).

One of the by-products of Scott's *Edinburgh Annual Register* involvement was a feud with Coleridge, which has been rendered largely invisible by Lockhart. Relations between the two poets evidently remained tense after the publication of the *Lay* (which Coleridge resolutely neglected to read), with mutual friends like Southey doing their best to smooth things over. It is significant that no record of any correspondence between the two remains, nor apparently did Scott meet Coleridge on his Lake District trips. Conversational records that have fragmentarily survived testify to a massive contempt on Coleridge's and Wordsworth's part for Scott's poetry. Coleridge told his friend Thomas Allsop, for instance, that 'not twenty lines of Scott's poetry will ever reach posterity; it has relation to nothing'. He told the same correspondent in 1820 about 'Wordsworth's contemptuous Assertions regarding Scott' (Griggs 4. 1229).

Coleridge on his part must have been vexed by a review-article (recognizably by Scott) in the November 1809 *Quarterly Review*, on the subject of Croker's new poem, 'The Battle of Talavera'. It was written, Scott declared, 'in that irregular Pindaric measure first applied to serious composition by Mr Walter Scott, and it is doing no injustice to the ingenious author [i.e. Croker] to say that, in many passages, we were, from the similarity of the stanza and the subject, involuntarily reminded of the Battle of Flodden in the sixth book of *Marmion*.' This was an extraordinarily impudent observation on Scott's part. The 'Pindaric measure', as he surely knew, was first applied by Coleridge to the narrative of 'Christabel'. It added salt to the wound to accuse *Croker* of plagiarism, when it was the author of the *Lay* who was the culprit.

A new salvo against Coleridge was launched by Scott in the *Edinburgh Annual Register* for 1808 (published in July 1810). In a long 'review of contemporary literature' the anonymous author (Scott) declared that 'we do not hesitate to distinguish as the three most successful candidates for poetical fame, Scott Southey, and Campbell' (*EAR*, 1808, 2. 419). This was the author who would write in his 1830 afterword to *The Lady of the Lake* 'I can, with honest truth, exculpate myself from having been at any time a partisan of my own poetry, even when it was in the highest fashion with the million' (JLR 275). Scott – under his mask of anonymity – went on to praise to the skies his own works, those of Southey (whom he was concurrently puffing in the *Quarterly*) and Thomas Campbell – who represented to Scott and his Pittite friends the acceptable face of Whiggery.

Himself apart, two worse poetic causes than Southey and Campbell it would have been hard to find in 1810. Turning to other contenders for poetical fame, Scott trotted out a list of his cronies (William Rose, John Leyden, Joanna Baillie, Richard Heber). He went on to accord Wordsworth some faint praise, but condemned Coleridge in violent terms. Among other criticisms, he cast aspersions on Coleridge's 'honour'. 'This author', Scott writes, 'has been uniformly deficient in the perseverance and the sound sense which were necessary to turn his exquisite talents to their proper use' (*EAR*, 1808, 2. 427). Coleridge is accused by Scott of perpetrating 'quaint and vulgar doggerel . . . we can hardly suppose the author who threw forth such crude effusions is serious.'

During the summer of 1810, at the precise moment that this attack was published, Coleridge was visited by Francis Jeffrey. Jeffrey apparently reminded the poet (as had Wordsworth) about the indebtedness of the *Lay* to 'Christabel'. He must surely have told Coleridge about the *Register* piece, whose authorship he would have penetrated. All this occurred at a particularly low point in Coleridge's fortunes. His weekly journal, the *Friend*, had collapsed after only 28 issues, never having achieved more than a few hundred subscribers. He had written the poems on which his subsequent fame rests – but in 1810 there was no suggestion that he was to be anything other than an obscure literary failure. In the *Edinburgh Annual Register* Scott had recorded, in his encomium on the poetic fame of Walter Scott, that *The Lay of the Last Minstrel* had sold 25,000 in six years. 'Christabel', the poem on which it was based, was still unfinished and unpublished. Coleridge was falling into hopeless drug addiction, his marriage had broken up, and there was a rupture with Wordsworth looming.

In this extremity, Coleridge was contemplating an approach to an old friend, Daniel Stuart, who had published his early poetry in the *Morning Post*, and was now proprietor of the *London Courier*. On 15 September 1810, there appeared over the signature of 'STC' a *Courier* article accusing Scott of plagiarism from dead and living poets. The author set out portions of the *Lay* and *Marmion* with a set of parallel passages which, it was alleged, Scott had illicitly drawn on. It was, of course, notorious among Coleridge's friends (among whom was the *Courier* editor) that the *Lay* was inspired by

Coleridge's unpublished work. It is inconceivable that Stuart did not appreciate the construction that would be put on an article signed by 'STC' alleging plagiarism by Walter Scott.

Scott was mortified and wrote to Southey as soon as the offending issue of the paper arrived in Edinburgh. Southey wrote back by return, reassuring him that Coleridge 'knows nothing of this petty and paltry attack' (*Lett*. 2. 373). On 20 September Stuart inserted in his paper, at Coleridge's request, a denial that the poet was the author of the attack on Scott (although the article did not identify who the offending 'STC' was). Scott declared himself relieved not to have to believe that 'a man of Mr Coleridge's high talents, which I had always been among the first to appreciate as they deserve ['vulgar doggerel'?], had thought me worthy of the sort of public attack which appeared in the Courier of the 15th' (*Lett*. 2. 373).

Coleridge did, in fact, take up employment with Stuart at the *Courier* a few months later. And in early October, he wrote to Wordsworth a scathing attack on *The Lady of the Lake* – a copy of which had apparently been given him by Southey. Coleridge begins:

> I am reading Scott's *Lady of the Lake*, having had it on my table week after week till it cried shame to me for not opening it. But truly as far as I can judge from the first 98 pages [Coleridge seems never to have read more than the first two cantos], my reluctance was not unprophetic. Merciful Apollo! – what an easy pace dost thou jog on with thy unspurred yet unpinioned Pegasus! – The movement of the Poem (which is written with the exception of a multitude of Songs in regular 8 syllable Iambics) is between a sleeping Canter and a Marketwoman's trot – but it is endless – I seem never to have made any way – I never remember a narrative poem in which I felt the sense of Progress so languid.

Despite his inability to read the poem, he nonetheless was keen to write on it at length. Coleridge notes, meaningfully, that the poem is 'not without it's peccadillos against the 8th Commandment à la mode of Messieurs Scott and Campbell', and he cites examples of illicit borrowings. It is the work of a 'Picturesque Tourist' and Scott is like a dog, mechanically lifting its leg six times to piss a canto. (*Critical Heritage*, ed. J. R. de J. Jackson, London, 1970, 56–61)

As a kind of antidote to the venomous rivalry which had sprung up between Scott and Coleridge, Lockhart publishes a happy anecdote, which he places in the biographical narrative for summer 1809 (i.e. shortly before the above quarrel). Johnson also places this episode in summer (more specifically June) 1809, and I quote his version as being shorter than Lockhart's, although it exactly follows him in all details:

> Scott's literary fame aroused no little jealousy. At a brilliant dinner party where Scott and Coleridge were among the men of letters encircling the table, there were signs of a desire to humble Scott by extravagantly eulogizing

poets of smaller renown. Several of those present recited poems they had not yet published and were enthusiastically praised; Coleridge repeated more than one and was lauded to the skies. Scott heartily joined in the applause. When he was asked to give them something of his own, he replied that he had nothing worth their hearing but that he had seen some verses in a provincial newspaper that he thought very fine. He then repeated a poem entitled *Fire, Famine, and Slaughter*. It was received with only faint approbation. Criticism followed; Scott defended the unknown author. Finally, a more bitter antagonist, fastening upon one line, cried 'This at least is absolute nonsense!' Scott denied it – the carper maintained his criticism – until Coleridge, who had been growing more and more uncomfortable, called out, 'For God's sake let Mr Scott alone – *I* wrote the poem.' (EJ 313–4, Lock. 2. 126–7)

It is a nice story that testifies to Scott's manly good taste, and the pettiness of the calumnies he had to put up with. It is, however, 'manipulated'. Writing a memoir to his eclogues in 1815 (as his editors guess), Coleridge confirms the general outline of the story. But according to Coleridge's account, the verses were originally published by Daniel Stuart in the *Morning Post*, January 1798, and republished in 1800. More significant, however, is the date of this encounter. It must (from the evidence of Coleridge's movements) have been in 1803, not 1809. 1803 was a sensitive period: Scott had written most of the *Lay*, but not published it. It seems that he was keen to flatter Coleridge at this juncture. (What, one wonders, did he say to the other poet about 'Christabel', if anything?) What is most significant is that Lockhart moves the story forward six years (to a period, incidentally, when the pacifist sentiment of Coleridge's poem would have been obnoxious to Scott). Clearly the intention was to repair any idea that there was a difference between the poets.

WINDING UP JOHN BALLANTYNE & CO.

All commentators agree that whatever his shortcomings as a publisher, John Ballantyne was good with figures. For three years he was able to invent paper profits – by valuing up book stock – but if that stock never sold, it was fairy gold. The amount that Scott poured into John Ballantyne & Co. is unknown, but can be guessed at. With the Judicature reforms and the retirement of Home in January 1812, his Clerkship salary was £1,300. So as Clerk and Sheriff, he was guaranteed £1,600 for life. The thousands of copies of *The Lady of the Lake* which were sold probably brought him £10,000. He had inherited £6,000 from his uncle, and could expect as much from his father's estate, whenever the trust was cleared up. Charlotte had some thousands from her brother. The Scotts were, until 1812, living virtually rent-free at Ashestiel. Yet when in June 1811 he bought the land on which he would build Abbotsford, Scott was obliged to borrow £2,000 (half the purchase price) from his brother John and have John Ballantyne raise the rest on the security of his next, unwritten, poem, *Rokeby*.

So precarious had John Ballantyne's affairs become by early 1813, that Scott was forced to turn to Constable. His first hope was that the publisher might offer financial aid. But Constable did not like the kind of books John Ballantyne & Co. published at Scott's commissioning. As he put it in one of his pungent similes: 'I like well Scott's *ain bairns*, but heaven preserve me from those of his fathering!' (EJ 415). John Ballantyne had, moreover, given injudiciously generous credit to booksellers in a reckless attempt to stimulate sales – bad debts were inevitable. Spring 1813, following a series of banking crises, was a bad time for the book trade. The war had made money scarce and loans hard to come by. Scott might conceivably have bolstered the firm's creditworthiness by revealing, if only to his banker Sir William Forbes, that he was an active partner in John Ballantyne. But such an admission would have been wormwood to him.

Nonetheless, Constable was inclined to be helpful – on his own strict terms and with the clear intention of bringing back to the fold 'the Earl', as Scott was called by Constable's young partner Robert Cadell (no relation of Scott's earlier publishers Cadell & Davies[6]). Constable offered in all £1,300 for a selection of Ballantyne's most saleable quire (i.e. unbound) stock. But there were two conditions to his offer. Scott must give him a quarter share of the copyright of *Rokeby*, for a further £700 (a low sum). Constable's £2,000 would not be cash, but bills payable at six, twelve and eighteen months. 'It *is* a sacrifice', Scott wrote to John Ballantyne, 'but being pennyless and without credit what could we do?' (EQ 64).

The actual crash was preceded by some desperate juggling and improvising and 'a Mickey Mouse pursuit of bills' (HG 109, EJ 411–5). Scott was assisted by loans from friends like Morritt and in August 1813 was obliged to ask the Duke of Buccleuch to guarantee a bank loan of £4,000 to keep John Ballantyne afloat until the end of the year. (Scott was on tenterhooks until the letter from the Duke, which had been misdirected, arrived; EJ 425.) Neither Morritt nor Scott's 'Princely Chief' were enlightened as to the full extent of Scott's involvement with the Ballantyne brothers.

Scott – despite his pride on the matter – was forced back into the arms of Constable, who had behaved throughout the separation with restraint. Scott had been less restrained, and sometimes downright provocative. (As recently as Christmas 1812, when James Ballantyne suggested that they give the publisher a share of *Rokeby*, Scott refused on the extraordinary grounds that Constable would underpay him.) It was some consolation that the odious Hunter was now gone. But Constable's new young partner (and son-in-law) Robert Cadell advised his chief to keep 'the Bard' in suspense. In June 1813 Scott offered Constable the *whole* copyright of his next poem (i.e. the poem after *Rokeby*), provisionally called 'The Nameless Glen' (eventually it emerged as *The Lord of the Isles*). Scott had £5,000 in mind – a sum directly inspired by the current needs of John Ballantyne and Co. Cadell was bitter about Scott's earlier 'usage and neglect' of their house (dragging his feet on Swift, 'humbugging' them by holding back supplies of *Rokeby* until John Ballantyne had creamed the market). He counselled keeping Scott in suspense about the unwritten poem (*Lett.* 3. 286).

In the last week of July 1813 Scott and the Ballantynes had some sharp reminders of the precariousness of their position. Their banker, Sir William Forbes, who had been squeezing them for some time, refused more credit and John Ballantyne (whose business habits were driving Scott crazy) omitted to inform Scott of the fact until the bills fell due. Scott lost a night's sleep and had to send off personal money orders by horse from Abbotsford at three o'clock in the morning. They were within hours of disaster. Scott wrote a sharp letter to his publishing partner. 'Suppose that I had gone to Drumlanrig?', he asked (Lock. 2. 237). Drumlanrig was the Inigo Jones castle where the Duke of Buccleuch resided and Scott was in fact due to go there on 26 July. The prospect of being discovered a bankrupt tradesman in that setting made his blood run cold.

The Ballantynes and Scott faced some very unpleasant choices in August 1813. If they remaindered their unsold stock, it would infuriate booksellers who had taken it in good faith and still had it in their inventory. If they sold some of their more marketable assets – such as James Ballantyne's printing equipment – it would be taking blood from their one milch cow. Scott had to face the prospect of winding up John Ballantyne's publishing business, with the hope that the forthcoming two poems would refloat his and James's finances.

Disposing of the vast quantity of unsold (and possibly unsellable) stock which they had accumulated posed great problems. Again Constable – with his background in retail bookselling – had to be applied to. The rival publisher was asked to draw up a thorough inventory of the firm in summer 1813. (That John Ballantyne could not be trusted to do this is some mark of his professional limitations.)

Constable worked quickly and gave his verdict on John Ballantyne to James Ballantyne in August 1813. It made grim reading. The firm's £18,000 of warehouse stock would realize a meagre £8,600. Of the £4,000 owed the firm, only £1,600 could be collected. The firm must raise £4,000 at once, or declare itself bankrupt. (This was the period when Scott was making his plea to the Duke of Buccleuch for just that sum for just that purpose.) Scott grumbled that Constable must be exaggerating the extent of John Ballantyne's liability for his 'own reasons'. But he reluctantly accepted the assessment and its drastic implications.

Constable's £2,000, the £4,000 which the Duke's guarantee enabled Scott to raise, together with other loans from friends like Morritt and Erskine, and the writing-off of the firm's debts to its principal creditor – James Ballantyne – just lifted them over the immediate rocks. But it was a very close thing. John Ballantyne & Co. was wound up without Scott being unmasked as a tradesman. Scott the poet (and embryonic novelist) returned to Constable. The partnership, forged anew in 1813–4, was to be glorious.

How culpable was Scott in the downfall of John Ballantyne & Co.? Lockhart blames John Ballantyne entirely (just as he blames James for the 1826 crash). Johnson passes no comment, other than to praise Scott's resilience under pressure. David Daiches alleges that Scott was dishonest and irresponsible:

> The whole affair should have been a lesson and an awful warning to Scott, but it wasn't. It did not even trouble his conscience that he had to borrow money from his friends under what were virtually false pretences. Neither Morritt [who was misled with the information that Scott stood only to lose his copyrights if Ballantyne went under] nor Buccleuch, nor anyone except the Ballantynes had the remotest idea that Scott's troubles were largely the result of his financial involvement with a publishing and a printing firm. (Daiches, 94)

Daiches ascribes Scott's misconduct to incorrigible 'impulsiveness'. But aspects of his involvement go beyond this. It is clear, for instance, that Scott borrowed money from Charles Erskine, his Sheriff Depute at Selkirk (HG 112). For an officer of the law to raise loans from his subordinates (for the purpose of business and land speculation) is very questionable. Nor, apparently, did Scott repay the loans until Erskine pressed him, in October 1814. Erskine had, apparently, advanced the money to John Ballantyne, ignorant of Scott's actual involvement, simply to please his chief.

8

Abbotsford and *Waverley* (1811–1814)

Scott's seven-year lease on the farm at Ashestiel was due to run out in May 1811. He could have stayed on year-to-year with a modest increase in rent. The house was adequate to the family needs and the landlord, his kinsman Colonel Russell, had no immediate intention of returning from service overseas. But Scott did not like being another man's tenant. He had a passion for planting trees – literally putting down roots wherever he lived. The notion of planting acorns for someone else's children to enjoy the oaks was not to his taste. In a dark moment Scott contemplated (perhaps not entirely seriously) the most drastic move of all – emigration. He wrote to his brother Tom in November 1810 that were Robert Dundas to go out as Governor General to India 'and were he willing to take me with him in a good situation, I would not hesitate to pitch the Court of Session and the booksellers to the Devil and try my fortune in another climate' (EQ 53).

Desperate remedies were rendered unnecessary when the 'Scotch Shylock' George Home, having vexatiously refused to die, consented to 'retire' in 1811 with an outrageously comfortable superannuation payment (EJ 366–7). After five years Scott was at last – in January 1812 – paid a salary for his work as Clerk of the Session. It meant a handsome increase to his annual income. With this life-income, his sheriff's stipend, his various inheritances (from his uncle, father, and Charlotte's brother), occasional thousands for his poems, regular hundreds for his reviews, and his dividends from the Ballantynes – Walter Scott was (if he could hold on to his money) a gentleman of considerable means.

On 1 July 1811, Scott told Morritt that he had just bought a small farm worth £150 in annual rent, 'with the intention of "bigging myself a bower" after my own fashion' (*Lett.* 2. 508). The property had belonged to a Galashiels minister, Dr Douglas, an old friend of the family. It was not as a farm that Scott bought the property, but as a potential estate. He had no interest in 'common vulgar farming', as he told Joanna Baillie (EJ 371). The property – which was beautifully situated but devoid of trees or any distinguished building – would serve as a *tabula rasa* for Scott's architectural and landscape visions. He could do in stone and oak what up to now he had only been able to do in words – build castles and paint scenery.

Scott bought the property after some hard bargaining for 4,000 guineas (£1,500 down – the rest payable by five-year mortgage). As John Buchan observes, the cost is 'astonishing' and reflects the sky-high value of farm land with the inflation of food prices during the Napoleonic Wars. 'Clarty Hole' (James Hogg tells us gleefully that the dialect name meant 'dirty puddle') comprised 110 acres with a half-mile frontage on the River Tweed, from which the land rose steeply. It was thirty-odd miles from Edinburgh; rather too far for regular working trips, but ideal for seasonal residence. When Scott purchased it, Clarty Hole comprised a single, humble farm structure. Scott promptly renamed the property Abbotsford (the land, he discovered, had once been owned by the abbots of Melrose). Soon after taking up residence, Scott began to title himself (at first in jest) 'Laird of Abbotsford'.

The family moved in May 1812, with a mighty train of two dozen waggons followed, as Scott recorded, 'by a horde of hooting children'. There was the inevitable bad-tempered chaos of settling into the original and rather poky farmhouse. This over, the proud owner began to 'big his bower'.[1] Scott possessed a strong compositional sense in architecture formed by considerable study and a number of educative influences from his friends. His connection with Morritt after 1809 introduced him to the amenities and finer points of the grand country house. Rokeby Park (the subject of his next long poem) confirmed his loyalty to the Vanbrugh style. Scott's friendship with Daniel Terry instructed him in decor – and was to give the interiors of Abbotsford a distinctly theatrical aspect.

To make the best of his new property Scott pored over guides like Uvedale Price's 'Essay on the Picturesque as compared with the Sublime and the Beautiful'. On 23 March 1813 he told Lady Abercorn, 'I have been studying Price with all my eyes' (*Lett.* 3. 240). In a letter of August 1825, to Sir George Beaumont, Scott called himself a '*pittore*, in the sense of plantations and buildings' (*Lett.* 9. 216). Scott's education in arboreal composition culminated with two authoritative essays in the *Quarterly* in 1827: 'On Planting Waste Lands' and 'On Ornamental Gardening' (both, ironically, were published at the moment when Abbotsford's outlying lands were lost to him and his heirs).

In his first few summer months in Abbotsford, Scott spent £1,000 on building and planting. Most expensive – and ultimately ruinous – was his aspiration to enlarge his property in terms of acreage, and make it a true estate. By 1816, it was five times as large and, at the zenith of Scott's lairdship, ten times the size of the original 'small farm'. It was his misfortune, as Buchan observes, to be surrounded by farmers and bonnet lairds only too willing to sell at the prices Scott would pay. Most of these purchases were made by mortgage, which involved high interest rates. Scott was still plotting the acquisition of bordering land as late as 1825.

The central element in making an estate worthy of the 'Laird of Abbotsford' was the structure of the house itself – his 'Dalilah', as he called it. When he first arrived it was, for a short time, Scott's intention to keep Abbotsford as a 'cottage' – like Wordsworth's Dove Cottage in Grasmere. He contemplated renovations costing a modest £1,500, which would have been well within his means (EJ 374). But his ideas soon expanded to a mansion, and ultimately a nobleman's 'castle'. Over the years of its building (1812–24) he composed Abbotsford in the same spirit as his 'imitations of the antique ballad'. Externally, the style was Scottish baronial: Abbotsford had towers with conical-roofed angle turrets, high chimneys, and a castellated fringe ('crow stepped gablets'). These purely rhetorical defensive features alluded to Britain's being still at war (until 1815, at least). In this time of military alarm, Scott naturally remained faithful to the fortified houses of the Scottish sixteenth century – the domestic establishment always on the *qui vive* for armed defence.

In building Abbotsford, Scott had the assistance of a series of architects. William Stark (about whom not much is known) was contracted in 1811–12. A young Glaswegian, he was suggested by Daniel Terry, and may also have had theatrical connections. Initially, he was contracted to draw up a design for an 'ornamental cottage' (Macaulay, 224). Scott relinquished Stark's plans as 'too expensive' in 1814 (EJ 461). Evidently this was a brief attack of prudence on Scott's part (Macaulay, 225). James Skene supplied the next ideas for the house. Then, at the close of 1816, Scott met Edward Blore, antiquarian and architect, and George Bullock, owner of a furniture warehouse in London (Macaulay, 224). With their suggestions, the scheme enlarged. Blore took over as principal designer in 1816 (EJ 556). He seems to have had a strong aesthetic theory of architecture, and to have pulled the design towards the picturesque folly. In their superstructural detail Blore's plans tended towards excessive castellation, 'in the old fashioned Scotch stile' (Macaulay, 225).

Blore's design was eventually 'thrown out' (EJ 567). According to Macaulay, he may have supplied his plans on a 'friendly' basis, and they were perhaps largely provisional. Terry subsequently procured another set of plans from the more famous William Atkinson. Atkinson supplied the full-blooded Gothic flavour (stained-glass windows, for instance) that Scott craved. He supported Scott's amiable kleptomania for borrowed, bought, or begged bric-a-brac. Atkinson was responsible for the most important phase of the construction of the house, 1822–3. He seems to have worked largely through Terry, in a kind of syndicate with Bullock until the salesman's death in 1818.

The final result was a miracle of eclecticism: combining Scottish Picturesque, Scots-Jacobean, English manor house, with Scottish Castle and monastic styles. Inside, Scott's imagination ran wild. Suits of armour and old weaponry (guns, pistols, targes, claymores, bugles, horns) covered the walls. He had a library-study, with secret recessed compartments (shades of

Northanger Abbey). His 'curio room' was dominated by Rob Roy's long-barrelled gun, pouch and dirk. Scott collected or commissioned paintings to celebrate his family history and lore. Heraldic devices were posted up in the main hall. Terry's theatrical touch is felt strongly in the interior decoration. And yet, for all the spurious antiquity, Abbotsford had queerly futuristic touches – such things as gaslighting, a pneumatic bell system and water closets.

Commentators like Virginia Woolf have seen this combination of the stylistic antique and the new technological as allegorical.[2] Ruskin, the prophet of pure Gothic, was disgusted and upbraided Scott for his miscegenations in *Modern Painters*: 'Scott reverences Melrose [Abbey], yet casts one of its piscinas, puts a modern steel grate into it, and makes it his fireplace.' Whatever else, Abbotsford was an immensely influential house – as influential on building styles as was *Waverley* on the Victorian novel. As Macaulay notes, 'Abbotsford is the unsung prototype of Scots-Baronial architecture which was to sweep across the country after the middle of the [nineteenth] century' – as such, it was both the culmination of a tradition and ahead of its time.

Everything that Scott did to and for Abbotsford cost a 'pouch of money' (EJ 375). These expenses eventually forced Scott more and more to write for quick cash. By committing himself to an ever more extravagant vision of his house, Scott ensured that literature would indeed be his crutch, despite his earlier resolve. The profits of *The Lady of the Lake* had inspired the purchase of Abbotsford. The costs of improving Abbotsford motivated *Rokeby* and every major work Scott would write for the next ten years. As Grierson puts it, 'The publication of *The Lady of the Lake* in May 1810 marked, I think, the culmination of Scott's good fortune' (HG 103). The purchase of Abbotsford, a year later, marked the beginning of much bad fortune.

THE VISION OF DON RODERICK AND ROKEBY

The conduct of the war in the Iberian Peninsula was for Scott an obsession of Uncle Tobyish proportions. Even on coach trips between Edinburgh and Ashestiel he is recorded as carrying 'the largest and best map he had been able to procure of the seat of war' marked by black and white pins 'showing the latest state of battle' (Lock. 2. 215–6). Mrs Scott complained, to no effect. The Peninsular Campaign was the direct inspiration for Scott's poem *The Vision of Don Roderick*. He began writing it in spring 1811, after the Court of Session retired. The poem was published (in quarto) a few weeks later in July. Scott dedicated the work, and the receipts from its sale, to the Portuguese War victims. Rather less philanthropically, Scott inserted the poem into the flagging *Edinburgh Annual Register* for 1809 (published in July

1811) noting that the publisher of the journal had paid a 'good sum' for it. Since Scott owned both the copyright and the *Register* it is not clear what money found its way from this transaction to the relief fund.

Scott was dismissive of *The Vision of Don Roderick* as he wrote it, complaining that he could not bring the verse to life. He later dismissed it as a 'Drum and Trumpet performance' (EJ 376). His friends, nonetheless, rallied round his latest effort. William Erskine reviewed the poem at length in the *Quarterly* (October 1811). His verdict was overpitched to the point of absurdity: 'We are inclined to rank *The Vision of Don Roderick*, not only above the Bard [i.e. Shakespeare], but (excepting Adam's vision from the mount of Paradise and the matchless beauties of the sixth book of Virgil) above all the historical and poetical prospects which have come to our knowledge.' That is, *The Vision of Don Roderick* was simply the best poem ever written in the English language. Posterity has generally agreed with Grierson, who judges the poem 'quite negligible' (HG 104).

The *Vision* has a long opening section, in which Scott debates what is the poetic mode adequate to modern war. He settles on the Spenserian stanza – a measure which rather clogs the natural brio of his verse. More closely, however, the *Vision* nods towards Southey, now Scott's closest poetic and political ally. Southey was an expert on Iberia. He could speak the languages and had visited Spain in 1795 and Portugal in 1800 – some time before the present hostilities blew up. In December 1809 Southey began his *Roderick, the Last of the Goths*, a work which was not published until 1814. Doubtless he mentioned the theme to Scott. Equally doubtless, when the work appeared most readers assumed that Scott had thought of the Roderick subject first. Southey did not mind Scott stealing his thunder (more so as his conception of Roderick was quite different). Scott's machinery in *The Vision of Don Roderick* was in turn borrowed by Southey for *A Vision of Judgement* in 1821, and promptly answered by Byron's *The Vision of Judgement* a year later. In this way, *The Vision of Don Roderick*, if not a good poem in itself, was the cause – ultimately – of good poetry in others.

Scott's poem fails on a number of counts. Inferior as Southey was to Scott as a versifier, at least he had been to Spain. Scott at this stage of his career had never in fact been outside Britain, and the provincialism shows. There were other causes for complaint. For contemporary readers the most controversial aspect of the *Vision* was the third of Roderigo's visions in the 'fated room' (the first two picturing the Moorish invasion, and the lecherous monarch's own well-deserved death on the field of battle). This third and last vision portrays – in the spirit of the propaganda newsreel – British battles and Spanish guerilla warfare against the French, climaxing with the recent allied victories.

In this section of his poem Scott indulges an admiration for the Highland regiments which verges on historical misrepresentation. The British forces initially appear under a Union Jack (from which the Irish cross is mysteriously absent). The focus narrows down, almost at once, to the

Scottish contingent, from which – equally mysteriously – the Lowland regiments are missing:

> But ne'er in battlefield throbb'd heart so brave
> As that which beats beneath the Scottish plaid. (II. 59)

Scott was wild about Scottish gallantry at this period. Even his new terrier (who sat on his lap while he wrote *The Vision*) was called 'Wallace'. Shortly after writing the poem (in April 1812) Scott purchased Rob Roy's gun ('a long Spanish-barrelled piece') and ammunition pouch. They took their place of honour over his writing desk.

The *Vision* ends on the highpoint of two acts of conspicuous (Highland) Scottish gallantry at Fuentes d'Honoro and Barossa. The first celebrates the memory of Colonel Cameron 'who fell at the head of his native Highlanders the 71st and 79th' (JLR 618). These wild warriors 'raised a dreadful shriek of grief and rage' on seeing their chief die, and promptly overwhelmed 'the finest body of French grenadiers ever seen', bayoneting their foes and tearing them to pieces in their fury. The second poetic citation for gallantry is to General Thomas Grahame, another leader of Perthshire Highlanders and a descendant of Montrose (whose sword Scott acquired at the same time he got Rob Roy's weapon; Lock. 2. 265). Grahame won the Battle of Barossa, but resigned his command when the Spanish generals claimed the whole honours of the victory.

Scott's climactic stress on Highland Scottish triumph in the *Vision* was tendentious, and in line with his fierce patriotism. Representatives of Lowland regiments have protested their erasure from the record. The *Edinburgh Review* focused attention on another tendentious omission – that of Sir John Moore, the martyr hero of Corunna, around whom a cult had formed in Britain. Moore was supposed to have died with the unlikely last words 'I hope the people of England will be satisfied' on his lips. England might have been satisfied, Scott and his Tory confrères on the *Quarterly Review* were not. Moore was deliberately blanked out of *The Vision of Don Roderick*. Scott giving the unconvincing explanation of insufficient space:

> Yes! hard the task, when Britons wield the sword,
> To give each chief and every field its name. (III. 33)

That is to say, the poet had stanzas enough for a relatively obscure Colonel [Cameron] but not for the country's most popular military hero since Nelson.

Of course, the omission of Moore was political – although the politics were not entirely discreditable to Scott. In 1811 reactions to the three-year old Peninsular campaign had not clarified. In March 1808, the French, under General Junot, had invaded Spain on the most cynically flimsy of pretexts. A British expeditionary force had been sent to Portugal under Sir Arthur Wellesley, arriving in August 1808. Later in the month, Wellesley won the Battle of Vimeiro and forced Junot to capitulate – triumphs which raised British hopes unduly. In September, the British forces invaded Spain. Napoleon, alarmed by his army's reverses and its poor leadership, took over command personally in November. At roughly the same period, after disputes with his Spanish and Portuguese allies, Moore took over command of the British forces. A cautious general, Moore chose at this point to execute a strategic withdrawal that his defenders saw as a skilful retreat, and his Tory critics as 'flight'. On 20 December, the French took Zaragoza. By January the British forces had withdrawn to Corunna. They were now pursued and harried by the French, under Marshal Soult. In the last stages of their retreat Moore's men had become disorganized and indisciplined – less an army than a rabble. Nevertheless, in a battle fought to protect the embarkation, the French were repulsed. The British force was evacuated safely but during the action Moore was fatally wounded. Was Moore's generalship craven, or wily?

Like other fire-breathing Tories, Scott felt Corunna to have been a national disgrace. His anger was increased by the fact that Moore was a Scot with strong Selkirk connections. The Sheriff-Depute of Selkirk complained incessantly through 1808 about Moore's cautious generalship (*Lett.* 2. 138, 140, 159, 543). Southey was equally critical in his private correspondence. In a letter to his brother Tom, Southey condemned Moore's retreat as 'one of the most disastrous and disgraceful flights upon record [which] would everlastingly have tarnished our army had he not luckily been compelled to fight at last' (Southey, *NL.* 1. 516).

The Vision of Don Roderick was the only major work Scott wrote in 1811. It was with a real sense of financial need (in the shape of Abbotsford bills and Ballantyne debts) that he turned to his new poem, *Rokeby*. The inspiration for the poem's subject was his four-year-long friendship with Morritt and his visits to Rokeby Park, Morritt's stately home. A magnificent pile, designed in the Vanbrugh style, Rokeby was situated in Yorkshire. The choice of an English setting for the poem was deliberate. Scott's first thought had been a poem on Robert Bruce (EJ 375). This would have suited the war mood of the country, but might have turned off his large English public.

Rokeby was conceived as 'a tale of the civil war of 1643 but [with] no reference to history or politics' (JLR 313). The poem was first mentioned to Morritt in December 1811 (HG 105). In March 1812, Scott reported that he had written the first canto, then torn it up. (This destruction or loss of the openings of his literary works recurs so often with Scott that one has to suspect it was a compositional ritual.) When the Court rose for its long break in July, he was able to compose in earnest – although the cramped and uncomfortable quarters of Abbotsford must have been a distraction. He went to Rokeby in September, where apparently Morritt saw or heard parts of the poem (EJ 400). Scott apparently wrote the magnificent country park vista opening to canto 2 during this visit. Having just purchased Abbotsford, his mind was full of 'capabilities' and the beauties of mature landscape. (Pedants who have perspectivally examined the prospect point out that Scott's description of the view is physically impossible, and he must have used a map.) By October, he was writing the impressive quantity of a hundred lines a day. Extracts of the poem in progress were read to Lady Louisa Stuart, now one of his close literary advisers. Scott did not quite make his target for delivery, Christmas 1812. *Rokeby* was finished on the last day of the year, in 'an odd and melancholy' mood, as he recorded (EJ 405). It was published on 10 January 1813.

The financial arrangements were complex. Initially, three-quarters of the poem was owned by John Ballantyne (as Scott's frontman) with a quarter sold off to Longman and Murray (EJ 397). But with Ballantyne's crisis, and the expense of Abbotsford, Scott and his partners were pressed to sell off other portions of the *Rokeby* copyright (HG 105). As Grierson notes, 'Few but Scott could have written a poem of this kind under the circumstances of distraction, haste, and increasing anxiety in which *Rokeby* took shape' (HG 106). He was buying a house he could not afford, and staring bankruptcy in the face with the imminent collapse of John Ballantyne & Co. Moreover, Britain itself seemed on the brink of unimaginable chaos and catastrophes. *Rokeby*'s opening – a man in a castle, waiting for news of a momentous battle being fought just over the horizon – was very much Scott's situation for most of 1812.

The times were anxious. In June 1812 America was added to Britain's enemies. The unnecessary war was triggered by American anger at the blockade of Europe, which damaged her international trade. Two years of nautical skirmishing precipitated a depression in the textile industry which, together with the inflation of food prices, led to civil disturbance. Glasgow was hit particularly hard, as was the whole of the industrial north. There was machine-breaking and rebellion. Scott told Southey in June 1812: 'You are quite right in apprehending a *Jacquerie*; the country is mined below our feet' (*Lett.* 3. 125). The Prime Minister, Spencer Percival, had been assassinated on 11 May 1812. Scott assisted in apprehending agitators ('rascals') among the weavers of Galashiels, the industrial town near Melrose, later in the same month (EJ 393–4).

Gradually, the tide of success on the mainland of Europe overtook domestic anxieties. Riding the crest of British victories, *The Vision of Don Roderick* went through three editions. The great victory of Salamanca was celebrated in August 1812 with bonfires and a fête at Abbotsford. 'The people – at least my subjects danced almost the whole night', Scott, already very much the laird, told Lady Abercorn (*Lett.* 3. 156). The retreat from Moscow and the final collapse of Napoleon in December confirmed a sense of total victory: 'Pereat iste!' Scott exulted (EJ 395). He charged at the last stanzas of his poem 'in my old Cossack manner' (EJ 397) with an honorary Russian simile.

Rokeby is the first of Scott's narrative poems in which a member of his family was not somehow woven into the action. Psycho-biographically, *Rokeby* is nonetheless among the most revealing of his works. Williamina

Belsches had died in 1810, and Scott depicts the 'lady who is now no more', his love of 1796, in the character of Matilda. Scott evidently felt old with the death of Williamina. In his 1830 afterword, he makes some symptomatic chronological errors describing the personal background to *Rokeby*'s composition:

> In the meantime years crept on, and not without their usual depredations on the passing generation; my sons had arrived at the age when the paternal home was no longer their best abode, as both were destined to active life. The field-sports, to which I was peculiarly attached, had now less interest, and were replaced by other amusements of a more quiet character. (JLR 379)

Scott was barely forty, and his sons were eleven and six years old when he wrote *Rokeby*. Scott misrepresents himself here as a man of sixty or more, and his sons grown up. What he implies by this (apparently unconscious) error is that in 1813 his sexual life was over. His marriage, after the birth of Charles in 1805 and Mrs Scott's invalidism, was blank, one guesses. The death of Williamina clinched this sense of premature superannuation.

The poetic materials out of which *Rokeby*'s narrative is put together are well below Scott's best. The verse is frequently abysmal, with clumping rhyme and syntax wrenched to get homophonic monosyllables to the end of the line. Compare the following passage from *Rokeby* with one from *The Lay of the Last Minstrel*:

> Now, through the wood's dark mazes past,
> The opening lawn he reach'd at last,
> Where, silver'd by the moonlight ray,
> The ancient Hall before him lay.
>
> *Rokeby*, V. 3

> Now, slow and faint, he led the way,
> Where, cloister'd round, the garden lay,
> The pillar'd arches were over their head,
> And beneath their feet were the bones of the dead.
>
> *Lay*, II. 7

The artful irregularity of the second passage with its meandering last line shows a poet trying harder than the author of *Rokeby*.

One is used to holes in Scott's poems, but those in *Rokeby* gape like chasms. It is impossible to work out the details of the poem's marriages (Rokeby's to Philip's sister, Philip's to his Irish princess). If Philip and Rokeby fought with Essex in 1599, they cannot have been much use to their respective commanders at the Battle of Marston Moor in 1644. (Philip, particularly, is an extremely vigorous seventy-year-old.) How, exactly, does Edmund of Winston – sly as he is – contrive to open the postern gate to Rokeby Hall while the whole company is watching him go through his extensive repertoire of Yorkshire ballads?

On the strength of Scott's name, *Rokeby*'s 'lumbering quartos' (EJ 408) sold well. According to Ballantyne virtually all the first edition of 3,250 copies were sold by the day after publication. Scott claimed that 10,000 'walked off . . . in about three months' (EJ 412). But the poem was notably less of a hit than its predecessor. Johnson estimates that its sales 'never amounted to more than half the dizzy heights that *The Lady of the Lake* attained.' Nevertheless, the Prince Regent admired *Rokeby* immensely and Scott was informed he might use the royal library 'whenever he comes to town' (EJ 409). Royal favour was further confirmed when Henry Pye died in 1813. Scott was offered the Laureateship. His patron, the Duke of Buccleuch, warned him against accepting the honour: 'The Poet Laureate would stick to you and your productions like a Piece of Court Plaister' he told Scott (EJ 427). Scott followed his chief's advice and declined gracefully. He suggested to the authorities that Southey 'my elder brother in the muse' should be considered (in fact, Southey was three years younger than Scott). Southey – who was much the poorer of the two – accepted the post with an effusion of vanity: 'We shall both be remembered hereafter, and ill betide him who shall institute a comparison between us. There has been no race: we have got to the top of the hill by different paths' (*PLB*, 80).

Alongside *Rokeby* Scott made time to write (or dig up from his earlier writing, as Grierson suspects; HG 105) an Arthurian fantasy, *The Bridal of Triermain*. A conscious exercise in 'romanticism', the poem has a complex narrative layering. In the present a poor young poet, Arthur, is wooing Lucy ('Noble in birth, in fortunes high / She for whom lords and barons sigh'). He hopes to marry her, and his poem is designed to further his courtship. An inset poem goes back six hundred years to the time of Sir Roland de Vaux, who falls in love with a fairy beauty. A second inset poem, told by the wizard Lyulph, pursues the maiden (Gyneth) back to the mythic age of King Arthur, whose half-fairy daughter she is. By a series of trials Roland releases his princess from her spell, and marries her. The poem ends with hope of the same matrimonial outcome for Arthur and Lucy. Triermain, where the poem is set, is a fief of the Barony of Gilsland (the 'place of valleys'). The poem's setting is exactly where, in 1797, Scott won his Charlotte. It requires no great ingenuity to see the poem as a recollection of the impecunious Walter's wooing of his rich and nobly connected sweetheart. Scott evidently chose to publish it as a counterweight to *Rokeby*, which celebrated the other – unsuccessful – love affair with Williamina. Possibly it was designed to mollify Mrs Scott.

Scott's reputation as a poet took some knocks over the years 1812–3. There was a general propensity to laugh at him. Tom Moore, for instance, wondered which rich friend's house Scott was going to versify next (EJ 409). Above all, his status as a poet was damaged by the first two cantos of *Childe Harold* – published on 10 March 1812, the morning that Byron awoke and 'found himself famous'. Scott was that much less famous. By comparison with other Romantic poets, Scott had begun to appear provincial and stay-at-home. He had seen very little of the world – even of his own country. He had never once set foot outside Britain. Strongly influenced by Germany, he had never (unlike Coleridge) gone to that country to absorb its literary culture at first hand. He was disgusted by French Jacobinism, but unlike Wordsworth had never set foot in France. Southey, like Scott, wrote a poem about the Goth king Roderigo, but with the difference that the other poet had spent long periods in Spain and Portugal and knew the languages. Byron – the most intrepid traveller of them all – hit the nail firmly on the head, writing to Moore after being told, in August 1814, that Scott was making a 'great voyage' – to northern Scotland:

> Lord, Lord, If these home-keeping minstrels had crossed your Atlantic or my Mediterranean, and tasted a little open boating in a white squall – or a gale in 'the Gut', – or the 'Bay of Biscay', with no gale at all – how it would enliven and introduce them to a few of the sensations! – to say nothing of an illicit amour or two upon shore, in the way of essay upon the Passions, beginning with simple adultery, and compounding it as they went along. (Byron, *Lett.* 4. 152)

Byron was seventeen years younger but infinitely more the man of the world (in travel and amours) than 'the home-keeping minstrel'. Scott had written a rousing poem about the Peninsular War – particularly the Battle of Albuera (15 May 1811) – without ever having been there. Byron, who had stood on the field of Albuera, was scathing on the subject of 'worthless lays' written about the battle. He disdained to write poems about such 'heroism':

> Enough of Battle's minions! let them play
> Their game of lives, and barter breath for fame:
> Fame that will scarce reanimate their clay,
> Though thousands fall to deck some single name. (I. 44)

As Ruskin pointed out, Byron 'was the first great Englishman who felt the cruelty of war, and, in its cruelty, the shame'. There is a maturity in Byron, for all his youth, that Scott could not aspire to. Of course, Scott did not lose all his readers in March 1812. But his standing was lowered, and his price was reduced. Constable was distinctly disappointed in *Rokeby*. In June 1813 he declined to give the £5,000 Scott asked for a new long poem (*The Lord of the Isles*, as it was to become). It was a new experience for Scott to have his price driven down (EJ 418).

EDITING SWIFT

On remaking his peace with Constable, Scott turned to Swift 'like a dragon' (or so he promised). Completion was, however, interrupted by the mental collapse of his assistant on the project, Henry [Heinrich] Weber. A young refugee who had studied at Jena,[3] Weber had arrived in Edinburgh around

1804 in a condition of abject poverty: he was taken under Scott's wing probably about three years later. He had been born in St Petersburg in 1783 into a community of Moravian Brethren. His mother, however, was English and he himself was apparently bilingual. Weber came to Edinburgh ostensibly to study medicine, although his hope was eventually to make a career in literature.

Weber acted as Scott's amanuensis until 1814, working on the same terms of domestic intimacy as had John Leyden. The Scott family were evidently as fond of him as they had been of his predecessor. He was well qualified to assist his patron. He had a German university background and Scott put numerous literary assignments his way – notably the editing or preparation for press of the works of the Jacobean dramatists, 'Northern Antiquities', heroic sagas, and eastern tales. These were principally intended as grist for James Ballantyne's mill, and Weber was a paragon of industry. Scott – who seems to have been extraordinarily kind and forbearing to his odd assistant – clearly anticipated that after his apprenticeship Weber would, like Leyden, graduate into dignified independence. In addition to his credited editorial tasks, Weber did research and secretarial work for his benefactor during one of the busiest periods of Scott's literary career. He was, apparently, efficient. On his own account, Weber published no less than 24 edited volumes between 1810 and 1814. Despite Lockhart's spiteful contempt ('a mere drudging *German*') Weber was extremely serviceable.

Although Weber may have lacked Leyden's genius he more than equalled his predecessor's eccentricity. After an epic walking tour around Scotland (covering some 2,000 miles as Scott reckons – a distance which strains credulity) Weber returned to Edinburgh at Christmas 1813. Early in the New Year, after the Scotts had returned to the city from Abbotsford, the young man suffered a spectacular nervous breakdown at 39 Castle Street:

> The two men were sitting quietly in the book-lined library at opposite sides of the great desk made on the model of Morritt's huge desk at Rokeby. The winter light began to fail; Scott was just about to ring for candles when he observed the German looking at him with a fierce intensity. 'Weber', he said, 'what's the matter with you?' Weber stood up. 'Mr Scott,' he said, 'you have long insulted me, and I can bear it no longer. I have brought a pair of pistols with me, and must insist on your taking one of them instantly.' (EJ 434, Lock. 2. 377)

According to Lockhart, Scott, with consummate coolness, persuaded the demented Weber to take dinner with the family, smuggled out a message, and eventually had his assistant apprehended and straitjacketed without Mrs Scott ever suspecting how close she was to widowhood. Scott, Lockhart tells us, subsequently supported Weber during the remaining five years of his life, which were passed in asylums for the insane.

There are grounds for being slightly suspicious of some details of the story which, as Gamerschlag notes, 'practically cries out for all sorts of wild

conjectures'. Gamerschlag tentatively fills in some of the gaps. He recon-
structs the long walking tour in the Highlands. It appears that Weber had
been recruited (together with a Gaelic-speaking piper) to accompany a rich
Jamaican gentleman called Johnstone who was an amateur mineralogist. It
was Weber's responsibility to make maps for Johnstone's itinerary in the
rocky Highlands. Scott probably got his amanuensis this commission
through Ellis (who had West Indian contacts). Scott also furnished letters
of introduction to grand people whom Weber and Johnstone might visit. It
seems, however, that Johnstone got drunk and disgraced himself. Scott, as
Gamerschlag deduces, was furious since it reflected badly on him. When
Weber returned to Edinburgh Scott was probably high-handed and ostentatiously curtailed Weber's access to drink at his house. The young man was
hurt, insulted, and ill with a mysterious 'fever'. This was the background to
the dramatic events at Castle Street. After Weber's breakdown, Scott acted
with his usual unobtrusive kindness (he may even have felt remorseful),
'paying the bill for Weber's hospitalization, amounting to eighteen shillings
a week for more than fifteen months' (Gamerschlag, 216–7).

Weber's outburst and collapse delayed Swift still further. Its nineteen
volumes were not finished until summer 1814 – four years past the contract
date. Nor, for all the time it took, did the edition do credit to Scott. His
heart had never been in the project. He originally agreed to do the work on
25 July 1808, undertaking to finish in two years. Almost immediately, he
regretted the commitment. Just four months after he is found telling
Murray 'I now heartily wish it had never commenced' (*Lett.* 2. 125). He
pictured the Swift edition as a second old man of the sea (the first being the
inconveniently long-lived Home.) Scott wilfully dragged his feet, either to
induce Constable to revoke the contract, or transfer it to John Ballantyne.
Constable, however, declined to unclasp his legs from Scott's neck.

Scott's procedures in preparing his edition hovered between the lazy
and the downright plagiaristic. John Nichols's third edition of Swift's works
had been published in 1808 in nineteen volumes. Presumably the only
justification for another nineteen-volume edition within two years was that
it should be different. But Scott reproduced the other scholar's texts 'almost completely untouched'.[4] Johnson's compliment that 'little scholarly
investigation had been done on Swift, and Scott's industry had achieved a
valuable pioneer job' (EJ 458) is very wide of the mark. Scott used the
actual printed pages of Nichols's edition and sent them – often virtually
unmarked – to his own printer. (It was a minor inconvenience that in places
he was obliged to use Nichols's earlier 1801 edition, because parts of the
'1808' were not available.) Scott also cannibalized Nichols's notes – often
without change, or with minuscule additions. As Lee H. Potter puts it, 'what
appears in Scott's edition to be Scott's work is not always his work at all.'
Scott's manipulation of Nichols's notes was, according to Potter, 'un-
seemly'. In his apparatus Scott made no acknowledgement of the extent of
his debt and to compound the offence misspelled 'Nichols' ('Mr Nicol') in
a perfunctory reference to the other scholar's 'labour' in his preface. When
he saw Scott's edition, Nichols was justifiably indignant at work which, as he

ironically understated it, 'is somewhat similar to mine' (Potter, 263) and had earned three times as much.

After Swift, and the completion of the thirteen-volume 'Somers's Tracts' (1809–12), Scott avoided such massive editorial tasks. Even his energies were insufficient to continue as a sideline what for lesser men would have been a full-time occupation. 'Massive' does not overstate the case. Dryden, Sadler, Somers, the volumes of drama on which he assisted Weber, Swift, and the 'Border Antiquities' (to take the multi-volume projects only) represented some sixty-three large volumes in less than ten years. Single-volume projects bring the number up to around seventy. Although he subsequently drew in his horns as an editor, Scott continued his editorial work virtually to the end (after 1822 mainly under the auspices of the Bannatyne Club.) In all, this department of his activities is equivalent to what G. A. M. Wood aptly calls 'an editorial factory'.[5]

As is evident from the Swift venture, Scott had his limitations as an editor. His interests were so widely dispersed that he could not be meticulous. He lacked the obsessive attention to detail that ruthlessly single-minded editors brought to their work. Scott's strongest achievements are where he had the work of a reliable predecessor to build on, such as Malone or Nichols. Alternatively, Scott scored high when he had resourceful scholarly assistants to help with editorial chores – such as Leyden, Weber or Arthur Clifford (Scott's collaborator on Sadler's 'Life and Letters').

Leyden was clearly the best of these 'coadjutors' and their *Sir Tristrem* is the most durable of Scott's scholarly editorial ventures. But even Leyden was not entirely reliable. His transcription of the romance has been found by later scholars to 'swarm with errors' (Ball, 35). Leyden it seems had a defective knowledge of Middle English, and allowed the printers to further botch the text. Moreover, the whole project was based on a false theory which originated with Scott.

Where Scott was working by himself, he could go very wrong indeed, as in his 1808 edition of the 'Memoirs' of Captain Carleton. Scott mistakenly presumed this narrative to be a genuine autobiography. Later scholars have identified it as a work of fiction and attributed it to Defoe (other authorities less plausibly attribute it to Swift). Scott's misunderstanding began with a scholarly howler. The book was originally published in 1728, but Scott used the 1743 text, which he erroneously took for the first edition.[6] By 1743 Defoe was long dead and Swift had lost his mind; so the possibility of attributing it to either of them did not occur to him. It is not a mistake Scott would have made had he been able to devote all, or even a worthwhile portion, of his time to scholarly editing.

MYSTERIES OF *WAVERLEY*

Towards the end of his life, in 1829, Scott was to launch his Magnum Opus – the 'improved' edition of the *Waverley* novels. Textual changes were made,

but mainly the well-loved stories were improved by publisher's embellish-
ment and by an *apparatus criticus* supplied by Scott, paternally surveying his
youthful ebullitions from the stance of the wisdom he had acquired after
the crash of 1826. In his afterwords, prefaces, appendices and notes Scott
made an elaborate show of opening up his bag of tricks to the reader. Now
the 'secret' of the *Waverley* novels could be told. 'It remains to be tried',
Scott noted wryly, 'whether the public (like a child to whom a watch is
shown) will, after having been satiated with looking at the outside, acquire
some new interest in the object when it is opened and the internal machinery displayed to them' (1. xxxiv).

As part of this opening-up Scott wrote a new introduction to *Waverley*,
explaining how the great work came into being. It is a remarkable document, if only for its fantastic modesty. As he tells it, Scott was the Inspector
Clouseau of fiction. He blundered into greatness looking – surreally
enough – for fishhooks. This, however, is to anticipate. Before one arrives
at the inspirational red hackle, there are some awkward chronological
contradictions. According to what Scott writes in 1829, 'the Highland
scenery and customs made so favourable an impression in the poem called
The Lady of the Lake that I was induced to think of attempting something of
the same kind in prose' (1. xx). But this must have been after May 1810,
when the Highland poem was published. Nevertheless, Scott claims that
'about the year 1805' (i.e. five years earlier) he 'threw together' some seven
chapters of *Waverley* – then a tale of '50 years since' (the numbers do not
add up – this would make *Waverley* a tale of 1755). 'A critical friend'
(William Erskine?) to whom he showed the draft did not like what he read
and it was 'thrown aside' (1. xx).

There is no clear suggestion in these early chapters that Edward
Waverley will go into the Highlands. And it is only by unconvincing artifice,
in chapter 16, that Edward goes to the far north: some of the Baron's cattle
are stolen by way of 'blackmail', there is some explanation of Celtic *mores*
and the young English hero 'inquired whether it was possible to make with
safety an excursion into the neighbouring Highlands, whose dusky barrier
of mountains had already excited his wish to penetrate beyond them' (1.
140). Common-sense suggests that a prudent host would respond, with
utmost firmness, 'No, by God, it is certainly not safe for English officers in
the dragoons to go visiting bandits in their lairs, or rebellious chieftains
meditating war against England.' But Edward is sent off. One can perhaps
make sense of the perplexing *Lady of the Lake* comment by supposing it to
refer to the later, Highland chapters of the novel, which were an afterthought (after May 1810, that is).

More accidents crowded in on the slow genesis of *Waverley*. In 1807–8,
Murray asked Scott to conclude Joseph Strutt's hyper-antiquarian novel,
Queenhoo Hall. (Strutt had died in 1802.) Reading Strutt's tale of fifteenth-
century England jogged Scott's memory about his own incomplete manuscript. The Dryasdust pedantry and didactic historicism of *Queenhoo Hall*
also suggested better ways of writing historical fiction. Scott revolved in his

mind 'a similar work', but one which might be 'more light and obvious to general comprehension' (1. xxiii).

There then occurred the famous episode of the 'old writing-desk'; one of the hoarier creation myths of nineteenth-century literature. When he decided not to proceed with the *ur-Waverley* Scott stored the manuscript (i.e. the opening seven-or-so chapters) in a writing desk. On taking up residence at Abbotsford in May 1812, new and more elegant furniture was procured for his study. The old writing desk was thrown into an attic. The manuscript was 'entirely forgotten' and 'mislaid for several years' (1. xxi). Fate, in the shape of uncaught salmon, intervened. In autumn 1813, as Scott recalls, 'I happened to want some fishing-tackle for the use of a guest [John Richardson, a fanatic angler] when it occurred to me to search the old writing-desk already mentioned, in which I used to keep articles of that nature. I got access to it with some difficulty; and in looking for lines and flies, the long-lost manuscript presented itself. I immediately set to work to complete it according to my original purpose' (1. xxiv).

The 'improved' Black edition of *Waverley* is embellished by a picture of the fateful writing desk by David Roberts, RA. The volume has another oil painting by C. M. Hardie, RSA, showing Scott rummaging. There is a ruminative look on his face as he gazes at the packet he has just redis-covered. The desk shares the foreground with rods and the faithful hound Maida. Lockhart gives a full genealogy of this cradle of nineteenth-century fiction. The piece was 'given to [Scott] by William Laidlaw . . . The desk is now a treasured possession of his grandson, Mr W. L. Carruthers, of Inver-ness' (Lock. 2. 392). Like Jack Worthing's handbag (which also once con-tained a three-volume novel), it is fondly enshrined.

The reading public have always loved the '*Waverley* and fishing tackle' story. Recently, however, scholars have become wary about taking Scott's and Lockhart's versions of such episodes too faithfully. One can point small-mindedly to some discrepancies in Scott's account. *Waverley* was adver-tised by Longman as forthcoming in August 1810 with a view, presumably, to bringing the work out that winter. James Ballantyne was seriously con-sulted in September 1810 on the Scotch novel project. He was not at all enthusiastic: 'Perhaps your own reflections', he told Scott, 'are rather too often mixed with the narrative' (Lock. 2. 307). (A sagacious observation, which Scott heeded in later composition of the novel.) Evidently, Ballantyne was shown the same old manuscript chapters – now rather dog-eared, one would think. If Scott is to be believed, they must have come out of the desk and gone back in again.

The critic Peter Garside has been most radical in discounting the re-ceived version of *Waverley*'s genesis.[7] From internal evidence (such things as Scott's opening allusions to current popular fiction, and watermarks on the manuscript paper) Garside deduces a two-part composition. *Waverley* was – he proposes – seriously embarked on in late 1810. Scott – as he records – was inspired by the success of the northern Scottish setting of *The Lady of the Lake*. He and Mrs Scott went to the scenes in which the Highland chapters of *Waverley* are set in summer 1810. The seven chapters – or possibly substantially more – were written, presumably shortly after the trip, shown to Ballantyne, disapproved of, put away; probably for rewriting rather than oblivion (hence Longman's August 1810 advertisement). The move to Abbotsford intervened, together with Tom's troubles and a thousand other things. In June 1811, Scott secured an offer of 3,000 guineas for *Rokeby*. 'Its relative failure two years later,' Garside surmises, '*pace* the legendary search for fishing tackle, determined that the "fragment" should be published' (Garside, 48).

Later stages of the novel's composition are less controversial. Scott confessed that he was 'too indolent . . . to attempt to write [the opening] anew' (EJ 429) and simply again dangled the yellowing pages, unchanged, in front of James Ballantyne's nose in 1813. This time he was given encouragement and he dashed off the first volume between October 1813 and January 1814. The proof sheets of this volume (which Ballantyne set up as they were written) were read aloud to a gathering of friends by William Erskine. It held them all night and Erskine reversed his earlier opinion and predicted that *Waverley* 'would prove the most popular of all [Scott's] writings' (Lock. 2. 390). On the basis of this first volume (transcribed by an unrecognizable hand) the project was sold to Constable in the new year of 1814. There was no indication of authorship – although the publisher was in no doubt that Scott was the man and would never have entertained the proposition otherwise. £1,000 was demanded and a cautious counter-offer of £700 returned. The parties eventually agreed on no advance and half profits for *Waverley*, the standard contract for works with uncertain prospects. The second two volumes were then written at blurring speed, in three weeks in June 1814. They were delivered on 1 July and published by Constable six days later. *Waverley* cost a guinea, and came out in three 12mo volumes (i.e. pocket-book size).

Scott told Morritt (one of his confidants as to 'the author of *Waverley*', the others being James Ballantyne and Erskine, but not, as yet, Constable) that he had 'fun' in the completion of *Waverley* (Lock. 2. 392). Perversely Lockhart's mythopoeia has enshrined a contrary image of Scott at work on *Waverley*, one of arduous, drudging labour. One June night in 1814, as Lockhart alleged, four years before he formally met Scott, he was visiting an advocate friend, William Menzies, in George Street, which cuts Castle Street (where Scott lived in town) at right angles. The young men made merry:

> When my companion's worthy father and uncle, after seeing two or three bottles go round, left the juveniles to themselves, the weather being hot, we adjourned to a library which had one large window looking northwards. After carousing here for an hour or more, I observed that a shade had come over the aspect of my friend, who happened to be placed immediately opposite to myself, and said something that intimated a fear of his being unwell. 'No,' said he, 'I shall be well enough presently, if you will only let me sit where you are, and take my chair; for there is a confounded hand in sight of me here, which has often bothered me before, and now it won't let me fill my glass with

a good will.' I rose to change places with him accordingly, and he pointed out to me this hand which, like the writing on Belshazzar's wall, disturbed his hour of hilarity, 'Since we have sat down,' he said, 'I have been watching it – it fascinates my eye – it never stops – page after page is finished and thrown on that heap of MS., and still it goes on unwearied – and so it will be till candles are brought in, and God knows how long after that. It is the same every night – I can't stand the sight of it when I am not at my books.' – 'Some stupid, dogged, engrossing clerk, probably,' exclaimed myself or some other giddy youth in our society. 'No, boys,' said our host, 'I well know whose hand it is –'tis Walter Scott's'. (Lock. 2. 394)

It is one of the most famous anecdotes in literary history. 'The Hand' went on to become an icon. It was taken over by the 'Waverley Pen' manufacturers, and for over half a century (well into the 1960s, as I recall) a huge billboard of Scott's dismembered writing hand stood on the firm's wall, just behind the Tron Kirk.

Even if Lockhart were not notorious for pious inventions about Scott, there would be something suspicious about the story. If you pace the distance between 39 Castle Street and the nearest houses in George Street, the angle means that the hand must have been hundreds of feet away. It is impossible clearly to perceive an object of nine inches or so from that distance without a telescope. Moreover, the friend Menzies whom Lockhart describes himself as visiting did not live in George Street until Whitsunday 1818, by which time Lockhart had met Scott and had visited 39 Castle Street (Hart, 237). There does, in fact, seem to have been a 'hand' episode (that is, Scott was often observed working by neighbours in his study). But it belongs to the period five years later, when he was writing three novels a year to pay for Abbotsford and when the no longer so young Lockhart was interested in another Scott hand – that of his future wife Sophia.

Not to pursue the matter, this must be a pious invention, like the famous deathbed speech ('Be good my dears . . .'). Why did Lockhart do it? By retrodating the event to 1814, he presumably intended to counteract the impression Scott gives in his 1829 introduction that his novel was dashed off (e.g. 'The tale of *Waverley* was put together with so little care that I cannot boast of having sketched any distinct plan of the work'; 1. xxiv). Lockhart wished to insert a corrective image of Scott into posterity: a writer who was a model of industry and application for thoughtless young dogs like himself.

One would rather retain Scott's version, that writing *Waverley* was fun. Poetry was no longer fun. *The Lord of the Isles* – his last effort in narrative poetry – was agonizingly hard work: 'The *peine forte et dure*', he told Terry, 'is nothing in comparison to being obliged to grind verses; and so devilish repulsive is my disposition, that I can never put my wheel into constant and regular motion, till Ballantyne's devil claps in his proofs' (*Lett.* 3. 514; Millgate, 64–5). The hand of the minstrel seems to have been very listless in 1814.

About one thing – the identity of the author – Scott was morbidly careful. It was his habit with novels to have Ballantyne copy the manuscript in another hand before it went to press. He explained that 'I have certain particular reasons for being secret over this' (EJ 436). What were his certain particular reasons? Constable was not fooled. Early reviewers were not deceived, nor were Jane Austen, Maria Edgeworth, nor most of the cultivated population of Edinburgh. The mystery about the author of *Waverley* is nothing compared to the mystery of why the author of *Waverley* persisted in the ruse. Anonymous authorship was not, of course, Scott's invention. It was a familiar gimmick in fiction.   J. M. S. Tompkins notes that it was routine in the preceding century for ' "gentlemen" dabbling in novels'. But Tompkins also notes that 'the practice gradually declined as the standing of the novel became more assured, and by the end of the [eighteenth] century the learned professions were cheerfully acknowledging their indiscretions.'[8]

Not so Scott. He gave a number of reasons at different times, most of which boil down to Shylock's surly 'it was my humour'. A number of explanations have been put forward on his behalf, none of which is absolutely convincing. (1) Scott hated criticism, and Jeffrey's criticism of *Marmion* had particularly stung him. (2) His father would have disapproved of his writing novels, and even as a forty-three-year-old he could not shake off this sense of filial guilt. (3) A sheriff like himself needed to observe 'some solemnity of walk and conduct'. (4) Anonymity was a useful sales gimmick. 'Humour' serves as well as anything.

Waverley and History

Waverley coincides with what Scott and his contemporaries saw as the greatest moment in European history: the allies' final (as they thought) victory over Napoleon in the spring of 1814. During this happy season Edinburgh, like all the cities of Britain, was in a fever of joy. Castle Street was incandescent with candles (EJ 437). Scott wrote of the episode as a Moses on Pisgah: 'My own eyes have seen that which I had scarcely hoped my son's should see, the downfall of the most accursed and relentless military despotism that ever wasted the blood and curbed the faculties of a civilized people' (*Lett.* 3. 428). The long war, which began in 1793 – Scott's first year as an advocate – was over; or so it was believed.

It is instructive to correlate the second burst of *Waverley*'s composition in June 1814 with the geo-political turmoil around Scott as he wrote his novel. The allies' triumphant entry in April into Paris – which Scott had feared would be defended to the last man – immediately preceded *Waverley*'s last chapters describing the victorious English campaign after Culloden. Napoleon abdicated unconditionally on 11 April. Scott clearly lusted for the trial and speedy execution of 'the arch enemy of mankind' (EJ 437). At the same time he was writing, or was about to write, the chapters describing the trial of Fergus by the victorious English at Carlisle. There is, of course, no symmetry here. Scott exulted at the overthrow of the Corsican tyrant while he was ambiguous about the execution of the rebel Highlander (Waverley's 'foster-brother') and the extinction of the Jacobite cause and clan culture. But he was ironist enough to know where he would have been seventy years before – slavering for rebel blood and judicial revenge.

All this is to emphasize that *Waverley* was a timely novel. That it was perceived by its makers to be so is the only explanation for Constable's having rushed it into print so promiscuously, less than a week after getting Scott's final copy, and at the 'dead' time of the year. August was, and is, a notoriously bad month to bring out fiction. In other ways *Waverley* resonates to events of summer 1814 and to Scott's personal dilemmas. It is, at heart, a novel about ideological unsettlement. Edward is a young man born under one flag – that of England and Hanover – who defects to Scotland and the Jacobites. The defection is the more serious, since the two countries are at war. Waverley's change of allegiance is justified by love. His head follows his heart and his attachment (unreciprocated) to Flora recruits him to the Chevalier's cause.

One can make a connection here with Scott's own case. He was British and excessively patriotic during the French wars. He proudly bore the English King's commission. Yet – at the same time – he had a French wife, to whom he was very attached. His son and heir, Walter, was half French. Both Mr and Mrs Scott maintained excellent relations with French officers, prisoners of war, held around Edinburgh during the hostilities. The sense of division must have inspired some curious speculations in Scott's mind.

Waverley hinges on a drama of political choice – 'under which king?' is its motto. The implication is that Edward is free to choose. The notion of ordinary citizens being able to select their rulers, their flag, their government, was something relatively new in historical terms and part of the general drift towards 'Reform'. That a man might – for rational or irrational reasons – turn his coat and not be for that reason a Judas, or a traitor, was relatively recent and still piquant in the early nineteenth century. One of the inescapable deductions from Edward Waverley's wavering character is that if all men were like him there would be no war. His being a Jacobite with Jacobites and a Hanoverian with Hanoverians recalls Buster Keaton's gag in *The General*. The comedian walks between the fighting lines in the civil war with a bisected uniform and flag showing Union colours one side and Rebel on the others. As he marches along, the shooting stops. But, of course, the majority of men in Waverley's (or Keaton's) world are not passive or pacific. They are filled with a passionate intensity. Or they are like the paranoid villagers in Cairnvreckan who want to lynch Edward on the mere ground that he is a stranger ('There was a pause and a whisper among the crowd – "Secretary Murray" – "Lord Lewis Gordon" – "Maybe the Chevalier himself!".'.) As a soldier, Waverley has something of Schweik about him. His main achievement is to survive the history which is being made around him, and which crushes more honourable men like Gardiner and MacIvor.

Scott, one may assume, felt similarly left out of things, but sneakingly glad for having been spared. What, after all, had he *done* with his life? It was a question which he often asked himself in later years. He was a gentleman. He had put his life and services at the disposal of his country, but they had not actually needed his military services or the ultimate sacrifice. He survived the Napoleonic War without a scratch (apart from being kicked in the leg by a horse and hit on the head by a rioter's stone in 1802.) Had he lived in interesting times like 1745 he might have done something great and died for it. But he was never called on. Scott, we may assume, experienced survivor's guilt. But like Waverley he had the consolation that he was at least alive to feel guilty. He took refuge in a therapeutic battery against Edward Waverley, his despised self who was, as he told Morritt, 'a sneaking piece of imbecility' (*Lett.* 3. 478–9).

One of the most extraordinary aspects of Waverley's imbecility is that – as far as one can make out – he wanders through the battlefield offering as little danger to his foe as a dormouse in a tiger's cage. Take, for instance, the highpoint in chapter 47 ('The Conflict') which describes the Battle of Prestonpans. Observing among the mêlée an English officer 'of high rank' Waverley is so struck by 'his tall martial figure' that he decides 'to save him from instant destruction' (2. 148), going so far as to avert the battle-axe of Dugald Mahoney, which is about to fall on Colonel Talbot's head. Waverley, who evidently has a keen eye for insignia of rank, then perceives another English colonel in trouble. 'To save this good and brave man became the instant object of his most anxious exertions' (2. 149). But try as he does, again apparently impeding his own sworn comrades, he can only witness the death of his commander Colonel Gardiner and suffer his *et tu Brute* look. What on earth, one wonders, is Waverley doing on this battlefield, scurrying around trying to save *enemy officers* from being killed? In fact, Scott's account of the battle is remarkably patchy and vague (the event is 'well known', he says by way of excuse). Yet, we learn, the Chevalier 'paid him many compliments on his distinguished bravery.' After the battle, Fergus tells Edward that 'your behaviour is praised by every living person, to the skies, and the Prince is eager to thank you in person, and all our beauties of the White Rose are pulling caps for you' (2. 166). He is a hero – what does this mean but that he did great slaughter among the enemy? 'You know how he fought', Rose later reminds Flora (2. 190). Would that we did. Scott's narrative begs the all-important question, did Waverley kill any Englishmen? Did he even draw English blood?

Either Edward Waverley is the most incompetent warrior who ever lived or – still bearing the King's commission – he killed the King's men. It is not forgivable, or it ought not to be. Had Scott not faded out the battlefield details, it would be very difficult to tolerate Waverley's surviving so comfortably. What reason does he have for turning his coat? He wants to make a good impression on Flora (who despises him) and the Chevalier who, skilled in the meaningless *politesse* of the French court, is civil to him. Before the skirmish at Clifton, Fergus foresees the genocide that will fall on his race: 'They will deserve the gallows as fools if they leave a single clan in the Highlands in a situation to be again troublesome to government. Ay, they will make root-and-branch-work, I warrant them!' (2. 240). And what does Edward do as his foster-family in the north – old men, women and children – are put to the sword in Perthshire? As Flora foresees, he settles down as a happily married and prosperous civilian. He has a full-length portrait of Fergus executed by 'an eminent London artist'. Doubtless, we are to apprehend that his eyes moisten whenever he looks at it after the port has passed once too often at Tully Veolan. 'Poor Fergus! Such a pity his head was cut off and stuck on a pike. And all those children starving. Bless my soul, is that the time? We must join the ladies.'

9

Guy Mannering to *The Antiquary* (1814–1816)

Scott had returned to Constable with considerable hard feelings on either side. Most of Constable's irritation went back to the ill-fated Swift edition. The publisher secretly believed that Scott 'did not choose to keep faith with us' on the Swift contract. He let them down on purpose: possibly, in his more paranoid moments Constable thought that Scott meant to ruin him, so as to advance the Ballantynes. Scott's dilatoriness about Swift was a life-and-death matter for Constable. Although Scott did not know it, the publisher was in terrible financial shape after 1812 and was in no condition to wait on slow authors. The purchase of the *Encyclopaedia Britannica* had involved him in the huge expense of revamping its contents, under Macvey Napier. By 1821, the property would be worth £75,000 and stand as one of the glories of Edinburgh culture. But that was nine years and 33,000 sales in the future. In April 1814, there were widespread failures in the Edinburgh business world which hurt Constable. The banks cut down the firm's credit savagely. It was one of the complex effects of the peace.

Among all this, when the nineteen volumes of the Swift edition finally appeared in July 1814, the response was poor. The London bookbuying world had been 'mad' for Scott when it was originally due. Now he was yesterday's author. Subscriptions for the 1,250 sets were slow in coming. In April, Constable was plotting with Cadell to unload £1,500 worth of 'this most vexatious of all books' (*Lett.* 3. 433) at up to 20 per cent discount on the trade price. To add to his woes, Constable's wife died on 28 October, while he was fighting to save his business in London. His health collapsed at this critical period: rheumatism and gout, exacerbated by alcohol, overeating and stress were the causes.

Constable & Co. was saved in 1814 by the steady sales of volumes like John Sinclair's statistical account of Scotland, a strong back list, the continuing appeal of the *Edinburgh* and – probably above all – by *Waverley*. The novel's success was a bolt from the blue. It had cost nothing other than its modest production costs. (Physically, the first editions are sub-standard and ugly-looking volumes.) Scott had not had a penny in advance. But if *Waverley* may be said to have saved Constable, he, correspondingly, *made* the novel. All through the summer and autumn of 1814, Constable had been slaving to sell shares of his books and copyrights to the 'leviathans of Paternoster Row'. Because he was in London, he contrived to sell *Waverley* there as well. Constable infected Longman, his London co-publisher, with excitement about the new novel and its 'mysterious' author. Of the first impression of 1,000 Longman took no less than 700. When Scott left on 29 July for a yacht trip around northern Scotland he did not apprehend any great thing for the novel. On 15 August, however, Constable shipped off 1,000 of the second edition (of 2,000) to Longman, and the novel at once became the book of the season. It is clear that *Waverley* owed much of its triumph to the skill with which Constable planted it in the English market.

In August 1814 Scott's mind was firmly on his 'great voyage' round northern Scotland, from Leith to Glasgow, taking in all the outlying islands. It would be the longest and most exciting journey he had ever taken in his life. He had free passage with an expedition of commissioners and marine engineers surveying Scotland's most remote lighthouses. Scott would see the far Highlands as a guest of the English government. The chief of the company was the engineer, Robert Stevenson, grandfather of the novelist and inventor of the Scottish lighthouse system. Their vessel, the 'Lighthouse Yacht', had a crew of ten and six guns. Britain was still at war with America (there were, in fact, a couple of alarms about Yankee privateers during the course of the voyage, and the guns were shotted for action). The company on board was distinguished, the most distinguished of all being Walter Scott. (At Greenock flags were flown when it was known that the author of *The Lady of the Lake* was on board; EJ 453.)

The shipboard company was all male. Scott's wife and children were left behind. The primary mission of the voyage was to inspect the safety of shipping lanes. (Scott, of course, was a passenger.) But the voyage also had a disciplinary purpose. The flag would be shown and some order imposed on the more unruly regions of the kingdom. Three of the company were absentee sheriffs of the northern territories, where day-to-day justice was normally delegated to resident substitutes. One of these lords of the Isles, 1814-style, was Scott's good friend William Erskine, Sheriff of Orkney and Zetland, who spent several days in his jurisdiction at Lerwick in the Shetlands. At the head of a contingent of soldiers from the local garrison, Erskine rounded up a selection of 'riotous' sailors who had gone on the razzle while their whaling boats were in port (EJ 443). They were duly punished.

Scott's attitude towards the Shetlanders was frankly that of the proprietor. They were a superior kind of stock. Noting that Shetland could support sheep, the winters being mild, he at once dismissed the idea because 'it would tend to diminish a population invaluable for the supply of our navy' (Lock, 2. 416). Scott, who had spent some two weeks before the mast, was already thinking like the leader of an Admiralty press gang. At other times, he was very much the laird. On Fair-Isle he registered eloquent disgust at the 'utter and inconceivable dirt and sluttery'. How could this peasant condition of life be 'improved'? By rational agriculture of course, and good landlordism. Whatever wastes Scott saw on the islands, his mind converted to rents. Clearance was necessary progress.

Scott made notes for *The Lord of the Isles* on his trip. But he seems never to have given a thought to the fortunes of *Waverley*. His major anxiety was quite other. At Portrush in early September, as the voyage was coming to an end, he heard the news that Harriet, the young Duchess of Buccleuch, had died on 24 August. His grief at the loss of his 'Chieftainess' – the inspirer of the *Lay* – was uncontrollable. 'I wake, or rather rise at six,' he wrote in his diary, 'for I have waked the whole night, or fallen into broken sleeps only to be hag-ridden by the nightmare' (Lock. 2. 505). The Duke, his 'chieftain', 'is more to be pitied than any human being living', he declared (EJ 452). It seems an excessive condolence. More so when one compares it to the phlegmatic way in which Scott accepted his parents' and his siblings' deaths.

The Lord of the Isles (originally 'The Nameless Glen') was actually planned before *Rokeby*, in the financial duress of summer 1813. Some parts of the poem were read to Morritt at an early stage, well before the 1814 voyage to the Isles, and a contract was made with Constable just before departure. The bulk of the six cantos was written in autumn and early winter 1814, on Scott's return in September from the voyage round northern Scotland that furnished much of the precisely observed scenic detail. Composition was finished by 16 December (EJ 465). The poem was published on 8 January 1815, only a few days after Scott penned the last lines.

Edgar Johnson's partisan image of the poem lying 'like a banked fire' (EJ 480) in the poet's mind until the voyage ignited it into roaring flame is flattering. *The Lord of the Isles*'s verses were 'ground' out (Scott's image) with an effort verging on physical pain. A writer famed for his fluency and extemporizing abilities, he was – for perhaps the first time in his life – wrestling with writer's block. Partly, the block was simply Scott's usual problem of having overwhelmed himself with literary commitments. He was writing the novel *Guy Mannering* at breakneck speed at the same time as finishing the poem. Switching between two major works in wholly different genres strained even Scott's facilities

Despite the grinding which went into its making, *The Lord of the Isles* has a clearer story-line than the ineffably opaque *Rokeby*. The reader at least knows what is going on. The origin of *The Lord of the Isles* is evidently the 'Bruce' poem that he had contemplated before embarking on *Rokeby* (EJ 480). There are in fact two plots to the poem – one historical and one romantic – whose imperfect mingling is a main flaw. There are other flaws. *The Lord of the Isles* is a poem of occasionally alarming technical badness. It is mainly written in couplets, the worst of which fall on the page like lead. Syntax is wrenched brutally to get the rhyme word at the end of the line. No extravagance of diction is spared to fill up the syllabic measure. An early

description of Edith, lovelorn Maid of Lorn, is representatively awful. She
is immune to her minstrel, grey Ferrand's, tuneful plucking, since Ronald
loves her not:

> Retired her maiden train among,
> Edith of Lorn received the song,
> But tamed her minstrel's pride had been
> That had her cold demeanour seen;
> For not upon her cheek awoke
> The glow of pride when Flattery spoke,
> Nor could their tenderest numbers bring
> One sigh responsive to the string. (I. 5)

The core of *The Lord of the Isles* is the sixth-canto battle. English readers
– who made up the bulk of Scott's contemporary readers – have never liked
to be reminded of Bannockburn. Nor do they like militant – as opposed to
picturesque – Scottishness. Initial sales were 'disappointing' (EJ 467). In
his 1830 afterword, Scott adopts a crying-all-the-way-to-the-bank attitude.
'Although the poem cannot be said to have made a favourable impression
on the public, the sale of 15,000 copies enabled the author to retreat from
the field with the honours of war' (JLR 474).

As this comment indicates, Scott saw *The Lord of the Isles* as marking the
'close' of his serious poetic career. In the envoi to the poem, he gives an
elegant explanation for hanging up his harp. His young and beautiful
patroness, the Duchess of Buccleuch, was dead – 'all angel now'. The last
two stanzas of *The Lord of the Isles* are a graceful gesture to this inspirational
woman who had given him the idea for his first ambitious narrative poem.
The Lord of the Isles was the minstrel's last lay to his Chieftainess and muse.
Like Greyfriars Bobby, mute devotion until his own death was all that
remained.

Guy Mannering

If we credit Lockhart, 1814 was a year of Herculean literary labour for Scott.
He reportedly polished off the greater part of the 'Life and Works of Swift',
Waverley, *The Lord of the Isles*, two essays for the *Encyclopaedia Britannica*
'Supplement', an edition of *Memorie of the Somervilles*, and *Guy Mannering*
(Lock, 3. 10–1). Grierson suspects some Lockhartian 'manipulation'. At
least one of the essays ('Chivalry') was not written until 1817. More perplexing is the composition of *Guy Mannering*. When he returned from his July
and August trip, Scott was encouraged to follow up *Waverley*'s triumph with
'a second attempt'. It was not merely authorial pride, his 'money troubles
were acute' (HG 123). In October 1814, James Ballantyne had come alarmingly close to being distrained for debt – something that might have
dragged his connection with Scott into public view (EJ 463). The winding

up of John Ballantyne was a slow and expensive business. Wrongly handled, it too might land Scott in the bankruptcy court.

According to Lockhart (drawing on a letter of James Ballantyne's), Scott originally had in mind another novel of 'more ancient manners' (Lock, 3. 12, HG 125). But this project (which sounds like *Old Mortality*) was set aside for *Guy Mannering*, a story of the 1770s. Lockhart lays stress on 'what I have often heard Scott say, that his second novel "was the work of six weeks at a Christmas"' (Lock. 3. 16). That is, *Guy Mannering* was started in mid-November 1814 and finished in time for publication on 24 February 1815 ('by the Author of *Waverley*'). This speed is the more astonishing since – according to Lockhart and Johnson – Scott did not finish composing *The Lord of the Isles* until 16 December (EJ 465). Lockhart asserts that 'it is certain that before *The Lord of the Isles* was published, which took place on the 18th of January 1815, two volumes of *Guy Mannering* had not only been written and copied [by an amanuensis with an unrecognizable hand] but printed' (Lock. 3. 12).

Grierson questions this sequence; more particularly he doubts the break-neck speed of the 'six weeks at Christmas' composition. He points out that Scott already had the name of the novel in mid-October 1814, and was putting it out to bid to publishers. Grierson believes that *The Lord of the Isles* was substantially completed earlier than Lockhart and Johnson assume, and that in the last months of 1814 Scott had only the proofs and notes of his poem to worry about – something that he never found arduous. In the six weeks during which Lockhart claims Scott wrote the whole of *Guy Mannering*, Grierson suggests that he was actually 'giving final form to a story over which he had been brooding for several months and probably composing in the intervals while he waited for the successive proofs of *The Lord of the Isles*' (HG 125).

There is another mystery attached to the origin of *Guy Mannering*. In his 1829 preface Scott ascribes 'the simple narrative on which *Guy Mannering* was originally founded [to] an old servant of my father's, an excellent old Highlander' (1. v). It was this John MacKinlay (about whom we know nothing else) who three decades before told the boy Walter Scott the astrologer's-curse story which opens the novel. Scott retails MacKinlay's story at vivid length in his preface. It later emerged, however, from Lockhart's biographical research, that Scott had the astrologer's story from Joseph Train, a Supervisor of Excise in Galloway. In his spare time Train was an enthusiastic antiquarian and a fanatic admirer of Scott's poetry. Scott came across some of Train's publications just before setting off on his summer voyage to the Isles. On his return, he opened correspondence with the exciseman (on the subject of notes for *The Lord of the Isles*, as Grierson surmises). In a packet sent in early November 1814 Train included the story of the astrologer 'almost in the words placed in the mouth of John McKinlay in the introduction to *Guy Mannering*' (Lock. 3. 4).

There are two possibilities: (1) Scott began *Guy Mannering*, using the John MacKinlay story, and coincidentally received the same story in 'the

1 Walter Scott, aged 6, at Bath, attributed to Abraham
Daniels, 1776. As Lockhart notes, the profile is
'wonderfully like what it was to the last'. (Edinburgh,
Scottish National Portrait Gallery.)

2 Portrait of Walter Scott, painted for his wife Charlotte, by James Saxon, 1805. Scott's bull-terrier Camp is sitting on his knee. This was Lady Scott's favourite representation of her husband. (Edinburgh, Scottish National Portrait Gallery.)

3 Portrait of Walter Scott, commissioned by his publisher Archibald Constable, following the success of *Marmion*, by Sir Henry Raeburn, 1809. Camp is again beside his master, with one of Scott's two greyhounds, either Percy or Douglas. The landscape is that of the Vale of Yarrow. (Edinburgh, Scottish National Portrait Gallery.)

4 Walter Scott finds the MS of *Waverley* by C. M. Hardie. The deerhound Maida is anachronistic. Scott acquired the beast in 1815.

5 'The Abbotsford Family' by Sir David Wilkie, 1817. Scott's family in peasant dress. From left to right: Maida, Mrs Scott, Sophia, Anne, the Laird of Abbotsford, Tom Purdie, Charles, Adam Ferguson (who commissioned the picture), Walter. Abbotsford can be seen distantly. (Edinburgh, Scottish National Portrait Gallery.)

6 'The Discovery of the Regalia of Scotland' by Andrew Geddes, probably 1818. The chest containing the regalia in the Crown Room of the castle was investigated on 4 February 1818 and formally opened the following day. (London, British Museum.)

7 Walter Scott by Sir Francis
Chantrey, 1820–1. According to
Lockhart, the most lifelike
representation of Scott as he was in
his prime. (In the collection of
Abbotsford: Mrs P. M. Maxwell-
Scott.)

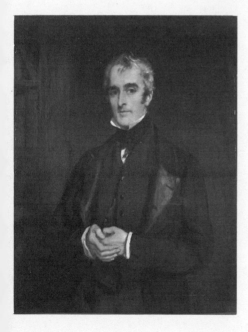

8 Portrait of John Gibson
Lockhart, Scott's son-in-law, by
Sir Francis Grant. (Edinburgh,
Scottish National Portrait
Gallery.)

9 Sir David Wilkie, *The Entrance of George IV at Holyroodhouse*, OM 1184, reproduced by kind permission of The Royal Collection © 1994 Her Majesty the Queen.

10 Walter Scott in 1823 by Sir Henry Raeburn. According to Lockhart, 'a massive strong likeness that grows into favour upon better acquaintance'. (Edinburgh, Scottish National Portrait Gallery.)

11 Walter Scott in 1824 by Sir Edwin Landseer. (Edinburgh, Scottish National Portrait Gallery.)

12 Walter Scott in 1830 by Colvin Smith. (Edinburgh, Scottish National Portrait Gallery.)

13 Walter Scott in 1832 by Sir Edwin Landseer. (Liverpool, Walker Art Gallery: with grateful acknowledgement to The Board of Trustees of the National Museums and Galleries on Merseyside.)

same words' from Train a couple of weeks later. The odds against this are astronomically high. (2) The 'old John MacKinlay' business is a 'fable of composition' (like the 'Gilpin Horner' origin of the *Lay*, or the fishhook genesis of *Waverley*). Scott had the story from Train, and invented the more colourful account involving an old Highland retainer for the delectation of his readers. Lockhart clearly believed the second of these hypotheses, hence his dating the start of the narrative in mid-November, after the point at which Scott is known to have been corresponding with Train. Hence, too, the improbable 'six weeks at Christmas' claim. The genesis of *Guy Mannering* is further complicated by the fact that having started on the astrologer plot (whoever suggested it) Scott promptly changed direction after 'three or four first chapters'. He apologizes elaborately for the alteration in his 1829 introduction without ever explaining what induced him 'to lay his purpose aside'.

Scott broke with Constable over the publication of *Guy Mannering*, despite the publisher's success in marketing *Waverley*. He determined on this occasion to take his goods to market himself and save paying Constable's commission. Via John Ballantyne Scott negotiated the sale of *Guy Mannering* directly with Longmans. It was his intention to wholesale a stock of books already printed by James Ballantyne. He accepted a price of £1,500 (EJ 464) for 2,000 copies (which in the event sold out on the day of publication). Scott added a clause requiring Longman to take £500-worth of John Ballantyne 'trash' (EJ 465). Constable, Scott stipulated, should have the Scottish market share of *Guy Mannering*. The break, he intimated, was nothing permanent.

It is said that the reviews of *Waverley* sold *Guy Mannering*. One could almost go further and say that the reviews of *Waverley* wrote *Guy Mannering*. It was a novel undertaken primarily because Scott wanted to exploit a volatile market while it was still receptive to his wares and while the shock of narrowly averted bankruptcy was still spurring him on. Getting the work on paper was everything. *Guy Mannering* is driven by generative devices whose primary purpose is to fill pages and keep the reader eagerly turning those pages. Mystery is the principal of these devices. *Guy Mannering* is a novel hinged on the outcome of enigmatic prophecy and the dénouement of dark mystery as to identity and the ultimate ownership of valuable property. The story is suspended from the first to the last chapter on the tantalizing question of what will happen and what has happened to the heir of Ellangowan – Henry Bertram alias Vanbeest Brown.

Another device, borrowed from Shakespeare (more particularly the camp scenes in *Henry V*) is rampant garrulity. The world of *Guy Mannering* is inhabited by pathologically talkative characters, each with their own tics, catchwords and formulaic expressions. The text of *Guy Mannering* is a maelstrom of languages, jargons, idiolects, and dialects: the genteel epistolary English of Julia and Matilda, Meg Merrilies's Romany (ancestor of 'flash' – the thieves' argot beloved by Victorian novelists), the racy Border dialect of Dandie Dinmont, Pleydell's playful lawyer jargon interspersed with broad Scots, Gilbert Glossin's legal bureaucratese (frigidly English, indicating a denial of his Scottish roots), Dirk Hatteraick's bastardized Dutch-English, Dominie Sampson's dog Latin (and his overworked catchphrase – 'prodigious!') and Guy Mannering himself, who speaks with all the mannerliness of a Restoration hero. It is astonishing that characters so idiosyncratic in their speech patterns can communicate with each other at all. In its review, the *Quarterly* rather bad-temperedly suggested that *Guy Mannering* might be translated into English (EJ 468).

Extraordinarily – given that he was in such a breakneck hurry to finish the novel – the one thing that Scott did not do in *Guy Mannering* was to imitate himself. It would have seemed easy enough merely to throw off a *Waverley II*. But in a letter Scott told Morritt (now one of his closest confidants) that 'I want to shake myself free of Waverley.' *Guy Mannering* he predicted would be 'much more interesting than Waverley. It is a tale of private life and only varied by the perilous exploits of smugglers and excisemen' (*Lett*, 4. 12–3). Interesting it certainly is, but as a narrative, *Guy Mannering* is one of the patchiest novels ever to enter the canon of British literature. The most intriguing hole in its patchwork is Colonel Mannering's twenty-odd years in India, a hiatus which contains any number of unwritten tales. Scott's declining even to summarize this phase of his hero's life – which comprises duels, adultery and native uprisings – is extraordinarily unsettling to the reader. The other great omission in *Guy Mannering* is world history. The action is set during the period of the climax of the American War, which is referred to only a couple of times in passing, and then in the most laconic way. It is a strange reticence, given the Colonel's military character.

There are other intriguing obliquities. Scott was writing *Guy Mannering* in the period when the Clearances had reached their awful climax. He had himself seen the effects on his northern voyage and was evidently conflicted on the subject. In the Orkneys he called the landowners' dilemma about whether to clear old tenants in order to farm efficiently 'the hardest chapter in Economics; and if I were an Orcadian lord, I feel I should shuffle on with the useless old creatures, in contradiction to my better judgment' (Lock, 2. 456). As a Roxburgh laird – albeit only of a couple of years standing – he should have been of the rational party that approved the evictions. But evidently Scott could not steel himself to the human suffering. This sympathy with the evicted is conveyed in the scenes of Ellangowan's 'root and branch' dispossession of the gipsies (and Meg Merrilies) from their traditional settlements.

> Every door in the hamlet was chalked by the ground-officer, in token of a formal warning to remove at next term. Still, however, they showed no symptoms either of submission or of compliance. At length the term-day, the fatal Martinmas, arrived, and violent measures of ejection were resorted to. A strong posse of peace officers, sufficient to render all resistance vain, charged the inhabitants to depart by noon; and, as they did not obey, the officers, in terms of their warrant, proceeded to unroof the cottages, and pull

down the wretched doors and windows – a summary and effectual mode of
ejection still practised in some parts of Scotland when a tenant proves refractory. (1. 67–8)

One has to wonder with Graham McMaster if the last sentence is an
example of Scott's irony at its bitterest.[1]

WATERLOO

In April 1815 Scott and his family made a long visit to London (EJ 488). It
was partly business. Scott was acting legally for his Highland friends the
Clephanes, one of whose daughters was marrying into the aristocracy (EJ
493). It was on this occasion that Scott met Byron for the first time face to
face. The affront caused by *English Bards* had by now been repaired by
Murray's good offices. Scott had been flattered by Byron's report (via the
publisher) of how much the Prince Regent admired 'the poet of princes'
(EJ 392). He was even more pleased by an inscribed copy of *The Giaour*
which Byron sent him a couple of years later (EJ 462).

There is, however, a misleading Lockhartian spin given to this episode.
According to Lockhart (adapting James Ballantyne's memorandum),
shortly after the publication of *The Lord of the Isles* (i.e. in January 1815)
James called at Castle Street:

> and found on the table a copy of the *Giaour*, which [Scott] seemed to have
> been reading. Having an enthusiastic young lady in my house, I asked him if
> I might carry the book home with me, but chancing to glance on the auto-
> graph blazon, 'To the Monarch of Parnassus from one of his subjects', in-
> stantly retracted my request, and said I had not observed Lord Byron's
> inscription before. 'What inscription?' said he; 'O yes, I had forgot, but
> inscription or no inscription, you are equally welcome.' I again took it up, and
> he continued – 'James, Byron hits the mark where I don't even pretend to
> fledge my arrow'. (Lock. 3. 22)

In 'January' according to Lockhart (Lock. 3. 22), Scott wrote to Byron
thanking the other poet for the *Giaour* ('your high-spirited Turkish fragment'), and the 'Parnassus' compliment. He was particularly glad to have
the presentation copy because 'I had lent my first edition' (Lock. 3. 25). He
had not replied earlier because he was away from Edinburgh. On the
following page, Lockhart records (without dating) a 'Homeric exchange'
of gifts: a gold-mounted Turkish dagger from Scott to Byron; a silver Greek
burial urn from Byron to Scott.

Lockhart's narrative should be read as follows: Scott received an
unsolicited report from Byron (via Murray) informing him of the Prince
Regent's high opinion of *The Lady of the Lake*. He subsequently received a
wholly unexpected gift from Byron (the inscribed *Giaour*) in January 1815,
shortly before going down to London. So unexpected was it, that he did not

realize he had it. He wrote to thank Byron, after Ballantyne accidentally brought the other poet's inscription to his attention. He was inspired by Byron's compliment (and his rudeness in failing immediately to acknowledge it) to reciprocate with an appropriate Turkish gift, starting the sequence of *politesse* that continued with Byron's urn, the meetings in London, and Scott's glowing review of the third canto of *Childe Harold* (a poem whose moral and political sentiments were anathema to him) in late 1816.

In fact, what can be guessed and shown to have happened is as follows. Scott (I guess) gave a copy of *The Lady of the Lake* (published by John Ballantyne, Bookseller to the Regent) to Murray to take to the Regent: Murray asked Byron to do the favour for him. Scott subsequently sent the Turkish dagger to Byron, unsolicited, in October 1814 (this date is known, from Byron records). On receiving this, Byron dispatched his presentation copy of the *Giaour* (a ninth edition), with the handsome inscription, and followed it up later with the Greek burial urn. The main point is that the initiative in all this came from Scott; he was, unlike the Scott of Lockhart's version, making conciliatory overtures to Byron, not receiving them.

An encounter in London crowned this elaborate minuet of courtesy. Writing in response to Moore's requests for information for his life of Byron, Scott a decade later described the episode as something extraordinarily intimate:

> It was in the spring of 1815, that, chancing to be in London, I had the advantage of a personal introduction to Lord Byron . . . I found Lord Byron in the highest degree courteous, and even kind. We met for an hour or two almost daily, in Mr Murray's drawing room, and found a great deal to say to each other. We also met frequently in parties and evening society, so that for about two months I had the advantage of a considerable intimacy with this distinguished individual. Our sentiments agreed a good deal, except upon the subjects of religion and politics, upon neither of which I was inclined to believe that Lord Byron entertained very fixed opinions. (Lock. 2. 28–9)

Together with a fleeting dinner party in September 1815 (on Scott's return from Waterloo), this spring 1815 encounter constitutes the only time the two most popular poets of the age met. On the basis of Scott's testimony, subsequent critics have deduced that – despite their extreme political differences – the relationship was exceptionally cordial. The evidence suggests it was polite, but tense and distant.

The immediate consequences of the spring encounter were, as it happened, embarrassing to Scott. On one meeting with Byron, just before he returned to Scotland, he evidently recited virtually the whole of 'Christabel' to the other poet, who was deeply struck by it. Byron also realized that Coleridge's 'Pindaric measure' had been picked up in his own *Siege of Corinth* – an influence he had legitimately (as he thought) taken from a published source, Scott's *Lay*. On 18 October 1815, Byron wrote to Coleridge, exculpating himself from plagiarizing 'Christabel' (and implicitly laying the offence at Scott's door). He explained to Coleridge that

'Last Spring I saw Walter Scott – he repeated to me a considerable portion of an unpublished poem of yours' (Byron *Lett.* 4. 318). Coleridge was evidently angry and accused Scott of plagiarism. Byron conceded, 'I cannot contradict your statement' (Byron *Lett.* 4. 321), although he went to great lengths to urge how well disposed Scott was towards the other poet. It was all patched up by Byron's generously using his good offices to persuade Murray to publish the incomplete 'Christabel' in 1816.

Byron was not the only celebrity Scott met on this jubilant London trip. He called on Wordsworth and the novelist Amelia Opie (EJ 493). He hobnobbed with the Prince Regent, to whom he had sent a copy of *The Lord of the Isles*. As a signal honour, the poet ('Walter') was invited to Carlton House and overwhelmed by the famous 'manners' at a 'snug little dinner' (EJ 489). Scott had the knack of flattering great men without seeming to fawn. His modest but manly manner, his braw Scotch stories, and his rollicking verse, above all his fealty to his 'Chief', all went down very well with the first gentleman in Europe. But, as with the Byron 'intimacy', one has to beware a retrospective glow cast over this encounter by Scott, anecdotalizing in later life, and by Lockhart. Lockhart got from Scott the information that the Prince had sung songs at the dinner. But the other guests at the function whom Lockhart contacted could not recall the episode (which is not entirely plausible). Having heard the information from Scott's own lips, however, Lockhart was loath to sacrifice it. So he invented – without any warrant – a second dinner at 'Carlton House, when the party was a still smaller one than before, and the merriment if possible still more free' (Lock. 2. 37). Johnson follows suit with his talk of 'an even more select dinner party, at which the Regent sang songs, told stories, and continued affectionately to call Scott by his first name' (EJ 491). There was, as Francis Hart has convincingly demonstrated, no such second dinner (Hart, 182–3).

Scott and his family returned to Scotland on 11 June, just seven days before the great battle in Belgium. After Waterloo he was 'set on fire' (Lock. 3. 40) by a letter shown him from a surgeon friend, Charles Bell. Bell vividly described post-battle Brussels, with its 20,000 wounded men, and soldiers everywhere. Scott saw a last opportunity to witness 'real warfare' (Lock. 3. 45) and wear his cavalry-officer's uniform. He resolved to make a trip to the field of combat, while it was still warm with battle.[2]

Scott was one of the first wave of British tourists. Like the whole of the British civilian population, he had been cooped up all his adult life by the Napoleonic Wars. Fluent in French, with a French wife, cosmopolitan in his culture, he had never been to France: had never in fact left Britain's shores except for his 1814 yachting expedition round Orkney and the Western Isles. On 27 July, he took a coach to Cambridge, hired a cutter from Harwich to Holland, travelling thence to Brussels and finally Paris. Scott took with him a retinue of three younger Scots: his kinsman John Scott of Gala, Alexander Pringle of Whytbank and the advocate Robert Bruce. Mrs Scott did not accompany him. Whether she did not care to return to her native country, was indisposed or too busy with the children is unclear.

Before he left, Scott arranged through John Ballantyne to subsidize his tour with *Paul's Letters to his Kinsfolk*, a travel book. It would comprise 'a series of letters on a peculiar plan'. The letters are sent by a shrewd but provincial Scot (a bachelor, oddly), writing home to a little group of congenial spirits in his 'old mansion house': a spinster sister, a statistical laird, a rural minister, and a brother who is a veteran on half pay (the last apparently based on John Scott). Scott's assumption of a country-bumpkin persona is symptomatic of a certain uneasiness at his unfamiliarity with foreign parts. But the general tone of *Paul's Letters* and their sentiments are indistinguishable from Scott's own, once they are into their stride. And – for all the ostentatious small-town eye-popping – they make lively reportage. Particularly effective is Scott's analysis of the battle itself in Letter 8. But the account is marred by the author's chauvinistic harping on the French atrocities. Napoleon's army, according to Scott, 'had renounced the common rules of war, and bonds of social amity, and become ambitious of distinguishing themselves as enemies to the human species' (*Prose* 5. 143).

More affecting is Scott's sheer wonder at the violence of modern warfare. The author of *Marmion*, and the avid collector of old weaponry, was genuinely appalled at the reality of what steel could do to flesh. 'Had not the ghastly evidences remained on the field,' he records, 'many of the blows dealt upon this occasion [of the early cavalry engagements] would have seemed borrowed from the annals of knight-errantry, for several of the corpses exhibited heads cloven to the chine, severed from the shoulders' (*Prose* 5. 116). The coolness and bravery of the British is everywhere extolled. Wellington's only problem, in Scott's analysis, was not to have enough of his countrymen to field against the French; 'with 80,000 British troops it is probable the battle would not have lasted two hours' (*Prose* 5. 122). The cowardice of 'les braves Belges' and the contemptible Hanoverians was, by contrast, total (*Prose* 5. 120). *Paul's Letters* finish with a revealing chapter in which Scott tendentiously contrasts the French system of 'free representation' with the more 'gradated' system of Britain suffrage, grounded as it was in property and land holding, and social rank. Like most of his middle-class countrymen, Scott conceived the British class system as having received a divine vindication by the victory of Waterloo. The letters were published in early January 1816, and healthily sold some 9,000 copies at 12s a volume (EJ 512).

In Paris Scott was swept up in the post-victory euphoria and celebration. There were daily parades, banquets, fêtes, presentations of honours. Kings and rulers had congregated to feast in the enemy's stronghold. The author of *The Lady of the Lake* had introductions to great people such as Lord Cathcart, the former ambassador to Russia, who could in turn introduce him to supremely great people, like the Czar and Wellington.

But there were uncomfortable rubs as well. Scott's air could be misleading in a city where every other man was a limping hero. Sometimes Scott, by rising to the occasion, could give quite the wrong impression. Among his luggage he had brought his territorial army uniform. At a dinner given by

Cathcart, he was presented to Czar Alexander. 'Scott appeared,' as Lockhart records, in the blue and red dress of the Edinburgh Light Horse:

> The Czar's first question, glancing at his lameness, was 'In what affair were you wounded?' Scott signified that he suffered from a natural infirmity; upon which the Emperor said, 'I thought Lord Cathcart mentioned that you had served.' Scott observed that the Earl looked a little embarrassed at this, and promptly answered, 'Oh yes; in a certain sense I have served – that is, in the yeomanry cavalry; a home force resembling the Landwehr, or Landsturm.' – 'Under what commander?' – 'Sous M. le Chevalier Rae.' – 'Were you ever engaged?' – 'In some slight actions – such as the battle of the Cross Causeway and the affair of Moredun Mill'. (Lock. 3. 60)

At this point, Cathcart intervened to change the subject. But Scott's private joke must have had a sharp edge for its maker. Crosscauseway was the street next to George Square where he fought bickers as a child. Moredun Mill was where he had helped put down starving and unarmed Scottish rioters.

The encounter with the Duke, the man whom Scott admired above all other mortals, was similarly tinged with author's embarrassment. Scott recalled the event for James Ballantyne, telling him

> that he might now say he had seen and conversed with all classes of society, from the palace to the cottage, and including every conceivable shade of science and ignorance, but that he had never felt awed or abashed except in the presence of one man – the Duke of Wellington . . . [Scott] said he beheld in him a great soldier and a great statesman – the greatest of each. When it was suggested [by Ballantyne] that the Duke, on his part, saw before him a great poet and novelist, [Scott] smiled, and said, 'What would the Duke of Wellington think of a few *bits of novels*, which perhaps he had never read, and for which the strong probability is that he would not care a sixpence if he had?'. (Lock. 3. 66)

Ballantyne stoutly denied that his friend had been 'sheepish or embarrassed in the presence of the Duke . . . but unquestionably [the feeling] did exist to a certain extent' (Lock, 3. 66).

In three months, Scott had met the three most famous Britons of the age. The Prince Regent ('Our fat friend') he rather despised, for all his deference now and – more ostentatiously – in 1822. Byron eluded him as a writer who was younger, nobler, worldlier, and even more successful than himself. The Duke put him in his place as a maker of 'bits of novels'. Scott was keenly aware that however successful he might be as an author, he would never matter in the real world, the world that Waterloo had transformed.

Donald Sultana is justified in making a whole book out of Scott's Waterloo jaunt. He was obliged after his 1815 experiences and his brush with world history to take stock, and to redefine himself. Self-administered humility was the main change. In *Guy Mannering* the Scott figure – his surrogate – is a saturnine, military man who has undergone the rigours of active service: a man of the world. In *The Antiquary* the Scott surrogate is a comical, superannuated, cranky windbag, Jonathan Oldbuck of Monkbarns, who has lived out of the main courses of history and society. 'Some years' after Waterloo, 'with gravity, and even sadness' (Lock. 3. 68) Scott told Lockhart an anecdote which symbolizes the change wrought by the Waterloo experience. Scott's sense of his manhood was intimately dependent on the military service that he began in 1797. His 'charger' – the dragoon's terrifying horse – proclaimed his military manliness to the world. One luckless groom had his arm broken and another his leg when they foolishly tried to saddle and ride Captain Scott's mount. But when Scott returned from Waterloo his charger Daisy (a white stallion) looked askance at his master, 'like a devil'. When Scott mounted the beast, he was thrown twice, heavily. But Daisy allowed Scott's man, Tom Purdie, to mount him 'with all manner of gentlemanliness'. 'The thing was inexplicable,' Scott told Lockhart, 'and wars and rumours of war being over, I resolved to have done with such dainty blood. I now stick to a good sober cob' (Lock. 3. 69). Daisy was sold off to John Ballantyne. One reads this as Scott's discharge from the military. He was a cavalryman no more. He made a joke of it, but it was a symbolic passage into fogeyhood.

THE ANTIQUARY

After what had been the longest trip of his adult life, Scott was back at Abbotsford in late September 1815. To commemorate his expedition he published in October a gaudeamus poem – *The Field of Waterloo*. The work was dedicated to the Duchess of Wellington and its profits went to the Waterloo subscription. Constable sold the pamphlet-sized volume at 5s. It was reviewed badly and probably did not relieve much suffering. Nonetheless, it certified Scott's standing as a kind of laureate without the laureateship.

On his return to Scotland, Scott threw himself into furious activity. 1815–6 is one of the most wonderful of his years. It saw the publication of three major works of fiction – *Guy Mannering, The Antiquary*, and the first series of *Tales of My Landlord*, in addition to *Paul's Letters*. In the same period Scott composed most of *Harold the Dauntless* (his last long poem). Eight volumes appeared under Scott's name, his pseudonym, or his anonym, in 1816 alone. He was also in full flow as a journalist. In the October 1815 issue of the *Quarterly* he published a long article that represented his most considered statement to date on the subject of Scotland and race. In the same journal at the same period he published his generous and perceptive review of Jane Austen's *Emma*, which survives to the present day in various anthologized forms as his best known piece of critical writing. Scott also did the 'History' section of the *Edinburgh Annual Register* for 1814–5 (published in 1816).

Need for cash was a main reason for this outpouring. As Eric Quayle puts it, 'the whips of financial necessity were the compelling reason why he drove himself to write ceaselessly in every spare moment he could snatch from his work in court and the social engagements that pressed increasingly upon him' (EQ 97). He was buying land and 'improving' Abbotsford all the time. And as late as 1815, he still had large financial obligations outstanding from the crisis of 1813. (The £4,000 guaranteed by Buccleuch was not yet repaid, for instance.) The neighbouring estate of Kaeside was bought at a cost of £3,400, £400 down, the rest on mortgage (EJ 509).

Scott had meanwhile assumed heavier business burdens. In February 1816 James Ballantyne married. His bride was twenty years younger than he. To put things straight with his wife's family, who were moneyed farmers and distrustful of city businessmen, James's uncleared debts to the printing firm (£3,000 or so, according to Lockhart; Lock. 3. 108) were transferred to Scott as notional 'credits'. Ballantyne then became a salaried 'manager', at £400 p.a. Scott was now drawing all profits, but in return had all the responsibility for uncleared stock and capital investment in the firm.

Scott was able to produce so fluently in 1816 because he had systematized his mode of composition and publication. Contract arrangements were a main part of the system. For the bulk of his novels after *Waverley* (and before the 1826 crash) Scott sold Constable the right to print two-thirds of an edition of 10,000 to 12,000 for a fixed sum (payable in money that Constable did not have, but which he could make out bills for, on the strength of the forthcoming *Waverley* novel). Up to 1822 that sum was usually £3,000; thereafter it was reduced to £2,500. The remaining one third went to James Ballantyne, but a half of this portion also reverted to Scott, as his printer's commission. The copyright also reverted to Scott, to sell again or otherwise 'work' as he saw fit (HG 146). Although Grierson believes that the system was intrinsically rotten – in that it encouraged Scott to draw excessively on future earnings and discouraged Constable from building up a financial core – there is no doubt that it suited everyone, particularly the effortlessly productive author of *Waverley*, extremely well.

Around him there was a protective apparatus which not only brought his wares to market, but acted as a screen to his identity. John Ballantyne served (for commission) as agent and his intermediary with the outside publishing world. James was Scott's editorial adviser and proof-reader. Sandy Ballantyne – a third brother – copied out the manuscripts. Constable, now officially informed of the identity of the author of *Waverley*, was a sworn co-conspirator. Scott had a council of privileged friends in the know, who advised him gratis – Morritt, William Erskine, Louisa Stuart. All were of his own class, or higher, and could be trusted. He himself was the mysterious ghost at the centre of the machine. If there was a fault, it was what Dickens diagnosed on reading Lockhart's *Life* in 1841, that Scott 'never left off'. That is to say, he never learned how to space his works so that his art might mature and his price be driven up by scarcity.

John Ballantyne – the bankrupt of 1813 – had bounced back spectacularly. He was now a successful auctioneer, Edinburgh's answer to Leigh and Sotheby. Auctioneering suited his opportunistic, immoralist character. He had premises and a magnificent counter in Hanover Street. He had built extensions to his 'marine villa' at Trinity (by the Forth) where he could indulge in some very dubious hospitalities (Lock. 3. 259). The stock of the old publishing house which had borne his name (but little of his capital) was being cleared, bit by bit, in codicils to successive deals with Constable and other luckless publishers, and in auctioned-off job lots.

Scott mentions first thoughts for *The Antiquary* in a letter to Morritt of December 1815. 'I have only a very general sketch at present,' he tells his friend, 'But when once I get my pen to the paper it will walk fast enough. I am sometimes tempted to leave it alone and try whether it will not write as well without the assistance of my head as with it – a hopeful prospect for the reader' (*Lett.* 4. 145). Composition of the new novel evidently started at some point just before this date, and proceeded very rapidly. The published work came out in early May 1816. After his flirtation with Longman Scott returned to Constable for this, his third novel, because, as he later put it, the Scottish publisher 'pushed' his books better.

The Antiquary is very much a middle-aged man's novel. The hero, Oldbuck, is a man whose loves and passions are all in the past. Events surrounding the composition of the novel must have made Scott feel even older than his forty-five years. In May 1816 Major John Scott – his last surviving older brother – died. This left only Walter and Tom (exiled in Canada) out of the thirteen children Mrs Scott had borne. At eighty-three, she herself was still alive and hale enough. Scott took his brother's death with his usual stoicism about such things. In a letter to Morritt he observed that '[John's] death under all the circumstances cannot be termd a subject of deep affliction and although we were always on fraternal terms of mutual kindness and goodwill yet our habits of life our taste for society and circles of friends were so totally different that there was less frequent intercourse than our connection and real liking to each other might have occasioned' (*Lett.* 4. 232). Scott and his brother Tom shared the £6,000 estate which their soldier brother left, most of the sum itself left from the legacy of their father (EJ 518).

The Antiquary was published on 4 May 1816. 'After a little pause of hesitation', the novel was a hit. It came to be Scott's favourite, and has always been among his best-loved tales. Jonathan Oldbuck, who dominates the action as the titular antiquary, is in large part a version of Scott himself, crossed with some external eccentricities drawn from George Constable, who had been kind to the little boy all those years ago at Prestonpans. Like Scott, Oldbuck began working life as a younger brother and an apprentice to a 'writer, or attorney' (2. 16). Again like Scott, he fell in love with a noble young lady, who jilted him for a better connected and richer lover.

Monkbarns, like Scott, retreated into antiquarian pursuits for consolation. His father and elder brother died, as did Robert and Walter Scott WS, leaving Oldbuck a modest competence to retire on. Monkbarns is what Scott might have become had he not, on being repulsed by Williamina, thrown himself into life with his rebound marriage to Charlotte. When as a seven-year-old boy Walter first hung on George Constable's extravagant stories, the forty-something gentleman must have seemed a figure of great antiquity. Now Scott himself was forty-something and in his old boyhood.

The laird of Monkbarns ('Monk's Barns' is, incidentally, analogous to 'Abbot's Ford') is, as his name implies, an old buck (as Lovel is both lovable and prone to fall in love). Oldbuck is a mine of queer erudition. By avocation a scholar-lawyer-laird, his energies discharge themselves with manic and self-deluding obsessiveness on minutiae. For Oldbuck the ditch at the Kaim of Kinprunes – on a meadow that he fortuitously owns – is a relic of Roman times, a fortification, and clear evidence that at this place, just outside Fairport [Dundee], there occurred 'the final conflict between Agricola and the Caledonians' (1. 40). He expatiates with great pedantry on the overwhelming evidence for his supposition: 'Yes, my dear friend [he tells Lovel], from this stance it is probable – nay, it is nearly certain – that Julius Agricola beheld what our Beaumont has so admirably described! from this very Praetorium', at which point he is interrupted by Edie Ochiltree, the mendicant, who has approached unnoticed and is listening to the two men talking (or one talking and the other politely listening): 'Praetorian here, Praetorian there, I mind the bigging o't' (1. 43). That is, Edie remembers the ditch's being dug about twenty years ago. Monkbarns, of course, will not be convinced. Who, then, knows more, the antiquarian scholar, or the oldest inhabitant? Scott's adolescent raids into the Borders with Shortreed had aimed to gather exactly the kind of lore (in the form of trophies and ballads) that Monkbarns devotes his life to. Was Scott too deluding himself? Was it *really* Rob Roy's gun hanging over his writing desk, at Abbotsford?

For all that one admires his mind and exuberant rhetoric, one recognizes (as does Edie) that Oldbuck is a wholly impotent figure. He lives out of history and out of society. He has never fought a war, nor even acted in a major court case. When his sister Griselda wakes him to tell him the French are about to invade, he sternly commands, 'Bring me my sword.' Which one? his sister asks, offering him 'a Roman falchion of brass with the one hand, and with the other an Andrea Ferrara without a handle'. Neither is the one he wants. 'Give me', he declares, 'the sword which my father wore in the year forty-five – it hath no belt or baldrick – but we'll make shift' (2. 294–5). His nephew comes on him in this shift, looking like a stage pirate, and tells him not be ridiculous, but to go to Fairport and act there as quartermaster (Scott's role, with the Light Cavalry). And then, after all, the invasion turns out to be a false alarm. History is determined to pass Oldbuck by. Heartbroken in early life when Eveline jilted him for

Glenallan, Oldbuck has no wife and no child. He is looked after by his comical sister, the faithful Grizel. Oldbuck is the end of his family line. His heir is the buffoonish Hector – a Celt.

Lovel is rather overshadowed by his friend. Formally he is the lost heir, journeying towards the discovery of his own identity, and the eventual restoration of order and of property to its rightful owner: but like many of Scott's young heroes after Waverley, he never quite succeeds in making an impression on the reader's mind. There is an emptiness at his core. A man without a name and without a past – he fights a duel on the question of whether or not he actually exists. (Hector M'Intyre, his rival in love, has questioned the absence of an address on the letter of introduction which Lovel carries with him.) When he goes to ground with Edie – who has a uniform, a past, and, as he proudly asserts, a mendicant profession – Lovel becomes literally a non-person.

The Antiquary's first volume contains some of the best episodes Scott ever wrote in fiction: the fare-stage scene at Queensferry; the rescue from flooded sands at Halket-head craigs (including the famous error in which Scott makes the sun 'sink below the horizon', on the east coast of Scotland); Lovel's terrific dream and its rational explanation; the scenes in the post-master's house at Fairport, in which a band of town gossips use the evidence of envelopes to construct what is going on in their neighbours' private lives with an efficiency that the KGB might envy.

The middle volume sags much less than the corresponding section of *Waverley*. The duel between Hector and Lovel may be factitious, but its bungling incompetence renders the scene pleasingly ironic (the crack shot misses; the unpractised marksman, who desperately does *not* want to kill his man, hits his target). Oldbuck's puncturing dialogues with the warlike Hector, about the 'phoca' [seal] and his heartless deflation of the young man's Highland pretensions are funny, and reflect on Scott's own *odi et amo* mixture of fascination and amusement at his country's Celtic heritage. It is in some sense himself he is laughing at (the Walter Scott, that is, who was to attend the Highland Society in chieftain's trews, and who went on to welcome his monarch in Campbell tartan).

The third volume shows signs of rush, and automatic plotting. The death at sea of Elspeth Mucklebackit's grandson leads – via death-bed confessions – into the gothic secret of the Glenallans. Scott's introduction of the incest motif was surely inspired by the Byron scandals. The revelation that Lovel is Neville (the names are equally empty and hollow-sounding) is artificial. But it does explain some aspects of the plot in terms of plausible psychology. Oldbuck's irrational 'love' for the young stranger he met for the first time at Queensferry is explained by the man's facial resemblance to Eveline Neville, his tragic mother, whom both Oldbuck and the young Glenallan loved.

What is most disquieting in *The Antiquary* is its oppressive paternalism. Although an unprecedented amount of the narrative is given over to humble, low or proletarian characters, Scott is very much the 'Shirra', or

'Laird' in his treatment of them. It arises from the narrator's tone and manner, and from the low characters' often implausible serviceability to their betters. Edie, for instance, is remarkable for his willingness to contradict his betters in conversation, but to serve them – typically without any thought of monetary reward and at the risk of his own skin – where their material interests are involved. His willingness to die to save Sir Arthur and Isabella from drowning is explained, rather unconvincingly, by his appreciation for the benevolence of the young lady: 'I couldna bide to think o' the dainty young leddy's peril, that has aye ben kind to ilka forlorn heart that cam near her' (1. 87). A flower or two on her grave would seem to be sufficient. So too Edie's assistance to Lovel after the duel is never justified (harbouring a murderer from justice is something any reasonably prudent beggar should avoid). Nor is his dedication to rescuing Sir Arthur from the duns explained. It seems that Edie never considers his own welfare where that of his superiors is threatened. At this historical point, it should be remembered, Edinburgh and North Britain generally were swarming with beggars and the disaffected unemployed, laid off after the Napoleonic War. Scott yearned, apparently, for the old class solidarity of 1797, when the country was unified by threat of war, and laird and man stood shoulder to shoulder against haughty Gaul.

10

'Tales of my Landlord' to
The Heart of Midlothian (1816–1818)

Scott was shrewd enough to realize that one of the advantages of anonymity was that he could forge for himself a writing personality other than 'the author of *Waverley*'. He was not tied to a single pen-name or pen-personality; he could invent another – or as many as he wanted. By this means he could keep Constable happy and supply other employers with slightly (or entirely) different lines of goods. James Ballantyne was duly instructed in April 1816 to open negotiations with William Blackwood – at this date a prosperous Edinburgh bookseller and the Scottish agent of Murray. To entice Blackwood, Scott projected something 'totally different in style and structure from [the other novels] – a new cast, in short, of the net' (EJ 549). Unsurprisingly, Blackwood (who immediately apprehended Scott's hand in the venture) would have been perfectly happy with another old cast, the familiar and ever-saleable 'author of *Waverley*' article. What Blackwood was offered instead was a four-volume, four-title, collection to be called 'Tales of My Landlord', with settings in all four corners of Scotland. Scott had been hugely amused in 1812 by the comic apparatus to Washington Irving's *History of New York* (1809) by 'Diedrich Knickerbocker'. Scott's new collection would make up 'four tales illustrative of the manners of Scotland in her different provinces' (EJ 548), with a pedantic explicator as outlandishly named as Irving's, Jedediah Cleishbotham. As Edgar Johnson points out, 'cleish' is Scots for flog, and the name translates as 'Thwackarse'. Jedediah is schoolmaster and parish-clerk of the equally pseudonymous Gandercleugh – 'the navel, *si fas sit dicere,* of this our native realm of Scotland' (*OM* 1. xxxix).

Something less than a cosmopolite, Jedediah has visited Edinburgh twice and Glasgow three times in his life. Cleishbotham's one virtue is clerical doggedness. He transcribes, with hound-like fidelity, the literary remains of his dead friend and fellow teacher, Peter Pattieson, whose funeral expenses he hopes to defray with his profits. Pattieson was everything that his disciple is not – sensitive, gifted, learned, and a dedicated local historian. But without the mindless secretaryship of Cleishbotham, Peter's compositions would never see print. The narrative device neatly prismatizes aspects of Scott's own literary character – the drudging 'clerk', and the genius man of letters.

The financial arrangements for the 'Tales' were simple. Ballantyne, of course, should have the printing work; whoever bought the right to publish 6,000 copies must take £600-worth of old Ballantyne stock. (The fact that he was obliged to accept this 'trash' confirmed for Blackwood that he had the genuine Scott article.) When it seemed that Blackwood might balk, Scott kept him to the mark by mounting what was essentially a rights auction among his old and new publishers. The deal was eventually agreed in August, Blackwood (with Murray as English co-publisher) having come through with the most acceptable bid. Scott had shown great adroitness in the negotiation: 'employing first James, then John Ballantyne, as his agents, Scott had managed to get Constable, Longman, Blackwood, and Murray all hotly bidding for the unknown novel. He had so adroitly balanced their claims that it was the author rather than the booksellers who commanded the situation' (EJ 550).

Scott was no better than other novelists in keeping to his blueprint and the 'Tales' eventually came out as two separate works in a four-volume set – *The Black Dwarf* making up the first volume and *Old Mortality* the remaining three. Scott's intention of covering the four quarters of Scotland got no further than *Old Mortality*'s western setting. In other ways the project went awry. The first 192 proof pages of *The Black Dwarf* were reassuringly good and Blackwood read them with the pleasurable sense of having made a bargain. But the novel's ending was something else altogether. The scene in the chapel in which the black dwarf is transfigured into a white knight is tosh. Blackwood was very worried when he received the complete text. But he did not entirely trust his own judgement in the matter. Perhaps it might go down well with readers. He asked for a second opinion from his co-publisher Murray who in turn consulted his editor, William Gifford. Gifford confirmed the publishers' fears: the end of *The Black Dwarf* was indeed sub-standard, well below what might be expected from the Author of *Waverley*, or even the author of *The Mysteries of Udolpho*. Armed with Gifford's verdict, Blackwood was emboldened to ask for the concluding sections to be rewritten. He made suggestions as to how it might be done, and offered to pay himself for the expense of reprinting (EJ 554).

Scott, when he learned about this conference, was furious. 'I have received Blackwood's impudent proposal. God damn his soul!' he ranted to James Ballantyne. 'Tell him and his coadjutor that I belong to the Black Hussars of literature, who neither give nor receive criticism' (Lock. 3. 114–5; this, as reported by Lockhart, probably catches Scott's speech more accurately than the toned-down version in *Lett.* 4. 276.). Scott was, of course, in the wrong. As the purchaser of the novel, Blackwood had a perfect right to demand that Scott write to his best abilities. What Scott meant by his rage was that no mere *tradesman* of a publisher could speak to him so. Blackwood was thoroughly cowed by the outburst, grovelled an apology to 'the author', and the novel remained unchanged. Privately, to Louisa Stuart (an equal), Scott confided that he had indeed 'bungled up [the] conclusion' (*Lett.* 4. 292–3, EJ 557).

Few read Scott today and those that do probably have *The Black Dwarf* well to the bottom of their list. It is a pity, since the novel has much to recommend it. Shortness is one recommendation; another is the striking treatment of deformity. Lockhart drops in passing a key to the narrative that he picked up from Scott talking about the novel:

> [*The Black Dwarf*], however imperfect, and unworthy as a work of art to be placed high in the catalogue of his productions, derives a singular interest from its delineation of the dark feelings so often connected with physical deformity; feelings which appear to have diffused their shadow over the whole genius of Byron – and which, but for this single picture, we should hardly have conceived ever to have passed through Scott's happier mind. (Lock. 3. 130)

Scott, as Lockhart reminds us, was as lame and potentially as prone to misanthropy on the score as Byron. But neither poet was as disabled as the hero of *The Black Dwarf* who (if he is a projection of their shared disability) is magnified into a monster of deformity. Scott's introduction to the novel recalls as Elshie's original an actual dwarf, David Ritchie – 'Bow'd (i.e. crooked] Davie' – a well-known Edinburgh character in the late years of the eighteenth century. A native of Tweeddale, who supported himself as a brush-maker, Ritchie eventually wearied of the taunts his appearance pro-voked and 'settled himself . . . upon a patch of wild moorland at the bottom of a bank on the farm at Woodhouse, in the sequestered vale of the small river Manor, in Peebleshire.' In his later years he became notoriously misanthropic. He 'detested children' and was generally 'reserved, crabbed and surly' (2. 182–3). People were frightened of him, and he gained a reputation for magical powers.

Scott saw Ritchie in autumn 1797, in the company of Adam Ferguson, on one of their 'expeditions'. It was, as Grierson reminds us, a very low point in young Walter's fortunes. He had been rejected by Williamina (quite likely because of his deformity) and betrayed by his whole-limbed friend, Forbes. The sections of *The Black Dwarf* which stick in the memory are Elshie's diatribes against mankind which may well express what the spurned Walter then felt, a desire to destroy the whole race of his fellow man: 'Why should not the whole human herd butt, gore, and gorge upon each other', Elshie asks, 'till all are extirpated but one huge and over-fed Behemoth, and he, when he had throttled and gnawed the bones of all his fellows – he, when his prey failed him, to be roaring whole days for lack of food, and, finally, to die, inch by inch, of famine? – it were a consummation worthy of the race' (2. 229). As we learn in the final, fantastic dénouement, the source of his misanthropic rage is his having been rejected in love by Isabella's mother for the whole-limbed Vere.

If *The Black Dwarf* was a dubious achievement, *Old Mortality* – the second of the 'Tales' – is generally rated (not least by the author himself) as one of Scott's best novels, although it has never been one of the more loved. As Lockhart reports, main ideas for the novel were supplied by Scott's fellow antiquarian and fanatic admirer, the Galloway exciseman Joseph Train, in May 1816. Train brought Scott a 'fresh heap of traditionary gleanings which he had gathered among the tale tellers of his district' (Lock. 3. 133). He also brought with him a document by a schoolmaster called Broadfoot, who signed himself, by way of joke, 'Clashbottom' (EJ 553), and Rob Roy's pouch which, as Lockhart speculates, was the germ of Scott's next but one big novel. If nothing else, Train directed the novelist's attention to the west of the country.

According to Train's recollection, years after the event, it was he who fed Scott the idea of John Grahame of Claverhouse, Viscount Dundee ('Bluidy Clavers'), as the hero for his novel in progress. Train also told Lockhart that it was he who had the inspiration that the story should be narrated by Robert Paterson, called 'Old Mortality', – a figure not unlike Scott's 'last minstrel', Train helpfully added (Lock. 3. 134). According to Train's recollection Scott was ignorant about Paterson and needed to be reminded of who the eccentric old man had been. If Train is to be believed, the Black Hussar had no scruples in taking advice from his antiquarian friends. But should we believe him?

Take the Robert Paterson detail. According to Scott he (unlike Train) had actually encountered Old Mortality in person, in 1793 (Lock. 1. 195–6). In a letter to John Murray, shortly after the novel's publication, Scott goes so far as to say: 'I knew Old Mortality very well' (*Lett.* 4. 318). Moreover, Scott's interest in the Covenanters was of very long standing. He and Leyden had included a group of five Covenanter ballads in the *Minstrelsy.* Scott was evidently fascinated by the complexities in Claverhouse's personality and had an enigmatic portrait of him prominently on his study wall. As another question mark over Train's claims to paternity, one should note a letter to him after the publication of *Old Mortality* in which Scott elaborately and with a very straight face disclaims his authorship of both the *Waverley* novels and the 'Tales' ('I get the credit of them and wish I deserved it but I dare say the real author will one day appear'; *Lett.* 4. 323). Why would he do this, if Train were himself 'all but the author of *Old Mortality*'?

Robert Paterson – the narrator who may or may not have been suggested by Train – was a fanatic Cameronian who devoted his old age to tending and mending the graves of otherwise forgotten covenanters, travelling to graveyards all over the Lowlands. He earned for himself a number of nicknames – 'the Hewer', 'the Letterer', 'the Headstone Man', and finally, that by which Scott calls him. As a type, Old Mortality recalls both the last minstrel (as Train supposedly pointed out) and the antiquarian who hunts for history in stones. In historical fact, Paterson had quite prosperous farmer sons, whom he disowned the better to follow his Sisyphean task of keeping the past new.

Using 'Old Mortality' as the 'source' was a brilliant stroke, but it is not easy to hold the resulting narrative framework in the mind while reading the novel. Scott, an Edinburgh lawyer, writes through the persona of the author of *Waverley*, a popular but anonymous novelist. For commercial purposes, the author of *Waverley* has disguised himself – but not so efficiently as to fool either his publisher or the reading public at large – as Jedediah Cleishbotham, a pedantic schoolteacher. Cleishbotham, however, is merely a conduit, transcribing the literary remains of Peter Pattieson. Pattieson, although a thoroughly literary (and strangely doomed) figure is not, however, the author. He has recorded stories taken from a fanatic and vagrant haunter of Scottish churchyards, Robert Paterson. And, if one thinks about it, Paterson himself must have had the story of Henry Morton from somebody who had it from, probably, Cuddie Headrigg. 'Chinese Whispers' might be a better title.

As Scott recalls in his 1830 'Introduction', it was at Dunnottar in the district of Mearns, 'about thirty years since, or more' (i.e. 1793) that he himself encountered Old Mortality (1. xxxvii). The old man was engaged in cleaning the inscriptions relative to the so-called 'Whig's vault'. In 1685 – when Argyle was threatening to invade Scotland, and Monmouth the west of England – a hundred or more Cameronians with their women and children were rounded up and driven northward 'like bullocks'. On the way, they were jeered at by the local population. Finally they were penned up in a dungeon in the Castle of Dunnottar. The guards made them pay for everything, including water, and when they brought it, threw the liquid on the floor with the savage jest that 'if they were obliged to bring water for the canting whigs, they were not bound to afford them the use of bowls or pitchers gratis' (1. xxxviii). Several died of disease, others suffered broken bones in futile attempts to escape, others were killed. After the 1688 Revolution, a monument to these 'saints' was erected in the grave-yard of the local church. It was this shrine that Scott saw Paterson cleaning. But he was bad-tempered, and would not speak to the young lawyer. In the fictional version, the more affable Peter Pattieson accosts Old Mortality in the same place, and much the same time, and succeeds in extracting from the old man sufficient anecdotage to make up the novel.

At the heart of *Old Mortality*, then, is not rebellion but war crime. Although the narrative avoids the Whig's Vault episode (it must be supposed to occur while Morton is on the Continent, in chapters 2. 16–7), atrocity runs through *Old Mortality* like a crimson thread. Again and again in the novel we encounter brutalities inflicted by an exultant military power over defenceless civilians. Both sides are guilty. The novel opens with a scene in which Life Guards terrorize cowering villagers, paying for their drinks with stolen cattle, forcing the God-fearing inhabitants to blaspheme (rape will come later, we apprehend). On their part, the Presbyterians plan a massacre once they have taken Tillietudlem; they shoot soldiers under flags of truce; they butcher churchmen with as much compunction as one would exterminate a rat.

Henry Morton is a variant of Edward Waverley: the pococurante young man who is politicized by an accidental collision with the forces of history and who is thereby recruited into a highly charged ideological cause of whose ultimate rightness he is never inwardly convinced. Stronger-spined than Waverley, Morton turns his coat twice – taking on the double character of a rebel against rebellion. The conflict between the Covenanters and the Crown is portrayed as entirely ideological: there is none of the glamorous nationalism which figured in *Waverley*.

Nor is there any of the honour that vindicated the savageries of battle in Scott's earlier novel. *Waverley*'s germinal anecdote – Invernahyle's honourable sparing of Whitefoord – is unthinkable in the ruthless and entirely sordid world of *Old Mortality*'s warfare. Scott in this later novel anticipates the horrors of total war – its systematic cruelties and ineradicable ignobility. Bothwell particularly is a depiction of the soldier as total brute worthy of Brecht. His death, which requires three thrusts of the sword by Balfour – all vividly described – is no more romantic than the slaughter of a pig in an abattoir. (To get the last thrust home, Balfour has to lean his foot on Bothwell's chest, to keep the body from rolling away from the blade; 1. 233.)

Claverhouse is a devil in armour – and like the devil, clever. His Covenanter opponents hopefully use silver bullets against him. War is, correspondingly, hell. After the rebels have been put to flight at Bothwell Bridge, the 'mild' Monmouth (Scott's ancestor) orders mercy, and an end to the indiscriminate killing. But Claverhouse and his troops pursue their foe relentlessly with the cry '"Kill! kill! no quarter!"' ... Their swords drank deep of slaughter among the unresisting fugitives. Screams of quarter were only answered by the shouts with which the pursuers accompanied their blows' (2. 138). Scott, one deduces from such passages, had been more morbidly affected by the field of Waterloo than the triumphalist poem dedicated to the Duchess of Wellington suggests. And after the battle, there follows the obscene torturing of Ephraim Macbriar (a minister of God) by the 'Scottish boot' (to force him to reveal the whereabouts of the escaped Balfour). As the prisoners are shot without ceremony in the courtyard below, Claverhouse offers the now rehabilitated Morton a horn of ale. 'Men die daily,' Claverhouse observes, 'not a bell tolls the hour but it is the death-note of someone or other; and why hesitate to shorten the span of others, or take over-anxious care to prolong our own' (2. 157). He shortly after asks a horrified Morton the extraordinary question, 'Did you ever read Froissart?' No, the young man replies. With what may be irony, or perhaps merely Napoleonic grandeur, Claverhouse proceeds to eulogize the laureate of chivalry:

His chapters inspire me with more enthusiasm than even poetry itself. And the noble canon, with what true chivalrous feeling he confines his beautiful expressions of sorrow to the death of the gallant and high-bred knight, of whom it was a pity to see the fall, such was his loyalty to the king, pure faith to his religion, hardihood towards his enemy, and fidelity to his lady-love! – Ah, *benedicite!* how he will mourn over the fall of such a pearl of knighthood, be it on the side that he happens to favour, or on the other. But, truly, for sweeping from the face of the earth some few hundreds of villain churls, who are born but to plough it, the high-born and inquisitive historian has marvellous little sympathy – as little, or less, perhaps, than John Grahame of Claverhouse. (2. 164–5)

One could substitute 'the author of *Waverley*' for Froissart. Scott, as a writer of martial fiction, has changed. *Old Mortality* conveys his darker, post-Waterloo view of warfare. Having seen the battlefield, and the still mangled bodies of the 20,000 walking wounded in Brussels, Scott had a less romantic view of fighting than in 1814, when his ideas of battle were still associated with charging up and down Musselburgh sands and lopping the tops off turnips.

It is easy to see why *Old Mortality* should be among the most admired of Scott's works; it is also easy to understand why it should not be his most loved work. One admires and shudders. The majestic achievement of *Old Mortality* is raised on the wreckage of the original 'Tales' conception. The novel outgrew its one-volume frame, expanding to a full-length three. With the expansion, the idea of four works representative of the four quarters of Scotland was sacrificed. Scott having begun *Old Mortality* in summer (the wettest Scotland could remember) finished the last half of the third volume in the usual rush, over 'four rainy days' (EJ 555) in November. The 'Tales' were published at the beginning of December, and sold well.

There was an odd follow-up. The 'Tales' were generally well received. One of the few astringent notices was in the *Quarterly* – penned by Scott himself (with the assistance of William Erskine). Scott wrote to Murray offering the piece on 18 December 1816. Ostensibly it was a 'Solomonic' gesture, aimed to show that the baby was not his – otherwise why would he consent to its being 'quartered'? The review began as another of the obfuscatory jokes which Scott and Erskine loved. But shortly after he received Murray's commission, Scott was attacked at immense length and considerable savagery by Thomas McCrie D.D. in a series of papers in the *Edinburgh Christian Instructor*, January–March 1817. McCrie was a formidable opponent – learned, eloquent and dignified. Grierson calls him 'a historian of principle and policy' (*Lett.* 4. 386). From his co-religionist's standpoint he considered Scott's depiction of the Covenanters as homicidal maniacs in *Old Mortality* to be a travesty.

Scott at first affected to be above McCrie's attack. 'I have not read it, and certainly never shall' (Hew. 115), he told Lady Louisa Stuart on 31 January 1817. But he did read it, and was stung. His part of the *Quarterly* review was largely devoted to replying to McCrie. A more positive response, and one which tacitly confesses to contrition, is the favourable depiction of the Cameronian fanaticism in the characters of David and Jeanie Deans, in the next series of 'Tales'.

HAROLD THE DAUNTLESS

Scott's departure from serious poetry – a field which he had dominated for a decade – is commonly explained by reference to self-deprecating comments in his letters, conversations, and in his 1829–30 prefaces that Byron had 'beat' him. Scott made other more or less cryptic remarks that he was 'too old and stupid' (EJ 563) for verse now that he was in his mid-forties. What then did that make the older Wordsworth and the stupider Southey? Scott's protestations are not entirely satisfactory. For one thing, he was assiduous in superintending reprints of his verse during his lifetime – he obviously cared about his reputation as a poet. For another he was still publishing poetry on an ambitious scale five years after the appearance of the first two volumes of *Childe Harold* (1812).

The *Bridal of Triermain* and *Harold the Dauntless* (the first reprinted from 1813) were put out in 1817 as a single octavo volume – a form which consciously imitated the Murray–Byron style of book (hitherto, Scott's major poems had appeared in the old-fashioned quarto form). The two works represent a thematic unit, and a departure from Scott's 'lays' commemorating fictional love and historical battle. Both contain an extraordinary variety of complex metres and stanza forms. Neither gives the impression of being dashed off, or a rehash of old successes. The poems were published anonymously, unlike their predecessors. They are, in short, experimental. It is the failure of the 1817 experiment that more plausibly explains Scott's leaving the field of poetry to Byron. He was never one to back losing horses.

Harold the Dauntless is the shortest of Scott's long poems. Although he never visited the country, he had a long-standing interest in Scandinavia, and the polemical racial theories that clustered around Vikings.[1] As early as 1790–1, he wrote a class paper for Dugald Stewart, 'On the Manners and Customs of the Northern Nations'. In October 1806, reviewing a volume of poetry that contained some Norse imitations for the *Edinburgh Review*, Scott noted that Scandinavia was probably 'the real source of many of the tales of our minstrels'. Scott's engagement with the ancient literature of the northern nations peaked in 1814, when he published his abstract of the 'Eyrbyggia-Saga' in Weber and Jamieson's *Illustrations of Northern Antiquities*. Scott's interest in the rugged culture of the north was also heightened by his sea trip to Ultima Thule and beyond in July 1814. (His fascination with the sagas features prominently in *The Pirate*, a work directly inspired by the trip.) There are some fifty volumes on Scandinavian subjects catalogued in the Abbotsford library.

There is uncertainty as to when Scott actually wrote *Harold*. Dating is complicated by references Scott made at the time, and in his April 1830, afterword, noting the unfortunate similarity in titles with *Childe Harold*. 'I am still astonished', he wrote in 1830, 'at my having committed the gross error of selecting the very name which Lord Byron had made so famous.'

In January 1817, when the poem was published, Scott told Morritt in a letter that *Harold the Dauntless* was 'partly printed before *Childe Harold* was in question' (*Lett.* 4. 383). He must have meant before the third volume of Byron's poem. He could not have meant the first two volumes, published in March 1812. Around November 1816 he had received the third volume of *Childe Harold* to review for the *Quarterly*. (The issue of the magazine in which Scott's review appeared was dated October 1816, but actually came out in February 1817. *Harold the Dauntless* was published on 31 January 1817.)

J. T. Hillhouse, who has studied the chronology of composition,[2] suggests that Scott began work on *Harold* in autumn 1815 and arranged to have early sections of the poem printed on the same stock of paper, watermarked 1812, as had been used for the 1813 publication of *The Bridal*. It may be that he wished to put on record – however spuriously – that he had come up with the 'Harold' title before Byron. This, however, would be such a devious way of establishing priority, that one cannot seriously uphold it. What seems more likely is that Scott chose 'Harold' as a good Saxon name some time after the first two volumes of Byron's poem appeared. 'Eric' was a possible alternative, but Harold had the added attraction of being the name of the last Saxon king of England, and would set up a desirable resonance with 'Arthur' in *The Bridal of Triermain*. Scott simply did not anticipate a third volume of Byron's poem clashing so closely with the publication of his own synonymous work.

Hillhouse plausibly argues that Scott wrote the poem in two sections, with a long break between cantos 1 and 2. There is a palpable loosening of mood, and a new flexibility in technique between these sections. It seems likely that the first canto was written shortly before October 1815, and sent to the printer then. On 22 December 1815 Scott told Morritt that the second volume of *The Bridal of Triermain* (i.e. *Harold the Dauntless*) was 'nearly finished'. But writing novels intervened. Almost a year later, on 14 November 1816 Scott told Louisa Stuart that he hoped to have *Harold the Dauntless* out of the way soon. He evidently wrote the remaining verses between November and December 1816, in between correcting the proofs of his 'Tales'.

ROB ROY

The first series of 'Tales of my Landlord' was hugely successful. Scott crowed to Morritt on 31 January 1817 that 'Jedediah carries the world before him. 6000 have been disposed of and 3000 more pressing onward which will be worth £2500 to the worthy pedagogue of Gandercleuch' (*Lett.* 4. 383). He would repeat the experiment – but not immediately. In early May 1817 an agreement was made with Constable for the new novel, *Rob Roy*. It would be a work by the 'author of *Waverley*', in the old style.

Scott's terms were higher than before, but not excessively so. For the right to print 6,000 copies £1,700 advance was demanded; additionally the publisher must take the 'usual quantity' of stock (£600-worth) in Hanover Street (EJ 570). Constable groaned, and acquiesced.

In late 1816 Scott had attempted to promote himself from his Clerkship of the Court of Session. The time was propitious. His party was in power and his reputation was at its zenith. What he had in mind was promotion to the Bench of the Scottish Court of the Exchequer. As a 'Baron of Exchequer' he would be a judge and Lord Scott. He applied in December 1816 to the Duke of Buccleuch who for once could not, or would not, help him (EJ 560–1). Why not? Because he was suspected of being a novelist? Because of the taint of jobbery in his favours for his brother Tom? Because of his persistent money troubles, news of which may have leaked out? Because of the growing power of the Whigs in Edinburgh? Buccleuch's excuse (and it sounds like an excuse) was that he did not at the moment have the power to help his kinsman.

Denied one promotion, Scott consoled himself with another – that of lairdship. There developed at this period the full fury of his lust for property. Abbotsford was erecting itself with great speed. His proprietary ideas were in constant change, and constantly grander. In late 1816 further 'improvements' were made with the aim of rendering the house something more in the nature of 'a small Scottish manor'. That winter there were some thirty labourers working at Abbotsford in Scott's employ. He believed in the Malthusian doctrine of relieving distress by having the unemployed beautify rich men's estates (EJ 568–9). Blore's improvements quickly ate up Blackwood's payments for the 'Tales' and Major John Scott's £3,000. It did not deter 'Abbotsford and Kaeside' (as Scott now called himself). In autumn 1817 Scott bought Toftfield, another neighbouring estate, for £10,000. It would make him 'a great laird', he jubilantly told John Ballantyne (EJ 586). In 1817 Scott had Wilkie paint himself and his family in the character of peasants (EJ 587). This Marie-Antoinettish exercise expressed Scott's firm belief in the identity of interest between Dives and Lazarus, laird and man, Oldbuck and Ochiltree, Abbotsford and Purdie.

Despite such confident proclamations Scott was not entirely sure of the invincibility of his Tory-laird philosophy. Fiction allowed him to ponder alternative theories, and to extend deviant aspects of his own personality under the perspectives of romance and irony. His next novel took as its subject one of Scotland's most renowned freebooters. Rob Roy was no respecter of any laird's property. He was a thief, a blackmailer, a smuggler, and a cattle-rustler – just the kind of person to give the Laird of Abbotsford nightmares, were he to come sweeping out of his Loch Lomond lair again.

Scott had been fascinated by Rob Roy for some time, an interest fanned by Joseph Train (who, as an exciseman, was another of Rob's natural enemies). Scott – the lawyer with a soft spot for outlaws – projected his own irrational pleasure in Rob's 'daft reiks' on to Nicol Jarvie, a character in the novel:

'It's a queer thing o'me, gentlemen, that am a man o' peace mysell, and a
peacefu' man's son, for the deacon my father quarrelled wi' nane out o' the
town-council, – it's a queer thing, I say, but I think the Hieland blude o' me
warms at thae daft tales and whiles I like better to hear them than a word o'
profit, Gude forgie me! But they are vanities, sinfu' vanities, and, moreover,
again the statute law – again the statute and gospel law.' (2. 121)

At the time that he was meditating *Rob Roy* Scott was acting for the Duke
of Buccleuch as a legal gamekeeper. The Duke was very worried about
poaching on some of his lands that lay around Yarrow. He had opened the
walks there to the common people of Selkirkshire (something that Scott
heartily approved of) and there had been some depredations of his game
and vandalism by local children. Scott was furious on his chief's behalf. As
a novelist, he might indulge Rob Roy. As a sheriff and a landowner, he
would prosecute all trespassers, poachers, and juvenile fruit scrumpers to
the utmost of the law. Britain in 1817 was – as prosperous landholders like
Scott and Buccleuch might think – going to the dogs. The euphoria of
Waterloo was now well in the past. There was much distress, particularly in
the Scottish countryside. Scott's friend Morritt was working on drafting a
new poor law, for the masses of new poor. Scott's old friend William Laidlaw
had been ruined as a farmer, and was taken on as an Abbotsford tenant and
factor (EJ 567). Harvests were successively poor, and British corn was
undercut by imports.

Scott had driven himself very hard over the last few years. Too hard, it
would seem, for his health broke in 1817. On 5 March at a 'merry dinner
party in Castle Street' he experienced an agonizing internal pain. He rose
'with a scream of agony which electrified his guests' (Lock. 3. 146) and left
the company. News of his illness swept through Edinburgh and even made
the national papers (Lock. 3. 151). Morritt, in England, read that his
friend's life was in danger. In reassuring him that he was still alive, Scott
divulged some details – not of his complaint, which eluded his physicians,
but of their brutal treatment. It involved a reprise of his early treatments for
lameness, a kind of homeopathy mixed with scarification. Heated salt was
applied to his body (EJ 566). It was so hot 'that it burned my shirt to rags.'
But Scott was in such pain that 'I hardly felt [it] when clapped to my
stomach. At length the symptoms became inflammatory, and dangerously
so, the seat being the diaphragm. They only gave way to very profuse
bleeding and blistering, which under higher assistance saved my life. My
recovery was slow and tedious from the state of exhaustion. I could neither
stir for weakness and giddiness, nor read for dazzling in my eyes, nor listen
for a whizzing sound in my ears, nor even think for lack of the power of
arranging my ideas' (Lock. 3. 152). A fortnight later he was still 'as weak as
water'. His friend R. P. Gillies, who saw him in Edinburgh in July, describes
a living corpse:

He was worn almost to a skeleton [and] sat slanting on his horse, as if unable
to hold himself upright; his dress was threadbare and disordered; and his

countenance, instead of its usual healthy colour, was of an olive-brown – I might almost say, black tinge . . . 'The physicians tell me,' [said he] 'that mere pain cannot *kill*; but I am very sure that no man would, for *other* three months, encounter the same pain that I have suffered *and live*. However, I have resolved to take thankfully whatever drugs they prescribe.' (EJ 572)

The cramps (which turned out to be gallstones; EJ 566) continued. Scott was put on a lowering diet and forbidden all stimulants by his physicians. Against the recurrent agony, he took large amounts of opium. The changes in mood which the drug induced, particularly the listlessness, he recorded in the melancholy, Coleridgean lyric composed in August, 'The Dreary Change'. That summer (1817) Scott had a strong presentiment of imminent death, the dreariest change of all. He meditated his own obituary, repeating in his letters to friends the motto 'sat est vixisse'.

Despite his illness Scott raced ahead with his novel. The first volume was written within the month, in August. According to Lockhart, the narrative was finished by the end of December 1817. Scott penned a little envoi for James Ballantyne:

> With great joy
> I send you Roy.
> 'Twas a tough job,
> But we're done with Rob.

In the meantime, Scott was doing his usual load of incidental work. He finished his chronicle of 1815 for the *Register*, which was published in August. He was preparing his article on 'Chivalry', for Constable's *Encyclopaedia*. He wrote an introductory essay on 'Border Antiquities' for a two-volume quarto, which came out in September 1817. All in all, it was a productive year for a man suffering unto death. Scott seems also to have served as usual in the Court of Session and done his usual review of cases from Selkirk. When the Court rose in July, he made a visit to Rob Roy's cave at the head of Loch Lomond (EJ 573).

Rob Roy is Scott's first novel to deal with the Highlands and their 'feudal' culture from below. His interest in the subject probably originated with his research for his very long article on the 'Culloden Papers', published in the *Quarterly* for January 1816. The article opens with the remark that 'everything belonging to the Highlands of Scotland has of late become peculiarly interesting'. What follows is Scott's most considered and deeply researched statement on such things as the character of the Chevalier (he generally admired his courage and daring as a commander), the military reasons for the failure of the '45 adventure ('French advisers'), and the peculiar sociology of the clans. He noted particularly their 'contempt of labour' and their military prowess, which under the command of Montrose showed them superior as soldiers to their Lowland countrymen. 'Clanship, however, with its good, and evil, is now no more', Scott concludes (*Prose* 20. 91).

Rob Roy Macgregor Campbell (Scott was remotely a Campbell) played an important, if unconscious, part in the survival of what was best in the Highland tradition, namely the Highland regiments of the British army. As the 'Culloden Papers' article records, he was the chief of a gang based at the head of Loch Lomond, preying largely on the estate of the Duke of Montrose. His bolt hole was in the estate of the Duke of Argyle, who hated Montrose. Rob Roy lived by blackmail, extortion, and coerced tribute. He 'summoned the people of Lennox to pay the blackmail with as much gravity as if it had been a legal demand' (*Prose* 20. 75). And he offered in return, protection. Rob Roy 'blended in his own character the capacity of a police officer and of a freebooter.' It was to control such predations that the Black Watch were formed, and following its model all the fifty-or-so subsequent battalions of Highland regiments that fought so gallantly in the Napoleonic Wars.

Despite the circumstances of its composition, there is no feel of weariness or sickness about *Rob Roy*. Nor is it (as an invalid's novel might be) a reprise of earlier successes. The most innovatory feature in *Rob Roy* is not the titular hero (who lurks around the edges of the action, for most of its length) but the leading lady, 'Di' Vernon. Di is a type of horsey, dashing heroine quite new to English fiction in 1817. The vivacious Miss Vernon's ancestress is, clearly enough, Millamant in *The Way of the World*. Di is the aggressive, saucy, perverse, coquettish (but inwardly pure), and finally submissive, heroine of Congreve's comedy transplanted across genres and time. Di Vernon radiates through subsequent Victorian fiction, as Beatrix Castlewood, Diana of the Crossways, Glencora Palliser, Estella, Bathsheba Everdene.

The other notably new thing in *Rob Roy* is found in the lower layer of subplot. Andrew Fairservice is a version of the buffoon-clown type of Scottish peasant whom Scott had introduced in Alick Polwarth and portrayed at much greater length in Cuddie Headrigg. Fairservice extends the characterization further. He is infuriatingly independent. It is he, in a sense, who controls his master, anticipating Sam Weller – the highest reach of the witty servant type who can be traced back genetically through Jonson, to Plautus. Fairservice is insubordinate but in important matters indomitably loyal to his master. The Fairservice comedy plot in *Rob Roy* (there is a lot of it) invokes all the contradictions of hierarchical class relations. How can one be a servant, yet one's own man? What 'freedoms' or licence can someone in a position of class inferiority and/or service claim?

The title *Rob Roy* was suggested by Constable, who had evidently noted the outlaw's pouch and gun at Abbotsford (EJ 570). Scott liked the suggestion but the tactician in him was averse to such a determinate title. Anyone coming to '*Rob Roy*' would know what to expect. 'Nay . . . never let me have to write up to a name. You well know I have generally adopted a title that told nothing' (Lock. 3. 161). Scott was also averse to write to his publisher's dictation, on principle. As he told Lord Montagu on 8 June 1817 (as he began to write *Rob Roy*): 'In bookselling matters an author must either be the conjuror who commands the devil or the witch who serves him and few are those whose situation is sufficiently independent to enable them to assume the higher character' (*Lett.* 4. 461). He found an ingenious way around the dilemma. He accepted Constable's suggestion and dutifully called his novel *Rob Roy*. But then he withheld the titular hero tantalizingly. Rob Roy ('Campbell') makes a brief appearance in disguise early in the narrative and re-enters, briefly and again incognito, in the middle sections. And his voice is heard (but he is not seen) in Glasgow. But the outlaw does not occupy front of stage until the last chapters. He is, for most of the narrative, the original absent presence.

Rob Roy is in fact two novels, and stretches to the utmost the looseness of the multi-volume form and Scott's essayistic narration. After the dismissal scenes between the waywardly poetic Frank and his dry merchant of a father, the novel concentrates on the Osbaldistone Hall episode. It is a prelude which goes on and on. Improbability is everywhere in these early sections of *Rob Roy*. It is never entirely clear, for instance, why Frank's father should have banished him to a place where he can hardly have expected to receive any correction. It is no more clear what Di – another cousin – is doing there. The arch-Jesuit Rashleigh is so unlike his five bucolic siblings that one must presume some misconduct on the part of his departed mother. And why Frank's father should select him, of all his young relatives, as the heir to Osbaldistone and Tresham is wholly mysterious. Andrew Fairservice, a Scot, is wholly out of place in this quintessentially English household. To compound improbability to the pitch of fantasy, this country estate, occupied by boors, sots and cretins, is, we are to believe, a centre of international intrigue and espionage. God help any rebellion with Osbaldistone Hall as its headquarters.

In 1817–8 Scott returned to make another stab at drama, with a 'goblin drama called the Fortunes of Devorgoil'. He wrote the play – which is short enough to be part of a double bill – to 'oblige' his friend Daniel Terry, currently making his way in the theatre world of London. The piece would have been a terrific success had the dramatist publicly revealed himself as the author of *Waverley*. But he was not inclined to drop his mask. Many years later, in January 1826, Scott recalled rather bitterly that 'Terry refused a gift of it but he was quite and entirely wrong' (Jrnl. 69). The 'gift' was ostensibly in honour of Scott's new godson, Walter Terry.

When Terry (for whatever reasons) turned down *Devorgoil*, the manuscript was apparently put away. In 1826, immediately after the crash, Scott resurrected it as a makeweight piece, that might 'be added to *Woodstock* as a fourth volume'. In the excitement of the crisis, the manuscript was mislaid yet again. Scott came across it in April 1829, became preoccupied with it, and 'out of mere contradiction' (Jrnl. 553) spent an evening rewriting 'the piece of nonsense'. That evening he read it 'to the girls [i.e. Anne and her cousin] who seemed considerably interested'. It was eventually published, renamed *The Doom of Devorgoil*, by Cadell in 1830, along with the later-written dramatic piece *Auchindrane*.

THE HEART OF MIDLOTHIAN: ROYALTY AND PATRONAGE

Constable published an initial 10,000 of *Rob Roy* – 4,000 over the originally agreed number (EJ 575). It was an unprecedentedly large first print run for a novel. And within a fortnight, 3,000 more were called for. Scott, naturally, was pleased and it confirmed his intention to return lock, stock and barrel to his old publisher. In November 1817 Scott negotiated a second series of the 'Tales'. A hard bargain was driven. Scott demanded an immediate £5,000 for the lease of an edition of 10,000 copies. Constable feared that Jedediah Cleishbotham might defect once more to Blackwood (currently riding high with his new magazine – which had the gall to lampoon Constable as 'the Crafty' in its early issues). He haggled Scott down a token thousand to £4,000 (EJ 583) but was induced to take the last of John Ballantyne's old stock (valued, if that is the word, at just over £5,000; EJ 584). Thus Constable secured four volumes of *The Heart of Midlothian*, and thus was the Augean stable in Hanover Street finally swept of its 'trash'. Enriched by this and other recent contracts Scott was finally able (after five years) to pay off 'the good Duke's £4,000' in January 1818 (Lock. 3. 205). Less prudently, he embarked on an orgy of Abbotsford building and land purchase.

Once again the plan was for a four-volume bundle of 'Tales'. As Scott foresaw it in late 1817, *The Heart of Midlothian* would be the three-volume main course (apparently with a gloomier ending, in which Jeanie would, like her original, Helen Walker, die single). The supporting item was to be a story about the Regalia of Scotland (crown, sceptre, sword of state). With the 1707 Union, Scotland had lost its traditional right to a Scottish monarch. An article of the treaty had stipulated that, as a salve to national pride, the Regalia should remain in Scotland. It was felt prudent to store these paraphernalia secretly, however, lest they be exploited by Scottish opponents to the Union (*Lett.* 5. 48–9, *Prose* 7. 341–2).

There were over the years persistent rumours that the Regalia had been smuggled to London – a symbolic mark of Scotland's humiliating colonial status. These baubles were much on Scott's mind in 1817. He had been lobbying for some years for a search and recovery operation. He brought up the subject of an official commission to do this on his first meeting with the Prince Regent, in 1815. What he had in mind was an official quasi-ceremonial opening of the Crown Room in Edinburgh Castle, and the investigation of the chest in which it was believed that the Regalia had been deposited in March 1707, at the behest of the last Scottish parliament.

The time, Scott felt, was symbolically right for Scotland to restore the Regalia to public display – not in a spirit of rebellion or national assertiveness, but as proof of the indestructibility of the Union. Displaying them now could cause no mischief. Scott lobbied and wrote tirelessly on the subject, and finally brought the authorities round. In an operation superintended by himself the dust-covered box containing the regalia was forced open on 4 February 1818. The relics were found to be intact. There was a formal ceremony of discovery the next day, again orchestrated and presided over by Scott. Lockhart records his father-in-law's overpowering emotions during this ceremony – particularly when some less overwhelmed member of the company playfully made as if to put the Crown of Scotland on his head (Lock. 3. 212–3).

Scott's idea for his Regalia story was outlined to Louisa Stuart in January 1818 (*Lett.* 5. 53–6). It would centre around some of the Regalia's earlier adventures. They had been 'lost' on an earlier occasion, at the time of the Commonwealth. Then they were hidden under the pulpit of the Church of Kinneff, in Kincardineshire, and later carried into safety by the minister's widow – a heroic and unchronicled Scottish woman. They were subsequently secreted in an oubliette in the house of Sir George Ogilvie. This would, Scott thought, make a 'capital' story for Jedediah. From clues in the correspondence it seems that as late as April Scott intended *The Heart of Midlothian* to extend over no more than two-and-a-half volumes, with 'The Regalia' as a one-and-a-half volume pendant.

'The Regalia' indicates Scott's addiction to things 'royal' at this period. By the original agreement of November 1817, the manuscript of the second series of 'Tales' was to be delivered in incredibly short order – for publication on 4 June 1818 (EJ 583). The date was significant as George III's official birthday and one of the great royalist holidays of the British calendar. Scott moreover consciously built his novel around an elaborate compliment to his monarch's grandmother, Queen Caroline, who is (wholly fictionally) portrayed as Effie Deans's saviour from the hangman and a fairy godmother to virtuous peasant girls. In the 'historical' anecdote on which *The Heart of Midlothian* was based it was the Duke of Argyle alone who won Isobel Walker's pardon. In Scott's version, Argyle is demoted to mere intermediary. Scott fictionalized Caroline as the granter of Effie's pardon and a friend to all Scots despite the historical fact that it was she who reprieved Porteous and who swore, after his lynching, that she would make her northern kingdom a hunting ground.

It seems that the vignette of the Queen was the central element in Scott's early thinking about the novel. Lockhart first met his future father-in-law at this period, around May 1818, and he heard James Ballantyne read out from proof sheets the interview between Jeanie and Queen Caroline in Richmond Park. Those sections in which Caroline appears in *The Heart of Midlothian* are notable for a greasily obsequious tone of narrative. Dealing with the touchy subject of Hanoverian girth and ponderosity, for instance, Scott shows all the tact of a haberdasher by royal warrant: 'Her [i.e. the regal] form, though rather *embonpoint*, was nevertheless graceful; and the elasticity and firmness of her step gave no room to suspect, what was actually the case, that she suffered occasionally from a disorder the most unfavourable to pedestrian exercise' (2. 188). In other words, the queen was fat and dropsical, like her grandson, Scott's fat and dropsical friend.

In order to understand the conception of *The Heart of Midlothian* one must look at Scott's own campaign for English favours over the years 1816–18. The facts of this campaign, which are misrepresented by Lockhart, have been dug up by Peter Garside.[3] Scott in the early years of the century neither admired, nor felt himself to be admired, by the occupant of Carlton House and his cabal. In 1811, however, the Prince Regent allied himself with the Tories. In 1812 Scott received Byron's flattering report of Royal favour, via Murray. This was followed in August 1813 by the offer of the Laureateship. In late 1813, Scott delivered a loyal address to the Regent, on behalf of the citizens of Edinburgh. In early 1815 Scott had his first encounter with the Prince, and learned that his 'Chief' (as he hailed him) was an admirer of the *Waverley* novels, and had no doubt as to who their author was.

At this point (April 1815) Scott made his direct proposals about the Regalia. It was something calculated to appeal to the Regent's interest in royal pomp. Scott, however, also had a personal agenda. By means of the Regalia process – and the custodial offices which their recovery would create – he intended to flatter the Prince and gain himself a baronetcy thereby. This contradicts the much repeated assertion that Scott's ennoblement in late 1818 was something 'neither begged nor bought' (*Lett.* 5. 263). Lockhart's bald statement that 'Scott's baronetcy was conferred on him, not in consequence of any Ministerial suggestion but by the King [i.e. the Prince Regent] personally, and of his own unsolicited motion' (Lock. 3. 447) is not true. As Garside shows, William Adam (Scott's friend, a senior Scottish lawyer and a Privy Councillor) lobbied the Prince in February 1818, immediately after the 'discovery' of the Regalia. Adam followed up with another application to the Home Secretary, Lord Sidmouth, in April.

Scott's pushiness was resented in high places. He was rebuked later in February by Alexander Maconochie, the Lord Advocate, for having presumed to make direct overtures to the Prince Regent. Scott was, according to Adam, enraged at Maconochie 'beyond what I could have imagined' (Garside, *MLR*, 21) for this rap over the knuckles. He nonetheless swallowed his rage and returned to his old friend – Melville. The supplication was at last successful, and by October Scott knew that his title was secure.

Scott's reason for wanting the '*petit titre*' was ostensibly to aid his son Walter's career in the army. But, as Scott informed Buccleuch, 'It may also help my own views towards the court of Exchequer' (EJ 637–8). This advancement was still Scott's ultimate aim. In early 1819, a vacancy arose. According to Lockhart, Scott now stood aside, in order to yield the position to his 'old friend' Sir William Rae. Garside quotes an unpublished letter by Adam Ferguson, of 9 January 1819, which contradicts Lockhart's flattering version. In the letter, Ferguson recounts a conversation with the Duke of Buccleuch in which the Duke reports raising Scott's claims with Lord Melville, only to be told rather sharply that 'Sir William Rae was first on the list'.

Scott prudently did as he was advised. Lockhart's and Johnson's version, that Buccleuch 'urged' Scott to accept the post and that he 'generously' yielded his place to a more needy friend as a kind of Sidneyesque gesture, is a distortion of the facts (EJ 638). As it happened, the resignation did not occur. William Rae took the higher promotion of Lord Advocate the following summer (1819). But the deaths of the Duke of Buccleuch in May 1819, and of Robert Dundas [of Arniston] Chief Baron of the Scottish Exchequer, in June 1819, effectively closed off Scott's main lines of patronage. There was no more serious talk of promotion for him.

THE HEART OF MIDLOTHIAN AND HISTORY

The Heart of Midlothian represents an impressive range of departures from the novels that precede it. It is the first novel Scott wrote which has a female protagonist, the first to cast a lower-class personage as protagonist – rather than as a comic Sancho Panzaish companion. *The Heart of Midlothian* is the first of Scott's novels to take Edinburgh – the author's 'own romantic town' – as its central location. As its name suggests, the novel's action pivots on the geometrical centre of the city: those few yards' radius in the High Street which at various times housed all the main arms of the Scottish state, before and after the union. And the centre of the official buildings around St Giles was the so-called 'Heart of Midlothian', the Tolbooth which over the years was Parliament House, College of Justice, Municipal Chambers and latterly City Prison. All these symbolic edifices were located only a few yards from where Scott was born, where he went to university, and where for most of his adult life he worked in the Court of Session. The fact that he could write a whole novel centred on 'his' Edinburgh suggests a new confidence in Scott.

For all its apparent novelty *The Heart of Midlothian* has close links with *Old Mortality*. One can plausibly interpret *The Heart of Midlothian* as the other shoe dropping on the question of Presbyterian rebellion against temporal authority. Both novels chronicle the consequences of ideological excess. *Old Mortality* anatomises Cameronian fanaticism – the sadism and inhumanity that accompany millennarian certainty. In *The Heart of Midlothian*, by contrast, Scott portrays the domestic, or virtuous aspect of the Cameronian faith; its staunchness in the face of temptation. In the later period of the novel's action Presbyterianism has been internalized as strenuosity of private moral conscience – rather than externalized as fanatic militancy. (The last relic of militancy is David Deans's comic battles with Reuben Butler in Knocktarlitie about the length of his sermons, and the propriety of Knockdunder's smoking in church; 2. 303).

This evolution is more striking in view of the historical continuity between the novels – a continuity which is set up by the long life of David Deans. Scott says the date of Davie's birth is unknown, but he dies in 1751,

aged upwards of ninety, as we are told (2. 343). This gives a birthdate in the
late 1650s. Although he is wary about admitting that he was a 'Bothwell-
Brigg whig', young David Deans evidently fought at that battle in 1679 and
must have presumably have known the famous Henry Morton, if only by
report and sight. From hints, we can reconstruct most of Douce David's
early and middle career. When he was fourteen, he was put in the pillory at
the Canongate 'for the cause o' the National Covenant'. Such punishment
was no joke (any more than the ducking that kills poor Madge Wildfire).
Pilloried victims were often blinded, disfigured, or brain-damaged by the
missiles thrown at them. As a young man, David fought for the Covenanters
not only at Bothwell Bridge, but presumably at Airdsmoss (1680) as well,
where Richard Cameron was killed. As far as one can make out (Scott gives
only a very oblique account, as a kind of pendant to that of the Butler
family) David then became a tenant farmer at Woodend, near Dalkeith.
Here he was persecuted by a loyalist landlord, the Laird of Dumbiedikes,
but staunchly maintained his independence and true-blue Presbyterianism.

The bad harvest years of 1700–1 ruined him (1. 106). Three years later,
on the point of being evicted, Douce David Deans was saved by the death of
the laird, his landlord. At this point, it is evident that David had a 'family'.
But since the only child of that union, Jeanie, was not born until 1708
(1. 113), family means 'wife'. The new Dumbiedikes was kinder but
an unenlightened agriculturist. His fields were unenclosed, his land
undrained, he did not 'improve'. Nevertheless, David Deans became a
shrewd and relatively wealthy farmer. His first wife died, and he married
again. His second wife was worldly. There was another daughter, Euphemia,
born in 1718. The laird fell in love with the growing Jeanie, and wished to
marry her. David's second wife died, and he moved from Woodend to a
small cottage on the edge of Edinburgh, at St Leonard's Crags, where – as
the novel opens – he tends a small herd of cows on the Royal Park common
land, supplying dairy produce to the city.

Although David is said to have some 'substance', he is clearly wholly
dependent on the labour of Jeanie who milks the cows and makes the
butter and cheese. She cannot marry. Effie goes into service in the city.
After the great trial of their faith which the novel recounts, from which they
emerge tested but true, the Deanses are adopted by the Duke of Argyle as
managers on his model estate in the Highlands. They are thus an advance
guard, and active agents in the Highland clearances. David is now entirely
loyal to the crown (he prays for the king and queen's preservation every
night) and a full – if somewhat balky – member of the parish kirk, officiated
over by his son-in-law Reuben. He dies, as has been said, in 1751, aged
'upwards of ninety years'. In fact, David has been made to seem younger
than his age for most of the novel because Scott wanted him both as a
father, and as the symbol of one hundred years of Presbyterian evolution,
from savagery to civilization.

In this second character, David Deans's career has a highly emblematic
aspect. As a boy, he is a martyr, and suffers torture. Then he is a rebel

warrior, and presumably kills his share of King Charles's men. He then enters on a feudal but independent relationship with the old landowning classes. As the old structures break down, he is pulled into the orbit of the newly emerging urban Scotland. Here he undergoes a terrible trial, in which his faith is almost destroyed. But he holds fast, and ends up integrated into the new, progressive Scotland. The Presbyterianism which was so horrifically anti-social in *Old Mortality* is now an energetic component in Scotland's modern progress. He is part of the new ascendancy. Jeanie's 'heroism' is merely a highly dramatized moment in David Deans's long domestication, his becoming at last 'useful' to his country.

David's story would have made a tedious saga. Scott chose to divert attention to Jeanie. The inspiration for her heroism was the story of Helen Walker, sent by an anonymous correspondent to the anonymous novelist, early in 1817. The letter-writer's hope was that a 'monument', in the form of a publication, might be erected to the memory of Miss Walker who – true to her name – had tramped down to London to save from the gallows a sister found guilty of infanticide. In Scott's 1830 preface the correspondent is revealed to be Mrs Thomas Goldie of Craigmuie (née Helen Lawson), wife of the Commissary of Dumfries. Mrs Goldie's *donnée* set up what is – even for Scott – a complicated narrative lead-in. Although Mrs Goldie met Helen Walker in 1790–1, just before her death, she would not speak of her heroic feat in the 1730s. The details were confided to Mrs Goldie by her husband who – as Helen enigmatically put it – 'kens weel about me'. Not many people knew the story. As an old friend put it, 'Helen was a wily body, and whene'er ony o' the neebors asked any thing about it, she aye turned the conversation' (1. xxxiii–iv).

Jeanie's tale is in most essentials parallel to that of her historical original. Helen Walker, born in 1712, was the daughter of a day-labourer at Dulwhairn. She and her much younger sister Isobel ('Tibby') were themselves field workers. They were orphaned early. Helen took over the care of the family. Isobel got herself pregnant, and killed her child by a river side, in autumn 1736. Tibby had kept her condition secret from her family. She was tried at Dumfries (well after the crime, oddly) in May 1738. Helen would not testify on oath that her sister had confessed her intention, which would have mitigated the crime. Helen Walker's act of heroism was provoked by the law of 1690 (abolished in 1809) which declared that murder should be presumed in cases where pregnancy was concealed and the child subsequently either died in mysterious circumstances, or disappeared. The aim was to put down infanticide and abortion. 'O Nelly! Ye've been the cause of my death,' the unlucky sister is supposed to have called out in court.

In Scotland, six weeks intervened between the passing of sentence and execution. In this interval, Helen tramped to London, presented herself to the Duke of Argyle in her tartan and won a pardon for her sister. Isobel subsequently married her seducer, and lived and died at Whitehaven. Helen never married and in old age had the reputation of being a 'pensy body' (i.e. slightly stuck up). She passed her later years in great poverty and died in December 1791, very shortly after Mrs Goldie came by her story while holidaying at Lincluden Abbey.

The novel changes and tones down certain details. Effie does not kill her child, nor does the thought cross her mind. It is the Queen in the novel, not Argyle, who grants the pardon. It is Jeanie, not Effie, who has the happy-ever-after marriage. In Scott's version – by a somewhat historically unconvincing prelude – Jeanie is a peasant (with all the peasant's bumpkin-virtues), living nonetheless in the largest city in Scotland. St Leonard's Crags, despite the implications of the story, is only ten minutes' walk from the Heart of Midlothian and about a quarter of an hour (for a healthy body like Mistress Deans) from the Grassmarket where the story opens with the hanging of Wilson. Of course, small-holding farmers did live like the Deanses, on the margins of the city. But it is unlikely that someone like Jeanie could have kept her countryfied personality intact living where she did.

THE HEART OF MIDLOTHIAN: GREAT AND LITTLE PEOPLE

Historically, John second Duke of Argyle and Greenwich (1678–1743), dominates the novel. A main architect of the Union in 1707, Argyle commanded loyal forces against the Scottish rebels in 1715 and won important battles. It is directly relevant to *The Heart of Midlothian* that Argyle mitigated Queen Caroline's wrath and her intention to strip Edinburgh of its ancient privileges, in her sympathy for Porteous's widow. By this date, Argyle was the most powerful aristocrat in Scotland and its principal lobbyist in England. A Scottish Quisling from one point of view, Argyle was an Enlightenment hero from another. Scott portrays him as a quick-footed opportunist, necessary to Scotland 'in a very precarious and doubtful situation', before the 'cement' of the Union had taken hold.

The Duke, among all his other 'patriotic qualities' is, as Scott puts it, a 'distinguished agriculturist' (2. 206). It is in this character that he recruits the Deanses to manage the land, and Reuben Butler to manage the labouring-class souls, on his model estate at Roseneath. The Duke's agriculturally scientific policies are shown to be historically prudent in *The Heart of Midlothian*. In parenthesis we learn that the 1745 Rebellion (two years after the Duke's death) washes over Roseneath without so much as a ripple of sympathy from the tenantry. This, we apprehend, is the direct result of the Duke's enlightenment. Argyle's practice of settling Lowlanders like the Deanses on the 'cleared' properties of shiftless Celts is similarly an intelligent anticipation of the Heritable Jurisdictions reform of 1748.

In one of its many aspects, *The Heart of Midlothian* is a novel about law and a whole range of related concepts: justice, mob-law, privilege, social discipline. One can put Scott's views on a scale. Clearly, he disapproves of the lynch law by which an English mob ducks Madge Wildfire to death in a muddy English village pond ('their favourite mode of punishment'), having just hanged her mother (who deserved to be hanged, but not for the offence of witchcraft). Like Argyle, Scott clearly disapproved of the Porteous riots, but could sympathize with the perverted civic pride that provoked the outburst. On the question of the law that condemns Effie to death, the narrative is inscrutable. There is no perceptible sentiment on Scott's part that the cruel and stupid *law* should be changed. Relaxing laws designed to instil discipline and wholesome fear in the lower classes was something not to be lightly undertaken. The judge at Effie's sentencing is sympathetic to her suffering, but inflexible:

> Young woman . . . it is my painful duty to tell you, that your life is forfeited under a law, which, if it may seem in some degree severe, is yet wisely so, to render those of your unhappy situation aware of what risk they run, by concealing, out of pride or false shame, their lapse from virtue, and making no preparation to save the lives of the unfortunate infants whom they are to bring into the world. (1. 355–6)

Scott has a similarly complex and enigmatic line on the 'moral courts' of the Kirk Session. These enforced good behaviour by humiliation. Offenders, especially sexual offenders ('for light life and conversation, and for breaking the seventh command'; 2. 196) were obliged to sit on the chair of repentance (the 'cutty stool') before the congregation. As Jeanie tells the Countess of Suffolk, the shame of this experience leads to much clandestine child murder. What Jeanie does not know is that she is talking to the King's mistress (in the company of a complaisant queen), the most exalted breaker of the seventh commandment in the land. When Effie – as the ruling belle of English society – goes into the upper-class world, she is appalled by their morality. Where does the novel stand on this? Is the cutty stool a cruel barbarism, like the ducking stool (in which Madge is slaughtered) or the pillory (in which young David was martyred)? When the Captain of Knockdunder – whose sexual morality is dubious – asks Butler to spare the public humiliation of a woman connected with him, Reuben acquiesces, but rather unwillingly. Knockdunder, after all, is the Duke's agent. One suspects that Scott believed that such draconian methods as the cutty stool and the 1690 infanticide statute were necessary for the strictly expedient purpose of keeping the lower classes in order – those members of the lower classes that is who had not, like Jeanie, internalized a strict morality.

It is significant in *The Heart of Midlothian* that Effie – the sister who rises in life and gets thereby a decent education – is wholly wretched. Jeanie, the sister who remains in her station and happily dusts her husband's books, is blissfully happy. Scott had a very limited belief in the virtue of educating the lower classes. Were it not that Reuben is too frail to work in the fields, his education might also be the waste of a good farmer. Scott satirizes self-improvement mercilessly in the person of Saddletree, with his buffoonish

Latin and law talk. Significantly, Saddletree's brain, addled with his self-taught learning, is dangerously radical.

It cannot be accidental that Jeanie's husband – the man who in some sense occupies the spot in the novel where a hero ought to be – is Reuben Butler. Scott, who called his wavering hero Waverley, his well-mannered hero Mannering, and his old buck of a hero Oldbuck did not, one can assume, choose Reuben's surname randomly. The name of Butler – a Scot of English descent – indicates that rank of servant which was particularly useful in intimate offices to the aristocracy ('MacJeeves'). Reuben is extraordinarily aware of his own place, and humble. Whatever spirit of rebellion once fired Bible Butler has been entirely bred out of his descendant. (Reuben, as Alexander Welsh notes, is symptomatically illness-prone.) He eventually rises by the machinery of aristocratic patronage. Who knows, perhaps one day his children will rise to be butlers by occupation, as well as by name.

The Heart of Midlothian is a very imperfect masterpiece. The novel contains, as the contemporary critic Nassau Senior complained, some half a dozen beginnings, all of them 'singularly careless' (Scott, *Critical Heritage*, 224). It opens with fifty pages of Jedediah at his most infuriatingly verbose. 'Begin at the third chapter' is the advice which many critics have given prospective readers. Once one gets into the story, it is extremely jerky and incoherent in its transitions. Senior complained that in the early parts of the novel Scott was like 'Humboldt examining the bifurcations of the Oroonoko'. And the story's coincidences were unlikely 'to a degree almost beyond the powers of numeration'. It beggars the imagination that on her random walk through England Jeanie should fall in with (1) a highwayman intimately friendly with Ratcliffe; (2) the woman who abducted Effie's child; (3) the seducer of Effie. No haystack but furnishes its pin.

Many hinges of the plot creak. How was it, for example, that no-one noticed that the Lily of St Leonard's was nine months pregnant? Scott skates over this general imperception among Effie's nearest and dearest very implausibly. It escapes 'the matronly eye of Mrs Sadletree' with whom Effie is in service because that lady is mysteriously 'confined by indisposition to her bedroom for a considerable time during the latter part of Effie's service' (1. 147). Mr Saddletree was, apparently, too obtuse to see or hear what all his neighbours were loudly joking about – 'the disfigured shape, loose dress, and pale cheeks of the once beautiful and still interesting girl' (1. 147). Why, above all, did Jeanie not notice? Rather lamely, the narrator informs us that – although she lived hardly a mile away – Jeanie was 'so occupied . . . with the concerns of her father's household, that she had rarely found leisure for a walk into the city' (1. 148). Equally unconvincing is the progress of her lover and husband, in his mutation from Gentle Geordie to Sir George Staunton. His assassination by his savage, unrecognized bastard, 'the Whistler', is poetically just but fantastically improbable.

As is often the case in Scott, one sees interesting novels just over the edge of what he actually offers us. Effie's seduction would be a banal novelette that one is relieved not to have. But the tricks, the education in the way of the world, and the transformations which made this unsophisticated Edinburgh servant, the daughter of a fanatic cow-feeder, the 'belle all London is talking about' would be a Pygmalion fable well worth reading. In four years, Effie is 'educated' at a French convent and emerges sufficiently sophisticated to delude even Argyle himself (who is sexually attracted, but haunted by a resemblance to Jeanie which he cannot explain; 2. 338). Reuben – the other husband – prudently does not educate Jeanie, even though teaching is his profession. As her letters reveal ('To prevent farder mischieves, whereof there hath been enough'; 2. 212) she is imperfectly literate. This, we apprehend, is the secret of her happiness.

Effie, on her part, is capable of writing a very creditable letter recounting, with occasional glancing wit, how miserable it is to live in high society and excoriating 'the cruel tone of light indifference with which persons in the fashionable world speak together on the most affecting subjects' (2. 330). In addition to being extraordinarily quick and intelligent, Effie has also mastered the very complex business of clothes, cosmetics, and jewelry: things that were not, presumably, taught at the convent. As the Duke records, Lady Staunton is 'the ruling belle – the blazing star – the universal toast of the winter . . . the most beautiful creature that was seen at court upon the [Royal] birthday' (2. 337). What, one wonders, should Effie have done? remained a disgraced ex-servant in her father's household, sitting week after week on the stool of repentance until all her brains and looks were decently extinguished?

No critic has a good word to say for Robertson (although I suspect many readers relish his gothic appearances in the action). His career would nonetheless make a good adventure story. A rector's son in Lincolnshire, and heir to the Willingham title, George sinks to the lowest levels of society: he becomes a smuggler. Here he finds true comradeship in Wilson and true love in Effie. Betrayed by the implacable mother of a woman he has wronged, he narrowly escapes terrible retribution. He rises to the highest rungs in society. He returns to the very city where he organized the riots, and was condemned to hang, as a government official. Finally, he is killed by his lost son. Similarly, the story of 'the Whistler', after he has run off to America, is volumes of romance compressed into two sentences:

> The young man had headed a conspiracy in which his inhuman master was put to death, and then fled to the next tribe of wild Indians. He was never more heard of, and it may therefore be presumed that he lived and died after the manner of that savage people, with whom his previous habits had well fitted him to associate. (2. 412)

On one level, the Whistler is a gothic monster: a kind of Frankenstein (Scott reviewed Shelley's novel in 1818; interestingly enough, he later declared it to be his favourite work of fiction.) On another, more political level, he is surplus population. *The Heart of Midlothian* is the first (non-pornographic) novel in the English language to deal with the tricky matters of contraception, infanticide, abortion and the embarrassing propensity of the working classes to breed. In the rather improbable eavesdropping scene at Gunnerby where Jeanie gets her 'dark insight' into the mystery surrounding her sister's condition, it is made clear that the horrific Meg Murdockson, among her other criminalities, is a professional abortionist and infanticide: when 'the hag' says that she cannot revenge herself against Staunton, having nursed him, Frank Levitt rejoins with the brutal jest: 'But, mother, they say you han'n't been so kind to other *bairns*, as you call them, that have come your way' (2. 80).

'Bairns', here, is a euphemism for bastards. How best to dispose of illegitimate offspring is a problem that recurs frequently in *The Heart of Midlothian*. The novel refers, on a number of occasions, to such unwanted children being thrown into the Nor Loch (as it is supposed happened to Effie's child, the loch being evidently a favourite resort of desperate mothers). Madge's bastard by George was done away with by Meg (so as to clear her daughter's marriage to a rich man). Meg sells the unwanted offspring of Effie to a beggar, who uses the child until it grows too big to appeal to passers-by in the street. At about the age of eight, the Whistler is sold to Donacha Dhu, who intends to sell the boy to the American slave trade. But perversely, he takes to the child, and adopts him as a trainee robber and murderer. There are even bastards in the Roseneath Arcadia. Knockdunder, for instance, during the upheaval of 1745, has the 'recorded foibles of a certain Kate Finlayson' (2. 304) erased by his accomplice Donacha Dhu, to save himself the expense of providing for the infant.

The upper classes treat their bastards better. One of the more interesting throwaway lines in the novel is spoken by Reuben, in an early conversation with the Saddletrees. 'Ye dinna ken whether ye are to get the free scule o' Dumfries or no,' asks the ever-inquisitive Mrs Saddletree, 'after hinging on and teaching it a' the simmer.' No, Reuben glumly answers, 'The Laird of Black-at-the-bane had a natural son bred to the kirk, that the presbytery could not be prevailed upon to license; and so . . .' (1. 67). Mrs Saddletree finishes the sentence for him. The Laird of Abbotsford, one may note, was also looking after the interests of *his* bastard nephew (Daniel's illegitimate son William) with some scrupulosity at this time.

Scott, at the period of writing *The Heart of Midlothian*, was influenced by Malthus's theories, and deeply worried about the problem of surplus working-class offspring. Like Malthus, he saw morality as primarily valuable as a check on vice and the surplus population arising from profligacy. This it is that accounts for the peculiar double morality of the story. Every night, David Deans prays for 'his Majesty' and, after the reprieve of his daughter, for the preservation of Queen Caroline as well. But the English king is spectacularly delinquent sexually: much more so than poor Effie Deans.

Why should Effie face the hangman and other lasses the cutty stool for what Lady Suffolk openly does at Windsor? Because, Scott might have replied, what is at issue is not general morality, but population.[4]

Better, of course, never to have bastards in the first place. Among Jeaine's other sterling virtues is that of marrying late. When she and Reuben marry she is just over thirty. Later, after they are prosperously set up, they have a modest brood of three children in the course of five years – two boys and a girl and 'all stout healthy babes'. Effie, by contrast, is eighteen and destitute, when she tragically adds to the British population. She evidently succumbs to the first man who makes an assault on her virtue. Jeanie, ten years her senior, resolutely keeps both Dumbiedikes and Reuben waiting years, before either may even consider proposal. Scott could quite effectively have kept to his source story, in which Helen Walker remained a life-long spinster. Mrs Goldie records an affecting retort that Helen made, on being told that she looked commendably cheerful: 'Mem, have ye na far mair reason to be happy than me, wi' a gude husband and a fine family o' bairns, and plenty o' every thing?' (1. xxxii). But Scott wanted to dramatize sexual prudence, not celibacy.

11

The Bride of Lammermoor to *The Abbot* (1818–1820)

The Heart of Midlothian appeared at the end of July 1818. The novel was popular to the point of mania, especially in England. The Scott–Constable axis had triumphed again. Lady Louisa Stuart reported being 'in a house where everybody is tearing [*The Heart of Midlothian*] out of each other's hands, and talking of nothing else' (Lock. 3. 268). Jeanie duly became the English public's favourite plebeian Scot, a position she has only briefly lost to Harry Lauder, Billy Connolly and Rod Stewart.

The Bride of Lammermoor, the partnering 'Tale', was written over 1818–19. It is hard to be more precise, although there are reasons for wishing one could be. As the novel's acutest critic, Jane Millgate, points out, it is possible that Scott began composition as early as May 1818. Certainly the novel was well underway in autumn 1818. Then, apparently, it was put aside for other tasks. It was, according to Millgate's guess, finished in March 1819, when Scott fell gravely ill again with his agonizing – and still undiagnosed – gallstones. He seems to have dictated the last section of *The Bride* (for which the manuscript does not survive) in some pain. Nevertheless, the novel was sent off complete to James Ballantyne 'by 2 May 1819' (Millgate, 170).

For a novel written by a dying man (as it was feared), *The Bride of Lammermoor* is an appropriately terminal work. Essentially, it is a romantic meditation on time's decay, and multiple *fins de ligne*. It chronicles the ruin of a race, the decay of a castle, the historical decline of a whole region (namely the Borders, which with the Union ceased to be a border). The narrative, as Robert Gordon perceives, is suffused with a 'Tory pessimism' about which there is 'nothing ambiguous'. Other critics (notably Andrew Hook), while concurring as to the generally pessimistic tone of the novel, have discerned some quite striking ambiguities.[1]

The Bride of Lammermoor is the darkest of Scott's novels. Its mood may have been artificially depressed by Scott's vast intake of opiate painkillers in early 1819. On 18 April, for instance, he told Daniel Terry: 'Conceive my having taken, in the course of six or seven hours, six grains of opium, three of hyoscyamus, near 200 drops of laudanum – and all without any sensible relief of the agony under which I laboured' (Lock. 3. 338). So debilitated was Scott that, for the first time in his authorial career, he (allegedly) dictated portions of *The Bride* to William Laidlaw and John Ballantyne (whom he preferred). According to Ballantyne, Scott's efforts were heroic: 'Though he often turned himself on his pillow with a groan of torment, he usually continued the sentence in the same breath' (Lock. 3. 343).

According to Scott, as relayed through James Ballantyne to Lockhart, so extreme was his pain and so drugged his condition while writing *The Bride of Lammermoor* that 'when it was first put into his hands in a complete shape, he did not recollect one single incident, character, or conversation it contained' (Lock. 3. 358). He then read the printed copy in a state of great uneasiness, 'lest [he] should be startled by meeting something altogether glaring and fantastic' (Lock. 3. 359). He affected to find the work 'monstrous gross and grotesque; but still the worst of it made me laugh, and I trusted the good-natured public would not be less indulgent.' Scott published with his 'ower true tale' an apology for its being 'overstrained, romantic, and composed by the wild imagination of an author, desirous of gratifying the popular appetite for the horrible' (2. 151–2).

This, of course, was the period in which Coleridge's most spectacular poetical experiments with drugs were published. 'Christabel', 'The Pains of Sleep', and 'Kubla Khan' (with its explanatory preface) came out in 1816. Scott would have read these works carefully. In light of remarks about his own intake of drugs and unconscious composition of the novel, one might well assume *The Bride of Lammermoor* to represent a uniquely Coleridgean phase of his artistry and James Ballantyne his person from Porlock. Taking Scott's cue, commentators have rhapsodized over the novel's Poe-like 'world of unrelieved darkness and nightmare'. Edgar Johnson seems himself to be under the sympathetic influence of Scott's laudanum in describing *The Bride of Lammermoor*: 'Page after page was written in a blurred trance of suffering in which he did not know what words he was putting down, images and dreamlike actions rising somehow out of unconscious depths of the imagination while he himself struggled through a drugged nightmare world' (EJ 646).

Jane Millgate, in a valuable debunking exercise, has looked at the manuscript of *The Bride of Lammermoor*, and disperses the wreath of Coleridgean fumes in a most business-like way. The four-fifths of the novel which survives in original form she notes to have been written by Scott in his usual neat hand. She detects no tremor of excitement, or transport in his script. She concludes: 'So far as the manuscript itself goes there is every reason to believe that Scott had completed most of the holograph before becoming seriously ill, and that even if one assumes that he did indeed dictate the final fifth of the novel in April 1819, his illness had by that time abated sufficiently for him to substitute the taking of hot baths for the frequent recourse to opiates that had been necessary earlier' (Millgate, 171).

Nevertheless, even after rejecting the drugged-trance myth, *The Bride of Lammermoor* remains a uniquely pessimistic effort. Its mood is a striking contrast to *The Heart of Midlothian.* 'Dismal' was Scott's term for *The Bride* (*Lett.* 5. 186), and the novel lives up to this description. Normally Scott's hero and heroine, as Alexander Welsh points out, end up with happy marriage, long life and a castle. *The Bride* ends with the hero being swallowed up in mud, the heroine dying mad (and possibly raped), the hero's castle falling into ruin, and his few remaining servants declining into hopeless destitution.

One of the things that makes *The Bride of Lammermoor* such an unsettling read is what James Kerr calls its 'weird amalgam of genres'.[2] The comedy of Caleb Balderstone (which Scott confessed to being overdone) clashes with the lurid gothic scene-painting. The balladic use of omens and a general mood of fatalism contradict the novel's superficial realism of narrative manner. Equally unsettling for the reader is the double time setting, which blurs the historical frame of the narrative, normally so firmly drawn in a Scott novel. Clearly the Union of the Parliaments in 1707 is the main pivot in the story, and is thematically central. But the narrative is ambiguous as to when exactly the principal events take place. Scott, in fact, wrote two *Brides*, one set before, the other after the crucial date of 1707. Again Jane Millgate was the first to register the importance of this, and again by a scrupulous examination of texts. As she observes: 'The manuscript of the novel, the first edition of 1819, and all subsequent editions for the next ten years set its events two or three years *before* the Union, the 1830 *magnum opus* edition transposes the action to two or three years *after* the Union' (Millgate, 172). The motive for this vacillation, as Millgate speculates, was not artistic but professional. In the first version, Ravenswood is engaged (albeit rather on the edge of the plot) with an appeal to the Scottish Parliament against the judgement of the Court of Session which has ruined his family. This represented a legal gaffe on Scott's part, so to protect his reputation (as a long-standing Clerk of Session) now that he was identified as the author of *Waverley,* he altered the novel when he revised it for the 1830 reissue. He did this by postdating events to after the Union, so allowing Ravenswood a legally plausible appeal to the British House of Lords.

Jane Millgate argues forcefully for the 'integrity' of the first, unrevised, version of *The Bride of Lammermoor* as possessing 'considerably greater coherence than its successor' (Millgate, 173). In her edition of the 'World's Classics' edition of the novel, Fiona Robertson makes an opposite argument for the revised, 1830 text, as representing Scott's mature preference. Robertson also denies that there is any satisfactory 'historical coherence' in either state of the novel. Both versions of the novel contain 'inconsistent historical references'. An aura of vagueness permeates the novel, and no editorial ingenuity can dissolve it.

Granting the existence of this vagueness, should one take it as a stroke of art, or the failing hand of a sick novelist? Consider, for example, the removal of Ravenswood from the action for a whole year at the critical moment when Lucy has to choose between two affianced lovers. It is hard to think of anyone less suited to be an envoy on the delicate diplomatic business for which the Marquis of A— has chosen Ravenswood. This, remember, is the man whose solution to a tricky legal problem is to lie in ambush and shoot his adversary dead. We are not told that he can speak French. Nevertheless, Edgar is sent on an embassy for the Marquis, for a whole year. He apparently writes no letters to his loved one. And what, we may ask, is the embassy? All the reader is told is that it is 'related to a secret and highly important commission beyond [the] sea, which could only be intrusted to a person of rank, talent, and perfect confidence, and which, as it required great trust and reliance on the envoy employed, could not but prove honourable and advantageous to him' (2. 54–5). What does this mean? Does Scott want to baffle his readers, or is he simply too exhausted to devise some plausible subplot?

Modern readings of *The Bride of Lammermoor*, particularly those which are alert to the unsettling and perplexing aspects of the novel, have generally ranged themselve against Gordon's assertion that the novel embodies 'unambiguous' Tory pessimism. The majority opinion is that the novel is extraordinarily riddling and undercuts itself at strategic points. The glamour of the Ravenswoods, for instance, is besmirched at crucial points in the narrative. Superficially, *The Bride of Lammermoor* seems to breathe a warm nostalgia for what the old cavaliers represent: grace, martial skill, indomitable courage, clan loyalty to family and feudal loyalty to retainers, physical handsomeness, gallantry. But at a number of points in the narrative the 'bonny' Ravenswoods are cast into a very dubious and unglamorous light. When Ravenswood goes to arrange for the burial of old Alice, the sexton, Mortsheugh, gives him a piece of his mind. Gravediggers, as in *Hamlet*, are no respecters of princes. The old man, it emerges, was a very unwilling bugler at Bothwell Brigg in 1679, where Edgar's family helped put down the Covenanters, and from which point (although it was in the short term a victory for their cavalier party) all the current Ravenswood misfortune sprang. From Mortsheugh's jaundiced angle (he had looked forward to something better in life than being a gravedigger) the battle was not the biblical massacre described in *Old Mortality*, nor the heroic trial of faith buried in David Deans's past. It was a shambles. Mortsheugh (the name means digger of the dead) is particularly scathing about Edgar's ancestors and their warrior posturing on the field of battle:

> There was auld Ravenswood [Edgar's grandfather] brandishing his Andrew Ferrara [sword] at the head, and crying to us to come and buckle to, as if we had been gaun to a fair, – there was Caleb Balderstone, that is living yet, flourishing in the rear, and swearing Gog and Magog, he would put steel through the guts of ony man that turned bridle, – there was young Allan Ravenswood [Edgar's father], that was then Master, wi' a bended pistol in his hand, – it was a mercy it gaed na aff, – crying to me, that had scarce as much wind left as served the necessary purpose of my ain lungs, 'Sound,

you poltroon! sound, you damned cowardly villain, or I will blow your brains out!' (2. 42)

Johnnie Mortsheugh was injured in the battle, and lost his place as Ravenswood's trumpeter. His verdict on the fall of the house of Ravenswood is uncompromising: 'When they had lands and power, they were ill guides of them baith, and now their head's down, there's few care how lang they may be of lifting it again' (2. 40). In the face of Ravenswood's protests about his father's bounty, and goodness to his 'vassals', the old man persists that 'he loot his affairs gang to the dogs, and let in this Sir William Ashton on us, that will gie naething for naething, and just removed me and a' the puir creatures that had bite and soup at the castle, and a hole to put our heads in, when things were in the auld way' (2. 44). In other words, the Ravenswoods are not victims of historical determinism; nor are they doomed by some ancestral curse; they are hereditarily stupid.

There may have been a private explanation for *The Bride of Lammermoor*'s melancholy vision of a ruined Scottish aristocracy. Scott was much worried by the Duke of Buccleuch's straitened circumstances in 1818–19. His Chief's estate was in some distress. Landowners in general had suffered in the post-war period, but none more than Charles, Duke of Buccleuch. It seemed like the end of an era for Scotland's great landlords. Nor was the Duke's health good. Always solicitous, Scott began in November 1818 to have serious apprehensions for the Duke's life. His absolute devotion to this very distant kinsman probably seems very odd to the modern reader. Scott clearly felt more depth of attachment to his Chief than to most members of his immediate family.

Scott wrote with extravagant dutifulness to his ailing Chief on 15 April 1819, 'God bless you, my dear, dear Lord. Take great care of your health for the sake of all of us. You are the breath of our nostrils useful to thousands and to many of these thousands totally indispensible' (*Lett.* 5. 343). What, one wonders, did 'totally indispensible' mean? Scott did what he could to rally his clearly dying Chief, writing a series of 'Edinburgh Gazettes Extraordinary', to raise his spirits. He evidently gave these epistles as much, or more thought than the fiction in hand. But all his encouragement and rallying was fruitless. The Duke went to Portugal in the vain hope of rescuing his health – pursued by any number of loyal communications from Scott – and died there on 20 April 1819. Scott was more distraught than at any time since the Duchess's death. 'To me', he told Lord Montagu (the Duke's brother), 'the world seems a sort of waste without him' (*Lett.* 5. 376).

A LEGEND OF MONTROSE

In December 1818 the Scotts learned of the death of Charlotte's nabob brother Charles Carpenter (EJ 635). Although married, he was childless, and his death meant a large bequest (some £40,000 as Scott initially thought) to the Scott children in course of time. The baronetcy (officially offered in October 1818) would also assist young Walter's career. He had elected to go into the cavalry – a notoriously expensive and snobbish branch of the military. Walter was duly gazetted as a cornet, or colour bearer, into the 18th Regiment of Hussars in July 1819, aged just eighteen.

Scott was misguided to set so much store on the Carpenter inheritance. The money was a widow's death away (she in fact outlived them all, lasting until 1863) and in the interim Walter would never support himself in the required style from his officer's salary – let alone buy the necessary promotions. (Johnson estimates that it cost Scott 'more than £1,300 to set Walter up as a cavalryman'; EJ 682.) Meanwhile, Abbotsford was entering its most expensive phase of construction and furnishing. Scott's appetite for land was proving insatiable. To raise money, he sold his literary copyrights, sixteen in all, to Constable for £12,000 in early 1819 (Lock. 3. 309).

Vast as the purchase sum was, it was to prove an underestimate of their worth when Constable promptly began to bring out collective reissues of the *Waverley* novels. Scott was ill-advised to part with these 'eild kye' (cows barren from age). A more prudent author would have 'worked his copyrights'. Scott himself probably realized the unwisdom of selling off his literary property (he had, for instance, told Blackwood just a year or so previous that he would see 'his nose cheese first' before parting with the copyright of the 'Tales'). But he needed ready money. Nor was Constable's £12,000 enough for his needs. Scott set to and wrote no less than fourteen full-length novels in the next six years – fiction to buy farms with, as Carlyle sardonically put it.

Scott's output between 1819 and the crash of 1826 is one of the wonders of literature. That he could publish three novels in 1819 verges on the miraculous, given the broken-down condition of his health. The mysterious stomach cramps had continued, and prevented his going to London in Easter 1819 to receive his baronetcy. His illness had in fact reached an acute stage in April 1819. As before, it took the form of agonizing spasms in the stomach, jaundice, 'tension of the nerves all over the body'. As before, the physicians treated the symptoms, not the (undiagnosed) ailment. He was overdosed with opiates, jolted with stimulants, given violent laxatives and soused 'like a salmon' in scalding water. Over the course of their twelve months' acquaintance, Lockhart observed a great change in Scott, as he now appeared in Easter 1819: 'He had lost a great deal of flesh – his clothes hung loose about him – his countenance was meagre, haggard, and of the deadliest yellow of the jaundice – and his hair, which a few weeks before had been but slightly sprinkled with grey, was now almost literally snow white' (Lock. 3. 344).

In June 1819 Scott suffered an attack which was so severe that he thought the end had come. He took his farewell from his family and turned his face to the wall. But, happily, he woke up again, having survived the crisis. Around this period he was treated by a new physician, Dr Dick, and made a gradual recovery over the next few months. Dick – who had gained his experience in the East India service – (mis)diagnosed liver problems, and prescribed small quantities of calomel and a changed lifestyle. By September 1819, according to Johnson, Scott's health was 'entirely restored' (EJ 683). It was nonetheless evident to his family and friends that he had aged twenty years. Scott, one presumes, must have been driven by financial demons, the evidence for which has been expunged, to have written and published seven volumes of fiction during this most tormented year of his life.

The Bride of Lammermoor and *A Legend of Montrose* were published together in four volumes as the third series of 'Tales of my Landlord', on 10 June 1819. *A Legend of Montrose* is generally judged to be sub-standard and has never enjoyed the acclaim of its partner. The inspiration for the tale was talismanic – as was frequently the case with Scott. He possessed a sword of Montrose's which adorned a wall at Abbotsford. The life of James Graham, 5th Earl and first Marquis of Montrose (1612–50), encompassed much Scottish history, as well as legend. Graham had made himself a champion of the New Covenant in 1638. In June 1639 he put down opposition to the Covenant at the Bridge of Dee, routing the Gordons. A year later Montrose headed the Scottish army that won the victory of Newburn, near Newcastle. In 1641, however, he was imprisoned in Edinburgh Castle. Liberated by the King, Montrose turned his coat and fought for the Royal cause. When the Scots invaded England in 1644, he was promoted Lieutenant-General and created a marquis. Montrose roused the Highlands and won a string of victories until he was surprised and defeated at Philiphaugh, in the Borders. The tide had turned. Montrose was taken prisoner, tried for treason and executed at Edinburgh in 1650. He was hanged and quartered, and his severed limbs were affixed to gates of principal towns in Scotland, a country which now loathed him.

Although the mid-seventeenth century was the furthest back he had taken his fiction, Scott found strong echoes of the present in the period of Britain's earlier civil wars. Both eras were marked by confusion, rebellion, and disorder. But the mid-seventeenth century upheaval was essentially different in England and Scotland. While a clear-cut civil war raged in England between the Crown and Parliament, Scotland was torn by more complex splits. The Lowlands and Highlands, the Covenanters and Royalists, and the feuding clans were all in conflict or opportunistic alliance. Montrose's own drastic changes of alliance reflect the complexity of Scottish politics, class allegiance and theology in the period. Montrose fought and killed for the Covenant, and for the King. He was at different times a patriotic Scottish soldier and a mercenary English General who killed Scots.

Although record of the family councils has not survived, Scott is known to have been disappointed that young Walter had not followed his father's 'selfish wish' and chosen law – like his father and grandfather – something that would have kept him within the frame of traditional Scottish culture.

The young man's wishes were, however, firm and probably he accepted his intellectual limitations more readily than his father. Walter resolved to be a soldier. That meant an English soldier and service abroad in England's colonial possessions (in fact, Walter was immediately posted to rebellious Ireland). He would be, that is, a mercenary. In *A Legend of Montrose* there is a revealing exchange between Menteith and Anderson, as they contemplate hiring Dalgetty – the ex-mercenary of the King of Sweden:

> 'I think this fellow Dalgetty is one of those horse-leeches, whose appetite for blood being only sharpened by what he has sucked in foreign countries, he is now returned to batten upon that of his own. Shame on the pack of these mercenary swordsmen! They have made the name of Scot through all Europe equivalent to that of a pitiful mercenary, who knows neither honour nor principle but his month's pay, who transfers his allegiance from standard to standard, at the pleasure of fortune or the highest bidder.' (35–6)

During the course of the narrative, the Ritt-master Dalgetty rises from Captain to Major and eventually becomes Sir Dugald. Then – with a final turn of his coat – he transfers to the Covenanters' cause after Philiphaugh. Finally, by calculated marriage, he reacquires his old patrimonial estate. How was young Walter Scott different from Dalgetty, fighting as he now was for an English king? Montrose himself – although his entries into the novel are somewhat incidental – is another turncoat. He had been a fierce Covenanter in his youth. Then he transferred to the Crown and fought bitterly against the Covenanters (his own people) in the service of an English king. By accepting his '*petit titre*', Scott himself (who liked to say that he would have ridden with the Pretender) had become an English knight – Sir Walter Turncoat.

In December 1819, Scott's mother died. With her, his allegiance to provincial Scotland seems to have died as well. From this point on, his principal fictional location was to be England. Scott evidently wanted a larger stage than the 'Tales' permitted. It is clear that he had tired of the Jedediah joke (probably rather later in the day than most of his readers). Gordon thinks Scott may also have tired of 'the muddy problems of his Scottish material' (Gordon, 117). For whatever reasons, with *A Legend of Montrose* a cycle in Scott's fiction came to an end. With his third novel of 1819, *Ivanhoe*, 'the author of *Waverley*' returned. And with this tale of 'not sixty, but six hundred years since' (Millgate, 191), a new cycle of novels opened.

IVANHOE

In 1819 Scotland's greatest novelist re-emerged as England's chronicler. *Ivanhoe* can be seen as tribute to Albion's growing cultural domination over its dependencies. Scott himself, rather unconvincingly, attributed the change in national subject matter to a fear that constant harping on

Scottish themes would 'wear out the public favour'. One can explain the Englishing of Scott in other ways. He spent much of his out-of-court time in London over the period 1808–20 and knew the literary market well (as did Constable, who spent a season every year visiting Paternoster Row). More importantly, perhaps, Scott always liked to place his authorial tribute at the feet of some patron, or chief. The death of Buccleuch had left him without a Scottish chief, and he evidently transferred his allegiance (at least nominally) to the Prince Regent, the monarch who would dub him knight.

Without too much ingenuity the plot of *Ivanhoe* can be construed as an elegant compliment to the Regent. In the novel, the English state is paralysed by a monarchic power vacuum. Prey to an uncontrolled oligarchy of barons ('Prince John's cabal'), the country must wait until its true king – Richard – returns to occupy his throne. This interregnant state of things is analogous to the current condition of England in 1819. It was titularly under the rule of a wholly disabled monarch, the mad George III, with a competent, masterful heir-presumptive in the wings waiting to sweep in like the black knight and rescue his country from scheming politicos. *Ivanhoe* could hardly but be flattering and Scott's royal friend was, it seems, captivated by the novel when he read it.

Scott had the first volume of *Ivanhoe* largely done by mid-July 1819 (EJ 680). The work was in the hands of a 'very slow transcriber' by early November and was published on 18 December. Appropriately, Scott invented an English alter ego as editor of the work – Laurence Templeton. Wholly unlike the provincial dominie Jedediah, Templeton is an urbane metropolitan lawyer. His dedicatory epistle to Dr Jonas Dryasdust (a friendly caricature of Morritt) constitutes the meatiest critical document Scott had incorporated into his fiction since *Waverley*'s Postscript (which should have been a preface). In his letter to the old pedant, Templeton justifies the artificial modernity of the idiom of *Ivanhoe*: its giving an artistic impression of being antique, without being authentically antique. Occasionally Scott makes anachronistic blunders of the De Mille 'wrist watch on the arm of a centurion' kind – as when, for instance, we are told that on learning the true identity of the Palmer (i.e. Wilfred) 'Gurth started up as if electrified' (1. 77); or when we are told that Isaac in the dungeon 'would have afforded a study for Rembrandt, had that celebrated painter existed at the period' (1. 279–80). But in general Templeton's theory is expertly put into practice by Scott.

Scott's first intention, he claimed in 1830, was to set up a third line of anonymous novels (following the 'author of *Waverley*' and 'Tales of My Landlord' lines). But he was talked out of this project by his publisher, who wanted the sales advantage of identifying *Ivanhoe* as by the author of *Waverley* (1. xxxi). As a kind of hallmark, Scott duly drew some lines of consanguinity with characters in *Guy Mannering*. *Ivanhoe* is supposed to be derived from an Anglo-Norman manuscript belonging to Sir Arthur Wardour, and Laurence Templeton is, we are told, an English antiquary friend of Oldbuck.

Strung as it is on three loosely connected episodes (the tournament at Ashby, the storming of Torquilstone, the trial of Rebecca by the Templars), *Ivanhoe* is one of the best 'combined' of Scott's works – to use his own term. It makes notably good use of suspense. Scott liked the title particularly because 'it conveyed no indication whatever of the nature of the story'. *Ivanhoe* has powerful scenes which climax in cliff-hanging situations (Isaac about to go on the toasting rack; Rebecca about to be deflowered, for example). Of all his novels it has kept its popularity best.

One can enjoy *Ivanhoe* even today as a good tale and nothing more. But fundamentally it asks to be read as a treatise on nationality. There had been 'national tales' in plenty before Scott: but *Ivanhoe* was something more – a novel about the making of England. Intermingled with the novel's nationalist themes was an investigation of race. The author of *Ivanhoe* was largely responsible for injecting consciousness of race (and a sizeable dose of racism) into the popular British mind. This injection took three general forms: (1) the propagation of polygenic rather than monogenic theories of race; (2) the popularization of the national myth of the 'Norman Yoke'; (3) the legitimation of anti-semitic stereotypes.

Both monogenic and polygenic theories of race were current in the early nineteenth century. Monogeny assumed that the human species, in all its national and social diversity, had the same racial origin: one race – the human race, as the later slogan was to put it. As a 'science' it devoted itself to the search for primal Adamic origins. Monogeny lent itself as a political ideology to philanthropic movements, such as abolitionism. Polygeny, by contrast, concentrated on physical differences and assumed separate racial origins for the major ethnic groups. It was the polygenic theory – particularly as popularized by Robert Knox in the 1830s – that helped found anthropology as a field of scholarly study and which, in the socio-political arena, sanctioned aggressive racism and imperialism in the nineteenth and twentieth centuries. And it was Knox, a rabid polygenist and a contemporary of Scott's in Edinburgh, who propagated the view that races stood in a hierarchical relationship to each other. The 'lighter' races were superior to the 'darker' races. And within the lighter division, blonds, like the Saxon, were superior to swarthier groups, like the Celts.

Scott adheres closely in the early chapters of *Ivanhoe* to Knox's light–dark hierarchy. The villainous Knight Templar, Brian de Bois-Guilbert, has an 'unusually swart complexion' with 'thick black features', and features 'burnt almost to Negro blackness' (1. 16). To emphasize the point he also has a couple of Negro attendants (an anachronism for which Scott apologizes in a later note). These subhumans relish the infliction of torture. They are not Scott's man and brother. Cedric, by contrast, has 'long yellow hair' (1. 34). Rowena has 'mild blue eyes' and hair 'betwixt brown and flaxen' and a pale complexion 'exquisitely fair' (1. 49). Wilfred has 'a profusion of short fair hair' (1. 174). These tints and pigments predict an inevitable marriage between Wilfred and Rowena.

Scott had introduced racial themes marginally into *The Antiquary*, where Jonathan Oldbuck is a proponent of Gothic supremacy, against the Pictophile supremacist Sir Arthur. Race is, by contrast, the primary issue in *Ivanhoe*. And Scott is firmly in the polygenist camp. Race dominates the prelude in the Yorkshire forest, where Wamba the jester and Gurth the swineherd discuss – like a couple of arcadian Jespersons – the archaeology of English, sometime around the end of the twelfth century. How is it that the language has two words for such things as swine and pork, bull and beef, calf and veal? This point of diction is explained by politics and race: the Normans see the meat on the dining table, the Saxons tend it in the pasture and the sty.

This leads on to the second of *Ivanhoe*'s major racial propositions – the so-called 'Norman Yoke Thesis'. As Christopher Hill has noted, Scott did not invent the myth that a 500-year-old Saxon democracy had been extinguished by the Norman Invasion, and that the next 700 years were absorbed in the recovery of those lost rights – a process gloriously consummated with the repulse of a second Norman (or Napoleonic) invasion.[3] But there is no doubt that *Ivanhoe* was the main popularizer of the myth among the English at large. One of the attractions of the Norman Yoke Thesis in the nineteenth century was its adaptability. All parties and interests could use it. Disraelian Conservatism was built on it. So too were Carlylism and muscular Christianity. Thomas Jefferson was a fanatic believer. Thomas Paine was a radical proponent of the thesis. Scott himself is what Hill labels a 'middle-class radical' proponent of the Norman Yoke Thesis.

One of the problems in the novel's exploitation of the Norman Yoke Thesis is the historical fact that – as Scott himself notes – the barons who established 'English' rights on 15 June 1215 were all of Norman extraction. Of course, Prince John can be portrayed as possessed of all the worst Norman features. But his brother Richard the Lionheart has the same Norman parentage. Scott gets around this by recalling that the Normans were 'a mixed race' – part French, part Viking. Even Normans might have some saving Saxon genes. There is also some allusion – by Cedric – to Richard's distant Saxon relations. But what really transforms the Black Knight into 'Richard of England' is his fighting shoulder by shoulder with the Saxons against his brother Normans at Torquilstone. By this act of fratricide, he becomes an adoptive Saxon. (Scott himself, we remember, had a French wife – dark as a blackberry – and was himself a straw-haired Border Saxon. His own children were, however, Saxon for all their Latin heritage.)

The most objectionable form of racism given currency by *Ivanhoe* is anti-semitism. Scott was not the first novelist to make fiction the vehicle for this form of bigotry. Richard Cumberland's *John de Lancaster*, which Scott reviewed for the *Quarterly* in 1809, is more virulent. (Like *Ivanhoe*, Cumberland's novel fed on dislike of the Rothschilds whipped up by the French Wars.) There is no evidence that Scott personally intended to

wound Jews as a group, but his depictions in *Ivanhoe* put into currency
stereotypes which might easily be exploited by racists. Like *The Merchant of
Venice, Oliver Twist,* or *Jew Süss, Ivanhoe* can be twisted into racist slander. And
even if he is not himself racist, there is a consistent undercurrent of
derogation in Scott's narrative which verges on the anti-semitic. In the
opening description of Isaac by the fire in Cedric's hall (where he receives
appalling treatment) we are told that it is 'perhaps' owing to universal
persecution that the Jews adopted 'a national character, in which there was
much, to say the least, mean and unamiable' (1. 55). Wilfred helps Isaac
escape the Knight Templar's clutches, which seems to imply that there will
be no state persecution under the Lionheart, once he regains his throne.
But shortly after this episode, at the beginning of chapter 7, the point is
made that the sad condition of England is directly attributable not to John's
misgovernment, but to Jewish financiers. Their loans to the nobles 'at
the most usurious interest . . . gnawed into their estates like consuming
cankers' (1. 87). Jewish bankers, even at this early date, are the cancer
eating away England. This race guilt on the part of the Jews extenuates the
obscenity of Isaac's torture scene in chapter 22. It is, after all, only a kind of
radiation therapy for the body politic, to cure its cancer. He is to be cooked
alive, Front de Boeuf's slaves basting him all the while with oil, lest 'the
roast burns'. Meanwhile, his daughter has been given to Bois-Guilbert as
a plaything.

Historically, few have spoken up for Jewish financiers (although it would
have been difficult to run the Napoleonic Wars without them). Jewish
doctors are something else. It is Rebecca who saves Wilfred after he has
been wounded winning the great tournament at Ashby. Scott notes the
proficiency of Jewish physicians – male and female – and notes, rather
sourly, that it is possible 'that the Jews possessed some secrets of the healing
art peculiar to themselves, and which, with the exclusive spirit arising out of
their condition, they took great care to conceal from the Christians among
whom they dwelt' (2. 267). Again one hears the note of racial derogation.

The Jewish plot of *Ivanhoe* was, apparently, suggested by James Skene,
who had observed Jewish communities 'when he spent some time in
Germany in his youth' (Lock. 3. 423). Prejudice against Jews in England was
hardened by the popular belief that the Rothschilds had enriched themselves immensely by early knowledge of the result of Waterloo. They were
the real victors, profiteers from the long war. It makes sense to see the
depiction of Isaac in the light of the popular Rothschild slander. Like the
later financiers, Isaac has amassed huge wealth as the direct result of
Europe's wars – the Crusades. When Front de Boeuf tortures him in the
dungeon, it seems that Isaac can, if necessary, come up with the fabulous
amount of one thousand pounds of silver. It is clear that this hoard has
been amassed by banking – more specifically loans at 'usurious' rates of
interest. At the end of the novel, the judgement on Isaac is no less interesting than that imposed on Shylock. Unlike Shakespeare's Jew, Isaac is not
obliged to convert. His beautiful daughter – unlike Jessica – is not given to

the Gentiles to enjoy sexually. He keeps his ducats, but only if he pays a heavy (not crippling) tax or ransom, of 1,000 crowns (2. 168). Scott's thinking seems to be racially tolerant, and he looks for a solution to the 'Rothschild problem' (i.e. profiteering) through what was currently the favourite panacea promulgated in his political writings, a rational income tax applied particularly on high earners. But then – in the most ambiguous aspect of this racial subplot – Isaac and Rebecca are made to leave the country: they are banished, presumably as racial contaminants. Subsequent adapters of *Ivanhoe* have never been happy with this conclusion. In the 1952 MGM film version Isaac and Rebecca finance the ransom of Richard through the Jewish community, and in return are pledged by the (proto-Zionist) King a homeland in Palestine, once the Crusades have succeeded.

The (threatened) rape of Rebecca in Torquilstone leads on to another extraordinary subplot in the novel. Repulsed but now an admirer of his victim's strength, the Templar confesses to Rebecca his plans to take over the world by means of his secret society, the Knights Templar. This guild of ascetic Christian Crusaders was one of a number of forerunners of the Masons. The Knights Templar now exist as a branch of the Free Masons (like the Societas Rosicruciana they apparently admit only Christians to membership). Once he has the 'batoon of the Grand Master' the Templar will be more powerful than kings. 'Our mailed step', he tells Rebecca, 'shall ascend their throne, our gauntlet shall wrench the sceptre from their gripe. Not the reign of your vainly-expected Messiah offers such power to your dispersed tribes as my ambition may aim at. I have sought but a kindred spirit to share it, and I have found such in thee' (2. 15).

The Mason and the Jew will thus achieve world conquest. In *Ivanhoe*, Scott sowed the paranoid seeds for any number of twentieth-century conspiracy fantasies. Without a potent monarch and a regenerated aristocracy, conspiracies like Bois-Guilbert's will thrive, together with the 'canker' of Jewish finance. One of the first things that happens when Richard resumes charge of his state is that Isaac is taxed into obedience and secret societies like the Templars are brought to heel. In historical fact, Scott wrote *Ivanhoe* at a time when the Masonry had immensely increased its power, with the union in 1813 of the 'Antients' and 'Moderns'. This laid the ground for the secret society's huge subsequent expansion. George IV was initiated (as Prince of Wales) into the Masons in 1787, and on his accession in 1820 became the first king of England to be a member.

POLITICS AND FAMILY

Scott's conservatism is never easy to pin down, but by 1819 he was on most matters a diehard reactionary. Of the Peterloo Massacre in August 1819, he told young Walter (since July a dragoon officer cracking other radical heads in Ireland) 'the Manchester Yeomen behaved very well . . . and notwith-

standing the lies in the papers without any unnecessary violence' (*Lett.* 5.
483). The eleven civilians killed and hundreds wounded might have dis-
agreed. As 'L.T.' (i.e. Laurence Templeton) Scott wrote a piece in the
Edinburgh Weekly Journal (which he co-owned) defending the authorities.[4]

Scott's ferocity against the Manchester pro-Reform demonstrators is not
creditable to him. But he was very jumpy and somewhat irrational about the
condition of the nation at this point of his life. Personally, he had always
been renowned for his affability to political opponents – the *Edinburgh
Review* Whigs for instance, some of whom were intimate friends. But now he
almost broke even with James Ballantyne over Peterloo when his old friend
(and co-proprietor) printed something critical of the Manchester magistrates in the *Edinburgh Weekly Journal.* 'I cannot continue a partner where
such mistaken views are inculcated', he declared (*Lett.* 5. 485). Eventually
he was talked out of resignation when a thoroughly browbeaten Ballantyne
'promised to be cautious' in future (EJ 688).

One assumes that Scott was worried about his property and his new
status as a laird. His lust for land had become ravenous. In summer 1820 he
bought for £2,300 a property called 'Heiton's grounds' (EJ 707). He was
toying with the idea of buying a neighbouring estate, Faldonside, for
£30,000 (EJ 685). As interior decoration for Abbotsford he was ordering via
Terry a museum of curios from the London salerooms. What, one wonders,
could Abbotsford want with 'an Esquimeaux jacket made of the intestine of
a whale' or 'Addison's velvet slippers' (EJ 684). Collecting property had
become Scott's mania and protecting it against revolutionary lower orders
was his obsession. 'You will succeed me in my landed property', Scott told
his son (*Lett.* 5. 497). But what if something like 1789 happened? Where
would the Walter Scotts' landed property be then?

There was in fact insurrection in the winter of 1819. The Government
introduced strict measures of control over assembly, the right to bear arms
and the popular press. Miners in Northumberland and weavers in the west
of Scotland had risen up. The Laird of Abbotsford was all for beating them
down again mercilessly (at the same time that as an author he was cheering
on the Saxon peasants storming Torquilstone Castle). In his panic, Scott
persuaded himself that 'upwards of 50,000 blackguards are ready to rise
between Tyne and Wear', – an army of Napoleonic size (EJ 687–8). 'The
Devil seems to have come up amongst us,' Scott declared, 'unchaind
and bellowing for his prey' (EJ 690). Glasgow was put under martial law
following the discovery in February of a radical plot to seize arms and take
over the city.

Alarming as the times were, Scott's alarm was excessive. So too was his
military zeal. 'The Highland chiefs', he told Morritt, 'have offered . . . their
clans' (*Lett.* 6. 58). The Highland chiefs were not (as they had been in
Montrose's time) called on by the English authorities, but Scott thought he
might usefully levy a company of Lowland reivers. With other like-minded
lairds he proposed 'raising a company of sharpshooters' from the loyal
Scottish peasantry. He became more and more excited by this idea, and

elaborated on it. They might be called, he suggested, the 'Buccleuch Legion' or 'The Loyal Foresters' (Lock. 3. 409). All this was over November and December 1819, while Scott was still labouring on *Ivanhoe* – a convalescent if not absolutely a sick man, of sedentary profession, with a lifelong disability, close on fifty. Nevertheless, he proclaimed himself ready to march at the head of his legion of Melrose Volunteers to Tynedale. Later in 1820 the corps of Foresters project collapsed when the government declined to finance it. Anyway the 'Radical row' had by summer of that year been put down by military force and judicial severity.

On finishing *Ivanhoe*, Scott had intended to go to London to receive his '*petit titre*'. In fact, he did not manage to do so until March 1820, when he was duly 're-edited' as Sir Walter Scott, Bart (EJ 701). Lady Scott, as she now was, did not accompany him, although young Walter was in London. Scott's was the first baronetcy of George IV's reign – something, the monarch said, that he would always reflect on with pleasure. Scott himself was pleased because he regarded the baronetcy as an order of chivalry (that is, an honour earned by feat of arms). Among other incidental honours at the time, Scott's bust was done by Francis Chantrey (EJ 703) on this London visit. It is the most circulated of the Scott icons, and according to Lockhart gives posterity its best impression of the author of *Waverley* in the flesh. His portrait was also painted at the new King's command by Sir Thomas Lawrence, and the picture hung in the great gallery at Windsor.

Scott's pleasure in these events, and in the triumph of *Ivanhoe*, was muted by the death of his mother on 24 December 1819. Aged eighty-seven, she had suffered a stroke earlier in the month, having just given a vivid exposition of the 'real story' of *The Bride of Lammermoor*. Scott's uncle, Dr Daniel Rutherford, who was attending her, died suddenly at the same time (EJ 692–3). A favourite aunt, Miss Chritty, went in the same awful month. All these old relatives were buried at St John's Chapel, at the west end of Princes Street. The reason given for Mrs Scott not being interred alongside her husband was that Greyfriars' graveyard was too crowded. Doctrinal difference may have come into it; Anne Scott may have preferred to await resurrection in the company of Episcopalians. As he had with his father twenty years earlier, Scott took his mother's loss stoically as 'the natural consequence of very advanced life' (*Lett.* 6. 117).

New generations came on to replace those departed. On 29 April 1820, Lockhart married Scott's daughter, Sophia. The young man was an advocate, a star writer on *Blackwood's Magazine*, a poet and a firm Tory. Scott had met his future son-in-law and biographer two years earlier, and liked him from the first. In 1819, the two of them had negotiated with Croker about the possibility of setting up a Tory newspaper – another 'Anti-Jacobin' – to oppose the *Scotsman* in the wake of the Peterloo furore (EJ 689). It was pleasing to Scott that Lockhart was a member of the volunteer corps of cavalry raised in response to the 1819 disturbances, doing what he himself had done as a young patriot in 1797.

'Perhaps Charlotte would have preferred a man of wealth or title', Johnson observes (EJ 697). Sophia herself told her former governess Miss Millar, on accepting Lockhart in January 1820, 'that I might have made a much higher marriage in point of rank and wealth I have little doubt.' On his part Scott thoroughly approved Sophia's choice. 'He will probably rise high, as his family are rich and his talents excellent and I have some interest', he predicted (*Lett.* 6. 189). Scott only worried about 'a certain rashness' in his future son-in-law, by which he meant the scorpion-like propensity to sting everyone he came into contact with in print. Scott's policy had always been more affable – to dine with his harshest critic on the eve of *Marmion*'s publication, for instance. Sophia and Lockhart married quietly at Castle Street and made 'rather a pretty couple' as Scott thought (EJ 706). The newly-weds settled down in Great King Street, a short walk from the Scotts' town house. Later they took up a roomy summer cottage, Chiefswood, on the Abbotsford estate.

THE MONASTERY AND THE ABBOT

Ivanhoe was hugely successful when it came out on 18 December 1819. A new Scott novel, Sydney Smith declared, was a 'holiday for the whole kingdom' (EJ 691). Having mined the 'Scotch' quarry to extinction, Scott had found a new and even more profitable literary vein. Constable had considerably improved the packaging of the '*Waverley* novel'. They were now finer made articles, and more expensive, having gone up from eight to ten shillings a volume. Sales of *Ivanhoe*, even at 30s, were immense – the first edition of 10,000 clearing in less than a fortnight (EJ 687). But, as Lockhart notes, this level of sale was not sustained in subsequent novels and Scott was (Lockhart alleges) somewhat deluded by booksellers on the subject (Lock. 3. 425). The success of *Ivanhoe* engendered hubris in Scott and confirmed his tendency to overspend in the belief that he could pay off any consequent obligation with so many strokes of his pen.

Scott's negotiations for *The Monastery* reflected his new sense of worth. For half profits on 12,000 copies he received an advance of £5,000 in 'Longman's beautiful and dutiful bills' (EJ 683), thanks to his 'brilliant little haggler' John Ballantyne. *The Monastery* was duly published in March 1820 – only three months after *Ivanhoe*. There is no clear record of composition, although the work seems to have been projected in July 1819, just before the contract was made. The extraordinarily short interval between two major works of fiction has led to speculation that Scott had written a substantial part of *The Monastery* some time before *Ivanhoe* (EJ 680, Lock. 3. 431).

The Monastery evidently began as a conventional Romantic *meditatio* – the contemplation of a ruin. The ruin was that of Melrose Abbey (archly called in the novel St Mary's or 'Kennaquhair' – 'I ken not where'). The Abbey was part of the furniture of Scott's childhood, and was rich with Buccleuch associations. He had incorporated a portion of its stonework into Abbotsford. As with Wordsworth's Tintern Abbey or Carlyle's meditation on the Abbey of Bury St Edmunds (in *Past and Present*), Scott's contemplation of Melrose's decayed structure inspired grand visions. Set in the later Elizabethan period, the novel's early sections revolve around the Lady of Avenel's 'Black Book' – the Bible in English, more dangerous to Catholic Scotland than any invading army. Border abbeys like Melrose were the Scottish Church's bulwark against reform. But Scottish Catholicism was now in its last days. Scott offers a fine description of the 'ancient system' towards the end of the novel as being like 'some huge leviathan, into which some ten thousand reforming fishers were darting their harpoons . . . actually blowing blood and water, yet still with unremitted, though animal exertions, maintaining the conflict with the assailants, who on every side were plunging their weapons into her bulky body' (2. 195). And alongside modern Protestantism seeping up from the south and eroding traditional Catholicism is a deeper, ineradicable layer of pagan folklore. At every important juncture of the novel, the White Lady of Avenel intervenes: a wraith whose existence is attested to even by the sceptical Father Eustace.

The execution of *The Monastery* does not do justice to the theological plot Scott devised. There are other flaws in the novel. After *Ivanhoe*'s mercifully brisk lead-in, the reader of the 'Magnum Opus' *Monastery* has to wade through almost a hundred pages of prefatory matter. Indeed, in this edition it opens with a preface which is so self-deprecatory as to discourage anyone from proceeding further. This is followed by an 'introductory epistle' from 'Captain Clutterbuck', a retired soldier turned antiquary, who has received the manuscript on which *The Monastery* is based from a mysterious Benedictine monk, visiting his Scottish homeland from France. This is followed by a letter from 'the author of *Waverley*' to Clutterbuck.

Nor, once the reader reaches the first page, is the story brisk. *The Monastery* begins with a historical essay on Catholicism in Lowland Scotland in the sixteenth century, the devastating effects on the nation of the battle of Pinkie, and a leisurely introduction to the parents of the characters who are to be heroes and heroine. It seems that Scott designed his novel around a set of dualisms: Protestantism, Catholicism; Father Eustace and the heretic preacher Henry Warden; Halbert and Edward Glendinning. The last of these was clearly intended to make up the main romantic plot. Halbert, the elder of the two, has 'hair as dark as the raven's plumage' and is a born fighter. His brother Edward is light-haired, blue-eyed and scholarly. One is destined to be a soldier, the other a monk. (Scott may have been thinking of the different temperaments of his own sons, Walter and Charles. While Walter had joined the Hussars, Charles – who was clever but idle – was clearly designed for university; EJ 681, 695.) Both brothers love Mary, the ward with whom they are brought up. This was evidently intended to come to fratricidal pitch, and Edward makes a few speeches of extreme turgidity about his Cain-like temptations. ('My fierce, turbid, and transitory joy discharged itself in a thirst to commit homicide, and now can I estimate the frenzy of my despair?'; 2. 217.) But the tension is never drawn tight, and indeed Scott seems as a narrator to avoid the more painful aspects of the brothers' rivalry. The result is a romance largely devoid of romantic interest.

Scott's relations with his publishers continued to be vexed – a vexation arising principally from the author's resolute disinclination to be anyone's sole property. Longman, not Constable, was entrusted with the first edition of *The Monastery*. Longman and Constable were permitted to combine on *The Abbot* – a venture which Constable proposed renaming 'The Nunnery', on the grounds that it would boost sales (EJ 700). Scott found the suggestion crass, and made one of his dinner-table jokes about it. But the publisher was correct in thinking *Waverley* novel titles too bland and enigmatic. Constable had better luck when he suggested the subject of Queen Elizabeth for Scott's next effort, which he was sketching out in 1820. The suggestion was taken up and the outcome, to Constable's immense pride, was *Kenilworth*. 'By God,' he liked to declare, afterwards, 'I am all but the author of the *Waverley* Novels!' (EJ 698).

Before he could get to *Kenilworth*, Scott had to dash off his sequel to *The Monastery*. That novel had not found favour with the critics when it was published in March. Normally Scott did not like repeating himself. But Edgar Johnson plausibly suggests that in writing *The Abbot* (*The Monastery* twenty years on), he was primarily motivated by a desire to 'bob it again' – to get the story of sixteenth-century Scotland right (EJ 700). Constable was sweetened into backing the venture by the offer of all future rights to profits from the 'Tales' (EJ 700). 'The Great A' was dashed down by August 1820 and published on 2 September (EJ 711–2).

The main plot of *The Abbot* revolves around a subject of much public interest in 1820–1 – that of an inconvenient queen. Although Scott avoids clear historical markers, both *The Monastery* and *The Abbot* take place during the early phase of Mary's decades of incarceration. She was imprisoned at Lochleven in June 1567 and escaped in May 1568 with the help of a youth called Willy Douglas (Roland Graeme in the novel). There ensued the Battle of Langside, which she watched. Imprisoned again, the luckless queen was executed nineteen years later on grounds of treason. The years of Mary's long crisis constituted a 'calamitous' period for Scotland, during which the country was turbulently tossed between old Catholicism and new heresies. And – with the succession crisis provoked by Elizabeth's childlessness – Scotland was, for once, central to the affairs of Britain. Like other romancers, Scott was drawn to Mary – the most glamorous of Scottish heroines – for her romantic associations. (It is significant that he makes her slightly younger and more sexually desirable than her actual age warrants.)

At the period dealt with in *The Abbot* Mary had become an embarrassment which had to be dealt with for reasons of state – but how? As the novel opens, Elizabeth, with the aid of Murray (Mary's half-brother), has shut her away. But, as Murray angrily corrects Roland, 'She is not imprisoned . . . God forbid she should be: she is only sequestrated from state affairs, and from the business of the public, until the world be so effectually settled that she may enjoy her natural and uncontrolled freedom, without her royal disposition being exposed to the practices of wicked and designing men' (1. 295–6). At Lochleven Mary is put under pressure to renounce all her claims on pain of death – for 'murder and adultery' (murder of Darnley, adultery with Bothwell).

It would have been hard for any moderately aware Briton reading *The Abbot* in 1820 not to think of Caroline – the most inconvenient queen in British history since Mary of Scotland. The Prince had married Caroline, a German aristocrat (at George III's instruction) in 1795. But he abandoned her a year later. She was denied access to her daughter in 1812–3, but allowed to travel abroad after August 1813. Over the intervening years she had lived scandalously in Italy, misconducting herself flagrantly with an Italian courier, Bartolomeo Bergami. She was in 1820 fat, middle-aged and consistently ridiculous. But she was determined. On the proclamation of George IV in February 1820, the 'Queen' announced her intention to return to her realm. She turned down an offer of handsome reward if she agreed to live abroad and surrender the title of queen.

Caroline duly returned to her 'realm', with much pomp, in early June 1820. Her cause was taken up by the Whigs (disaffected by the Prince's backing of the Tories). Caroline was fêted, given loyal addresses, pageants, and had bonfires lit in her honour by an opportunistic alliance of politicians, political groups, and mobs antagonistic to the King. There were many of them. It was an extraordinary spectacle. The King's lawyers mustered sordid evidence of his wife's misdoings. The Prime Minister, Lord Liverpool, dug up a cumbersome legal instrument, a Bill of 'Pains and Penalties' against Caroline which, if carried, would enable the King to divorce his wife. Essentially, it was a trial of her sexual morality in the House of Lords. Caroline was served (brilliantly) by Brougham as her Attorney-General and Thomas Denman as her Solicitor-General.

The trial began in the third week of August 1820 (as Scott was finishing *The Abbot*) and was an orgy of prurience. Stained bedclothes, brimming chamberpots, and groping in carriages featured prominently in the parade of evidence from Italian servants. The Bill mustered a tiny majority, but it was clear that it had no chance in the Commons. It was abandoned by Liverpool in early November, who feared revolution if the divorce were somehow forced through. Mobs roamed the London and Edinburgh streets, breaking windows that like Scott's had no celebratory candles in them (his glass, however, was spared). On 30 November the 'Queen' was cheered by a huge mob when she went to St Paul's to give thanks to God for her deliverance. She was denied a palace, but Parliament voted her an annuity of £50,000. She was physically barred from the Coronation in July 1821. She died in the same year and was buried without state at Brunswick.

Granted that one was tragedy and the other ripe farce, there were obvious parallelisms between Caroline and Mary Queen of Scots – two adulterous women extremely vexatious to their sovereign. Scott, like everyone else, was entranced by the 'extraordinary pas de deux' (EJ 721). He was not, of course, intending to satirize the Hanoverian divorce circus in *The Abbot* (he was far too loyal to the monarch who had knighted him). Nor was he advising George IV to chop off Caroline's head – much as the Hanoverian may have yearned for the arbitrary powers of the Tudors in such domestic matters. But in a year dominated by hysteria on the subject of inconvenient queens, Scott's novel (whose composition and publication shadow the divorce proceedings almost to the day) was clearly topical and its topicality must have enhanced its sales. Scott, this is to say, had established an intimate reverberation between his fiction (now coming out as regularly as a quarterly magazine) and the events of the day. It is one of the reasons why the novels of this period (unlike the Scottish novels) have not 'lasted' critically.

The Abbot was published on 2 September, 1820 and had a mixed reception. The *Edinburgh Review* was unimpressed and *Blackwood's* (probably through the Lockhart connection) was very favourable. The *Quarterly* was enthusiastic. The novel had a huge influence in making Loch Leven attractive to tourists – recalling the cultural impact of *The Lady of the Lake*. In the long term, *The Abbot* glamorized posterity's image of Mary Queen of Scots to the point where it can now never be deglamorized. As the first sequel novel in English, *The Abbot* was to be immensely influential. Thackeray's vast webs of consanguineous fiction, Trollope's Barsetshire and Palliser sagas, Oliphant's Carlingford Chronicles, together with a multitude of other Victorian sequence novels (not to mention Balzac)[5] can be traced back to the *Monastery–Abbot* combination. Scott himself, however, never tried the experiment again. His writing *The Abbot* in the same mould as *The Monastery* had not been consciously innovative, but an attempt to mend the faults in the earlier novel. This aim achieved, Scott had no more interest in the sequel form.

12

The Tory Grandee (1820–1822)

Scott's fame was consolidating. In May 1820, he was offered honorary degrees by both Oxford and Cambridge. (He was unable to attend the ceremonies, and gracefully declined, Lock. 3. 459.) In November 1820, he was elected President of the Royal Society of Edinburgh – an institution devoted to the furtherance of science. He accepted and gave a puckishly unscientific inaugural address (EJ 721). Nonetheless those who chose him knew what they were doing. The 'practical' Scott had a keen interest in technology, and in 1823 he was put on the board of a new company set up to extract gas from oil – a process for which he became an energetic evangelist. A 'century of inventions' was installed at Abbotsford – about which Lockhart is amusingly unimpressed.

Scott was at the age when honours came unsought. He now wielded considerable patronage in Edinburgh and was instrumental in getting John Wilson ('Christopher North', of *Blackwood's Magazine*) the chair of Moral Philosophy at Edinburgh University. It was Lockhart who in March 1820 asked him to intervene on his comrade's behalf with the Tory ministers, in whose gift the chair was. Scott complied – with the proviso that Wilson restrain some of his 'eccentricities' and drink less. It was an appointment of Caligula-like inappropriateness, more so as Wilson's opponent was the distinguished metaphysician, Sir William Hamilton. Scott's support of the wholly unqualified Wilson can only be justified on the grounds of Tory solidarity and Wilson's convivial – if reckless – wit.

Scott had made Wilson – one of Blackwood's wild men – a respectable citizen. He was eager to do the same for Lockhart – another wild man. Lockhart's early relationship with Scott can only be reconstructed hypothetically from a few known facts. The son of a rigid Glaswegian minister, John Gibson Lockhart ('JGL') had distinguished himself by intellectual merit at Glasgow and Oxford. A saturnine, rather sinister, figure (Scott nicknamed him 'the Hidalgo') Lockhart combined deep misanthropy with the knack of forming intense friendships with a few chosen comrades. John

Wilson (another Glaswegian) and Jonathan Christie – both of whom he met at Oxford – were two such comrades. When Lockhart returned to Edinburgh in 1815 as a young lawyer, he and Wilson gravitated to *Blackwood's Magazine* (known among its contributors as 'Maga'). After the journal's tepid start they, together with James Hogg, gave it a sensational relaunch with 'The Chaldee Manuscript' (October 1817). A panoramic, spoof-antiquarian, and hilariously irreverent conspectus of the Edinburgh literary world, the 'Manuscript' was notably tender of Scott's reputation. (JGL, nonetheless, gave himself in it the masochistic nickname that stuck through life – 'Scorpion'.)

Scott was nervous about the satirical play with personality, but enjoyed the 'Manuscript'. In the wake of its sensational impact, JGL (assisted at every step by Wilson) embarked on what his biographer calls 'the year of disgrace' – 1818. Its low point was the 'revolting' multi-article attack on Leigh Hunt and the 'Cockney School of Poetry' (a term which JGL invented). His campaign of scurrility – which included blackguarding his victim's sexual proclivities, class origins and learning – scraped its lowest level with the assault on Keats's *Endymion* in August 1818. Keats hated Lockhart to his (arguably accelerated) dying day.

Lockhart first met Scott at the General Assembly of the Church of Scotland (a public holiday) in May 1818. Scott had evidently noted the young man as a rising star. Shortly after their introduction he recruited him to do the history section of the *Register* for 1816 (a job long since resigned by Southey). It was a valuable piece of patronage – worth around £400. But it was conspicuously non-satirical. Scott intended the work to be corrective of Lockhart's 'tomahawk' propensities. JGL was briefed at a meeting at 39 Castle Street in summer 1818, and was invited to Abbotsford in October 1818, in company with Lord Melville, the grand panjandram of Scottish Toryism.

The Abbotsford visit was the turning point in the young man's life. It is unlikely that he fell in love with Sophia Scott on this first meeting, but he certainly lost his heart to Walter Scott. In the immediate aftermath JGL proposed to William Blackwood his first book, *Peter's Letters to his Kinsfolk*. It was transparently a homage to *Paul's Letters to his Kinsfolk* and it was designed – as JGL's synopsis to Blackwood indicated – to climax with an account of the author's glorious visit to Abbotsford in October 1818. The book would frame Scott as the tutelary spirit of Scottish Toryism, and its finest flower. The descriptions of Scott himself in the *Letters* soared past sycophancy into idolatry.

After they became intimate Scott warned his future son-in-law against 'Maga's style of brutal personal satire, which made lifelong enemies and provoked blood feuds that could ruin a man's career. That he should mend his ways was imperative after New Year 1820, when Sophia (and Scott – who superintended all the lovers' correspondence) accepted JGL's proposal of marriage. Scott saw JGL as the adoptive son he had longed for and never found in his own male offspring. As he told Morritt: 'To me as it seems neither of my sons have a strong literary turn the society of a son in law possessed of learning and talent must be a very great acquisition' (*Lett.* 6. 188–9). JGL it would seem was marrying more than one Scott.

Scott's warnings about reckless satire proved true in 1820 when the editor of *Baldwin's London Magazine*, John Scott (no relation) wrote a series of articles accusing Lockhart of being the secret editor of *Blackwood's Magazine* and a libeller. There was a tangled background to the dispute going back years. John Scott's magazine had been a champion of the 'Cockney School' which Lockhart had held up to scorn in 'Maga'. In an article published in November 1820, John Scott extended his censure to Sir Walter himself as the malicious mastermind of *Blackwood's* anonymous ruffianism and its penchant for 'hoaxing and masquerade'. In the context of Scott's recent ennoblement these were hard words. And they put Lockhart in an excruciatingly difficult position. He was, under Scott's tutelage, a reformed man. But his Hidalgo's pride would never allow him to disavow comrades like Wilson. Nor did Scott help. Infuriated by John Scott's animadversions on himself, he abused the other man as an 'absolute dunghill' and poured contempt on him. Instead of calming Lockhart, and advising contrition (or failing that dignified silence) he fired his son-in-law up. It was the more unwise since Sophia was in the later months of what was proving a difficult pregnancy.

Threats were returned to John Scott, who refused to retract his allegations unless Lockhart testified that he was not *Blackwood's* editor. Formally he was not. But effectively the magazine was edited by a coterie of whom 'the scorpion' had been a founder member. Moreover, in a letter to Coleridge of 8 June 1819 (written with malicious intent), Lockhart had informed the poet unequivocally that he was 'the editor of Blackwood's Magazine' (Griggs 934, 1199). It must have caused Lockhart agonies that he did not know who had seen that letter or whether John Scott might even have it in his possession. Lockhart finally went down to London in January 1821 to force an apology or fight a duel. He can only have done so with his father-in-law's acquiescence, Scott's honour having also been impugned in the *London Magazine.*

Lockhart's 'friend' (i.e. second) in the affair was Jonathan Christie, his old Oxford classmate. In the face of JGL's bullying, John Scott continued to demand an 'assurance' as to his not being the editor or a salaried member of *Blackwood's* staff. With a duplicity which seems to have been habitual to him, Lockhart had two statements printed. That which was distributed to selected other parties declared, unequivocally, that he was not the editor of *Blackwood's Magazine*, nor an employee. That which was dispatched to John Scott had this vital section missing (Lockhart evidently feared that his opponent had the June 1819 letter to Coleridge in his possession.) When John Scott did not immediately respond, Lockhart publicly branded him coward and liar – clear provocation for a duel. Still receiving no immediate response, he scuttled back to Edinburgh. He may have been recalled by Scott, on behalf of a distraught Sophia.

Sir Walter Scott's own position was murkier than his supporters then and now have conceded. He was at this period the patron of Blackwood's three main 'Mohocks' – literary hatchetmen: Wilson (for whom he got the Edinburgh chair in 1820), Lockhart (whose career he was bringing on as fast as he could) and Hogg (for whom he had done innumerable favours). The author of *Waverley* – as John Scott rightly pointed out – had made anonymity in authorship a Scottish cult; and it was anonymity which added the razor-edge of malice to 'Maga's satire. Sir Walter Scott's role could easily be seen as Cato-like: 'without sneering, teach the rest to sneer' – and then load the sneerers with all the rewards that the bulging coffers of Tory patronage could supply.

There was a tragic conclusion to the affair. At some point after Lockhart's return, in early February 1821, John Scott was alerted to the difference in the texts that his antagonist had printed. The word 'lie' was uttered. Lockhart, whose wife was seriously ill, was detained in Edinburgh. His luckless second, Jonathan Christie, was drawn into an actual moonlight duel, on behalf of his friend. John Scott was shot in the stomach and lingered in agony for ten days before dying. Christie surrendered himself and was subsequently acquitted, although no-one (other than his father-in-law) has had a good word for Lockhart then or since. Walter Scott was in London at the time of the duel, and must have been in agonies of apprehension (although he showed very little sympathy for John Scott, even on his deathbed).

Scott used this sordid affair, from which neither he nor Lockhart emerged with credit, to press his son-in-law still more urgently to give up all connexion with 'Maga', the 'Mother of Mischief' (*Lett.* 6. 363–4). Apart from anything else, JGL was now a family man. On 14 February, while the John Scott affair was reaching its bloody conclusion, Sophia gave birth to Scott's first grandchild – John Hugh Lockhart. The birth was a month premature, and may have been brought on by the mother's anxiety about the child's father having his head blown off. Lockhart duly mended his ways and turned his hand to writing the excruciatingly dull classical romance *Valerius* (1821), a work in which only Scott seems to have found much merit.

In subsequent years, Scott worked to promote his son-in-law as a respectable London editor and to insinuate him into the echelons of Tory power. Lockhart's career – although modestly distinguished – never reached the heights he, or his father-in-law, hoped for. For all his outstanding gifts, he ascended no higher than the eventually embittered editor of a decayed *Quarterly Review* – an editorial rule marred by ineradicable outbreaks of his 'scorpion' venom. For posterity Lockhart's only lasting literary distinction is that he wrote his father-in-law's life. One wonders if he might not have prospered better had he had not been smothered so benignly by Scott's patronage and paternalism. It is likely too that the grandees of the Tory party were quite willing to turn a blind eye (or even condone) one of their young bucks fighting a duel; but having your best friend do it for you was something else.

Scott's own unrespectable connections died with John Ballantyne. He
had been ailing for some time, and intimating a desire to retire to Kelso on
what remained from the sums he had made as Scott's adviser and secret
partner. He gave up auctioneering at the end of 1820. But his 'Parisian
tastes' had been expensive and he did not find himself well provided
for. Scott contributed free of charge a set of introductions to '[John]
Ballantyne's Novelists' Library' which began publication from February
1821 onwards. By the time it limped to its conclusion, in 1824, the series
had covered most of the fathers and mothers of English fiction.

Scott's motives in giving John Ballantyne this set of introductions
are not entirely clear. It was a sizeable gift – almost 200,000 signed words –
at a period when every spare minute was needed to keep up the golden
flow of fiction for Constable. It may have been that Scott intended to
provide a pension to his dying friend. Eric Quayle perceives a more sinister
motive. He believes that Scott offered the introductions to entice
the tubercular John out of retirement in Kelso's clear cold air back
to the 'smoke and fogs of the city' (EQ 147). To return to Edinburgh
was, Quayle further alleges, 'suicide' on John's part (EQ 151), and
little better than homicide on Scott's. But with up to three novels appearing
a year and Constable embarked on ambitious collective reissues of his
fiction and poetry, Scott needed John Ballantyne's magic with figures. The
'author of *Waverley*' could not, of course, deal directly with publishers,
printers, and booksellers without an intermediary agent. There was also all
the complicated business of confidential bill discounting, money-changing,
loan raising and double accountancy for which John (and his unscrupulosity) was irreplaceable. Scott must have an agent. If his agent were
dying (Quayle implies) that was unfortunate, but Scott still had
need of his services.

Some seven weeks before Ballantyne's death, on 28 April 1821, Scott
positively insisted that John drag his dying body to Edinburgh, to keep his
[Scott's] financial affairs in order (HG 194). Grierson indicts Scott for
cruelty in this summons, a recurrent cruelty which mars his relationship
with both Ballantynes (HG 87). Johnson suggests, unconvincingly, that
Scott did not know, until a few days before his friend died on 16 June 1821,
that he was seriously ill. It is more likely, as Grierson claims, that Scott knew
but felt his own concerns came first.

Quayle elaborates on Scott's selfishness towards the Ballantynes. At
exactly the same time that John was dying – and thus becoming
unserviceable – Scott invited (lured, as Quayle implies) James back into
partnership. He had resigned in 1816, at the instigation of his wife's family
– more particularly her lawyer brother, who prudently doubted Scott's
financial solidity. As Quayle points out, if James had not been 'inveigled'
back in June 1821 he would never have been engulfed in the crash four
years later, with all its calamitous consequences for him. Johnson retorts
that Scott allowed James to return on extraordinarily advantageous
financial terms and that in 1821 the Printing Office was booming with the

reprint orders that Constable was issuing for reprints of *Waverley* novels (EJ 764). On this point, Johnson seems in the right.

John Ballantyne wrote a gallant letter to Scott two weeks before his death: 'A spitting of blood has commenced, and you may guess the situation into which I am plunged. We are all accustomed to consider death as certainly inevitable; but his obvious approach is assuredly the most detestable and abhorrent feeling to which human nature can be subject' (Lock. 3. 534). He thanked Scott for his friendship over the years. He was forty-seven and had travelled lifetimes since he was a shopkeeper in Kelso in 1801. Scott told Lockhart that after John's death, 'I feel as if there would be less sunshine for me' (Lock. 3. 537). As a last irony, Ballantyne left Scott a non-existent £2,000 in his will. Lockhart scoffs at this testamentary gesture, and presents it as typical of John Ballantyne's inextinguishable self-importance. Even of the brink of eternity, he could not repress his own grandiosity. Quayle, who has looked carefully at John's finances, suspects that he died not all that badly off, but that his assets were misappropriated by his wife and family to protect them from creditors. (Scott would probably not have objected.) Whatever the financial facts, Scott behaved very generously towards John Ballantyne's surviving family.

Scott's involvement with John Scott's death was hard enough to live down. But it was compounded by another scandal which again identified him in the public mind as the provocateur of unprincipled literary ruffians. In December 1820 Scott had become, with other prominent Tories, a secret financial backer of a new journal which, at Scott's suggestion, was called the *Beacon* (EJ 773). The aim was to fight Radical-Whig fire with Tory fire. Edinburgh Tories, once the absolute rulers of the country, now felt themselves sadly beleaguered, and in imminent danger of rout.[1] The Tories desperately needed counter-propaganda and the *Beacon* was to be its vehicle. The first weekly issue duly appeared in early January 1821.

The early numbers of the *Beacon* quickly earned the paper a reputation for libellous invective against political opponents, and its attacks on Edinburgh Whigs provoked a predictable rumpus. In August, a slighting reference to James Stuart of Dunearn (a fiery Fife Whig) apropos Queen Caroline led to his thrashing the *Beacon*'s printer in the public street. The Laird refused the subsequent challenge of the tradesman to fight a duel, on grounds of class difference. The *Beacon* meanwhile conducted a long series of slanderous attacks on another Whig, James Gibson.

Gibson got wind of the existence of certain backers in high places and confronted Sir William Rae, the Lord Advocate, asking if it were true that he – one of the senior law officials in the land – was involved. Rae, evidently rattled by Gibson's ferocity, protested weakly that he had indeed put up £100, but his involvement extended no further. He foolishly showed Gibson a list of the other backers. They included besides himself the Solicitor General (James Wedderburn), two Advocates-Depute (John Hope and Henry Home-Drummond), the Sheriff of Perth (John Hay Forbes) and two Clerks of Session – Colin Mackenzie and Walter Scott. It was astounding intelligence. A group of the highest Law Officers of the Crown were involved in the most scurrilous journal in Scotland. Gibson had no doubt as to who the mastermind was, and threatened Scott with a duel. As Robert Chambers (who was in Edinburgh at the time) recalled, Scott was 'loudly blamed' for his conduct in the *Beacon* affair.

The duel would have been serious and possibly fatal for Scott. He was willing enough to fight, but the ground was cut from under him when the other law-officer backers collectively withdrew their financial support and gave an assurance that they had nothing to do with the content of the paper. Scott felt impotent, humiliated, and very angry. He branded his colleagues cowards. But he had to go along, unless he was to fight duels with them as well. Following Rae's revelation, the *Beacon* was extinguished after a ten-month run. But it flared up again in Glasgow with the same corps of contributors, now called the *Sentinel*. The attacks on Whigs were resumed. James Stuart of Dunearn, unable to find anyone else to flog, instituted a libel suit against the Glasgow publishers. To forestall the action, the publishers opened their contributors' files to the plaintiff. To his astonishment, Stuart discovered that his principal tormentor was Sir Alexander Boswell of Auchinleck, son of the biographer and a very close friend of Sir Walter Scott's. A duel ensued on 22 March 1822, in which Boswell was mortally wounded. Stuart stood trial in June, defended by Edinburgh's most distinguished Whig advocates and 'Edinburgh Reviewers', Francis Jeffrey and Henry Cockburn. Stuart was acquitted, and Walter Scott's reputation fell that much lower.

Scott's position in this affair is equivocal. His apologists suggest his connection with the *Beacon–Sentinel* was simply an error of judgement. He had, as it were, thrown a hundred pounds in a collecting box without thinking what the money was to be used for. According to Grierson 'the fault of the trustees [was] want of control, not an active part in the campaign.' According to Lockhart Scott 'never even saw the journal' (Lock. 3. 613). He himself protested to Heber that he had never caught sight of it, even 'by chance' (HG 195–6).

This defence is not entirely convincing. It is clear that Scott played a formative part in founding, designing, and launching the *Beacon*. He complained in some detail, for example, at its references to the John Scott affair (*Lett.* 6. 377) – how did he know what it was writing if he was not reading? There are references to his being friendly with the editors (*Lett.* 6. 346). Common sense suggests that he would, however cursorily and uneasily, have scanned the contents. And if he didn't read it, Lockhart must have done so, and reported to him. As Scott recalled more than once in later life, Alexander Boswell had actually dined with him a couple of days before the duel: 'That evening was, I think, the gayest I ever spent in Castle Street', Lockhart recalled (Lock. 4. 23). Although he could contemplate the death of John Scott as the disposal of so much dung, the shooting of his nobleman friend affected Scott deeply (the duel in *Saint Ronan's Well* reproduces the event 'exactly', according to Lockhart; 4. 23.) It is inconceivable that Scott did not know what Boswell was doing in the *Sentinel.* And as someone who had himself been challenged a few months earlier, it is hard to believe that – on this last convivial meeting with Boswell – he had not caught wind of what was going on.

The world of early nineteenth-century journalism was so scummy that no-one should hold Scott to the highest ethical standards. But two deaths, even if they are not to be laid at Abbotsford's gates, could have been prevented by Scott. He should have restrained Lockhart (whose moral case was untenable) in the John Scott affair. He should either never have backed the *Beacon,* or having backed it he should have exercised more control or publicly detached himself with a statement of censure. It is true that Scott never personally wrote lampoons, or libels. But on too many occasions for it to have been coincidence, he was an accomplice before and after the fact and bestowed favours on those who did his party's dirtiest work.

KENILWORTH

Scott worked on *Kenilworth* through the summer and autumn of 1820. The novel was published in January 1821 as the work of six otherwise distracted months. Momentously, *Kenilworth* was retailed by Constable in three 'luxurious' volumes, octavo, at a guinea-and-a-half. It thus set the pattern for fiction for the next three-quarters of a century. As the first 'three decker', if for no other feature, *Kenilworth* was one of the most influential novels ever published in English. It was also a supremely influential text for what was to become a Victorian industry – the lusty Elizabethan romance. *Kenilworth* raised to a new level what was later to be called 'tushery' ('Tush' is, in fact, Richard Varney's favourite ejaculation) or 'gadzookery'.

Thematically *Kenilworth* was a celebration of English nationhood – a pageant in prose. The narrative is constructed around a great 'Queen's Festivity' in July 1575.[2] Scott was inspired by the build-up to the Coronation of July 1821 – the most flamboyant festivity of its kind that modern Britain had seen. As such *Kenilworth* has no more artistic durability than a 1953 Coronation mug. The novel also shows him for the first time measuring himself as the modern Shakespeare – his nation's laureate in fiction. It all went down extremely well. Scott had caught the national mood perfectly. *Kenilworth* was a main source of the cult of Elizabethanism that was to flourish in nineteenth-century Britain and which is still periodically revived by opportunistic politicians and nostalgists.

Scott's novel popularized the Elizabethan age by a set of tableaux which have entered folklore, where (thanks to Hollywood's enthusiastic revivals) they still have currency. They include Ralegh hurling down his cloak into the mud for his monarch to tread on (earning himself a knighthood thereby); the court of brilliantly clad wits and poets, dominated by a fiery beautiful queen; the set of cunning astrologers lurking on the edge of things; an entourage of Flynn-like buccaneers, half-courtiers, half-lovers of their glamorous monarch. Above all, Scott associated the Elizabethan age with the bounding energies of English chauvinism – the qualities which made tiny Britannia mistress of the world. Although Scott presents the royal portraits as logical partners, that of Elizabeth glows with a patriotic lustre entirely lacking in the lachrymose presentation of Mary Queen of Scots in *The Abbot*.

Even more than the previous novel, *Kenilworth* is shot through with what Grierson calls 'a noble contempt' (HG 200) for chronology and the finer points of historical fact. Scott's Elizabethanism is no slave to literalism. There is, for instance, heroic anachronism in the walk-on parts given Edmund Spenser and the 'player' Shakespeare in *Kenilworth*. Scott specifically identifies the period of the action as July 1575, when the great pageant took place at Kenilworth Castle. At that date, Shakespeare was eleven, and the poetry (including snatches from one of his last plays, *The Tempest*) which is so popular with Elizabeth and her court in the novel was decades in the future. Nor had Spenser begun to write seriously in 1575. Ralegh is congratulated by the Queen on his daring in Ireland five years before he went there. And Fuller's story about the cloak is almost certainly apocryphal. Amy Robsart died in 1560 – fifteen years before the action of the novel in which she is the main character. The pageant at *Kenilworth* which provides the background to the climax of the novel is similarly glossed. Scott describes it as a sumptuous affair. In fact, it seems to have been a familiar kind of English summer shambles. The main dramatic representation was rained off. The poet Gascoigne practically killed his monarch by having a 'wild man' leap out to present his poem of welcome, and terrifying her horse.[3] It is not, one must hasten to say, a question of ignorance on Scott's part. As David Daiches graphically shows (by a pictorial representation of Scott's working materials for *Kenilworth*, Daiches, 104), he undertook careful historical research for those parts of the novel which interested him. It was his choice, apparently, to take his liberties with fact. It indicates something like scorn for his public. It was *Kenilworth*, as Grierson tells us, that led Goethe to repudiate Scott in 1823 with the lofty declaration, 'I can learn nothing from him. I have time only for the most excellent' (HG 201). The issue is, however, more complex than whether or not we have 'time' for novels like *Kenilworth*. Canonically, of course, the novel is an outcast. There cannot be a graduate course in the Western World where it is taught, and the MLA bibliography confirms that few modern scholars have wasted their valuable time on the novel. And yet, as a mass-produced article of fiction *Kenilworth* did exactly what Scott required of it; that is to say, it pleased discriminating critics (his close friends), it caught the mood of the day (and would appeal to the brazen nationalism of the later century), it made pots of money, and it left his tens of thousands of readers eager for more of the same post haste. It is an achievement as worthy of studious examination as the inner meaning of *Elective Affinities*.

THE PIRATE

In early February 1821 Scott was again resident at the Waterloo Hotel, Jermyn Street, London, lobbying (together with Sir William Rae) on behalf of the Clerks of Session in a Bill currently being debated in Westminster. The reform they wanted was designed 'to relieve [the Clerks] from a considerable part of their drudgery, in attesting recorded deeds by signature' (Lock. 3. 511). Scott remained in the capital until April. It was an eventful period. Although Lockhart (for obvious reasons) does not mention it, Scott must have been agonized by the Scott–Christie duel and its sensational aftermath. When John Scott died on 27 February, Walter Scott had to wonder whether his son-in-law would be dragged through the criminal courts as an accomplice to murder. Scott was also anxious about the condition of his pregnant daughter, Sophia, whom he had left in Edinburgh in a precarious state of health. He was still in London when on 14 February she gave birth, prematurely.

In London Scott met for the first time the widow of his brother-in-law, Charles Carpenter, who was back from Madras. Charles's will had stipulated that Mrs Carpenter should live on the interest of his fortune, and that after her death the capital should be divided equally between Charlotte's children, the Carpenters being childless. As David Daiches points out, 'Scott grossly over-estimated what the amount turned out to be . . . it is interesting evidence of the way Scott was becoming more and more obsessed by money that he should have written cheerfully to several of his friends crowing about the expected £30,000' (Daiches, 108–9). Scott now learned from his sister-in-law that his Indian fortune was considerably less than he and Charlotte had hoped for (EJ 726). As it happened Mrs Carpenter would outlive both Scott parents and all their children.

Scott continued to be preoccupied by the expenses and affairs of his son, Ensign Walter Scott, currently on active duty in the Irish countryside (EJ 766). The unruliness and riots of the Irish insurgents were worrying. He warned his son that 'the Irish of the lower ranks are a vindictive people' (EJ 767). These were not the paths of glory which Scott had in mind for the ennobled heir to Abbotsford. And there were other hazards than Irish of the lower ranks. There were reports of 18th Hussar officers drinking heavily and misconducting themselves – even introducing prostitutes into their mess. A punishment posting to India was on the cards for the unruly cavalry unit (EJ 733). Scott was hugely alarmed in February on hearing from an informant (of whom, he warned his son, he had many) that Walter was 'paying rather particular attention' (Lock. 3. 515) to a lady. If this were true, he told the young dragoon, 'it would excite my *highest displeasure*' (*Lett.* 6. 359). Sir Walter Scott was not going to play the part of Mr Osbaldistone.

Duty, duty, duty is the whole refrain in Scott's letters to his son (*Lett.* 6. 389). Particularly, Walter must have no political opinions. 'A democrat', he tells the young man, 'in any situation is but a silly sort of fellow but a democratical soldier is worse than an ordinary traitor by ten thousand degrees as he forfeits his military honour and is faithless to the Master whose bread he eats' (*Lett.* 6. 426). The King's patronage, in other words, was a paramount consideration. Scott was meanwhile carefully introducing young Walter's name to HRH the Duke of York, who was reported to be 'most obligingly disposed'. An exchange was arranged which enabled the young officer to study at Sandhurst while the rest of his regiment went to India (EJ 766). At the military college Walter would not be led into temptation by Irish whores and the 'sotting' of his bibulous comrades (*Lett.* 6. 438). This royal favour to his son strengthened Scott's sense of the power of monarchs, which is one of the main themes of *Kenilworth* and its successors. Kings – so weak or remote in *Waverley* – are now truly sovereign presences in his fiction.

The great public event of 1821 was the Coronation. The ceremony had necessarily been delayed by the sordid business of the Queen's Trial, but was finally set for 19 July 1821. Scott of course would attend. Bizarrely, it was his first intention to take James Hogg with him, as a kind of Wamba. 'The great Caledonian Boar' (Lock. 3. 547) demurred on the sublimely irrelevant grounds that attending the enthronement of his monarch would mean missing the annual Border fair at St Boswell's Green on the 18th of the month.

Scott duly went to Westminster unattended. He travelled down by the new steamship, the 'City of Edinburgh'. The modern age had arrived. Despite its foul clouds of engine smoke (it should be renamed the 'New Reekie', he informed the Captain), Scott liked the new conveyance enormously. It combined 'the speed and certainty of the mail-coach with the ease and convenience of being on shipboard' (Lock. 3. 546). It was progress, in a word. Once arrived in the capital Scott ('An Eye-Witness') wrote up a very literal account of his impressions of the Coronation – the great National Solemnity, as he called it – for the *Edinburgh Weekly Journal.* George IV, he loyally averred, looked 'every inch a King' (especially around the waist, one presumes). Scott was rather squeezed out by the host of lords and ladies clustered round the jubilee, the first coronation in most citizens' living memory (Lock. 3. 351, EJ 769). But the author of *Waverley* (as he was now universally assumed to be) was not entirely forgotten by his royal patron. The Chantrey bust was finished on this trip and one of the three copies was dispatched by royal command to a place of honour at the monarch's gorgeous new palace at Windsor. On the way back to Scotland at the end of July Scott and his friend William Stewart Rose stayed in Stratford-upon-Avon, and Scott inscribed his name on the wall of the room in which Shakespeare is supposed to have been born.

Lockhart, Sophia and their child were now established every summer at Chiefswood – the nearby cottage loaned them by the Laird of Abbotsford. Scott visited and stayed regularly, and it was at Chiefswood that he wrote much of *The Pirate* (Lock. 3. 584). Scott dashed off the novel with the same haste as its immediate predecessors. Originally entitled 'The Buccaneer', the work came from an idea suggested by Constable as early as December 1820 (*Lett.* 7. 12). Scott received a generous £4,500 advance on his half share from the publisher. He had the first volume done by 9 August, and by 30 September reported himself as 'cracking on well' with the remainder. He finished the second half of the novel by October 1821 and it was published in early December (EJ 773).

Piracy in the seventeenth century had traditionally had a base in the Northern Isles where *The Pirate* is set. But Scott had another reason for choosing that location. William Erskine – former Sheriff of Orkney and Zetland and a companion on the 1814 trip – was invited by Scott to Abbotsford in September 1821 because 'I want to talk to you about the locale of Zetland, for I am making my bricks with a very limited amount of straw' (*Lett.* 7. 12). 'The Counsellor' as Scott called his sedentary and rather retiring friend was a mine of information. No man of action himself ('He would,' Lockhart observed, 'have as soon thought of slaying his own mutton as of handling a fowling-piece'; Lock. 3. 587), Erskine knew all about the Orkney wilderness, and the farthest of the Northern Isles, Shetland. It was Erskine who supplied – or checked – all the anthropological material on such things as fishing for 'finners', and the Norse lore with which Scott packed his narrative.

Scott antedated the action of his novel to the seventeenth century because he loved those threshold eras in history when (as he put it in the preface to *The Fortunes of Nigel*) 'the ancient rough and wild manners of a barbarous age are just becoming innovated upon, and contrasted, by the illumination of increased or revived learning, and the instructions of renewed or reformed religion' (1. xxv). The threshold era in Shetland – which took the form of a clash between old Norse paganism and Enlightenment Scotland – had occurred very late. Scott read up on Viking and Norse lore, supplementing what Erskine told him. From his few days in the region in summer 1814 Scott remembered such details as the Orcadian superstition that it was bad luck to rescue a drowning man, because on being saved he was bound to do his rescuer great harm. This was woven deep into the fabric of the novel. (Mordaunt and Cleveland rescue each other from drowning, and do each other mortal harm.) Unfortunately, Scott had no nautical 'Counsellor', and *The Pirate* has never impressed readers who know about the sea. Fenimore Cooper (in all else Scott's most devoted American disciple) was so enraged by the landlubberliness of *The Pirate* that he wrote a corrective tale the following year, *The Pilot* (1823).

Edgar Johnson praises *The Pirate* as 'a penetrating exploration of its theme. Nowhere has Scott shown more clearly his profound understanding of the organic role of tradition in a culture' (EJ 821). Well and good, except that Scott had undertaken what amounted to no more than a day trip to the culture which he is congratulated on for understanding so 'profoundly'. Scott, it must be said, was becoming in his haste an increasingly superficial novelist. It is extraordinary that with such brief acquaintance as his 1814 tour (even assisted by Erskine) Scott felt confident to reconstruct the life and society of the northernmost islands with the clear implication to his readers that he knew them intimately. As with the blatant anachronisms in *Kenilworth,* one detects something very like contempt in Scott's attitude to his public – why bother to spend a few weeks gathering local colour, or even travelling north (which would not have been impossible)? There has also been an ingenious attempt by Judith Wilt to reassess *The Pirate* in terms of Norna's 'female counterrevolution' (Wilt, 120). But Scott the novelist seems to have known as little about militant women as he knew (at first hand) about the Northern Isles or life on the ocean wave.

THE FORTUNES OF NIGEL

Lockhart has left a revealing vignette of Scott starting work on his next novel:

> I well remember the morning that he began *The Fortunes of Nigel* . . . I went over to Abbotsford before breakfast, and found Mr Terry (who had been staying there for some time) walking about with his friend's master mason [inspecting progress on Abbotsford]. While Terry and I were chatting, Scott came out, bare-headed, with a bunch of MS. in his hand, and said, 'Well, lads, I've laid the keel of a new lugger this morning – here it is – be off to the waterside and let me hear how you like it.' Terry took the papers, and walking up and down by the river, read to me the first chapters of 'Nigel'. He expressed great delight with the animated opening, and especially with the contrast between its thorough stir of London life, and a chapter about Norna of the Fitful-head, in the third volume of *The Pirate,* which had been given to him in a similar manner the morning before. I could see that (according to the Sheriff's phrase) *he smelt roast meat*; here was every prospect of a fine field for the art of *Terryfication.* (Lock. 3. 603)

The presence of Terry accounts for the ostentatious theatricality of *The Fortunes of Nigel* – its close dependence on such sources as Dekker's *The Shoemaker's Holiday* (which Terry would have immediately picked up in the first chapters) and Shadwell's *The Squire of Alsatia* (1688).

The reading public concurred with Terry. When *The Fortunes of Nigel* was published in late May 1822 Constable saw people devouring the novel in the London streets on the morning it was published (EJ 787). By ten o'clock in the morning, 7,000 copies had been sold from Constable's London outlet in Cheapside. Scott had triumphed again. By now, Scott was the most accomplished historical novelist who had ever put pen to paper. He had invented a literary form, perfected it, and now excelled in it. He had also evolved a grand theory of the value of historical understanding, more so when it was delivered by a system of mass communication, like popular fiction. Scott believed, and could persuasively argue, that an aware-ness of history was the locomotive of social progress (that elusive pot of

gold at the end of the Scottish Enlightenment rainbow). Historiography
added to the sum of human good. He made the point in an otherwise
rather nagging letter to his younger son Charles, currently drudging away
with a tutor in distant Wales:

> The son of the learned pig if it had one would be a mere brute fit only to
> make bacon of. It is not so with the human race. Our ancestor[s] lodged in
> caves and wigwams where we construct palaces for the rich and comfortable
> dwellings for the poor. And why is this but because our eye is enabled to look
> back upon the past to improve on our ancestors' improvements and to avoid
> their errors[?] This can only be done by studying history and comparing it
> with passing events. (*Lett.* 7. 734)

The Fortunes of Nigel had a closer inspiration in Scott's experiences at the
Coronation in July 1821. He had been very much the Scottish alien in the
English capital, an experience which he incorporates into the misfortunes
of the humble Scot Richie Moniplies, who is promptly beaten up and left
for dead when he ventures on the London streets. Scots are foreigners in
their own (British) capital. But Scott's meditation on the Coronation led to
some more solemn thoughts about his own country's economy. He could
not but observe that Scottish technological skill – embodied in the person
of David Ramsay the watchmaker and horologer – was being sucked south.
As the crown had gone to London, so had Edinburgh's weal. As Moniplies
puts it: 'The King's leaving Scotland has taken all custom frae Edinburgh;
and there is hay made at the Cross, and a dainty crop of fouats in the Grassmarket. There is as much grass grows where my father's stall stood, as might
have been a good bite for the beasts he used to kill' (1. 28). This of course
is the early seventeenth century. But it had clear analogies with the 1820s.
Looking around London during the Coronation, Scott could not but register how much more dynamic, bustling and crowded it had become than the
other royal burgh, Edinburgh. It was at this time, presumably, that his
intention to bring the King to Edinburgh formed. The royal visit would
generate a new confidence and vitality in the Scottish capital.

It is significant that *The Fortunes of Nigel* is a novel which pivots on
unimaginably huge debt – Nigel's 40,000 marks. Although biographers
routinely present the years 1821–4 as the 'crest of the wave', Scott had
gnawing anxieties about money. As Eric Quayle calculates, by May 1822 the
debts of the Printing Office (of which Scott had been sole owner from 1816
until James Ballantyne rejoined at Whitsunday 1822) amounted to over
£36,000 – and after all receipts came in, £27,000 (EQ 160). According to
Quayle, Scott had milked the firm ruthlessly and starved it of capital in
order to build Abbotsford. And when James Ballantyne rejoined as equal
partner, his understanding was that Abbotsford represented part of the
firm's security (it did not, as he discovered to his cost in 1826). Scott, as
Lockhart points out, was gambling everything on his ability to turn out two
or three bestsellers a year. On the strength of this very precarious golden
stream, he was incurring huge costs in the building of Abbotsford, his

lairdly lifestyle, the extension of his estate, the promotion of his children's welfare and careers.

It was a mark of Scott's evident desperation for cash that he was willing to part with copyrights long before he had exhausted their value. On his part, Constable was eager to buy, having in mind plans for a cascade of collective reissues. He had bought sixteen copyrights for £12,000 in 1819. In 1821, he bought rights to the four most recent copyrights for 5,000 guineas. In April 1823, Scott sold for another 5,000 guineas (EJ 807) rights to *The Pirate, The Fortunes of Nigel, Peveril of the Peak* and *Quentin Durward*.

These sales of barely exploited property, together with advances for work as yet unwritten, meant a satisfying bundle of cash in hand. Scott made £10,000 from 'scarcely more than twelve months' labour' in 1822. As a statistic, it is breathtaking; for comparison, Maria Edgeworth, in the course of her eighty-one years, only earned a life-time total of £11,000 from her pen. But Scott's policy of writing two or three novels a year and never holding on to his copyrights was madness in the long term. He was doing with his manuscripts what he (disastrously) did with bills of accommodation – letting them go at much less than their face value for ready money. And a hairline crack had already appeared in the foundation on which his economy was based. Although he did not know it, did not care to know it, or was not told, title for title 'the sale of his novels was rather less than it had been in the days of *Ivanhoe*' (Lock. 3. 425). Evidently his backers, particularly James Ballantyne, held the risky view that any small shortfall could be made up by even faster increased production.

Scott understood only one pace – the gallop. Before *The Fortunes of Nigel* was finished, in spring 1822, Scott made agreements and took advance payments for four more works of fiction, each to be at least three volumes. Three of them were written within the year (EJ 772, 788). In March 1822, over the course of 'two rainy mornings', Scott polished off the dramatic sketch *Halidon Hill*. According to Lockhart, Constable, without seeing the manuscript, offered £1,000 for the two-act scrap. This 'wild bargain' (Lock. 4. 13) was evidence of a loss of control on both sides. Constable was so ecstatic with his purchase – Lockhart adds – that he proposed that Scott write four such bagatelles a year (there was that much rain at Abbotsford, surely) beginning with a sketch of Bannockburn and going on to Hastings, Crécy, Bosworth (EJ 785–6). Lockhart spitefully implies that the digitalis he was taking for his heart must have over-excited Constable's brain. Or perhaps he had caught the Abbotsford fever. As Lockhart notes, 'he, too, had considerably before this time purchased a landed estate in his native Fife [his] own rural castle *in petto*' (Lock. 4. 18). He was now 'Archibald Constable of Balniel'. Lockhart is spiteful about this pretension on the part of a mere tradesman. As for Scott of Abbotsford, Constable's paying him £500 a day raised his mood to 'a degree of almost mad exhilaration, near akin to his publisher's' (Lock. 4. 17). In a spasm of gratitude, he gave Constable all his *Waverley*-novel manuscripts in March 1823 (EJ 806). As he showed Maria Edgeworth around his estate in July 1823 he confided that 'the best of it is, it is all paid for, and all paid for by Constable' (EJ 841). This *folie à deux*, with ever more grandiose expectations, would continue until January 1826.

13

The Royal Visit and *Redgauntlet*
(1822–1823)

In January 1822 Scott's oldest friend William Erskine was promoted to a newly vacated seat on the Bench of the Court of Session, as Lord Kinnedder (EJ 780–1). Lockhart records that Scott took 'great pleasure' in his comrade's good fortune. Doubtless he did, but he must nevertheless have experienced some pangs of envy. It was the promotion he had solicited for himself four years earlier and 'conceded' to Rae (who leap-frogged it into a higher post). Sir Walter Scott, apparently, was stuck at the respectably middling level of Clerk of Session and provincial sheriff. He would never, it seemed, wear the Baron's gown and preside over a court. Being passed over intensified a gloomy sense that he was getting old. 'I did indeed rejoice at Erskines promotion', he told Joanna Baillie, '[but] there is a degree of melancholy attending the later stage of a barristers profession which though no one cares for sentimentalities attendant on a man of fifty or thereabout in a rusty black bombazeen gown are not the less cruelly felt. Their business sooner or later fails for younger men will work cheaper and longer and harder' (*Lett.* 7. 60–1).

Like other ageing men, Scott fretted about the decline of the world and the culpable impotence of Britain's rulers: 'They are acting weakly', he complained to Lord Montagu (*Lett.* 7. 110–1). There was a clear line of ominous insurrections in Scott's mind, from the Spa Fields Riots in 1816, the Peterloo Massacre (or insurrection, as he saw it) in 1819, the Cato Street Conspiracy of 1820, when Arthur Thistlewood and thirty others, enraged by the government's resistance to Reform, plotted to blow up the whole cabinet with gunpowder. Above all, Scott was alarmed by the 'Radical War' which had raged in Scotland since 1819 and climaxed in the proclamation of a general strike (answered by 60,000 workers) and insurrection at Bonnymuir in April 1820. Three men were killed in the affray, 26 radicals tried, and 24 sentenced to death (only three eventually suffered execution, the remainder being transported).

Scott favoured three measures for restoring order and stability to the British nation. The first was military coercion laced with punitive terror. 'The dogs', as he called the Radicals, should be taught a lesson they would remember for 'half a century'. The second measure was Braxfieldian judicial severity – the kind of thing that had worked so well in 1794. Scott heartily approved of the executions and wholesale transportation following Bonnymuir, and would have liked more of it. The third measure was massive public ceremonies designed to bind the country's wounds, and rally the populace around its traditional governors in emotional displays of regimented unity.

It is not clear where the idea of the King's visit to Scotland originated (Maria Edgeworth thought the inspiration must have been *Kenilworth*, which had gone down very well with its royal reader, *Lett.* 7. 25). Probably the scheme was hatched by Scott, Lord Montagu (with whom Scott acted as tutor to the young Duke of Buccleuch) and Melville. Montagu was in a position to promote the 'King's Jaunt' (as Scott called it) in London. Apart from anything else, these three Scottish Tories must have felt it would be one in the eye for the Edinburgh Whigs, still off balance from the death of Queen Caroline. Of course, when he came, the King must stay in a Tory palace (in the event, the Buccleuchs' Dalkeith was chosen).

The King's advisers were keenly aware of the benefits of the monarch's being seen by his subjects. Among a string of other royal visits, tours and progresses, he had honoured Ireland in 1821. Once the decision was taken to visit Scotland, Sir Walter Scott was the obvious person to be 'adviser general' (EJ 790). He was an expert on the intricacies of public ceremony – what Bagehot would call the 'ornamental' aspects of the British constitution. Since boyhood, he had been fascinated by heraldry, genealogy, pageant and pomp. Scott had studied with a scholar's care the pageantry of the Elizabethan era for *Kenilworth*. And he had been an interested student of all the 'invented traditions' of George IV's coronation – the first of its spectacular kind. Over the years, his association with Terry and the Theatre Royal had trained his eye for spectacle. Now, in 1822, he was invited by a desperate Lord Provost to paint on the largest canvas Scotland could supply – the Royal Burgh. As his right-hand man, Scott selected the actor-manager of the Theatre Royal, William Murray. His other principal assistant was Colonel Stewart of Garth, a wounded veteran of the Peninsular Wars and a student of Highland culture and Highland Regiments. Theatrical effects and tartan were to be the themes of the programme he devised.

That the visit would take place was not confirmed until the last minute (Scott privately thought the chances were against it, and had made plans for a holiday in Tweeddale.) The announcement on 22 July gave Scott barely more than a fortnight to organize the most lavish public pageant the city had ever seen. Probably no-one other than he could have masterminded the Jaunt as imaginatively; certainly no-one but the Wizard of the North could have done it in such amazingly short order. Writing *Guy Mannering* in six weeks over Christmas was child's play by comparison.

The theme of the visit had been devised in Scott's dinner party with the monarch in 1815, when he evidently persuaded his Prince that he was the last of the Stuarts, a truly Scottish monarch and – in spirit at least – a Jacobite. Scott was keen to stress the point that unlike Ireland – a mere lordship – Scotland was a kingdom. He took the strategic decision to make Highland culture (with all its associations of recent British military triumph in the Great War) the keynote of the Pageant. The most momentous words for his country that Scott ever penned were his instruction in the 1*s* booklet of *Hints addressed to the Inhabitants of Edinburgh and Others in prospect of His Majesty's Visit by an Old Citizen*: 'No gentleman is allowed to appear in anything but the ancient Highland costume.' Thus an item of clothing for the wearing of which a Scotsman could face execution until 1782 became the uniform of Lowland gentlemen who before August 1822 would no more have thought have wearing a kilt than a suit of medieval armour. On his part, the monarch ordered from the Royal tailors (George Hunter & Co., Edinburgh and London) a full Royal Stewart tartan outfit and accoutrements costing £1,354 18*s*.[1]

George IV's ceremonial visit to Edinburgh took place over two weeks in August 1822. He was the first Hanoverian to set his foot on Scottish soil since 'Butcher' Cumberland, and the first reigning monarch to do so since the 1630s. By now the last Stuart in direct line had died, giving George a tenuous, but heraldically plausible claim to be a legitimate king of two kingdoms. His visit could thus partake of the flavour of a royal installation. But even if he could get the ceremonies arranged in time, Scott's task was fraught with problems. Edinburgh was not sure it wanted to dance to his tune. There was opposition and widespread indifference to the Royal Visit. The Tories approved of it, naturally enough since George was their man. But the Whigs, Hanover-haters and Radical-sympathizers (a majority of Edinburgh's middle classes) still represented themselves as disgusted by George's treatment of the just dead Caroline. And as Lockhart notes, in view of the clearances which were reaching their painful crescendo in 1822, 'it almost seemed as if there were a cruel mockery' in the Great Jaunt (Lock. 4. 35).

Scott's strategy was to drown out critics by a deafening barrage of pomp and reach over the heads of the Whig middle classes to the populace. He embarked on what Lockhart calls 'an orgy of Celtification': a shameless parade of kilts, bagpipes, sporrans, claymores, and the panoply of Old Gael, all of dubious accuracy but picturesque enough to establish the image of Scotland in the non-Scottish mind for all time. He invented 'traditions' as freely as anything in the plots of his novels. (One of these inventions, that the Company of Archers were the 'ancient bodyguard of the Kings of Scotland', inspired his next novel, *Quentin Durward*.) Underlying everything Scott invented for the occasion was the grand fiction that the Scots are a nation of Highlanders. The '*Waverley* and *Rob Roy* animus' and an 'air of ridicule and caricature' permeated the whole of what Lockhart contemptuously called 'Sir Walter's Celtified pageantry' (Lock 4. 46).

Lockhart might sneer but Scott's populist strategy worked. The masses loved the programme Scott had devised for them. Linda Colley quotes an eyewitness to the effect of the King's Visit on the common folk of Edinburgh:

A continued line of pale faces, with expectation wound up to actual pain, and a sort of bewildered smile on their first glimpse of that being called a king – Britain's king – Scotland's king – their own king! The moment come, the first in their lives, when they could compare the actual thing called Majesty, with all they had from childhood dreamed and fancied of it. (Colley, 235)

The programme Scott devised was varied, exhausting (as the fat, ailing, heavy-drinking king complained) and designed to expose him to all levels of society: a ceremonial landing at Leith, various progresses through the city, a Royal Levee and Drawing Room at Holyroodhouse, Royal Balls, a grand review of Horse and Foot at Portobello, a display of the Regalia ('the Honours of Scotland') and their solemn transportation between the Castle and Royal Palace, a 'Gathering of the Clans' in loyal allegiance to the Chief, and to cap it all, there was a Royal Command performance of the 'Terryfied' *Rob Roy*. All this was to be interspersed with quiet, conspiratorial dinners with Tory grandees at Dalkeith Palace.

George arrived in the rain on 14 August. Scott, who had an audience with the king on board the Royal Yacht, immortalized his loyalty by first secreting the glass from which his monarch drank in a hip pocket and then later, at Castle Street, sitting on the sacred vessel. (He was not, fortunately, injured.) During the festivities that followed, George displayed himself in the tartan of the Stuarts and Scott himself wore the 'Garb of old Gael' – Campbell tartan by courtesy of his great-grandmother (EJ 792). The sight of the King at the Holyrood Levee, bekilted but with flesh coloured tights over the massive royal pins, provoked almost irrepressible mirth among Edinburgh's genteel classes and was gratefully seized on by caricaturists. Crabbe – whom Scott had long admired as the greatest poet of his age – was visiting and thought himself lost among a wilderness of savages. Baffled by the Edinburgh burr he addressed his kilted company, hopefully, in French. It is an indication of how busy Scott was in these weeks that Crabbe never once saw Abbotsford. Nor did the King, who lodged at Dalkeith Palace, seat of the Buccleuchs.

The visit went well, defying incessantly bad weather and the ill omen of the Foreign Secretary, Lord Castlereagh, cutting his throat at the precise moment that his monarch set foot on his northern realm. Scott's efforts were evidently approved by George and he was granted three royal boons. He requested that the great cannon Mons Meg (carried off in 1754) should be brought back from the Tower of London to Edinburgh Castle (in the event the return was delayed by red tape until 1829). Secondly, he requested that the Scottish peerages, forfeited in 1715 and 1745, be restored. And thirdly, he contrived to have his old friends Henry Raeburn and Adam

Ferguson knighted by the king during his visit. Surprisingly, perhaps, there was no further ennoblement for Scott himself, who might legitimately have expected some such mark of favour.

Scott worked himself ragged to make the royal visit a success. There were a thousand things to distract him. Abbotsford was in the last stages of completion; the Scotts 'lived to the music of the hammer and the saw' (Lock. 4. 79) and every detail required a decision from Sir Walter. He was in the middle of writing a new novel, *Peveril of the Peak*. Most distressingly, his oldest and dearest friend, William Erskine, died on the very day of the King's arrival (and Castlereagh's suicide). In any circumstances it would have been a heavy blow. But it was the more painful since Scott's friend had been killed by 'a fatal calumny' – a baseless allegation of adultery with an apothecary's wife. Erskine (who was an eminently respectable widower) was driven into deep depression. His physicians compounded his melancholy by excessive bleeding. As Scott reported to Joanna Baillie (with an account of the 'calumny'): 'On the day of the Kings arrival he waked from sleep and took a kind leave of his servants (his family were not allowed to see him) orderd the window to be opend that he might see the sun once more, and was a dead man immediatly after' (*Lett.* 7. 223–4).

There are mysterious aspects to Erskine's death, as it is reported. It is odd that a Scottish judge (not a species famous for their sensitivity) should have succumbed to a 'canard'. Did he kill himself? (Scott's '[he] was a dead man immediatly after' leaves the possibility open). All Scott's letters to his friend were burned (HG 198). Chronically shy, Erskine erased himself from the record: 'For Scott's biographers he counts for nothing', Grierson adds. There are similar mysteries surrounding Lady Scott. Henry Fox, who visited early in 1822, dined with the Scotts and observed that she was 'nearly an idiot with great marks of her love for the bottle on her face'. This was probably unfair. But she may well have been in the grip of another addiction. In an injudicious and suppressed passage in his memoir, Hogg observed that Lady Scott was, towards the end of her life, addicted to opium (Mack, 22–3). Later in 1822, she developed a serious (but vaguely described) asthmatic complaint, compounded by 'water on the chest' (EJ 804). If she were befuddled by her intake of pain-killers (which seems very plausible), it cannot have made Scott's life any easier at this frantic period.

During and for two months after the Royal Visit, Scott himself suffered agonies from what was diagnosed as 'prickly heat' (EJ 796). Eric Quayle claims that the rash was 'alcoholic' in origin – precipitated by the vast amount of malt whisky Scott was obliged to drink in company with his over-indulgent monarch. In a letter to Terry of the period, he himself talked of 'a whoreson thickness of the blood' (*Lett.* 7. 281) and mentioned 'apoplexy'. Lockhart takes this to be the first symptoms of the blood pressure that would eventually lead to the strokes of 1826 and after (Lock. 4. 77). Grierson, however, points out that the apoplexy reference by Scott in a letter to Terry is a Shakespeare allusion, and merely indicates that he was out of sorts (HG 209). If so, the remark was uncannily premonitory. And it would have been odd for Scott to jest in this way about the disease that killed his father.

Meanwhile, over this most eventful of summers, Scott was writing *Peveril of the Peak* – his longest novel since *The Heart of Midlothian*. Despite all the distraction it appeared, promptly enough, in January 1823, in an initial print run of 10,000 (now routine for a Scott novel). *Peveril* returns to the setting of *Rokeby*, the north country (here Derbyshire) in the period of the Restoration. Like the poem, *Peveril* clearly owes its origin to Morritt, who is gently poked fun at as 'Jonas Dryasdust of York' in the preface. Thematically, the novel is a sequel to *The Fortunes of Nigel*, continuing the saga of the Stuart dynasty. Like James, Charles II – who appears at full length in the conclusion of the novel – is portrayed negatively. Scott is critical of Restoration moral laxity, and London's libertinism in the period. The Popish plot, which makes up the main business of the novel (once it gets started), clearly echoes the Cato Street outrage of 1820, and the panic it inspired.

Lockhart justly criticizes the story of *Peveril* as 'clumsy and perplexed' (Lock. 4. 86). There are at least three plots, none of which is properly worked out. Is Edward Christian the villain? or is it the increasingly fanatic Ralph Bridgenorth? or the lecherous Duke of Buckingham? There is no centre to the novel's action. Despite the promise of the title the Peaks hardly figure. The Isle of Man setting is abandoned, just as it promises to get interesting. And a corrupt London ('the grand central point of intrigues') – infested with pimps and libertines and bravos and brutal citizens – is never more than sketched. The novel is too long (something that gave Constable and Cadell anxiety; they were not sure that the market would bear four volumes and two guineas.) It is very hard to get a fix on some of the main characters. Bridgenorth, for example, at some points seems a religious maniac. But at other points he is eminently pragmatic in his political views (see, for instance, his remarks in chapter 14 – 'even war is not in itself unmixed evil . . .').

The most pervasive fault in *Peveril of the Peak*, however, is the muddy writing. (Take, as a representative instance, chapter 39, which opens with a whirling 134-word sentence which a cryptographer would have difficulty following.) Although his diagnosis may have been medically premature, Lockhart can be forgiven for thinking that Scott's brain was damaged by apoplexy when he wrote *Peveril* and that it anticipates that 'clouded writing' which is seen at its most terrifying in *The Siege of Malta*. In Grierson's view *Peveril* 'is the most complete failure of all the novels before the final breakdown' (HG 209).

For all its faults, there is a haunting aftertaste to *Peveril of the Peak*. The Manx chapters are clearly a hankering after Tom Scott, Walter's errant but loved brother. Scott himself never went to the island, easy as a trip would have been. He absorbed all his local colour from secondary sources and (as he records in his notes) from recollections which Tom entrusted to him. Scott was very fond of his brother. But there was no disguising that Tom was a black sheep. He had fled to the Isle of Man in disgrace, to avoid possible criminal proceedings. Scott used Tom as an example to his son Charles in 1823, as an example of what happened to young men who neglected their talents, took up 'idle and intemperate habits' (*Lett.* 7. 357) and generally went to the bad. Tom was, in fact, dying as Scott wrote his novel. He had been in trouble for some months. Predictably it had to do with funds entrusted to him. The £2,100 Scott remitted as his brother's share of their mother's estate did not apparently clear the problem (EJ 814); nor did the sums which Scott had put up as security so that Tom could take up his post as paymaster of the 70th. Representations were made to Scott by Tom's in-laws in November. But Scott felt he could help no further. Mercifully Tom died in mid-February 1823. At the same period, a committee of investigation discovered £600 adrift in his accounts. A court-martial might have followed, which would not have been helpful to Lieutenant Walter Scott's career. While mourning his best-loved brother, Scott must have felt a shameful pang of relief. He took on the responsibility of his sister-in-law's affairs, which involved the delicate business of getting her a War Office pension without provoking further inquiry into Tom's derelictions. Scott also took a particular interest in advancing the career of his nephew, another Walter Scott (EJ 804).

QUENTIN DURWARD

Peveril of the Peak was published in four volumes, at two guineas, in January 1823. It apparently sold well, despite Cadell's anxieties. But, according to Lockhart, it received a cooler reception from the critics than its predecessors. It was followed by a finer work, *Quentin Durward*. Scott evidently conceived the idea of 'a young Scotchman going to France to be an archer in the Scots Guard tempore Ludovici XImi' (EJ 802) in November 1822. He embarked on the new novel immediately after *Peveril,* and had it finished by April 1823.

Quentin Durward had a number of detectable inspirations. Scott was rereading Smollett at this period. Despite its tight, one-month narrative time-frame, *Quentin Durward* is an experiment in Smollettian picaresque, as Scott's young soldier of fortune bounces all over late medieval Europe. Another inspiration was Scott's 'invented tradition' for the King's Jaunt, that the ancient company of Edinburgh bowmen had in times of yore been the royal bodyguard. A third inspiration was his paternal anxieties and hopes for Walter. Having transferred from Ireland the young man travelled to Germany in February 1822. The aim was that he should study military tactics and European languages. After a year or so, he would return to Sandhurst that much better equipped for rapid promotion (EJ 804). Walter sent his father regular bulletins – including reports of his meetings with German royalty. Clearly Scott's story of a young Scottish soldier learning his craft in Europe draws on his preoccupations with his own young Scottish soldier.

Quentin Durward had a continental setting, something quite new for Scott. His own experience of Europe was limited to the few weeks he had spent there after Waterloo. This did not daunt the author of *Waverley*. His friend Skene had recently undertaken a tour in France, and kept a journal which he put at Scott's disposal. This document served the same function as Tom's Manx registers had for *Peveril of the Peak*. Scott also undertook research in the Advocates' Library, on maps and historical accounts of medieval France and Flanders (EJ 802). The ground had been broken by the research he had undertaken for the 1817 *Britannica* essay on 'Chivalry' for Constable.

After a preface which is unusually riddling, even for Scott, *Quentin Durward* opens with a scene of fine brio. Louis, disguised as the merchant 'Maitre Pierre', watches the young Quentin save himself from drowning in a ford. The spectacle amuses the 'Mephistophelean' monarch, and he stands the ingenuous young Scot a meal, pumping him all the while for information. Near-escape from death is to be a recurrent feature of Quentin's career. Quentin's wide-eyed innocence and innate chivalry are set against a world of utter political corruption. Scott portrays the fifteenth century as the fag-end of feudalism; the codes of chivalry have decayed and survive merely as the arrogance of rank. Nationalism is emergent, but it has not yet formed as an ideology which can bring the best out of men. Religion is a racket. Louis appoints bishops as managers of his estate, and takes what spiritual counsel he requires from his astrologer Galeotti Martivalle. Political counsel he takes from his barber. The world of *Quentin Durward* is an ideological vacuum. Louis is ruthless craft personified. His every act is a deception, a ruse or a betrayal. In the central strand of the novel's plot, he dispatches Quentin on a mission to 'protect' Isabelle by lodging her at the palace of the Bishop of Liège. He has meanwhile set up an ambush and – should the ambush fail – has arranged the destruction of the Bishop at the hands of the inhumanly 'Wild Boar of the Ardennes', William de la Marck. All this, it emerges, is a cunning scheme to destabilize his own realm, the better to gain sole sovereignty. One of the novel's bitter aftertastes is that finally Quentin recognizes the moral worthlessness of Louis but nonetheless elects to serve on as an honest servant of a dishonest king.

Quentin Durward remains the most readable of Scott's novels. And beneath the rollicking action there are some tantalizing obliquities. The career of the Durwards describes a poignant curve, from ruin to ruin. Quentin – we learn from the Preface – is forced to leave his native Glen Houlihikan by the feud enmity of the Ogilvies. (He also escapes monasticism, which would have meant the end of his line.) He makes his fortune by daring and honour. He wins a noble bride and promotion (as Scott hoped would happen to Walter). His family reaches the highest ranks – and where does it all end? A childless old aristocrat, in a dilapidated château, ruined by revolution. Viewed in this light, *Quentin Durward* shows Scott ironizing his own ambitions to 'plant a lasting root'.

Quentin Durward was published in May 1823, barely four months after *Peveril of the Peak*. Perhaps because the two novels were competing with each other it hung fire – despite being a far better work. It nonetheless enjoyed a surprising success in the country where it was set. As Hesketh Pearson describes:

> *Quentin Durward* was rather coldly received in England, probably because people had not yet digested *Peveril of the Peak* and were not ready for another novel from the same pen. But suddenly it created a furore in France, making the same sort of sensation there that *Waverley* had made in Scotland and *Ivanhoe* in England. French women began to wear gowns of the Stuart tartan *à la Walter Scott*, strings of carriages waiting near the shop where they were on sale. The author became the talk of Paris, and his book sold by the thousands. (Pearson, 189)

Gratifying as this international fame was, there was no real money in exports – Europe and America were havens for piracy. The domestic market was what counted and *Quentin Durward*'s relative failure was alarming. Perhaps the author of *Waverley* had glutted his market. Constable was particularly nervous. He had paid Scott over £22,000 for copyrights of written *Waverley* novels and some £10,000 in advances for works as yet unwritten and unspecified. Moreover he and the Ballantyne Press had exchanged 'paper' (i.e. accommodation bills) to the value of £30,000 or more, in order to raise capital for which there was no security other than Scott's saleworthiness. Publisher and author were very exposed.

St Ronan's Well

Lockhart gives a richly anecdotal account of the birth of Scott's next novel, *St Ronan's Well*:

> As [Scott], Laidlaw, and myself were lounging on our ponies one fine calm afternoon, along the brow of the Eildon hill where it overhangs Melrose, he mentioned to us gaily the *row*, as he called it, that was going on in Paris about *Quentin Durward*, and said, 'I can't but think that I could make better play still with something German.' Laidlaw grumbled at this, and said, like a true Scotchman, 'Na, na, sir – take my word for it, you are always best, like Helen MacGregor, when your foot is on your native heath; and I have often thought that if you were to write a novel and lay the scene *here* in the very year you were writing it, you would excel yourself.' – 'Hame's hame,' quoth Scott, smiling, 'be it ever sae hamely. There's something in what you say, Willie. What suppose I were to take Captain Clutterbuck for a hero, and never let the story step a yard beyond the village below us yonder?' – 'The very thing I want,' says Laidlaw; 'Stick to Melrose in July 1823'. (Lock. 4. 122–3)

It is a fine story, but unfortunately it must be one of Lockhart's inventions. The setting is self-evidently July 1823 – after Scott had finished the summer session of Court, and moved to Abbotsford. Yet it is on record (although

Lockhart did not register the fact) that Scott began writing *St Ronan's Well* in mid-May 1823. (Edgar Johnson, who is unwilling to lose the story, redates it as 'one calm May afternoon' – which given Scott's movements between the city and the country is unlikely; EJ 807.)

The question arises why Lockhart should have invented scenes like the above. Probably he wanted to dramatize his sense that connection with Laidlaw had a strong effect on Scott's fiction. And, as with his habit of splicing together separate letters or episodes, Lockhart evidently allowed himself a novelist's licence to project the image of the Scott he knew better than anyone living.

The early composition of *St Ronan's Well* was interrupted by a long-awaited visit. In the first week of June 1823 Scott met Maria Edgeworth for the first time, having long been an admirer of her Irish fiction. The fifty-six-year-old Miss Edgeworth ('a little, dark, bearded, withered, active, laughing, talking, impudent, fearless, outspoken, honest, Whiggish, unchristian, good-tempered, kindly, ultra-Irish body' in Lockhart's tumultuous description; HG 214) and her two thoroughly overshadowed half-sisters descended on the Scotts in Edinburgh for two weeks, on route for a northern Scottish tour. On their return from the north, in late July, the Edgeworth party paid another congenial visit to Abbotsford. The two novelists took to each other. Edgeworth left some sharp portraits of the Scotts: Anne she did not much like; Lady Scott ('a Frenchwoman much dressed') she found alarmingly rouged but apparently grew to like.[2] Sir Walter she declared 'one of the best bred men I ever saw' (EJ 813). But Edgeworth did wonder 'WHEN has he time to write' (EJ 842–3). July 1823 – with the completion of Abbotsford at last in sight – was certainly a crowded season. In addition to the Edgeworths Walter had returned from Germany and Charles from Wales (it was now decided that he should go to Oxford rather than take up the place offered him in India). The Lockharts (JGL, Sophia and their son John Hugh) were nearby at Chiefswood. Grierson deduces, in answer to Edgeworth's query, that Scott did the bulk of his writing by getting up several hours before the rest of the household.

St Ronan's Well is the first (and only) novel of Scott's set in the near present day, the action taking place 'about twenty years' since' (1. 1) at the height of the Napoleonic War. Austen-fashion, however, the hostilities do not intervene. *St Ronan's Well* was intended, Scott declared, '*celebrare domestica facta*' (1. xvii). It is domestic not only in its homely plot, but in the scale of its national concerns. Scott is again the 'Scotch novelist', but it is a new and very tame Scotland that he describes. This is not the world of *Waverley* – the northern cauldron where the destiny of the United Kingdom is being decided. Nor is it the Scotland of *The Antiquary*, with the threat of invasion at its shores. St Ronan's is a small village which has fallen into decay like many Border villages with the dwindling of the cattle-droving trade. Luckier than other villages, St Ronan's has the good fortune to be sitting on top of curative springs – a 'salutiferous fountain', as Scott archly calls it. The waters have brought a third-rate prosperity, tourism, and a wave of ugly speculative building. Nabobs, with their copper faces and their lakhs, settle in St Ronan's. Students and young lawyers wanting to taste the fashionable life at affordable prices (and possibly to find a rich wife) pass the summers there.

Against this seedy backdrop of arrivistes, parasites, nouveaux riches, and gimcrack gentry the old order – the Lowland lairdocracy – is in terminal decline. A cunning lawyer, Saunders Meiklewham ('large belly') leeches the wealth of the local laird (now known by the 'knapping English' title 'squire'), whose son is addicted to gambling and whose daughter is 'touched'. No hope of regeneration from these shoots. In the distant past the Mowbrays were a powerful family, allied with the 'heroic race' of Douglas. But they backed the wrong side in James II's reign, and their castle was pounded into dust by Cromwell's cannon. The family then built a large mansion in the centre of the village. But some fifty years before the story opens, it was burned down. Now the family lives like any other middle-class family of moderate means in an undistinguished house some three miles outside the village. The old Mowbray mansion has been converted into an inn. 'The Cleikum' (i.e. 'catch 'em') is managed by a former Mowbray retainer, the formidable Meg Dods. If anyone carries on the traditions of the family, it is she. But Meg's custom has been sadly depleted by competition from the new hotel built by subscription ('tontine'), and by the newly built Assembly Rooms and Pump Rooms where the tourists congregate. To Meg's disgust, even the Mowbrays patronize the 'hottle' keeping 'company wi' a' that scauff and raff of physic-students, and writer's prentices, and bagmen, and sic-like trash' (1. 37).

It is tempting to see *St Ronan's Well* as a kind of hangover from the Royal Visit, a painful coming down to earth. The Scotland it portrays is hopelessly seedy, and a backwater. The novel is shot through with a peculiar kind of Scottish *honte*, a sense of national inferiority. There is, for instance, a bitter passage in which the young and arrogant Earl of Etherington confides his contempt for the Scots in a letter to his fashionable friend, Captain Jekyl:

> Excellent bankers the Scots may be, for they are eternally calculating how to add interest to principal; – good soldiers, for they are, if not such heroes as they would be thought, as brave, I suppose, as their neighbours and much more amenable to discipline; – lawyers they are born; indeed every country gentleman is bred one, and their patient and crafty disposition enables them, in other lines, to submit to hardships which other natives could not bear, and avail themselves of advantages which others would let pass under their noses unavailingly. But assuredly Heaven did not form the Caledonian for the gay world; and his efforts at ease, grace, and gaiety resemble only the clumsy gambols of the ass in the fable. (1. 301)

Was this how Scott thought himself talked about by his London friends behind his back?

More than other novels of this period, *St Ronan's Well* seems to be driven by paternal preoccupations. The novel's strong propaganda against gam-

bling – in the feckless person of John Mowbray, and his despairing father –
may signal some recent alarms of Scott's. One of the few things we know
about young Walter Scott is that he had a dangerous love of the gaming
table. Germany, where he had just been, would have been an easy place to
have picked the habit up. Scott, uncharacteristically, made the point in his
preface that part of his motive for writing *St Ronan's Well* was to warn young
men against the vice of play – more particularly piquet, 'the most beautiful
game at which a man can make sacrifice of his fortune'. *St Ronan's Well* is
also a novel obsessed with duelling, and its invariably fatal outcomes for
young men. There are two duels between Frank and Etherington; one
(aborted) between Bingo and Frank; and a final, bloody encounter between John Mowbray and Etherington. No great detective effort is required
to work out why this theme should have been preying on the novelist's
mind in 1823.

Perhaps because he was in the new field of contemporary fiction, Scott
listened rather more attentively than he should have to his adviser, James
Ballantyne. In the manuscript and proof versions of the novel, Scott indicated (as Lockhart records) that 'Miss Mowbray's mock marriage had not
halted at the profane ceremony of the church' (Lock. 4. 151). That is to say
she was seduced after Etherington's marriage trick.[3] James Ballantyne, now
himself a married man and more prudish than he used to be, took 'vast
alarm' at this episode. Constable was called in and Scott was prevailed on to
'cancel and rewrite some twenty-four pages'. But, of course, this makes
Clara's madness, and death, that much less plausible. Scott complained that
James was acting like a snob – he would never have complained had Clara
been 'a girl in gingham', and not a squire's daughter (EJ 853). But he
nonetheless submitted to his printer's wisdom on the matter.

Scott finished writing *St Ronan's Well* in late November. The novel duly
appeared in December 1823, to crown the heaviest year in his authorial
career (there were three full-length novels, comprising ten volumes). As
Lockhart records, 'in its English reception there was another falling off'
(Lock. 4. 159). More pungently, in his 1832 preface Scott recalled that 'the
English critics . . . pursued *St Ronan's Well* with hue and cry and declared it
was 'a literary suicide' ' (1. xxi). Scott did not attempt a modern tale again.

REDGAUNTLET

Redgauntlet was apparently contracted for as early as May 1822 (HG 230).
Grierson assumes that Scott must have begun writing the novel in
November 1823, as the final proofs of *St Ronan's Well* were being corrected.
Other scholars have subsequently suggested that actual composition began
slightly later. It was a crowded and authorially hectic period. Scott was
preoccupied in the last months of 1823 with his *Britannica* article on
'Romance', and the 'Richardson' volume for Ballantyne's Library. Orig-

inally the new novel was entitled 'The Witch' and – as a throwaway remark by Cadell records – it was to contain 'Goblins'. It was James Ballantyne who advised changing the novel's second proposed title, 'Herries', on the (plausible) grounds that it gave too much away. Scott came up with the more enigmatic *Redgauntlet* – whose meaning is not unveiled until late in the action.

Despite the relatively long gestation, Scott never resolved what remains the principal weakness in *Redgauntlet*. The clearly autobiographical recollection in the first thirteen chapters sets the action in the early 1790s. That is where one *feels* the novel is, historically. But the fact that the plot involves a second, forlorn, attempt by the Chevalier and his followers has – for reasons of historical plausibility – to place *Redgauntlet*'s action well before the Prince's death in 1788. The narrative is chronically foggy as to its exact historical period. The young men's letters, which make up the opening sections, are studiously undated. Clear historical markers are avoided in the narrative. But at one point, we are given a provisional setting of 'not twenty years since [1745]' (2. 20). And later in the narrative, we are told that the Chevalier is now twenty years older than he was in 1745. This fits in with Scott's 1832 afterword (which is partly written to defend *Redgauntlet* against the widespread accusation that its rebellion plot was wildly unhistorical). There, Scott recalls the folklore that the Pretender made one last clandestine visit to England in 1753; this, with fictional licence, the novel postdates to 1765. Nevertheless, the ambience of the novel is the early 1790s, when Scott was Alan Fairford's age, and when his WS father was the image of Saunders Fairford.

Redgauntlet is, once again, a 'Scotch novel' of the last century. As Grierson puts it, 'the author is once more upon his native heath and breathing the same historic air' (HG 234). But *Redgauntlet*'s Scotland is a country left over by history. If *St Ronan's Well* chronicles the comedy of national exhaustion, *Redgauntlet* dramatizes its pathos. This pathos is particularly poignant in the novel's climax, when it emerges that George III's efficient 'secret police' (Scott uses this term, interestingly enough) have kept the authorities fully apprised of Redgauntlet's uprising. But the conspiracy is judged to be a negligible threat. The rebels are not worth crushing. The on-the-spot amnesty delivered by General Campbell is the death blow, or, as the Pretender himself puts it, the 'copestone'. There will be no martyrs. Redgauntlet's anguished 'the cause is lost for ever' resonates after the novel is closed. And in the mind's eye there lingers the final vignette, of Pretender and arch-revolutionary, making their way to Nanty Ewart's brig:

> The last heir of the Stewarts leant on Redgauntlet's arm as they walked towards the beach; for the ground was rough, and he no longer possessed the elasticity of limb and of spirit which had, twenty years before, carried him over many a Highland hill, as light as one of their native deer. His adherents followed, looking on the ground, their feelings struggling against the dictates of their reason. (2. 333)

Scott alludes, with masterly effect, to the last lines of *Paradise Lost*, and Adam and Eve leaving Eden, 'hand in hand, with wand'ring steps and slow'.

The Gilsland recollections in *St Ronan's Well* suggested a nostalgic turn in Scott. Nostalgia was further indulged in *Redgauntlet*. In this novel he delved a few years farther back into the 1789–90 period – his own student and apprentice-lawyer years. As critics have noted, the two young heroes, Darsie and Alan Fairford, represent dual sides of Scott's early character: the vagabond and the 'douce' scrivener. There was the Walter who dutifully wanted to follow his father's profession and wishes; and there was the Walter who wanted to roam the countryside like a 'gangrel gut-scraper', collecting tales and ballads and lore. *Redgauntlet* also introduces from the early 1790s 'Greenmantle', in the person of Lilias (whom Alan, luckier than Walter, eventually marries). Peter Peebles, the proverbially drunken litigant who is Alan's first client, was (Scott's 'Note 30' tells us) based on one of young Walter's earliest clients in 1792, when the inebriate served as an 'assay piece', or hurdle, for all tyro advocates.

The early sections of *Redgauntlet* are most notable for the tender depiction of Walter Scott WS as he was in 1790:

> Punctual as the clock of Saint Giles tolled nine, the neat dapper form of the little hale old gentleman was seen at the threshold of the Court hall, or at farthest, at the head of the Back Stairs, trimly dressed in a complete suit of snuff-coloured brown, with stockings of silk, or woollen, as suited the weather; a bobwig, and a small cocked hat; shoes black as Warren would have blacked them; silver shoe-buckles, and a gold stock-buckle. A nosegay in summer, and a sprig of holly in winter, completed his well-known dress and appearance. (1. 212–3)

Edgar Johnson, like other biographers, reproduces this as a virtual photograph of Walter Scott WS.

Scott penetrates deep into his father's complicated politics. Fairford is 'zealous for King George and the government even to slaying, as he had showed by taking up arms in their cause' (when the rebels marched on Edinburgh; 1. 213). But at the same time, he is courteously deferential to Jacobites, Tories and die-hards. This courtesy extends beyond the lawyer's self-serving prudence. Scott notates the precise euphemisms ('out in 45', e.g., for 'rebel') that Fairford uses. In all this, we may assume, Scott was recollecting his father. Some less lovable aspects of his father are also recalled. Saunders is dictatorial: it is by the 'path of law alone' that he would have Alan rise. 'I wish my father would allow me a little more exercise of my free will', Alan complains (1. 18). Perversely Saunders good-naturedly tolerates the scapegrace antics of Darsie, as Walter Scott WS (with occasional grumbling) tolerated his son's vagabondage. Significantly, Saunders Fairford is presented as a highly competent lawyer – not the 'Uncle Toby' bumbler Scott elsewhere satirizes. All in all, this is a much more respectful picture of his father's professional abilities than that offered in the Ashestiel fragment, written in 1808, when Scott was vexed at the confusion in which his parent had left his business affairs.

There are some symptomatic distortions in the *Redgauntlet* version of Scott's young manhood. There is, for instance, nothing about the mother, Mrs Fairford – an odd omission. Alan has no siblings. He is the only child that Walter may often have wished to be. (Ironically, perhaps, he was now in 1823 the only child – but only in the sense that he had survived longest). Scott rewrites family history with himself as apple of his father's eye. As part of this rewriting, Saunders Fairford is so solicitous about his son's health that he moves from the old to the new town, on a hint from 'Dr R—'. In biographical fact, little Walter was moved to Sandy Knowe on the advice of Dr Rutherford, his maternal grandfather, at least a year before the Scotts moved to George Square, in 1774. There is no suggestion that Walter Scott WS made the move to George Square in the interests of the youngest of his five children. Scott is recasting family history with himself at the centre of things, rather than the unconsidered fringe.

Redgauntlet, particularly in its early chapters, is an extraordinarily intro-spective work, and one which mulls over a whole range of 'family' issues. As Grierson notes, the two heroes, in addition to recalling Scott's confusion in the 1790s, also reflect what was happening with Scott's sons in the 1820s. Walter had become a man of action, an English soldier – eventually, like Darsie, he would inherit an English title. It had been decided that the introverted Charles, like Alan, should make his career at the Scottish bar.

How had Scott produced such very different sons? It was as if his own personality had split into two. The novel also ponders Scott's own national-ist dilemma – was he a Scots laird, or an English baronet? It is a symbolic moment when Darsie – now Sir Arthur Redgauntlet, inheritor of a violent Borders tradition of rebellion – decides that after all he is English. It is only proper that Darsie should finally be introduced at court (to be for-given and rehabilitated by his Hanoverian monarch) by the General Campbell who had earlier delivered the *coup de grace* to the Pretender's plot. It is significant, too, that this Campbell was Scott's own ancestral relative, via Beardie, who married a lady of that clan. (It was on the strength of this connection that Scott wore the Campbell tartan during the King's jaunt and on his evenings at the Celtic Society.) Darsie's appearance at the English court may be viewed as either selling out, or political realism. *Redgauntlet* suggests that Scott had not entirely worked the problem out for himself in 1823–4.

For all its faults of structure, *Redgauntlet* is the last great novel Scott wrote. His next works went consciously downmarket (for younger readers, mainly) and were feebler and at times downright cynical in conception. What raises *Redgauntlet*, like *St Ronan's Well*, to a higher level is its rich vein of introspection and retrospection – Scott looking into himself and into his past. One suspects, too, that writing *Redgauntlet* was therapeutic for its author, an activity which relieved the increasingly urgent stress of his money concerns, which had reached crisis proportions by 1824. A passage in

Redgauntlet is highly relevant to the journal Scott was to begin in November 1825 (Darsie is writing):

> There is at length a halt – at length I have gained so much privacy as to enable me to continue my Journal. It has become a sort of task of duty to me, without the discharge of which I do not feel that the business of the day is performed. True, no friendly eye may ever look upon these labours, which have amused the solitary hours of an unhappy prisoner. Yet, in the meanwhile, the exercise of the pen seems to act as a sedative upon my own agitated thoughts and tumultuous passions. I never lay it down but I rise stronger in resolution, more ardent in hope. A thousand vague fears, wild expectations, and indigested schemes, hurry through one's thoughts in seasons of doubt and of danger. But by arresting them as they flit across the mind, by throwing them on paper, and even by that mechanical act compelling ourselves to consider them with scrupulous and minute attention, we may perhaps escape becoming the dupes of our own excited imagination; just as a young horse is cured of the vice of starting, by being made to stand still and look for some time without any interruption at the cause of its terror. (2. 41)

Scott's best writing after June 1824 is diverted into the journal. He had outgrown fiction. And the above passage would seem essential to a true literary valuation of the journal. Commentators have argued that Scott's journal was inspired by Lockhart's giving him *Pepys's Diary* to review in the *Quarterly* in July 1825. But it seems clear from Darsie's comments (written at some point before June 1824) that the 'Journal' was born out of Scott's internal evolution as a writer and his need to find new forms for self-expression.

Redgauntlet was published in June – when, like its predecessor, it was received a little coldly, according to Lockhart (4. 154). It was Scott's only novel in 1824, following the avalanche of fiction the previous year. Although he was thinking of the 'Tales of the Crusaders' as early as December 1823 and spelled out the two-volume format to Terry, in February 1824, that project was held back (HG 231). Scott was evidently again conscious of the danger of 'overcropping'.

14

The Crash (1824–1826)

After some vacillation, Charles, Scott's younger son, was entered at
Brasenose College, Oxford in October 1824 (Lock. 4. 193). The offer of an
East India place which Lord Bathurst had made was declined. Scott decided
instead that Charles should, after Oxford, become a Scottish advocate. The
choice of an English university for his son was carefully considered. Scott
was internationalizing his 'line' of 'Scotts of Abbotsford'. In November
1824, Walter – having finished his course at Sandhurst – was purchased a
captaincy in the 15th Hussars for £5,000 (EJ 883). He was on course
eventually to command an English regiment. On his part, Charles would
now be formed intellectually by English dons. Scott justified his choice to
Lord Montagu (apropos young Buccleuch, who was also sent to school in
England): 'I am more and more convinced of the excellence of the English
monastic institutions of Cambridge and Oxford . . . If a man is poor, plain,
and indifferently connected, he may have excellent opportunities of study
at Edinburgh; otherwise he should beware of it' (Lock. 4. 183). In his
enthusiasm for youthful monasticism Scott, of course, was thinking of his
own High Street dissipations as a university student.

Had Scott had his wits about him, there were other dangers to beware of
in 'English monastic institutions'. Charles's main patron at Oxford was
Scott's old friend, Richard Heber, now MP for the city. It was he, in fact, who
had suggested that Charles join him there (EJ 778–9) and it was Heber who
secured the young man a place at his own college, Brasenose. Heber took
an avuncular interest in Charles Scott. But in summer 1826, the distinguished don and MP was forced to flee the country in scandal when he
was discovered in homosexual practices. In his journal Scott alludes to the
'degrading bestiality' of Heber's secret life, in such a way as to make it clear
that the discovery of his friend's preferences was a bolt out of the blue.
Where did it leave Charles? For much of his adolescence, he had been
brought up in Wales with a clergyman (to keep him away from Glaswegian
street-women). Had he, horrible thought, been corrupted by Heber's

'bestiality'? Charles never subsequently married. His manner as it is described to us was one of excessive reserve, moroseness and secrecy. When he eventually entered the diplomatic service it was at his request that his father pulled strings to have him posted as a junior *attaché* to Naples. Charles liked the posting, despite its dead-end prospects, and made determined efforts to stay there on the grounds that the warmth was good for his rheumatism. It was also a city where sexual alternatives could be discreetly indulged.

One of Scott's happiest concerns in summer 1824 was tending his woods. They were now sufficiently grown to need thinning, a chore which he undertook vigorously with Tom Purdie. And in autumn 1824, as the leaves fell, Abbotsford was at last finished. Soft furnishings, decor, room layout and a thousand finishing touches obsessed Scott. He composed Abbotsford more carefully than any of his poems. It was, as John Buchan calls it, 'his romance in stone' (JB 260). It comprehended an anthology of civilization, from the symbolic Wallace chair made of wood from Robroyston (where the Scottish hero fell) to the progressive flues. Scott was forever writing to Daniel Terry, his sales-room agent in London. Nothing was too insignificant. On one occasion he asks for 'a parcel of old caricatures, which can be bought cheap, for the purpose of papering two *cabinets à l'eau*' (Lock. 4. 172). Water closets were, of course, as new-fangled as the caricatures were antique.

On his part, Daniel Terry's ambitions had also reached their dizziest height, with the proposed purchase of a lease on a London theatre, the Adelphi (EJ 896). He opened the scheme to Scott in May 1825. Sums as high as £30,000 were mentioned. Scott and his *protégé* encouraged each other in a kind of *folie à deux*. Scott – with what, if it were not irony, was extraordinary self-delusion – chose to lecture the younger man on fiscal responsibility, when asked to stand guarantor for a loan of £1,250 (which he did): 'The best business is ruined when it becomes pinched for money and gets into the circle of discounting bills . . . besides the immense expense of renewals, that mode of raising money is always liable to some sudden check which throws you on your back at once' (Lock. 4. 264–8). At the time he wrote this sage advice, Scott probably had some £40,000 outstanding in 'fictional' paper. He was using Ballantyne's credit as a personal bank. (Daniel Terry was to be ruined shortly after Scott. He never got out of the morass of his Adelphi lease and died prematurely and exhausted by money troubles in 1829.)

Christmas 1824 took the form of a gigantic housewarming. Scott, the Laird of Abbotsford at last, presided over the kind of traditional festivities which he had immortalized in *Marmion*. Plum pudding was devoured and favours distributed. He read the ghostly *Christabel* to the company and recited seasonal stories and ballads (Lock. 4. 213). Captain Basil Hall, a guest at these 1824–5 festivities, vividly describes Scott's charitable 'boxes' to 'his people' and his public double act with Tom Purdie, 'his man' (Lock. 4. 225–6). The twelve days' celebration were succeeded by a great ball at Abbotsford on 7 January – 'the first and last ball which Scott saw in Abbotsford' (JB 259). It was an occasion to crown Scott's family ambitions, commemorating the completion of his house, and the engagement of his heir Walter to a supremely eligible heiress.

According to Lockhart summer 1823 was the happiest period of his father-in-law's whole life and 1824 was 'his last year of undisturbed prosperity' (Lock. 4. 130). He seemed to the visiting Captain Hall radiant with his sunny good humour and serene modesty. Wherever Scott went, Hall observed, 'there was a sort of halo of fun and intelligence around him.' Scott's public self was now majestic. In 1823 'the great well-known Unknown' (Hall's description; Lock. 4. 230) had assumed the mantle of Henry Dundas, as 'the manager of Scotland'. His list of social honours was unequalled – given the few advantages he had started with.

None of this entailed any let-up in his writing. In 1824 Scott was preparing a new edition of Swift, and after the burst of fiction writing over 1823–4, he embarked on what was the single most strenuous effort of his career – *The Life of Napoleon*. No British writer had attempted anything so grand since Gibbon. How did he intend to find time to carry out this scheme, while keeping up his social obligations? Hall ruminated, as had Edgeworth the year before, 'It becomes a curious question to know when it is that he actually writes these wonderful works which have fixed the attention of the world' (Lock. 4. 239).

Onlookers like Hall assumed that someone so worldly wise must also be money wise. 'He is too prudent and sagacious a man not to live within his means', Hall wrote (Lock. 4. 239). In fact, Scott was living wildly beyond his means. In a letter to Tom's widow at this time, he was eerily prescient: 'The real road to ruin 1st is to have an improveable estate with a taste for building – 2ndly to have your son marry a wealthy heiress and call on you for outfit and marriage presents, and if over and above you can manage to have a troop to buy for him in a crack regiment of cavalry you will find the bottom of the purse with a vengeance' (HG 237). His intention may have been to tactfully head off any request from his sister-in-law for further assistance. But the word 'ruin' was ominous.

He could see what was coming, and could even – at this late date – have averted at least the worst of the catastrophe. But he did not. Indeed, he seems recklessly to have surrendered to the mood of 'speculation' and commercial mania that swept across Britain in 1824–5. We find him throwing £1,500 into railway shares (good technology, but years away from being a good investment; EJ 896.) He was similarly involved in oil-gas projects (the wrong technology, as it turned out). As has been said, he guaranteed Terry £1,250 for his new theatre, and was pensioning a regiment of friends and relations down on their luck. And in May 1825, on the eve of destruction, he was still toying with the idea of buying the adjoining estate of Faldonside for some £33,000 (EJ 901).

Scott's floating debt in the intricate paperwork dealings between Ballantyne and Constable at this period is not easy to work out, but

Grierson (who contracted an accountant to look into it) estimates it as something around £30,000 in bills 'for value received' (i.e. in payment for copyrights or printing services) and about the same amount in 'accommodation bills' – or mutually guaranteed loans between the firms. The danger of these bills – as Scott later discovered – was that they could exact a double repayment if, instead of being held as security, they were passed on to raise still more money (HG 221). Constable and Cadell were nervous about the huge quantity of bills to which they had put the firm's name. But they 'had staked too much' in Scott to frighten him away by making him retire bills when what he wanted was more loans.

In his partial account of this phase of Scott's life, Lockhart paints Constable as something little better than a lunatic. Take, for instance, the famous meeting on a Saturday in May 1825 at Abbotsford, with Scott, JGL, Constable and James Ballantyne in attendance:

> Constable was meditating nothing less than a total revolution in the art and traffic of bookselling; and the exulting and blazing fancy with which he expanded and embellished his visions of success, hitherto undreamt of in the philosophy of the trade, might almost have induced serious suspicions of his sanity, but for the curious accumulation of pregnant facts on which he rested his justification, and the dexterous sagacity with which he uncoiled his practical inferences. He startled us at the outset by saying: 'Literary genius may, or may not, have done its best; but printing and bookselling, as instruments for enlightening mankind, and, of course, for making money, are as yet in mere infancy. Yes the trade are in their cradle.' Scott eyed the florid bookseller's beaming countenance, and the solemn stare with which the equally portly printer was listening, and pushing round the bottles with a hearty chuckle, bade me 'Give our twa *sonsie babbies* a drap mother's milk.' (Lock. 4. 270–1)

Fortified by more drink, the already drunken publisher went on to outline his dream of 'Constable's Miscellany' (as it was to become), 'a three shilling or half-crown volume every month, which we must and shall sell, not by thousands, or tens of thousands, but by hundreds of thousands – ay, by millions!' Millions of copies of reprints of *Waverley* novels were what Constable principally had in mind. Scott rejoined by saluting the publisher as 'the grand Napoleon of the realms of *print*' and went on:

> 'I am willing to do my part in this grand enterprise. Often, of late, I have felt that the vein of fiction was nearly worked out; often, as you all know, I have been thinking seriously of turning my hand to history... What say you to taking the field with a Life of the *other* Napoleon?' (Lock. 4. 273–4)

It is a famous and much quoted scene. But there are reasons for being slightly sceptical. The dates do not quite fit. Lockhart gives two markers: the Abbotsford meeting took place (1) between 5 May and July, when Terry's Adelphi business was going forward; (2) 'on the eve of publication' of 'The Tales of the Crusaders', in early June (Lock. 4. 270, 274). But as early as 5 May, Scott writes to Lockhart that Constable's 'Miscellany' project 'is the cleverest thing that ever came into the head of the cleverest of all bibliopolic heads' (HG 240). This anomaly does not discredit JGL's account. But what makes one suspicious (apart from the extraordinary theatricality of the dialogue) is the stress on Constable's reckless drunkenness (a favourite theme of Lockhart's), set off by Scott's cool, ironic judiciousness. As the note to Lockhart suggests, Scott seems to have been as excited as Constable by the 'Miscellany' idea. He would hardly have hazarded the most ambitious piece of writing of his life were he not. What seems as plausible is that Scott was keen to raise vast new sums for the purchase of Faldonside (which he was discussing with Walter in the last week of April 1825) and proposed the idea of *The Life of Napoleon* to Constable rather more aggressively than Lockhart suggests.

A MATCH FOR WALTER

Scott arranged his heir's marriage as carefully as he supervised his army career. A suitable bride was found in spring 1824, when Sir Adam Ferguson and his wife brought their exceedingly shy niece, Jane Jobson, to Castle Street. Walter was twenty-three. Miss Jobson was a teenaged heiress from Lochore in Fife and carried, as Scott put it, 'gold in her garters' (*Lett.* 8. 487) – around £70,000. Her father was dead, but her mother was alive and 'difficult'. Mrs Jobson was strategically kept out of the picture at this early meeting. According to Scott, the idea that Jane and Walter might make a match originated with her uncle (EJ 861). It was as likely to have been hatched between the two old friends. Ferguson owed Scott a favour for arranging his knighthood, as one of the three boons granted by the monarch on his August 1822 jaunt (EJ 795).

Walter's first enquiries on being told about his future wife were very much to the point. Was she of good family (no 'trade', if you please), how much money did she have, and was it understood that he would not, under any circumstances, give up the army? On being reassured on all points, he consented to be at Abbotsford that summer. The young people were duly introduced to each other in August 1824, but did not fall in love as intended. Mrs Jobson, when she was finally informed later in the year about arrangements which had been made for her daughter, proved difficult indeed. She disapproved of soldiers and poets on religious grounds. On grounds of rank, she despised new baronets (EJ 884–5). A round of hard bargaining ensued, interspersed by tantrums on Mrs Jobson's part and (private) anger on Scott's. As requested, Scott informed the lady's legal representatives that the rent rolls of Abbotsford came to £1,680 a year, and that the house itself was worth some £50,000. He did not, as Grierson observes, enlighten the Jobson lawyers about the mountain of unpaid loans lying in the Ballantyne and Constable files. It may be true that Mrs Jobson was 'fat and vulgar' (Jrnl. xxxii), but her suspicions were not groundless. Scott's finances were not sound.

Things evidently picked up in December after Scott had purchased Walter's captaincy (this may have been required by the young man as a price for going forward). Miss Jobson was the guest of honour at the great Christmas and Hogmanay celebrations in 1824. Scott did everything he could to foster romance and Jane and Walter did, in fact, get on better than they had in the summer. Or, as Edgar Johnson puts it, 'the enchantment that had failed to burgeon under the leafy boughs of August burst into flower in the crisp air of winter and the festive season' (EJ 884).

Despite this burgeoning (of which, incidentally, there is no objective evidence), the engagement was not formally announced at Christmas. Before this could happen, there was more horse-trading. Scott was eventually obliged by the Jobson lawyers to make over Abbotsford to Walter and his heirs male. Scott was permitted to keep the rents during his life and to raise a mortgage on the property not greater than £10,000. So, having owned his house in its complete form for three months, Scott signed it away. He did so with admirable generosity of spirit (EJ 886). But, culpably, he did not inform the Ballantynes of what he had done (EQ 179).

The wedding took place on 3 February 1825, as a quiet domestic affair at Mrs Jobson's Edinburgh house. It was a highpoint in Scott's life. Walter – the English cavalry officer – was as much his creation as Abbotsford or *Redgauntlet*. He had now married money, and would inherit a title and a large estate. Scott had managed things with consummate skill, and he was genuinely fond of his new daughter-in-law. But his conduct in prosecuting the match verged at times on the unscrupulous. He evidently felt so himself, and circulated among all his friends and acquaintance – including the Duke of Buccleuch and Lady Louisa Stuart – the falsehood ('pretty story' as Johnson euphemistically calls it) that Walter and Jane had met and been attracted to each other two years earlier (EJ 886–7). Although she had money, there is no evidence that Jane was the kind of woman that a man-of-the-world like Walter would fall in love with at first sight. According to W. E. K. Anderson, she was 'a humourless, insipid girl ... neither the Lockharts nor Anne [Scott] enjoyed her company' (Jrnl. xxxii). From what scanty evidence there is, one suspects that the childless marriage of the younger Walter Scotts was not passionately happy. It is reported that after being widowed Lady Scott declined ever to speak of her husband, or his family. It would be unkind to stress that Scott's part in his son's marriage arrangements ran flat against the romantic tendency of such novels as *The Bride of Lammermoor*. The writer who could create Lucy Ashton's wedding night could mate his son and daughter-in-law like a bull and heifer on one of his farms.

'Tales of the Crusaders'

Scott began the series that was to be marketed (somewhat misleadingly) as the 'Tales of the Crusaders' in winter 1824–5. According to Edgar Johnson, he started *The Betrothed* as soon as *Redgauntlet* was off his hands in June 1824. James Ballantyne was, however, critical of the samples shown him and progress on the novel was intermittent. At some point in the new year 1825, Scott turned to another 'Tale', *The Talisman* (EJ 895). This went more fluently. But in May 1825, with the end of the second novel in sight, Scott was persuaded to go back (rather reluctantly) to *The Betrothed* and finish it so the works could be published together as a package in June.

The title *The Betrothed* was evidently intended as a compliment to Scott's son and new bride (of February 1825). His writing the novel straddled the period of the engagement and marriage. The novel's plot is something of a tour de force in that the heroine, Eveline Berenger, is a 'betrothed' (to three different suitors) for all the novel's 300-odd pages and over a period of four years. This extends the elasticity of what is normally a brief interval in life to the breaking-point of credulity. It is, however, significant that *The Betrothed* begins with what was probably Scott's January 1825 nightmare, an arranged marriage that falls through at the very last moment. One does not know; but the fact that Walter's engagement to Jane was not announced at the Abbotsford ball of 7 January suggests that there was some very hard bargaining between the families, right up to the public announcement.

The Betrothed is set in Wales, a country with which Scott had little acquaintance, and at the most remote period – the mid-1100s – he had hitherto chosen for his fiction. Ingenuity can link *The Betrothed* with novels like *Rob Roy* via chauvinist theories of pan-Celticism – there is, for example, a small disquisition in chapter 1 on the Welsh kilt. But Scott himself does not seem to have been very excited by such connections. Nor does he have any obvious inwardness with Wales, and if anything seems to favour the view that the Welsh are so many 'wolves' – savages like Gwenwyn or cowardly assassins like Cadwallon. There is no-one in *The Betrothed* who has the status of a Welsh folk hero (a Rob Roy) or a noble servant (an Evan Dhu).[1]

It is indicative of Scott's general indifference to racial and national themes in *The Betrothed* that he makes no attempt to render the richness of the characters' dialect. The dramatis personae are a *mélange* of racial and national types. There are Normans, Saxons, Flemings, Welsh and the bastardized 'Britons'. In the novel all speak the sub-Shakespearian fustian that was first devised for *Ivanhoe*. This is convenient to Scott, in that it enabled him to write almost with his left hand, automatically.

If the dialogue is 'written by steam' (as the preface self-mockingly tells us), Scott gives the reader, by way of compensation, some fine action writing. *The Betrothed*'s defects and compensating strengths are evident in the passage describing the death of Sir Raymond outside the walls of his ominously named castle, Garde Doloureuse:

> The combat . . . had raged for more than half an hour, when Berenger, having forced his horse within two spears' length of the British standard, he and Gwenwyn were so near to each other as to exchange tokens of mutual defiance.

'Turn thee, Wolf of Wales,' said Berenger, 'and abide, if thou darest, one blow of a good knight's sword! Raymond Berenger spits at thee and thy banner.'

'False Norman churl!' said Gwenwyn, swinging around his head a mace of prodigious weight, and already clotted with blood, 'thy iron head-piece shall ill protect thy lying tongue, with which I will this day feed the ravens!'

Raymond made no further answer, but pushed his horse towards the prince, who advanced to meet him with equal readiness. But ere they came within reach of each other's weapons, a Welsh champion, devoted like the Romans who opposed the elephants of Pyrrhus, finding that the armour of Raymond's horse resisted the repeated thrusts of his spear, threw himself under the animal, and stabbed him in the belly with his long knife. The noble horse reared and fell, crushing with his weight the Briton who had wounded him; the helmet of the rider burst its clasps in the fall, and rolled away from his head, giving to view his noble features and grey hairs. He made more than one effort to extricate himself from the fallen horse, but, ere he could succeed, received his death's wound from the hand of Gwenwyn, who hesitated not to strike him down with his mace while in the act of attempting to rise. (48–9)

Since the 'exchanges of defiance' were uttered one in Norman, the other in Welsh, how *could* the combatants exchange anything except blows? One is reminded of the film *Where Eagles Dare*, in which when the characters go into guttural stilted English, the audience is to understand that fluent German is being spoken. But the action describing Raymond's death which follows is grittier than anything Hollywood has produced. The decencies of screen performance (not to say the American Humane Society) would never allow a horse to be stuck in the belly. But the underhand stroke and the killing of the old man when he is down capture the nastiness of warfare, even in the age of chivalry.

Scott did not think at all well of *The Betrothed* while writing it, or after. Reportedly, he wanted to burn the manuscript. But it was preserved, so as to give ballast to *The Talisman*. Not that the two works went all that well together. According to Scott's 'Magnum' preface the blanket title, 'Tales of the Crusaders', was 'determined on rather by the advice of the few friends whom death has now rendered still fewer than by the Author's own taste' (1. xvi). He further records in the preface to *The Talisman* that perversely – having talked him into the blanket title – these same 'friends' objected that *The Betrothed* was like *Hamlet* without the Prince – a tale of the Crusades which never left Wales.

This omission was corrected in *The Talisman*, which opens in the sands of Syria. Scott cheerfully concedes in his preface that he had never seen the East. But despite this handicap, he contrived to create a garishly effective desert setting for *The Talisman*'s opening chapters. Under the 'burning sun', a knight of the Red Cross paces slowly on his overburdened charger, across the 'sandy deserts which lie in the vicinity of the Dead Sea' (1). In the distance, he sees a form moving quickly towards him. ' "In the desert", saith the proverb, "no man meets a friend" '. It is a 'Saracen cavalier' on a light horse which he manages 'more by his limbs and the inflection of his body than by the use of his reins' (6). The lightly armed but nimble Arab and the heavily armoured Christian fight.

After sparring and proving each other's mettle, the Scottish knight Sir Kenneth of the Leopard Couchant and the Saracen Ilderim make peace, and adjourn to a nearby oasis, debating the differences in their religions and social codes. Scott stresses his conviction that ideological opponents (Saracen and Christian, Whig and Tory) are capable of chivalric, or 'gentlemanly' intercourse, on the basis of shared ideals of supra-ideological honour. Mark Girouard has recently shown how influential Scott was with novels like this in redefining the ideal of the Victorian gentleman in terms of idealized medieval chivalry. This advocacy of chivalry – an 'open' and transcendent set of values, to which all classes and even opponents can subscribe – is opposed in *The Talisman* (as earlier in *Ivanhoe*) to the closed system of masonry, or the Templars, whose knights are initiates and whose membership is exclusive. The Templars are the source of plots, underhand intrigues and dishonourable conspiracy.

The Talisman is rich in scenes which have entered folklore, often detached from the novel which originated them. One such is the climactic encounter of Richard and Saladin, and their demonstrations of the respective powers of their swords. Richard, with a mighty blow of his two-handed sword, severs a bar of metal. The more dextrous Saladin cuts through a cushion with his shimmering scimitar, and then does the same with a silk veil. At another point in *The Talisman*, Scott put his originator's mark (although he rarely receives credit) on a gimmick which was to become a universal standby in the detective novel. Some traitor desecrates the English standard – wounding Sir Kenneth's faithful Roswal in the process. Richard brings the hound to a general meeting of knights. The dog unerringly goes for Montserrat's throat. He, of course, denies his guilt (he is, in fact, hand in glove with the Templars, who are plotting to frustrate Richard). The King orders Conrade to stand forth, and if he dares

> 'deny the accusation which this mute animal hath in his noble instinct brought against thee, of injury done to him, and foul scorn to England?'
> 'I never touched the banner,' said Conrade, hastily.
> 'Thy words betray thee, Conrade!' said Richard; 'for how didst thou know, save from conscious guilt, that the question is concerning the banner?' (368)

So are clichés born.

The Talisman bequeathed a wealth of machinery and scenarios to boys' fiction of the nineteenth century and after. But the novel also has its adult aspects, dealing as it does, obliquely but powerfully, with anti-Scots prejudice in the British armed forces. Sir Kenneth is subjected to a constant barrage of insults, slights, and racial jeers from his comrades (but not, as they make only too clear, his compatriots). Lord Thomas Vaux's spiteful catchphrase, 'Scots, ever fair and false' rings through the novel (and is even glossed by Scott in a defensive note). Richard's queen amuses herself by indulging her wit 'at the expense of the garb, nation, and, above all, the poverty' of the Scottish knight (246). All this must have been brought to mind – consciously or unconsciously – by Walter, Scott's Scottish son, currently serving in the English army.

The 'Tales of the Crusaders' were published in June 1825 and sold well. They are efficient novels, and on the level of purely entertaining romance *The Talisman*, at least, is one of the most successful works Scott wrote. But the question remains: how could Scott write such unambitious work, after *St Ronan's Well* and *Redgauntlet*? He was still at the height of his powers. These tales are a huge comedown. (Hesketh Pearson goes so far as to claim that they could win a prize in any competition for the dreariest and stupidest books by a great writer with all his faculties intact; Pearson, 206.)

THE ONSET OF THE CRASH

There were few precedents for a biographical work on the scale of *The Life of Napoleon*. Something much grander than Southey's bestselling *Life of Nelson* (1813) was foreseen, and a design more extensive even than the other writer's history of the Peninsular War (begun in 1823). Napoleon had emerged from the period of Scott's own adult life as the greatest, if most perverse, man of the time. With his premature death in 1821, the Corsican was (just) far enough away to be seen historically. Over the years Scott's attitude to Napoleon had matured. Once upon a time he had hated him viscerally, like all right-thinking Britons. Now his hatred had cooled into a kind of wonder.

For the publisher and author *The Life of Napoleon* would be a long-term seller (and if the 'Miscellany' took off, as Constable fondly hoped, a million-seller). Scott embarked on a programme of deep research. His nearly thirty years of marriage (and Lady Scott's difficulties with English) had rendered him conversant in French, and he began by calling up (via Constable) a mass of primary materials on the Revolution. Because they regarded it as potentially a useful piece of Tory propaganda the government (via Croker) gave Scott access to official documents. Whatever else, this biography would be a Herculean literary labour. 'He read, and noted, and indexed with the pertinacity of some pale compiler in the British Museum', Lockhart records (Lock. 4. 337). Lockhart also detected signs of weariness as Scott bent to the labour. As Buchan puts it, 'He was as much a slave of the pen now as he had been when he copied legal documents' (JB 275).

The Life of Napoleon was written up with the usual speed. The first volume was finished by October 1825 (EJ 948). By July 1825, Scott had written the greater part of his Introduction on the French Revolution (HG 241). With his two latest novels recently published and selling well he was free to visit Ireland to see his son Walter and his daughter-in-law. Scott seems genuinely (unlike others in his family) to have doted on Jane, and clearly anticipated from her the male heir (Walter the fourth) who would carry on the line at Abbotsford.

It was his first visit abroad since 1815 – if Ireland in 1825 counted as abroad. He took Lockhart and his daughter Anne with him (it was her first visit abroad ever). Lady Scott, as always nowadays, was indisposed and did not accompany them (EJ 902). The family group left on 9 July and reached Dublin some five days later (EJ 906). Lockhart gives a vivid description of Scott on the voyage over, 'as full of glee . . . as a schoolboy' (Lock. 4. 297). On shore, Ireland was a triumphal progress. He dined at his son's table at St Stephen's Green where the newly married Scotts were sharing quarters with another married officer. They all visited the Edgeworths at their model community Edgeworthstown (EJ 909). Scott was awarded an honorary doctorate of laws at Trinity College and visited Swift's tomb. He was fêted as never before. The Irish middle classes were famous booklovers and no-one had any doubt that Scott was the author of *Waverley*. His carriage was cheered in the street (EJ 908) and theatrical performances were halted when it was discovered that Walter Scott was in the audience. The Viceroy dined him. When, on the way to Wicklow, the Scotts had their way barred by an ugly mob of laid-off paperworkers, Scott solemnly thanked his hosts for getting up a 'rebellion' for his benefit (EJ 908). The visit, which lasted a month, was, as Grierson puts it, 'an ovation and a picnic'. Above all, it was a family occasion. As Scott put it, 'We had Lockhart to say clever things, and Walter with his whiskers to overawe postillions and impudent beggars, and Jane to bless herself that the folks had neither houses, clothes nor furniture, and Anne to make fun from morning to night' (*Lett.* 9. 185). But for all the rosy aura round the trip, there may have been some secret sadness. Scott's happiness would have been crowned if there had been news that Jane – now married for six months – was pregnant. In a letter of February 1826 to Lord Montagu Scott made the enigmatic remark 'My estate of Abbotsford is secured on my son and his family *if he has one*' (*Lett.* 9. 408). It's an odd thing to say of a couple one year married unless the doctors had pronounced on the unlikelihood of Jane's producing the desperately wanted heir.

The Scott party left Ireland on 18 August. They returned to Scotland via North Wales, visiting interesting people, places and grandees at every stop of the way. Most memorably, they dropped in on Wordsworth at Rydal and 'the great Laker' Southey at Keswick. Wordsworth, according to a profoundly unimpressed Lockhart, was 'absurdly arrogant beyond conception' (EJ 913). The Scotts arrived back at Abbotsford on 26 August. The Irish jaunt was the last family occasion, as such, in Scott's life.

The summer gave way to what Buchan calls 'a somewhat shadowed autumn' (JB 275). It was a season marked by loss and separation. Lockhart, with whom Scott was now very intimate, was the principal loss. Scott evidently accepted that his oldest son, Walter, was a soldier with the indelibly unliterary tastes of his profession. All Captain Scott required now was a handsome allowance from his father and – in the fullness of time – his title. Charles was something of an idler, cultivated but remote from his father. Anne was the cleverest of his children, but only a woman.

It was Lockhart into whom Scott poured his vicarious ambitions. His first intention had been to prise his son-in-law away from 'Maga' – to raise him above the gutter of Scottish magazinery (which was, in point of fact, the line in which Lockhart excelled). Reforming JGL was not easy; his reputation had been permanently scarred by the John Scott affair, and by his 'Scorpion' writings in the 'year of disgrace', 1818. On his marriage, Scott had (as he told Maria Edgeworth) exacted a promise that there should be no more 'satire'. But the novels that JGL wrote between 1820 and 1824 had not taken the world by storm.[2] His career at the Scottish Bar had not advanced. On meeting him in June 1823, Harriet Edgeworth bluntly observed that 'Mr Lockhart practises at the bar but does not get on as he is idle.'[3] He was also 'rather deaf' – which made him forbidding company. His volunteer service in the yeomanry had not brought him the kind of contacts Lieutenant Walter Scott had made in the 1790s: his off-putting 'hidalgo' air did not make for mess-room intimacies. An attempt in June 1825 to secure for him the Sheriffdom of Caithness or of Sutherland failed (HG 248). There was the added complication that Lockhart's young son, 'Hugh Littlejohn', on whom Scott doted, was evidently too frail for northern winters. In January 1824 another child, a daughter, died two days after birth, leaving Sophia on the verge of invalidism. Everything pointed to a move south.

The year 1825 was one of wild expansiveness in the magazine and literary world. Like Constable, John Murray was caught up in this mood. The London publisher proposed nothing less than to launch a rival to *The Times*. On 27 September Murray's 'confidential friend', the young dandy Benjamin Disraeli, came to Chiefswood on a fortnight's embassy, dazzling Scott and his son-in-law with the offer of the editorship of this new 'Thunderer' (to be called 'The Representative'), and the inevitable seat in Parliament that would accompany it. A munificent salary of £1,000 was mentioned (EJ 944). Lockhart was sufficiently tempted to make a trip to London, in October. There was, as it turned out, a more appropriate vacancy on the *Quarterly*, Murray's other organ. Gifford had given up the editorship in 1824, after an undistinguished tenure. John Taylor Coleridge (a nephew of the poet) had taken over in a temporary capacity. On 15 October it was settled that JGL should be the new editor of the *Quarterly*. The emolument was huge: almost £3,000 if Lockhart agreed to work for the *Representative* as well.

Lockhart's acceptance of the *Quarterly* post was blemished by the scheming that preceded it. Coleridge, the incumbent, was not told of his replacement until the day before the official announcement in *The Times* on 17 November, a full month after Murray clinched his agreement with JGL (Shattock, 47). There were protests by regular contributors, some of whom despised Lockhart for his role in the Scott–Christie duel and his 1818 antics in *Blackwood's Magazine*. Scott weighed in with a circulated letter of support for his son-in-law, who was, he said, a reformed man and had left his earlier satirical excesses behind him. Lockhart eventually secured the *Quarterly* editorship by some very unscrupulous manoeuvres, and a spectacular stabbing of his old friend Croker in the back. As Joanne Shattock records: 'Lockhart's toadyism to Murray, coupled with the abrogation of friendship with Croker, a *volte face* accomplished within a matter of days once he had sensed the direction in which events were moving, presents him in an extremely unattractive light' (Shattock, 51).

In Scott's eyes, to be editor of a quarterly was eminently respectable and appropriate for his son-in-law. For JGL, it looked like a huge step up in life. Scott wrote around to powerful friends in London, promoting his son-in-law. Lockhart and Sophia must make a mark in 'the great world', he resolved (Shattock, 53). But the move to London was, in the event, to prove disastrous for Lockhart. Socially, his reserved sarcastic manner went down badly with 'magnificoes' (Shattock, 54). His inability to speak well in public and his deafness (something that had impeded his career as an advocate) stood in the way of any parliamentary prospects. The coolness with Croker put Lockhart at odds with the Conservative establishment. The *Representative* was destroyed by the financial panic at the end of 1825 (the same cataclysm that would bring down Scott and Constable). It ceased publication in July 1826, having cost Murray a small fortune (Shattock, 55). It was also JGL's bad luck that in 1825 the quarterlies were no longer in the vanguard of British literary culture.

Overshadowing everything in 1825 was the volatile British economy. The year saw one of the country's periodic manias, a frenzy of commercial bubbles and over-optimistic speculation. Scott wrote to Maria Edgeworth as early as 23 March that 'the people are all mad about joint-stock companies' (HG 247). He too was infected – having invested 'only a few thousands' (as he understated it) in the oil-gas venture, the Berwick-to-Kelso railway project, and a local glassworks (EJ 941). He was also contemplating an outlay of over £30,000 for the Faldonside property. Speculation reached its peak in summer 1825. Booksellers, in order to raise quick cash, were speculating wildly in non-book commodities. Hurst & Robinson – the London publishers on whom Constable had staked his commercial future – had attempted to corner the market in hops (of all things) with an outlay, as JGL reported, of £100,000. In the same expansionist spirit, they had also just opened opulent new premises in Pall Mall. Murray had money involved in mining shares. Sensing that a crash was coming, the Bank of England attempted to cool down the economy with an autumn squeeze on loans.

It was in this inauspicious period (around October 1825) that Constable was prospecting for funds with which to launch his great 'Miscellany' scheme. As was his wont in autumn, he was down in London, visiting his colleagues in Paternoster Row. But he returned in ill health (gout, exacerbated by drink and stress) to Polton on 7 November. Lockhart was meanwhile moving between Edinburgh and London, arranging his *Quarterly* business. This was the setting for one of the more notorious sections of Lockhart's narrative, the so-called 'Polton Ride'.

According to the *Life*, 'a few days after my arrival at Chiefswood' (i.e. on his return from London, in November, having accepted Murray's offer) JGL received a letter from his London adviser, the lawyer William Wright. Wright informed JGL 'that Constable's London banker [Dixon] had thrown up his book.' The letter arrived at about five and JGL immediately rode over to Abbotsford where

> I found Sir Walter alone over his glass of whisky and water and cigar . . . I gave him Mr Wright's letter to read. He did so, and returning it, said, with his usual tranquil good-humour of look and voice, 'I am much obliged to you for coming over, but you may rely upon it Wright has been hoaxed. I promise you, were the Crafty's book thrown up, there would be a pretty decent scramble among the bankers for the keeping of it'.

With more of the same airy assurance, Scott lit another cigar and declared, 'I shan't allow such nonsense to disturb my *siesta*.' Seeing Scott's coolness, Lockhart returned home, 'relieved and gratified'. The next morning on rising, however, he was astonished to find Scott at his door in his carriage:

> his horses [were] evidently off a journey, and the Sheriff [was] rubbing his eyes as if the halt had shaken him out of a sound sleep. I made what haste I could to descend and found him by the side of the brook looking somewhat, worn, but with a serene and satisfied countenance, busied already in helping his little grandson to feed a fleet of ducklings. 'You are surprised,' he said 'to see me here. The truth is, I was more taken aback with Wright's epistle than I cared *to let on*; and so, as soon as you left me, I ordered the carriage to the door, and never stopped till I got to Polton, where I found Constable putting on his nightcap. I staid an hour with him and I have now the pleasure to tell you that *all is right*. There was not a word of truth in the story – he is fast as Ben Lomond; and as Mamma and Anne did not know what my errand was, I thought it as well to come and breakfast here, and set Sophia and you at your ease before I went home again.' We had a merry breakfast, and he chatted gaily afterwards as I escorted him through his woods, leaning on my shoulder all the way, which he seldom as yet did, except with Tom Purdie, unless when he was in a more than commonly happy and affectionate mood. (Lock. 4.353–5)

Despite the extraordinary specificity of detail (the cigar, the ducklings, etc.) and the vividness of the dialogue, Grierson shows – by reference to dates and Scott's movements – that this episode must be a fabrication (HG 253, EJ 1300).

What actually happened was that Scott returned to Edinburgh on 11 November, and learned about the rumour from JGL on 18 November. Lockhart, who was indeed at Chiefswood, did not apparently see Scott personally, but dispatched Wright's letter, or a summary of it. Scott, in Edinburgh, went immediately (that is, on 18 November) to see Cadell, not Constable (who was, indeed, *hors de combat* at Polton). Scott did not disclose the source of his information that Constable & Co. had been thrown over by their London banker Dixon (EJ 950).

When Scott came to see him on 18 November Cadell reassured him, saying that the firm 'had not engagements either present or future that they were not amply prepared to fulfill' (*Lett.* 9. 292). Cadell (not Constable) had already embarked on a cunning campaign of disinformation which extended to refusing a loan of £2,500 from Scott – which the firm in fact desperately needed – so as to allay the author's (entirely justifiable) nervousness (EJ 950). On being informed of Wright's fears, Cadell showed Scott a reassuring letter 'received that very morning' from Dixon, the firm's London bankers (EJ 950). Cadell also led the way in deceiving the firm's Edinburgh bankers (something for which they bore a mighty grudge later). By his soothing diplomacy, it was Cadell who evidently lulled Scott into signing a £5,000 bond at the end of November for Hurst & Robinson (EJ 951). That same night (24 November) Scott coming home from a party had a bad fall – he may have drunk too much in his anxiety. But the next day Cadell cheered him up with news that the Royal Bank had come through with another £4,000 loan. There was also cheerful news from Robinson, he added. In all this, it was Cadell, not Constable, who was weaving a complex web to deceive Scott.

Why did JGL mask Cadell's deceptions by inventing the Polton ride? It involved more than merely 'novelizing', or 'Scottifying' – more, that is, than the usual biographer's licence which he allowed himself. It should be remembered that Lockhart wrote the *Life of Scott* for Cadell – his paymaster in the mid-1830s. When he invented the Polton episode, he knew and Cadell knew that it was a lie. Moreover, it was a lie designed to shift the burden of principal responsibility from Cadell squarely onto Constable's shoulders. Had Scott and Ballantyne acted decisively in November 1825 – with the asset of Scott's huge credit with Edinburgh's financial establishment – they could have averted disaster. According to Lockhart's *Life* it was Constable who – face to face with Scott, armed with Wright's information – denied the firm was in trouble. In fact, as Lockhart and Cadell knew, it was Cadell who had reassured Scott in November 1825, and thus made inevitable the catastrophe. In other words, Lockhart was rewriting history so as to smear the dead Constable and exonerate the living Cadell.

Lockhart was also under the awkward necessity of sustaining the line of defence which Scott himself staked out in the preface to *Chronicles of the Canongate*: 'I bought, and built, and planted, and was considered by myself, as by the rest of the world, in the safe possession of an easy fortune'. The calamity fell on him, Scott claimed, 'almost without a note of premonition'. As early as 1834, the biographer George Allan had poured scorn on this defence. 'The *pus*', Allan observed, 'had been accumulating for years, and Scott *could not* but have been perfectly aware of it' (Allan, 463).

Lockhart's account of the Polton ride is concluded by an extraordinary disavowal: 'That Sir Walter was [in 1825], and had all along been James's partner in the great printing concern, neither I, nor, I believe, any member of his family, had entertained the slightest suspicion prior to the coming calamities which were now "casting their shadows before"' (Lock. 4. 356). This is an astounding proposition. JGL had been a confidential member of the Blackwood's set for ten years – and William Blackwood was a regular customer of James Ballantyne (particularly over the five years between 1816 and 1822 when Scott had been sole proprietor of the firm). JGL had been present at the great May 1825 meeting when Ballantyne, Constable, and Scott cooked up the 'Miscellany' project. That he had no 'suspicion' that Scott was commercially involved with the Printing Office is incredible.

The 'Polton Ride' episode crystallizes a defensive strategy in the *Life* designed to protect Cadell, Lockhart and the memory of Scott. A main element in the strategy was the scapegoating of Constable, who is portrayed as being in a state of alcoholic megalomania in the period 1825–6. Another element in the strategy is Lockhart's portrayal of James Ballantyne as having been culpably disorganized in his office-keeping, and as having kept facts from Scott. There may be some substance in this. But in his account of the crash, Lockhart savagely overstates the case against James Ballantyne, 'the most negligent and inefficient of master-printers . . . he never made even one serious effort to master the formidable balances of figures thus committed to his sole trust' (Lock. 4. 359–60). Trust is the wrong word here – the truth is that both he and Scott neglected their business accounts. Lockhart overlooks the fact that Scott was the senior partner; that for six years (1816–22) Scott had been the sole proprietor; and that he – Walter Scott – was the lawyer and James Ballantyne the printer (a function which he carried out very competently; at the time of the crash the firm had more orders on its books than it could handle).

Much of Ballantyne & Co.'s problems arose from the peculiar status of Abbotsford. Having built it, and paid from his own pocket for the work as it was done, Scott regarded the property as his. But since Scott's pocket had been regularly replenished by subventions from the firm, James and John Ballantyne regarded Abbotsford as a Printing Office asset. This leads on to the most serious allegation made against Scott in the *Refutation* of the account in Lockhart's *Life*, a pamphlet published by Ballantyne relations in 1838. Namely, that Scott allowed James to believe, even after 1824, that the Abbotsford house and estate were security for the bills which the printing firm was issuing (EQ 178). The allegation is not that Scott lied to his partner, but that he did not enlighten him until too late. Eric Quayle is eloquent on the point:

> The fact that his friend and confidant did not see fit to divulge to him the news that Abbotsford and its estate had been transferred to the ownership of another man, and that it no longer stood as a bastion supporting the tottering walls of the Ballantyne Press, was later to come as a shock that [James] and his brother [Sandy] felt very deeply. For the present [i.e. spring 1825] the two were kept in blissful ignorance of the action the senior partner had taken, but their awakening a few months later was to be a rude and hurtful one. (EQ 179)

In a letter as late as 4 January 1826 to George Hogarth (James's brother-in-law and legal adviser) Scott implies that Abbotsford is his (not his son's) to do as he wants with: 'The property has cost me more than £50,000, and it agrees as well with my own purpose as with Mr Dunlop's wish that it should not be burthened beyond the extent of £10,000' (*Lett.* 9. 360). Anyone reading this would assume that Scott was the owner of Abbotsford, and that his partners could, in extremity, rely on it as an asset of the firm. Lockhart's defence of Scott in this matter in 'The Ballantyne-Humbug Handled' pamphlet (1839) is very unconvincing.

As a third element in Lockhart's defensive strategy Cadell is consistently portrayed as having been the 'sober' partner, the pendulum to Constable's spring. This overlooks, as Grierson points out, that Cadell was in point of fact the more reckless of the partners (it was he, for instance, who offered Scott £1,000 for *Halidon Hill*). Moreover it was Cadell who aggressively pursued the 1825 policy of insisting, until it was too late, that Constable & Co. 'were rooted, as well as branched, like the oak'. It was this high-risk tactic which eventually multiplied the losses to astronomic proportions. If Scott had been thinking clearly, it was Cadell with whom he should have refused to shake hands after the crash, not the luckless Constable. Cadell consistently secured financial advantage for himself after the crash. JGL consistently glosses Cadell's unscrupulosity in such matters. Cadell was, of course, paying for Lockhart's *Life of Scott*, and his version of events is skilfully inserted into the biographical narrative. As Grierson points out from his more objective standpoint, Cadell's final coup was to cheat Lockhart out of the family's half of the copyrights in 1847 and 'Lockhart, who was not an acute business man, thanked him for his generosity!' (*Lett.* 9. 401).

THE WITNESSES OF THE CRASH

November 1825 was an event-filled month. Scott began a new novel in late October. Initially titled 'Woodstock: A Tale of the Long Parliament' it was changed (on the sage advice of James Ballantyne) to the more romantic *Woodstock: The Cavalier, a Tale of 1651*. Scott was having some difficulties with the second volume of *The Life of Napoleon*. But it is likely that *Woodstock* was embarked on as a kind of insurance in case the worst happened. The 'Tales of Crusaders' had done well and another quick £10,000 might be very useful, if 1825 boom turned to 1826 bust.

At this critical period of his life Scott began his journal, what JGL calls 'perhaps the most candid diary that ever man penned' (Lock. 4. 358). The first published version of Pepys's 'Diary' had come out in summer 1825, and Lockhart sent an early copy to Scott for review in the *Quarterly*. (JGL records his father-in-law reading it avidly in Ireland. The review was published in January 1826.) As David Daiches shrewdly suggests, the urge to

keep a journal was probably also motivated by the loneliness consequent on
the Lockharts' leaving for London (Daiches, 113). Other old friends, like
Erskine, were no longer alive to confide in. Lady Scott's health deteriorated
sharply in October 1825 (EJ 946). She suffered from asthma, heart problems, dropsy and, probably, opium addiction. Scott did not want to burden
her with his intimate thoughts.

As Grierson notes, the journal marks the end of Scott's 'compartmental
arrangement of his interests and activities'. The lawyer, the novelist, the
tradesman, the Scot – all are integrated on the page. The essence of the
entries is spontaneity. Scott throws aside 'all pretence to regularity and
order and marking down events just as they occurrd to recollection' (Jrnl.
1). Since it was not 'taskwork', he could turn to the journal when he should
really be doing more important things. In this way, he would profit from his
own vices. It was what he called 'concentric' composition. Scott clearly did
not want to have the journal published in his lifetime, but he saw it as an
eventual public record – a critical last act in the eventual unmasking of the
author of *Waverley*. As it happened, the journal coincided with greatest trial
of Scott's life – the crash of Ballantyne and Constable. In these appallingly
humiliating circumstances it evidently became more important than ever
that he should preserve a noble image of himself *in extremis* for posterity.

On 5 December 1825 the Lockharts returned to London, to take up
permanent residence (EJ 952–3). They sneaked away, without painful fare-
wells. 'This was very right,' Scott noted, 'I hate red eyes and blowing of
noses' (Jrnl. 25). It marked the end of an era at Abbotsford. Scott was no
longer the grandfather. And with Lockhart's departure, the last act of
Scott's ruin began. The alarms of late November had been lived through,
and although Scott constantly cheered himself in his journal as to the tide
turning, anxiety remained. On 14 December he announced in his journal
his intention to raise the £10,000 which his son's marriage contract allowed
him on the Abbotsford estate. It is clear that Cadell was instrumental in this
decision, by putting pressure on James Ballantyne, who in turn put pressure
on Scott, telling him that their bills were only covered for a week more. In
a letter to William Laidlaw, two days later on 16 December, Scott made clear
that the mortgage would be raised to 'protect my literary commerce'.

This, however, is not how Scott records the mortgage business in his
journal entry of 14 December:

> Affairs very bad in the money market in London. It must come here and I
> have far too many engagements not to feel it. To cut the matter at once I
> intend to borrow £10,000 with which my son's marriage contract allows me to
> charge my estate – at Whitsunday and Marts I will have enough to pay up the
> incumbrance of £3,000 due to old Moss's daughter and £5,000 to Misses
> Ferguson in whole or part. This will enable us to dispense in a great measure
> with Bank assistance and sleep in spite of thunder. (Jrnl. 37)

This entry must have been disingenuous. In the first place, Scott does not
record the primary fact – that it was impending disaster at James Ballantyne

& Co. (only a week off) that was forcing his hand. 'Old Moss', however, refers to the outstanding Kaeside mortgage of £3,000 which he had to pay off if he was to raise the £10,000 mortgage allowed him by the Jobson lawyers. The implication in the journal is that he will use the bulk of the remaining £7,000 to repay the Misses Ferguson the £5,000 he owed them. That he owed these ladies (aunts of his daughter-in-law) such hefty sums is indicative of how reckless his borrowing had become in later years (HG 257). But it is clear that neither before nor after was repaying the Misses Ferguson the real motive for raising the mortgage, as he implies in the journal. The £7,000 was promptly sucked into the accounts of Ballantyne and Constable, and the Misses Ferguson were not paid off until years later, with other creditors after the crash. But why did Scott, talking to himself in the Journal, suggest that he was going to repay the Misses Ferguson? Was he deluding himself? More likely, he was covering his tracks. If it all blew over, no-one should know how dangerous the Ballantyne game was, not even posterity when it 'uncovered' his private papers.

Scott's confidence only lasted a few days. On 18 December, he heard 'all but positively' that Hurst & Robinson had failed. Ballantyne brought the news, which he had heard from Cadell. 'Venit illa suprema dies', Scott wrote in his diary. Anne took the news well. Lady Scott, he recorded tightly, 'did not afford me all the sympathy I expected' (Jrnl. 40). There are accounts of food being brought and taken away again by the servants, untasted. At the end of the awful day Cadell came with (false) good news – Hurst & Robinson could stand, if they had a little more money from Scotland (EJ 956). Cadell also insinuated the reassuring sense that Hurst and Robinson – with a property holding of £350,000 – were too large to fall. It was at this period, Scott's most vulnerable, that Cadell wedged Constable away and himself into Scott's favour. Under this see-sawing strain Scott was seduced by the manly support of him 'who I thought had no more [feeling] than his numeration table' (Jrnl. 42). Constable meanwhile was still out of play, ill with gout.

Scott laboured to create 'the tone of mind with which men should meet distress'. Stoicism came naturally to him. It was a matter of pride that in the extremity of his suffering, on 22 December, he could write the poem 'Bonnie Dundee' (like a bird in a storm, as he noted; Jrnl. 46. The poem celebrates Claverhouse's defiance of the Whig Provost of Edinburgh – 'Away to the hills, to the caves, to the rocks – Ere I own a usurper, I'll couch with the fox.') Scott went on to have a reasonably merry Christmas at Abbotsford; he was not yet exiled to the hills. But immediately after the holiday he was afflicted with kidney trouble, and ended the year on a diet of calomel. On 1 January 1826 he confided to his journal that 'to me this New Year opens sadly' (Jrnl. 53). 'Pecuniary difficulties' were, of course, the primary cause of sadness. But he also feared that Walter might be posted to India, and he would never see him again. His manner remained self-controlled, even in the privacy of his journal entries. But the physical strain was immense. On 5 January he suffered what was clearly a minor stroke (EJ

959). For a few hours he could not write coherently nor spell correctly 'but put down one word for another and wrote nonsense' (Jrnl. 55). All three major players in the drama were suffering from stress-related illness. At Polton, Constable was bedridden by gout (brought on by drink, as Lockhart unkindly suggests); Scott was experiencing the ominous cerebral symptoms mentioned above; and Ballantyne had developed ulcers and was, as Eric Quayle deduces, on the verge of a nervous breakdown (EQ 207).

There was another interval of wild hope. Scott and Cadell believed that if only Constable could haul his gouty carcass to London, all could be put right by a quick sale or mortgage of the firm's literary property. But Constable could not move until 13 January. Lockhart was at this period in London, and in the *Life* he pens a poisonously slanderous picture of Constable:

> It was there [i.e. London] that I, for the first time, saw full swing given in the tyrannical temper of *the Czar*. He looked, spoke, and gesticulated like some hoary despot, accustomed to nothing but the complete indulgence of every wish and whim, against whose sovereign authority his most trusted satraps and tributaries had suddenly revolted – open rebellion in twenty provinces – confusion in the capital – treason in the palace. I will not repeat his haughty ravings of scorn and wrath. (Lock. 4. 422)

Lockhart goes on to describe Constable as requesting he come to the Bank of England and support him (as a confidential friend of the Author of *Waverley*) in his application for a loan of as much as £200,000 on the strength of the security of the copyrights in his possession. Lockhart comments: 'It is needless to say that, without distinct instructions from Sir Walter, I could not take upon me to interfere in such a business as this. Constable, when I refused, became livid with rage. After a long silence, he stamped upon the ground, and swore that he could and would do alone' (Lock. 4. 424). According to JGL the hoary old despot 'lingered on, fluctuating between wild hope and despair, until, I seriously believe, he at last hovered on the brink of insanity. When he returned to Edinburgh, it was to confront creditors whom he knew he could not pay' (Lock. 4. 425).

All this has been refuted. What evidence there is suggests that Constable went down with a plausible rescue package worth some £50,000 (made up of *The Life of Napoleon* property, his accumulated Scott copyrights, the *Encyclopaedia Britannica*, the *Edinburgh Review* and various life insurances). The subsequent value of this property was vast. Apart from anything else, Constable had well-formed ideas for the edition of Scott's works that became in Cadell's hands the Magnum Opus. In London there is absolutely no evidence that he behaved like the despot or madman JGL describes. His letters are, as Quayle notes, 'perfectly coherent' (EQ 204). He seems, in fact, to have come tantalizingly close to saving the business (EJ 961), but Hurst & Robinson's debts proved too vast. Edgar Johnson convincingly dismisses the Bank of England story as a JGL invention, fabricated to portray Constable as a megalomaniac (EJ 1301–2). And far from 'lingering' in London the publisher set back on 19 January, barely five days after his arrival.

Scott himself returned from Abbotsford to a bitterly cold Edinburgh on 16 January, to discover from Ballantyne that Hurst & Robinson had allowed a bill to return to Constable unaccepted. It was the final blow, and guaranteed the public 'ruin of both houses' (Jrnl. 60). The next morning he greeted his friend Skene with the salutation: 'My friend, give me a shake of your hand – mine is that of a beggar' (EJ 961). He had invited Skene particularly – both as a close friend and as someone who would spread the news through Edinburgh without malice.

Financially, Scott had four options in late January 1826. He could (1) declare personal bankruptcy (2) apply for trade bankruptcy (3) effect a trust deed or (4) apply to his friends and relatives for short and medium-term loans, with the understanding that he would repay them over the next ten years which – as a fifty-four-year-old man – he might confidently expect to live.

The last option would have been in many ways the easiest. Scott was overwhelmed with offers of help in the immediate aftermath of the crash. Walter (for whom the news of his father's plight was a wholly unexpected thunderbolt) would happily have surrendered his ownership of Abbotsford, or have taken out a £50,000 mortgage on it. He could have raised a few thousands more on his Carpenter expectations. Walter's wife, Jane, immediately offered her £14,000 in the funds and even volunteered to sell Lochore to help her father-in-law (EJ 964). Since the cumulative debts Scott was held liable for were initially under-assessed at around £30,000 (Jrnl. xxiv),[4] family aid alone would have been enough to see Scott through the black weeks of early 1826. And there were substantial outside offers of help: from the Buccleuchs, from Morritt, from an unknown admirer who claimed to be good for £30,000. The Duke of Somerset offered a loan of the same amount. Nearer home, Skene and Scott's fellow Clerk of Session, Colin Mackenzie, were prepared to make over sizeable sums. His daughters' music teacher offered his few hundreds of life's savings (EJ 964). The Scotts' butler, Dalgleish, threw in his mite in the form of a willingness to work for no wages (EJ 962). Only half facetiously, the Earl of Dudley observed that if Scott received 6*d* from everyone to whom he had given pleasure he would be as rich as Rothschild. A public subscription (as there was a subscription some years later for the Scott monument in Edinburgh) would certainly have raised thousands.

Touching as these gestures were, Scott was appalled at the thought of charity. His reaction when he received Jane's offer was 'God Almighty forbid!' In his journal he proclaimed 'a penny I will not borrow.' He repeated over and again, his favourite vaunt: 'My own right hand shall do it' (Jrnl. 65). But Edgar Johnson is not correct to claim that Scott accepted 'no aid from anyone, rich or poor' (EJ 964). He several times applied for discreet loans from his lawyer Gibson (Jrnl. 78). He had another sizeable loan from William Forbes (his old rival in love) which he supposedly did not know about. And there is the rather uncomfortable business about the money he took from Alexander Ballantyne, to which Eric Quayle devotes much space. The episode can be briefly summarized: in May 1826 Scott discovered by conversation with James that Sandy Ballantyne (a printer and co-proprietor of the *Kelso Mail*) had saved some £500 from the general wreck. Alexander's plight was extreme – he had a wife and eight children. In the face of an unknown quantity of accommodation notes bearing his name, he thought at first of fleeing to the Continent. But his creditors allowed him to resume management of the *Edinburgh Weekly Journal* and like his brother James he soldiered on in Edinburgh in a much reduced style of life. He nonetheless offered to make his £500 available to James, who was the more distressed of the two. Scott learned of the offer, and himself applied to Alexander requesting this last £500 as a loan to himself. He was impelled to do so since Daniel Terry was in trouble, and he was legally the actor-manager's guarantor for the lease of the Adelphi theatre – for which a payment was now required (Jrnl. 143). Scott's lawyer Gibson had been unable to help in this matter.

Scott clearly felt guilty about squeezing Sandy for his rainy-day money, and wrote in his journal a memorandum that, should he die, 'I request my son Walter will in reverence to my memory see that Mr Alexr. Ballantyne does not suffer for having obliged me in a sort of exigency' (Jrnl. 143). Excuses can be made for Scott – he had, after all, shielded the two living Ballantynes from the worst of the storm and had helped Mrs John Ballantyne in her widowhood; the family owed him a lot. But the episode does not show him in a noble light, even if one parts company with Quayle who thinks that it 'betrays a selfishness that is hard to forgive' (EQ 221). Scott, one deduces, was prepared to borrow from the humble printer but not from the Duke of Buccleuch.

This left the hard road of bankruptcy, or the very complex business of setting up of a trust. *Cessio* – or private bankruptcy – was, as W. E. K. Anderson points out, 'not the best solution, since it would have entailed the loss of his library, his furniture, and his life-rent of Abbotsford' (Jrnl. xxv). He would have had to decamp to Boulogne, or the Isle of Man, like Tom. Sequestration, or trade bankruptcy, was what Scott's lawyer, John Gibson, advised and the course that Scott himself would have advised a client to take (EJ 961). It gave the debtor an absolute discharge, so long as four-fifths of the creditors went along with the arrangement. Such was sympathy for Scott that the majority of his creditors would certainly have settled for seven shillings or so in the pound. Once cleared he could, in a matter of months, set up in business again. This facility was available only to commercial bankrupts, but the bulk of Scott's obligations had been incurred via his trade partners James Ballantyne and Constable. Only a sixth of the £121,000 claims that were finally laid to him were 'personal' debts, and he had funds enough to cover them (Jrnl. xxiv). Why then did Scott not take this route? As Anderson argues, the problem was psychological: 'he could not take advantage of it without sinking himself forever, in his own eyes, and in the eyes of his friends, to the level of a shopkeeper' (Jrnl. xxv). It would confirm the worst impression made by the crash (an impression that Scott laboured to erase through friends like Skene). Cockburn testifies to the horror with which the initial revelation was received by genteel Edinburgh: 'Ballantyne and Constable were merchants, and their fall, had it reached no further, might have been lamented merely as the casualty of commerce. But Sir Walter! The idea that his practical sense had so far left him as to have permitted him to dabble in *trade*, had never crossed our imagination'. Lady Scott was apparently equally mortified at being branded a tradesman's wife. One remembers that young Walter's first question on being told of the eligible Miss Jobson was whether the family was 'trade'?

The last option – that of the trust deed – was favoured by Cadell and James Ballantyne. By this device, the creditors would syndicate themselves and agree to hold back their legal claims on Scott's assets, allowing him time to pay off his debts. The terms under which he might work were negotiable. The advantage of the trust method was that Scott would retain his honour and many of his baronet's perquisites. In return for a little patience, his creditors on their part would get a good return on their 'paper'. The trust arrangement would allow Scott to bring to fruition the high-yield long-term ventures Constable had commissioned or envisioned – *The Life of Napoleon* and the 'Magnum Opus' collective reissue (outlined by the publisher to Scott at Christmas 1825). It was, of course, now necessary that Constable – discharged after his sequestration – be cut loose from these brainchildren and that Cadell take them over, an operation which was carried out with all ruthless efficiency.

A main disadvantage of effecting a trust deed was that the creditors, in return for their forbearance, would expect total repayment – twenty shillings in the pound. Over the years, the arrangement would cost Scott two or three times as much as sequestration. In the short term, it also involved him in minor dishonesty as to his physical condition. Clearly the trust was only attractive to the creditors insofar as they believed that their investment was in good health. They bought Scott's existing life insurances, and took out another – making £22,000 benefit in all.[5] Scott cannot have informed the trustees, or the examining physician, of his small stroke on 5 January 1826.

It is not entirely clear who devised the exact terms of the trust. Quayle believes that it was the wily Scott himself and that he imposed the scheme on his creditors with a mixture of promised bribes (full repayment) and threats to declare bankruptcy and 'bid [them] defiance' (EQ 212). As the journal informs us on 17 January 1826, Cadell, James Ballantyne and George Hogarth (James Ballantyne's legal adviser), together with Scott's lawyer, John Gibson, made the recommendation to Scott – but the idea seems to have been fairly well advanced by this point and Scott may have well have introduced it in earlier conversations. He was, after all, a lawyer and familiar with trustee arrangements through his father's estate. Whoever was its originator, on 26 January Gibson came 'with a joyful face announcing all the Creditors had unanimously agreed to a private trust' (Jrnl. 69).

It was not even now entirely clear sailing. The Bank of Scotland – the oldest banking institution in the country – had proved obstinate because it felt that Scott's contracts with Constable should be honoured, and that the money from the works in hand should go to the publisher's estate and creditors. They were also unhappy about Scott's having alienated his creditors' claims on Abbotsford. Scottish law was firmer on this point than English. One of the reasons put forward by the Commission reporting on the 1825 crash for no Scottish bank having collapsed (while hundreds went under in England) was Scotland's practice of 'attaching a debtor's property, whether it consist[ed] of land or movables, and making it available to his debtors'. There were evidently those in the Bank of Scotland who felt that if they were aggressive about it they could recover Scott's major asset for their creditors. But they were eventually won over (although they remained vindictive towards Cadell, who had vexed Edinburgh bankers by raising loans by false claims until almost the eve of the Constable collapse).

Sir William Forbes – Scott's old rival for the hand of Williamina – was a main agent in executing the trust arrangement, and was evidently instrumental in talking his banking colleagues round. The private banking firm Forbes & Herries, which he now headed, was Scott's largest single creditor and was owed nearly a tenth of his total debts, £13,846 (EJ 967).[6] It is curious that Forbes's firm found itself in this position, and one wonders when and why they invested so heavily in Scott's paper. But however it happened, the irony was painful. Williamina was long dead, and Forbes behaved as Scott's best friend might have done. But for the second time in his life, 'dot and carry' had proved the better man. 'Down – down – a hundred thoughts' (Jrnl. 70), Scott commanded in his journal.

As Eric Quayle remarks 'It is doubtful if any other debtor in Britain would have been let off the hook in quite so generous a fashion as Scott was by the bankers and moneylenders of London and Edinburgh in the spring of 1826' (EQ 218). Affection played its part. But it was also a calculated gamble which did pay off – if not quite to the degree that Scott promised. The trust enabled the family to continue living rent-free at Abbotsford, among the Laird's own books and furniture, as if nothing had happened. He kept his £1,600 income from the law. He was allowed to earn sizeable sums by literary work in his 'own time'. He had more of his own time, because he was no longer obliged to manage his farms (something he admitted now he had loathed) or Ballantyne's printing works. That firm and its bulging order-books were also taken over by the trust, James Ballantyne having followed his master and eschewed the easy option of sequestration. He was employed at a salary of £400 and allowed to continue living in his old house in St John Street.

Generous as they were, the trustees were not going to allow Scott to live like a baronet in town as well as in the country. In February 1826, 39 Castle Street was put up for sale and its furnishings auctioned. It fetched £2,300. Henceforward when legal duty called him to Edinburgh Scott would live in lodgings. Although friends (Skene, for instance) offered him appropriately plush quarters, Scott took rooms at Mrs Brown's, in North St David Street.

It was, apparently, bug-ridden and barking dogs kept him awake at night doubtless also waking his butler, Dalgleish, who accompanied his master, before suffering a total health breakdown. Scott may well have wanted to be seen as down on his luck in Edinburgh, lest questions were asked about Abbotsford, where he was still the landed baronet. Scott would wittily dramatize his descent to Mrs Brown's in Chrystal Croftangry's decision to move into lodgings with Janet MacEvoy, in the extended preface to *Chronicles of the Canongate*. On the whole, Scott seems to have liked the bachelor simplicity of lodgings; and he referred to Mrs Brown's as my 'Patmos' (EJ 992).

According to Edgar Johnson, the trust 'was the course that *honour* dictated' (EJ 962). Jane Millgate puts a similar moral stress on Scott's nobility (the italics are again mine): 'only about £20,000 [of the £120,000] could *properly* be considered Scott's private debt', she points out: 'Unwilling to take the escape route of bankruptcy, Scott determined on the *honourable but foolhardy* course of attempting to pay off everything that was owed by Ballantyne and Co., including, of course, the bills of Constable and Co. that the printing firm had backed' (*SLE*, 5).

Stressing Scott's 'honourable' conduct is as unsatisfactory a way of dealing with the crash as the mudslinging that Lockhart and the Ballantyne descendants resorted to in the late 1830s. The best place from which to get a clear view is James Glen's 'Sir Walter Scott's Financial Transactions', which prefaces Grierson's edition of the letters. Glen blows away most of the partisan allegations, special pleading and name-calling, leaving the clear impression that blame was pretty evenly decided and muddle was the chief villain.

It helps at this point to step back and consider the three careers of the principals. In 1800, Walter Scott was a not very successful advocate and antiquarian. In 1826 the author of *Waverley* was the most successful man of letters Scotland had ever known. He had single-handedly made the novel the most potent form in literature. In 1800, Constable was a second-hand bookseller. By 1826, he was the most powerful and innovative publisher Scotland had ever known and had revolutionized the British bookworld. In 1800 James Ballantyne was the editor of a small-town newspaper. By 1826, he was head of Edinburgh's largest and most advanced printing factory (with an annual payroll of £4,500) and – as proprietor of the *Edinburgh Weekly Journal* and the *Kelso Mail* – a major Scottish newspaper magnate.

Three such careers in the short space of a quarter of a century could not have been achieved without capital. But none of the trio began with any other patrimony than their skills. All three tried traditional means of raising capital. Constable tried rich partners and co-publishing with longer-established houses. Neither served. He was too headstrong to work with equals. Scott tried marrying money (in the shape of Miss Belsches) and writing for the theatre. Neither Cupid nor Drury Lane smiled on him. James Ballantyne – in the years of the John Ballantyne & Co. venture – tried the experiment of setting up a publisher with which to feed the printing office.

He got his presses going, but could not sell the mountain of stock the experiment produced.

Two methods did produce the required capital. One was the advance system of authorial payment, which Constable pioneered in 1808 with *Marmion*. In later years, Scott would sell a literary property to Constable before it was written. Constable on his part would sell a portion of the copyright in advance to other publishers. The advance system worked very well for Scott, but it put a huge pressure on Constable, who was also having to invest huge sums in re-editing the *Encyclopaedia Britannica*. There is no question that Scott used his indispensability with Constable (and the threat of his freedom as an author to take his wares elsewhere) to force Constable into a dangerous expenditure on unwritten work. At the time of the crash, Scott had contracts for no less than nine works outstanding with Constable, going back a dozen years. In his journal, he records himself as £10,000 in debt to the firm for advances taken.

The other effective instrument for raising capital was the accommodation bill. As Constable & Co. and Ballantyne & Co. worked it, 'A' would make out a credit note for a sum to be repaid at a certain number of months endorsed by 'B'. In return 'B' would make out a counter-bill endorsed by 'A'. The primary bill (and sometimes the secondary bill) would then be cashed at a bank or discounter to be redeemed or retired in the specified number of months. These bills were an invaluable means of raising large amounts of capital on sound businesses. Banks, of course, would not look at bills from shaky enterprises. The primary advantage of James Ballantyne & Co. for Scott (and Ballantyne) was that it was known to be a sound and profitable business concern. It would have been impossible for Scott to raise these bills as a private individual.

Convenient as it was to great men in a hurry like Scott, Constable and Ballantyne, the accommodation bill system had disadvantages. First, bills had to be discounted; in the process a percentage (often usurious) was taken by the discounter. When bills were retired, they had to be repaid in full. It was an expensive way to raise cash. Second, bills tied in one firm with another, in a rickety house of cards structure. In 1826 James Ballantyne was brought down by Constable who was brought down by Hurst & Robinson. There was no intrinsic reason why Ballantyne and Constable should have fallen in 1825–6. Both were trading successfully.

Thirdly, and insidiously, bills were too easy a method to raise money. All three players, Constable, Scott and Ballantyne, fell into the habit of using accommodation bills to raise funds for non-commercial purchases: notably houses – at Polton, Abbotsford, and Heriot Row. The understanding was that at a pinch these properties were realizable assets, or mortgageable securities. But it was hard to realize such assets quickly enough to be useful. Fourthly, and most dangerously, the bills and counterbills had two sets of names on them, those of the acceptor (or endorser) and of the drawer. In the primary transaction, only one sum of money was to be raised. But where the counterbill was passed on (or scooped up by bankruptcy proceedings) a signatory could find himself responsible for double payment on a single sum for which he had already paid a heavy discount. In the final reckoning of Scott's debts, something over £20,000 was listed as private debts; £12,615 as bills due by James Ballantyne; £9,129 as bonds for which Scott was liable 'but which were the proper debts of Archibald Constable and Co.'; and some £75,000 as 'bills discounted and in the hands of third parties' (Daiches, 119). It was this last category, with some £29,000 worth of bills and £29,000 worth of counterbills, that revealed the horrific consequences of the accommodation system, should the house of cards collapse.

Despite what Lockhart implies, there is no doubt that all three knew exactly what they were doing. Scott was a lawyer; printers and publishers of decades' standing such as Ballantyne and Constable would know all about credit. All three principals had come perilously near to bankruptcy in the years 1814–6, and were intelligent enough businessmen to learn from the experience. There is evidence that around 1823 Scott, Cadell, and Constable audited their firms and made efforts to retrench. Unfortunately, it was too late and too little.

Was Scott dishonest? Is he to be blamed for coming out of the catastrophe so comfortably? Eric Quayle certainly thinks so, and stresses what other biographers underplay – namely that the Ballantynes did not know that Abbotsford had been transferred just before the storm broke. Scott was not evicted from his new home, as James Ballantyne was (and Ballantyne could complain that he had only been a partner for four years). Abbotsford was left to Scott as a refuge from the financial blasts that destroyed Constable and a host of minor tradesmen whose names are lost to literary criticism. (David Daiches notes, as Lockhart and Edgar Johnson do not, Scott's incidental callousness in this regard; Daiches, 119.)

In his ruin, Scott contrived to live comfortably. When he moved from Castle Street in March 1826, over 4,000 bottles of wine and some 400 bottles of spirits were moved from the house's cellar to Abbotsford (already well stocked). This was ruin in style. Within a few months of his 'fall' he was off on a journey to Paris (in part to raise money for his children). Meanwhile, Constable was stripped bare. Within weeks all his possessions and his grand house at Polton (about which Lockhart was pleased to sneer) were sold. He, his wife and eight children moved to squalid rooms. His eldest son, David, went mad with shame. Constable himself died (apparently of dropsy) on 21 July 1827. Constable's final misery is not pictured in Lockhart's or Johnson's account.

15

Working for the Creditors (1826–1827)

Throughout the worst weeks of the crash Scott worked furiously on his latest romance, writing one whole volume in fifteen days (EJ 972). By the end of March he had finished *Woodstock*. Scott began writing it in November, at the time of the painful separation from the Lockharts and the first intimations of disaster. The bulk of the novel was written in the awful months of December and January. He began *Woodstock* as the Laird of Abbotsford and finished it as a 'beggar', knowing that any money it made (it eventually made around £7,000) would go to satisfy his insatiable creditors – and, as a final twist of the knife, probably not *his* creditors but Constable's. In the background of the novel's composition was the terminal condition of his wife – who actually died a couple of weeks after publication. As painful was the lingering weakness of his beloved grandson, Hugh Littlejohn, who was clearly not long for the world. And lowering over everything was the condition of Britain question, the growing tide of reform. Given the circumstances of its writing, it would be a wonder had *Woodstock* been merely competent. That it is an effectively theatrical and readable piece of work is little less than miraculous.

Fragments of Scott's own anxieties find their way into *Woodstock*. The backbone plot of the novel is an instance. Sir Henry Lee of Ditchley is a gallant old ranger on the royal park of Woodstock. As the novel opens, this veteran royalist is alone in the world with only his loyal daughter Alice for companion. His soldier son is away in the wars, fighting for the king. Sir Henry – a fanatical lover of Shakespeare despite his condition as country gentleman – faces eviction from his lodge, and indeed under threat of sequestration is actually forced to take refuge in a loyal servant's hovel. All this translates fairly directly into Sir Walter Scott, with only his faithful daughter Anne for companion, fearful of eviction from Abbotsford. Scott even gave Sir Henry his own 'gallant hound', Maida ('Bevis' in the novel). Woodstock itself is a kind of original of Abbotsford, 'an old Gothic building, irregularly constructed, and at different times, as the humour of the

English monarchs led them to taste the pleasures of Woodstock Chase, and to make such improvements for their own accommodation as the increasing luxury of each age required' (1. 48).

The setting of *Woodstock*, England in the unsettled period after the Battle of Worcester and before the Restoration (where the plot ends), reflects Scott's firm conviction that the 'republican' forces of 1820s radicalism were, like the Commonwealth, an aberration. No more than in the late seventeenth century could Radical Democracy last. The natural body of Britain would resist such levelling tendencies. The novel is shot through – blemished, in fact – with the harsh conservatism of Scott's post-ruin period. Much of his immediate misery he projected onto Jewish merchants and the irresponsible levellers at work in England (Jrnl. 14). The Civil War background ties in with Scott's worried reflections in his Journal entries about 'combinations of workmen' (Jrnl. 12) and his pervasive unease (going back to the 1817 Radical agitations) about 'mechanics' and the mischievous machinations of their middle-class allies, the Whigs. The dispassionate even-handedness of *Waverley* seems gone forever from his writing.

AFTER THE FALL

Scott's fall polarizes the emotions that posterity has towards him. There have been those who blame him squarely for the disaster and resent his getting off so lightly. The most stridently prosecutorial voice is that of Eric Quayle who, as a descendant of James Ballantyne, has an inherited family grudge to pay off. Quayle's sympathy is reserved for the principal commercial casualties of Scott's fall: his partners (the Ballantyne brothers), his publisher (Constable but not Cadell), and the numberless and mainly nameless tradesmen who were ruined. One could extend the casualty list into Scott's own family. Lady Scott died a few months later of a vaguely diagnosed combination of serious, but not necessarily fatal ailments (one of which was, allegedly, drug addiction). She was just fifty-six. It is likely that she was hurried into her grave by disgrace. All Scott's children developed chronic physical ailments in the years immediately following the crash: with Charles and Sophia it was crippling rheumatism and gastric pains. Anne too began to display gastric symptoms which were apparently nervous in origin but wholly prostrating when they struck. Walter the heir took to drink and tobacco so heavily that his health broke down in 1829, requiring a long furlough from the army to recuperate in the south of France.

None of Scott's children – nor Lockhart, his favoured son-in-law – was able to realize their early promise or to make anything great of their lives. Anne, though attractive and vivacious, never married. Walter neither achieved high rank in the army, nor managed to produce an heir. Charles had a disappointing career in the Foreign Office, and never married. Sophia, Scott's favourite, was, apparently, bedridden and petulant in her last years. The Scott children seem, after the crash, to have got on badly with each other and squabbled (something that is reflected in Anne's often spiteful letters). All the principals in the crash – Constable, James Ballantyne, Scott himself – died prematurely: but so too did all Scott's children. Against the genetic odds, none of the four lived as long as Lady Scott (fifty-six), Scott (sixty-one), Scott's father (seventy), let alone Mrs Anne Scott, who lasted into her eighties. Walter died in 1847, aged forty-six; Sophia died in 1837, aged thirty-eight; Anne died in June aged thirty; Charles died in 1841, aged thirty-six. Given the care that was lavished on them in childhood, it is an astonishing catalogue of premature decease. Scott's principal business associates also died prematurely: Constable in 1827, aged fifty-three; and James Ballantyne in 1833, aged sixty-one. Even Robert Cadell died aged only sixty-one. The servant who loved Scott most, Tom Purdie, who had lived the healthiest of lives, died of a heart attack in 1829, well before his time. Scott's devoted butler, Dalgleish, was forced into premature retirement by illness in 1830.

The pro-Scott faction – represented most staunchly by Lockhart and Edgar Johnson – picture their subject quite differently. They highlight his nobility of character under intolerable stress. 'Chivalry' is the term which is used to plate Scott's actions with shining nobility. 'His spirit', Johnson tells us, 'was that of an aristocrat. He, who had been the first citizen of Scotland, would not behave like a bankrupt tradesman in the Luckenbooths' (EJ 971). Chivalry was, of course, a favourite allusion of Scott's own in the period after the crash. He converted bankruptcy into a 'debt of honour' with his defiant champion's boast – 'My own right hand shall do it.' He would wield his author's pen like Excalibur.

Scott's chivalric pose presupposed that bankruptcy, sequestration, paying whatever he could in the pound, and discharge, would have been the far easier option. Declaring bankruptcy, Scott claimed, was 'the course I [as a lawyer] would have advised a client to take . . . But for this I would in a court of Honour deserve to lose my spurs' (Jrnl. 68). Such protestations are magnificent, but do not ring true. It was quixotic for a fifty-five-year-old Scottish lawyer to claim in 1826 that his actions (actions which had damaged many people less chivalrously inclined) were being judged in courts of honour rather than courts of law. Nor was bankruptcy obviously the more attractive option for Scott and his dependents. He might well have avoided the huge burden of total financial repayment, but he would have incurred other burdens. His sons' (and possibly his son-in-law's) careers might well have been injured, as well as Anne's marriage prospects. As a bankrupt he would not have been able to hold on to Abbotsford, nor could he have looked forward (as he could in 1832) to his ennobled progeny living there forever. He would probably have had to spend his last years in lodgings in Boulogne, or the Isle of Man: free but broken.

It was not sentimentality that made Scott's creditors deal tenderly with him. His undamaged assets – namely his earning potential as a bestselling author – made him a sounder horse to back if the creditors wanted more than the two-and-ninepence in the pound that Constable's estate had paid. And, as a sounder horse, he could be allowed a more comfortable stable. With Scott's copyrights the sequestered Constable *might* also have recovered. But he was less robust: and publishers of Napoleonic vision with a weakness for the bottle are less bankable than authors of proven genius. But if Scott had a debt of 'honour' to his creditors, did he not owe an even greater moral obligation to Constable, with whom he had signed contracts and from whom – for many years – he had taken large advances? Did he not have contracts outstanding for no less than nine works, pending or unfulfilled?[1] Had he not given Constable all the manuscripts in his possession, in 1823, as a warrant that he was to be responsible for the great task of the collected edition? The implication of these advances, contracts and gifts was that Constable trusted Scott and was trusted in return. This was not a fair-weather thing.

Scott extricated himself from his moral dilemma by the usual strategy. He demonized Constable, made him in his mind the root of all his misfortunes. He developed an invincible resentment against the publisher for having induced him to make over the useless £5,000 to Hurst & Robinson in November 1825, and the equally useless £7,000 a month later. He blamed Constable for not having gone down to London earlier in January, overlooking the unfortunate man's illness (which, following Lockhart, he may have put down to drink). Scott thus justified dooming his sick old friend to ruin and premature death. Without apparently admitting to himself what precisely he was doing, Scott cleaved to the younger, healthier man – Cadell – who would faithfully carry out Constable's long-laid plans more reliably than their original architect and moral owner.

Guarded as the journal is (despite its disarming veneer of candour) one can see how the operation was carried through. As a first step Scott (who had been buoyed up by Cadell's sympathy in the hours after the crash) listened to the other publisher's poisonous tattle-tale about his partner and former father-in-law. As early as 21 January 1826 one finds Cadell blackguarding Constable, alleging that his partner's high-living had destabilized the firm (Jrnl. 64). On 23 January there was a frigid meeting between Scott and Constable, in which the publisher was rudely rebuffed when he attempted friendship. On 24 January Scott warned Constable that he was disposed 'to regard the present works in progress [i.e. *The Life of Napoleon, Woodstock*] as my own'. This disposition hardened as Scott allowed himself to fall further under Cadell's spell. By February 1826, Scott had contrived to convince himself that Constable's timbers were 'rotten from the beginning' (Jrnl. 81). (Were they rotten in 1808, when he offered Scott 1,000 guineas for *Marmion*?) Scott's heart was hardened. On 8 March, on hearing of Constable's plight, Scott wrote: 'I have succeeded in putting the matters perfectly out of my mind since I cannot help them' (Jrnl. 107). At the end of March 1826 Scott learned (presumably from Cadell, who was now always at his side) that Constable would not pay above three or four shillings in the pound (Jrnl. 122). By 24 April 1826, Scott's attitude had hardened further to anger. '[Constable's] conduct has not been what I deserved at his hand', he protested (Jrnl. 135).

This anger was the prelude to the deed of blood: reneging on his contract to deliver the manuscript of *Woodstock* in the short-term and that of *The Life of Napoleon* in the long-term. (Scott had taken a £1,000 advance for this second work in 1825; EJ 901.) Again the deed was done in a number of steps: an initial scepticism as to whether these works in progress were the author's, or his publisher's property; next a deliberate go-slow on the completion of *Woodstock*. By June, Scott's legal advisers were actively fending off the claims of 'Constable's people', something they eventually succeeded in doing partly by delay, partly by ingenuity. Of course, Scott's position had a moral basis and some strong legality to it. As Johnson points out, the bills with which Constable had paid for the works in hand were virtually useless (EJ 965). But it is not clear whether Scott had already discounted some of those bills. The matter was sufficiently obscure legally for the profits of *Woodstock* to be put in escrow, pending the decision of an arbiter. (He eventually came down in favour of Scott – but by that time, Constable was dead.) The most upsetting aspect of Scott's behaviour to Constable was the last act (unmentioned by Lockhart or Johnson). As George Allan records, on the publisher's death 'Scott neither attended the funeral, nor returned the slightest acknowledgement to the cards of intimation and invitation sent to him' (Allan, 471). It was a repeat of his behaviour to Daniel.

Cadell duly rose as his former partner fell. 'Constable without Cadell', Scott reassured himself, 'is like getting the clock without the pendulum – the one having the ingenuity – the other the caution of the business' (Jrnl. 67). Now, of course, was the time for caution. It is a nice image. But, as Grierson points out, it was *Cadell* who had been the reckless partner in the past. It is true that after the events of 1826, Cadell learned some salutary lessons. (Three lessons, in fact: always take cash, only publish the works of Scott, and never experiment.) But he was no pendulum in 1824, just the opposite.

A number of commentators have wondered why Scott allied himself so wholeheartedly with the wily – and wholly unlovable – Cadell. The question is given point by the fact that it was Cadell who eventually coined most profit from the *Waverley* novels. The simple answer is that Scott always needed a business factotum and in such circumstances his choice was invariably pragmatic. John Ballantyne was amoral and possibly criminal as a book-keeper. But he served Scott's purposes admirably over the years 1809–21. The moment John died, Scott brought James back into partnership to fill his brother's vacancy. James of course survived 1826, and so did Scott's affection for his 'honest' comrade. 'We must in some sort stand or fall together', he declared (Jrnl. 411). But James lacked the guile Scott needed to extricate himself from the unimaginably large debts he inherited. He continued to be of use as an agent and adviser (and he actually prospered as a printer after 1826 on the work that Scott insisted Cadell give him). But James could not be Scott's right-hand man. He needed someone ruthlessly efficient. Cadell fitted the bill.

Scott duly helped Cadell evade the nets of bankruptcy (as he did not help Constable). It was not easy. There were stormy meetings at banks. It was not until April 1829 that Cadell was finally discharged, on the eve of the publication of the first 'Magnum Opus' volume (HG 281). At one low point in February 1826 Cadell was actually forced into sanctuary at Holyrood to escape his creditors (like Chrystal Croftangry). In all these trials, Scott used his powerful connections to protect and finally liberate Cadell. He also assumed a huge quantity of Cadell's debt, disguised as Constable's bills (HG 271).

It would be an error to assume that Scott was Cadell's dupe. It is quite likely that Scott contrived to keep Cadell undischarged from his debts until April 1829, the better to control him during the long and arduous preparation for the 'Magnum Opus'. The project could not, of course, have gone forward without a skilled publisher to bring it to fruition. As the first volume came off the presses, Cadell was cleared from the obligation to repay his debt. In the years immediately after the crash, Scott handled Cadell with consummate skill and imperious authority. Above all, he ensured that Cadell took on no work but Sir Walter Scott's. Cadell had learned some lessons from 1826, but so had Scott. He now kept his publisher on a very tight rein. It was not Scott but Scott's heirs who let themselves be cheated by Cadell, in selling the *Waverley* copyrights for the same £10,000 that Scott had raised on Abbotsford in 1825. In the long run, Cadell (and after him, Adam and Charles Black) collected the greatest harvest from the *Waverley* novels. Whether Cadell would have succeeded in 'cuckooing' the heirs out of their nest (his image) had Scott lived longer with an unclouded mind is something else.

RECOVERY

Scott's rebound from the 1826 crash was the combination of the shrewdly-devised trust, his realignment of publishing alliances, and – not least – the fact that his health kept up moderately well. In 1825 he had experienced some premonitory tremors which he described in the journal as: 'A touch of the *morbus eruditorum*... It is a tremor of the heart, the pulsation of which becomes painfully sensible – a disposition to causeless alarm – much lassitude – and decay of vigour of mind and activity of intellect' (Jrnl. 34). Over 1826, he experienced some recurrence of these 'mulligrubs' and on 14 March 1826 another 'fluttering of the heart'. 'It is entirely nervous', Scott reassured himself, without going into why his nerves were bad (Jrnl. 113). Scott also suffered what looked like symptoms of high blood pressure: a 'thickness' in his mental processes. He felt himself dull and may have suffered some small strokes. On one occasion in his journal he catches himself repeatedly writing one word for another. On the whole, however, his mind held up admirably. (It is evident that he was taking pains to keep it clear by abstinence from drink and tobacco.)

Scott's recovery from gloom was aided by a new distraction – namely the plight of the Scottish currency. The general slump of 1825–6 put in train a number of far-reaching banking reforms. Among them was an English proposal to abolish idiosyncratic Scottish notes and currency – to create a true British money. Private banks would no longer be allowed to issue their own notes: even the Bank of England would be restricted to notes of £5 and up. This proposed measure provoked a storm of nationalist protest in Scotland (where not a single bank had gone under in 1825–6). It was, as Scott observed, a panic measure that would cause hardship in Scotland, where there was a shortage of coinage. In February, Scott declared himself 'horribly tempted to interfere in this business of altering the system of Banks in Scotland' (Jrnl. 93). Malachi Malagrowther's first 'Letter on the Proposed Change of Currency' was begun the next day, 18 February.[2]

The pseudonymous author is a supposed descendant of Sir Mungo Malagrowther in *The Fortunes of Nigel* – the King's whipping boy. As Scott saw it, England had created the 1825–6 catastrophe and had decided to punish Scotland for it. In his first letter Scott (who in the past had done so much to extend the provisions of the Union) protested 'the late disposition to change everything in Scotland to an English model'. His motto in the Malagrowther letters harked back to 1745:

> Out claymore and down wi' gun,
> And to the rogues again.

He was now, however, no longer the English-honorary-Scot Edward Waverley, but a Highland cateran battling the Southron. He now knew, Besonian, under which King he served. Gratitude for recent favours partly inspired the 'Letters'. They were a small return to the Scottish banks (more particularly his principal creditors, Forbes and the Bank of Scotland) who, as he recorded, had exercised 'lenity towards me' in the trials of early 1826.

Malagrowther's first letter was published in the *Edinburgh Weekly Journal*. Scott argues that the Scottish banks are perfectly sound, as witnessed by the low rate of failure in the recent crash. The measure proposed by Parliament is moreover illegal, under the terms of the Union. It might be justified in England, as a deflationary measure, but not in Scotland, where the economy is healthy and the banks efficient. Scott was encouraged to write another Malachi letter at the end of February. In it he appeals to all Scottish representatives in Parliament to combine and resist the 'reform'. There is a hint of military rebellion, if they do not. The two letters, which had caused a great flutter among the Whigs, were then put out as a pamphlet by Blackwood. Although he felt his second epistle had been 'perhaps too peppery' (Jrnl. 99), Scott went on to write a third in early March ('which I don't much like'; Jrnl. 106). In this last instalment, Scott points to the inefficiency of replacing paper with coinage, and the credit shortage it will surely create. The tone is markedly more conciliatory than its predecessors, although still firm.

In their severity the Malachi Malagrowther letters were out of character – a measure of the changes wrought in Scott by the crash. One cannot imagine him writing them had that catastrophe not occurred. They were felt in some quarters to be positively revolutionary and lost him – at least temporarily – former friends like Lord Melville, who took it on himself to dispatch a forty-page rejoinder via his relative Sir Robert Dundas, the Chief Clerk of Court (the messenger was presumably chosen to remind Scott who his masters and patrons were). Scott penned a rebuttal. It is a mark of his recklessness that he would now go against the Dundas faction, the source of so much patronage for him over the years. Another former ally, Croker, published a refutation of the Malagrowther letters under the pen-name 'E. Bradwardine Waverley'. (Neither Scott's authorship of the letters or the novel was much of a secret, apparently.)

The Malachi Malagrowther letters were strikingly effective. On 13 May Scott noted that 'The projected measure against the Scottish bank notes has been abandond the resistance being general' (Jrnl. 143).[3] He had mounted a one-man campaign against a powerful government lobby, and won. Victory was sweet, but also had its ominous side. It encouraged Scott to believe that he could hold back political reform ('Democracy' as he pejoratively called it) as effectively as he had banking reform. It was to prove a dangerous illusion. Conservatism about Scottish pound notes was one thing. Withholding the franchise from all but landholders was another.

While throwing off the Malachi Malagrowther letters Scott deliberately held off completing *Woodstock*. He finished the second volume of the novel on 11 February and then called a deliberate halt to give John Gibson more power in negotiation with 'Constable's people' and the 'Yorkshire tyke', Robinson. Terms were not at issue. He wanted the whole property of the novel. 'A finished work might be seized under some legal pretence', he feared. So *Woodstock* was not finished until the end of March, when it was clear that Constable was out of the picture. Gibson went to London to sell the *Woodstock* copyright and on 3 April a gleeful Scott was informed that it had been bought by Longman for £8,228 in 'ready money'. This included £1,728 payable to Ballantyne for printing and paper. It was 'a matchless sale for three months work', as Scott rightly observed (*Lett*. 9. 496).

Scott now returned to his larger project, *The Life of Napoleon*, reassured that his magic wand was still unbroken. Domestic happiness was evidently a more intractable problem in the months following the crash. Things were broken there that would never mend. It is clear from passing and guarded remarks in the Journal that Lady Scott did not take the change in her status well. Nor, it would seem, did Scott take her distemper well. Even Herbert Grierson – who is one of Scott's stoutest partisans – applies the word 'heartless' to Scott's conduct towards Lady Scott during her last wretched months of existence (HG 267). An invalid for some years, she began to decline sharply in mid-March. Scott's Melrose doctor, John Abercrombie, diagnosed asthma and 'water on the chest' (EJ 979). She was also taking digitalis, presumably for a weak heart. 'Wasting attacks' are mentioned. And as Lockhart notes (and Scott does not), 'it seems but too evident that mental pain and mortification had a great share in hurrying her ailments to a fatal end' (Lock. 4. 513).

There may have been other sources of friction between husband and wife. On 3 May, Scott tersely mentions in his journal that investigations into his wife's family background have turned up the mysterious business of a 'Mr Owen' (i.e. one of Lady Scott's four putative fathers) in Chancery Records. In March, he had received a letter from Thomas Handley, a solicitor for the Marquess of Downshire (another of Lady Scott's putative fathers, as was *his* father). Handley informed Scott what he apparently did not know before, that there was a large fund in Chancery to which Lady Scott might be entitled. There were complications: one of the people who knew about the fund was demanding half-profits in it – which might be criminal extortion (EJ 1003). To authorize payment it would be necessary to establish Lady Scott's parentage, a point that was still sore even after all these years. At this stage, Scott thought the mysterious bequest would be a fortune large enough to set up his children for life. That would be very desirable. But claiming the money would raise publicly the question why a dissolute Welshman should have left such provision for Lady Scott's mother? Why were the Downshires involved? If Scott now learned of Owen's connection with the Charpentiers for the first time, he would surely have questioned his wife closely on the matter: there was already extortion threatened, might not blackmail follow?

If Scott interrogated his sick and fractious wife on this most sensitive of subjects it is likely that emotions ran high. (Her daughter claimed that on her death bed, a few days later, Lady Scott's last words were 'Lord Downshire' and 'father'; EJ 985.) Whatever their final relationship, it is clear that Scott left Abbotsford on 11 May 1826 without taking any farewell of Charlotte, who was apparently sinking fast and either in a 'deep sleep' or too overcome to talk to him. Why? The reason he gives for not waking her in the journal for 11 May is singularly unconvincing. 'Perhaps it was as well – an adieu might have hurt her' (Jrnl. 142; JGL changes this to 'Emotion might have hurt her'). Edgar Johnson asserts that Scott was 'forced' to go to Edinburgh (EJ 984). It is true that routine business of the court called him, but it was not so pressing that he could not absent himself, pleading his wife's condition. Scott nonetheless went to the city and took up his place in Mrs Brown's lodgings. The night after his departure Charlotte was taken very ill: her physician, Dr Clarkson, thought she would not last the night (EJ 985). But Scott was not summoned home, nor apparently informed that his wife was dying. For a nightmarish three days, Lady Scott hovered between life and death. Her daughter Anne, who was bearing the brunt of her mother's suffering, was prostrated with fainting fits and hysteria. The experience of watching her mother die is said to have shortened her own life.

Scott (three hours' gallop away) was still not contacted, apparently. At five in the afternoon of 14 May, Lady Scott began to sink. She died that night. On the same evening, Scott made a cheerful entry in his journal, unaware of what was happening just thirty miles away. It would seem that for four days Scott – within very easy reach of Abbotsford – was not informed that his wife was dying agonizingly and that his daughter was collapsing under the strain. Only after Lady Scott's death did anyone send him a note (which seems to have reached him within a few hours). On 15 May, Scott noted tersely 'Received the melancholy intelligence that all is over at Abbotsford' (Jrnl. 144). Why had he not been at her side?[4]

He now left for Abbotsford at once and the family were summoned for the funeral which took place on 22 May. (Sophia was too unwell to attend: she was still recovering from the birth of her latest child, Walter, born in mid-April.) Having seen his wife's corpse, Scott recorded one of the most memorable passages in the journal:

> I have seen her – The figure I beheld is and is not my Charlotte – my thirty years' companion – There is the same symmetry of form though those limbs are rigid which were once so gracefully elastic – but that yellow masque with pinchd features which seems to mock life rather than emulate it, can it be the face that was once so full of lively expression? I will not look on it again. (Jrnl. 145)

Scott bore up remarkably well. Between 1 June and 12 June he wrote manuscript equivalent to a hundred printed pages of *Napoleon* (EJ 990). At the same period, he engaged into an agreement with Cadell for *Chronicles of the Canongate*. He makes much of the simplicity of his ploughman's meals but he relished them. He mentions his widowed couch, and alludes to the black dog and black horse – depression. But at the same time his moods are shot through with what he calls 'a kind of buoyancy'. He threw himself into the struggle with Boney and a new union with 'Mrs Duty'. He resumed something like his bachelor's life, with its familiar dining, drinking, and conversation rituals. Ever since the crash, he had benefited from a strange access of energy, connected it seems with his diminished social responsibilities. On 23 February he had written: 'The fact is that the not seeing company gives me a command of my time which I possessed at no other period of my life' (Jrnl. 96). With Charlotte's death (and the departure of his sons after the funeral) these responsibilities diminished still further. He had yet more time to command. Thus it was that through the tempests of 1826, Scott produced a torrent of articles and reviews, fiction and biography.

At the end of July, with the rising of the court, Scott left Mrs Brown's 'Patmos' (for good as it turned out) for his annual long break at Abbotsford. It was a social summer. Charles came home in July. Walter visited in August with his wife and mother-in-law ('the old *torment* as the sharp-tongued Anne called her; Jrnl. 190). Anne Scott had been joined in

May by her Canadian cousin Anne Scott (Tom's twenty-four-year-old daughter) as a semi-permanent companion. There was the usual round of visits from dignitaries and friends. Scott had originally aimed to skip his summer in Abbotsford and go down to London (and thence to Paris) as soon as his legal duties finished. This plan was frustrated by an obdurate creditor, Abud & Sons, who declined to accept the terms of the trust, and were apparently bent on forcing Scott into bankruptcy (EJ 998). The Abuds were goldmerchants and moneylenders, and they had bought some of Constable's paper cheap as a speculation. Scott hated them ('They are Jews I suppose; the devil baste [them] for fools with a pork griskin'; Jrnl. 209). As late as October 1826 Scott was not sure he could venture to London without the risk of being arrested for debt.

Scott was not a well man; he had had a wretched year – losing all his money, his wife, and some of his mental capacity. A summer in the bosom of his family at Abbotsford would have seemed the sensible course of action. Why then trail off to London and Paris beyond the care of doctors who knew him? The ostensible reason for the trip was that he needed to do research on Napoleon. He also wanted to see his London family, particularly his beloved grandson, Johnnie. But since it was the Lockharts' habit to come north in summer (the father following the family for a shorter stay) grandfatherly motives were not clearly compelling. Nor, if one thinks about it, was 'research' a plausible motive. *The Life of Napoleon* was going to press in a few months; a week before he left for London, Longman had offered Scott 10,500 guineas for the copyright. The project would seem to have been wrapped up. The logical time to have done archive research was at the beginning, not the end, of the writing process.

One assumes that Scott's real reasons for spending an arduous (and possibly life-threatening) summer away from home were twofold. In London, he hoped to get patronage for his son Charles, about whose future he was increasingly worried. Secondly, he wanted to turn up as much as he could of his wife's background in London and Paris, so as to secure the Chancery money. (At the very least, he would have to prove his wife's legitimacy.)

There was a premonitory panic on the eve of Scott's departure south. He thought he could see in his mind's eye Charlotte standing before him and saying 'Scott, do not go' (a spectral echo, perhaps, of that last unspoken farewell on 11 May). He defied her advice in death as he had doubtless often defied it in life, and left on 12 October, by coach. Anne (who, incredibly, had never seen London, although her sister lived there) accompanied her father. A call was made on Morritt on the way down at Rokeby. In London he dined with assorted grandees and men of letters, and went to Terry's theatre, the Adelphi. He did research on Napoleon in Foreign Office archives, and read the latest historical and silver-fork romances. He had a meeting with the King on 20 October. It was all gratifying, particularly the audience with his monarch who was as flattering to 'Walter' as ever. 'He is, in many respects', Scott recorded with a return of his earlier loyalty, 'the model of a British monarch . . . I am sure such a man is fitter for us than one who would long to head armies or be perpetually intermeddling with *La grande politique*' (Jrnl. 218). More to the point, Sir William Knighton, the King's secretary, indicated that there would be royal patronage for Charles in the diplomatic service, after he had taken his degree (EJ 999).

From London, Scott and his daughter travelled on to France, which he reached in the last days of October. In Paris, Scott met, among many others, the American novelist Fenimore Cooper. They got on well and Cooper (a self-proclaimed disciple) offered to be helpful about American copyright problems. He saw Rossini's *Ivanhoe* at the Odéon. Gallic civility was less pleasing than his monarch's had been. Scott declared himself driven half mad with greasy French compliments. He longed 'for a little of the old Scotch causticity' (EJ 1001). Nevertheless, on leaving France on 10 November he declared himself refreshed: 'The effect of a succession of new people and unusual incidents has had a favourable effect [on my mind] which was becoming rutted like an ill kept highway' (Jrnl. 235). In London, on the way back, he dined with a congenial band of Tory men of letters – Lockhart, Croker and Theodore Hook. Malachi Malagrowther was, apparently, forgiven. Thomas Lawrence painted yet another portrait of 'the Great Unknown' for George IV. Scott poked some more among official documents and had an interview with the Duke of Wellington about the Great War. On 16 November he dined at the Admiralty with no less than five Cabinet Ministers. This hobnobbing with greatness suddenly made Scott feel diminished. Why was *he* not a great man, a temporal lord? On 15 November, he noted ruefully 'I might have been a Judge of Session [by this time] – attain in short the grand goal proposed to the ambition of a Scottish lawyer.' Where had he gone wrong? 'It is better however as it is', he concluded, with his invariable stoicism (Jrnl. 239).

In London, Scott continued his investigations into the Owen trust. It seemed that his children could look forward to £4,000, if Charles and Charlotte were ruled legitimate (EJ 1004). It was less than he had hoped for. He left London on 19 November. On the way back to Abbotsford, Scott called on his son Charles at Brasenose (EJ 1005). Oxford was now dead to him since Heber's disgrace. After a rather unpleasant winter trip through the industrial North, Scott and Anne reached home on 25 November. The 'skirmish' had cost some £200 (EJ 1004). It was, Scott noted, humiliating to have to take note of such tiny outgoings but 'I wished to get information and have had to pay for it' (Jrnl. 246). He also paid in a currency he could less well afford, his health. Over the winter of 1826–7 he was to experience severe attacks of rheumatism (for which a chauvinistic Lockhart blames wet sheets in French inns). Prudently, he moved his Edinburgh lodgings from 'bug haunted' Mrs Brown's to a furnished house in Walker Street (HG 270). But negotiating Edinburgh pavements was becoming increasingly difficult. His bad knee had worsened. He was afflicted with chilblains which restricted his mobility still further. Immobility led to piles. 'My journal is getting a vile chirurgical aspect,' he noted dryly. 'I shall never see the threescore and ten', he concluded (Jrnl. 254).

CHRONICLES OF THE CANONGATE

By 12 June 1826 Scott had finished the third volume of the ever-expanding *Life of Napoleon*, and the fourth by 13 August. On 9 September he recorded, 'I begin to fear *Nap* will swell to seven volumes' (nine, as it eventually turned out; Jrnl. 195). By 22 June, with *Woodstock* out of the way, he was well into the first volume of his new series of Scottish tales. *Chronicles of the Canongate* was the first of Scott's literary ventures to be hatched exclusively for and with Cadell as publisher. Cadell evidently suggested the joint venture in early summer 1826. It was shortly before October (HG 271) that Scott made his financial arrangement for *Chronicles of the Canongate or the Traditions of the Sanctuary by the author of Waverley* with his new partner. (The 'author of *Waverley*' tag was an important concession on Scott's part; the work had originally been planned as anonymous.) Cadell engaged to pay Scott £500 for himself – these receipts to come from first sales. Scott needed the money for expenses arising from Lady Scott's last illness (*SLE* 42).

The original idea was that the *Chronicles* should be a one-volume venture. Later Cadell suggested they be expanded to two volumes (EJ 997). It was thought prudent not to expand the collection to three volumes, however, lest the property be seized as one of the unnamed three-volume novels for which Scott had made contracts with Constable. The trust pronounced it 'highly reasonable' that Scott should have £500 for himself (EJ 998). (The creditors would receive at least three times as much for their fund.)

First entitled 'Baliol's Lodgings, or Traditions of the Sanctuary,' *Chronicles of the Canongate* cemented a fellowship between Scott and his publisher – bankrupts both. Shortly after Charlotte's funeral, on 27 May, Scott mentions 'The Highland Widow' ('Mrs Murray Keith's Tale of the Deserter') and describes the work as an *hors d'oeuvre* to be written 'between the necessary intervals of *Nap*' (Jrnl. 150). He dashed off a few pages for James Ballantyne's opinion. Reassured that the project was worthwhile, Scott wrote his new story quickly and (as he anticipated) found it a refreshing break from the biography. The first third of the first volume (i.e. most of 'The Highland Widow') was finished by the July 1826 vacation.

What strikes the modern reader of *Chronicles of the Canongate* most forcefully is their Scottish nationalism. The first three stories in the series all present the Scot as tragic victim. As in the Malachi Malagrowther letters, Scott was still angry against the 'Southron' for the events of 1825–6. All during 1826 – at least until his trip south at the end of the year – Scott indulged a vein of Anglophobia and Scottophilia unique in his writing career. In *Chronicles of the Canongate* he selected for his subject-matter the most badly-done-by of his compatriots, the Highlanders after 1745. The story of 'The Highland Widow' draws directly on the Glencoe massacre – one of England's most disgraceful acts in her dealings with Scotland. Scott describes the massacre in a long footnote which goes into the most nauseatingly violent details of the affair. He lingers, for instance, on the Crown soldiers' treatment of the Macdonald chieftain's wife, after he had been shot in the back by Campbell: 'She was stripped naked by the soldiers, who tore the rings off her fingers with their teeth' (*CC* 344).

Although it is not mentioned directly, the plot of 'The Highland Widow' is clearly allusive to the Glencoe affair. The massacre was officially justified by the Macdonald clan's failure to meet an arbitrary English deadline. The Campbells were acting directly under English orders in carrying out their slaughter. So too in 'The Highland Widow' Hamish Bean is shot under English law because he fails to meet an arbitrary deadline and is deemed – quite unjustly – a 'deserter' for being a few hours late to return to his barracks (just as – to be fanciful – Scott was ruined because Constable was a few days late getting to London in January 1826).

Even by Scott's standards, *Chronicles of the Canongate* has a grotesquely long introduction. At seven chapters' length, it dwarfs the narrative of 'The Highland Widow' which it ostensibly introduces. The introduction is, in fact, best read as a long short story in its own right. As he tells us, the *donnée* for 'The Highland Widow' had come some time ago from Scott's friend, Mrs [Anne] Murray Keith – the Mrs Martha Bethune Baliol who is Chrystal Croftangry's friend. Scott had, as he recalled in the opening epistle, 'on many occasions been indebted to her vivid memory for the *substratum* of [my] Scottish fictions' (*CC* xxxiii).

The descent of *Chronicles of the Canongate*'s narrative is devious: it is Elspat Mactavish's story, divulged by herself in conversation, via the bilingual Highlander Donald MacLeish as local guide or 'conductor' (and possibly translator; it is not clear if Elspat can speak English), with Mrs Bethune Baliol as recorder, and Chrystal Croftangry as 'editor'. The author of *Waverley* takes title-page credit and behind that unknown is Sir Walter Scott. The narrative line to the reader runs: actor, conductor, recorder, editor, author, laird. The dominant voice in this chorus is Chrystal Croftangry, an amalgam of Scott himself and R. P. Gillies, the bankrupt editor and wayward German scholar who was one of Sir Walter's lame dogs at the period.

Croftangry is described as a man around sixty, 'a Scottish gentleman of the old school' (*CC* 2). In his youth he was a prodigal who lost his patrimony. He has since raised himself – by industrious application to the law, we discover. He is writing around the present time (a fact that emerges more clearly from the introduction to 'The Two Drovers'). At one period of his early manhood, Chrystal was obliged to retreat to the Canongate (i.e. Holyrood) to find sanctuary from his creditors. This, of course, is what had happened to Cadell a few weeks before and what Scott feared in the early months of 1826 might happen to him as well.

Before his fall, Chrystal's family had been 'old proprietors in the

Upper Ward of Clydesdale' (*CC* 17). He ran through the fortune they left him and the estate was bought up by *nouveaux riches* cotton mill owners. But they too fell on hard times, in their turn, in the post-Napoleonic-War slump. Chrystal, who is now prosperous again from his law practice, toys with the idea of resuming his patrimonial heritage. Incognito, he visits an old and crusty family servant – Christie Steele – who now keeps an inn in the former jointure-house of Duntarkin. This formidable lady – who is as hard and sharp as her name – penetrates Chrystal's disguise and flatly discourages his returning 'home'. The clock cannot be turned back.

For all his jauntiness there is something defeated in Chrystal's retreating to Canongate's sanctuary – half-prison, half-asylum – for the second time in his life. Like Byron's Prisoner of Chillon, he cannot accept the freedom his wealth bestows. Nor can he reassume his lairdship. His only recourse is to retreat to a sentimentalized 'old' Scotland; romantic antiquarianism. The telling of old second-hand stories becomes his occupation. Chrystal loathes the new world. He bemoans the desecration of old monuments ('betwixt building and burning, every ancient monument of the Scottish capital is now likely to be utterly demolished'). But he is incapable of halting the new world's march.

Chyrstal's condition of life is one of emblematic loneliness. His two brothers died in childhood; he was brought up the only child by a doting widowed mother, who has also since died. He has never married. His only friend, Mrs Bethune Baliol, sends him as a packet to be dispatched after her death the story of Elspat MacTavish. Chrystal has no family, and no old friends. Above all, no children. His only friendly human contact is his landlady, Janet MacEvoy, who remembers him fondly for overpaying her fifteen shillings in his youth (something that Chrystal, of course, has forgotten).

'The Two Drovers' (which made up the first volume of the two-volume *Chronicles of the Canongate*) has a shorter introduction than 'The Highland Widow'. There is no Mrs Bethune Baliol, a printer's devil waits impatiently for copy at the door, and Chrystal has only Janet for inspiration. (She, incidentally, had not been at all impressed with 'The Highland Widow': 'It was but about a young cateran and an auld carline, when all's done.' Like James Ballantyne, she probably preferred chivalry to Highlands realism; *CC* 200). The story which Chrystal comes up with under this pressure is imbued with a fatalism worthy of Hardy. Death is predicted from the first page. And the densely informed description of the eighteenth-century drovers' way of life, and their place in the old Borders economy, makes 'The Two Drovers' one of the gems in Scott's later fiction. This *was* a world which Scott knew intimately (unlike the clan world of 'The Highland Widow'). As John Buchan observes, 'The Two Drovers' offers 'an unforgettable picture of the old world of the drove-roads' (JB 314).

'The Surgeon's Daughter', which is a longer short story than its predecessors, made up the second volume of the *Chronicles of the Canongate* set, which was published in late 1827.[5] 'The Surgeon's Daughter' may have been inspired by a visit to Abbotsford in January 1827 by Dr Joshua Marshman, 'a great Oriental scholar' and, as Scott recalled, an old friend of 'poor John Leyden' (Jrnl. 271). For the substantial Indian part of the story, Scott borrowed notes from his friend Colonel James Ferguson (Jrnl. 350). But since that gentleman's experience was of a different area of the subcontinent from that in which 'The Surgeon's Daughter' is set, the result was some egregious errors (EJ 1070).

'The Surgeon's Daughter' opens with the now familiar scenario of the desperate editor scrabbling for inspiration. Chrystal finds his publisher (i.e. the dour Cadell) no help: 'He understands his business too well, and follows it too closely, to desire to enter into literary discussions' (*CC* 236). Would that Constable ('I am all but author of the *Waverley* novels') had been so professionally circumspect, is what Scott implies. In his desperation for a story, Chrystal resorts to his lawyer, Mr Fairscribe. He makes the point that the first two chronicles have succumbed to 'tartan fever'. Highlanders are a drug on the literary and artistic market. Fairscribe advises Chrystal to send his 'Muse of Fiction' to India, fifty years since: 'That is the true place for a Scot to thrive in' (*CC* 248).

It is astonishing that in this terminal phase of his writing career, and in the decay of his later years, Scott can still surprise the reader. 'The Surgeon's Daughter' is a 'page-turner'. It has a gothic climax set in an orient which Scott had never seen, but where – as a younger man – he had once thought of emigrating. The design of the novel is extraordinarily glum, like all *Chronicles of the Canongate*. There is a lot of death, much gothic violence, and no happy ending to sweeten the last page. The plot is impelled by a number of strong, diffused drives which one can relate to Scott's own condition in 1826–7. As the preface to 'My Aunt Margaret's Mirror' makes clear, Scott was haunted at this period of his life by survivor's guilt, the feeling that all his siblings were gone – why should he remain, more so as he had been the weakest of the brood? He pictures himself a lonely old man, limping by the new buildings alongside the meadows – those fields where he had played as a child, and been mocked for his lameness by his better-made brothers. Scott's dead siblings inhabit *Chronicles of the Canongate* like unexorcized ghosts.

'The Surgeon's Daughter' also has one of the most obviously incestuous of Scott's plots. Richard Middlemas and Menie Gray are brought up as sister and brother, and become affianced. There is a strong suggestion that Richard seduced her (why did Gideon Gray die prematurely, apparently of a broken heart? Why does she feel unfit to give herself to any decent suitor after her eleventh-hour rescue from the clutches of Tippoo?) The ending defies Scott's normal narrative conventions. Adam and Menie do not marry and live happily ever after as do their *Waverley*-novel predecessors. 'Her feelings', we are told, 'were too much and too painfully agitated, her health too much shattered.' Adam survives only two years before dying heroically (and probably suicidally) in an epidemic. Menie thereafter retires into seclusion in her Lowland village. In this sequence of events one catches tantalizing glimpses of Scott's mysteriously unfortunate sister Anne. Had *she* been seduced?

One is on clearer ground with the overt anti-semitism of 'The Surgeon's Daughter'. The main strut of the plot – the antagonism, twinned careers and moral opposition of Adam and Richard – draws on two main sources. One, clearly enough, is Hogarth's series of prints of idle and industrious apprentices. The other is Scott's own pattern of racial dualism in *Ivanhoe*. Adam, the industrious hero, has an 'open English countenance, of the genuine Saxon mould' and 'chestnut locks'. He is a male equivalent of the fair Saxon beauty, Rowena. The idle apprentice Richard Middlemas, by contrast, is 'dark . . . with high features, beautifully formed, but exhibiting something of a foreign character' (CRP 308). Middlemas is half-Jewish by blood, and wholly Jewish by nature (Jewish, that is, by Scott's prejudiced definition). Richard is swarthy, treacherous and greedy. He will sell the woman who loves him to the embraces of a sub-human oriental for gold. He will sell his country to its treacherous enemy – the Hyder Ali – for gold. Gold is his God.

Physically, Richard is the equivalent of the dark beauty, Rebecca. But he is a xenophobic and frankly anti-semitic creation. The reason for the sinister and racially caricatured Richard is found in events of 1826–7 and Scott's persecution by the Jewish gold merchant, Abud & Son. Scott seriously feared Abud would drive him to bankruptcy and flight – either abroad or to Holyroodhouse, like Chrystal. Scott's remarks in the journal about 'the Jew broker' are venomously racist. In the end, the obdurate Abud ('Abut', 'Ahab', as Scott contemptuously misnamed him) was paid off by Sir William Forbes. But the odious Richard Middlemas survives as Scott's counter-attack against his Jewish tormentor. In his three-volume *History of Anti-Semitism* (New York, 1975), Léon Poliakov calls 'The Surgeon's Daughter' 'historically the first lesson in the dangers of a "mixture of blood"' (p. 327). In the next hundred and fifty years it was to be a fertile theme in the hands of authors more bigoted than Scott.

1827

After a very low point over Christmas 1826, Scott's health improved slightly. But his journal for this year remains a catalogue of chronic ailments. The trip to Paris had been bad for him – something that his friends should have noted carefully, but apparently did not. He was afflicted in the new year with bowel complaints, together with blood in his stools and urine (EJ 1008). He was particularly bothered by a near crippling rheumatism which afflicted his hands. His writing had become like a 'kitten's scratch', he ruefully observed (Jrnl. 300). His bad knee also suffered terribly. He could barely stand at Christmas. Nonetheless, he had recovered sufficiently to walk two miles on 7 January with Skene, nowadays his closest friend.

The Life of Napoleon was meanwhile outgrowing its planned four volumes. Like *Tristram Shandy*, the more Scott wrote the more he found to write. He enlarged the project to seven and – finally – to a massive nine volumes. There was a certain commercial risk in this expansion, but it was the one work of whose bestsellerdom the author was confident. He hired the services of an amanuensis, James Hogg's nephew Robert, to help him with the herculean labour of writing up a massively long work in an absurdly short period. Scott did Waterloo by April 1827. He killed Napoleon on 3 June. And by the end of that month the huge work was in the bookshops and selling in unprecedented numbers under the joint imprint of Longman in London and Cadell in Edinburgh. As Edgar Johnson calculates, 'the actual writing of the whole stupendous undertaking, done amid financial ruin, pain, and sorrow, had taken little more than twelve months' (EJ 1012). And in the two years that *The Life of Napoleon* had been on the stocks Scott had also written *Woodstock* and a mass of other incidental work. The first printing of 8,000 was cleared instantly. The first two editions produced £18,000 for the trust. Scott fairly gloated: 'I question if more was ever made by a single work or by a single author's labours in the same time', he wrote in his journal (Jrnl. 272). More soberly, John Buchan notes that 'No one can read the nine volumes without a good deal of admiration and a good deal of boredom' (JB 312).

Most commentators have concurred with Buchan – often, one suspects, to spare themselves the labour of reading Scott's text. In fact, the work – while undeniably long – is anything but boring. The tactical decision to begin explosively with the Revolution was very canny. Scott's account is uncompromisingly Tory. The Revolution was nothing less than the dismantling of everything that makes society social:

> France [in 1792] had lost her King and nobles, her church and clergy, her judges, courts, and magistrates, her colonies and commerce. The greater part of her statesmen and men of note had perished by proscription, and her orators' eloquence had been cut short by the guillotine. She had no finances – the bonds of civil society seem to have retained their influence from habit only. The nation possessed only one powerful engine, which France called her own, and one impulsive power to guide it – These were her army and her ambition. (*LN* 142)[6]

And this engine, of course, was incarnate in Bonaparte – a monster of 'insatiable' ambition. Scott demonizes Napoleon , while fairmindedly allowing that he rationalized many aspects of French life and had good personal qualities (there is a moving passage on the 'sterility of Josephine' which may reflect some of Scott's worries about Walter and Jane). Chapter 89, on Waterloo, is a masterpiece of rapid and economical narration. Chauvinist as ever, Scott forcefully denies the assertion 'of almost all the French, and some English writers, that the English were on the point of being defeated, when the Prussian force came up' (*LN* 612). The most useful section of *The Life of Napoleon* from the British authorities' point of view was the last, in which Scott stoutly defends the conditions of 'General' Bonaparte's non-imperial residence and life-style at St Helena (chapters 95, 96), the subject of much Radical attack. Scott specifically refutes the canard that the privations of St Helena prematurely killed Napoleon, bringing on his fatal cancer. Scott finishes his massive narrative with a peroration which begins by stressing Napoleon's personal amiability and kindness to dogs and climaxes in violent denunciation:

> The consequences of the unjustifiable aggressions of the French emperor were an unlimited extent of slaughter, fire, and human misery, all arising from the ambition of one man, who, never giving the least sign of having repented the unbounded mischief, seemed, on the contrary, to justify and take pride in the ravage which he had occasioned. This ambition, equally insatiable and incurable, justified Europe in securing his person, as if it had been that of a lunatic. (*LN* 668)

Three classes of readers have never liked Scott's *Life of Napoleon*: the French, radicals and professional historians. Yet the book effectively appropriated the Napoleonic myth for a Tory party fighting an aggressive rearguard action against Reform. On the other side, Hazlitt's *Life of Napoleon* is comprehensively outgunned. Although they started at the same time, and both authors were equally handicapped by age and physical decay, Scott got his nine volumes out in June 1827, while Hazlitt could only manage two of his four by February 1828. Moreover, while Scott's *Napoleon* sold like hot cakes, Hazlitt's was a flop. And, to cap it all, Hazlitt was driven to furtive plagiarisms of Scott – whose Tory propaganda he had set himself up to controvert.[7] On their part, professional historians dismiss *The Life of Napoleon* as popular history written for money. This may be so, but Scott carved out the genre later exploited by Carlyle's *The French Revolution* and Macaulay's *History of England*.

One of the uncomfortable features of the *Napoleon* triumph was that it coincided with the death of the work's other 'author', Constable. When 'the Crafty' finally died on 21 July 1827, Cadell delivered himself of a vicious obituary. Constable according to his former pupil, partner, and son-in-law was 'one of the vainest and most absurd men . . . ill-educated [he] died a Bankrupt from want of knowledge of business and calculation' (EJ 1020–1). Although he did not attend the funeral nor condole with the Constable family, Scott was more generous than Cadell in his obituary remarks, but studiously offhanded: 'Constable's death might have been a most important thing to me if it happened some years age and I should then have lamented it much.' Now, however, he did not much lament. 'I have no great reason to regret him yet I do – if he deceived me he also deceived himself' (Jrnl. 331–2). But Constable had not deceived Scott in the original planning sessions for *The Life of Napoleon*; without him would it have ever come into being? On the same day that Constable died, Scott learned that the court had decided that *The Life of Napoleon* and *Woodstock* were indeed his own property, not the dead publisher's (EJ 1021). The erasure was complete. A huge flood of pent-up earnings was released into the Trust. A dividend was paid to the creditors, releasing him of a third part of the burden of his debt.

On 23 February 1827, at an otherwise routine benefit dinner for the Edinburgh Theatrical Fund, Scott at last allowed the great secret to be publicly divulged. Lord Meadowbank, in proposing one of innumerable toasts, declared – with a truly cosmic flourish – 'the *darkness visible* has been cleared away – and the Great Unknown – the minstrel of our native land – the mighty magician who has rolled back the current of time, and conjured up before our living senses the men and the manners of days which have long passed away, stands revealed to the hearts and the eyes of his affectionate and admiring countrymen' (CC1 xlv). He was the 'small known now', Scott urbanely retorted (CC1 xlvii). It was not, as far as one can see, a calculated move. Scott had given Meadowbank permission to unmask him in the anteroom, just before the dinner started. Nor had the audience expected the announcement. There was a huge uproar and the 300 guests stood on chairs and tables in their excitement. The papers took up the matter with similar furore. It was one of the great discoveries of the time. Scott, however, scoffed at the 'farce' in his Journal. 'That splore is ended', he declared (Jrnl. 282).

Scott missed the Lockharts – particularly his beloved Johnnie. The ache was relieved in June when Sophia and her children came to Portobello (the seaside resort just outside Edinburgh) for the summer. They declined to stay at Abbotsford, which suggests tension between Anne and her married sister. The boy was strong enough to ride with Scott, and they saw a lot of each other. In the updraft from the triumph of *The Life of Napoleon* Scott resolved to write an anecdotal history of Scotland 'for little Johnnie Lockhart' – something that would remind the little Londoner of his Scottish roots. (Scott was inspired by Croker's *Stories from the History of England*, 1817). This eventually became the *Tales of a Grandfather*. Scott began work in earnest on the project in July 1827. It was subsequently expanded to four successive series, published 1827–30. It is one of the most tender of Scott's productions and also one of the most useful since it crystallizes, in the most grand-paternally comprehensible form, Scott's feelings about the evolution of his country. According to Andrew Lang 'of the little that the world used to know about Scottish history, three-quarters were learned from *Tales of a Grandfather*.'[8] At Cadell's urging, it was conceived as something to be done in his free time, and 'not for Mr Gibson's money bags' (EJ 1013). The trust conceded the point (although they did not have to). There was a thriving market for improving children's books and the project turned out to be a money-spinner. Reportedly, Johnnie Lockhart was entranced by the work and so excited by its battle scenes that he 'set out to dirk his young brother with a pair of scissors' (JB 313).

For Scott 1827 was a year of hard, well-rewarded work and recovery. The summer, after the court recessed, was especially delicious. Charles was awarded his degree in June; in the same month Walter was posted back to the mainland and he and Jane projected a visit in September. Scott indulged his old bibliophile habits, cataloguing his books. He wrote a number of mellow essays and reviews, including his two major statements on landscape gardening: 'On the Planting of Waste Lands,' and the 'Essay on Ornamental Gardening'. Having saved Abbotsford's library and its grounds from the wolves, he was glorying in their repossession. He looked forward to editing Shakespeare with Lockhart, as an old man's labour of love.

In autumn 1827, however, a number of upsets conspired to jolt Scott out of his good temper. In September trouble blew up over his portraiture of General Gaspard Gourgaud in *The Life of Napoleon*. This episode is more complicated than Lockhart (and following him, Johnson) makes it. Gourgaud was a young artillery officer close to Napoleon at Waterloo who subsequently followed the Emperor into exile at St Helena. His diary and recollections are a main primary source for that episode. On the island, however, Gourgaud quarrelled with other of Napoleon's retinue, threatening one of them with a duel. He was encouraged in early 1818 to leave and return to Europe.

Lockhart's account clearly states that the issue between Scott and Gourgaud concerned the latter's contradictory statements about Napoleon's health and ill treatment by the English governor of St Helena, Sir Hudson Lowe:

> Among the documents laid before Scott in the Colonial Office, when he was in London at the close of 1826, were some which represented one of Buonaparte's attendants at St Helena, General Gourgaud, as having been guilty of gross unfairness, giving the English Government private information that the Emperor's complaints of ill-usage were utterly unfounded, and yet then, and afterwards, aiding and assisting the delusion in France as to the harshness of Sir Hudson Lowe's conduct towards his captive. (Lock. 5. 105)

Johnson follows this, with minimal paraphrase: 'In the *Life of Napoleon* Scott had quoted official records of General Gourgaud's testimony that Napoleon had not been ill-treated at St Helena. This contradicted Gourgaud's later statements portraying Napoleon as a pathetic victim of Sir Hudson Lowe's persecutions' (EJ 1025). In fact, as Lord Rosebery points out in *Napoleon, the Last Phase* (London, 1928), Scott's charges were much more serious than that Gourgaud had said different things on different occasions. In chapter 94 of *The Life of Napoleon* Scott (hinting at information in official documents) alleged that Gourgaud had been a spy for Napoleon's English captors. There was no ambiguity – Scott bluntly accused Gourgaud (an officer of proven battle field gallantry and fanatic loyalty) of having betrayed his Emperor, of being a Judas. Rosebery – having looked at the matter more carefully than Scott's biographers – concludes: 'We do not believe that Gourgaud, an honorable and distinguished French General, long attached to the person of Napoleon, would wantonly reveal to Lowe, Bathurst, or Sturmer the real secrets of the

Emperor's intimacy' (p. 56). Unless he could cite his evidence (which he never did) Scott's actual allegations were outrageous – which is probably why Lockhart masks them.

Not unreasonably, Gourgaud protested at Scott's misrepresentations. Scott responded with an article denouncing the 'long moustachoed son of a French bitch' (Jrnl. 309) in the *Edinburgh Weekly Journal*, on 14 September. Gourgaud (who was ten years younger than Scott and had actually fought duels) threatened to come over to London and call his tormentor out. On his part, Scott declared himself very willing to meet the Frenchman – and defend his honour, if need be, with one of Napoleon's own pistols (a pair of which decorated Abbotsford's walls; EJ 1026). It would never have been allowed to happen, of course. Scott was fifty-five, and all but crippled. In the event no actual challenge was received, although the French newspapers ranted. Gourgaud comes out much better from the affair than Scott's chauvinistic biographers have allowed.

The other upset came at the end of October with the climax of the Abud & Sons affair. They had been persecuting Scott, on and off, since the early days after the crash and had acquired two of Scott's bills made out to Hurst & Robinson for £1,760 (EJ 1031). Obdurately they held out for cash. Although Edgar Johnson (following Scott) calls the demand 'legal blackmail' and 'extortion', Abud were quite within their rights. The trust was a voluntary arrangement among the creditors, which they were under no obligations to join. For a sum of this kind, if he did not pay up, Scott might well have gone to prison. As he had with Gourgaud, he nonetheless faced his antagonists down. If necessary, he declared, he would let himself be sequestered, which would mean all creditors would have equal shares of a relatively small pie.

The situation was complicated in early November by what looks like some very murky involvement on Cadell's part. Scott learned that his 'partner' had held back some vital information: namely that Abud had acquired Scott's bills from Robinson in return for overvalued gold ingots, which he had then sold at under value to an Abud frontman. 'If this were proved,' as Edgar Johnson points out, 'Abud might not merely be unable to collect the debt but be convicted of usury himself' (EJ 1032). Cadell knew about this, but had not given Scott the information that might have saved him – until Scott threatened the sequestration proceedings that would surely pull down Cadell as well. 'What made [Cadell] keep Robinson's secret? – *Cela donne à penser*', Scott wrote in his journal (Jrnl. 373). What it made one think was that Cadell had passed on to Abud (via Robinson) the inside information that Scott had been earning money of his own. Robinson, Abud and Cadell may have calculated that rather than face gaol, Scott would pay the £1,760 out of his private earnings and could be milked for further sums in course of time. When it was clear that Scott would rather go to the wall than pay up, Cadell came clean rather than go to the wall with him.

Scott did not flinch – even when the courts decided that Abud must be paid in full. Eventually, according to Lockhart, his old friend Sir William Forbes privately paid the £2,000-odd debt. According to Lockhart 'it was not until some time after Sir William's death [in 1828], that Sir Walter learned what he had done on this occasion' (Lock. 5. 132–3). There is, apparently, no corroborating evidence for this act of gallantry of Forbes's in the journal or Scott's correspondence. The episode does not ring entirely true. The trustees would hardly have lied to Scott on such a matter and he must surely have asked some direct question as to who had paid the £2,000 and he must regularly have checked his list of creditors. Either he chose not to know or this is another Lockhart fabrication.

The first series of *Chronicles of the Canongate* was published in November. Sales were disappointing, confirming Ballantyne's scepticism about the attractions of Scottish tales. The Highlands were passé – as Scott himself concedes rather too often in his prefatory rambles around the stories. *Tales of a Grandfather*, on the other hand, sold brilliantly when it came out as a Christmas book in December, and was in a second edition by the end of the month. As Johnson records, Scott was frequently prey to 'black dog', at the end of 1827. Nonetheless it was the best of his post-crash years. The trust paid its first dividend, six shillings in the pound, in December (Jrnl. 388), representing revenue of some £40,000 generated by Scott's pen. It was an astounding achievement. The dividend coincided with another piece of good news; Charles was notified at the end of November that the first vacancy in the Foreign office was earmarked for him. Walter (although his health was not all it should be) was up for promotion, and Sophia was expecting her third child by the end of the year.

On the strength of his improved financial state Scott had moved into more salubrious lodgings at 6 Shandwick Place. These quarters boasted a water closet, and no bugs. The property belonged to Mrs Jobson, his in-law, who may have taken a grim pleasure in being Sir Walter's landlady. Nearby, in Maitland Street, there lived another old lady, the mother of Williamina (now dead seventeen years). At the end of November, Lady Jane Stuart found a pretext for meeting Scott in some old albums of her daughter's, containing poems he had copied out as an eager lover thirty years ago. The ensuing letters and interviews, in which she seems to have apologized for sabotaging his suit in 1795, were extraordinarily painful to Scott. He confesses to weeping like 'an old fool' (Jrnl. 375).

16

The 'Magnum Opus' (1828–1829)

Scott did what Ballantyne roared for and turned to chivalry. His new *Chronicle of the Canongate* would be set in the reign of Robert III, and would feature swordplay and tushery. The journal records that in mid-October 1827 a Captain Mackenzie of the Celtic Society had told Scott about the clan chief, Hector, whose bodyguard were all killed protecting their leader (Jrnl. 365). At about the same time, Scott became interested in the legendary Harry Wynd, an armourer in Perth who had joined the soon-to-be-exterminated Clan Chattan (a theme which must have been suggested by Fenimore Cooper's *The Last of the Mohicans*).

We find Scott on 5 December sketching out ideas for his tale of Perth centred on 'a difference between the old highlander and him of modern date' and the paradox of the 'brave coward' (Jrnl. 389–90). Originally this new work was titled 'St Valentine's Eve' – which was, on reflection, too suggestive of a fluffy gift-book poem. Scott had the second volume done by March 1828. The novel (and the 'Canongate' series – which Ballantyne and Cadell had never much liked) was finished on 14 April 1828: 'So there's an end of the *Chronicles*', Scott recorded by way of obituary (Jrnl. 457). Thanks to some quick work by Cadell the three-volume novel went on sale in May 1828.

For modern readers *The Fair Maid of Perth* remains the most admired of Scott's later fictions. Like other 'Chronicles' the narrative is replete with disappointing, or weak sons. Richard Middlemas and young Armstrong (in 'The Death of the Laird's Jock') are joined in their gross filial shortcomings by Conachar – the Highland chief with nerves of jelly – and Rothsay, the dissipated prince who womanizes and drinks his way into premature death. All these weak sons betray strong, potent, admirably decent, hard-working fathers (or father figures) like the Laird, Dr Gray, Simon Glover, and Torquil of the Oak. One can detect a submerged resentment on Scott's part that Walter, Charles (particularly) and even Lockhart had let him down.

Charles, the least satisfactory of his children, was in Edinburgh from December 1827 until February 1828 polishing his command of modern languages, preparatory to the career in the Foreign Office which had been procured by Royal favour towards his father. Even after graduation, Scott was still obliged to pay the young man an allowance of £150. Later in 1828, after some nail-biting, Walter (now twenty-seven) had his promotion to Major purchased for him, by the assistance of the three Misses Fergusson at Huntly Burn. (They loaned Walter back the £1,500 which they received from the dividend, on account of the £5,000 which they had loaned Scott in 1825 – thus multiplying the family's obligation to them.) Scott had interceded with Wellington, among others, to further Walter's career. And by early summer Major Scott was stationed with his regiment at Hampton Court, where a clever young officer might make a reputation for himself. But it was clear that, as with Charles, the eldest son was wholly dependent on his father to provide the wherewithal for a brilliant career. Scott was still having to 'bustle' to keep Lockhart's star in the ascendant. When, Scott might have wondered, would these sons and son-in-law fend for themselves? Was this the 'lasting root' for which he had ruined his health, his happiness and his financial security?

The chronology of *The Fair Maid of Perth* is unusually tight knit for a Scott novel. Its events are all packed into a few days around 14 February. *The Fair Maid of Perth* is also by far the most bloody novel Scott had hitherto written. The bloodiness is particularly striking in the key scene where Oliver Proudfute picks up a severed hand (in fact lopped from Sir John Ramorny) after the night skirmish and proceeds to pore over it as an angler might examine a particularly interesting fish: 'It is large, indeed, and bony, but as fine as a lady's', he muses (1. 73). Later Oliver himself will have his head bashed in by the psychopathic assassin, Anthony Bonthron. The sadistic starving to death of Rothsay is lingered on with extraordinary detail. And looming over the last volume is the gory battle of sixty champions which climaxes the story. The novel slithers to its conclusion on a carpet of blood.

The Fair Maid of Perth was conceived in the aftershocks of 1826 and the end of the longest Tory administration in history, that of Lord Liverpool, 1807–27. In January 1828, the 'old Tories' came back, with Wellington at their head. It was reassuring but Scott, like others of his party, had been very disturbed by the political convulsions and *The Fair Maid of Perth* is a novel which shows its author reaching for political panaceas. In its quieter moments, *The Fair Maid of Perth* promotes what was – with Ruskin, Carlyle, and Morris – to become a Victorian political platitude: namely the idealized medieval utopia. The way forward for Britain was back to the guilds and the caste system of the fifteenth-century town. Perth in Scott's novel has solved its class problems entirely. There is no 'agitation', no unhealthy yearning for 'Democracy'. Artisans are happy, and they are organically defined by their work. Glovers in *The Fair Maid of Perth* are called 'Glover' and smiths 'Smith'. (Poets would doubtless be called 'Rhymer'.) The middle-class heroes, Simon Glover and Harry the Smith, are defiantly content with their place in society. Nor would they change it for a coronet. After the great battle, when the Earl of Douglas offers Harry a knighthood, he turns it down, almost contemptuously.

The narrative stresses images of energetic harmony, such as the panorama of Shrovetide ('Fastern's E'en') at the beginning of chapter 16:

> The common people had, throughout the day, toiled and struggled at football; the nobles and gentry had fought cocks, and hearkened to the wanton music of the minstrel; while the citizens had gorged themselves upon pancakes fried in lard, and brose, or brewis – the fat broth, that is, in which salted beef had been boiled, poured upon highly toasted oatmeal, a dish which even now is not ungrateful to simple, old-fashioned, Scottish palates. (1. 295)

What Scott pictures here is the perennial British weekend: the proles siphoning off their disruptive energies at the 'Fu'ba''; the gentry at their golf and theatre: the middle classes feeding their faces at the restaurant.

Perth in the fifteenth century represented for Scott a representative nexus of class, social codes, and race. Glover and Smith are situated between the Highland clans and Douglas's lawless Lowland gang. Presiding over all is a weak king (such as those Scott himself had lived under for all his life). The fibre of Perth is entirely in the freeman artisans, with their rituals, societies, and proudly idiosyncratic mores. How to rediscover that in an age when weavers were burning everything they could torch in industrial Britain?

After the relative failure of the first series of 'Chronicles', their author, printer and publisher were uncertain as to *The Fair Maid of Perth*'s prospects. Ballantyne had gone off Scottish subjects altogether, and predicted that the 'Ossianick monotony' would tell against the work. (In his journal, Scott noted that Mr Cadell was 'less critical than James Ballantyne' – or perhaps, being Cadell, he was merely more diplomatic.) Nevertheless, as Scott records, the novel 'had a favourable reception'. This was confirmed when Cadell offered £4,200 (£12,600 in all) for each of three future novels over the next eighteen months (EJ 1045). In his journal for 23 March Scott noted complacently that if he could continue at the present rate of earning '£10,000 a year for the Creditors I think I may gain a few hundreds for my own family at bye hours' (Jrnl. 447).

Incredibly, Scott was setting himself up to pay off the trust and – on the side – earn a second income for himself. The sums were not trivial. The £500 he got from the *Keepsake* was his own (EJ 1041); the £1,600 which Cadell offered in January 1828 for 20,000 copies of a second series of *Tales of a Grandfather* would also be his, as were the payments for the pieces he wrote for Lockhart and other editors. The result was a late flowering of Scott the essayist.[1] To 1827 belong some of his finest magazine writings: his essay on landscape gardening and its partnering piece, 'On Planting Waste Lands', his review of Mackenzie's life of Home (all were supplied to Lockhart's *Quarterly*). Occasional writing was also the currency by which Scott could do the kind of favours for which he had earlier used banknotes or bills drawn on Ballantyne. In this spirit he donated two sermons ('religious discourses') which he wrote in the last weeks of 1827, to an unliterate and deaf friend about to take orders, George Huntly Gordon. In 1827, R. P. Gillies founded the *Foreign Quarterly Review* and Scott helped his penurious friend with literary pieces. Gillies was a pioneer of German writing in Britain and renewed Scott's interest in German literature. Scott gave him, *ex gratia*, a piece on the novels of Hoffmann (published in July 1827), although he took £100 for a piece on Molière, published the following January.

Scott's literary activities over 1827–8 are breathtaking. He was essentially providing lavish incomes for three masters: the trust (for whom he was writing £10,000 worth of fiction a year), Cadell (for whom he was embarking on the massive task of revising and writing apparatus for the Magnum Opus – the project that would in time make Cadell the richest publisher in the country), and for himself (he must have been making some £2,500 a year – enough to maintain himself as Laird of Abbotsford). And all this while, he was still serving as Clerk and Sheriff. 'Was ever willing horse so driven?' (HG 275) Grierson asks. Grierson blames Cadell particularly for encouraging Scott in this punishing and life-shortening regime.

TRASH FROM A GOOD NAME

Scott embarked on a six-weeks' trip to London on 3 April 1828, the last such jaunt he was to undertake in good health. On the way down he and Anne took a week and made a tour of English castles. In London he had a host of things to do. Most urgent was legal business to do with Lady Scott's Chancery suit. To secure Owen's bequest he needed an affidavit as to Charlotte's legitimacy from the now aged Jane Nicolson (a lady some gossips assumed to be Scott's mother-in-law). There was a new administration and Scott was keen to put in good words for Lockhart and Walter with the Duke of Wellington, Sir William Knighton (the King's private secretary) and Peel. He also wanted to deviate the route of a new turnpike that might cost him a 'good field' (Jrnl. 463), and to secure cadetships for the two sons of his friend, Allan Cunningham. In London Scott had his picture done by Haydon and Northcote. He was now the most pictured and busted man of the age, apart from the Great Duke. His wax effigy, lavishly bekilted and sporraned, was the pride of Madame Tussaud's. He ate and drank too much, and was warned by his physicians. He breakfasted and dined with everyone – not excepting his old poetic rival Coleridge, who 'bethumped' him with his Homeric learning, and the King, who on 11 May entertained him 'in a very private party' (EJ 1053). Scott successfully proposed dedicating the 'Magnum Opus' to his sovereign on this trip. He was introduced to Princess Victoria and hoped 'they will change her name' (Jrnl. 478).

There was as much of a family reunion in London as the Scotts could now muster. Charles and Walter were in town, as were Morritt and the Lockharts. Sophia (about whose health Scott was anxious) had given birth to a daughter in January (EJ 1038). There was even more anxiety about Scott's favourite, Johnnie, who was apparently sinking fast, and being nursed at Brighton. On 20 June, two weeks after he had returned to Edinburgh Scott received a letter from Lockhart, removing 'the last hope of poor Johnnie's recovery' (Jrnl. 492). Scott took it, as he seems to have taken all such blows, with exemplary stoicism: 'It is no surprize to me. The poor child . . . was not formed to be long with us' (in fact, he lingered on three more harrowing years).

Scott was similarly stoical about Daniel Terry's long-expected bankruptcy, news of which reached him shortly after his arrival in London. The actor-manager had fled to Boulogne and then returned at Scott's prompting 'to stand the storm' (EJ 1050). He had let debts accumulate at interest and was liable for £7,000, £500 of which was owed Scott – 'but that is the least of my concern', he declared (Jrnl. 458). Terry's debt was a drop compared to Scott's £120,000. But the actor had no comparable means of paying it off. Scott ruefully noted that 'It is written that nothing shall flourish under my shadow – the Ballantynes, Terry, Nelson, Weber, all came to distress'.[2] It was a gallingly unnecessary disaster, since Terry's theatre was in profit. He eventually paid eleven shillings in the pound and by the end of the year was acting again at Drury Lane. But, aged just forty-nine, he suffered a series of paralytic seizures which left him unable to remember lines. He died in June 1829. It was ominous for Scott, subject to even greater stress than his young friend. Scott's own health took a turn for the worse in summer, with a crippling rheumatic attack. This was perhaps to be expected in someone pushing himself as hard as he was. More worryingly, over the autumn his son Walter fell ill (EJ 1087). Over-indulgence in food, drink, and tobacco seems to have been at fault – although he too must have been reacting to post-crash stress. He was sent to the South of France to recuperate.

The second series of *Tales of a Grandfather* was finished in September, bringing Scottish history up to 1707 and the Act of Union. This was where Scott had originally intended to end. But the work had sold remarkably well (to its author's, not the trust's profit). Scott was now thinking about four instalments.[3] Cadell was pleased with the sales of *The Fair Maid of Perth* (EJ 1054), which had been published on 15 May. Work on the 'Magnum Opus' continued steadily. In September Scott began serious work on a new full-length novel, *Anne of Geierstein*. It would have a Swiss landscape that he had never himself seen. Cadell rather worried about this but Scott retorted that 'if I have not seen the Alps, I have seen Salvator Rosa's pictures' (EJ 1084). It was to Skene that Scott owed some of the best things in the novel, notably René, the troubadour king of Provence and 'the amusing ceremonies of the Fête Dieu' (EJ 1091). Scott hoped to finish in November, but his progress was slowed somewhat by James Ballantyne's criticisms in October and by difficulties in integrating Skene's material. He had the second volume done by 27 January 1829.

On 10 January 1829 Scott resumed his journal after a six months' lapse. 'During this period nothing has happend worth particular notice', he bleakly noted (Jrnl. 502). His entries are now perfunctory. In addition to twinges (mainly rheumatism and chilblains) there were many deaths to record. Sir William Forbes – his old rival in love and head of the bank which was Scott's largest creditor – died in October 1828; his old Liddesdale guide, 'poor Bob Shortreed', died in July; Terry on 22 June; and most painfully, his faithful Tom Purdie on 29 October. 'There is a heart cold that loved me well', Scott told Laidlaw (Lett. 11. 256). Purdie was only four years older than his master. His grandson Johnnie visited with his mother in summer. He too was clearly dying.

Scott was less sentimental in February 1829 when James Ballantyne's wife died. His reaction to his friend's distress verged on the callous. On 14 February, he noted that he was 'twenty leaves before the Printers but Ballantyne's wife is ill and it is his nature to indulge apprehensions of the worst, which incapacitates him for labour. I cannot help regarding this amiable weakness of the mind with something too nearly allied to contempt' (Jrnl. 519). Despite Scott's suspicions, Mrs Ballantyne died three days later. James was too distressed to attend the funeral and he secluded himself in deep mourning. Six weeks later, on 9 April, with Ballantyne still not returned to his 'labour', Scott's tone turned savage. Ballantyne was 'Hypochondriack . . . and religiously distressd in mind' (Jrnl. 544). On 13 April, he wrote 'a painful letter to J. Ballantyne'. By the 18th, with James still not returned to work, Scott reported that 'My pity begins to give way to anger. Must he sit there and squander his thoughts and senses upon cloudy metaphysicks and abstruse theology till he addles his brains entirely and ruins his business?' (Jrnl. 549). Scott apparently hinted that he might lose the lucrative 'Magnum Opus' printing commission. Two days later, James returned to work.

Scott's behaviour towards his oldest business friend can be read in different ways. As he saw it, he was merely shaking James out of a paralysing and potentially self-destructive lethargy of grief. But the two men had drifted apart politically, and Scott evidently despised Ballantyne as a Whig turncoat and a religious dupe. It may be, too, that Scott felt rebuked by the depth of the other's widower's grief. It showed up his own 'stoic' recovery from the death of Lady Scott as unfeeling. (It is significant that Scott's fiction of this period abounds in widowers with forgotten wives: Gideon Gray, Simon Glover and John Armstrong, for instance.)

Edinburgh had something other than the fall of Sir Walter to talk about in 1829. William Burke and William Hare had been apprehended for murder in the service of Edinburgh University anatomy classes. They would get their victims drunk, smother them (so as not to damage the commodity) and deliver the corpses to the College surgeons (notably Robert Knox), no questions asked. Scott was obsessed with the case, and wore his eyes out reading newspaper accounts. His letters of late 1828 and early 1829 are full of the 'horrid business'. Hare turned King's evidence and escaped the rope. Knox claimed ignorance, and was cleared. Burke was sentenced to public execution on 28 January. Scott and Charles Kirkpatrick Sharpe were spectators at the hanging (EJ 1094). Scott, in fact, bought a share of a bookseller's window overlooking the Lawnmarket gibbet. He evidently felt somewhat guilty about his fascination with the affair, making a vague and misleading entry in his journal entry for the day (Jrnl. 512, 720).

Anne of Geierstein was finished by the end of April. Its birth was not easy. Scott himself did not think well of his novel, admitting in his journal on 25 February that 'there is too much historical detail and the catastrophe will be vilely huddled up' (Jrnl. 524). He was confident his materials were excellent, 'but the power of using them is failing' (Jrnl. 502). His advisers agreed. In early March, Ballantyne 'totally condemned' the manuscript portion of the narrative shown him. (The severity of the opinion may have sharpened Scott's asperity at the printer's grief on losing his wife.) Cadell was more diplomatic in his criticisms (EJ 1099). At a 'privy council' meeting between Cadell and Scott on 9 March it was decided to 'refer the question whether *Anne of Geierstein* be sea worthy or not to further consideration' (Jrnl. 530). It might be wise to hold it back 'during the full rage of the Catholic [emancipation] question'. Grierson points out how dependent on his advisers Scott had become. He was no more the 'Death's Head Hussar' who neither took nor gave criticism. The novel was duly set aside, and when Scott looked over it again in mid-April, he found it better than he remembered (Jrnl. 546). Ballantyne 'is not infallible', he decided, 'and has been in circumstances which may biass his mind.' But finishing the story proved burdensome. 'I hate Anne', he wrote on 27 April (Jrnl. 533).

He dashed the last sections down with the air of a man carrying out a peculiarly distasteful chore. 'The story will end, and shall end', he wrote on 28 April, 'because it must end, and so here goes' (Jrnl. 553). On the eve of publication in mid-May, Cadell developed 'apprehensions', and deepened Scott's gloom about the thing. Nevertheless, when *Anne of Geierstein* was published, it confounded everyone by enjoying a huge success with the reading public. Scott thought that much less of their taste: 'Get a good name and you may write trash', he concluded (Jrnl. 554).

John Buchan calls *Anne of Geierstein* 'the last of the novels written under anything like normal conditions' (JB 321). It was, however, written in the bustle of Edinburgh, not quietly in the country. Scott apologizes in his introduction for having no library to consult, and the history was done from memory. In *Anne of Geierstein* he returned to the era and subject-matter of *Quentin Durward* – but now from the Burgundian side. The French King Louis does not appear; but Charles the Bold plays a leading role. The action is set against operatic Alpine scenery, leading one to wonder whether Scott had been taking lessons from his admirer Rossini, who had produced *La Donna del lago* in 1819 and *Ivanhoé* in 1826. What is initially striking in the plot of *Anne of Geierstein* is the importance and potency of old men. Early sections of the narrative are dominated by scenes in which the wise old John Philipson (who at fifty-five is near enough Scott's age) and the Landamman Biederman (i.e. a magistrate, or sheriff) interrupt the duel between their murderous young followers, with irresistible patriarchal authority: ' "Rudolph Donnerhugel," said the Landamman, "give thy sword to me – to me, the owner of this ground, the master of this family, and magistrate of the canton" ' (1. 104). When Rudolph consents, as he must, and when Arthur similarly defers to his father they are commanded: 'Now join hands my children, and let us forget this foolish feud' (1. 105). This is a book in which fathers and father-figures are honoured and obeyed. Later in the novel it is the oldsters who plot great affairs of state – notably the conspiracy by which Edward IV will be bled to death in France, allowing the house of Lancaster to restore itself. And it is the superannuated Oxford who baffles the deadly Vehmgericht. One is only surprised that it is not an old man who finally wins the hand of the heroine.

THE 'MAGNUM OPUS'[4]

The founding idea for the 'Magnum Opus' was Constable's, although the act that put the idea in his head was apparently Scott's. As a token of gratitude in March 1823, the author of *Waverley* had presented his publisher with all the novel manuscripts in his possession. It was a graceful gesture, but it could also be interpreted as Scott's signalling that he desired some monument to himself. Pondering on the gift, it struck Constable that an illustrated, annotated collective reissue would both sell well and honour the author. His firm now owned most of the copyrights. He acquired the bulk of them in 1819. He bought further parcels in September 1821 and April 1823 (*SLE* 5). He was now owner of all the early and middle-period novels. (*St Ronan's Well*, *Redgauntlet* and the 'Tales of the Crusaders' remained in Scott's hands.)

Scott was interested in Constable's idea for a collective, edited and embellished reissue of his fiction. But he was not particularly encouraging. He was in 1819–25 furiously turning out new fiction at the rate of two or three novels a year. The idea lapsed. The publisher returned to it in late 1825 – a period when his superheated brain was teeming with projects. One which particularly gripped him was the monthly 'Miscellany'. Concurrently with the 'Miscellany' – which would offer the *Waverley* novels in cheap and cheerful form for the millions – Constable thought he might put out a collected issue of the same texts 'in superior stile at £1.1s. a volume' (*SLE* 5) – an *édition de luxe* for the discriminating purchaser. But, as a sales incentive, it should have 'a new feature . . . Notes and Illustrations'.

Constable's 'Napoleonic' plans were overtaken by the January 1826 crash. Skilfully working through the wreckage, Robert Cadell took over the reissue projects, merging them into one grand idea: a cheap, total edition of Scott's work, embellished with new authorial apparatus (much easier to introduce once the author of *Waverley* had revealed himself). Bringing this scheme to fruition required ruthlessness and far-sighted planning. First, Cadell had to separate Constable and Scott. It was a great help that in the blackest days of January 1826 Constable was in London and he, Cadell, in Edinburgh with access to Scott's ear.

At the same time that he was blackguarding Constable, Cadell gave Scott genuine sympathy. But Scott needed more than sympathy in the aftermath of the crash, if he was to survive as anything more than an object of pity and casual charity. Shrewdly, James Ballantyne (who had no great reason to love Cadell) advised him to go with the junior partner rather than stick with Constable. Cadell was, Ballantyne declared, the more 'able' of the two (*SLE* 40). Cadell demonstrated that ability by using his family and his wife's family to give him the money to set himself up in business again, only weeks after the crash and two years before he was free of the stigma of bankruptcy.[5] Although Cadell was still undischarged, and the affairs of Constable & Co. highly confused, by June 1826 Cadell & Co. was trading. Nominally, he served as a clerk in his firm – actually, he was its sole head with much more sovereignty than he had ever enjoyed as a partner in Constable and Co.

Cadell became the primary publisher of Scott's new work with *Chronicles of the Canongate*, later in 1826. These were a wholly independent Cadell–Scott venture, designed as a new line of goods by the Author of *Waverley*. The first series of the *Chronicles* forged a necessary bond between Scott and his new publisher. Cadell's next step was to interest Sir Walter again in the idea of a collective reissue, as a means of raising the huge amounts of money needed to clear his debt. This he did. The third step, and in many ways the trickiest, was to repossess the copyright material to which Constable's estate could lay claim. This comprised: (1) *The Life of Napoleon*, and *Woodstock* – Scott's work-in-progress at the time of the crash and that for which he was contracted. Scott and his trustees claimed that the contract was void because Constable could not (as a bankrupt) fulfil his part of the agreement. The arbitrator, Lord Newton, eventually found in favour of Scott. (2) The six-volume 'Prose Works', which Constable was in the process of publishing at the time of the crash. Newton found in favour of the Constable estate. (3) The copyrights of the earlier novels (from *Waverley* to *Quentin Durward*), sold by Scott to Constable but for which he claimed that full payment had not been received. Newton found in favour of Constable. (4) The manuscripts of the novels. Scott claimed that the terms on which the gift had been made – that Constable keep his authorship secret – had been betrayed. Newton found in favour of Constable (Jrnl. xxix).

On the face of it, these legal manoeuvres against the distressed Constable were cruel – particularly the attempted repossession of the manuscripts which had been given years earlier as a gesture of grateful friendship. Nor were Scott's private remarks on the matter endearing. On learning that Newton's judgement had gone against him, he declared that he considered himself 'swindled out of my property' (Jrnl. 646).

It was clear in 1827 that Lord Newton would need many months to make his adjudication (years, in the case of the manuscripts). In the interim, it was decided that – as a wasting asset – the copyrights of the earlier *Waverley* novels should be sold so that they might be reprinted, whoever the ultimate beneficiary should be. The money from the sale would be held in escrow until Newton arrived at his final determination. It was decided that the copyrights should be auctioned. Scott, initially, had been in favour of waiting for Newton's decision (*SLE* 7) but was persuaded by Cadell to join with him to bid for the copyrights at the auction. Neither Scott nor Cadell – both still under the stigma of indebtedness – were free agents. And it was Scott (briefed by Cadell) who persuaded the Trustees at the end of November 1827 as to the 'propriety of the project' (Jrnl. 387). As much as £10,000 might be made in two years for the Trust from the exploitation of the copyrights in the 'Improved Edition', he promised.

Assent was given. Scott and Cadell were allowed to bid as partners for Constable's copyrights. Scott's stake came from money recycled by the trust from recent and imminent sales of the two series of *Chronicles of the Canongate*. (If Newton determined the copyrights were Scott's the Trust would get its money back.) Cadell raised more money from Simpkin & Marshall, the London publishers and wholesaler (*SLE* 9).

The auction took place on 19 December 1827. The upset price was £4,200, but the bidding went up to double that sum, £8,500 (as Scott had predicted). Cadell made the successful bid and rushed round, breathless, to inform Scott at the Bannatyne Club (Jrnl. 400). Having secured their prize, Cadell, Scott, Alexander and James Ballantyne devised the form of the 'Magnum Opus'. It should be a handsomely uniform set of 18mo, 5*s*, embellished and annotated volumes, issued serially at monthly intervals over 32 months (*SLE* 10). This proposal was put before the trustees six months later in June 1828. A large tranche of cash was required to launch the project – something over £15,000 as Cadell estimated (*SLE* 11). The trustees took advice, and advanced the start up money. Cadell exercised overall production control, but Scott insisted on James Ballantyne being the sole printer. This was contrary to Cadell's wishes. He had never been much impressed with the work of James Ballantyne & Co. In January 1828 Scott bluntly informed his publisher (who intended to put the 'Magnum Opus' work out to a variety of printers, for greater speed) that the three of them should consider themselves like three shipwrecked men clinging to the same plank (*SLE* 30). Despite Scott's firmness, there was a series of rows in the first year of production about the quality of Ballantyne's work, the price he charged, and problems with the new steam presses which he had introduced (*SLE* 32–5).

Having received the go-ahead from the trustees in June 1828, Cadell displayed great energy in getting the Magnum Opus underway, masterminding the production and recruiting a band of distinguished illustrators. On his part, Scott began the work of annotating at the beginning of 1828, just after the copyrights were purchased (*SLE* 19). His work was methodical, and in places inspired. He inserted his notes on interleaved editions of the novels specially prepared for him by Cadell. As always, Scott enjoyed the labour of commentary and introduction.

The printing of the 'Magnum Opus' (as it was now called) began in autumn 1828. Cadell had wasted no time. Scott had the proofs of *Waverley*, the first volume, by early October. A prospectus was issued in February 1829, and there was intensive advertising. In response to bookseller interest, the per-volume print run was raised to 20,000 from the 7,000 originally projected. *Waverley* came out on 1 June. A first complimentary copy from the Press was dispatched (via Sir William Knighton) to the King, the series's dedicatee. Scott initially had his doubts: 'How can men [buy] Waverley Novels when they are going mad about the Catholic question?' (Jrnl. 529), he asked. But from the first, sales were 'prodigious'. The only problem, as Scott observed, 'is to satisfy the delivery fast enough.' Cadell had visions of an 'El Dorado' (Jrnl. 564). Eight volumes (*Waverley* novels in chronological order) came out in the first year. According to Lockhart, by the end of 1829 Ballantyne was printing 35,000 a month. At this rate, Scott calculated he could pay off his debt in six years (EJ 1109). He had the 'Pisgah prospect' of being a free man again within his lifetime.

Scott had arranged Cadell's discharge from bankruptcy in April 1829, using his immense personal influence with Sir William Forbes (before he died in October 1828) and the trustees to mollify the still angry Royal Bank of Scotland. In August 1829, he set up again as unfettered proprietor of his own publishing house – Robert Cadell Bookseller. Scott voluntarily took over as his own responsibility some £40,000 of Constable and Cadell debts (HG 279). In May 1829 (a month after Cadell) Ballantyne was also discharged (although, like Scott, he was technically never a bankrupt).

Cadell's subsequent career is marked by two unswerving features: a total dedication to marketing the works of Scott, and an inexorable prosperity. His progress may be charted. In 1827, he was able to come up with the £4,000-plus to buy his half share of the copyrights. At the end of 1828 (while still formally a bankrupt) Cadell declared himself 'prosperous' on the profits of selling Constable stock of *Waverley* novels acquired at knock-down price (*SLE* 43). In the same year he offered Scott £4,200 for *Anne of Geierstein* and similar amounts for later, as yet unplanned, novels. In 1829, he advanced £7,000 for the half profits in the 'Poetical Works' (newly copyrighted by Scott's added apparatus; *SLE* 47). By July 1831 Cadell was well enough off to give £10,000 to complete his half-share in all the novel copyrights (*SLE*, 46).

The 48 volumes of the 'Magnum Opus' issued from 1829–33, comprising novels, poetry, miscellaneous prose, and the uniform accompanying ten volumes of Lockhart's *Life*, would eventually run to a 98-volume set – published exclusively by Cadell. The 1842 copyright act was a godsend to him. When Scott's son Walter died in 1847 Cadell paid off the £10,000 mortgage on Abbotsford (outstanding since 1825) so that Lockhart's son Walter could inherit his grandfather's property unencumbered with debt. In return Cadell was given sole ownership of the *Waverley* copyrights, which were now protected into the 1870s. As Jane Millgate calculates, in 1848 Cadell was worth 'at a conservative estimate, almost £121,000' (*SLE* 51). He died in January 1849, rich and honoured; after which the copyrights of the 'Magnum Opus' were sold to Adam and Charles Black for £27,000 (*SLE* 53).

Despite devastating strokes (three between February 1830 and April 1831) Scott worked on introductions and notes until the last conscious moments of his life. As late as February 1832 he was sending material from Naples to Cadell (*SLE* 26). The only novel not to appear in the Magnum Opus is *Count Robert of Paris* ('appropriately', as Millgate points out, since the novel was largely Lockhart's composition; *SLE* 27.)

DRAMA

In 1829 Cadell was desperate to reissue anything he could find with the golden name of Sir Walter Scott on it. A collected edition of the poetry was put in hand. The copyrights were recovered from Longman in June 1829 for £7,000. (Murray returned his share of *Marmion* free of charge; *SLE* 47, EJ 1110.) As with the fiction copyrights acquired at auction, ownership was divided between Cadell and Scott in alliance with his trustees. Scott set to and wrote a new apparatus for his verse.

Cadell suggested that one volume of the new poetry edition might be devoted to poetic drama. The unlucky *Devorgoil* was duly resurrected from 1817–18 and refurbished, as was *Macduff's Cross* (written for Joanna Baillie in 1823) and *Halidon Hill* (EJ 1117). These works did not, however, constitute a volume's worth. So in autumn 1829 Scott dashed out a verse drama, *Auchindrane, or the Ayrshire Tragedy.*[6] It was inspired by a case in Robert Pitcairn's *Scottish Criminal Trials*, which Scott was reading for the author. Pitcairn's chronicle referred to 'the extraordinary case of Mure of Auchindrane, AD 1611'. Around this Scott framed a dramatic sketch ('in no particular, either designed or calculated for the stage') which Lockhart judges 'a composition far superior to any of his previous attempts of that nature' (Lock. 5. 252).

Auchindrane was a wholly unnecessary chore from every point of view, except bulking out Cadell's volumes and earning private income for its author. But Scott was only too willing to be exploited. 'Must I not make hay while the sun shines?' he asked, 'Who can tell what leisure, health, and life may be destined to me?' (Jrnl. 548). In his wilder moments he thought that if the sun continued shining he might not only wipe out his debt, but regain his fortune. He even began to fantasize about more land purchases. On 25 May 1829 he predicted that 'I shall be much better off in two or three years than if my misfortunes had never taken place' (Jrnl. 565).

Wearing another of his many hats, Scott was active as an historian. In March 1829, he wrote a review of Fraser Tytler's *History of Scotland* for the

Quarterly. In May he did a review of a travel book, *Le Duc de Guise à Naples* for Gillies. In June he examined and sceptically commented on the *Vestiarium Scoticum* (the garb of Scotland) manuscript with its 'strange averment that all the low Country gentlemen and Border clans wore tartan' (Jrnl. 571). In April 1829 Scott had a letter from Sir James Mackintosh ('the Whig Cicero') inviting him to write a survey of Scottish history for Lardner's *Cabinet Cyclopaedia* (EJ 1105), to be published by Longman. The work could be easily spun off from the research for the *Tales of a Grandfather*. 'I have the whole stuff in my head' Scott told himself (Jrnl. 547). The first volume was half finished (despite illness) by June, but as he worked on the project Scott found he would need two volumes. The first of these was published in winter 1829, and the second in 1830 (EJ 1117–8). Lardner's history earned Scott £1,500 in all, which was very welcome. He was also receiving for his own pocket fees for his historical review-articles, regular £50 payments for the historical apparatus to the 'Magnum Opus' novels, and substantial sums for *Tales of a Grandfather*, of which he began a fourth series in early 1830. He also had £700 from Murray for a volume of 'Letters on Demonology and Witchcraft'. Scott was putting together what for other men would have been a whole income from his history writing alone.

He would perhaps have been wiser to have protected his health. He found himself passing a 'formidable quantity' of blood in his urine in June 1829 (EJ 1112). 'When a man makes blood instead of water,' he told Walter, 'he is tempted to think on the possibility of his soon making earth' (EJ 1113). Walter himself was still recovering from his breakdown. On his part, Charles was extremely unwell. His rheumatism became acute in the second half of 1829 and he had applied for a Foreign Office posting in the warmth of Naples (EJ 1128). As a semi-invalid in his early twenties, Charles could not look forward to any great career in diplomacy, any more than could his semi-invalid soldier brother. Anne was suffering from gastric illness. Sophia was iller with every childbirth. In summer 1829 she was bedridden. When she returned to London in November 1829 after her annual holiday in Scotland she was so lame that she had to be lifted into her carriage (EJ 1122). As for John Hugh, Scott feared that the little boy had come 'to lay his bones in his native land' (EJ 1113). The deaths of Daniel Terry in June, Bob Shortreed in July, and Tom Purdie – on whose shoulder he was used to lean when walking – in October lowered Scott's spirits still further (EJ 1121).[7] His condition in winter 1829 terrified Cadell, who foresaw the 'Magnum Opus' – with only eight volumes edited – left in the lurch (EJ 1119).

17

The Last Years (1830–1832)

Scott dropped his journal from late July 1829 to late May 1830 'because I thought it made me abominably selfish' (Jrnl. 590). There were other distractions. On the early afternoon of 15 February[1] Scott returned to Shandwick Place from court and had some conversation with a Miss Young of Hawick about a sheaf of MS memoirs of her late father, a dissenting minister. Scott had engaged to revise these papers for the elderly lady. It was an act of characteristic civility, which would have gone unrecorded were it not for the fact that while talking to Miss Young he suffered a severe cerebral seizure. He staggered to the drawing room and collapsed apparently choking at his daughter Anne's feet. She was appalled and assumed he had received information that her sister, Walter or Johnnie had died (her first thoughts are an interesting indication of the general level of anxiety in the household). As Scott later recalled to Lockhart, 'I lost the power of articulation or rather of speaking what I wishd to say' (Lett. 11. 297). This speechlessness lasted some ten minutes.

Scott's doctors were called. In the evening, after being bled and cupped, he recovered his faculties. Knowledge of the episode was apparently kept within the family and no physical after-effects were observable, other than what Lockhart describes as 'a nervous twitching about the muscles of the mouth' (Lock. 5. 268). Lockhart also discerned a 'cloudiness' in Scott's prose after the attack (Lock. 5. 255). As John Buchan puts it, 'Scott was suffering now not only from disease but from decay' (JB 322). The entries in the Journal (which resume on 23 May 1830) although cogent are notably thinner in texture, lacking the buoyancy and rich allusiveness of earlier years. This attenuation may be as much the consequence of reduced energy as trauma. Scott was put on a severely lowering diet, his doctors having told him that the attack was 'from the stomach'. His private diagnosis was more honest (as doubtless was theirs): 'It lookd woundy like palsy or apoplexy. Well be it what it will, I can stand it' (Jrnl. 591). It was ominous in the extreme. As he later 'told Cadell, 'the deaths of both my father and mother [were] preceded by a paralytick shock' (*Lett.* 11. 436).

Although he could not but concede that 'I am not the man that I was' (EJ 1158), Scott continued to work at full steam, producing as much as he had in 1829. Within a fortnight he embarked on a long-meditated demonology volume for Murray's 'Family Library'. He was aided by Lockhart, who had originally suggested the scheme to the publisher – to distract Scott from the dangerous exertions of a new full-length novel, as Edgar Johnson shrewdly suggests (EJ 1126). It was the kind of roundabout essay on antiquarian themes which came as easily as talking to Scott. But, despite his longstanding fascination with the subject, Scott was in no condition to enjoy writing even a chatty book on the supernatural. 'I must finish it though for I need money', he grimly noted (the payment – £600 – was to be his own; Jrnl. 591, EJ 1126). The resulting book is a readable work of popular anthropology (one of the many new genres Scott opened up in his amazingly diverse writing career). Shrewdly, Murray published the demonology volume as a Christmas book in 1830 – when public appetite for things ghostly was highest – and it enjoyed a warm reception. Main selling points were the twelve illustrations by George Cruikshank which Murray commissioned. Had Scott been a younger author, he would surely have latched on to the vogue for German supernaturalism which Cruikshank was pioneering.

Over the same period, and again for his private purse, Scott began a Fourth Series of the bestselling *Tales of a Grandfather* (now devoted to French history). It too was published towards the end of 1830, making twelve volumes of the project in four years. Scott was still ploughing ahead with Lardner's history (of which the second volume was published in May 1830) and sundry reviewing chores. Lockhart, particularly, was putting substantial amounts of work his father-in-law's way.

As W. E. K. Anderson points out, these 'by-jobs' were dubiously honest if Scott intended to observe the terms of his agreement with the Trust. In the six years that he worked for them, Scott made £50,000 for his creditors. But he also made some £6,000 for himself – something over £3,000 from *Tales of a Grandfather*, £1,500 from Lardner, £500 from Cadell for *Chronicles of the Canongate*, '£100 or £50 for every lengthy review for the *Quarterly* or *Foreign Quarterly*' (Jrnl. xxvii). The thorniest issue was *Tales of a Grandfather*: 'Scott kept the proceeds for himself, without a word to the Trustees, other than a remark "in a jocular manner" to Gibson, "Remember I do not mean to give you this little Book, I must keep it for myself to pay my current expenses and for my family"' (Jrnl. xxviii).

The discovery that Scott was writing *Tales of a Grandfather* for his own pocket caused consternation among the trustees. Nevertheless, after 'anxious discussion' they did nothing. They could not kill their goose for keeping a few golden eggs to himself. But with his £1,600 income, rent-free accommodation in one of the finest private houses in the Lowlands, and his £1,000 a year income from his pen (including the legitimate stipend from the Magnum Opus), Scott was a very odd kind of bankrupt.

Of course, not even Scott – having sustained a major stroke – could keep up this gruelling literary regime as a sideline to his professional legal work. Something must give. In spring 1830, he made arrangements to retire as Clerk of Court from the end of the summer term. Lockhart records that the move was 'acceptable to the Government' and that Peel reacted courteously to the proposal. Sir William Rae, the Lord Advocate, was also favourable. In addition to a natural solicitude for his old friend's health, there was government pressure to reduce the number of Clerks from six to four (EJ 1127). Sir Robert Dundas would retire with Scott, it was agreed. Scott made his last appearance in court on 10 July 1830. His retirement officially took effect on 12 November.

The terms of Scott's retirement were generous: he would receive an allowance of £864, in recognition of his twenty-four years' service (six of them without remuneration). Scott was slightly disappointed; he had initially expected three-quarters of his salary – £975 (EJ 1147). But he declined Peel's magnanimous offer to raise his pension to full salary level, on the grounds that it would bring 'obloquy' on his friends. Nor did he want to be obliged to the incoming Whig ministry (EJ 1147). Scott cleared his refusal of Peel's offer with the Trust first, punctiliously regarding his income as their property. They 'handsomely' acquiesced in his decision.

Pensioned retirement entailed no great loss. Liberated from attendance at court, he could write (and earn) more. Thanks to the trustees he would have the services of William Laidlaw (once more at Kaeside as Tom Purdie's replacement) as factor and amanuensis, the company of his old friends the Fergusons at Huntly Burn, and annual summer visits from the Lockharts at Chiefswood. All these would add to his comfort, efficiency and productiveness. There were, however, domestic repercussions. Could the Scotts keep up two establishments – one in town and one in the country? Scott was in favour of retrenchment. In March 1830 there had been rows about Anne's overspending her household expenses (Scott believed she had inherited extravagant habits from her mother; Jrnl. 550, EJ 1129). Scott was obliged to ask Cadell for a subvention of £180. On her part, Anne evidently did not relish rustication, as the companion of 'a lame Baronet, nigh sixty years old' and nothing more. She had, evidently, refused all offers of marriage as part of her daughterly duty (EJ 1139). Her comments on the luckier Sophia and Walter were increasingly tart. A clever and frustrated woman, she was resentful at having her narrow orbit narrowed even further by Scott's retirement from Edinburgh. 'We see nobody but the dogs', she complained, with characteristically mordant wit (EJ 1148).

When Scott resolved to retire it was in the hope that his health would pick up. It did not. That summer the Lockharts found him 'jaded and worn' (Lock. 5. 267). Lockhart observed that despite his condition, Scott was neurotically addicted to work: 'Nothing could keep him from toiling many hours daily at his desk.' He would not be distracted (although ingenious ways were tried) and must be humoured, although his perceptions were becoming increasingly unstable. He was convinced that he would soon be free of debt – the six years which Cadell predicted in 1829 had shrunk and continued to shrink in his mind. Wildly optimistic speculations as to earnings speckle the journal in late 1830. 'The year 1833 may probably see me again in possession of my estate', he fondly told himself in December (Jrnl. 614). It was this delusion that drove him. In October, the trust paid a second dividend of 3s. It was a magnificent achievement, but only half as much as the first dividend, and left the original debt still less than half-paid.[2] Scott was humoured in his delusion 'that he had already all but cleared off his encumbrances' and he resumed entertaining at Abbotsford 'as in the golden days of 1823 and 1824' (Lock. 5. 268).

Physically Scott's exertions were taking a terrible toll. On 28 October 1830 he told Sophia 'I believe I have grown older in the last year than in twenty before' (EJ 1146). There was another stroke in November – 'another slight touch of apoplexy', Lockhart calls it (Lock. 5. 287). Judging by other evidence (not least the quality of the Journal entries) it was calamitous. As Anderson observes (and as his faithful transcriptions only too painfully show) 'the entries which follow [the second stroke], full of omissions and mis-spellings, muddled and almost illegible, are clear about one thing only: this second warning must soon be succeeded by incapacity and death' (Jrnl. 612).

As Edgar Johnson records, the stroke occurred in the middle of November, two days after the fall of the Duke of Wellington's administration and the obnoxiously liberal Earl Grey becoming Prime Minister. It is a fair assumption that excitement (and possibly too much consolatory whisky) played a part in the episode. Scott was alarmed to hysterical pitch by the politics of the time. Since 1827 the Tory party had been in disarray. In August 1830 a new Parliament promised unprecedented reforms (EJ 1158). There was fear of further bank failures and sporadic violence was reported all over the British Isles. Europe was in upheaval. Walter, recovered in health, had been stationed with his hussars at Nottingham and Sheffield in spring 1830, charged with keeping the agitated workers in order (EJ 1130). He received the inevitable death threats from 'Captain Swing' (EJ 1149). His son's being in the front line of the civil conflict inflamed Scott's apprehensions as to general rebellion and reform.

Scott gives a brief account of his November stroke in one of the last summary accounts in the journal for that year. After taking a glass of whisky (with Lord Meadowbank, as Johnson guesses) Scott retired and sank stupefied on his dressing room floor. Some time later he came to himself. Not even his family were told of the episode, although he consulted his doctors. They again told him his condition could be stabilized by a strict dietary regimen. Scott was not duped. The biographer of Swift, he was terrified that he too would 'linger on an idiot and a show' (Jrnl. 615). But he was even more terrified by the financial consequences if he did not overwork. Distress was heightened by a 'constant increase of my lameness. The thigh joint knee joint and ancle joint' (Jrnl. 615). If madness was one horror, destitution a second, being a total cripple (something that had haunted him since childhood) was a third.

The subsequent events of December 1830 have been subjected to considerable obfuscation in Lockhart's biography. The motives for concealment clearly originate in a collective guilt among Scott's family and advisers for not having done more to prolong his life. The starting point is the new novel, *Count Robert of Paris* as it was to be. Scott had the idea for a story set in Byzantium as early as February 1826 (Lock. 4. 491). He had the 'new novel' (Jrnl. 548) clearly in his sights in April 1829, at a period when (following *The Fair Maid of Perth*) Cadell was hungry for such wares. The first mention of the 'Romance of the Lower Empire' is found in Cadell's notebook for 20 May 1829 (Gamerschlag, *SSL* 97).[3]

It seems, however, that by mid-1830 Cadell, Ballantyne and Lockhart (all of whom knew about the February stroke) were conspiring to dissuade Scott from the labour of a new novel, which they felt might either kill him, or disable him from preparation of the all-important 'Magnum Opus', now approaching its twentieth volume. As Lockhart records, Cadell came to Scott in early September 1830 and informed him that by 'October the debt will be reduced to the sum of £60,000, half of its original amount' (Lock. 5. 269). This was an optimistic assessment, clearly intended to relieve Scott so that he might give up his exhausting range of writing commitments and concentrate on the annotation, which he found easy and therapeutic. But, as Lockhart goes on to record, 'Cadell found his friend . . . by no means disposed to adopt such views'. 'Ingeniously and kindly' (as Lockhart, with Cadell over his shoulder, phrases it) the publisher then suggested that, if he wanted extra work, Scott might go on to catalogue the rare and interesting items in his library – work which, as he perceived, had a soothing effect on Scott. He offered £750 for these 'Reliquiae Trottcosienses' (money which would, of course, be Scott's own).

This new suggestion caught Scott's fancy, 'but after a few days he said he found this was not sufficient – that he should proceed in it during *horae subcesivae*, but bend himself to the composition of a romance, founded on a story which he had more than once told cursorily already, and for which he had been revolving the various titles of Robert of the Isle – Count Robert de l'Isle – and Count Robert of Paris. There was nothing to be said in reply to the decisive announcement of this purpose. The usual agreements were drawn out; and the Tale was begun' (Lock. 5. 269).

Lockhart and Cadell (Lockhart's accomplice in the biography) are so unreliable about this section of the life that one has to be suspicious. There is a large gap in Scott's Journal between 5 September and 20 December. But in the 5 September entry, Scott refers to the above meeting with Cadell. It seems that the publisher's main business was something Lockhart omits to mention – namely that Cadell tried to persuade Scott to part with a half share of the *Waverley* novel copyrights after *Quentin Durward* so as to complete his (Cadell's) set (Jrnl. 611). Scott was wary of this proposal. He in fact held out against Cadell until July 1831, when he made the reluctant publisher cough up £10,000 for the property that he lusted after. In the same (5 September) entry Scott mentions in passing his intention to write 'four novels betwixt 1830 and 1834' (intending, apparently, to finish *Count Robert of Paris* by 31 December 1830).

Scott, as letters suggest, had actually been working on *Count Robert of Paris* for some time (HG 292, EJ 1143). On 6 September, he wrote to Cadell agreeing to the 'Reliquiae', but insisting that it not 'appear till after the publication of *Count Robert of Paris*' (HG 293). He was determined to write the novel, it seems, so as to prove to himself that he had not collapsed mentally. It was a matter of pride to him, and on such things he was always peremptory. He may also have resented the transparent attempts to manipulate him 'for his own good'. On his part, Cadell was painfully aware that Scott was no longer the novelist that he had been. A poor new novel, he feared, would cast a fatal blight over the 'Magnum Opus' (and at the very least might fatally distract Scott from keeping up with the monthly printing schedule). He was also aware that he had committed himself on 21 March 1828 to paying £4,200 apiece for three new novels which increasingly looked as if they might be substandard (*PLB* 362).

The 'slight touch of apoplexy' occurred in November and seems to have made Scott even more determined to write *Count Robert of Paris* (and keep Cadell to his rash agreement). By the end of November 1830 he had written three chapters for the printer (Gamerschlag, 97). Although they did not know about the second stroke, Scott's friends and acquaintances had observed that he was thinner, more distracted and less articulate in his speech. They could not but detect the gross deterioration in his handwriting. Cadell, watching Scott like a hawk, must have been surer than ever by December 1830 that Scott would never again write a novel worth £4,200 of his money.

Cadell evidently persuaded James Ballantyne to deliver a damning verdict on the opening sample of proofs which Scott sent them around the beginning of December. Cadell while reporting Ballantyne's devastating opinion diplomatically restricted himself to mild criticisms (*PLB* 365–6). Scott evidently suspected he was being disingenuous. The intention was to discourage Scott by a two-pronged attack from continuing with *Count Robert of Paris*. But James's 'candour' (as Scott drily called it in the journal; Jrnl. 616) produced a much more violent reaction than was desired. Scott wrote back to Ballantyne on 8 December stoically accepting the criticism as to the inferiority (and unpublishability) of *Count Robert of Paris* and adding the bombshell: 'My present idea is to go abroad for a few months, if I hold together as long. So ended the fathers of the Novel Fielding [who died in Portugal] and Smollett [who died in Italy] and it would be no unprofessional finish for . . . Walter Scott' (*Lett.* 11. 432). Clearly unsure how much the two men were conspiring, he wrote the same day to Cadell, rubbing in the same ultimatum: 'I have lost it is plain, the power of interesting the country by surprizes [?] and ought in justice to all parties to retire while I have some credit . . . I may perhaps take a trip to the continent for a year or two if I find Othellos occupation gone rather Othellos *reputation*' (*Lett.* 11. 433). Scott was calling Cadell's bluff. If the publisher would not let him write fiction, heigh ho, he would leave for a sunny clime and let his copyrights pay off his debts and the 'Magnum Opus' (now just under half-way through, with a twentieth volume in December) could go hang. Cadell would lose tens of thousands.

Cadell and Ballantyne took terrible fright at losing their principal asset, as Scott evidently intended they should. James instantly recanted his criticisms (EJ 1155). Nothing was further from his mind than any suggestion that Scott's powers were failing. On his part, Cadell also replied post haste: 'You have taken the matter too seriously... We agree that laying aside Count Paris is out of the question.' (Cadell, as it happened, had a number of further tricks up his sleeve as to the novel, but he kept those to himself.)

Now firmly in the ascendant, Scott wrote a letter on 12 December, confiding to Cadell (what he may already have deduced) that he had recently had another stroke, and that it had made him touchy about criticism reflecting on his mental abilities. But he carefully understated the episode: 'One day when I had a friend with me . . . I had a slight vertigo when going to my bed and fell down in my dressing-room though but for one instant I wrote to Dr Abercromby . . . in consequence of his advice, I have restricted myself yet further and have cut off the Segar and almost half of the mountain [dew]' (*Lett.* 11. 437). Reading this, someone less canny than Cadell might well assume that Scott was confessing to a drinking bout – many Scotsmen have an occasional slight vertigo after over-indulgence in the mountain dew.

It was a masterly power play by Scott. He had both confessed the November stroke to Cadell, and at the same time elicited from him and Ballantyne written assurances that he was in no way disabled. His negotiating position was as strong as before. His ascendancy was crowned on 17 December when the trustees unanimously adopted the resolution that 'Sir Walter Scott be requested to accept of his furniture, plate, linens, paintings, library, and curiosities of every description, as the best means the creditors have of expressing their very high sense of his most honourable conduct, and in grateful acknowledgement for the unparalleled and most successful exertions he has made, and continues to make for them' (Jrnl. 613). He could now, as he said, 'eat with my own spoons, and study my own books.' The property which the trust had made over to him was worth, as Scott calculated, £10,000 and would enable him to leave Anne and Charles provided for (Lock. 5. 293, 295). This was immensely gratifying to him, and he immediately began a flurry of will-making and letters to Walter on the disposition of legacies. He was now more sure than ever that he would be entirely free and easy by 1833. There can be little doubt that the trust's gift originated with Cadell, who had passed on to them the alarming news that Scott was seriously contemplating leaving Scotland. The gift was designed to anchor Scott to Abbotsford and his library by bonds of ownership. And, in his library, he should continue working on the 'Magnum Opus'. When the forty-eighth volume was finished, then he might go off and die in the sun.

Had the trust and Cadell had Scott's interests at heart they would have encouraged him to go at once abroad and recuperate, and forget all idea of clearing himself in two years. There was, as it happened, a third and even more calamitous stroke to come in April 1831. It could well have been averted, or postponed, by a regime of sun and relaxation. Lockhart, with manifest bad faith, congratulates Cadell for his benevolence in encouraging Scott to continue with *Count Robert of Paris*. 'If we did wrong,' he quotes Cadell as saying, 'we did it for the best: we felt that to have spoken out fairly [about the defects of *Count Robert of Paris*] would have been to make ourselves the bearers of a death warrant.' Lockhart adds, 'I hope there are not many men who would have acted otherwise in their [Cadell's and Ballantyne's] painful situation' (Lock. 5. 297). This is extremely dishonest. The dilemma was not between Scott's writing *Count Robert of Paris* (the slow death warrant) or being told the truth about his impaired abilities (the instant death warrant). It was between him leaving Scotland and all writing labour for the sake of his health, or staying behind to grind like Samson in Gaza at the 'Magnum Opus'. What Cadell (backed by Ballantyne, Lockhart and the trust) should have done, had they had Scott's best interests at heart, was to confirm that *Count Robert of Paris* showed clear symptoms of mental decay, persuade Scott to give up all literary work and recuperate abroad, and hire someone else to do the apparatus for the 'Magnum Opus'.

COUNT ROBERT OF PARIS

Once he had assent from Cadell and Ballantyne Scott forged ahead with *Count Robert of Paris*. By mid-March 1831 he had the second volume finished and was half way through the third volume on 6 April (Gamerschlag, *SSL* 104). Writing was a struggle and he needed considerable help. Laidlaw was again his amanuensis (Scott's fingers were chilblained, and his penmanship had deteriorated). There was great uncertainty whether with the impending General Election and the attendant Reform uproar anyone would want to read novels, even by Sir Walter Scott (EJ 1174). Meanwhile Cadell and Ballantyne were reading the proofsheets with 'increasing anxiety' (Gamerschlag, *SSL* 105). Their anxiety peaked into panic when they encountered Scott's 'highly offensive' descriptions of Brenhilda's pregnancy (Gamerschlag, *SSL* 106).

At meetings on 9–10 April Scott declared himself adamant against removing 'the incident'. The following weekend, however, he had yet another stroke. On his recovery, he continued with the novel as best he could. There ensued yet more to make Cadell and Ballantyne nervous. Scott now intended the third volume to climax on a combat to the death between Anna Comnena (the Emperor Alexius's daughter) and Brenhilda – still in her interesting condition. On 6 May Cadell warned Scott that this episode 'will injure all your work [he meant the Magnum Opus] to the extent of many thousand pounds' (Gamerschlag, *SSL* 109). Under this pressure, Scott put the novel aside in favour of *Tales of a Grandfather*, which he was concurrently dictating to Laidlaw. In June–July, his thoughts turned towards a new novel, *Castle Dangerous*.

Scott never finished *Count Robert of Paris*. By mid 1831 it was clear that he was so incapacitated that solving the narrative problems of the final volume (more particularly, the women's gladiatorial combat) was beyond him. The final trip to the Mediterranean intervened. While the Scotts were waiting to embark in London Lockhart suggested that the complete *Castle Dangerous* and the incomplete *Count Robert of Paris* be knit together as a fourth series of 'Tales of my Landlord'. Scott duly resurrected Jedediah. Meanwhile, Cadell and Lockhart conspired together and 'decided that once the author was safely out of the way on his trip to the south they would go over his last two novels again and correct them according to their own lights' (Gamerschlag, *SSL* 113). In October 1831 Lockhart (who had not travelled with the Scotts) began his revisions to *Count Robert of Paris* and *Castle Dangerous* and rewrote Scott's 'Jedediah introduction'. All Lockhart's improvements were kept from the increasingly ill and confused Scott. *Count Robert of Paris* was revised so heavily that, as Gamerschlag judges, 'it cannot any more be called Scott's.' Nor can one accept Lockhart's declaration that his own contributions to the novel were 'merely editorial, all the essential achievement is Scott's own' (EJ 1207). In fact, Gamerschlag estimates, 'nearly one-third of *Count Robert of Paris* was rewritten by Lockhart against the express wishes of its original author who, in the end, almost certainly never realized what had become of his novel' (Gamerschlag, *SSL* 93).

Abortion as it was, *Count Robert of Paris* turned out to be an influential work. In terms of literary history, it emerges as the first of the nineteenth century's muscular novels. In the character of the Varangian Hereward, and the clash of Saxon heroism and imperial Byzantine dissipation, Scott lays the ground for Charles Kingsley's *Hereward the Wake* and *Hypatia*. *Count Robert of Paris* deals with the clash of two huge ideologies, the classical world, now in decay and capable of supporting itself only by guile and conspiracy, and the crusades, with their new chivalrous energy. As always, Scott is firmly on the side of chivalry. But at the heart of *Count Robert of Paris* is a core of Gibbonian uncertainty. Scott was nervous about the demise of his own class. The Tories had ruled, triumphantly – imperially, one might say – for twenty years. Opposed by the apparently irresistible forces of Reform, the Tory hegemony was crumbling. But did it not deserve to fall? In *Count Robert of Paris* the Holy Roman Empire is a shadow of its former imperial self; full of grand memory, but impotent and corrupt at its core (as Canning represented the rotten core of conservatism). Images of degeneration proliferate in the novel. We are told that 'the race of the Greeks was no longer to be seen, even in its native country, unmixed or in absolute purity' (1. 219). Shortly after their arrival at Constantinople, Count Robert and his lady, Brenhilda, discover:

a party of heathen Scythians [who] presented the deformed features of the demons they were said to worship – flat noses with expanded nostrils, which seemed to admit the sight to their very brain; faces which extended rather in breadth than length, with strange unintellectual eyes placed in the extremity; figures short and dwarfish, yet garnished with legs and arms of astonishing sinewy strength, disproportioned to their bodies. (1. 219)

The late-imperial Scythians on whom Robert and Brenhilda look with scorn are only one step up from the wholly degenerate organ-utan or 'man of the woods', Sylvanus. Sylvanus is the most extraordinary creation in the novel and figures in scenes of nightmarish and surreal ingenuity, such as that in which he strangles Agelastes in full philosophizing flow. There are other garish conceptions in *Count Robert of Paris* – the tiger in the bedroom, for instance, or Ursel's pain on having his dungeon blindness lifted (a kind of reverse stroke). All these are as strange as anything Scott created. Although *Count Robert of Paris* is undoubtedly marred by Scott's post-traumatic 'clouded' style, and watered down by Lockhart's 'improvements', it remains Scott's most powerful exercise in grotesquerie.

1831

Lockhart complains that most of the journal in 1831 is too 'medicinal' to quote in a biography. Scott's brain was increasingly clouded, his voice – as he put it – 'sunk', and his gait encumbered. A prosthetic device – or brace – was acquired in February from a 'skilful mechanist' (EJ 1169): it proved to be of rather dubious use. Scott could now manage only half-a-mile or so on foot and two miles on his pony, Douce Davie. In Edinburgh that winter Scott was reduced to making social calls in a sedan chair. Even his pen 'stammered' when he wrote. It was now certain that he had suffered a 'paralytic touch' (Jrnl. 621). He did not delude himself that death was far off.

Thanks to the (somewhat forced) generosity of the trustees, Scott had something to leave after death. At Christmas 1830 he informed Walter that he was drawing up his will, which he duly did on 4 February. He deposited the document not with his lawyer or Lockhart, but with Cadell (Lock. 5. 306), putting the well-being of his surviving family in the rapacious publisher's hands. The will contained bequests to the amount of £5,000 executed via Walter, who had the security of the furniture of Abbotsford for making various small payments to immediate family, of which the largest were £2,000 each to Anne and Charles (EJ 1160).

Scott, despite Cadell's desperate attempts to restrain him, continued to overwork and to excite himself about the political crisis. His Toryism had reached the point of mania. Infected by her father's excitement, Anne feared in February 1831 that 'Captain Swing' was about to descend on Abbotsford and put it to the torch (EJ 1163). Walter was meanwhile opposing Swing at Sheffield with his hussars and the naked sword. Throughout the year, Scott's imagination ran wild. In his Journal, in October 1831, he had visions of the Royalists retreating north to the Scottish Borders with 'the Princess Vittoria... setting up the banner of England [!] with the Duke of W[ellington] as Dictator' (Jrnl. 664). Scott's mind recurred frequently to 1792 and Braxfield's short way with radicals. Repression was one remedy. The other – more humane remedies – were income tax (of which Scott was an early and rational advocate) and military-police service by the middle classes of the kind he had undertaken himself in the militia as a young man. Somewhat reluctantly, Scott conceded 'I am too old to fight' (Jrnl. 644).

In early March 1831 Scott was requested by friends, including Alexander Pringle of Whytbank and the Duke of Buccleuch, to speak at an anti-Reform meeting at Selkirk. Local feeling in Selkirkshire had been heightened by a new severity in the salmon-poaching laws (Scott, of course, had a long stretch of the Tweed in his estate; EJ 1159). Politically incautious, it was madness from a medical point of view for Scott to attend such a function. Excitement was dangerous and might even be fatal. Scott's strokes invariably coincided with some unusual stimulus to his mind. Although he suspected he was being used as a 'catspaw', Scott nonetheless acceded to his friends' request. He wrote a powerful speech that – to his joy – could not 'be said to smell of the apoplexy' (Jrnl. 636). But in the event he was not called on to deliver it. There were only six present at the meeting, and Scott kept his peace.

Silence was one thing, absence another. He would not desert what he took to be his place of duty. There was another meeting of freeholders (i.e. voters) later in March at Jedburgh, where he had held his Sheriff's Assizes for thirty years. Athough Anne frantically begged him not to go (EJ 1165), he insisted on being present and on proposing one of the Tory resolutions. But he did so 'in a tone so low, and with such hesitation in utterance, that only a few detached passages were intelligible to the bulk of the audience' (Lock. 5. 313). He got lost in meandering reflections which infuriated his disenfranchised (and if Scott had his way never to be enfranchised) hearers – 'unwashed artificers', as he scornfully termed them (Jrnl. 641).

The outcome was disastrous and was to haunt Scott to his last glimmer of conscious life. 'My friends', he said, 'I am old and failing, and you think me very full of silly prejudices, but I have seen a good deal of public men, and thought a good deal of public affairs in my day, and I can't help suspecting that the manufacturers of this new constitution are like a parcel of schoolboys taking to pieces a watch . . . in the conceit that they can put it together again far better than the old watchmaker.' This provoked more furious outbursts. Scott put his resolution and turned to the noisy rabble with the dismissal 'I regard your gabble no more than the geese on the green' (Lock. 5. 314). On leaving he returned the hisses of the audience with an icy 'Moriturus, vos saluto.'[4] On 22 March, the first Reform Bill (or as Scott called it, 'Revolution Bill'; EJ 1167) passed its second reading, by one vote.

'It is vain to mourn what cannot be mended', he declared (Lock. 5. 316). But he continued to fret.

On 17 April Scott suffered a violent stroke in his dressing room, after which he hovered between life and death for three hours. The family were summoned, evidently thinking it might be the end. It was not easy for Walter, who was delayed for ten days by civil insurrection in Sheffield (EJ 1173). Nor was it easy for Sophia, who was recovering from a bout of rheumatic fever. Least of all was it easy for Anne, who recorded that her father, on his recovery, 'is irritable to a degree that is dreadful' (EJ 1173). Scott's doctors bled and blistered him, and lowered his diet still further. They advised the insertion of a seton in his neck, to drain off fluid. Understandably, Scott put off the dreadful operation, and submitted only when Walter insisted. 'I cannot hold out against my son' (Lock. 5. 330 – Jrnl. has 'against every one'). The treatment was agony. On 27 April he observed that 'dying like an Indian under tortures is no joke' (EJ 1173). That he was dying he was sure. 'The plough is coming to the end of the furrow', he wrote on 4 May (Jrnl. 651). He toyed with ideas of suicide (EJ 1177).

Meanwhile things went from bad to worse with politics. On General Election day at Jedburgh on 18 May, three troops of dragoons were called out to keep order. Scott was spat at, abused and pelted with stones. His staunchly anti-Reform relative, Henry Scott (who had tried to persuade him to keep away), was nonetheless re-elected – 'for the last time, I suppose', Scott sardonically noted (Jrnl. 656). 'Troja fuit', he added. His carriage left Jedburgh followed by hoots and stones. The mob's shout of 'Burke Sir Walter' stuck indelibly in Scott's mind, and was to resurface almost to his dying hour in dreams and delirium. Nonetheless, he stoically shrugged it off in the journal: 'Much obliged to the bra[ve] lads of Jeddart'. At the end of May, Scott sustained another, milder attack which left him temporarily speechless (EJ 1179). The seton, which he had agreed to on Walter's insistence, was inserted at this period.

Incredibly, Scott was still forging ahead with *Castle Dangerous*. He confided its outline to Lockhart, shortly after JGL's arrival at Abbotsford in May. Like *Kenilworth*, it would be a topographical work, based on Douglas Castle during its heyday in the fourteenth century. Scott began writing in late June. By 3 July (EJ 1183) he had completed the first volume. Cadell came through with a £1,200 advance five days later, and Scott proposed finishing the whole work by August. For the first time Ballantyne was not consulted as critic or adviser. The split between the two men was now complete (originally, Scott intended that Ballantyne should not even be the printer, but he finally relented; EJ 1186). After July 'They never met again in this world' (Lock. 5. 340). It was partly politics: Ballantyne and his paper were Whig and had espoused Reform. But so was Cadell a Whig. The main offence was Ballantyne's wounding criticism of *Count Robert of Paris*.

To prepare for the new novel Lockhart (who had arrived back from London on 13 July) took Scott on an expedition to the Douglas castle in Lanarkshire ('which he had never seen but once when a schoolboy'; Lock.

5. 340). A vivid and movingly pathetic description is given of the jaunt in the *Life*. As Lockhart recalled, 'he seemed constantly to be setting tasks to his memory.' The visit inspired 'some passages in *Castle Dangerous* which might almost have been written at the same time with Lammermoor' (Lock. 5. 344). He finished off the narrative in a couple of weeks, dictating rapidly to Laidlaw, racked all the while with rheumatic pains. The narrative was completed by the second week in September.

In design *Castle Dangerous* represents a nice circularity of subject-matter. Scott's novel writing career began with *Waverley*, a novel whose subject is English victory and English chivalry (in the person of Colonel Whitefoord). His career ends with a novel chronicling a Scottish victory (under Bruce and Douglas) and chivalrous behaviour by the victorious party. There is combat by champions, but not to the death. Honourable withdrawal is permitted to the vanquished English. *Castle Dangerous* is the final point on Scott's drift towards a mildly aggrieved Scottish chauvinism. The mutilated Ursula speaks for him when she says. 'If *your* [English] friends, whom I should term oppressors and tyrants, take our land and our lives, seize our castles and confiscate our property, you must confess that the rough laws of war indulge *mine* with the privilege of retaliation' (CD 306). Scott's cycle of fiction thus concludes with a hurrah for Scotland and 'the privilege of retaliation'.

Castle Dangerous, like the other very late works, bears signs of Scott's declining powers, and the disastrous strokes of November and April. It opens in the by now sadly familiar 'clouded' style. There are interminably long looping sentences (up to 170 words in places) which veer all over the place, and forget where they started. There are dialogues which go on too long and ramble away from the plot. The plot itself gets lost, and subplots (such as the quarrel between De Walton and De Valence) are introduced, only to be dropped. The spectre knight is the most unconvincing of his kind in all of Scott. All readers will guess that it is Sir James Douglas in disguise. *Castle Dangerous* starts with one hero and heroine and ends with another set. Principal characters are left off stage too long.

Nevertheless, through all this cloudiness shafts of brilliant clarity break through. Notably clear is chapter 7, with its superbly detailed description of the medieval Scottish hunt, written in as crisp a style as Scott in his heyday. Winter is the leitmotif of *Castle Dangerous*, a novel set between February and March, the bleakest Scottish months. There are some wonderful descriptions of raw morning mist, and smoky unwarming fires. One feels Scott aching to get away to warmer climates – even though he might die there. Perhaps he knew he could not stand another Scottish winter.

Doctors, family and friends also doubted that Scott could stand another winter at Abbotsford. The first thought was to make an overland tour to Naples and visit Charles, passing through Weimar and the Alps. There was discussion between Lockhart, Cadell and powerful political friends like Croker. Eventually, their discussion came to the ears of the amiable busy-body and retired naval officer, Captain Basil Hall. He went in person to the

Admiralty, and confided the fears of Scott's family to the government. The admiralty declared itself willing to give Sir Walter free passage to Malta in one of their warships, the *Barham*. He could travel on from there to Naples where Charles – now a twenty-five-year-old bachelor in poorish health himself – had been appointed to the British legation.

'The entire country rang with applause at the generous offer,' Edgar Johnson records (EJ 1191). It was the more generous in coming from Scott's political rivals, the party of Reform under Lord Grey. Scott, who was deeply gratified, 'exclaimed that things were yet in the hands of gentlemen' (Lock. 5. 348). Malta was a place he had always longed to see. He had also, ever since Cadell's rash £12,600 offer in March 1828, intended to write a novel set there. Scott's finances were in reasonably good order, thanks to the Magnum Opus. On the strength of its sales Cadell could be drawn on (although he was later to protest vociferously at Sir Walter's drafts). Nonetheless Scott was more sanguine about his finances than the situation warranted. 'It was about this time', Lockhart notes, 'that we observed Sir Walter beginning to entertain the notion that his debts were paid off. By degrees, dwelling on this fancy, he believed in it fully and implicitly. It was a gross delusion – but neither Cadell nor anyone else had the heart to disturb it by any formal statement of figures' (Lock. 5. 352–3).

Scott secured a £500 line of credit from the Trust. Walter arranged leave to accompany his father. This was a great assistance since Lockhart could not get away from the *Quarterly* during the Reform hurly-burly. Scott's favourite child, Sophia, could not leave her three children one of whom, Johnny, was terminally ill. There was, however, the possibility that some of the Lockharts might join up with the Scott party on the return journey, overland. It was thought for a while that Scott's daughter-in-law, Jane, would accompany her husband. But this fell through at a late date because she was, as she said, too prone to sea-sickness (she may have been anxious about likely rows between the Scott children, who did not get on well together). Anne would thus serve as nurse. She, however, was not well. Her stomach gave her trouble whenever she travelled and she slowed the family's progress down to London (Sultana, 12). With two invalids it did not promise to be an easy trip.

THE LAST VOYAGE

The decision to transport Scott across Europe to avoid the hardship of a Scottish winter in his own home was a grievous error. The consequences were disastrous not just for him, but for the members of his family who accompanied him. Walter and Anne quarrelled (she died, exhausted, shortly after the trip). The easier-going Charles suffered horribly from the rows and his own feeble health deteriorated under the strain. Flattered as he was by official largesse, Scott thought the trip ominous. He alluded again to Smollett and Fielding – fathers of the British novel who had died on final journeys to the sun.[5]

Before he left, there was a last visit from Wordsworth. It was a noble gesture from one poet to another, and inspired Wordsworth's lyric 'Yarrow Revisited', written a few days after their excursion by carriage to Newark Castle. The Scott party with Lockhart in charge arrived in London, via Rokeby, on 28 September. Scott looked on things with the acuity of a man who might not see them (or old friends like Morritt) again. On arrival, they were told that the *Barham*'s departure had been put back a week. The capital was seething over the Reform Bill, which had been rejected in the House of Lords on 8 October. Riots were a nightly event. Scott saw with his own eyes the Duke of Newcastle's house after it had been attacked by infuriated pro-Reform agitators. England was undergoing, Scott thought, 'one of those crises by which Providence reduces nations to their original Elements' (Jrnl. 669). More passionately, when his old friend Dr Ferguson came to take farewell, in London, Scott shouted 'England is no longer a place for an honest man. I shall not live to find it so; you may' (Lock. 5. 371). He expected the Reform Bill to be voted down, Parliament to be dissolved, and all hell to break loose. Walter (who had left the party at Rokeby to return to his military unit) was still cracking radicals' heads in the north (there had been serious riots at Derby and Nottingham). He only reached London on 17 October and there was some doubt up to the last minute as to whether his four months' leave would be withdrawn on account of the state of national emergency.

While they passed their time in London, Scott seems to have been social and even to have enjoyed himself. Dr Abercrombie, his Scottish physician, had advised against literary work. But Scott could not restrain himself. There was plenty on his plate. In addition to revision and annotation to the poetry (for a 12-volume supplement to the 'Magnum Opus'), Cadell had acquired the copyright of the 'Essays', or prose works, which would make up another multi-volume supplement (Sultana, 10). Scott's editing chores stretched out – even at one volume a month – for years ahead. He and Cadell had now recovered all his copyrights: a unique achievement for a writer who had been so prolific (and in his youth so careless of his property).

In the idle days in London Scott decanted his learning into the notes for the 'Magnum Opus' *Woodstock*. He was now writing his journal again. (Cadell had offered £1,000 for the copyright, thinking it would make a travel book.) He was contemplating another volume of 'Lives of the Novelists', which had proved successful when gathered into a volume in 1825. His main problem was physical debility. His voice, Ferguson thought, 'was so thick and indistinct as to make it very difficult for any but those accustomed to hear it to gather his meaning' (Lock. 5. 372). And his face was increasingly paralysed-looking. The condition of his brain continued to worry him most. He detected 'muddiness of mind' in himself and he was prone to uncontrollable fits of anger. 'There is beside some mental confusion,' he

noted, 'with the extent of which I am not perhaps fully acquainainted [sic].
I am perhaps setting . . . like a day that has been admired as a fine one
the light of it sets down amid mists and storms' (Jrnl. 659). In a spirit of
final valediction he wrote a general preface, in which he declared:
'The gentle reader is acquainted, that these are, in all probability, the last
tales which it will be the lot of the Author to submit to the public.' In this
preface he alluded publicly to his hope that his mind would not go before
his body.

The *Barham* was a frigate and a fifty-gun ship of war. The commander was
Captain Hugh Pigot – who impressed Scott very favourably and whom he
may have marked down as a possible husband for Anne. Much of the fretful
business on shore before embarkation was smoothed by the ever serviceable Captain Basil Hall. Scott admired such efficiency. It reminded him of
Cadell, who was similarly serviceable. He told Hall, 'If I had been in my
excellent friend Cadell's hands during all the course of my writing for the
public, I should now undoubtedly have been worth a couple of hundred
thousand pounds, instead of having to work myself to pieces to get out of
debt' (EJ 1199). But instead of really useful men like Cadell and Hall, he
had been mishandled by Constable and the Ballantynes.

There was a tedious delay of a week at Portsmouth, where Scott held
court in a small way. Meanwhile Parliament was prorogued for a month to
allow the Whigs to bring a third Reform Bill. The *Barham* finally sailed 29
October and reached Malta on 22 November, having voyaged past Trafalgar
and Cape St Vincent (stirring experiences for patriots like Scott). The
Scotts were barred from landing at Gibraltar because of the raging cholera
epidemic and – once arrived at Malta – the party was delayed another ten
days at Fort Manoel. Scott examined a new volcanic landmass, Graham
Island, between Malta and Sicily. As President of the Edinburgh Royal
Society it was his responsibility to report on it for his fellow scientists. Scott
was enlivened by these new sights and by the many visible remains of the
Knights of Malta. He was charmed by the 'Gothic' aspects of the island,
which he felt would be more to his taste than the Graeco-Roman classicism
to come later in the tour. Scott was at this stage in good health partly
(Donald Sultana suggests) because the abstemious Pigot forbade drinking
and cigar-smoking on board his ship.

Having undergone their period of quarantine (where Scott did some
serious thinking for a new story, *The Siege of Malta*) the party was installed in
a converted palazzo of the Knights, now called Beverley's Hotel. Scott had
the freedom of the island, and enjoyed the status of its most famous
resident visitor. He was offered every courtesy by order of the (currently
absent) governor. Through it all he stalked like the ghost of the author of
Waverley. He wore his Lowland plaid trews and carried his staff like a
shepherd's crook. In Malta Scott was described as 'an old gentleman'
(although he was just sixty) and he described himself (echoing Lear) as an
'old lame man' (Sultana, 50). His principal host in Malta was the congenial
John Hookham Frere, diplomat and poet.

Scott evidently rather overindulged in food, drink, company. He lost his temper when his daughter attempted to regulate his diet and restrict his frequent dining out. Their relationship was obviously tense. In his journal, Scott refers critically to her 'spirit of satire', and she may have had a sharp tongue when her father disobeyed the medical advisers she approved of. Her own health was delicate. Drink seems to have been particularly dangerous for Scott, and he was evidently encouraged by Cadell's offer of £1,000 into working too hard on the journal. He suffered a series of malaises from 5 December onwards. He nonetheless recovered from these reverses, and was to recover even more strikingly later in Naples. But there was a cumulative increase of confusion in his brain. His writing betrayed a symptomatic 'cloudiness of words and arrangement' (Sultana, 59). His hold on idiom and on long-stored literary allusion was still sure. But he forgot names (even that of the 'Irish lady', his friend Maria Edgeworth).

Scott was anxious to get to Charles in Naples where he would, in a sense, be at home. On his part, Charles was worried about receiving his father and was keen for him to come quickly, before stringent quarantine restrictions were imposed. (Charles had also been recalled to London, which was an added complication.) Anne and Walter were meanwhile squabbling. Walter was alarmed by reports which he heard about disorder in England and could not but feel that he had deserted his post under fire. His manners were rough. Anne complained about his swearing at waiters and his preference for dining with fellow officers at the garrison mess. Her health continued fragile. Perhaps, too, she was disappointed in the progress of her relationship with Captain Pigot (Sultana, 59). Scott, on his part, was worried, as always, about money.

On 13 December they sailed in the *Barham* for Naples and arrived on the 17th. Anne suffered horribly from her stomach disorder on the voyage. Charles was evidently shocked at the wasted appearance of his father when he first saw him. Scott, however, rallied and under the auspices of his younger son even appeared in the Neapolitan Court for a presentation to King Ferdinand II. He was decked out in 'the uniform of a brigadier-general in the ancient Body-Guard of Scotland – a dress of light green, with gold embroidery, assigned to those *Archers* by George IV at the termination of his northern progress in 1822' (Lock. 5. 390). It must have been a sight, and was evidently satirized. He remained chronically anxious about money and feared that the political upheaval might produce another trade catastrophe, such as that of 1825 which had ruined him. In fact, his last two 'apoplectic' novels were selling brilliantly, as was the Magnum Opus. On being informed in December of this fact, Scott declared 'I think it is the publick that is mad' (EJ 1228).

On 16 January came the sad news that Johnnie had finally died. He was just ten. Scott took the news stoically. 'Against all remonstrances', he was writing a full-length novel called *The Siege of Malta* and was well into its second volume by February. He was also jotting down a shorter tale called 'Il Bizarro'. Although Lockhart hoped that 'Neither of these novels will ever see the light' (Lock. 5. 391), *The Siege of Malta* has, in fact, been ingeniously exhumed by Donald Sultana. According to Sultana the story was planned to feature 'a range of original and swift-moving scenes, marked by heroism, tenderness, drama and intrigue in action.' It was compared by Scott himself to *Ivanhoe*, 'but perhaps [is] more reminiscent of the oriental atmosphere of *The Tales of the Crusaders*' (Sultana, x).

Scott undertook research into the island's fortifications, and began writing his new novel in late November and early December. When he arrived at Naples on 17 December, Scott had about a quarter finished *The Siege of Malta* (Sultana, 54). Cadell offered £2,000 for the first edition, although he privately thought it would be 'next to a miracle' if the new novel were publishable (Sultana, 55). Scott apparently destroyed some of his first draft (possibly accidentally) and rewrote it in Naples, where his health and energy temporarily took a turn for the better. He sent the first volume back in March to Cadell in piecemeal parcels. In early April, he dispatched the second section of the novel, which he now evidently considered to be finished. From the first, however, Cadell was resolved that *The Siege of Malta* could not be the last (forty-eighth) 'Magnum Opus' volume. In fact, in his mind, he had evidently written off Scott's last effort altogether. He delayed reading the segments of *The Siege of Malta*, the whole narrative of which was complete by the time that Scott reached Rome. It was at this point (without apparently having looked over the text) that Cadell pronounced that the novel 'cannot be published'. Scott, however, never lived to hear this verdict. It seems that Lockhart too, who was fearfully preoccupied with the Reform Bill, never read the manuscript. Grierson, who did look at the manuscript a century later, concurred with Lockhart's wish that *The Siege of Malta* should be suppressed. (Sultana suggests that Grierson may have been disturbed by what struck him as plagiarism from the Abbé Vertot's *Knights of Malta* in the last pages.)

In its serial dispatch by different messengers the manuscript of *The Siege of Malta* became dreadfully disordered. It was not until Sultana's examination of the novel in the 1970s, and his rearrangement of it, that the narrative could even be sensibly described. Sultana disinters 77,000 words comprising, in its unsorted form, 'a literary jig-saw puzzle'. Reconstruction is not helped by the fact that many pages – especially in the early sections – were given away to souvenir hunters. Nonetheless Sultana maintains that *The Siege of Malta* is, indeed, 'finished'. As he goes on to show, the novel – while not exactly publishable in its present form – is a remarkably coherent piece of work for a man in Scott's condition.

In Naples, Scott saw much of the classical topographer Sir William Gell. This gentleman (who was confined to a wheelchair) left a memorandum, extensively drawn on by Lockhart (Sultana, 61). Scott managed to work in the National Library, and they made numerous expeditions, notably on 9 February to Pompeii. One comment by Scott survives – 'the City of the dead'. He was overjoyed at this time to hear that *Count Robert of Paris* and *Castle Dangerous* had gone into a second edition. He was now intermittently deluded that all his debts had been paid in full. Sultana points out that Scott was, in fact, inexorably sinking into further debt (Sultana, 108–9). He had overspent on the trip. Cadell had poured money into the open accounts that Scott was drawing on and informed Walter: 'Your father is coming home to misery – yes, positive misery' (Sultana, 109). No one had the heart to tell Scott the true state of his finances.

As Sultana records, Scott's health improved markedly in Naples. He was considering a return to poetry, now that the financial need to write fiction was gone (as he fondly thought). Why had he ever given poetry up? Gell asked. 'Byron *bet* [i.e. beat] me', Scott wryly replied (Sultana, 77). In his Neapolitan upturn Scott felt he might manage Greece after all and a leisurely trip home through the Tyrol, detouring to meet Goethe at Weimar. Charles who was observed to be 'silent' and 'emaciated looking' (Sultana, 99) was extremely nervous at his father's more ambitious projects.

Walter left for home and his regiment on 6 March. He had been very restless and was probably not much missed – at least not by Anne who had found his behaviour 'unkind' (Sultana, 61). According to Lockhart, Scott was told at Naples that Goethe had died on 22 March: he took the news with the exclamation: 'Alas for Goethe – but he at least died at home – Let us to Abbotsford' (Lock. 5. 410). And at that point, he began his *via dolorosa* back to Scotland. If we believe Lockhart, Goethe's death suffused Scott with a yearning to return, so that he too might die under his own roof. But, as Sultana points out, there is no evidence whatsoever that Scott knew about Goethe's death while he was at Naples, nor that it demoralized him and filled him with homesickness (Sultana, 89). It remains one of the more beautiful of JGL's inventions.

On 17 April Walter Scott went with Charles, Gell and Anne to Rome during holy week. By now Scott was virtually immobile. Nonetheless he was socially active. And unfortunately he had lost his self-discipline over his intake of food and drink. There are many records of his conversation from this period – most of them noting his obstructed speech. His talk was still at times vivacious. And if Edward Cheney's testimony is to be believed, Scott's mood at this period was serene. Cheney, a retired army officer and art collector resident in Rome, reports Scott as telling him:

> I am drawing near the close of my career; I am fast shuffling off the stage. I have been perhaps the most voluminous author of the day; and it *is* a comfort to me to think that I have tried to unsettle no man's faith, to corrupt no man's principle, and that I have written nothing which on my death bed I should wish blotted. (Sultana, 107)

Sultana records that at this period Scott's mind alternated between lucidity and cloudedness. Sometimes he was confused and at others 'little remained of his illness, except a consciousness of his state of infirmity' (Sultana, 107). Anne however was fractious and Charles seems to have been very morose (Sultana, 85). Both were clearly unwell (Sultana, 94).

On 11 May, the Scott party left Rome for Florence, Bologna and Venice. Scott was never a tranquil traveller and he was now particularly difficult. But, as Sultana observes, he probably took more interest in Venice than Lockhart suggests. According to JGL 'he showed no curiosity about anything except the Bridge of Sighs and adjoining dungeons' (Lock. 5. 424). Sultana disputes this convincingly (Sultana, 112). If anything, Scott seems to have been stimulated by Venice, which they left on 23 May under some pressure of time since Charles's leave from the Foreign Office was running out. Scott was worried about his son's timetable, and may have hurried himself injudiciously.

On the journey through Germany Scott became progressively more ill. In Frankfort, on 5 June, he was offered a lithographed print of Abbotsford. The bookseller did not recognize its owner (Lock. 5. 425). Because of the never-ending business of the Reform Bill, Lockhart could not come to meet them. In Mainz he wrote his last letter: a reply declining an invitation from the philosopher Schopenhauer ('I am far from well'). A couple of days later, on 9 June, at Nijmegen, Scott sustained a shattering stroke – 'the crowning blow', as Lockhart calls it (Lock. 5. 425). Sultana reckons it was the fourth such major episode. Nevertheless, when he recovered consciousness, Scott insisted on travelling on. They made their way back to England, via Rotterdam, arriving on 11 June. Scott recognized Lockhart and Jane, but he was clearly disturbed and wandering in mind. The party reached London on 13 June, where the still stupefied Scott was lodged at St James's Hotel, Jermyn Street. It was a kind of lying-in-state. When he attended him Dr Robert Ferguson thought he had never seen 'anything more magnificent than the symmetry of his colossal bust, as he lay on the pillow with his chest and neck exposed' (Lock 5. 428). Walter and Cadell rushed down to London. The newspapers carried bulletins and reports.

Scott took farewell of his children on 18 June, believing he was dying. Cadell declared 'the great mind of the Author of *Marmion* is prostrated, gone past rallying' (EJ 1264). One thought remained. He was desperate to get home and die at Abbotsford. After three weeks the doctors consented to his departure. The party left by steamboat on 7 July; in addition to the recumbent Scott it contained Sophia, Lockhart, an invalid Anne, Cadell, Dr Thomas Watson and Scott's servant Nicolson (Lock. 5. 429). He was unconscious on arrival at Edinburgh on 9 July and was hoisted on shore like so much cargo. Two days later, on 11 July, he left for Abbotsford by carriage. According to Lockhart he sprang up with cry of delight when he recognized the landscape. He displayed an 'agitation almost uncontrollable' (Lock. 5. 430) and had to be physically restrained from leaping from the moving vehicle. When after some difficulty he recognized his factor, he exclaimed: 'Ha! Willie Laidlaw. O man, how often have I thought of you!' (Lock. 5. 430).

As Lockhart remarks, 'Recovery was no longer to be thought of: but there might be *Euthanasia*' (Lock. 5. 431). There was, in fact, a brief respite. Scott was heard to say, complacently, from his wheelchair, 'I have seen much, but nothing like my ain house.' He made some small expeditions in a bath-chair. Lockhart read the Bible and Crabbe to him. On hearing a passage from Crabbe's *Borough* – which he had known by heart many years – Scott thought he was hearing a new poem. 'Crabbe has lost nothing' (Lock. 5. 432), he declared. There were three good days. His memory seemed to clear. Scott even tried to write again. But he collapsed, and implored: 'Friends, don't let me expose myself – get me to bed – that's the only place' (Lock. 5. 434).

In darker moments (unrecorded by Lockhart – whose account must be suspected as highly embellished) Scott made 'unintelligible but violent reproaches' (EJ 1267) against those who were trying to help him. In his delirium, he would mutter 'Burke Sir Walter' – 'in a melancholy tone' (Lock. 5. 435). Scott died slowly. 'The process was long', as Lockhart drily puts it (Lock. 5. 434) – weeks long. Scott at one point screamed for twenty-six hours at a stretch (EJ 1276). He finally died, after two months' suffering, on 21 September. Lockhart's account of Scott's last lucid statement is controversial:

> As I was dressing on the morning of Monday the 17th of September, Nicolson [Scott's servant] came into my room, and told me that his master had awoke in a state of composure and consciousness, and wished to see me immediately. I found him entirely himself, though in the last extreme of feebleness. His eye was clear and calm – every trace of the wild fire of delirium extinguished. 'Lockhart,' he said, 'I may have but a minute to speak to you. My dear, be a good man – be virtuous – be religious – be a good man. Nothing else will give you any comfort when you come to lie here.' (Lock. 5. 438)

That Scott said any such thing is effectively disproved by Grierson, by reference to a letter in which an evangelical lady asks Lockhart to confect a pious scene and dialogue just like this. The probability is that Scott never regained consciousness in his last days (HG 300, EJ 1276).

Newspapers in Scotland and England displayed 'the signs of mourning usual on the demise of a king' (Lock. 5. 438–9). On 23 September, Scott's brain was anatomized. The physician discovered that the organ 'was not large – and the cranium thinner than it is usually found to be' (Lock. 5. 439). There was an unostentatious funeral at Dryburgh Abbey on Wednesday 26 September 1832. As Lockhart records,[6] 'The day was dark and lowering, and the wind high.'

Appendix
Map: Scott and the Borders

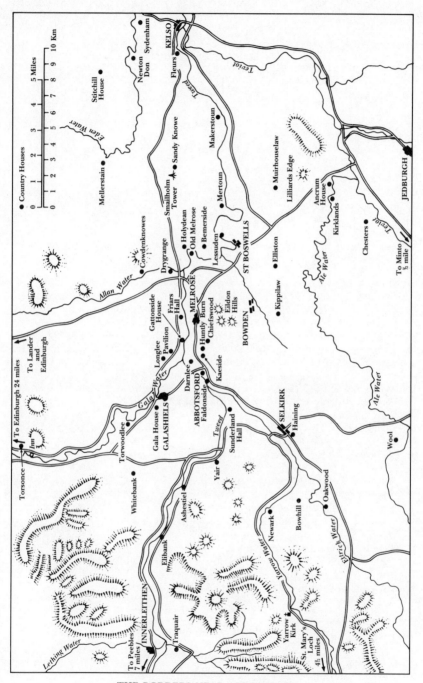

THE BORDERS NEAR ABBOTSFORD

Notes

Chapter 1   Scott among the Scotts (1771–1783)

1   This fragmentary autobiography, or 'Memoirs', was never published in Scott's lifetime. It is preserved in the 'Ashestiel' manuscript, named after the house Scott lived in, 1804–11. The memoir has been edited by David Hewitt (see *Scott on Himself*, ed. David Hewitt, Edinburgh: Scottish Academic Press, 1981, 1–44).

2   There is a less dramatic version of this episode, given by Scott in an 1816 memorandum of his family, quoted in *Lett.* 4. 153, which does not mention Anne.

3   As William Fraser (*The Scotts of Buccleuch*, Edinburgh, 1872) records, the match between Murray and Scott was in fact coldbloodedly contracted by lawyers of both families.

4   See Hewitt, 4. This detail about turning Whig on the spot was added by Scott in 1826.

5   See Robert C. Gordon, 'The Year of Sir Walter Scott's Birth: A Question Reconsidered', *Notes and Queries*, 21 (1974), 163–71.

6   Scott touches on his sister Anne's 'peculiar' temper in the 'Memoirs'. He describes the series of accidents she suffered as a child which seem to have left her chronically weak and neurotic.

7   Grierson seems to have originated this fallacious and much repeated story (see HG 11–2). It is repeated by Daiches (p. 32) and has been authoritatively contradicted by Donald Sultana in his two books on Scott.

8   See F. A. Pottle, 'The Power of Memory in Boswell and Scott', *Scott's Mind and Art*, ed. A. Norman Jeffares (Edinburgh, 1969), 240.

9   See William Falconer, *The Shipwreck* (1762, revised 1769), canto 3.

Chapter 2   Student and Apprentice (1783–1790)

1   According to Johnson (EJ 57, 64) this illness happened in the 'middle of' Scott's second session. There is, however, great uncertainty about how often Scott fell ill at this period, and Lockhart is confusing on the matter.

2   Lockhart locates this serious serious illness in the second year of Scott's university career, 1785. Johnson assumes that there were two subsequent bouts of illness. The more dangerous one that Scott describes in the memoir occurred, as Scott implies, in 'spring 1787' (EJ 64).
3   *The Diary of Frances Lady Shelley*, ed. R. Edgecumbe (London, 1912), 1, 139. This was not, of course, the poet's wife.

Chapter 3   Getting Forward (1790–1797)

1   See J. M. Levine, *Humanism and History* (Ithaca, 1987).
2   See *New Love Poems*, ed. Davidson Cook, F.S.A. (Oxford, 1932).
3   Ground-breaking work was done on the Scott–Belsches affair by Lord Sands in *Sir Walter Scott's Congé* (London, 1931), which remains a fascinating work of literary detection. See also Herbert Grierson, 'The Story of Scott's early Love', *Blackwood's Magazine*, 24 (Feb. 1937), 168–79; Donald A. Low, 'Walter Scott and Williamina Belsches', *Times Literary Supplement* (23 July 1971), 865–6.

Chapter 4   *The Minstrelsy of the Scottish Border* (1798–1802)

1   M. R. Dobie, 'The Development of Scott's *Minstrelsy*: An Attempt at a Reconstruction', *Transactions of the Edinburgh Bibliographical Society*, 2, 1 (1940), 66–87.
2   Edith C. Batho, *The Ettrick Shepherd: James Hogg* (Cambridge, 1927), 22.
3   *Scottish Literary Journal*, 10 (May 1983), 30–41.
4   In the following comments I draw on *Sir Walter Scott as a Freemason*, A. M. Mackay, PM (Edinburgh, 1928).

Chapter 5   Ashestiel and *The Lay of the Last Minstrel* (1802–1805)

1   'Cadyow Castle' has received an informative reading by Jane Millgate in *Walter Scott: The Making of the Novelist*, 17–8, to which I am indebted in what follows. I am also indebted to Nancy Goslee's illuminating discussion of 'Thomas the Rhymer', as pivotal in Scott's poetic evolution, in *Scott the Rhymer*.
2   Scott's and Leyden's work on *Sir Tristrem* is authoritatively discussed in Arthur Johnston, *Enchanted Ground: The Study of Medieval Romance in the Eighteenth Century* (London, 1964), 177–94.

Chapter 6   The Scott Brothers and *Marmion* (1806–1809)

1   This chapter in the Scott family history is uncovered in an article by 'H. G. L. K[ing]' in *Notes and Queries*, 181, 23 (August 1941), 102–4.
2   *The Life and Correspondence of Robert Southey*, ed. R. C. Southey (6 vols, London, 1850), 3, 140.

3 Sister Rose Marie Grady, *The Sources of Scott's Eight Long Poems* (Illinois, 1934), 6.
4 Robert Graves, *Goodbye to All That* (New York, 1930), 364.
5 Louis Crompton, *Byron and Greek Love* (Berkeley: California, 1985), 110.
6 Constable sold off shares in the *Marmion* copyright, as was normal practice with expensive properties. William Miller took one quarter and John Murray another.
7 *The Life and Letters of Thomas Campbell*, ed. Thomas Beattie (2 vols, New York, 1852), 1, 424.

Chapter 7 The Complete Author (1809–1811)

1 The authoritative account of Scott's involvement with the Edinburgh theatre is given in Christopher Worth, ' "A Very Nice Theatre at Edinburgh": Sir Walter Scott and Control of the Theatre Royal', *Theatre Research International*, 12, 2 (1992), 86–95.
2 Scott reviewed his own work, the first series of *Tales of My Landlord*, in the anonymous columns of the *Quarterly Review*, January 1817 (issued April 1817). William Erskine collaborated in the jape.
3 In April 1801, writing to John Thelwall, Coleridge warned his friend against calling a poem 'The Lady of the Lake'. It was, Coleridge pointed out, 'rather an unlucky title; as since the time of Don Quixote the phrase has become a cant word in almost all European languages for a Woman of Pleasure' (Griggs, 2. 723).
4 Caroline Bingham, *James V* (London, 1971), 90.
5 The authoritative account of the journal's career is given by Kenneth Curry, *Sir Walter Scott's Edinburgh Annual Register* (Knoxville: Tennessee, 1977).
6 Robert Cadell came into Constable's firm in 1807, and later married his daughter – she, however, died within the year. By 1811, Cadell was a partner.

Chapter 8 Abbotsford and *Waverley* (1811–1814)

1 For the authoritative account of Abbotsford and its precursors, see chapter 12 of James Macaulay's *The Gothic Revival, 1745–1845* (Glasgow and London, 1975).
2 Virginia Woolf, 'Gas at Abbotsford', *New Statesman and Nation*, 19 (27 January 1940), 108–9.
3 A brilliantly researched account of Weber is given by Kurt Gamerschlag in, 'Henry Weber: Medieval Scholar, Poet, and Secretary to Walter Scott', *Studies in Scottish Literature*, 25 (1990), 202–17.
4 See Lee H. Potter, 'The Text of Scott's Edition of Swift', *Studies in Bibliography*, 22 (1969), 240–55, for a full description of Scott's obligation to Nichols.
5 For a full listing of Scott's major editorial ventures see Margaret Ball, *Sir Walter Scott as a Critic of Literature* (New York, 1907). G. A. M. Wood has four highly informative articles on the Sir Ralph Sadler project (1809), *Studies in Scottish Literature*, 1969–71.
6 See Ball, 68.
7 See Peter Garside, 'Popular Fiction and National Tale: the Hidden Origins of Sir Walter Scott's *Waverley*', *Nineteenth Century Literature*, 46, 1 (June 1991), 30–53.

On the early composition of *Waverley* see also Garside's 'Dating *Waverley*'s early Chapters', *The Bibliotheck*, 13, 3 (1986), 61–81.

8   J. M. S. Tompkins, *The Popular Novel in England: 1770–1800* (London, 1932), 20.

Chapter 9   *Guy Mannering* to *The Antiquary* (1814–1816)

1   McMaster, *Scott and Society*, 158–6.
2   The authoritative account of Scott's journey to Waterloo is given in Donald Sultana, *From Abbotsford to Paris and Back* (Bristol, 1993).

Chapter 10   *Tales of my Landlord* to *The Heart of Midlothian* (1816–1818)

1   See Paul R. Lieder, 'Scott and Scandinavian Literature', *Smith College Studies in Modern Languages*, 2 (October 1920), 10–21.
2   See J. T. Hillhouse, 'Sir Walter Scott's Last Long Poem', *HLQ*, 16 (1952–3), 53–73.
3   See Peter Garside, 'Patriotism and Patronage; New Light on Scott's Baronetcy', *MLR*, 77 (1982), 16–28.
4   Graham McMaster gives an informed and succinct account of Scott's interest in Malthus in *Scott and Society*, 83–4.

Chapter 11   *The Bride of Lammermoor* to *The Abbot* (1818–1820)

1   Gordon and Hook argue their respective readings of the novel in a series of articles in *Nineteenth-Century Fiction*: Robert C. Gordon, '*The Bride of Lammermoor*. A Novel of Tory Pessimism', *NCF*, 12, 2 (September 1957), 110–24; Andrew Hook, '*The Bride of Lammermoor*. A Reexamination', *NCF*, 22, 2 (September 1967), 112–26; Robert C. Gordon and Andrew Hook, '*The Bride of Lammermoor* Again: An Exchange', *NCF*, 23, 4 (March 1969), 493–99.
2   See Kerr, *Fiction against History*, 90.
3   See Christopher Hill's essay on the Norman Yoke Thesis in *Puritanism and Revolution* (London, 1968).
4   This article is identified by Graham McMaster as by Scott, and is reprinted as an appendix to *Scott and Society*, 228–41.
5   See H. J. Gurnand, *The Influence of Walter Scott on the Works of Balzac* (New York, 1926).

Chapter 12   The Tory Grandee (1820–1822)

1   See J. Gordon Weir, 'The Case of the *Beacon* and the *Sentinel*', *Sir Walter Scott Quarterly*, 1, 4 (January 1928).
2   As he records in his note 16 to the Magnum Opus edition, Scott drew on Robert Laneham's 'Account of the Queen's Entertainment at Killingworth Castle'

and other historical accounts of Elizabeth's royal progresses and public processions.

3 See C. T. Prouty, *George Gascoigne* (New York, 1942), 88–90.

Chapter 13   The Royal Visit and *Redgauntlet* (1822–1823)

1 Its full hideousness is described by John Prebble, *The Great Jaunt* (London, 1990), 74.

2 On the return trip, in July, Edgeworth declared that Lady Scott 'has been in my opinion much belied and misrepresented' (EJ 842) as regards the widespread rumours of her drunkenness and/or laudanum addiction.

3 From examination of surviving proof sheets of the suppressed episode Andrew Lang points out that 'it seems that Lockhart forgot the original plan of the novel. The mock marriage *did* halt at the church door, but Clara's virtue had yielded to her real lover, Frank Tyrrel, before the ceremony' (1, xiii).

Chapter 14   The Crash (1824–1826)

1 In 1829, Scott declared himself 'totally ignorant' of Wales and things Welsh (*Lett.* 11. 85).

2 Fiction did, however, earn well for JGL. He got between 400 and 1,000 guineas from Blackwood for each of his four novels.

3 R. F. Butler, 'Maria Edgeworth and Sir Walter Scott: Unpublished Letters, 1823', *Review of English Studies*, 9 (February 1958), p. 31.

4 Claims stood at £104,081 51s 6d, funds at £69,456 2s 4d, amount outstanding £34,625 13s 2d (Jrnl. xxiv).

5 Scott had three policies with Constable, and two with Ballantyne (EJ 969).

6 The total debt was not yet capped: it would eventually rise from £104,000 to £127,000 after all the bills came in (EJ 970). Had Scott known the final size of the debt he might have thought again about sequestration.

Chapter 15   Working for the Creditors (1826–1827)

1 The contracts are listed in *ACLC*, 3.442. They comprise three novels, the *Life of Napoleon*, a history of Scotland contracted for in 1816, and an edition of Shakespeare contracted for in 1824.

2 The Malagrowther Letters have been edited by P. H. Scott (London, 1981) who stresses their nationalistic impulse. For a modern (and technical) evaluation, see George Hogg, 'Malachi Malagrowther 150 Years On', *Scottish Bankers' Magazine*, 68 (May 1977), 33–6.

3 The measure was at first postponed six months, then six years, then indefinitely (EJ 976).

4 There are two different accounts of Lady Scott's death (see EJ 984–5, Jrnl. 144–5). I follow Johnson.

5   In the editorial introduction Chrystal declares confusingly that 'The Surgeon's Daughter' was a follow-up volume called for by the success of the first two stories, suggesting that the volumes were published serially.
6   *The Life of Napoleon* (Philadelphia, 1842).
7   See R. M. Wardle, *Hazlitt* (Lincoln: Nebraska, 1971), 449.
8   Andrew Lang, *Sir Walter Scott* (New York, 1906), 107.

Chapter 16   The 'Magnum Opus' (1828–1829)

1   This profitable sideline was further encouraged by the success of the 'Miscellaneous Prose Writings', published by Cadell in six volumes in 1827. Scott hoped the trust would let him have the profits of this venture, which they declined to do.
2   Nelson was one of Scott's amanuenses. He fell into drunkenness and destitution in later life.
3   The Third Series of the 'Tales' would bring the narrative up to the John Paul Jones invasion of Edinburgh, and was finished by Christmas 1829. A Fourth Series was embarked on, and in a dedicatory letter Scott indicated his intention to move to French history. In May 1831, Scott was working on a fifth series of 'Tales', which he never finished, although some 100,000 words survive in manuscript and have been examined by William Baker. The topic covered in the unfinished fifth series is French history from the beginning of the eleventh century.
4   As will be clear this section is heavily indebted to Jane Millgate's exemplary *Scott's Last Edition, A Study in Publishing History* (Edinburgh, 1987). See also Iain Gordon Brown, *Scott's Interleaved Waverley Novels* (Edinburgh, 1987).
5   The Edinburgh Banks, particularly the Royal Bank of Scotland, were savage against Cadell because he had brazenly reassured them until the last minute that Constable & Co. was sound, and had made a £1,900 withdrawal on the eve of the disaster.
6   In addition to making up the dramatic volume in the poetry reissue, *Auchindrane* was published in 1830 together with the much worked-over *Devorgoil* as an independent production. *The House of Aspen* was similarly farmed out for reprinting in the 1829 *Keepsake*.
7   To replace Purdie the trustees installed William Laidlaw at Abbotsford (*Jrnl.* 589).

Chapter 17   The Last Years (1830–1832)

1   Scott later placed the episode in the morning (EJ 1123). In his journal, after a second stroke in November, he distractedly misremembered it as happening in 'summer'.
2   This was to prove the last dividend paid in Scott's lifetime. At a reckoning, on 29 October 1832, the creditors made do with 18s in the pound as their final settlement. The remaining 2s was written off as the value of Abbotsford library and furnishings given to Scott in 1830. Cadell eventually paid off the mortgage

on Abbotsford for the surviving family, as part of his purchase of all rights in Scott's work.

3   See Kurt Gamerschlag's 'The Making and Unmaking of Sir Walter Scott's *Count Robert of Paris*', *Studies in Scottish Literature*, vol. 15 (1980), pp. 95–123. Hereafter, 'Gamerschlag'. I draw heavily on Professor Gamerschlag's most informative article in later discussion of the novel.

4   Scott's journal suggests a rather messier, less nobly valedictory scene than Lockhart has left us. Peter Garside in 'Scott's Political Speech', *Scottish Literary Journal* (December 1980), suggests that Scott's oratory at this period was 'in no way impressive'.

5   The definitive account of Scott's final journey is given in Donald Sultana's *The Journey of Sir Walter Scott to Malta* (New York, 1986). Parenthetic references in this chapter to 'Sultana' refer to the reconstruction of *The Siege of Malta* by Dr Sultana.

6   Lock. 5. 440; for an analysis of accounts of Scott's funeral see Hamish Miles, 'William Allan's Description of Scott's Funeral', *Scottish Literary Journal*, 3, 1 (July 1976), 56–71.

Bibliography

Secondary materials on Scott are vast. A valuable guide to and synopsis of criticism published between 1932 and 1977 is furnished in Jill Rubinstein, *Sir Walter Scott: A Reference Guide*, Boston, 1978. This supplements James Corson's *A Bibliography of Sir Walter Scott* (Edinburgh, 1943). For material published between 1977 and the present day the MLA annual bibliography (now available in searchable, database form) should be consulted. Valuable notes and indexes will be found in W. E. K. Anderson (ed.), *The Journal of Sir Walter Scott*, Oxford, 1972 and James Corson, *Notes and Index to Sir Herbert Grierson's Edition of The Letters of Sir Walter Scott*, Oxford, 1979.

For consistency, references in the text here are to the 'Border Edition' of the *Waverley Novels* (48 vols, ed. Andrew Lang, 1892–94). In the near future Scott's major works of fiction will be available in both newly edited expensive and cheap forms. As I write, three volumes of the Edinburgh and Aberdeen Universities' Edition (general editor, David Hewitt) have appeared. By the end of the century, all of Scott's fiction will be available in this authoritative series. Meanwhile, 'World's Classics', 'Penguin Classics' and 'Everyman Paperbacks' are well on the way to providing texts of all the major novels, valuably annotated and at very reasonable price. Volumes which I have found particularly useful here are: Kathryn Sutherland's *Redgauntlet* (World's Classics, Oxford, 1985); Susan Manning's *Quentin Durward* (World's Classics, Oxford, 1992): A. N. Wilson's *Ivanhoe* (Penguin Classics, London, 1982); Fiona Robertson's *The Bride of Lammermoor* (World's Classics, Oxford, 1991); Claire Lamont's *The Heart of Midlothian* (World's Classics, Oxford, 1982); Angus Calder's *Old Mortality* (Penguin Classics, London 1975, reprinted 1985); Andrew Hook's *Waverley* (Penguin Classics, London, 1972); and Claire Lamont's *Waverley* (World's Classics, Oxford, 1986).

There is, apparently, no move to re-edit the letters, and the student must make do with Herbert Grierson's twelve-volume *Letters of Sir Walter Scott* (London, 1932).

Alexander, J. H., '*The Lay of the Last Minstrel*: Three essays', Salzburg, 1978.
Alexander, J. H., 'The major images in *Kenilworth*', *Scottish Literary Journal*, 17, 2, November 1990, 27–35.
Alexander, J. H., *Two Studies in Romantic Reviewing*, in *Romantic Reassessment*, ed. James Hogg, Salzburg, 1976.

Allan, George (continuing work begun by William Weir), *The Life of Sir Walter Scott, Baronet*, Edinburgh, 1834.

Anderson, James, 'Sir Walter Scott as historical novelist: Part VI, Alterations to historical fact in the *Waverley* novels: a caution', *Studies in Scottish Literature*, 5, 3, January 1968, 143–66 (this is part of a six-part series, July 1966 to January 1968).

Andrews, Malcolm, *The Search for the Picturesque: Landscape, Aesthetics, and Tourism in Britain*, Aldershot, 1989.

Ash, Marinell, *The Strange Death of Scottish History*, Edinburgh, 1980.

Aspinall, A., 'Walter Scott's Baronetcy: Some new letters', *Times Literary Supplement*, (25 October 1947), 556.

Ball, Margaret, Sir Walter Scott as a Critic of Literature, New York, 1907.

Batho, Edith C., *The Ettrick Shepherd: James Hogg*, Cambridge, 1927.

Beattie, Thomas (ed.), *The Life and Letters of Thomas Campbell*, 2 vols, New York, 1852.

Beiderwell, Bruce, *Power and Punishment in Scott's Novels*, Athens: Georgia and London, 1992.

Buchan, Alexander M., 'Jeffrey, *Marmion* and Scott', in *Studies in Memory of F. M. Webster*, St Louis: Missouri, 1991, 34–40.

Buchan, David, *The Ballad and the Folk*, London, 1972.

Buchan, John, *Sir Walter Scott*, London, 1932.

Buck, H. Michael, 'A message in her madness: socio-political bias in Scott's portrayal of Mad Clara Mowbray in *St Ronan's Well*', *Studies in Scottish Literature*, 24 (1989), 181–93.

Butler, R. F., 'Maria Edgeworth and Sir Walter Scott: unpublished letters, 1823', *Review of English Studies*, new series 9 (February 1958), 36.

Butterworth, Daniel S., 'Tinto, Pattieson, and the theories of pictorial and dramatic representation in Scott's *The Bride of Lammermoor*', *South Atlantic Review*, 56, 1 (January 1991), 1–15.

Bryson, Gladys, *Man and Scoiety: The Scottish Inquiry of the Eighteenth Century*, New York, 1945.

Cairns, John W., 'A note on *The Bride of Lammermoor*: why Scott did not mention the Dalrymple Legend until 1830', *Scottish Literary Journal*, 20, 1 (May 1993), 19–36.

Carlyle, Thomas, *Critical and Miscellaneous Essays*, 7 vols, London, 1888.

Chambers, Robert, *Memoir of Sir Walter Scott*, Edinburgh, 1872.

Clark, Arthur Melville, *Sir Walter Scott: The Formative Years*, New York, 1970.

Cockshut, A. O. J., *The Achievement of Sir Walter Scott*, London, 1969.

Constable, Thomas, *Archibald Constable and his Literary Correspondents*, 3 vols, Edinburgh, 1873.

Cook, Davidson (ed.), *New Love Poems*, Oxford, 1932.

Cooney, Seamus, 'Scott and Progress: the tragedy of "The Highland Widow"', *Studies in Short Fiction*, 11 (1974), 11–6.

Cooney, Seamus, 'Scott's anonymity: its motives and consequences', *Studies in Scottish Literature*, 10, 4 (April 1973), 207–18.

Cottom, Daniel, *The Civilized Imagination: A Study of Anne Radcliffe, Jane Austen and Walter Scott*, Cambridge, 1985.

Cowley, John, 'Lockhart and the publication of *Marmion*', *Philological Quarterly*, 32, 2 (April 1953), 172–83.

Craig, David, *Scottish Literature and the Scottish People*, London, 1961.

Crawford, Cedric E., 'Sir Tristrem, Sir Walter Scott, and Thomas of Ercildoune', *Studies in Medieval Literature and Languages in Memory of Frederick Whitehead*, ed. W. Rothwell and W. R. J. Blamires, Manchester, 1973.

Crawford, Robert, *Devolving English Literature*, London, 1992.

Crawford, T. C., *Scott*, Edinburgh, 1965 (repr. London, 1985).

Criscuola, Margaret M., ' "Originality, realism, and reality": three issues in Sir Walter Scott's criticism of fiction', *Studies in Scottish Literature*, 16 (1981), 26–49.

Criscuola, Margaret M., 'The Porteous Mob: fact and truth in *The Heart of Midlothian*', *ELH*, 22, 1, 1984, 43–50.

Crockett, W. S., *The Scott Originals*, Edinburgh, 1912.

Cross, Walter L., 'An earlier *Waverley*', *Modern Language Notes*, 17 (1902), 87–8.

Curry, Kenneth, *Sir Walter Scott's Edinburgh Annual Register*, Knoxville: Tennessee, 1977.

Daiches, David, *A Companion to Scottish Culture*, London, 1981.

Daiches, David, 'Scott and Scotland', *Scott: Bicentenary Essays*, ed. Alan Bell, Edinburgh, 1973, 38–60.

Daiches, David, 'Scott's achievement as a novelist', *Nineteenth-Century Fiction*, 6 (1951), 80–95 and 153–73.

Daiches, David, 'Scott's *Waverley*: The presence of the author', *Nineteenth-Century Scottish Fiction: Critical Essays*, ed. Ian Campbell, Manchester, 1979.

Daiches, David, *Sir Walter Scott and his World*, London, 1971.

Dale, Thomas R., '*Anne of Geierstein*: a political testament', *Scottish Literary Journal*, 7, 1 (May 1980), 193–201.

Dale, Thomas R., 'From epic to romance: Barbour's *Bruce* and Scott's *The Lord of the Isles*', *Studies in Scottish Literature*, 26 (1991), 515–21.

Dale, Thomas R., 'The jurists, the dominie, and Jeanie Deans', *Scottish Literary Journal*, 11, 1 (May 1984), 36–44.

D'Arcy, Julian M., 'Davie Deans and Bothwell Bridge', *Scottish Literary Journal*, 12, 2 (November 1985), 23–34.

D'Arcy, Julian M., and Kristen Wolf, 'Sir Walter Scott and the Erbiggja Saga', *Scottish Literary Journal*, 22 (1987), 30–43.

Davie, Donald, *The Heyday of Sir Walter Scott*, London, 1961.

Davie, Donald, 'The poetry of Sir Walter Scott', *Proceedings of the British Academy*, 47 (1961), 61–75.

Davis, Jana, 'Landscape images and epistemology in *Guy Mannering*', *Scott and his Influence*, ed. J. H. Alexander and David Hewitt, Edinburgh, 1983, 118–28.

Davis, Jana, 'Sir Walter Scott's *The Heart of Midlothian* and Scottish commonsense morality', *Mosaic*, 21 (1987), 55–63.

Devlin, D. D., *The Author of Waverley*, London, 1971.

Dickson, Beth, 'Sir Walter Scott and the limits of toleration', *Scottish Literary Journal*, 18, 2 (November 1991), 46–62.

Dobie, M. R., 'The development of Scott's *Minstrelsy*: an attempt at a reconstruction', *Transactions of the Edinburgh Bibliographical Society*, 2, 1 (1940), 66–87.

Duncan, Ian, *Modern Romance and Transformations of the Novel*, Cambridge, 1992.

Edgecumbe, R. (ed.), *The Diary of Frances Lady Shelley*, London, 1912.

Elbers, Joan, 'Isolation and community in *The Antiquary*', *Nineteenth-Century Fiction*, 28 (1973), 405–23.

Eller, Ruth, 'Themes of time and art in *The Lay of the Last Minstrel*', *Studies in Scottish Literature*, 13 (1978), 111–24.

Emerson, O. F., 'The early literary life of Sir Walter Scott', *JEGP*, 23, January 1924, 28–62; April 1924, 241–69; July 1924, 389–417.

Ferris, Ina, *The Achievement of Literary Authority: Gender, History and the Waverley Novels*, Ithaca and London, 1991.

Fleishman, Avrom, *The English Historical Novel*, London and Baltimore, 1972.

Forbes, Duncan, 'The rationalism of Walter Scott', *The Cambridge Journal*, 7 (1953), 20–35.

Forster, E. M., *Aspects of the Novel*, London, 1927.

Franklin, Caroline, 'Feud and faction in *The Bride of Lammermoor*', *Scottish Literary Journal*, 14, 2 (November 1987), 18–31.

Fraser, William, *The Scotts of Buccleuch*, Edinburgh, 1872.

French, Richard, 'The religion of Sir Walter Scott', *Studies in Scottish Literature*, 2, 1 (July 1964), 32–44.

Gamerschlag, Kurt, 'Henry Weber: medieval scholar, poet, and secretary to Walter Scott', *Studies in Scottish Literature*, 25, (1990), 202–17.

Gamerschlag, Kurt, 'The making and unmaking of Sir Walter Scott's *Count Robert of Paris*', *Studies in Scottish Literature*, 15 (1980), 95–123.

Garside, Peter, 'Dating *Waverley*'s early chapters', *The Bibliotheck*, 13, 3 (1986), 61–81.

Garside, Peter, 'Early accounts of David Ritchie', *Scott Newsletter*, 11 (1987), 8–14.

Garside, Peter, '*A Legend of Montrose* and the history of war', *The Yearbook of English Studies*, 4 (1974), 159–71.

Garside, Peter, '*Old Mortality*'s silent minority', *Scottish Literary Journal*, 7, 1 (May 1980), 127–44.

Garside, Peter, 'Patriotism and patronage; new light on Scott's Baronetcy', *Modern Languages Review*, 77 (1982), 16–28.

Garside, Peter, 'Popular fiction and national tale: the hidden origins of Sir Walter Scott's *Waverley*', *Nineteenth Century Literature*, 46, 1 (June 1991), 30–53.

Garside, Peter, 'Scott and the "philosophical" historians', *The Journal of the History of Ideas*, 36 (July 1975), 497–512.

Garside, Peter, 'Scott and the regalia', *Scott and his Influence*, ed. J. H. Alexander and David Hewitt, Edinburgh, 1983, 218–33.

Garside, Peter, 'Union and *The Bride of Lammermoor*', *Studies in Scottish Literature*, 19 (1984), 72–93.

Garside, Peter (ed.), 'Scott's *The Visionary*', Cardiff, 1984.

Gaskill, Howard (ed.), *Ossian Revisited* (Edinburgh, 1990).

Gaston, Patricia, *The Waverley Prefaces: A Reading of Sir Walter Scott's Prefaces to the Waverley Novels*, New York, 1991.

Gordon, R. C., '*The Bride of Lammermoor*: a novel of Tory pessimism', *NCF*, 12, 2 (September 1957), 110–24.

Gordon, R. C., 'Scott and the Highlanders', *The Yearbook of English Studies*, 6 (1976), 120–40.

Gordon, R. C., *Under Which King? A Study of the Scottish Waverley Novels*, Edinburgh, 1969.

Gordon, R. C., 'The year of Sir Walter Scott's birth: a question reconsidered', *Notes and Queries*, 21 (1974), 163–71.

Goslee, Nancy, *Scott the Rhymer*, Lexington: Kentucky, 1988.

Grady, Rose M., *The Sources of Scott's Eight Long Poems*, Illinois, 1934.

Grant, Douglas, *Private Letters of the Seventeenth Century, by Sir Walter Scott*, Oxford, 1947.

Grierson, Herbert, *Sir Walter Scott, Bart.*, London, 1938.

Grierson, Herbert, 'The story of Scott's early love', *Blackwood's Magazine*, 24 (Feb. 1937), 168–79.

Harkin, Patricia, 'The Fop, the Fairy, and the Genres of Scott's *The Monastery*', *Studies in Scottish Literature*, 19 (1984), 177–93.

Hart, Francis R., *Lockhart as Romantic Biographer*, Edinburgh, 1971.

Hart, Francis R., *Scott's Novels: the Plotting of Historic Survival*, Virginia, 1966.

Hayden, John O., 'Jeanie Deans: the big lie (and a few small ones)', *Scottish Literary Journal*, 6, 1 (1979), 34–44.

Hayden, John O., *Scott: The Critical Heritage*, London, 1970.

Hewitt, David (ed.), *Scott on Himself*, Edinburgh, 1981.

Hillhouse, J. T., 'Sir Walter Scott's last long poem', *HLQ*, 16 (1952–3), 53–73.

Hobsbaum, Philip, 'Scott's apoplectic novels', *Scott and his Influence*, ed. J. H. Alexander and David Hewitt, Edinburgh, 1983.

Hogg, George, 'Malachi Malagrowther 150 years on', *Scottish Bankers' Magazine*, 68 (May 1977), 33–6.

Hook, Andrew, '*The Bride of Lammermoor*: a reexamination', *NCF*, 22, 2 (September 1967), 112–26.

Howard, Donald S., 'Napoleon and Sir Walter Scott: a study in Propaganda', *Proceedings of the Annual Meeting of the Western Society for French History*, 9 (1982), 133–4.

Johnson, Edgar, *Sir Walter Scott: The Great Unknown*, 2 vols, New York, 1970.

Johnson, Richard E., 'The technique of embedding in Scott's Fiction', *Studies in Scottish Literature*, 13 (1978), 67–71.

Johnston, Arthur, *Enchanted Ground*, London, 1964.

Jordan, Frank O., 'Scott's last and best narrator', *Scottish Literary Journal*, 7, 1 (May 1980), 185–92.

Kelly, Gary, *English Fiction of the Romantic Period: 1789–1830*, London, 1989.

Kerr, James, *Fiction against History*, Cambridge, 1989.

K[ing], H. G. L., 'Daniel Scott', *Notes and Queries*, 181 (23 August 1941), 102–4.

Kroeber, Karl, *British Romantic Art*, Berkeley: California, 1986.

Kroeber, Karl, *Romantic Narrative Art*, Madison: Wisconsin, 1960.

Lackey, Lionel, '*The Monastery* and *The Abbot*: Scott's religious dialectics', *Studies in the Novel*, 19 (1987), 46–65.

Lamont, Claire, 'Literary patronage in late eighteenth-century Edinburgh', *Scottish Literary Journal*, 2 (1975), 17–26.

Lang, Andrew, *Sir Walter Scott*, New York, 1906.

Lang, Andrew, *Sir Walter Scott and the Border Minstrelsy*, London, 1910.

Lascelles, Mary, *The Storyteller Retrieves the Past*, Oxford, 1980.

Levine, J. M., *Humanism and History*, Ithaca, 1987.

Lieder, Paul R., 'Scott and Scandinavian literature', *Smith College Studies in Modern Languages*, 2 (October 1920), 10–21.

Lochhead, Marion, *John Gibson Lockhart*, London, 1954.

Lochhead, Marion, 'Victorian Abbotsford', *Quarterly Review*, 301 (January 1963), 57–66.

Lockhart, J. G., *Memoirs of the Life of Sir Walter Scott*, 5 vols, 1837–8, repr., Boston and New York, 1902.

Low, Donald A., 'Walter Scott and Williamina Belsches', *Times Literary Supplement*, (23 July 1971), 865–6.

Lukács, G, *The Historical Novel*, London, 1962.

Macaulay, James, *The Gothic Revival, 1745–1845*, Glasgow and London, 1975.

McClatchy, J. D., 'The ravages of time: the function of the *Marmion* epistles', *Studies in Scottish Literature*, 9, 4 (April 1972), 256–63.

MacDonald, T. P., 'Sir Walter Scott's fee book', *Juridical Review*, 62 (1950), 288–316.

Mack, Douglas (ed.), *James Hogg's Anecdotes of Sir Walter Scott*, Edinburgh, 1983.

Mack, Douglas, 'Bringing Scott back to life,' *Scottish Literary Journal*, 9 (Autumn 1993), 1.

Mack, Douglas S., 'Hogg, Lockhart, and the family anecdotes of Sir Walter Scott', *Scottish Literary Journal* (May 1983), 5–13.

Mackay, A. M., *Sir Walter Scott as a Freemason*, Edinburgh, 1928.

Mackenzie, M. L., 'The great ballad collectors: Percy, Herd and Ritson', *Studies in Scottish Literature*, 2, 4 (April 1965), 213–33.

McMaster, Graham, *Scott and Society*, Cambridge, 1981.

MacQueen, John, *The Enlightenment and Scottish Literature*, Edinburgh, 1989.

Manning, Susan, 'Ossian, Scott, and nineteenth-century Literature', *Studies in Scottish Literature*, 17 (1982), 39–54.

Manning, Susan, *The Puritan Provincial Vision*, Cambridge, 1990.

Mayhead, Robin, 'The problem of coherence in *The Antiquary*', *Scott Bicentenary Essays*, 134–46.

Mennie, Duncan M., 'Sir Walter Scott's unpublished translations of German plays', *Modern Language Review*, 33 (April 1938), 57–63.

Miles, Hamish, 'William Allan's description of Scott's funeral', *Scottish Literary Journal*, 3, 1 (July 1976), 56–71.

Miller, Karl, *Cockburn's Millenniums*, London, 1976.

Miller, Karl, *Doubles*, Oxford, 1983.

Miller, Karl, *Rebecca's Vest*, London, 1993.

Millgate, Jane, 'For lucre or for fame', *Review of English Studies*, 44, no. 174 (May 1993), 187–203.

Millgate, Jane, 'Guy Mannering in Edinburgh: the evidence of the manuscript', *The Library*, 5, 32 (1977), 238–45.

Millgate, Jane, '"Nought of the Bridal": narrative resistance in *The Lay of the Last Minstrel*', *Scottish Literary Journal*, 17, 2 (Nov. 1990), 16–26.

Millgate, Jane, 'Scott and the dreaming boy', *Review of English Studies*, 32, 127 (August 1981), 286–93.

Millgate, Jane, 'Scott and the law', *Rough Justice*, ed. M. L. Friedland, Toronto, 1991.

Millgate, Jane, *Scott's Last Edition*, Edinburgh, 1987.

Millgate, Jane, *Walter Scott: The Making of the Novelist*, London, 1984.

Mitchell, Jerome, *The Walter Scott Operas*, Alabama, 1977.

Moir, Esther, *The Discovery of Britain: The English Tourists, 1540–1840*, London, 1964.

Montgomerie, W., 'William McMath and the Scott ballad manuscripts,' *Studies in Scottish Literature*, 1, 2 (October 1963), 93–8.

Morgan, Peter F., 'Lockhart's Literary Personality', *Scottish Literary Journal*, 2 (1975), 27–35.

Nicolaisen, W. F. H., 'Sir Walter Scott: the folklorist as novelist', *Scott and his Influence*, ed. J. H. Alexander and David Hewitt, Aberdeen, 1983, 169–79.

Nixon, Ingeborg, *Thomas of Erceldoune*, Copenhagen, 1980.

Ochoiski, Paul M., 'Sir Walter Scott's continuous interest in Germany', *Studies in Scottish Literature*, 3, 3 (January 1966), 164–73.

Oman, Carola, *The Wizard of the North*, London, 1973.

Overton, W. J., 'Scott, the short story and history: "The Two Drovers"', *Studies in Scottish Literature*, 21 (1986), 210–25.

Parsons, C. O., *Witchcraft and Demonology in Scott's Fiction*, Edinburgh, 1964.

Partington, Wilfred (ed.), *Sir Walter Scott's Postbag*, London, 1932.

Pearson, Hesketh, *Sir Walter Scott*, New York, 1954.

Phillipson, N. T., 'Scott as story-teller; an essay in psychobiography', *Scott Bicentenary Essays*, ed. Alan Bell, New York, 1973, pp. 87–100.

Pikoulis, John, 'Scott and Marmion: the discovery of identity', *Modern Language Review*, 66, 4 (October 1971), 738–50.

Politi, Jina, 'Narrative and historical transformation in *The Bride of Lammermoor*', *Scottish Literary Journal*, 15, 1 (1987), 70–81.

Pope-Hennessy, Una, *Sir Walter Scott*, Denver, 1949.

Potter, Lee. H., 'The text of Scott's edition of Swift', *Studies in Bibliography*, 22 (1969), 240–55.

Pottle, F. A., 'The power of memory in Boswell and Scott', *Scott's Mind and Art*, ed. A. Norman Jeffares, Edinburgh, 1969.

Prebble, John, *The Great Jaunt*, London, 1990.

Quayle, Eric, *The Ruin of Sir Walter Scott*, London, 1968.

Reed, James, *The Border Ballads*, London, 1973.

Reed, James, *Sir Walter Scott and Scotland*, London, 1980.

Rogers, Charles, *Genealogical Memoirs of the Family of Sir Walter Scott, Bart*, Edinburgh, 1877.

Rubinstein, Jill, 'The dilemma of history: a reading of Scott's *Bridal of Triermain*', *SEL*, 12, 4 (Autumn 1972), 721–34.

Rubinstein, Jill, ' "This applause is worth having": Lady Louisa Stuart as a critic of Sir Walter Scott', *Scottish Literary Journal*, 7, 1 (1980), 19–30.

Ruddick, William, 'Sir Walter Scott's Northumberland', *Scott and his Influence*, ed. J. H. Alexander and David Hewitt, Aberdeen, 1983, pp. 20–30.

Ruff, William, 'A bibliography of the poetical works of Sir Walter Scott, 1796–1832', *Transactions of the Edinburgh Bibliographical Society*, 1936–7, 99–239.

Ruff, William, 'Deceptions in the works of Scott: or, lying title-pages', *Scott Bicentenary Essays*, ed. Alan Bell, Edinburgh, 1973, 176–87.

Ruff, William, 'Walter Scott and the Erl King,' *Englische Studien*, LXIX (1934), 106–8.

Sands, Lord, *Sir Walter Scott's Congé*, London, 1931.

Shattock, Joanne, *Politics and Reviewers*, Leicester, 1989.

Smith, D. J., 'Sir James and Sir Walter: Scott and James of Douglas', *Scottish Literary Journal*, 8, 2 (December 1981), 24–37.

Smout, T. C., *A History of the Scottish People*, New York, 1969.

Southey, R. C. (ed.), *The Life and Correspondence of Robert Southey*, 6 vols, London, 1850.

Spink, Gerald W., 'Sir Walter in Yorkshire', *Studies in Scottish Literature*, 10, 2 (October 1972), 103–20.

Sroka, Kenneth R., 'Wealth and illth in *St Ronan's Well*', *Scottish Literary Journal*, 7, 1 (May 1980), 167–84.

Sultana, Donald, *From Abbotsford to Paris and Back*, Bristol, 1993.

Sultana, Donald, *The Journey of Sir Walter Scott to Malta*, New York, 1986.

Sultana, Donald, *The Siege of Malta Rediscovered*, Edinburgh, 1977.

Sultana, Donald, 'Sir William Gell's correspondence on Scott from Naples and his "Reminiscences of Sir Walter Scott in Italy, 1832"', in *Scott and his Influence*, ed. J. H. Alexander and Donald Hewitt, Edinburgh, 1983, 243–54.

Sutherland, Kathryn, 'Defining the self in the poetry of Scott and Wordsworth', *Scott and his Influence*, ed. J. H. Alexander and David Hewitt, Edinburgh, 1983, 51–62.

Sutherland, Kathryn, 'Fictional economies: Adam Smith, Walter Scott, and the nineteenth-century Novel', *ELH*, 54 (1987), 97–127.

Sutherland, Kathryn, 'Travel books, fishing manuals, and Scott's *Redgauntlet*', *Scottish Literary Journal*, 13, 2 (November 1986), 20–30.

Sutherland, Kathryn, 'Walter Scott and Washington Irving: "Editors of the land of Utopia"', *Journal of American Studies*, 10, 1 (April 1976), 85–90.

Sutherland, Kathryn,'Walter Scott's Highland Minstrelsy and his correspondence with the Maclean Clephane Family', *Scottish Literary Journal*, 9, 1 (May 1982), 48–67.

Tompkins, J. M. S., *The Popular Novel in England*, London, 1932.

Trevor-Roper, H, 'Sir Walter Scott and history', *The Listener* (19 August 1971), 225–32.

Trumpener, Katie, 'National character, nationalistic plots, national tale and historical novel in the age of *Waverley*, 1806–30', *ELH*, 60, 3 (Fall 1993), 685–731.

Vincent, Esther H., 'Scott of Abbotsford', *Surgery, Gynecology, and Obstetrics*, 96, 1953, 629–33.

Waterston, Elizabeth, 'Beginning a life: opening movements in Scott's *Napoleon* and Galt's *Byron*', *Scottish Literary Journal*, 7, 1 (May 1980), 41–50.

Weinstein, Mark A., 'Scott's French Revolution, the British conservative view', *Scottish Literary Journal*, 7, 1 (May 1980), 31–40.

Weir, J. Gordon, 'The Case of the *Beacon* and the *Sentinel*', *Sir Walter Scott Quarterly*, 1, 4 (January 1928).

Weir, J. L., 'A Letter to Archibald Constable', *Notes and Queries*, 191 (August 1946), 78–80.

Welsh, Alexander, 'A Freudian slip in *The Bride of Lammermoor*', *Etudes Anglaises*, 18 (April 1965), 134–6.

Welsh, Alexander, *The Hero of the Waverley Novels*, New Haven, 1963.

Williams, Ioan (ed.), *Sir Walter Scott on Novelists and Fiction*, London, 1968.

Wilson, A. N., *The Laird of Abbotsford*, Oxford, 1980.

Wilt, Judith, *Secret Lives: The Novels of Walter Scott*, Chicago, 1985.

Wood, E. H. H., 'Scott's foreign contacts', *Scott Bicentenary Essays*, ed. Alan Bell, New York, 1973, 238–59.

Wood, E. H. H., 'Scott and Jamieson: the relationship between two ballad collectors', *Studies in Scottish Literature*, 9, 2–3 (October–January 1971), 71–96.

Wood, G. A. M., 'Sir Walter Scott and Sir Ralph Sadler: a chapter in literary history, Parts I–IV', *Studies in Scottish Literature*, (August 1969–April 1971).

Woolf, Virginia, 'Gas at Abbotsford', *New Statesman and Nation*, 19 (27 January 1940), 108–9.

Woodring, Carl, 'Three poets on Waterloo: Scott, Southey, and Byron', *The Wordsworth Circle*, 18 (1987), 54–7.

Worth, Christopher, 'A very nice theatre at Edinburgh', *Theatre Research International*, 17, 2 (1992), 86–95.

Zug III, Charles G., 'Sir Walter Scott and ballad forgery', *Studies in Scottish Literature*, 8, 1 (July 1970), 52–64.

Zug III, Charles G., 'The ballad editor as antiquary: Scott and the Minstrelsy', *Journal of the Folklore Institute*, 17, no. 1, 57–7.

Index